FinTech Regulation

Valerio Lemma

FinTech Regulation

Exploring New Challenges of the Capital
Markets Union

Valerio Lemma
Marconi University
Rome, Italy

ISBN 978-3-030-42349-0   ISBN 978-3-030-42347-6   (eBook)
https://doi.org/10.1007/978-3-030-42347-6

This Palgrave Macmillan imprint is published by the registered company Springer Nature Switzerland AG.
The registered company address is: Gewerbestrasse 11, 6330 Cham, Switzerland

CONTENTS

CHAPTER 1

Introduction

1.1 THE AIM OF THE BOOK

The identification of new market failures due to the combination of globalization, financialization and digitalization has led to the identification
of new needs for regulating finance. Policymakers are becoming aware
that new networks cross all jurisdictions, new dynamics move capital and
new devices support business and affairs. Hence, new directions arise for
both regulators and supervisors in order to improve market functioning,
ensuring the smooth circulation of capital, and to ensure the protection of
individual rights.

The scope of this research, then, refers to the phenomena that have
been driven by deregulation and have resulted in the creation and diffusion of extremely structured and complex financial instruments. If, at first,
all this may have favoured the development of the economy, it has also
encouraged reckless behaviour, unsound management and unscrupulous
speculation; and this comes at the risk of the reliability of trade, the stability of the entire financial sector and, as a result of contagion, the growth
of the entire economic system.

Therefore, this research aims to identify the regulatory interventions
that arise from the directions of policymakers and from understanding the
effects of the oversight of the use of technology for improving banking
and finance. Indeed, the investigation has a twofold orientation: on the
one hand, towards the verification of the contents of the activities that

© The Author(s) 2020
V. Lemma, *FinTech Regulation*,
https://doi.org/10.1007/978-3-030-42347-6_1

exploit technology and, on the other hand, of the failures that such activities may incur (if carried out in the absence of appropriate corrective measures).

All the above serve to point out the core elements of fintech as a concept that refers to "new business models, applications, processes or products with an associated material effect on financial markets and institutions and the provision of financial services" (as FSB stated in 2019 in the document named "Monitoring of FinTech"). It is worth anticipating that the link between finance and technology began many years before the rise of home banking, and certain experiences have been strictly regulated already in the twentieth century. However, the aforementioned scope considers the evolution of such a link towards an individualized, privatized, uncertain, flexible, vulnerable reality, in which a previously unexperienced freedom let the market participants to develop for new business models able to manage an increasing and shapeless set of relationships. Thus, the results of the analysis of the FSB (and the ones of other international organizations that will be examined below) represent a concrete starting point for identifying the implications of fintech innovations for both financial stability and individual rights.

In the course of past research, doubts had been repeatedly encountered and they, tenaciously avoiding a disciplinary solution, concerned the status of the technical-financial entrepreneurial condition of banks, financial intermediaries and alternative operators to them. These doubts were perhaps an anticipation—in a transitional phase—of the issues that are addressed in this book with regard to the challenges of business coexistence in an automated environment. To date, the current regulatory framework has not come any closer to resolving this dilemma, but tends to regulate a period of interregnum: one of those moments in history when the ancient ways of acting no longer work, the rules of the past are no longer appropriate to the current conditions of the market, but more appropriate rules still have not been designed, written and implemented in order to ensure civil coexistence.

In defense of the regulator, however, it should be noted that even businessmen are struggling in this middle ground. Even more important is the conviction that, unlike in the past, the legislative bodies do not have a clear vision of the destination of finance, which cannot aim to support the current unsustainable model of society, economy, market and bank. In reality, it seems that these bodies can only react to the emergence of each new problem, in full experimentation, without expressing a clear political choice on the relevant matter.

It can be also warned that the power (i.e. the ability to act) has been separated from the politics (i.e. the ability to decide how and when to act), so that in addition to the doubts of 'to do' are those concerning the identification of the subjects responsible for the decision, the regulation and the supervision. Today, more so than in the past, the two terms of the regulatory problem, freedom and well-being, appear more than a dichotomy, a couple linked to the idea that the limitation of freedom to ensure social welfare is not an opponent but an effect of the same freedom: the democratic character of the growth to ensure an inclusive effect. If there is anything that makes it possible to distinguish the free market from the regulated market (and to order these in sequence), it is precisely the change in the purpose of public intervention. Thus, if in the recent past the heart of public intervention resided in the capacity of control/definition (of actions, risks and of the future), in the current phase of evolution of finance, the main concern should be not to prejudice development and instead to mitigate any risk of frustrating the unknown opportunities expected for the future.

1.2   The Technology, the Market and the Law

The purpose of this book is to provide a view of the role of the law in the technological environment, whose functioning is driven by rules encrypted in algorithms, software and any other provision used to set up any automation. This would change the way policymakers and programmers intervene on a number of important matters in the microeconomic sphere of individuals using high-tech devices and autonomous tools based on machine learning and artificial intelligence.

Most of the contents refer to the need for regulating technology, as the use of algorithms makes the foundation of reasoning visible: programmers and coders have written the logical sequence underlying the high-tech decision-making; hence, it is possible to predict how software will adopt a decision in front of certain inputs. This suggests new ways of regulation, more effective than the strategy based on the provision of incentive or disincentive (used for direct humans' behaviour). Ahead of these hoped-for unknowable ways, the expectation concerns new regulatory and supervisory tools that add algorithms to the software used by market operators, projecting public intervention towards a coercive role that risks crushing innovation under the loss of slow-to-adapt public routines, not always in line with the speed of market operators.

As it is emphasized in the book, fintech distinguishes itself from finance because of its compulsive/obsessive modernization: as finance has looked for efficiency, fintech is looking for a solution aimed at reducing human effort; as risk has been a preliminary and temporary status (in the path towards a return), innovation is a step towards profit. Hence, this research analyses fintech as a movement towards a self-regulating system, able to overcome any possible perturbation by returning to an original state of maximization of well-being due to the ability to manage the asymmetry of probabilities.

Therefore, the technology as it has been proposed may be investigated as a support capable of ordering economic growth, bringing to mind the theories of nineteenth-century economists who called for a time when all human needs would be satisfied and growth replaced by a stable economy. Anyway, the arrival of technology is far from synchronized, as is the context in which it is applied and differentiated. This arises from the polycentrism of a market that is integrated by a relatively long and dispersed web of interdependencies, whose complexity refers to the evidence that—within this market—states, the individuals and their fortunes are inextricably tied together. Hence, the application of new software architectures (including blockchain technology) is overcoming the standardization that has characterized the 'mass market', and the relations between companies/intermediaries and customers are projected beyond the multilateral exchange of this type of market (and, in the end, are taking as reference a 'mass of markets').

In this context, technology is the means that exploits the relations between ends and scarce means that have alternative uses; and it supports human choice and usage of such means. This makes the technology the object of law and economics studies, and it increases the interest for the effects of its innovations over the functioning of the market. Accordingly, the focus goes to the organizations and the processes that support the transformation of inputs into outputs, both as a rationale for the regulations and as the range of activities it influences. Thus, the book considers technology as both an input and an output, provided that its development can be carried out in a completely decentralized (i.e. cloudy) way by means of relationships between individuals.

This continuous evolution of relationships means that, in the fintech environment, relationships do not normally maintain their own structure, do not fix their own structure and do not fix flows. As fluidity may be a feature of fintech, the policymakers are called to understand the nature of the current evolution of the market for capital. They need to adopt a new approach when considering the regulatory intervention, as the interrelationships between the technological system and the legal system are extremely complex, and many of the effects of the high-tech developments are still too far off to predict. Hence, the policymakers cannot predict the future of financial evolution and they should not repeat the mistake of formulating utopian excogitations, but should enact the law to solve the issues due to the technological evolution and the difficulties that affect individuals in the wired economy. Indeed, this research will address problems that do not arise within the political and legislative system, but come from the market. In this context, fintech—considered the end of a long-lasting tendency—requires an exogenous process of regulation to safeguard individual freedom within the globalized, financialized and digitalized society.

1.3   Innovation and Regulation

In recent years, the forms of capital circulation have expanded beyond the dynamics experienced during the twentieth century. Actually, the technological evolution has made possible the circulation of wealth through new types of systems (the so-called platforms), based on the possession of a compatible device, on the use of a software and on the access to an intangible network. In other words, through technological solutions, a platform allows for the execution of exchanges or the use of services that in the past were reserved to credit institutions, financial intermediaries, asset managers, insurance companies, and so on. After all, if the management of platforms were to be included among the non-reserved activities, an asymmetry (in terms of costs and safeguards) would be admitted and it would be difficult to justify with regard to effectiveness (of rights) and efficiency (of the market).

In this investigation, it is important to consider the interference between the provision of services and the management of the infrastructure supporting such provision; both are integrated in a digital complex that gives content to the system described above as a platform. This, of course, is a context that—still today—needs the safeguards provided by the system for the protection of savings, price stability and competition. The result is a specific significance of the technology with respect to the exercise of individual rights (of customers), and this must be taken into consideration by the regulator in order to ensure that the choice of a medium does not affect the public safeguards and backstops.

Therefore, it is necessary to start from the consideration that the diffusion of platforms broadens the scope of public intervention beyond the marks made during the twentieth century (during which the movement of capital was achieved through the intervention of an intermediary or the direct access to regulated trading venues, in a context that required compliance with standards of specific rigor). Indeed, in the context of a general use of information communication technology (ICT) tools and the affirmation of a 'digital single market', intermediaries are faced with new types of competitive pressures due to the alternatives that are spreading in the financial industry and that induce market participants to overcome the concentration of relationships (for credit and debt), as it was the case in the bank-centred system or in the first experiences of the stock exchanges.

At an operational level, in fact, the book will explore the ways in which innovations allow the matching of supply and demand formulated by subjects in surplus with those of others in deficit, through alternative services to traditional intermediation. It is worth noting that, before the advent of the new economy, the capital market was characterized by static contents and by minimal interactivity (between companies and customers). Only in recent times, in fact, has the orientation of market participants gone towards the integration of mechanisms able to personalize the activity and the service and, in particular, to the systematic use of ICT tools for the management of the contents of the relative relationship (from the new infrastructures, to the new devices, to the new software).

The above feeds the interest of this research towards the current trend of banks to process automation and innovation in their information systems in order to improve their operational conditions: 'fintech solutions' are now beginning to be commonly and widely used, by application of digital identification, mobile applications, cloud computing, big data analysis, artificial intelligence, blockchain and distributed ledger technologies.

From another point of view, the speed of application of the results of scientific research to the forms and methods of carrying out reserved activities must be considered equally significant. Devices and needs are becoming elements that—as a result of technological innovation—determine the performance of activities that allow operators to do business in innovative ways (sometimes less expensive than traditional affairs). Thus, there is evidence of activities (i) alternative to the banking system (the -called shadow banking), (ii) instrumental to the latter (aimed at improving the use of traditional services, e.g. comparison website) or (iii) similar to banking (which should require a special authorization, e.g. fintech banks).

1.4   THE INFINITY OF DATA
AND THE SOFTWARE-TO-SOFTWARE PARADIGM

Reasoning on data and big data, two modes of representation appearing in the law come to mind. The first is when a rule describes a case: it is a complete and enclosed form in which the legislator has represented all that has been known and that must be considered about a thing, a behaviour, a relationship. The other way is manifested when the legislator is not able to say who (and how many) were the subjects of the regulatory action, but it must be limited to an illustrative catalogue, which ideally leads to an *etcetera*.

There are lists and databases that have a practical purpose and are finished, such as the list of customers of a bank or the one of their operations; but there are others that want to suggest undeniable quantities and that stop uncompleted or grow to the limits of the indefinite. As this book and its anthology of rules show, technological innovations are infinitely rich in possibilities that can enrich lists with data circulating in the infosphere. Often they are aggregated data for the very taste of enumeration and tracking or, again, for the hope of bringing together elements without an apparently specific relationship, as happens in the so-called chaotic enumerations and as Alban William Phillips did in the twentieth century. However, this book does not only show that programmers have rarely analysed technology in its legal-economic implications, but it also highlights that the legal system should be able to direct the management of data in ways useful to society.

In this respect, the data is the economic goods and the unifying element of a decentralized set of algorithms and information: hence the analysis of the need for creating and defining property rights that would regulate the use of such valuable resource in the fintech environment. However, the technology makes such rights more exclusive and universal, as they would be cheaper to enforce by means of software (than it was in the traditional banking).

Traditionally, property rights have been correlated with scarcity, in order to avoid an extended use of a resource in a way that is not valuable; this leads to the appropriation. On the contrary, in the digital environment, property rights do not fulfill the same function, as the use of data does not prevent others from exploiting the same. Data is a resource that is valuable, but not scarce; it does not require an economizing intervention. Nevertheless, it is worth investigating the rules that would be able to maximize the social utility of data, enacting new rules for compensation, inhibition, and inalienability. Indeed, property rights help in controlling the flows of data, and allow for the remuneration of inventors and inter-mediaries: policymakers have to consider these features, and regulators have to try to minimize these problems. This refers also to secrecy figures in privacy law, whose limits will be shown in the book with respect to the inefficiency of the current mechanisms of information sharing: any user is selling himself/herself by remunerating his/her counterparties with any data they require (that is much more than the usual way to inform anyone about his/her honesty, loyalty, trustworthy, creditworthiness, etc.).

This point suggests the need to qualify the network and its nodes and to understand if and how the law has to protect the access to them. A related point is that the scope of property and contractual law reflects the need to balance the interests of the providers and the ones of the users. In this respect, it is worth considering that the costs refer to tracing, negotia-tion and allocation, and that certain users will pay more than others will for accessing the networks. This reflects the problems related to the need for speed (of transactions) and for avoiding the risk of congestion (in the flows of data).

All the above lead to consider the negotiation in the fintech environ-ment, and the possibility that users will not conduct them, but will run software able to compare the supply and place the demand on terms that are most favourable to the user. At the same time, providers will run soft-ware able to offer their services in a way that is most suitable to the afore-mentioned comparison software. Thus, fintech negotiation will refer to a software-to-software (S2S) context, and the law must address such trading practices, provided that the reliance on the good faith of the programmers is possible and does not guarantee the level of prudence set forth for bank-ing and finance. Moreover, in the interest of an effective implementation of the law, it is worth considering the risk of unfair trading practices in software-to-software relationships in the fintech supply chain (including the threats of collusion, interdependencies or sharing of data).

The main doubt may concern if this is the end of negotiations, as there has been a remarkable consensus concerning the legitimacy of the algo-rithms and artificial intelligence as a support to dealing that has emerged throughout the financial market over the past few years. More than that, however, the book argues that software-to-software may constitute the end point of businessmen's professional evolution and the final form of negotiation and, as such, may constitute the end of market as we know it;

that is, while earlier forms of market dealing were characterized by grave defects and human irrationalities that led to their eventual inefficiency, S2S is disputably based on (all the available) logic and data and, thus, free from such fundamental internal contradictions. This is not to say that today's software is stable and effective. But its problems have been ones of incomplete implementation of the algorithms on which comparison software is founded, rather than of flaws in the use of algorithms itself. However, this book will not question the evolution of the financial market (which may be endless), nor the possibility to satisfy any needs of the society without competing for the scarce resources. It will present the unfolding of technology and finance, which has had a uniform effect on all societies that have experienced it, and then it will summarize the view of a uniform horizon of economic possibilities, as technology does not make possible the limitless accumulation of wealth, but it helps in the homogenization of the market functioning, regardless of the market participants' historical origins or cultural inheritances.

CHAPTER 2

General Observations

This research starts addressing the definition of the fintech and its fundamental elements: modernization of the environment, business innovation of supervised entities and new supply to the financial market. This assessment introduces the analysis of the definitions provided by international bodies (FSB, G20, etc.) in order to understand the usefulness of such definitions for regulatory purposes. Indeed, public intervention will consider the impact of the fintech on the supply and demand of credit, financial services and insurance in order to set up the supervision required to correct market failures and protect individual rights.

Taking into account the most recent market trends, this chapter will also consider the U.S. regulation of fintech (or rather deregulation of the alternatives to banking), in order to offer a more comprehensive view of the subject matter. A close look will take into account also the British approach, considering Brexit and its consequences, and the interest of Switzerland for establishing a regulatory haven for 'fintechers'.

Whether the post-crisis reforms seem to enhance the soundness of the financial system, then the task of supranational institutions and supervisors will be the monitoring of the adjustments of this system.

© The Author(s) 2020
V. Lemma, *FinTech Regulation*,
https://doi.org/10.1007/978-3-030-42347-6_2

2.1   A Closer Look at the Regulation
of Innovation in the Banking and Financial Industry

The current recovery is leading financial markets to new equilibriums, while the research for an effective way to operate within these markets is driving banks and financial firms towards a *material* technological shift in their business model, in order to improve their efficiency and reducing costs to compensate for the decrease of margins due to the current level of interest rates (EBA 2018).[1] This lies under the wider application of innovations made by credit institutions, aimed at gaining productivity and then at operating in the globalized market (Draghi, M. 2018b).[2] In the meantime, the rising of new (fully technologically driven) firms is increasing the number and the type of operators that let their capital circulate outside of a regulated financial market or without the involvement of a credit institution, by means of algorithms, software and platforms that are not referable to a single jurisdiction, nor to a specific system of supervision.[3] Henceforth, the legal and economic effects of widespread high-tech mechanisms within the banking and financial industry, as well as within the shadow banking system (and then within the whole market for capital), are going to be analysed. Therefore, it will be verified whether and how the policymakers consider these mechanisms, and then will be investigated the actual regulatory framework applicable to the innovation in the capital market. Thus—it is worth anticipating—the results will show the applicability of the current law and regulations to a large number of activities that are occurring on line, as well as to the organization of the firms that are managing platforms and running software able to support the circulation of capital, the provision of payment and financial services, to insure risks. Hence, the question on the need for supervising the programmers and coders that are developing the previously mentioned innovative mechanism.

Conceived during the monitoring of the shadow banking system (and, more in general, the nonbank financial intermediation that occurs on a market base), fintech has been defined by Financial Stability Board (FSB) as the technologically enabled innovation in financial services that could result in new business models, applications, processes or products with an associated material effect on financial markets and institutions and the provision of financial services (FSB 2019c, 2020).

As highlighted by the FSB, market operators are gradually replacing the top managers' decision-making process with automation due to the design of adaptive software by means of algorithmic processes (FSB 2017d).[4] The same is true for the analysis of the market trends, where human examination has been supplanted by automatic scrutiny of huge amounts of data collected in the relevant environment.[5] Both of these innovations have rapidly increased productivity to new, previously unimagined heights. Financial institutions started shifting from the offering of mass-market products (referred to a specific target market) towards the application of self-executing strategies to be able to amend their offering programmes and products in connection with the evolution of the target-market trends (by means of adaptive software and analytics algorithms), so that each specific client relationship is a market.[6]

Next chapters show these innovations and the leveraging of technology; both of them challenge the current set-up of the regulatory framework. Moreover, the rules due to the application of algorithms seem to qualify as a new form of 'soft law', which influences the behaviour of individuals that are making affairs with the support of decision-making software, business analytics and big data (EBA 2020).[7] Indeed, according to the most recent economic analysis, fintech seems to qualify as a paradigm shift, rather than a technological improvement of the banking and finance business models.[8]

From a regulatory perspective, this shift is going to have a fundamental impact on the effectiveness of the regulatory framework based on a licensing process that takes into account a 'programme of activity' setting out—inter alia—the organizational structure of the firm (as the ones implemented in the most advanced countries are) (Capriglione 2018). The same is true for the current supervisory practices, based on the analysis of the corporate structure, internal rules and human resources of the supervised entities (having regard to a set of information, the results of specific inspections and the prudential set up of their assets and liabilities).[9]

Regulators have been called to action.

Fintech empirical manifestation calls for, on the one hand, the adoption of new rules (able to avoid asymmetries in the market for capital and financial services) and, on the other, the alignment of the supervisory methodology (with the new way of carrying out banking and financial activities) (Huang, X. et al. 2009).[10] Thus, there is the opportunity for focusing the scope of this research, aiming at understanding the effectiveness of the regulatory policies adopted by governments and central banks in the recent years after the financial crises of this new millennium.

Henceforth, in the European Union (EU), article 9(2) of the European Banking Authority's (EBA's) Founding Regulation provides that this

Authority has to monitor new and existing financial activities, and this duty includes the field of activities of credit institutions, financial conglomerates, investment firms, payment institutions and electronic money institutions (considered within the EBA's FinTech Roadmap). Moreover, it refers also to any activity that qualifies as a perfect substitute of the ones aforesaid (even if such area has not been fully assessed yet) (EBA 2019b).[11]

In this context, it can be easily assumed that the regulation of fintech does not refer only to the rules provided for the application of technology by banks and other supervised firms (in order to improve the performance of their affairs), but it will also consider the opportunity of regulating any activity aimed at proposing any solution alternative to the supply of traditional banking and financial services industry.[12]

After the non-standard operations made to support an expansionary monetary policy, and under the current market conditions (related to the interest rates), traditional banking does not lead to *margins* (and revenues) able to support the costs of the organizational structure and to repay the cost of capital required to perform such activity (as equity or debt) (Draghi, M. 2018a). Economic scholars have highlighted that banks are not changing their business model, but they are restructuring themselves for the purpose of making their business more sustainable (at least in the long run) (Onado, M. 2017). A simplistic solution suggests the growth of the firms for operating the banking business,[13] but a clever analysis would probably show that this path leads to a market failure, by reaching a size the regulator should consider 'too big to be'.

Nowadays there is no doubt that the financial industry is looking at certain tech-fuelled activities that represent an alternative to banking and finance and that certain big-tech companies are trying to access the financial markets (both on the supply and the demand side). It is clear that, in the last years, the shadow banking system satisfies the needs of several firms, investors and savers (Padilla, J. and de la Mano, M. 2018). Nevertheless, the perspectives of fintech go far beyond the shadow credit intermediation process.

Besides activities and firms staying in the financial market (competing with regulated firms for the supply and demand of investing or raising capital), the priorities set forth under the German G20 presidency referred to the opportunity of transforming the shadow banking system into a resilient form of market-based finance, by addressing structural vulnerabilities in asset management through a comprehensive oversight. This supported full and consistent implementation of post-crisis reforms provided by the Directive (EU) 2019/878 (the fifth Capital Requirements Directive, CRD V) and the Regulation (EU) 2019/876 (the second Capital Requirements Regulation, CRR II), including the development of a structured framework for post-implementation evaluation of the effects of these reforms. As outlined in the EBA 2020 Work Programme, this Authority will continue delivering its fintech roadmap by monitoring financial innovation and ensuring that regulation remains technologically neutral while assessing the impact on business models and the regulatory perimeter. This requires that the existing rules will be interpreted as applicable to any entity that raises savings and provides credit and that new institutions would foster cooperation and facilitate scalability across the EU.[14] Thus, it can be expected that developed countries will promote a harmonized framework on cyber resilience testing.

It follows the intention to highlight that the most recent rules governing banking, financial services, asset management and insurance set forth the boundaries of an environment where any technology-enabled innovation in financial services cannot result in new activities (out of the scope of the above rules), but in innovative business models based on applications, processes or products that go beyond the operative standards of traditional banks and intermediaries (FSB 2017b).

However, the aforesaid rules do not address new and emerging vulnerabilities due to the technologically enabled financial innovation that results in new business models, applications, processes, products, or services with an associated material effect on financial markets (including misconduct threats and software-related operational risks) (Barnett, J. 2013).[15]

In brief, the regulator will face the fact that the traditional supervised entities have not yet changed their business model (Cantú G. et al. 2019).[16] In the meanwhile, as it will be shown with regard to fintech firms, other companies are going to compete with banks and other financial intermediaries (by performing activities alternative to those regulated in a way able to provide a *substitute* for the customers, for example the solution for financing their business, the raising of the capital to be stored for their future needs and the fulfilment of payments obligations) (Braun, B. and Deeg, R. 2019).[17] And this competition will occur whilst recent reforms have not transformed shadow banking into resilient market-based finance.

2.2   THE PATH TOWARDS A DEFINITION OF FINTECH

Beginning by summarizing that the definitions provided by international bodies clarify the characteristics of fintech, it must be considered that this phenomenon, with regard to its empirical manifestation, arise from the choice of individuals to leverage technology in order to boost their financial business. This suggests that fintech can result from the application of a discontinuous set of heterogeneous processes and equipment, resulting in an automatized coordination of financial and non-financial operations.

Doubts will be cast in the next chapters about the need to implement a systemic oversight on fintech, having (the supervisors) to provide a set of incentives and safeguards that must prevent the use of software and big data in order to take advantage of individual customers or venture into risks excluded by prudential supervision.[18] Certainly, the absence of a global legal system justifies the non-appearance of an univocal definition of fintech and a boundary of its contents, and this is an obstacle to the affirmation of a supervisory system over entities with a tech-fuelled business model.[19]

It goes without saying that at a global level there are only 'soft law based institutions' that can lightly influence this phenomenon, and that only at a regional level are there authorities entrusted with the power necessary to regulate and control such business (Cassese, S. 2000). After all, this research is looking for the proper regulation of the essence of the banking and financial business, as well as with the optimal application of the fintech innovation to the operators of the market for capital.

That said, it must be considered that the *route* towards the regulatory analysis of fintech starts from the FSB monitoring of technologically enabled innovation in financial services that—in 2016, at the time the FSB started it—has been summarized with respect to "new business models, applications, processes or products with an associated material effect on financial markets and institutions and the provision of financial services" (FSB 2019c).

It is acknowledged that the link between finance and technology began many years before the rise of the home banking,[20] and certain experiences had already been strictly regulated in the twentieth century. Anyway, nowadays, the need for new business models able to manage the tangle of relations underlying globalization has increased the use of fintech innovations, and the competition among traditional supervised entities and fintech firms is going to affect many different areas of the market for capital.

Thus, the results of the analysis of the FSB (and the ones of other international organizations that will be examined below) represent a concrete starting point for identifying the implications of fintech innovations for both financial stability and individual rights. And this will support a call to action to the supervisors, as well as the identification of the rules required for avoiding asymmetries, protecting individuals and containing the risk of defaults and contagious. From another perspective, supervisors will also consider providing specific incentives (such as the reduction of capital constraints) to support the application of fintech innovations that support financial stability (or rather to avoid the engendering of new systemic risks).

As shown in the next chapter, the common definitions of fintech include the application of autonomous or semi-autonomous systems able to make available business assistance (with one or more automated system to manage a foreordained affair or transactions, i.e. a capital call, a sale of assets, etc.), provided that the management bodies can override the aforesaid systems and take control of the firm at any time (through the execution of their powers) (FSB 2017c). In particular, fintech also provides "environmental detection capabilities" (Arner, D. W. et al. 2016), so that the software can make informed decisions for itself, such as dismiss a customer, but—nowadays—the regulatory provisions still require human overriding. The corporate bodies of management and control are still necessary; the human resources must remain alert and ready to take control of the business if the software is unable to execute the task (or if the relevant bodies decide on other actions).

It is expectable that higher levels of technology also provide the possibility to have a fully automated business, whereby a firm does not require human attention with respect to the performance of the ongoing activities, but the prompt intervention of programmers and coders to support its development or any unforeseen (or rather unprogrammed) event (Pasquale, F. A. 2019). Despite the gains in efficiencies, the exclusion of the human intervention suggests that this set-up does not comply with the current legal frameworks of the most advanced countries in the world (which provides for a management body), anyway it is not possible to exclude that it can be enacted and the existing supervisory praxis are not able to detect it (Alexander, C. and Sheedy, E. 2008).

It is also known that the "FSB's Financial Innovation Network" has been interested in fintech with respect to its potential impact on financial stability; however, the areas being analysed by FSB include credit, digital currencies, distributed ledger technology, artificial intelligence and machine learning.[21] Indeed, this analysis shows the benefits and risks of the innovation due to an increase in technology, automation and analytics, while the capital markets are still recovering from the last crises.[22] Thus, according to the law and economic approach, it is clear that the regulation of fintech may aim at helping markets in functioning satisfactorily.[23]

Financial markets are competitive, and their competition is based on the quality of the assets and the transparency of the information. Although these features are not always accurate, many analysts question what could be traded (by means of a platform) and what should be disclosed (to inform the parties that accede to such platform).[24] It is expectable that innovations enabled by the use of new technology will be recognized as a driver of change in the financial system, and the first researchers highlighted that their importance will inevitably increase, and new and emerging risks will come with them (Andresen, S. 2016).

Furthermore, technology will increase the velocity of transactions, and therefore these changes pose more frequently risks that are already effectively regulated. However, economic analysis has shown that those innovations also lead to financial stability benefits, such as automatic systems of contingency or recovery based on the analysis of big data made by predictive software.[25]

Therefore, from a legal standpoint, it is important to highlight that the first analyses did not provide a clear input to regulate *against* fintech, nor to *limit* innovation in banking and finance. Addressing the examination of this phenomenon from such perspective, it appears possible to highlight the need to balance risk and benefits, as well as the need to avoid an unfair competition among banks and financial intermediaries, on the one side, and non-supervised entities, on the other.

Be proportionate. The aforementioned considerations lead us to the conclusion that the policymakers will articulate a position on fintech, so that the regulator would be in the position to allow the development of technologies that can provide real benefits for society, whilst acting on the management of risks as they emerge.

2.3   Fintech Firms and the Unbundling of Banking, Financial Services and Insurance

The material effects of fintech have highlighted, since the early observation of this phenomenon, the possibility that innovation allows a greater efficiency of supervised entities, as well as a greater access to and convenience of services alternative and substitutional to banking, financial services and insurance (FSB 2019b).[26] This suggests the possibility that the first outcome would be a more decentralized network, in which fintech firms may satisfy a portion of the *demand* for investment, credit or risk mitigation.

Scholars have made some empirical observations of these effects (Dhar, V. and Stein, R. 2016); therefore, there is the need for a comprehensive assessment of the applicable regulatory framework, in order to verify the envisaged efficiency of the latter and suggest the opportunity to extend the scope of supervision and the task of the authorities.[27] It is worth anticipating the need for a form of supervision aimed at monitoring the development of the technological equipment both dedicated to reserved activities and able to supervise its programmer and coder.

Significant, in this regard, is the fact that fintech firms can *supply* financial services supporting lower (operating) expenses and transaction costs, due to the flexibility of their organizational structure (Lemma, V. 2016).[28]

As the following chapters show, the presence of many tech-fuelled firms operating in the market for capital is outstanding evidence, recorded by the press and relevant institutions. Anyway, it is important to outline now that the mere application of software (in lieu of an organizational structure of people and own funds) (Belleflamme, P. et al. 2013) does not have effects on the qualification of the activity as banking or finance (and therefore on the duty to request a license related to the *reserve of activity* provided in favour of *supervised entities*).[29] It is also useful to anticipate that these firms cooperate with other companies through networking web-based platforms,[30] and they offer operational solutions to their customers in order to satisfy the demand of capital, maturity transformation and risk mitigation, usually by means of special purpose vehicles (SPVs) or contracts able to link demanders and suppliers.

Oddly perhaps, considering such fintech firms, platforms and SPVs as a whole (a sort of 'black box'), the regulator shall take into account their alternative nature with respect to their referability to the business of banks, financial firms, asset managers and insurance companies.

It has been stated that "to its advocates, this wave of innovation promises a fintech revolution that will democratise financial services … and most fundamentally, financial services will be more inclusive; with people better connected, more informed and increasingly empowered" (Carney, M. 2017). However, it should be clear that, within the system under consideration, any "business entity" needs a license to perform reserved activities (Cranston, R. 2002),[31] even if a set of independent companies whose software work together can supply substitutes for such activities. Therefore, from a law and economics perspective, it is possible to consider on autonomous entities and, as such, on fintech firms operating in any sector of the financial market (as long as they do not perform reserved activities or obtain a license) (FSB 2019a).

Hence, the research for a common definition of fintech highlights the need for identifying the authorities entrusted with the task to supervise a rapidly expanding landscape where certain firms perform activities (outside the boundaries of the traditional supervision) that concerns savings, credit and money (FSB 2017b). Above and beyond, it is worth anticipating that European Central Bank (ECB) considers fintech bank those having "a business model in which the production and delivery of banking products and services are based on technology-enabled innovation" (ECB 2018b).

That said, it is important to think through the possibility that the activities of such fintech firms will unbundle banking into its core functions of: settling payments, performing maturity transformation, sharing risk and allocating capital. This possibility suggests the opportunity to assign each function to an independent fintech firms, such that they act as payment service providers, aggregators and robo-advisors, peer-to-peer lenders and innovative trading platforms: entities that are adopting new technologies in an effort to reinforce the economies of scale and scope of their business models.[32]

Despite this, after any unbundling, a chain is weaved and a new market arises.

In this perspective, the investigation will refer to the juridical order of this new market for fintech goods (e.g. cryptocurrencies), information (e.g. big data) and services (e.g. analysing, programming and coding) keeping in mind that demand and supply will look for the elements required to develop an integrated process able to perform activities related to investments, credits/debits and risks. As shown in the following paragraphs, the regulators have not yet approached the web-based platforms able to support the trading of big data, application programme interfaces (APIs), algorithms and decision-making software.[33] Moreover, it has to be verified if the current approach based on disclosure and transparency can last or rather there is the need for specific rules aimed at regulating this sort of the customers' delegation of their decision-making process to machines set up by third parties (with respect to the investment of their funds or request for loans, even if the provision of an initial comparison can be qualified as advisory or brokerage).[34]

This leads to the analysis of the ways to this 'market for fintech' used by credit institutions, financial firms and insurance companies.[35] The focus on the demand placed by such supervised entities suggests the need for accurate internal controls, designed to avoid that a business model (drawn on certain machinery management mechanisms) allows the abuse of their bargaining power, in lieu of using big data and advanced analytics to *tailor* their products and services on the customers' needs (EBA 2020).[36] Indeed, it is clear that the involvement of supervised entities requires also public intervention, which must take into account that the reserved activities are not simultaneous, continuous or permanent, but rather they follow the course of a chain made by the sequential stages provided by the software. Thus, this leads to oversight programmers and coders, which shall not be considered as mere third-party providers, but as the professionals able to support the unbundling of the reserved activities into stages, as well as the suppliers of the tools required for the functioning of the 'fintech chains'.[37]

This helps in identifying a new industry, whose radical innovations challenge the capacity of the current supervisory authorities to regulate and control their high-tech business, even if it refers to well-known supervised activities (such as banking, financial services, asset management and insurance).[38] At the same time, it shall be considered that large, established technology companies ('BigTech') are the new entrants into the financial services sector, and that such BigTech firms could be in position to alter the universe of financial services providers (due to their bargaining power and customer knowledge, based on the intense use of business analytics and big data).[39] The same is true for the legal sector, where the BigTech shall provide standardized contracts and services, whose quality would be granted by the coding of the software and not by the professionalism of human lawyers (even if the latter could advise the programmers).[40]

Transaction costs will often enter into this analysis. Generally, they are used to explain the prevalence of firms over the individual in the market (Posner, R. 2007).[41] The impact of fintech on the negotiation of the suppliers' performance, their duration and payments is relevant. And it reduces the costs of buying an output in a market system (Pinna, A. and Ruttenberg 2016). It is not possible to extend such consideration to the direct employment of subordinate workers, whose burden involves compensation, incentives, information and educational costs. So fintech boosts financial activities that can be coordinated by a combination of market transactions between separate firms, and high-tech tools can command these firms within an informal organization (of money, people and data).

This casts the doubt that market-based intermediation processes are not an efficient method of coordination. Surely, the possibility to link independent firms through the *use* of decision-making software and business analytics overrides the consideration that a central planner could coordinate economic activities better than the market can (Posner, R. 2007).[42]

Bearing in mind that the ultimate goal of unbundling should be to increase efficiency, the will of supervised entities can be easily understood with respect to the possibility of increasing their profit.[43] However, it is important to consider that economic scholars suggested that business is organized in firms because inputs are primarily labour and capital, and these inputs could be organized as a whole under the current well-experienced schemes provided by the legislators.[44] Therefore, it is convenient to assume that firms operate under a sort of 'standard contract', and this economizes the transactions costs. Hence, question whether the leveraging of digitalization would promote a change in the operational structure of firms, and how the regulatory approach will go straight to this point.

On the other hand, it shall be considered that in wholesale markets, banking and financial services have already moved from intermediated trading (involving 'dealers', either via voice or electronically) to non-intermediated trading (based on a fully electronic order-driven mechanism of inputs and feedbacks) (FSB 2017b). Algorithmic trading and high-frequency trading software grow rapidly; as a result, the most recent technological improvements have led not only to the growth of multilateral trading venues, but also to changes to wholesale payment, clearing and settlement infrastructure.[45] Hence, it is possible to show the possibility of new regulatory standards set forth for blockchain applications and distributed ledgers, and firms involved in their functioning. These standards should ensure gains in the accuracy, efficiency and security of processes across payments, clearing, and settlement (and then the supervision of certain specific financial stability issues created by these developments, as shown in the next chapters).[46]

It is good to point out, then, that unbundling will influence the extent to which certain financial technologies are adopted and the system is transformed. Therefore, this analysis can easily focus on the role of regulators in seeking to ensure that standards provided for reserved activities (by the current regulatory framework) are upheld and that the integrity of the market will be protected by any threat arising by the use of new technologies.

2.4   The Regulation of Business Analytics: From Risk Assessment and Threat Detection to Decision-Making Using Big Data

In recent years, regulatory challenges have also arisen from the use of data science, with a particular boost due to the application of software able to collect, analyse and develop data and, therefore, to *support* the management and/or to *execute* its tasks.[47] In general, economic scholars refer to this aspect as an outcome of 'business analytics', and the study of the latter suggests to the policymakers the directions useful to restate rules that were formulated in light of older technologies and systems.[48] Anyway, from a regulatory perspective, it must be borne in mind that the use of such software follows a choice of the managers (and in particular the ones entrusted with strategic supervision), and that any software follows directions provided by its programmers and coders (or rather the management of the company that set the exact rules and specifications for the computer by writing the relevant source codes).[49]

This allows us to question the mere classification of the software-houses as ancillary service providers,[50] which is critical to develop a clear, rational legal scheme for the various decisions that emerge from the use of these software-based business analytics (Grossman, R. and Siegel, K. 2014).[51] Indeed, it is likely that the current regulatory standards of banking and finance provide that the corporate governance and the actions of management are placed under the monitoring of the relevant supervised authorities.[52] These regulatory standards take into account that the supervised entities were able to directly manage their business and that their employees were fully responsible for the *identification* of the target market, the *design* of the products and the *relationships* with the customers (Allenspach, N. and Monnin, P. 2006).

Now, these standards must be challenged by considering that the banking and finance 'value chain' is now being impacted across its components by fintech (FSB 2017d).[53] This refers to the choice of the target market, the structuring of the products and way of enacting the relationships with the costumers (European Banking Federation 2018). The following chapters will show the role of business analytics in the structuring of the supply curve of the supervised entities (with respect to the market share and the product features), and therefore the relevant need for regulation in order to safeguard the financial stability from the risk of correlation (arising from the widespread use of the same software by such entities). However, it is appropriate to anticipate that—with respect to the customer relationships—the current rules do not take into account the externalities produced by the software applied for identifying the customer, detecting his/her needs (by analysing the traces he/she involuntary left on the web) and leveraging these needs to sell bank products and services (EBA 2019b).[54]

It is worth highlighting that the common approach to business analytics focuses on the consideration of the issues around data protection. Since the last century, the first analysis concerned the mis-protection of the customers' data, as well as the new way of gathering a broad range of financial and non-financial data of the customers from, and sharing across, a wider set of sources (as it happens by collecting the data of a payer by analysing the account of the beneficiary).[55] All these aspects have been amplified by the digitalization of such data.[56]

The first findings with respect to the compliance of the business analytics with civil liberties, privacy rights and data-gathering laws (Rodotà, S. 1973) will be taken into account (but the analysis will not be limited to consider). From this perspective, the research for the legal standards—able to protect data (and the relevant individual rights), in a way able to increase financial stability, according to the principle of the regulation of the security and data-protection standards—will also support the protection of customers, savings and market functioning. Hence, it is possible to expect that the legislator will enact a form of cooperation (or coordination) among authorities entrusted with the task of data protection and financial supervision, as well as the provision for a new supervisory task, focused on the capacity to control the software used for business analytics.

In general, the recent researches did not challenge the actual capacity to understand the current technological elements of banking and finance business (Sacco Ginevri A. 2017).[57] However, this research highlights that such developments change potential macroeconomic and macrofinancial dynamics.[58] Therefore, there is the need that specific resources support the understanding and assessment of new risks (associated with the increase of tech-fuelled systems and the evolution of reserved activities that will emerge from the latter) and disruptions to systemically important markets.

The various considerations made so far concerning the regulation of business analytics follow the idea that programmers are rational operators. Therefore, the research is based on the 'if-thenness' of the mechanisms involved in decision-making processes. It is possible that certain software would include deviation from these mechanisms, being based on a randomized approach to the market opportunities or rather on an arbitrageur access to the financial market.[59] Therefore, the regulator will take into account the possibility that the fondness (of the result arising from the fintech mechanisms) is lacking. This challenges the key assumption of absolute efficient and rationale functioning of business analytics. Anyway, to the extent that these deviations from rationality are unclear, it is important that supervisors have access to the source code of such software, and it is important that the regulation does not assume that software is any more rationale than its programmers are (Cave, J. 2016).

Despite the fact that the general principles underlying financial market regulation suggest avoiding asymmetries, the proposal for a 'sandbox' able to accomplish the performance of business analytics and its implications for the aggregate level of cyber and operational risk in the financial system must be taken into account.[60] Indeed, business analytics models could become a source of systemic threats because they provide self-responses to critical economic choices based on what could be highly correlated to the ones provided by other operators who use the same software or rely on the same data. While a regulatory 'sandbox' would help in exploring such capacity experimentally, a prompt intervention should verify whether the use of such business analytics can be fully implemented within traditional banking activities and if it should be regulated as such. It is easy to understand the differences between the systemic risks associated with human management and the ones due to the self-executing credit intermediation process (that follows the directions of a programme) and to credit algorithms (Fenwick, M. et al. 2017).

This evidence advocates a *chain of questions* with regard to the protection of individual rights (related to savings), the safety and soundness of existing supervised entities, the mandate of the relevant authorities (both for financial stability and monetary purposes) (Draghi, M. 2017), in order to understand the incentives and the burdens able to drive business conduct towards the maximization of wealth.

At the same time, however, customers have access to comparison tools, such that they can rely on the support of business analytics, so the relationship seems to shift from a business-to-consumer (B2C) to a software-to-software (S2S) paradigm.

In emphasizing this point of view, it is important to observe an important threat with respect to the provision of software both on the buy-side and the sell-side. This is not dealing only with the risk of *infidelity*, but with the opportunity that the knowledge of the customer of one side will influence the provision of services to the other customers.[61] Indeed, this could lead to the risk that the software house will look to increase its profits without taking care of the social welfare and market stability. Therefore, a good reason to support regulatory intervention aimed at supervising firms providing business analytics in order to prevent, monitor and pursue any abuse of their fintech capabilities.

In this process, as the following analysis on fintech operations will show, systemic risks will evolve due to the interaction of the software used by both supervised entities and their customers. And, as the relevant economic analysis suggests, the probability of loss refers also to a disparity between the estimated and actual correlation between the results of such software. To conclude by summarizing: changes to customer selection of their 'home bank' could influence the stability of funding; self-executing programmes for risk assessment and threat detection could affect market functioning; investment choices made by software and models could affect macroeconomic dynamics. This requires a common regulatory framework, to ensure that these innovations develop by maximizing the wealth and minimizing the systemic risks.[62]

2.5   The Interest in Cryptocurrencies

The scope of this analysis also includes the use of technological innovation able to support the circulation of cryptocurrencies alternative to the money issued by central banks. Within this scope, the research will refer to such cryptocurrencies as assets, tokens or goods in order to distinguish their difference to sovereign currencies, legal tender or money.

It is worth declaring now that the analyses on the shortcomings of cryptocurrencies and on the difficulties in considering them as "money"[+] will not be repeated. [63] As the next chapters show, we'll take into account that individuals could use these assets with the expectation of storing value or enacting payments, although (generally) they are not backed by any public authority (Scitovsky, T. 1969),[64] nor supported by the legal duty to accept them as form of payment; however, they are as volatile as any other speculative asset. This approach helps the development of the research on both the regulatory approach to the activities of the operators that digitally issue and withdraw non-sovereign cryptocurrencies (and on the legal framework applicable to such business), and the responsibility to ban or regulate cryptocurrencies with respect to consumer protection, saving safeguards and financial stability.[65]

Moreover, quite recently, a new private cryptocurrency has been announced (scheduled to be offered in 2020) which has caused concern for the threats resulting from the handling of an asset able to record the personal data connected with is circulation (see Mersch, Y. 2019; Ang, A. and Piazzesi, M. 2003). Hence the need for clarifying the legal and regulatory challenges that cryptocurrencies pose, as well as the position of any central bank, in light of its mandate.

Indeed, currently, the interest in the effects of fintech arises with respect to the relevance of individual rights involved in the transaction of the cryptocurrencies, rather than the possibility that these would influence the effects of the monetary policies.[66] In other words, this research will go deep into the topic of cryptocurrencies in order to understand whether (and how) governments are going to oversee private cryptocurrencies. There is the possibility that—although entering into circulation via the retail trade—these cryptocurrencies could support the collection of savings (to be protected) or the granting of credit (to be controlled) (Troisi, A. 2014).[67]

In this respect, it will be taken into account the need for protecting savings and for controlling credit (as the functioning of most advanced economies requires), not only with respect to their (currently low) monetary significance nor to their capacity to influence the effectiveness of sovereign monetary policies (EBA 2019a).[68] On the contrary, regulators must take care of the individual rights of people who invest in such assets, considering also the influence of artificial intelligence and machine learning in portfolio management (IMF 2016; FSB 2017a).[69]

Furthermore, this research will consider the rights of end-users to spend online and in any other places that accept cryptocurrencies or deposit such money (in any virtual warehouse eligible for such a goal), in order to verify whether the use of these currencies can rely on the same rights that people exercise with the sovereign ones.[70] In this context, the analysis will be extended to the current regulation of the shared record-keeping and processing system, and to the possibility of the introduction of a 'global ledger account' as a form of public intervention aimed at reducing the regulatory asymmetries in the market for money.

These analyses lead us to clarify the possibility that the technology applied in the cryptocurrencies would be useful for anti-money laundering oversight, due to the possibility to record every digital transaction that occurs (kept secure through cryptography). Thus, it is possible to anticipate the expectation that the resilience of the financial system should take advantage of a system that records the exchange of payments down in a ledger (even if there is not yet a central authority or official body assigned with the task of updating this ledger and keeping track of all the transactions). It seems that, in this system, public intervention shall control a peer-to-peer network, being maintained in terms of strict protocols and multiple copies of the same ledgers. This leads to a positive judgement on the envisaged effects of an un-centralized system and a set of information shared among an indefinite number of private operators because this system seems to provide more data than the current one (based on national central 'financial intelligence units' cooperating with other authorities).

Therefore, the additional regulatory task of monitoring these multiple ledgers and their synchrony will be investigated, taking into account the risk arising from the lack of safeguards when a digital currency transaction is made (which shall be announced in the network so that any particular transaction can be recorded by all the operators, making the ledger verifiable). It seems expectable that a deeper analysis will reveal the need for other interventions (such as any improvement in the anti-money laundering regime of fintech firms) related to the regulation of the records made by every digital currency transaction that occurs (kept secure through cryptography) (Blemus, S. 2017; Trautman, L. J. 2016).

In addition, it will be verified whether central banks can apply fintech to sovereign money, in order to increase the efficiency of their traditional activity. It shall be borne in mind that the Euro itself was initially an electronic currency used by financial markets and for cashless payments (in 1999). Only three years later euro banknotes and coins entered into circulation in the form of physical notes, with physical security features regarding their authenticity (different from cryptography) and centralized ledgers (for dematerialized transactions, to ensure the possibility of circulating or stoking them with the traditional mechanisms and to avoid that payments are not made to different parties using the same money). Hence, the evolution of personal devices, new software, blockchain technology and cryptography will be considered as a whole, and as a whole it requires both regulation and control. This would help in ensuring that fintech and cryptocurrencies would not be able to put people's savings at risk, jeopardize monetary policies, reduce transparency, security, and the efficiency of transactions that occur in the capital market (ECB 2020).[71]

From a regulatory standpoint, it is possible to observe that the FSB undertakes regular monitoring of the financial stability implications of cryptocurrencies and other crypto-assets. It is worth recalling the conclusion (published in 2018) of the FSB on the absence of a material risk to global financial stability due to such assets and on the speed of market developments.[72]

However, the FSB's analysis did not conclude for the absence of a need for protection (FSB 2017b), but it also pointed out that crypto-assets raise several broader issues that require public intervention in order to ensure (together with consumer and investor protection) strong market integrity protocols, incentives for tracking their circulation and international measures to prevent tax evasion or forum shopping. Hence, Let us restate the above by highlighting the need for the safety and soundness of any platform or channel that offers the possibility of supporting the exploration of further innovations in the use of legal tender.

2.6   INDIVIDUAL RIGHTS, SOCIAL WELFARE AND REAL ECONOMY AS BENEFICIARIES OF FINTECH

The goals of public intervention in capital markets have been analysed since the beginning of studies on public policy (Green, A. R. 2016). There is no doubt that nowadays such intervention aims at improving the social welfare, the development of the real economy and the safeguarding of financial stability (Lagarde, C. 2019). This research will not recall the generally agreed-upon conclusions of the governments in the countries with the most advanced economies after the end of the 'short twentieth century', nor the instances for the 'enlightenment now'.[73] However, these goals must be achieved also in the fintech environment, even if their safeguards require actions different from those developed for traditional banking and finance (Lemma, V. 2018).

This perspective implies that public interventions look for a greater resilience of the global financial system. With respect to the technological shift, this also requires verifying whether the previous safeguards need to be extended to the new fintech business models or rather they require new rules and supervising methodologies.[74]

Bearing in mind that regulatory action could achieve inefficient results if the cost of the supervision is more burdensome than its benefits (Cooter, R and Ulen, T. 2008), this analysis started by considering that the mere extension of the prudential regulation, to operators who are engaged in the market-based operation (of banking, finance or insurance) through fintech, involves a commitment of "own funds" and therefore the burden of additional transactional costs.[75] The same is true for the duty to employ resources with a minimum level of technical ability and financial professionalism.[76] In this context, fintech is growing under an unjustified asymmetry between the pervasive controls on supervised entities and the absence of supervision on market-based mechanisms of credit intermediation (Bessone, M. 1978). (Hence, it will be highlighted that public intervention cannot consider fintech out of the scope of financial supervision and, at the same time, cannot exempt it from the backstops ensuring the smooth functioning of the market).[77]

It must be mentioned the assessment on fintech market developments made by the FSB, with respect to the potential implications for social welfare. The material effect associated with fintech has the potential to increase market access, the range of product offerings and convenience while also lowering costs to customers (FSB 2019a). Consequently, it is conceivable to imagine an increase in the aggregate outcome of the market, as well as a more efficient and resilient financial system (because of both greater competition and diversity in lending, payments, insurance and trading). However, this will also put pressure on supervised entities, and this pressure could lead to additional risk-taking by their managers.[78]

Thus, it is also expectable that the regulator will select those incentives that promote a relationship between the aforementioned supervised entities and fintech firms able to be complementary and cooperative in nature. Indeed, the implementation of new regulatory systems will increase the possibility of reaching gains in efficiency, which warrants ongoing attention from authorities.

All the above leads to the need for considering the access to fintech services and to the new networks as a right or a freedom.[79] According to this consideration, the duty (to secure such a right or to place restraints on governments) requires action, probably in the form of legislation. As previously mentioned, the further evolutions of the European Union might be more favourable to the supervision over fintech, given that a clear separation between the tech-fuelled business and the traditional one does not exist, nor is there any gateway able to prevent the relations between fintech firms and supervised entities. The political choice to make the banking sector safer than others (even if the "bail-in" of Directive 2014/59/EU has jeopardized this safety) and the success of the shadow banking system (due to spontaneous forces of the market and the free decisions of investors) are acknowledged.[80] However, any entities dealing with fundamental individual rights (as savings and property) would not proceed with the deliberate assumption of high levels of risks that are incompatible with the overall stability of the financial system (Alpa, G. and Bessone, M. 1976).

This is the background of a regulatory analysis of—useful or necessary—public supervision over fintech in order to ensure that the freedom of setting up the business model should not allow any damage to the market or the customers. It can be easily anticipated that this analysis leads to the identification of the need to restructure the current authorities, in order to be able to control the tech-fuelled solutions applied by supervised entities (based on big data and software) and the supply of high-tech assets and services (alternative and substitutional to the reserved activities). Hence, the following chapters will show the key economic drivers and technological mechanisms that are boosting the market-based financing, whose contents suggest that the efficiencies of fintech should be the rationale for the development of the new intermediation process. Therefore, there is the need to focus on the role of the international bodies, national governments and central banks in the oversight of financial innovation and its application through tools and instruments provided by the evolution of personal devices, network infrastructures and software. Focusing on innovation in banking and finance, the research will highlight that the evolution of the European regulation suggests that public intervention will extend its scope beyond the use of new technologies by supervised entities towards credit intermediation involving entities and activities outside the regular banking system.

Common drivers of fintech innovations suggest the development towards an ever-evolving ecosystem of financial institutions and markets, whose institutional forms vary over time and across borders (Merton, R. and Bodie, Z. 2005). Other innovations are seeking to change how information is shared within the industry, and smart contracts seem to be able to support automatic transactions, business analytics and self-executing operations. With these changes come predictions that direct finance will be simplified and will avoid the transactional costs of intermediation as well as the social welfare.

Shifting consumer preferences and evolving technological tools may have implications for the future structure of the financial market; anyway, these could lead to a more efficient provision of financial services (although asymmetric pricing strategies could benefit one side of the market more strongly). This is the first rationale background for promoting by regulating the application of fintech to banking and non-bank financial industry (Evans D. and Schmalensee R. 2007).

Individual rights can benefit from the reduction of costs, as far as they support the access to, and convenience of, financial services, with obvious positive effects on the financial inclusion of customers (including savers, consumers and small-medium enterprises) and on the sustainable economic growth of the real economy.[81] These conditions show that innovations in financial services have the potential to lead to greater efficiencies, by means of productivity enhancing technologies, such as robo-advice and other tools that are able to strengthen business models in dealing with financing issues and facilitate improvements in decision-making processes.[82] From this perspective, the consideration above refers to the models that supervised entities and customers use, with respect to the use of algorithms to assess risks, creditworthiness and investment opportunities.[83]

Let me state in my own terms what now seems to be the agreeable elements in the benefits arising from fintech. I will then compare these benefits with the actual assumptions of both global regulators and other international supervisory bodies about the broader benefits and risks (to be evaluated and weighed against one another) in order to identify the potential implications of further developments of fintech for individuals' rights, social welfare and the real economy. It should be clear that, within the innovations under consideration, the worthiness of fintech depends on the actual advances in market trends, as well as on the net effects of the trade-offs inherent in innovation. However, the concept of fintech can be helpful in any accurate analysis of the forthcoming regulation, as it can help in measuring the impact of innovations on the methods of business models in use and, in particular, on the interconnections between the progress in finance and the output of the market for capital.

2.7   Financial Recovery and Innovation: The Need for a Regulatory Assessment of Fintech

From a regulatory perspective, the analysis of this phenomenon will verify whether a *wider* application of financial technology will promote an increase in the efficiency of the market for capital, provided that it protects the relevant individual rights and financial stability.[84]

As anticipated at the beginning of this chapter, nowadays, the current economic and financial recovery is turning the *cycle*, and this suggests to firms the exploration of a new path for growth, through the leverage of technology innovations and financial opportunities.[85] Therefore, this research aims at understanding the regulatory framework able to avoid asymmetries in the previously mentioned innovations and opportunities.

According to the results of the recent economic analysis of regulation enacted after the crises of this third millennium,[86] fintech alternatives (to banking and finance) will compete in the financial market for both the supply of services and the demand for capitals. Hence the need for understanding the rights to protect, and then—as anticipated in the previous paragraph—the role of the international bodies, national governments and central banks (in the supervision of the new market trends, assets and tools that follow the evolution of personal devices, network infrastructures and software). This leads to the opportunity for an assessment on the 'legal status' of fintech firms, as their intensive use of financial technology should reduce the effectiveness of the current public supervisory mechanisms.

In light of the above, the current assessment will consider the role that the programmers and coders are playing in the financial market, and then identify the legal requirements capable of applying accurate control over the risk-taking and moral hazards of such players.[87] Taking into account the results of the recent research on the shadow banking system published by ECB, the efficiencies of fintech should be the rationale for the development of the market-based intermediation processes (Ordonez, G. and Piguillem, F. 2019).[88] Hence, those technological mechanisms should be the key economic drivers for the success of the aforementioned system, but cannot be the technique to *decrease* the burden of the requirements set forth by the regulator for the performance of the reserved activities.[89]

It is essential to underline that a coherent legal framework has not been established yet. According to this perspective, the regulator will be called to select its approach to fintech, by considering to standardize the application of high-tech mechanisms to the processes of financing and credit transformations, to supervise the programmer and coder of such mechanisms and/or to prearrange the allocation of risks and benefits among the intermediaries and their customers (Lastra, R. 2013).

With respect to the allocation of risks and benefits, it is important to highlight that the regulator would address the responsibility of individuals in developing the fintech business, as well as ban the use of bargaining power by one firm to exert influence over others (FSB 2017d), so that the outcomes of this business will improve the social welfare (Simoncini, A. 2016).

According to the above, the choice of regulators is not between free market and public regulations, because fintech is not a failure of the market's self-regulation, but a feature that can both increase the output of the market and jeopardize its stability.[90] These essential (and related) characteristics helps in understanding whether national governments will enact public supervision or provide for a compensation in case the use of fintech damages the customers. Indeed, it is difficult to doubt that a fintech firm would be able to compensate its victims (in case a systemic risk occurs due to its conduct). This doubt suggests that public supervision over fintech should be more effective than compensation, if the cost of prevention does not overcome the benefit of financial innovations.

Moreover, the preference for public supervision is strengthened by the possibility that the risks and the losses are very small in individual value, but very large in number. This event is likely in the financial market, due to the high frequency of operations and the huge amount of operators. Besides, the connection between the loss of a particular customer (or a class of customers) and the default of a fintech tool may be difficult to ascertain or its causal relationship may be attenuated by other events that occur in the relevant market. Furthermore, losses and instability should be due to a combined effect of numerous fintech tools and operators applying different fintech solutions.

Consequently, these problems support preventive regulation and control.[91] Such kind of intervention must be continuous and, therefore, may be costly. Even if there are difficulties in measuring the cost of financial instability, there is no doubt that this cost is a burden more than the one of supervision. Hence, this suggests to focus on future consequences of un-regulation of fintech by aggregating risks over time, and the relevant clarification will cast the doubt that the limits of cost-benefit analysis (as a regulatory tool) prevent us from concluding for the need of public intervention.

The normative use of economics should lead governments to consider the strengths and weaknesses of fintech. This suggests the use of the criterion of wealth maximization in order to use its results in the regulatory decision-making process, but the application of such criterion to fintech is foreseeable, because of the choice of the discount rate (while the commercial interest rates are negative).

Although there are fintech tools able to give supervising authorities enough information about their functioning, the underlying problem is the capacity to operate with cognitive limitations in cases of proliferation of data, warnings and communications (from the supervised entities to the supervisors).[92] This problem is not limited to the capacity of collecting and analysing data, but it extends its relevance to the costs involved in organizing the supervisory mechanisms required for providing an adequate response to the input received.

In brief, the evidences recorded during the current financial recovery seem to suggest setting new principles (or rather the opportunity to recast the current ones) to ensure that software pursues the safe and sound management, as a means to increase the outcome of the market within the limit of financial stability and inclusion. It is worth to anticipate that the following chapters will remark the opportunity that national government reserves the provision of 'high-tech services' to supervised entities that fulfil certain requirements.

Anticipating another conclusion, additional economic determinants for the regulation of fintech are going to be shown in the next chapters, given that the financial crisis—in intensifying the opportunities for interaction and dialogue between policy and administrations—has constituted a factor of acceleration for an intervention aimed at stabilizing the supervisory devices that, now, ensure the regularity of finance and the effectiveness of its relationship with the real economy.

2.8   Fintech as an Alternative to Banking and Finance

The following chapters will represent the results of research started by addressing the questions about the usefulness of a *common* definition for 'fintech' and its fundamental elements (the acts of fintech, the organizational structures of fintechers, etc.). This is the reason why this book is taking into account the digitizing of finance with respect to the increasing use of technology (in the production and commercialization of financial instruments and banking activity).[93] This will help us in understanding the public intervention executed during the years of the financial recovery and the perspective of a wider supervision on the alternatives to banking and finance (ECB 2018d).

This should not be surprising, given the fact that those innovations were disseminated more recently than the others were. However, given the growth of this type of financial technology in recent years, it is important to address any threats to financial stability. It is important to highlight that, since the beginning of the rise of fintech, scholars expected further regulatory updates, and in this respect specific areas were mentioned as priority: activities (i.e. issuance of e-money and its systems of transfer, mobile payment accounts and services), tools (i.e. means of identification and certification, passwords) and agreements (with respect to interoperability, confidentiality and integrity of information, securing applications, security infrastructure and follow-up, security system assessment). Besides that, the common approach provided that these areas may refer to specific procedures for obtaining a license (ECB 2018b). [94]

As a preliminary remark, it is important to investigate the points of observation chosen by the regulators, in order to get information on the developments of fintech and its economic relevance.[95] Sharing these points of observation will help us in understanding the definitions provided by international bodies and European authorities, in order to assess their attitude to drive professional and supervisory entities in dealing with this phenomenon. In this regard, the consideration of the US regulatory (or rather de-regulatory) approach to Fintech is offering a more comprehensive view of the subject matter. In this context, it is essential to outline that, given the efforts at the supra-national level (i.e. the ones consolidated in the European Commission's Action Plan on FinTech, dated 8th March 2018), a uniform legal framework has not been established yet, neither in the European Union, nor in the countries included in the Group of Twenty (G20).

This analysis began from the results of economic scholars interested in understanding the key economic drivers and technological mechanisms of market-based financing structures that rely on tech-fuelled tools (taking into account the results of the most recent research on the latest developments of the shadow banking system). In this context, financial innovation will improve the opportunities in banking and finance, as well as in the performance of activities alternative to them. This implies taking into account the role of hardware, software and technology used to support or enable such opportunities and alternatives.[96]

All the above suggests analysing the regulations on the application of technology to the intermediation processes that occur in the capital market (directly or through the intervention of an intermediary).[97] It also highlights the need for clarifying the current legal principles applicable to fintech within the EU internal market. As shown in the following chapters, the underlying idea refers to a lawful use of technology, and therefore it excludes any alternative or substitute that is able to avoid the prudential standards and constraints set by the regulator. Hence, this idea allows us to welcome fintechers that are willing to enter in the financial market by applying for a traditional license, even though they support the production and delivery of banking products and services with technology-enabled innovative business models (ECB 2018b).[98] This is not the proposal of an extensive interpretation of the Article 14 of EU Regulation no. 1024 of 2013, but a prudent approach to the capital markets would suggest presenting the programme of the fintech activities to the competent authority in order to verify whether such programme represents banking or not.[99]

Indeed, the rules set forth by EU regulator do not approach fintech as a new industry, but as a new business model for firms operating in the market for capital (Lener, R. and Parrillo, G. 2018). Therefore, the ECB's role will ensure that fintechers are properly authorized and have in place risk-control frameworks for anticipating, understanding and responding to the risks arising by executing their operations through tech-fuelled tools.

From a regulatory perspective, the role of the Financial Stability Board is remarkable, and its monitoring is supporting the analysis (on the technologically enabled innovation in financial services), which relates to the material effects of fintech on financial markets. Such monitoring helped scholars to identify the areas of financial services that could be affected in the coming years and in understanding the relevant implications for financial stability. It follows the need for setting up the regulatory principles that shall protect the benefits of fintech and contain its risks.

Consequently, there is the possibility that fintech provides the possibility to perform certain activities alternative to banking without setting up a bank. In addition, this allows that such activities fall outside the scope of prudential supervision (by going through the shadow credit intermediation processes). Therefore, the analysis of the relevant contractual arrangements will help in understanding the application of high-tech mechanisms to the processes of financing and credit transformations, and this will clarify the allocation of risks and benefits among the firms and their customers. This requires us to highlight the role of private law, in order to weigh the responsibility of individuals in developing the 'acts of fintech' (taking into account the sanctions provided in order to avoid that the outcomes of these operations go against the common benefit). Hence the need to verify the level of protection (of individual rights or market stability), and therefore the possibility to conclude that those activities require specific constraints, in order to oversight and limit a complex situation that can repeat an indefinite number of operations (in a specific sequence, which goes from lending or financing to asset management, risk mitigation, credit enhancement and maturity transformation). Indeed, this repetitiveness is able to produce individual damages, as well as domino effects and systemic risks.

It goes without saying that fintech business models require the application of a special procedure. Indeed, fintech innovations do not affect only the need for protection (of the market stability, the individual rights and the money's value), but they imply also the application of new high-tech mechanisms to several stages of capital circulation, and therefore this influences the way supervision on these institutions is to be executed.[100]

According to the above, there is no doubt that fintech firms performing supervised activities fall within the scope of the current supervision (even if such activities rely on tech-fuelled tools).[101] Indeed, there are difficulties in excluding a priori inefficiencies due to the operational risk arising from third-party fintech service providers, cyber risks and, more in general, macrofinancial risks due to fintech activities.

The same should be true for fintechers that provide services or perform activities that have not been considered by the regulator, such as the management of web-based platforms supporting individuals in trading credits or sharing financial opportunities, and whether or not such activities can jeopardize the rights of individuals or the market stability.[102] From this perspective, it is necessary to address the corporate governance of fintechers, provided that the criterion of the safe and sound management of 'other people's money' shall be applied to any automatized decision-making processes and therefore to their programmers or coders (i.e. people who create the relevant software).[103]

That said, it is necessary to investigate the impact of the financial technology evolution on the market for money, by considering that central banking is not yet driven to use fintech to support their monetary policies, nor to hinder the development of tech-fuelled instruments alternative to sovereign money (i.e. cryptocurrencies). Whether fintech will lead the tools used in monetary policymaking, then it will be necessary for banking and finance.[104]

Therefore, nowadays, it is useful to move from the consideration that fintech provide the opportunity of executing initial coin offerings of non-sovereign cryptocurrencies in exchange for goods or sovereign money. This implies a clear commitment to adopt measures for protecting savings invested in such kinds of instruments, and therefore the choice to supervise the entities that *promise* that cryptocurrencies will preserve their value, together with the adoption of backstops required for avoiding theft, plagiarism and fraud.[105]

Indeed, this study aims to achieve a better understanding of the regulatory intervention on the credit transformation processes that find direct execution by means of any fintech mechanism, transaction or firm. It is useful to conclude this chapter by anticipating that the findings shown in the following ones will suggest that fintech benefits the business related to the circulation of capital, even if this circulation flows in the shadow banking system (i.e. it circulates according to different set of parameters from those established by prudential supervision).

NOTES

1. European Banking Federation. 2018. "The Future of the Banking Industry. Dialogue with the Banking Industry on ESCB Statistics", Frankfurt, 16 march, where it has been represented that "Further digitisation is needed to provide better services and financing to consumers & businesses".

2. Draghi, M. 2018. "Monetary policy in the euro area", Speech by the president of the ECB, ECB Forum on Central Banking, Sintra, 19 June, where the author highlights, "In 2017, growth in the euro area turned out stronger than we had anticipated: the annual growth rate in the fourth quarter was the fastest for a decade. But in 2018, growth has moderated and, so far, has come in below our expectations. In the latest Eurosystem staff projections, growth for 2018 has been revised down by 0.3 percentage points This has prompted some questions about the sustainability of the ongoing expansion, which is unusual at such an early stage of the cycle."

    See also Lagarde, C. 2019. "Transcript of International Monetary Fund Managing Director Christine Lagarde's Opening Press Conference, 2019 Spring Meetings", Washington D.C., 11 April, who begun by recalling: "I was reminded by my staff of a lovely line by Mark Twain. Bear with me." "In the spring, I have counted 136 different kinds of weather inside of 24 hours." "I am not suggesting that the global economy is going through the 136 different iterations, from synchronized growth, to synchronized slowdown; but it feels a little bit like that at this point in time."

3. This analysis follows my previous study on the shadow banking system, as to be the outcome of the deregulation process begun in the twentieth century, whereby my conclusion summarizes that, even if this phenome-

non was aimed at reanimating the real growth of the economy and speeding up the circulation of money, the underlying idea was that a highly regulated financial market slowed down business and decreased the wellness of society. See Lemma, V. 2016. "The Shadow Banking System. Creating Transparency in the Financial Markets". London. p. 182.

4. It is worth summarize the publications that, since 2017, are sharing the results of FSB's monitoring on fintech. The research refers, in particular, to FSB 2017. "Chair's letter to G20 Finance Ministers and Central Bank Governors ahead of their Baden-Baden meeting", 17 March where the following priorities have been outlined: "Transforming shadow banking into resilient market-based finance, including by addressing structural vulnerabilities in asset management; making derivatives markets safer by progressing the post-crisis reforms to over-the-counter derivatives markets and delivering coordinated guidance on central counterparty resilience, recovery and resolution; supporting full and consistent implementation of post-crisis reforms, including the development of a structured framework for post-implementation evaluation of the effects of reforms; and addressing new and emerging vulnerabilities, including misconduct risks, as well as those stemming from the decline in correspondent banking and from climate-related financial risks".

5. It is worth considering FSB. 2017. "FinTech credit. Market structure, business models and financial stability implications". Report prepared by a Working Group established by the Committee on the Global Financial System (CGFS) and the Financial Stability Board (FSB), 22 May, whose initial remark pointed out that "FinTech credit—that is, credit activity facilitated by electronic platforms such as peer-to-peer lenders—has generated significant interest in financial markets, among policymakers and from the broader public. Yet there is significant uncertainty as to how FinTech credit markets will develop and how they will affect the nature of credit provision and the traditional banking sector".

6. The above consideration may be completed by recalling Chen, J. M. 1996. "The Last Picture Show (On the Twilight of Federal Mass Communications Regulation)", Minnesota Law Review, Vol. 80, No. 6, who highlighted that the regulators ignored the economics of a technologically driven industry at their peril. So, in this article, the author outlines antitrust-inspired regulatory principles for designing tomorrow's mass media markets, by considering that the emergence of gargantuan media conglomerates, each large enough to control vast amounts of programming but none powerful enough to conquer the entire industry, requires a comprehensive rethinking of mass communications and its regulation.

7. This research remarks the results of Lemma, V. 2006. "Soft law e regolazione finanziaria," Nuova giurisprudenza civile commentata, f. 11,

p. 600 ff.; see also Gersen and Posner. 2008. "Soft Law", U. of Chicago, Public Law and Legal Theory Working Paper, no. 213, where the authors clarify that soft law consist of "rules" issued by bodies that do not comply with procedural formalities necessary to give the same an "hard legal status," but nonetheless these rules may influence the behaviour of other law-making bodies and of the public.

8. It is worth adding that the current topic is addressed by European Commission's Action Plan on how to harness the opportunities presented by technology-enabled innovation in financial services (FinTech), 8 march 2018.

9. This research includes a reference to ECB 2018. "Banking Supervision publishes results of 2018 SREP"; and EBA 2014. "Guidelines on common procedures and methodologies for the supervisory review and evaluation process (SREP)", which—drawn up pursuant to Article 107(3) of Directive 2013/36/EU—are addressed to competent authorities and are intended to promote common procedures and methodologies for the supervisory review and evaluation process (SREP) referred to in Article 97 et seq. of Directive 2013/36/EU and for assessing the organisation and treatment of risks referred to in Articles 76 to 87 of that Directive 2013/36/EU. See also EBA 2018. "Final Report. Guidelines on the revised common procedures and methodologies for the supervisory review and evaluation process (SREP) and supervisory stress testing".

10. This analysis recalls Huang, X. and Zhou, H. and Zhu, H., 2009. "A Framework for Assessing the Systemic Risk of Major Financial Institutions". "*Journal of Banking and Finance*", Vol. 33, No. 11, pp. 2036–2049; the authors propose a framework for measuring and stress testing the systemic risk for a group of major financial institutions. The authors expressly stated: "Our methodology is closely related to but in sharp contrast with the Financial Stability Assessment Program (FSAP) conducted by IMF in recent years, the Supervisory Capital Assessment Program (SCAP) implemented by the U.S. regulatory authorities earlier this year, and the European-wide stress testing program sanctioned by the Committee of European Banking Supervisors (CEBS). These supervisory stress testing programs are primarily based on confidential banking information and adopt the historical stress scenarios as adverse as in the Great Depression era. In contrast, it is possible to rely on public banking information from the financial markets and use the statistical bootstrapping method to consistently assess the downside extreme outcomes. Therefore our approach is more applicable by the private sector in measuring and managing the systemic risk exposures of large complex banking institutions."

11. In particular, EBA. 2019. "The EBA 2020 Work Programme" shows an output related to: (i) thematic reports on the monitoring of financial innovation and targeted reports on new developments; (ii) thematic reports on business model changes, and risks and opportunities from FinTech, innovative products and emerging trends; (iii) activities regarding the FinTech Knowledge Hub (workshops, round tables, seminars); (iv) delivering regulatory products and technical advice to the Commission on the topics requested, particularly those included in the Commission's FinTech action plan; (v) supporting the forum of European Innovation Facilitators and related Activities.

12. The text recalls the considerations of Allen, F and Babus, A. 2008. "Networks in Finance", "Wharton Financial Institutions Center Working Paper" No. 08-07, who remark that "Modern financial systems exhibit a high degree of interdependence. There are different possible sources of connections between financial institutions, stemming from both the asset and the liability side of their balance sheet. For instance, banks are directly connected through mutual exposures acquired on the interbank market. Likewise, holding similar portfolios or sharing the same mass of depositors creates indirect linkages between financial institutions. Broadly understood as a collection of nodes and links between nodes, networks can be a useful representation of financial systems".

13. It is worth adding to the above considerations that Levine, R. and Lin, C. and Peng, Q. and Xie, W., 2019. "Communication within Banking Organizations and Small Business Lending". "NBER Working Paper No. w25872", investigated how communication within banks affects small business lending and exploits shocks to evaluate the impact of within bank communication costs on small business loans.

14. It is possible to add a reference to EBA. 2019. "The EBA 2020 Work Programme", whereby it is expressly mentioned that EBA will continue to strengthen the European Forum of Innovation Facilitators (EFIF), and will also develop thematic work on crypto assets and distributed ledger technology, and assess the potential implementation of a harmonised framework on cyber resilience testing.

15. It refers to Barnett, J. 2013. "Copyright Without Creators". "USC Law Legal Studies". Paper No. 13-7 whereby is clarified that "copyright is justified by an alternative rationale: it supports the profit-motivated intermediaries that bear the high costs and risks involved in evaluating, distributing and marketing content in mass-cultural markets. This 'authorless' rationale is consistent with the intermediated structure of mature mass-cultural markets and accounts for long-standing features of copyright law that have conventionally been dismissed as mere transfers from consumers to media interests. The digital transformation of mass cultural mar-

kets, which has been accompanied in some media by a decline in production and distribution costs but no change or even an increase in screening and marketing costs, challenges and clarifies the intermediary-based rationale for copyright. Even in digitized content markets, copyright plays a critical role by enabling intermediaries to select freely from the full range of transactional structures for most efficiently bearing the costs and risks of screening, producing, distributing and marketing content to a mass audience".

See also Krainer, R. 1999. "Banking in a Theory of the Business Cycle: A Model and Critique of the Basle Accord on Risk Based Capital Requirements for Banks". *SSRN Research Paper no. 177708.*

16. In addition, Cantú G. and Claessens, S. and Gambacorta, L. 2019. "How Do Bank-Specific Characteristics Affect Lending? New Evidence Based on Credit Registry Data from Latin America". "BIS Working Paper No. 798", which focuses on the recent changes in banking systems and how bank-specific characteristics have affected credit supply in five Latin American countries.

See also Arnaboldi, F. and Claeys, P. 2008. "Financial Innovation in Internet Banking: A Comparative Analysis" Available at SSRN 1094093.

Recently, Choi, B. 2019. "What is the Social Trade-off of Securitization? A Tale of Financial Innovation". *SSRN Research Paper no. 3440653,* which conducts a macroeconomic welfare analysis of securitization in a real business cycle model with a banking sector, besides the fact that the author models securitization as an optional interbank funding channel that credibly reduces the diversion ability on borrowed funds and increases operation costs on loan assets. It shows that securitization allows banks to increase the asset size while sacrificing the rate of return per unit of assets.

17. Moreover Braun, B. and Deeg, R., 2019. "Strong Firms, Weak Banks: The Financial Consequences of Germany's Export-Led Growth Model". *SSRN research Paper no. 3395566,* which shows that business lending by banks has increasingly been constrained on the demand side, reducing the power—and relevance—of banks vis-à-vis German industry.

18. This path will go through all the following chapters and will be developed in the final chapter, Chap. 7. Underlying this analysis there is a clear reference to the current actions of the main regulators, that is, EBA. 2019. "The EBA 2020 Work Programme".

19. All the above recalls Zaring, D. and Bignami, F. 2016. "Comparative Law and Regulation. Understanding the Global Regulatory Process". Northampton, MA, USA; the authors highlighted the regulatory state across the globe, focusing on American exceptionalism, EU regulation and East-Asian perspective and represents that "the domain of regulation has expanded dramatically over the past decades. In the United States,

regulation—defined as rules that govern private market and social activity and that are made and enforced largely by specialized administrative agencies—has always been a prominent mode of state action. By contrast, in Europe, Latin America, and other parts of the globe, regulation has only recently become a pervasive and distinct form of government activity with the retreat of both state ownership of industry and the taxing and spending policies of the welfare state. At the same time the regulatory process has become global".

20. It is clear that self-executing customer access to banking has been opened up with the introduction of the first automated teller machines of the 1960s, the arrival of online banking and brokerage in the 1980s, and the rapid rise of mobile banking since the new millennium begun, as pointed out by Carney, M. 2017. "The Promise of FinTech—Something New Under the Sun? Speech given by the Bank of England Chair of the Financial Stability Board Deutsche Bundesbank G20 conference on Digitising finance, financial inclusion and financial literacy", Wiesbaden 25 January.

21. See FSB. 2017. "Artificial intelligence and machine learning in financial services. Market developments and financial stability implications", 1 November, where this board highlights that "AI and machine learning tools are being used to identify new signals on price movements and to make more effective use of the vast amount of available data and market research than with current models. Machine learning tools work on the same principles as existing analytical techniques used in systematic investing. The key task is to identify signals from data on which predictions relating to price level or volatility can be made, over various time horizons, to generate higher and uncorrelated returns".

   See also Andersen, T. G., Bollerslev, T., Diebold, F. X., Labys, P., 2003. "Modeling and forecasting realized volatility". "Econometrica", 579–625.

22. This part of the research refers to Andresen, S. 2016. "Remarks given by the Secretary General of the Financial Stability Board, at the Chatham House conference on The Banking Revolution: Global Regulatory Developments and their Industry Impact", whereby it is represented that "in September 2008 in a building minutes from here, 4000 people at Lehman Brothers cleared their desks following the bank's failure. Much worse was to come for millions of others, with the events at Lehman Brothers precipitating a significant economic crisis the costs of which we are still feeling today. These costs include significantly higher public debt, increased unemployment and substantial, and likely unrecoverable, output losses, particularly for advanced economies. It is with this background that the FSB was established by the G20 in 2009 to coordinate the work

of national authorities and international bodies to promote financial stability at a global level".

23. See, in addition to the above, in general, Krugman, P. 2012. "End This Depression Now!", New York for an effective review of the "economic slump" that has afflicted the US, the European Union, and many other countries in the recent years; see also Posner, R. 2009. "A Failure of Capitalism". Cambridge. p. 41 ff. on the banking crisis of 2008 and the descent into depression.

  See also Posner, R. 2007. "Economic Analysis of Law", New York, p. 419 ff. and p. 465 ff., and Cooter, R and Ulen, T. 2008. "Law and Economics", Boston p. 91, where there is an analysis of the key elements of transaction costs, and p. 95 ff., where the authors focus on the level of them and the appropriate legal rule.

24. Let us add that Moenninghoff, S. and Wieandt, A. 2013. "The Future of Peer-to-Peer Finance". "Zeitschrift für Betriebswirtschaftliche Forschung", p. 466 ff. noted that "the financial risks stemming from peer-to-peer financial transactions are borne by the participants and span all major financial risk types. The effect of this risk assumption by individuals on economic growth and stability and required regulation will decide over the future of peer-to-peer finance. If it is not desirable, peer-to-peer finance requires a risk management mechanism—either funded or unfunded. The increasing use of peer-to-peer finance by institutional investors indicates a gradual movement towards funded risk management, transforming peer-to-peer platforms into institution-to-peer platforms".

  In this respect, Evans, D., 2014. "Economic Aspects of Bitcoin and Other Decentralized Public-Ledger Currency Platforms". "University of Chicago Coase-Sandor Institute for Law & Economics Research Paper No. 685" recalled that "a number of internet-based digital currency platform based on decentralized public ledgers have started since the introduction of the blockchain concept by the founder of Bitcoin in 2008" and represented that". "It is possible that public ledger platforms are more efficient than other alternative platforms for conducing financial transactions, but as of now the proposition is based on apples-to-oranges comparisons compounded with speculation. Competition will lead to better incentive and governance systems for public ledger platforms".

25. This analysis includes also the considerations of Angel, J. J. and Harris, L. and Spatt, C. S. 2010. "Equity Trading in the 21st Century". "School of Business Working Paper No. FBE 09-10"; the authors suggested that "Increasing automation and the entry of new trading platforms has resulted in intense competition among trading platforms. Despite these changes, traders still face the same challenges as before. They seek to

minimize the total cost of trading including commissions, bid/ask spreads, and market impact". And concluded that "'Front running orders in correlated securities should be banned' because of 'Make or take' pricing, the charging of access fees to market orders that 'take' liquidity and paying rebates to limit orders that "make" liquidity, [which] cause distortions that should be corrected".

26. Furthermore FSB. 2019. "Implementation and Effects of the G20 Financial Regulatory Reforms. 5th Annual Report" highlights that "the global financial system has continued to grow and the supply of financial services has also become more diversified, including through the expansion in NBFI and through financial technology (FinTech) innovations".

27. All the above recalls that Dhar, V. and Stein, R., 2016. "FinTech Platforms and Strategy". "MIT Sloan Research Paper No. 5183-16" refers that "a major consequence of the Internet era is the emergence of complex 'platforms' that combine technology and process in new ways that often disrupt existing industry structures and blur industry boundaries". The effects mentioned in the body of the text refer also to the evidence that "these platforms allow easy participation that often strengthens and extends network effects, while the vast amounts of data captured through such participation can increase the value of the platform to its participants, creating a virtuous cycle. While initially slow to penetrate the financial services sector, such platforms are now beginning to emerge". It is worth highlighting that the authors provide "a taxonomy of platforms in Finance and identify the feasible strategies that are available to incumbents in the industry, innovators, and the major internet giants".

28. As highlighted before, this is a system in which a process takes place that can provide further (and additional) funding than that allowed by banking (subject to the constraints of prudential regulation); together with the possibility of increasing the resources available to meet the needs of the real economy (without undermining the global financial stability); see Lemma, V. 2016. "The Shadow Banking System. Creating Transparency in the Financial Markets". London. p. 38.

29. In particular, ECB. 2018. "Guide to assessments of licence applications. Licence applications in general" expressly clarifies that "Licensing of credit institutions is essential for the public regulation and supervision of the European financial system. Confidence in the financial system requires public awareness that banks can only be operated by entities that are licensed to do so. ... At the same time, licensing should not hinder competition, financial innovation or technological progress. ... This Guide applies to all licence applications to become a credit institution within the meaning of the Capital Requirements Regulation (CRR), including, but not limited to, initial authorisations for credit institutions, applications

from fintech companies, authorisations in the context of mergers or acquisitions, bridge bank applications and licence extensions".

ECB. 2018. "Guide to assessments of fintech credit institution licence applications" whose background refers to the fact that the ECB considers fintech banks to be those having "a business model in which the production and delivery of banking products and services are based on technology-enabled innovation".

30. In addition, Allen, F and Babus, A. 2008. "Networks in Finance", "Wharton Financial Institutions Center Working Paper" No. 08-07, reviewed the recent developments in financial networks, highlighting "the synergies created from applying network theory to answer financial questions". Further, the authors propose several directions of research, by expressly remarking the following: "First, we consider the issue of systemic risk. In this context, two questions arise: how resilient financial networks are to contagion, and how financial institutions form connections when exposed to the risk of contagion. The second issue we consider is how network theory can be used to explain freezes in the interbank market of the type we have observed in August 2007 and subsequently. The third issue is how social networks can improve investment decisions and corporate governance. Recent empirical work has provided some interesting results in this regard. The fourth issue concerns the role of networks in distributing primary issues of securities as, for example, in initial public offerings, or seasoned debt and equity issues. Finally, we consider the role of networks as a form of mutual monitoring as in microfinance."

31. See also Capriglione, F. 2019. "Fonti Normative" In *Manuale di diritto bancario e finanziario*, Padova; Giorgianni, F. 2005. "Definizione di attività bancaria e analisi del linguaggio" *Rivista del diritto commerciale e del diritto generale delle obbligazioni*, pt. 1, p. 897 ff.; Molle, G. 1978. Review at "Francesco Capriglione, Intervento pubblico e ordinamento del credito" *Banca borsa e titoli di credito*, 1978, p. 123.

32. Once again, this analysis refers to Carney, M. 2017. "The Promise of FinTech—Something New Under the Sun? Speech given by the Bank of England Chair of the Financial Stability Board Deutsche Bundesbank G20 conference on Digitising finance, financial inclusion and financial literacy", Wiesbaden 25 January.

33. See Benzell, S. and LaGarda, G. and Van Alstyne, M. W. 2018. "The Impact of APIs in Firm Performance". "Boston University Questrom School of Business Research Paper No. 2843326", which—using proprietary information from a significant fraction of the API tool provision industry—explores the impact of API adoption and complementary investments on firm performance and include external as well as internal

developers. The authors, in particular, represent that "Categorizing APIs by their orientation, we find that B2B, B2C, and Internal API calls are heterogeneous in their association with financial outcomes" and "the fact that API calls are associated with contemporaneous increases in firm value suggest that data flow at the boundary of the firm can predict financial performance".

34. See Baker, T. and Dellaert, B. G. C. 2018. "Regulating Robo Advice Across the Financial Services Industry" "Iowa Law Review", p. 713; the authors highlight the potential to lower the cost and increase the quality and transparency of financial advice for consumers. However, they conclude that such tools "pose significant new challenges for regulators who are accustomed to assessing human intermediaries. A well-designed robo advisor will be honest and competent, and it will recommend only suitable products. Because humans design and implement robo advisors, however, honesty, competence, and suitability cannot simply be assumed. Moreover, robo advisors pose new scale risks that are different in kind from that involved in assessing the conduct of thousands of individual actors". This leads the authors to questioning that regulators need to be able to answer about them, and the capacities that regulators need to develop in order to answer those questions.

35. This part of the research considers also Zetzsche, D. A. and Buckley, R. P. and Arner, D. W. and Barberis, J. N., 2017. "Regulating a Revolution: From Regulatory Sandboxes to Smart Regulation" *Fordham Journal of Corporate and Financial Law* represented that "financial regulators are increasingly seeking to balance the traditional regulatory objectives of financial stability and consumer protection with promoting growth and innovation".

36. The above considerations may include the conclusion of Meyer, T. 2014. "From Contract to Legislation: The Logic of Modern International Lawmaking" in *Chicago Journal of International Law*, p. 559 ff.; the author argued that "In contractual lawmaking, states are free to expel holdouts from negotiations and make commitments among a smaller group of the willing. Moving from contract to legislation removes this freedom. … The increased holdup power created by legislatures is a feature, not a bug. This holdup power is beneficial because it allows states to enforce legislative bargains: deals in which a state makes concessions in one negotiation in exchange for another state's concessions in a later related negotiation. Such iterative negotiations—found in free trade talks, environmental regimes, and efforts to establish a robust international criminal law—are a hallmark of modern international law-making. … This rationale for holdup power explains a number of puzzles in international law. In particular, it explains why international legislatures have not

adopted robust majoritarian voting and further clarifies how international institutions enforce international law, which critics often claim is unenforceable".

It is useful to recall Barnhizer, D. D. 2007. "Bargaining Power in Contract Theory". "MSU Legal Studies Research Paper No. 03-04", which analysed the role that legal conceptions of bargaining power play in defining the jurisprudence of contract law. In particular, the author highlighted that "contract law cannot ignore bargaining power asymmetries", and from this consideration he highlighted that "unchecked power imbalances in the bargaining context soon become indistinguishable from naked coercion, and at some level the imbalance undermines both the consent of the weaker party and the legitimacy of the resulting bargain". This helps us in recalling the debate over the role of the legal doctrine of inequality of bargaining power that has largely focused on whether and how the government should intervene in individual private agreements to correct perceived power disparities. Hence, it is worth quoting again the author: "While bargaining power disparities may be difficult to analyse in these individual cases, legal conceptions of bargaining power may also be useful in defining the boundaries of contract law. Specifically, where both parties to a transaction possess some ability to affect the outcome of that transaction, they may take advantage of the relatively flexible and unregulated regime of private contract. ... At this macro level, bargaining power provides both a positive and normative explanation for why some promises are enforceable in contract and others are regulated under relatively more intrusive public orderings."

See also Spence, D. B. and Gopalakrishnan, L. 1999. "The New Political Economy of Regulation: Looking for Positive Sum Change in a Zero Sum World". "University of Texas at Austin, Graduate School of Business Working Paper No. 990415"; the authors argue that in the context of political conflict over policy changes, participants in these bargaining processes view positive sum policy changes in zero-sum terms. That is, they bargain strategically, using their power to veto these positive-sum changes in order to extract further policy concessions from other stakeholders. This revelation has important implications for the future of the regulatory reform concerning fintech.

37. It starts from the approach published by ECB, Pinna, A. and Ruttenberg, 2016. W., "Distributed Ledger Technologies in Securities Post-Trading Revolution or Evolution?" "ECB Occasional Paper No. 172", whose paper analyses the main features of distributed ledger technologies that could influence their potential adoption by financial institutions and discusses how the use of these technologies could affect the European post-trade market for securities. In particular, this paper discusses three

potential models of how market players could adopt DLTs for performing core post-trade functions. The DLT could be adopted: (i) in clusters, (ii) collectively, or (iii) peer to peer. Indeed, according to the authors, the evaluation of the three adoption models assumes that they are all equally compatible with the regulatory framework. It shows that, assuming this to be the case, they would each have different advantages and costs.

However, this analysis will move forward and will look to the supply due to DLTs' application, which will be considered as the output of a 'chain' rather than a mere 'black box', even if certain evidences suggest that it comes from the output of a 'chain of black boxes'.

38. Let us recall the outcome of de Weijs, R. J., 2011. "Harmonisation of European Insolvency Law and the Need to Tackle Two Common Problems: Common Pool & Anticommons", "Centre for the Study of European Contract Law Working Paper Series No. 2011-16"; the author's results can be considered in order to highlight that 'anticommons' present themselves in a situation in which there are several owners or entitled parties, and each of the parties has it within its power to block the use by others. Should anticommons behaviour in fintech chains go unchecked, creditors as a whole will be harmed. So, there is the need for understanding that this collective process may not be sabotaged by a single party.

39. The text considered that Carney, M. 2017. "The Promise of FinTech— Something New Under the Sun? Speech given by the Bank of England Chair of the Financial Stability Board Deutsche Bundesbank G20 conference on Digitising finance, financial inclusion and financial literacy", Wiesbaden 25 January pointed out that "the result has been a significant expansion of credit availability with low default rates (albeit ones not yet tested by an economic downturn)" by considering the following evidences: "In a number of G20 countries, new business models draw on big data and advanced analytics to tailor products and services to customers and discipline credit underwriting. For example, peer-to-peer ('P2P') lending has grown rapidly in recent years from a small base. In the UK, P2P lending now represents about 14% of the new lending to SMEs. Estimates suggest that more than half of these credits were unlikely to have been provided by existing banks. Other platforms are allowing firms to borrow against invoice receivables, drawing on data gathered directly from software their customers use to manage their accounts payable. Some of the more radical innovations underway are in emerging economies. E-commerce platforms in China, for example, are using algorithms to analyse transaction and search data to improve credit scoring."

40. See Simshaw, D. 2018. "Ethical Issues in Robo-Lawyering: The Need for Guidance on Developing and Using Artificial Intelligence in the Practice

of Law". "*Hastings Law Journal*"; the author noted that "Among other impacts, AI has the potential to increase access to justice in the self-help, individual, and corporate law firm markets by lowering costs and expanding services to untapped markets".

According to the author, a prominent question in early literature on AI in law is whether these services constitute the unauthorized practice of law, and "there is currently no comprehensive guidance for attorneys on how AI should be developed, adopted, and used in ways that conform to a lawyer's ethical obligations".

41. It recalls Posner, R. 2007. "Economic Analysis of Law", New York, p. 419, footnote 1.

42. This is remarked by Posner, R. 2007. "Economic Analysis of Law", New York, p. 420.

43. See Hughes, J. P. and Mester, L. J., 2008. "Efficiency in Banking: Theory, Practice, and Evidence", which gives an overview of two general empirical approaches to measuring bank performance and discusses some of the applications of these approaches found in the literature.

See also Albertazzi, U. and Gambacorta, L. 2006. "Bank Profitability and the Business Cycle" *Bank of Italy Economic Research Paper No. 601*, which—before the last crises—studied the link between business cycle fluctuations and banking sector profitability and how this link is affected by institutional and structural characteristics. This work estimated "a set of equations for net interest income, non-interest income, operating costs, provisions, and profit before taxes, for banks in the main industrialized countries and evaluates the effects on banking profitability of shocks to both macroeconomic and financial factors". They also identified differences in the resilience of the Euro and non-Euro banking systems and related them to the characteristics of their financial structure.

44. Let us recall the classic Keyenes, J. M., 1953. "The General Theory of Employment, Interest, and Money" (San Diego, edition 1964), p. 158.

45. The reference goes to Harvey, C. R. and Rattray, S. and Sinclair, A. and van Hemert, O., 2017. "Man vs. Machine: Comparing Discretionary and Systematic Hedge Fund Performance" *Duke I&E Research Paper No. 2017-01*; the authors analyse and contrast the performance of discretionary and systematic hedge funds starting from the evidence that systematic funds use strategies that are rules based, with little or no daily intervention by humans. They found out that "for the period 1996–2014, systematic and discretionary manager performance is similar, after adjusting for volatility and factor exposures, i.e., in terms of their appraisal ratio. It is sometimes claimed that systematic funds' returns have a greater exposure to well-known risk factors ... however, ... for discretionary funds (in

the aggregate) more of the average return and the volatility of returns can be explained by risk factors".

Kakushadze, Z. and Yu, W. 2019. "Machine Learning Risk Models" *Journal of Risk & Control*, p. 37 ff.; the authors give an explicit algorithm and source code for constructing risk models based on machine learning techniques (in which the resultant covariance matrices are not factor models).

In this respect, Creamer, G. G. and Freund, Y. 2010. "Automated Trading with Boosting and Expert Weighting" *Quantitative Finance*, Vol. 4, No. 10, p. 401 ff., proposed a multi-stock automated trading system that relies on a layered structure consisting of a machine learning algorithm, an online learning utility and a risk management overlay. The authors highlighted that "One of the strengths of our approach is that the algorithm is able to select the best combination of rules derived from well-known technical analysis indicators and is also able to select the best parameters of the technical indicators".

It has also to be recalled Golub, A. and Glattfelder, J. and Olsen, R. B., 2017. "The Alpha Engine: Designing an Automated Trading Algorithm" *High Performance Computing in Finance, Chapman & Hall/CRC Series in Mathematical Finance*, which proposed a new approach to algorithmic investment management that yields profitable automated trading strategies. This paper shows that a trading model design can be the result of a path of investigation that was chosen decades ago. In particular, the authors represent the following: "Back then, a paradigm change was proposed for the way time is defined in financial markets, based on intrinsic events. This definition lead to the uncovering of a large set of scaling laws. An additional guiding principle was found by embedding the trading model construction in an agent-base framework, inspired by the study of complex systems. This new approach to designing automated trading algorithms is a parsimonious method for building a new type of investment strategy that not only generates profits, but also provides liquidity to financial markets and does not have a priori restrictions on the amount of assets that are managed."

46. In this respect, it is worth considering that Yadav, Y. 2014. "How Algorithmic Trading Undermines Efficiency in Capital Markets" *Vanderbilt Law Review* and *Vanderbilt Law and Economics Research Paper No. 14-8* argues that "the rise of algorithmic trading profoundly challenges the foundation on which much of today's securities regulation framework rests: the understanding that securities' prices objectively reflect available information in the market".

In particular, the author made two claims "First, complex algorithms foster a separation between the trader and her ability to fully control the operation of the algorithm. Algorithms can execute many thousands of trades in milliseconds, crunching vast quantities of data and dynamically interacting with other traders in the process. This intelligence makes it difficult for a trader to fully predict how an algorithm might behave ex ante and near-impossible for her to track and control its activities in real-time. Secondly, though markets have traditionally relied on informed fundamental traders to decode complexity, these actors now possess reduced incentives to perform this function in algorithmic markets."

47. It should be added a reference to FSB. 2017. "Financial Stability Implications from FinTech. Supervisory and Regulatory Issues that Merit Authorities' Attention", 27 June, with respect to the fact that "The majority of regulatory changes and clarifications have been made in the areas of payments, capital raising, and to a lesser extent investment management as many of these economic functions naturally fit within existing regulatory regimes".

48. In particular, Ezrachi, A. 2018. "EU Competition Law Goals and the Digital Economy". *Oxford Legal Studies Research Paper No. 17/2018* goes deep into new competition dynamics in the digital economy, and raises doubts on the normative scope of competition enforcement. In brief, the competition nature of these doubts has become common in the face of new business strategies, new forms of interaction with consumers, the accumulation of data and the use of big analytics. Indeed, the author seeks to outline the goals and values advanced by European Competition law, and their application to digital markets.

49. Moreover, Mittelstadt, B. and Allo, P. and Taddeo, M. and Wachter, S. and Floridi, L. 2016. "The Ethics of Algorithms: Mapping the Debate" *Big Data & Society* highlighted that "more and more often, algorithms mediate social processes, business transactions, governmental decisions, and how we perceive, understand, and interact among ourselves and with the environment. Gaps between the design and operation of algorithms and our understanding of their ethical implications can have severe consequences affecting individuals as well as groups and whole societies."

50. See the results of Lemma, V. and Thorp, J. A. 2014. "Sharing Corporate Governance: The Role of Outsourcing Contracts in Banking" *Law and Economics Yearly Review*, Vol. 3, pt. 2, p. 357 ff., with respect to a specific conclusion highlighting that the principles set by the European regulation appear to be designed to prevent that outsourcing translates into an 'escape from responsibility', and then that competent authorities shall make further steps towards a proper configuration of supervisory practices on outsourcing.

51. Moreover, Grossman, R. and Siegel, K. 2014. "Organizational Models for Big Data and Analytics" *Journal of Organization Design*, p. 20 ff.,

introduced a framework for determining how analytics capability should be distributed within an organization. According to the interpretation of the authors, this "framework stresses the importance of building a critical mass of analytics staff, centralizing or decentralizing the analytics staff to support business processes, and establishing an analytics governance structure to ensure that analytics processes are supported by the organization as a whole".

52. See Mülbert, P. O. 2010. "Corporate Governance of Banks after the Financial Crisis—Theory, Evidence, Reforms" *ECGI—Law Working Paper No. 130/2009*; the author presents "the supervisors' financial stability perspective as illustrated by the Basel Committee's guidance, and concludes with a discussion of the functional relationship between corporate governance and banking regulation/supervision: Whereas banking regulation/supervision acts as a functional substitute for debt governance, equity governance benefits less from such regulation/intervention. Put succinctly, shareholder interests and supervisors' interests do not run exactly parallel, not even from a long-term perspective".

53. In particular, it should be noted that FSB. 2017. "FinTech credit. Market structure, business models and financial stability implications". Report prepared by a Working Group established by the Committee on the Global Financial System (CGFS) and the Financial Stability Board (FSB), 22 May, explains in more detail that "the nature of FinTech credit activity varies significantly across and within countries due to heterogeneity in the business models of FinTech credit platforms. Although FinTech credit markets have expanded at a fast pace over recent years, they currently remain small in size relative to credit extended by traditional intermediaries. A bigger share of FinTech-facilitated credit in the financial system could have both financial stability benefits and risks in the future, including access to alternative funding sources in the economy and efficiency pressures on incumbent banks, but also the potential for weaker lending standards and more procyclical credit provision in the economy".

54. Furthermore, EBA 2019. "The EBA 2020 Work Programme", which anticipates that "the EBA will continue delivering its FinTech roadmap by doing further work on the monitoring of financial innovation, continuing to strengthen the network of innovation facilitators, doing thematic work on open banking and distributed ledger technology, and implementing a harmonised framework on cyber resilience testing".

55. Let us recall some relevant papers on this topic from the twentieth century in order to point out the grounds of this analysis: Giorgianni, M. (1970). "La tutela della riservatezza" *Rivista trimestrale di diritto e procedura civile*, 1970, fasc. 1, p. 13 ff.; Graziadei, E. 1971. "Privatezza: rimedi vecchi e offese nuove" *Giurisprudenza italiana*, fasc. 1, pt. 4,

p. 1 ff.; Bessone, M. 1973. "Segreto della vita privata e garanzie della persona. materiali per lo studio dell'esperienza francese" *Università di Genova Facoltà di giurisprudenza Annali*, p. 1 ss.; Perlingieri, P. 1974. "Intervento alla tavola rotonda di bari su tecniche giuridiche e sviluppo della persona", *Diritto e giurisprudenza*, fadc. 2, p. 17 ff.; Consolo, G. 1975. "Informazione, riservatezza e calcolatori elettronici. aspetti sociologici e giuridici" *Amministrazione e politica*, fasc. 2–3, p. 240 ff.; Ichino, P. "Diritto all' informazione, diritto alla riservatezza, e diritto al segreto nei rapporti di lavoro" *Rivista giuridica del lavoro e della previdenza sociale*, 1977, fasc. 9, pt. 1, p. 541 ff.; Bevere, A. 1978. "Il caso della Banca d'Italia e la legalità del sistema economico" *Critica del diritto*, fasc. 15, p. 84 ff.; Martorano, F. 1978. "Convenzione di assegno e segreto bancario" *Banca borsa e titoli di credito*, fasc. 2, pt. 1, p. 217 ff.; Alpa, G. 1979. "Privacy e statuto dell'informazione" *Rivista di diritto civile*, fasc. 1, pt. 1, p. 65 ff.; Nuzzo, A. "Sul c.d. diritto alla riservatezza. Nota a pret. roma 25 gennaio 1979" *Rivista di diritto industriale*, 1979, fasc. 2, pt. 2, p. 25 ff.; Ferri G. B., 1981. "Privacy e identità personale. nota a Pret. Roma 30 aprile 1981. Pret. Roma 11 maggio 1981" *Rivista del diritto commerciale* fasc. 7-12, pt. 2, p. 379 ff.; Gambaro, A. 1981. "Falsa luce agli occhi del pubblico" *Rivista di diritto civile*, 1981, fasc. 1, pt. 1, p. 84 ff.; Marchetti, P. 1981. "Le offerte pubbliche di sottoscrizione e la legge 216" *Rivista delle società*, fasc. 6,pp. 1137 ff.; Zaccaria, R. 1982. "Diritto all'informazione e riservatezza" *Il diritto delle radiodiffusioni e delle telecomunicazioni*, fasc. 3, p. 527 ff.; Zeno Zencovich, V. 1983. "Telematica e tutela del diritto all'identità personale" *Politica del diritto*, fasc. 2, p. 345 ff.; Flick G. M., 1988. "Informazione bancaria e giudice penale: presupposti di disciplina, problemi e prospettive" *Banca borsa e titoli di credito*, fasc. 4-5, pt. 1, p. 441 ff.; Clarich, M. 1996. "Diritto d'accesso e tutela della riservatezza: regole sostanziali e tutela processuale" *Diritto processuale amministrativo*, 1996, fasc. 3, p. 430 ff.; Markesinis, B and Alpa, G. "Il diritto alla "privacy" nell'esperienza di "common law" e nell'esperienza italiana" *Rivista trimestrale di diritto e procedura civile*, fasc. 2, p. 417 ff.; Ubertazzi, L. C. 1997. "Riservatezza informatica ed industria culturale" *AIDA*, pt. 1, p. 529 ff.; Salanitro, N. 1998. "Privacy e segreto bancario", *Banca borsa e titoli di credito*fasc. 2, pt. 1, p. 228 ff.; Bianca, C. M. 1999. "Tutela della privacy (l. 31 dicembre 1996, n. 675). Note introduttive (Pt. I). Commento alla l. 31 dicembre 1996, n. 675." *Le nuove leggi civili commentate*, fasc. 2-3, p. 219 ff.; Stagno d'Alcontres, A. 1999. "Informazione dei soci e tutela degli azionisti di minoranza nelle società quotate" *Banca borsa e titoli di credito*, fasc. 3, pt. 1, p. 314 ff.

56. See Chap. 4.

57. All the above suggests to consider the approach of Sacco Ginevri A. 2017. "Proxy Advisors, attività riservate e conflitto di interessi" *Contratto e impresa*, p. 11 ff.

58. See Cortina Lorente, J. J. and Schmukler, S. 2018. "The Fintech Revolution: A Threat to Global Banking?" *World Bank Research and Policy Briefs No. 125038*; the author's paper highlights that "pushing digital transformation and exerting pressure on the global financial sector, their services appear to be highly complementary to the ones provided by the more established banks, which are also embracing these technologies".

   See also Grey, R. and Dharmapalan, J., 2017. "The Macroeconomic Policy Implications of Digital Fiat Currency" *'The Case for Digital Legal Tender' Paper Series*, which articulates a vision for how widespread adoption of fintech may affect the macroeconomic levers a nation has at its disposal to steady economic growth.

59. The consideration above includes a reference to Creamer, G. G. and Stolfo, S., 2009. "A Link Mining Algorithm for Earnings Forecast and Trading" *Data Mining and Knowledge Discovery*, which presented an algorithm that selects "the largest strongly connected component of a social network and ranks its vertices using several indicators of distance and centrality".

   See also Cave, J. 2016. "Regulation by and of Algorithms" *SSRN Research Paper no. 2757701*; the author pointed out the rationale of an increasing range of important decisions that are being made by algorithms, and an extensive literature that has emerged on the extent to which they can be monitored and regulated by adapting the mechanisms that have been used for human behaviour, in particular by some form of transparency.

   In particular, the author represented that "at the same time, algorithms are becoming ever more central, entrusted with vital decisions and even serving on corporate Boards of Directors (thus holding delegated authority). Automated processing of data and automated decision rules operating on these data are becoming ubiquitous, and in many settings sophisticated models capable of deep learning and machine intelligence are being out-competed by faster, simpler models whose structure gives no clue as to their collective behaviour and provides neither useful insight nor effective points of control. Moreover, the interaction of developments on the compute side with those on the network side is becoming ever-more intricate".

60. See Zetzsche, D. A. and Buckley, R. P. and Arner, D. W. and Barberis, J. N., 2017. "Regulating a Revolution: From Regulatory Sandboxes to Smart Regulation" *Fordham Journal of Corporate and Financial Law*,

which represented that "the resulting regulatory innovations include technology (RegTech), regulatory sandboxes and special charters". This authors analyse possible new regulatory approaches "ranging from doing nothing (which spans being permissive to highly restrictive, depending on context), cautious permissiveness (on a case-by-case basis, or through special charters), structured experimentalism (such as sandboxes or piloting), and development of specific new regulatory frameworks" and then they conclude that a new regulatory approach should drive to a 'smart regulation'.

61. This remarks the conclusion of Arner, D. W. and Barberis, J. N. and Buckley, R. P., "FinTech, RegTech and the Reconceptualization of Financial Regulation". *University of Hong Kong Faculty of Law Research Paper No. 2016/035*; the authors proposed new solutions to identify and address risk while also facilitating far more efficient regulatory compliance.

62. After all, the history of financial innovation is littered with examples that led to early booms, growing unintended consequences and eventual busts; see Carney, M. 2017. "The Promise of FinTech—Something New Under the Sun? Speech given by the Bank of England Chair of the Financial Stability Board Deutsche Bundesbank G20 conference on Digitising finance, financial inclusion and financial literacy", Wiesbaden 25 January.

63. See Grey, R. and Dharmapalan, J., 2017. "The Macroeconomic Policy Implications of Digital Fiat Currency" 'The Case for Digital Legal Tender' Paper Series; and Tiwari, N. 2018. "The Commodification of Cryptocurrency" *Michigan Law Review*, 117(3), p. 611ff.

See also Mersch, Y. 2018. "Virtual or virtueless? The evolution of money in the digital age", lecture at the Official Monetary and Financial Institutions Forum, London, 8 February. Szörfi, B. and Tóth, M. 2018. "Measures of slack in the euro area", Economic Bulletin, Issue 3.

64. In 1787, during the debates on adopting the U.S. Constitution, James Madison stated that "[t]he circulation of confidence is better than the circulation of money". It's telling that Madison chose to use public trust in money as the yardstick for trust in public institutions—money and trust are as inextricably intertwined as money and the state. Money is an "indispensable social convention" that can only work if the public trusts in its stability and acceptability and, no less importantly, if the public has confidence in the resolve of its issuing authorities to stand behind it, in bad times as well as in good.

Madison's eighteenth-century remark on the link between money and trust has lost none of its relevance in the twenty-first century. The issue of trust in money has resurfaced in the public debate on privately issued, stateless currencies, such as bitcoin, and their promise to serve as reliable substitutes for public money.

65. In this respect, please see also the approach of Keynes, J. M. 1930. "A Treatise on Money", London, Macmillan, I, chapter 1; Hicks, J.R. 1937. "Mr. Keynes and the "classics"; a suggested interpretation", *Econometrica. Journal of the Econometric Society*, 5(2), p. 147 ff.; Hansen, A.H. 1953. "A Guide to Keynes", New York. It is worth considering the Italian approach to this topic; see Ascarelli, T. 1928. "La moneta", Padua; Savona, P. 1974. "La sovranità monetaria", Rome; Stammati, S. 1976. "Moneta", *Enciclopedia del Diritto*, vol. XXVI, Milan; Capriglione, F. "Moneta", *Enciclopedia del Diritto*, Milan, p. 747 ff.

66. As ECB highlighted, private cryptocurrencies have little or no prospect of establishing themselves as viable alternatives to centrally issued money that is accepted as legal tender; see Mersch, Y. (2019), "Money and private currencies: reflections on Libra". Speech by the Member of the Executive Board of the ECB, at the ESCB Legal Conference, Frankfurt am Main, 2 September.

   See also Draghi, M. 2018. "Monetary Policy in the Euro Area", speech at the ECB and Its Watchers XIX Conference organized by the Institute for Monetary and Financial Stability, Frankfurt, 14 March.

67. Furthermore, any money follows a specific path through the economy: people spend (online and in any other places that accepts virtual currencies) or deposit it (in any virtual warehouse eligible for such a goal); see Plassaras, N. A. 2013. "Regulating Digital Currencies: Bringing Bitcoin within the Reach of the IMF" *Chicago Journal of International Law*, p. 377 ff.; Pozsar, Z. 2014. "Shadow Banking: The Money View", *OFR Working Paper*.

   See also Ricks, M. "Regulating money creation after the crisis" *Harvard Business Law Review*, 2011, 1, p. 75 ss. The author represented that "the (non-government) issuers of money market instruments-almost all of which are financial firms, not commercial or industrial ones-perform an invaluable economic function".

68. It refers to EBA 2019. Report on crypto-assets and to FSB. 2017. "FinTech credit. Market structure, business models and financial stability implications". Report prepared by a Working Group established by the Committee on the Global Financial System (CGFS) and the Financial Stability Board (FSB), 22 May; and Coenen, G. et al. 2017. "Communication of monetary policy in unconventional times", Working Paper Series, No. 2080.

69. See IMF 2016. "Virtual currencies and beyond: Initial considerations", IMF Staff Discussion Note, January 2016. See also FSB 2017. "Artificial intelligence and machine learning in financial services. Market developments and financial stability implications", 1 November.

70. It is worth recalling Zetzsche, D. A. and Buckley, R. P. and Arner, D. W., "Regulating LIBRA: The Transformative Potential of Facebook's Cryptocurrency and Possible Regulatory Responses" *European Banking Institute Working Paper Series 2019/44*, which highlights that the question will be not whether, but how, to regulate these cryptocurrencies.

71. It is worth recalling that the euro was initially an electronic currency used by financial markets and for cashless payments (in 1999). Indeed, three years later, euro banknotes and coins entered into circulation in the form of physical notes, with physical security features regarding their authenticity (different from cryptography), paper or centralized ledgers (for dematerialized transactions), to ensure that payments are not made to different parties using the same money and the possibility to circulate or stoke them with the traditional mechanisms; see Pellegrini, M. 2003. "Banca Centrale Nazionale e Unione Monetaria Europea. Il caso italiano", Padova.

72. Hence, the need for new rules related to this technology should be verified and, furthermore, if they shall be able to ensure that (public or private) cryptocurrencies will not put savings at risk, jeopardize the monetary policies or reduce transparency, security and efficiency (of transactions that occur in the capital market).

73. It refers to the issue arising from the "social revolution" developed between 1945 and 1990; see Hobsbawm, E. 1997. "Age of Extremes. The Short Twentieth Century" (Milano, Italian edition), p. 339 ff. and to the conclusions of Pinker, S. 2018. "Enlightenment now" (Milano, Italian edition), p. 88 ff.

74. The above consideration recalls FSB. 2017. "FinTech credit. Market structure, business models and financial stability implications". Report prepared by a Working Group established by the Committee on the Global Financial System (CGFS) and the Financial Stability Board (FSB), 22 May, whose conclusion led to the consideration that "the emergence of FinTech credit markets poses challenges for policymakers in monitoring and regulating such activity".

75. In addition, EBA. 2019. "The EBA 2020 Work Programme", whereby it is expressly provided that "the EBA will continue with its activities concerning the FinTech Knowledge Hub, in order to facilitate information and experience sharing, to raise awareness and to support the transfer of knowledge on FinTech, and to support information sharing among national innovation facilitators under the Forum of European Innovation Facilitators".

76. Furthermore Mittelstadt, B. and Allo, P. and Taddeo, M. and Wachter, S. and Floridi, L. 2016. "The Ethics of Algorithms: Mapping the Debate"; Big Data & Society contributed to clarify the ethical importance of algo-

rithmic mediation, provided a prescriptive map to organize the debate, reviewed the current discussion of ethical aspects of algorithms, and identified areas requiring further work to develop the ethics of algorithms.

77. By way of example, it is worth recalling Siclari, D. 2015. "Introduction". "Italian Banking and Financial Law. Regulating Activities", London; the author expressly mentions: "In the Italian regulatory system, the supervisory model, where the Bank of Italy is entrusted with the prudential supervision over credit institutions, investment firms and all other financial intermediaries to ensure the stability of the financial system while Consob is responsible for the transparency and conduct of investment services and for the disclosure of information made available by issuer, led to a potential conflict between the different objectives of the regulation and supervision. For long, in fact, primacy was given to the objective of financial stability at the expense of the objective of competition between intermediaries. This is also why those two objectives (financial stability vs. competitiveness of the financial system) were assigned by the law to the same supervisory authority. Recently, however, the Italian system of regulation has not been inclined only to the financial stability of banks but also included other purposes (competitiveness of the financial system, investors' protection) under the impetus of the EU law to achieve protection of all public interests involved in regulating banking and finance."

78. In particular, it refers to Khan, A. A. 2016. "Changing Banking for Good: Counting the Costs of Market Misconduct", which explored ethical dilemmas and conduct and technology-related themes in the wider arena of banking and financial services.

79. Let us recall Bobbio, N. 1993. "Teoria generale del diritto", Torino on the rights as rule of conducts, whose considerations link the freedom to a very dense network of rules of conduct, which from birth to death direct any action in this or that direction.

80. See Rossano, D. 2017. "La nuova regolazione delle crisi bancarie", Torino, in which the author—following the recent debate on the regulation of banking crisis—questions whether the objectives set by the European legislator can be pursued, and then analyses in a critical key the articulated interventionist techniques made by Directive 2014/59/EU and Regulation No. 806 of 2014 (which outline a regulatory framework that inevitably interacts with the discipline on state aid to the banking sector).

See also Binder, J. 2014. "Resolution: Concepts, Requirements and Tools" *Bank Resolution: The European Regime*, Oxford; the author represented that "with a harmonised 'toolbox' of instruments for the resolution of banking institutions, the European Bank Recovery and Resolution Directive of 2014 (Directive 2014/59/EU, 'BRRD') significantly widens the range of policy options available to national resolution authorities in accordance with international best practice". Indeed, this paper analyses the "harmonised toolbox" and focuses on the relevant policy objectives, conditions and requirements for resolution, and the five resolution tools prescribed by the BRRD, (i.e., the sale of business, bridge institutions, asset separation and bail-in tools).

81. In addition, it can be recalled Jagtiani, J. A. and Lemieux, C. 2017. "Fintech Lending: Financial Inclusion, Risk Pricing, and Alternative Information" *FRB of Philadelphia Working Paper No. 17-17*, whose considerations suggest that fintech has been playing an increasing role in shaping financial and banking landscapes. In particular, the authors represent that "banks have been concerned about the uneven playing field because fintech lenders are not subject to the same rigorous oversight. There have also been concerns about the use of alternative data sources by fintech lenders and the impact on financial inclusion".

It refers to the use of account-level data from the Lending Club and Y-14M bank stress test data, which have been used for finding out that "Lending Club's consumer lending activities have penetrated areas that could benefit from additional credit supply, such as areas that lose bank branches and those in highly concentrated banking markets" and "a high correlation with interest rate spreads, Lending Club rating grades, and loan performance".

82. Moreover, the conclusion of Arner, D. W. and Buckley, R. P. and Zetzsche, D. A., 2018. "Fintech for Financial Inclusion: A Framework for Digital Financial Transformation" *UNSW Law Research Paper No. 18-87* represents that specific regulatory changes are a major journey for any economy, but one that increasingly suggests has tremendous potential to transform financial inclusion and support digital economic development.

83. See Guild, J. 2017. "Fintech and the Future of Finance" *Asian Journal of Public Affairs* where the author shows that "the successful adoption of Fintech to increase financial inclusion is highly dependent on competent regulatory oversight". He reached this conclusion by examining the adoption of Fintech services in Kenya, India and China, and he argues that "adopting a responsive regulatory approach, rather than an overly interventionist one, is the most suitable framework for boosting financial inclusion through technological innovation".

84. It is remarkable the consideration on the 'ongoing changes' to the current business models of fintech firms; see Engst, A. and Lemma, V. 2018. "Insurtech and interoperability of Fintech firms", *Open review of management, banking and finance*, para. 2, where it is highlighted that "regulatory issues are related to the algorithms supporting the partially automated

activities in insurance undertaking (and other advanced technique of risk mitigation)".

In general, see Lagarde, C. 2019. "Transcript of International Monetary Fund Managing Director Christine Lagarde's Opening Press Conference, 2019 Spring Meetings", Washington D.C., 11 April.

85. See Beltratti, A. and Stulz, R. M., 2009. "Why Did Some Banks Perform Better during the Credit Crisis? A Cross-Country Study of the Impact of Governance and Regulation" *Fisher College of* Business *Working Paper No. 2009-03-012*, which highlighted that "large banks with more Tier 1 capital and more deposit financing at the end of 2006 had significantly higher returns during the crisis". See also Capriglione, F. 2018. "Considerazioni a margine del volume: il tramonto della banca universale?", *Rivista Trimestrale di Diritto dell'Economia*, p. 22 ff.; Capriglione, F. 2004. "Etica della finanza mercato globalizzazione", Bari, Chapter V.

86. See Gurdgiev, C. 2016. "Is the Rise of Financial Digital Disruptors Knocking Traditional Banks Off the Track?" *International Banker*, the author began his analysis considering that the long-term fallout from the 2008 global financial crisis created several deep fractures in traditional-banking models. Moreover, in the view of the author, a two-pronged challenge has a disruptive potential and is a challenge that today's traditional banking institutions are neither equipped to address nor fully enabled to grasp.

87. See Panetta, F. 2018. "Fintech and banking: today and tomorrow. Speech by the Deputy Governor of the Bank of Italy", Oxford, where the author highlights that "the progress recorded in the last few years is astonishing: for example, the amount of data exchanged internationally is now 45 times greater than in 2005, while the cost of storing information is 10 times lower than in 2010. It is against this backdrop that fintech comes into the equation".

See McKinsey 2016. 'Digital globalization: The new era of global flows'.

See also the conclusion reached by Engst and Lemma, *Insurtech and interoperability of Fintech firms*, in *Open review of management, banking and finance*, 2018, para. 2, on the absence of significant changes of the national legislative framework, which "should suggest a complete freedom in starting up a fintech firm that would support the business of insurance companies or distributors".

88. It refers to the conclusion of Ordonez, G. and Piguillem, F. 2019. "Retirement in the Shadow (Banking)" presented at ECB. 2019. "Fourth ECB Annual Research Conference", 5 and 6 September.

See also Banca d'Italia 2017. "FinTech In Italia. Indagine conoscitiva sull'adozione delle innovazioni tecnologiche applicate ai servizi finanziari", Roma; Panetta, F. 2017. "L'innovazione digitale nell'industria finanziaria italiana", Milano.

89. Let us recall again Engst and Lemma, *Insurtech and interoperability of Fintech firms*, in *Open review of management, banking and finance*, 2018, para. 2, on both the consideration that "the current legislative path for the adoption of a EU directive would not be timely for driving the innovation in this industry, anyway new rules should be able to set common standards (in order to ensure a fair competition in this market)" and the doubt "that new technologies and different business models are spreading in the insurance business, so the monitoring of outsourcing (and then the perspective of certain developments in licensing the ancillary service provided to traditional insurance companies) should allow the starting of new form of supervision without jeopardizing the market for servicing".

90. Once again, reference is made to the analysis of FSB 2017. "Artificial intelligence and machine learning in financial services. Market developments and financial stability implications", 1 November, with respect to the risk that "Use of AI and machine learning for trading could impact the amount and degree of 'directional' trading. Under benign assumptions, the divergent development of trading applications by a wide range of market players could benefit financial stability".

91. The analysis may be extended to consider also Coffee, J. C., "Bail-Ins Versus Bail-Outs: Using Contingent Capital to Mitigate Systemic Risk" *Columbia Law and Economics Working Paper No. 380*, which shows that the Dodd-Frank Act invests heavily in preventive control and regulatory oversight, but this paper argues that the political economy of financial regulation ensures that there will be an eventual relaxation of regulatory oversight ("the regulatory sine curve").

92. In this respect, it is possible to note that Arner, D. W. and Barberis, J. N. and Buckley, R. P., 2016. "FinTech, RegTech and the Reconceptualization of Financial Regulation" "University of Hong Kong Faculty of Law Research Paper No. 2016/035" argued that "the transformative nature of technology will only be captured by a new approach that sits at the nexus between data, digital identity and regulation" and therefore exposed "the inadequacy and lack of ambition of simply digitizing analogue processes in a digital financial world" by considering that "the development of financial technology ('FinTech'), the rapid developments in emerging markets, and the recent pro-active stance of regulators in developing regulatory sandboxes, all represent a unique combination of events, which could facilitate the transition from one regulatory model to another".

   All the above suggest to verify whether a public intervention could benefit regulators, industry and entrepreneurs in the financial sector.

93. According to FSB, "many jurisdictions have amended or clarified existing rules for equity crowdfunding and for online marketplace lending, which

have also been a significant focus of IOSCO"; see FSB. 2017. "Financial Stability Implications from FinTech. Supervisory and Regulatory Issues that Merit Authorities' Attention", 27 June. See also IOSCO. 2015. "Crowdfunding 2015 Survey Responses Report," December.

94. In addition to ECB 2018. "Guide to assessments of fintech credit institution licence applications", let us recall Zetzsche, D. A. and Preiner, C. 2017. "Cross-Border Crowdfunding—Towards a Single Crowdfunding Market for Europe" *European Banking Institute Working Paper Series* with respect to "how European regulators could facilitate a Single European Crowdfunding Market while limiting both the risks for investors and the regulatory burden for crowdfunding platforms and recipients. In light of the regulatory experience with other financial products and the segregating effect of product-based approaches, many of which exist in the EU/EEA Member States, we believe existing product regulation is insufficient to enable a European cross-border crowdfunding market. Instead, regulation based on the 'MiFID light' framework could function as basis for a cross-border crowdfunding manager passport, given the minimum protection it affords both investors and the financial system, and the low costs it imposes on the platform".

95. In this respect, it is possible to include a reference to Allen, F and Babus, A. 2008. "Networks in Finance" *Wharton Financial Institutions Center Working Paper* No. 08-07; the author remarked that "by providing means to model the specifics of economic interactions, network analysis can better explain certain economic phenomena".

96. See Yadav, Y. 2014. "How Algorithmic Trading Undermines Efficiency in Capital Markets" *Van-derbilt Law Review and Vanderbilt Law and Economics Research Paper No. 14-8*; the author argued that algorithmic trading is transforming how markets process and interpret information, and then represented that conventional assumptions in securities law doctrine and policy also break down, in order to offer a new framework to thoroughly revaluate the centrality of efficiency economics in regulatory design.

97. In particular, Zetzsche, D. A. and Arner, D. W. and Buckley, R. P. and Weber, R. H. 2019. "The Future of Data-Driven Finance and RegTech: Lessons from EU Big Bang II" *European Banking Institute Working Paper Series 2019/35*; the authors analyse these four pillars and suggest that together they will underpin the future of digital financial services in Europe, and—together—will drive a Big Bang transition to data-driven finance. Moreover, they conclude by arguing that "Europe's financial services and data protection regulatory reforms have unintentionally driven the use of regulatory technologies (RegTech) by intermediaries, supervisors and regulators, thereby laying the foundations for the digital trans-

formation of both EU financial services and financial regulation. The experiences of Europe in this process provide insights for other societies in developing regulatory approaches to the intersection of data, finance and technology".

98. See also Barbagallo, C. 2019. "Fintech and the future of financial services. Speech by Director General for Financial Supervision and Regulation Bank of Italy" who shows that "the licencing process affords the Bank of Italy unique insight into Fintech developments. Licencing is when the push for innovation—arising from the market—first meets the need to protect public interest—in the remit of the supervisor. The licencing function represents, in a nutshell, the entry point for innovative projects that might give rise to new financial players or lead to new products and services for customers".

99. On this point, see Australian Securities and Investment Commission 2017. "Regulatory Guide 257: Testing FinTech Products and Services Without Holding an AFS or Credit License".

100. Chapter 7 will go deep into this topic. However, it is worth anticipating that policymakers are called to develop regtech and suptech, in order to satisfy the needs of market participants; see Tsang, C., 2019. "From Industry Sandbox to Supervisory Control Box: Rethinking the Role of Regulators in the Era of FinTech" *Journal of Law, Technology and Policy.*

101. See Buchanan, B. and Cao, C., 2018. "Quo Vadis?: A Comparison of the Fintech Revolution in China and the West" *SWIFT Institute Working Paper No. 2017-002*; the authors show that "China's Fintech success derives not just from a technological advantage and unprecedented innovation, but also from integrating finance and real-life needs", so this paper links "differences in the Chinese and Western Fintech sectors to variations in legal, political and cultural regimes".

102. Obviously, the text refers only to platforms that do not act as an agent, broker or intermediary that falls within the scope of the well-known legal reserves.

103. See Packin, N. G., 2017. "Regtech, Compliance and Technology Judgment Rule" *Chicago-Kent Law Review*; the author shows that "RegTech is not a panacea for all corporate governance challenges", by considering the following reasons: "First, there are certain barriers to the adoption of RegTech. Second, RegTech alone cannot extirpate undesired and unethical business practices, or resolve ethical issues resulting from corporate culture. Moreover, technology can be used by businesses to evade regulations and frustrate regulators, a phenomenon referred to as anti-RegTech. Third, technology can hinder good judgement and human input in the governance and risk management decision processes, which operate based on opaque programmed reasoning that is often biased and

reflects altered interpretations of the law. Fourth, given the high stakes, financial institutions must be careful when partnering with third party firms, and include regulators in the conversation before entering into such partnerships, especially given the increasing cyber risks. Lastly, many of the RegTech's automation and efficiency gains have been offset by the costs of expanded regulatory requirements, such as the increasing number of information requests from regulators".

See also Pasquale, F. A., 2019. "A Rule of Persons, Not Machines: The Limits of Legal Automation" George Washington Law Review for a critique to the "technophiles [that] promote substituting computer code for contracts and descriptions of facts now written by humans".

104. In particular, Nabilou, H., 2019. "Central Bank Digital Currencies: Preliminary Legal Observations". *Journal of Banking Regulation* shows that central banks have been investigating and experimenting with issuing central bank digital currency.

105. The will to deal with the various problems raised by the non-sovereign cryptocurrencies should support the application of the cryptography's innovation to the money issuing activity of central banks. This would imply the possibility to promote new systems of payment, whose exchange could benefit distributed ledgers, blockchain, cryptography and other tools developed in recent years.

REFERENCES

Albertazzi, U. and Gambacorta, L. 2006. "Bank Profitability and the Business Cycle" *Bank of Italy Economic Research Paper No. 601.*

Alexander, C. and Sheedy, E. 2008. "Developing a stress testing framework based on market risk models", *Journal of Banking and Finance.*

Allen, F and Babus, A. 2008. "Networks in Finance" *Wharton Financial Institutions Center Working Paper No. 08-07.*

Allenspach, N. and Monnin, P. 2006. "International integration, common exposures and systemic risk in the banking sector: An empirical investigation". *Working paper, Swiss National Bank.*

Alpa, G. and Bessone, M. 1976. "Disciplina giuridica delle carte di credito e problemi di controllo del credito al consumo" *Giurisprudenza italiana.*

Alpa, G. 1979. "Privacy e statuto dell'informazione" *Rivista di diritto civile.*

Alvaro, S. 2015. "Listed Companies", *Italian Banking and Financial Law,* London.

Andersen, T. G., Bollerslev, T., Diebold, F. X., Labys, P. 2003. "Modeling and forecasting realized volatility", *Econometrica.*

Andresen, S. 2016. "Remarks given by the Secretary General of the Financial Stability Board, at the Chatham House conference on The Banking Revolution: Global Regulatory Developments and their Industry Impact".

Ang, A. and Piazzesi, M. 2003. "A no-arbitrage vector autoregression of term structure dynamics with macroeconomic and latent variables". *Journal of Monetary Economics.*

Angel, J. J. and Harris, L. and Spatt, C. S. 2010. "Equity Trading in the 21st Century", *School of Business Working Paper No. FBE 09-10.*

Arnaboldi, F. and Claeys, P. 2008. "Financial Innovation in Internet Banking: A Comparative Analysis", SSRN Research Paper No.1094093.

Arner, D. W. and Barberis, J. N.and Buckley, R. P. 2016. "FinTech, RegTech and the Reconceptualization of Financial Regulation", *University of Hong Kong Faculty of Law Research Paper No. 2016/035.*

Arner, D. W. and Buckley, R. P. and Zetzsche, D. A. 2018. "Fintech for Financial Inclusion: A Framework for Digital Financial Transformation" *UNSW Law Research Paper No. 18-87.*

Ascarelli, T. 1928. "La moneta", Padua.

Australian Securities and Investment Commission. 2017. "Regulatory Guide 257: Testing FinTech Products and Services Without Holding an AFS or Credit License".

Baker, T. and Dellaert, B. G. C. 2018. "Regulating Robo Advice Across the Financial Services Industry", *Iowa Law Review.*

Banca d'Italia. 2017. "FinTech In Italia. Indagine conoscitiva sull'adozione delle innovazioni tecnologiche applicate ai servizi finanziari", Roma.

Barbagallo, C. 2019. "Fintech and the future of financial services. Speech by Director General for Financial Supervision and Regulation Bank of Italy".

Barnett, J. 2013. "Copyright Without Creators", *USC Law Legal Studies, Paper No. 13-7.*

Barnhizer, D. D. 2007. "Bargaining Power in Contract Theory", *MSU Legal Studies Research Paper No. 03-04.*

Bavoso, V. 2019. "The Promise and Perils of Alternative Market-Based Finance: The Case of P2P Lending in the UK" *Journal of Banking Regulation.*

Belleflamme, P. and Lambert, T. and Schwienbacher, A. 2013. "Individual Crowdfunding Practices". "Venture Capital: An International Journal of Entrepreneurial Finance", p. 313.

Beltratti, A. and Stulz, R. M. 2009. "Why Did Some Banks Perform Better during the Credit Crisis? A Cross-Country Study of the Impact of Governance and Regulation" *Fisher College of Business Working Paper No. 2009-03-012.*

Benzell, S. and LaGarda, G. and Van Alstyne, M. W. 2018. "The Impact of APIs in Firm Performance", *Boston University Questrom School of Business Research Paper No. 2843326.*

Bessone, M. 1978. "Responsabilità civile, diritti della personalità e droit au respect de la vie privee. Nota a cour de cassation 26 novembre 1975", *Il foro italiano.*

Bessone, M. 1973. "Segreto della vita privata e garanzie della persona. materiali per lo studio dell'esperienza francese" *Università di Genova Facoltà di giurisprudenza Annali.*

Bevere, A. 1978. "Il caso della Banca d'Italia e la legalità del sistema economico" *Critica del diritto.*

Bianca, C. M. 1999. "Tutela della privacy (l. 31 dicembre 1996, n. 675). Note introduttive (Pt. I). Commento alla l. 31 dicembre 1996, n. 675." *Le nuove leggi civili commentate.*

Binder, J. 2014. "Resolution: Concepts, Requirements and Tools" *Bank Resolution: The European Regime*, Oxford.

Blemus, S. 2017. "Law and Blockchain: A Legal Perspective on Current Regulatory Trends Worldwide" *Revue Trimestrielle de Droit Financier.*

Bobbio, N. 1993. "Teoria generale del diritto", Torino.

Braun, B. and Deeg, R. 2019. "Strong Firms, Weak Banks: The Financial Consequences of Germany's Export-Led Growth Model". *SSRN research Paper no. 3395566.*

Buchanan, B. and Cao, C. 2018. "Quo Vadis?: A Comparison of the Fintech Revolution in China and the West" *SWIFT Institute Working Paper No. 2017-002.*

Cantú G. and Claessens, S. and Gambacorta, L. 2019. "How Do Bank-Specific Characteristics Affect Lending? New Evidence Based on Credit Registry Data from Latin America", *BIS Working Paper No. 798.*

Capriglione, F. 1999. "Moneta", *Enciclopedia del Diritto*, Milan.

Capriglione, F. 2004. "Etica della finanza mercato globalizzazione", Bari.

Capriglione, F. 2018. "Considerazioni a margine del volume: il tramonto della banca universale?", *Rivista Trimestrale di Diritto dell'Economia n.1/2018.*

Capriglione, F. 2019. "Fonti Normative", *Manuale di diritto bancario e finanziario*, Padova.

Carnevali M. and Petrocelli, E. 2015. "Inv estment services or Activities", *Italian Banking and Financial Law*, London.

Carney, M. 2017. "The Promise of FinTech – Something New Under the Sun? Speech given by the Bank of England Chair of the Financial Stability Board Deutsche Bundesbank G20 conference on Digitising finance, financial inclusion and financial literacy", Wiesbaden 25 January.

Cassese, S. 2000. "Quattro paradossi sui rapporti tra poteri pubblici ed autonomie private", *Rivista trimestrale diritto pubblico.*

Cave, J. 2016. "Regulation by and of Algorithms" *SSRN Research Paper no. 2757701.*

Chen, J. M. 1996. "The Last Picture Show (On the Twilight of Federal Mass Communications Regulation)", *Minnesota Law Review, Vol. 80, No. 6.*

Choi, B. 2019. "What is the Social Trade-off of Securitization? A Tale of Financial Innovation", *SSRN Research Paper no. 3440653.*

Clarich, M. 1996. "Diritto d'accesso e tutela della riservatezza: regole sostanziali e tutela processuale" *Diritto processuale amministrativo.*

Coenen, G. et al. 2017. "Communication of monetary policy in unconventional times", *Working Paper Series, No. 2080.*

Coffee, J. C. 2010. "Bail-Ins Versus Bail-Outs: Using Contingent Capital to Mitigate Systemic Risk" *Columbia Law and Economics Working Paper No. 380.*

Consolo, G. 1975. "Informazione, riservatezza e calcolatori elettronici. aspetti sociologici e giuridici" *Amministrazione e politica.*

Cooter, R and Ulen, T. 2008. "Law and Economics", Boston.

Cortina Lorente, J. J. and Schmukler, S. 2018. "The Fintech Revolution: A Threat to Global Banking?" *World Bank Research and Policy Briefs No. 125038.*

Cranston, R. 2002. "Principles of Banking Law". Oxford.

Creamer, G. G. and Freund, Y. 2010. "Automated Trading with Boosting and Expert Weighting" *Quantitative Finance, Vol. 4, No. 10.*

de Weijs, R. J. 2011. "Harmonisation of European Insolvency Law and the Need to Tackle Two Common Problems: Common Pool & Anticommons", *Centre for the Study of European Contract Law Working Paper Series No. 2011-16.*

Dhar, V. and Stein, R. 2016. "FinTech Platforms and Strategy", *MIT Sloan Research Paper No. 5183-16.*

Di Pietropaolo, M. 2015. "Regulation of banking activities", *Italian Banking and Financial Law*, London.

Draghi, M. 2017. "Accompanying the economic recovery", Speech at the ECB Forum on Central Banking, Sintra, 27 June.

Draghi, M. 2018a. "Monetary Policy in the Euro Area", speech at The ECB and Its Watchers XIX Conference organised by the Institute for Monetary and Financial Stability, Frankfurt, 14 March.

Draghi, M. 2018b. "Monetary policy in the euro area", Speech by the President of the ECB, ECB Forum on Central Banking, Sintra, 19 June.

EBA. 2014. "Guidelines on common procedures and methodologies for the supervisory review and evaluation process (SREP)".

EBA. 2018. "Final Report. Guidelines on the revised common procedures and methodologies for the supervisory review and evaluation process (SREP) and supervisory stress testing".

EBA. 2019a. "Report on crypto-assets".

EBA. 2019b. "The EBA 2020 Work Programme".

EBA. 2020. "EBA Report on big data and advanced analytics", January.

ECB. 2018a. "Banking Supervision publishes results of 2018 SREP".

ECB. 2018b. "Guide to assessments of fintech credit institution licence applications".

ECB. 2018c. "Guide to assessments of licence applications. Licence applications in general".

ECB. 2018d. "SSM Supervisory Manual. European banking supervision: functioning of the SSM and supervisory approach".

ECB. 2020. "Central bank group to assess potential cases for central bank digital currencies", Bruxelles 21 January.

Engst, A. and Lemma, V. 2018. "Insurtech and interoperability of Fintech firms", *Open review of management, banking and finance.*

European Banking Federation. 2018. "The Future of the Banking Industry. Dialogue with the Banking Industry on ESCB Statistics", Frankfurt, 16 march.

European Commission. 2018. "Action Plan on how to harness the opportunities presented by technology-enabled innovation in financial services (FinTech)", 8 March 2018.

Evans D. and Schmalensee R. 2007. "The industrial organisation of markets with two-sided platforms" *Competition Policy International.*

Evans, D. 2014. "Economic Aspects of Bitcoin and Other Decentralized Public-Ledger Currency Platforms". *University of Chicago Coase-Sandor Institute for Law & Economics Research Paper No. 685.*

Ezrachi, A. 2018. "EU Competition Law Goals and the Digital Economy". *Oxford Legal Studies Research Paper No. 17/2018.*

Fenwick, M, and Kaal, W. A. and Vermeulen, E. P. M. 2017. "Regulation Tomorrow: What Happens When Technology is Faster than the Law?" *American University Business Law Review*, Vol. 6, No. 3.

Ferri G. B. 1981. "Privacy e identità personale. nota a Pret. Roma 30 aprile 1981. Pret. Roma 11 maggio 1981" *Rivista del diritto commerciale.*

Flick G. M. 1988. "Informazione bancaria e giudice penale: presupposti di disciplina, problemi e prospettive" *Banca borsa e titoli di credito.*

FSB. 2017a. "Artificial intelligence and machine learning in financial services. Market developments and financial stability implications", 1 November.

FSB. 2017b. "Chair's letter to G20 Finance Ministers and Central Bank Governors ahead of their Baden-Baden meeting", 17 March.

FSB. 2017c. "Financial Stability Implications from FinTech. Supervisory and Regulatory Issues that Merit Authorities' Attention", 27 June.

FSB. 2017d. "FinTech credit. Market structure, business models and financial stability implications". Report prepared by a Working Group established by the Committee on the Global Financial System (CGFS) and the Financial Stability Board (FSB), 22 May.

FSB. 2019a "FinTech and market structure in financial services: Market developments and potential financial stability implications".

FSB. 2019b. "Implementation and Effects of the G20 Financial Regulatory Reforms. 5th Annual Report".

FSB. 2019c. "Monitoring of FinTech", available on fsb.org.

FSB. 2020. "Global Monitoring Report on Non-Bank Financial Intermediation 2019", 19 Jannuary.

Gambaro, A. 1981. "Falsa luce agli occhi del pubblico" *Rivista di diritto civile.*

Gersen, J. E. and Posner, E. A. 2008. "Soft Law", *U. of Chicago, Public Law and Legal Theory Working Paper, no. 213.*

Giorgianni, F. 2005. "Definizione di attività bancaria e analisi del linguaggio", *Rivista del diritto commerciale e del diritto generale delle obbligazioni.*

Giorgianni, M. 1970. "La tutela della riservatezza" *Rivista trimestrale di diritto e procedura civile.*

Golub, A. and Glattfelder, J. and Olsen, R. B. 2017. "The Alpha Engine: Designing an Automated Trading Algorithm" *High Performance Computing in Finance, Chapman & Hall/CRC Series in Mathematical Finance.*

Graziadei, E. 1971. "Privatezza: rimedi vecchi e offese nuove" *Giurisprudenza italiana.*

Green, A. R. 2016. "History, Policy and Public Purpose: Historians and Historical Thinking in Government", London.

Grey, R. and Dharmapalan, J. 2017. "The Macroeconomic Policy Implications of Digital Fiat Currency", *The Case for Digital Legal Tender Paper Series.*

Grossman, R. and Siegel, K. 2014. "Organizational Models for Big Data and Analytics" *Journal of Organization Design.*

Guild, J. 2017. "Fintech and the Future of Finance" *Asian Journal of Public Affairs.*

Gurdgiev, C. 2016. "Is the Rise of Financial Digital Disruptors Knocking Traditional Banks Off the Track?" *International Banker.*

Hacker, P. and Thomale, C. 2018. "Crypto-Securities Regulation: ICOs, Token Sales and Cryptocurrencies under EU Financial Law" *European Company and Financial Law Review.*

Hansen, A. H. 1953. "A Guide to Keynes", New York.

Harvey, C. R. and Rattray, S. and Sinclair, A. and van Hemert, O. 2017. "Man vs. Machine: Comparing Discretionary and Systematic Hedge Fund Performance" *Duke I&E Research Paper No. 2017-01.*

Hicks, J. R. 1937. "Mr. Keynes and the "classics"; a suggested interpretation", *Econometrica. Journal of the Econometric Society.*

Hobsbawm, E. 1997. "Age of Extremes. The Short Twentieth Century" (Milano, Italian edition).

Huang, X. and Zhou, H. and Zhu, H. 2009. "A Framework for Assessing the Systemic Risk of Major Financial Institutions", *Journal of Banking and Finance, Vol. 33, No. 11.*

Hughes, J. P. and Mester, L. J. 2008. "Efficiency in Banking: Theory, Practice, and Evidence".

Ichino, P. 1997. "Diritto all' informazione, diritto alla riservatezza, e diritto al segreto nei rapporti di lavoro" *Rivista giuridica del lavoro e della previdenza sociale.*

IMF. 2016. "Virtual currencies and beyond: Initial considerations", *IMF Staff Discussion Note*, January.

IOSCO. 2015. "Crowdfunding 2015 Survey Responses Report," December.

Jagtiani, J. A. and Lemieux, C. 2017. "Fintech Lending: Financial Inclusion, Risk Pricing, and Alternative Information" *FRB of Philadelphia Working Paper No. 17-17.*

Kakushadze, Z. and Yu, W. 2019. "Machine Learning Risk Models" *Journal of Risk & Control.*

Keynes, J. M. 1930. "A Treatise on Money", London, Macmillan.

Keynes, J. M. 1953. "The General Theory of Employment, Interest, and Money", San Diego, edition 1964.

Khan, A. A. 2016. "Changing Banking for Good: Counting the Costs of Market Misconduct".

Krainer, R. 1999. "Banking in a Theory of the Business Cycle: A Model and Critique of the Basle Accord on Risk Based Capital Requirements for Banks". *SSRN Research Paper no. 177708.*

Krugman, P. 2012. "End This Depression Now!", New York for an effective review of the "economic slump" that has afflicted the United States, the European Union, and many other countries in the recent years.

Lagarde, C. 2019. "Transcript of International Monetary Fund Managing Director Christine Lagarde's Opening Press Conference, 2019 Spring Meetings", Washington, DC, 11 April.

Lastra, R. 2013. *"The Globalization Paradox: Review of Dani Rodrik, The Globalization Paradox: Democracy and the Future of the World Economy"* *International Journal of Constitutional Law.*

Lemma, V. and Thorp, J. A. 2014. "Sharing Corporate Governance: The Role of Outsourcing Contracts in Banking" *Law and Economics Yearly Review.*

Lemma, V. 2006. "Soft law e regolazione finanziaria," *Nuova giurisprudenza civile commentata.*

Lemma, V. 2016. "The Shadow Banking System. Creating Transparency in the Financial Markets". London.

Lemma, V. 2018. "Fintech Regulation: The Need for a Research" *Open Review of Management, Banking and Finance.*

Lener, R. and Parrillo, G. 2018. "Quali Regole per Fintech?", *Fintech: diritto, tecnologia e finanza*, Roma.

Levine, R. and Lin, C. and Peng, Q.and Xie, W. 2019. "Communication within Banking Organizations and Small Business Lending", *NBER Working Paper No. w25872.*

Marchetti, P. 1981. "Le offerte pubbliche di sottoscrizione e la legge 216" *Rivista delle società.*

Markesinis, B and Alpa, G. 1997. "Il diritto alla "privacy" nell'esperienza di "common law" e nell'esperienza italiana" *Rivista trimestrale di diritto e procedura civile.*

Martorano, F. 1978. "Convenzione di assegno e segreto bancario" *Banca borsa e titoli di credito.*

McKinsey. 2016. 'Digital globalization: The new era of global flows'.

Mersch, Y. 2018. "Virtual or virtueless? The evolution of money in the digital age", lecture at the Official Monetary and Financial Institutions Forum, London, 8 February.

Mersch, Y. 2019. "Money and private currencies: reflections on Libra". Speech by the Member of the Executive Board of the ECB, at the ESCB Legal Conference, Frankfurt am Main, 2 September.

Merton, R. and Bodie, Z. 2005. "Design of financial systems: Towards a synthesis of function and structure," *Journal of Investment Management*.

Meyer, T. 2014. "From Contract to Legislation: The Logic of Modern International Lawmaking", *Chicago Journal of International Law*.

Mittelstadt, B. and Allo, P. and Taddeo, M. and Wachter, S. and Floridi, L. 2016. "The Ethics of Algorithms: Mapping the Debate" *Big Data & Society*.

Moenninghoff, S. and Wieandt, A. 2013. "The Future of Peer-to-Peer Finance", *Zeitschrift für Betriebswirtschaftliche Forschung*.

Molle, G. 1978. Review at "Francesco Capriglione, Intervento pubblico e ordinamento del credito" *Banca borsa e titoli di credito*.

Mülbert, P. O. 2010. "Corporate Governance of Banks after the Financial Crisis – Theory, Evidence, Reforms" *ECGI – Law Working Paper No. 130/2009*.

Nabilou, H. 2019. "Central Bank Digital Currencies: Preliminary Legal Observations". *Journal of Banking Regulation*.

Nuzzo, A. 1979. "Sul c.d. diritto alla riservatezza. Nota a pret. roma 25 gennaio 1979" *Rivista di diritto industriale*.

Onado, M. 2017. "Alla ricerca della banca perduta", Bologna.

Ordonez, G. and Piguillem, F. 2019. "Retirement in the Shadow (Banking)" presented at ECB. 2019. "Fourth ECB Annual Research Conference", 5 and 6 September.

Packin, N. G. 2017. "Regtech, Compliance and Technology Judgment Rule", *Chicago-Kent Law Review*.

Padilla, J. and de la Mano, M. 2018. "Big Tech Banking" *SSRN Research Paper no. 3294723*.

Panetta, F. 2018. "Fintech and banking: today and tomorrow. Speech by the Deputy Governor of the Bank of Italy", Oxford.

Panetta, F. 2017. "L'innovazione digitale nell'industria finanziaria italiana", Milano.

Pasquale, F. A. 2019. "A Rule of Persons, Not Machines: The Limits of Legal Automation" *George Washington Law Review*.

Pellegrini, M. 2003. "Banca Centrale Nazionale e Unione Monetaria Europea. Il caso italiano", Padova.

Perlingieri, P. 1974. "Intervento alla tavola rotonda di bari su tecniche giuridiche e sviluppo della persona", *Diritto e giurisprudenza*.

Pinker, S. 2018. "Einlightenment now" (Milano, Italian edition).

Pinna, A. and Ruttenberg, W. 2016. "Distributed Ledger Technologies in Securities Post-Trading Revolution or Evolution?", *ECB Occasional Paper No. 172.*

Plassaras, N. A. 2013. "Regulating Digital Currencies: Bringing Bitcoin within the Reach of the IMF" *Chicago Journal of International Law.*

Posner, R. 2007. "Economic Analysis of Law", New York.

Posner, R. 2009. "A Failure of Capitalism". Cambridge.

Pozsar, Z. 2014. "Shadow Banking: The Money View", *OFR Working Paper.*

Ricks, M. 2011. "Regulating money creation after the crisis" *Harvard Business Law Review.*

Rodotà, S. 1973. "Elaboratori elettronici e controllo sociale", Bologna.

Rosa, H. 2003. "Social acceleration: ethical and political consequences of a desynchronized high-speed society", *Constellations.*

Rossano, D. 2017. "La nuova regolazione delle crisi bancarie", Torino.

Sacco Ginevri A. 2017. "Proxy Advisors, attività riservate e conflitto di interessi" *Contratto e impresa.*

Salanitro, N. 1998. "Privacy e segreto bancario", *Banca borsa e titoli di credito.*

Savona, P. 1974. "La sovranità monetaria", Rome.

Scitovsky, T. 1969. "Money and the balance of payments", *The Economic Journal, 79(316).*

Siclari, D. 2015. "Introduction", *Italian Banking and Financial Law. Regulating Activities.* London.

Simoncini, A. 2016. "The Constitutional Dimension of the Internet: Some Research Paths", *EUI Working Paper Law.*

Simshaw, D. 2018. "Ethical Issues in Robo-Lawyering: The Need for Guidance on Developing and Using Artificial Intelligence in the Practice of Law", *Hastings Law Journal.*

Spence, D. B. and Gopalakrishnan, L. 1999. "The New Political Economy of Regulation: Looking for Positive Sum Change in a Zero Sum World", *University of Texas at Austin, Graduate School of Business Working Paper No. 990415.*

Stagno d'Alcontres, A. 1999. "Informazione dei soci e tutela degli azionisti di minoranza nelle società quotate" *Banca borsa e titoli di credito.*

Stammati, S. 1976. "Moneta", *Enciclopedia del Diritto,* Milan.

Szörfi, B. and Tóth, M. 2018 "Measures of slack in the euro area", *Economic Bulletin, Issue 3.*

Taylor, R. C. and Wilson, C. and Holttinen, E. and Anastasiia M. 2020. "Institutional Arrangements for Fintech Regulation and Supervision", 10 January.

Tiwari, N. 2018. "The Commodification of Cryptocurrency" *Michigan Law Review.*

Trautman, L. J. 2016. "Is Disruptive Blockchain Technology the Future of Financial Services?" *The Consumer Finance Law Quarterly Report.*

Troisi, A. 2014. "Crowdfunding e mercato creditizio: profili regolamentari", *Contratto e impresa*, Padua.

Tsang, C. 2019. "From Industry Sandbox to Supervisory Control Box: Rethinking the Role of Regulators in the Era of FinTech" *Journal of Law, Technology and Policy*.

Ubertazzi, L. C. 1997. "Riservatezza informatica ed industria culturale" *AIDA*.

Walter, I. 2009. "The New Case for Functional Separation in Wholesale Financial Services" *SSRN research paper no. 1442148*.

Yadav, Y. 2014. "How Algorithmic Trading Undermines Efficiency in Capital Markets" *Vanderbilt Law Review* and *Vanderbilt Law and Economics Research Paper No. 14-8*.

Zaccaria, R. 1982. "Diritto all'informazione e riservatezza" *Il diritto delle radio-diffusioni e delle telecomunicazioni*.

Zaring, D. and Bignami, F. 2016. "Comparative Law and Regulation. Understanding the Global Regulatory Process". Northampton, MA, USA.

Zeno Zencovich, V. 1983. "Telematica e tutela del diritto all'identità personale" *Politica del diritto*.

Zetzsche, D. A. and Arner, D. W. and Buckley, R. P. and Weber, R. H. 2019a. "The Future of Data-Driven Finance and RegTech: Lessons from EU Big Bang II" *European Banking Institute Working Paper Series 2019/35*.

Zetzsche, D. A. and Buckley, R. P. and Arner, D. W. and Barberis, J. N. 2017. "Regulating a Revolution: From Regulatory Sandboxes to Smart Regulation", *Fordham Journal of Corporate and Financial Law*.

Zetzsche, D. A. and Buckley, R. P. and Arner, D. W. 2019b. "Regulating LIBRA: The Transformative Potential of Facebook's Cryptocurrency and Possible Regulatory Responses" *European Banking Institute Working Paper Series 2019/44*.

Zetzsche, D. A. and Preiner, C. 2017. "Cross-Border Crowdfunding – Towards a Single Crowdfunding Market for Europe" *European Banking Institute Working Paper Series*.

CHAPTER 3

Fintech and Market-Based Financing

This chapter considers the impact of fintech on the key economic drivers of market-based financing, taking into account the opportunity that new business analytics offer in the 'shadow banking system' (or, rather, 'non-bank financial intermediation'). New evidence shows that the efficiencies due to the application of technology-enabled innovation and the proliferation of innovative market participants can contribute positively to the functioning of banking and its substitutes.

As the results achieved in the analysis of the shadow credit intermediation processes suggest that a chain of operations is able to replicate the supply of banks and other supervised financial intermediaries, it is expectable that the development of web-based platforms is going to support the circulation of capital (without the involvement of any intermediary). Hence the perspective of an increasing the relevance of such phenomenon, with effects on financial inclusion and stability.

Assuming that the current regulatory framework will be able to avoid the recurrence of a financial crisis, the conclusion will not be its success to be sufficient to prevent new turbulences (due to the negative externalities of the fintech mechanisms). Indeed, this chapter will analyse the need for introducing adequate prudential standards that consider the innovation provided by fintech business models (and prevent any opportunistic behaviour hidden behind algorithms and software). Hence the conclusion that there is the need for new forms of public supervision over fintech

© The Author(s) 2020
V. Lemma, *FinTech Regulation*,
https://doi.org/10.1007/978-3-030-42347-6_3

mechanisms, to avoid asymmetries, reduce risks and promote financial stability, taking into account the role of information disclosure and transparency in a market driven by automatic tools and self-executing processes.

3.1   FROM THE SHADOW CREDIT INTERMEDIATION PROCESS TO FINTECH CHAINS

The Financial Stability Board's (FSB) monitoring exercise to assess global trends and risks from the 'shadow banking system' highlighted (since 2017) the rapidly increasing role of fintech applications made by non-supervised firms in order to facilitate credit creation (FSB 2018, 2020).[1] These firms have been employing a variety of fintech solutions and business models, including ones related to the access of web-based platforms, used for providing a market place on which a borrower and lender can match their supply and demand (FSB 2018 and ESRB 2018).

In order to introduce the impact of fintech innovations on the business of market-based financing, it is possible to highlight that capital and its circulation require operators to afford two kinds of expenses: a sort of factor cost (due to the amounts paid out to collect the money from the investors) and a sort of user cost (due to the amounts paid out for the required work including financial services) (EBA 2018).[2] In this respect, automation in finance drives new kinds of processes, whose relations will be enacted by software and not by human dealings. So that the increase in the use of comparison tools will override the personal relations and the human tendency to rely on a limited number of experienced counterparts.

Nowadays in credit markets, fintech firms are becoming important in both supporting supervised entities and providing various mortgage facilitation services.[3] Furthermore, it appears that fintech credit platforms are growing rapidly, actively using business analytics and big data (by means of artificial intelligence such as neural networks for credit assessment) to match supply or demand, and they are developing automatic tools for collecting documentation and closing transactions (EBA 2020b).[4]

With respect to the direct usage of such matching platforms by banks and investment funds, it is also possible to highlight the possibility of liquidating loans and other assets. This usage has differentiated and increased the connections of shadow business with reserved activities, even if—in 2017—the size was still quite small. Moreover, it should also be considered that 'corporate treasurers' should shift from banking cash-pooling products to these recent technological innovations (i.e. matching web-based platforms) to reduce the costs of their cash management. It must be borne in mind that both banking loans and corporate cash holdings represent an increasing source of funds that could be invested in non-bank instruments based on new fintech solutions (IOSCO 2017).[5] With respect to Alternative Investment Funds (AIFs), it is useful to anticipate that empirical evidence indicates that this sector has got bigger, more risk-taking and interconnected on a global scale; therefore, AIFs may ultimately produce aggregate externalities to financial markets as an effect of their portfolio flows (and then of the investment policies).[6]

It is worth recalling that every stage of the shadow credit intermediation process repeats the issuing of financial instruments backed by several assets stored together in the special purpose vehicles (SPVs), bringing to the table a 'mixture of assets' that are continuously repeated, and ultimately, composed the underlying set of different debt situations. In this respect, such a process is based on the presence of one or more SPVs, in the legal form of companies, designed for the acquisition of assets (i.e. the credits arising from banking loans) and for the offering of financial instruments (i.e. ABCP, ABS and CDO).[7]

This best introduces what needs to be said on the fintech innovations for market-based financing by highlighting that the arrangers of the shadow banking operations both collect assets and issue financial instruments in order to match the financial market demand and supply. As it has been anticipated in the previous chapter, the basis for the lawfulness of fintech in these shadows refers to the compliance of its application with the limits set forth to reserve certain activities to supervised entities.

There is no doubt that the non-bank financial intermediation is the outcome of the deregulation process begun in the twentieth century. It is possible to consider the possibility that fintech will increase the success of such phenomenon. Hence, the threats due to an acceleration in the dynamics able to generate systemic risk should also be taken into account, because without any regulation, the number of transactions will increase (with no backstops against the lack of transparency and the absence of backstops against the lack of transparency; there will be regulatory arbitrage and a lack of resilience, which were some of the degenerative elements of an advanced (securities based) capitalism (ESMA 2020).

Difficult questions have arisen, after the growth of the shadow banking system and the decline of financial regulation, and having lived through the crises of this new millennium and their consequences. This is why this research is now focusing on the evidence that the market for credit, before reaching its maximum, splintered into two channels: the supervised activities (for safer collection of savings and monetary policy mechanisms) and the non-bank financial intermediation (for supporting the real economy with resources exposed at higher risks).[8] Indeed, the next steps will verify the possibility that fintech can reduce safety costs, and then increase the possibility of financing the real economy. New tools will be able to increase transparency, avoid information asymmetries and—more generally—introduce a system of data management (Lemma, V. 2016a). Thus the need for understanding the role of the regulation in respect of the exploitation of personal data and information.[9]

In brief, business analytics will be able to set up new chains of financial operations (for lending, warehousing and issuing), based on the correspondence of the reachable counterparty to the standards provided by its programmers. This set-up would change at any variation in market conditions or modification in programming, so that there will be a flow (of money and backed assets) that is going to change its path continually. Therefore, there is need for classifying these kinds of operational sequences as 'fintech chains', in order to remark the differences between them and the ones set up directly by humans (on the basis of their preferences, experiences and individual preferences, as well as on irrational components that cannot be excluded in human behaviour).

3.2   Fintech Chains, Efficiency Consequences and Vulnerabilities

Fintech chains show that the output of the shadow banking system could increase. This consideration is related to evidence that business analytics are able to find cheap sources of capital and profitable ways of lending, as well as reduce the costs of executing the operations required for raising capital and transferring securities.[10] Indeed, customers value the products of these shadows as a substitute to banking and therefore are ready to change their consumption.[11] It is possible this increase will imply a *surplus* in this market, and this would not infer *ex se* a transfer of wealth from borrowers and savers to fintech firms, but a challenge to retain such surplus or share it with customers.

Although this surplus can partially turn into producer surplus for the benefit of the aforesaid firms, it is likely to produce social costs (due to the increase in the systemic risk). Provided that—in non-bank financial intermediation—external players fix a minimum price for the output (equal to the interest rates set forth on an interbank basis or by the central bank) (FSB 2019c),[12] the competition among non-bank fintech firms will result (more and more) in an increase in quality and quantity, and that it continues until additional expenditures (due to such increases) rise to the amount that they will yield a loss (for the above firms). All the above requires a regulatory intervention, as there are no evidences that the free market would be able to maximize the social welfare (Van Loo, R. 2018).

Considering this process of non-price competition has been boosted by the technological swiftness of fintech innovation, it will continue until the benefit of such innovation expires or rather firms reach an agreement to limit such competition.[13] Therefore, the need for control that the programmers or coders (i.e. the firms that produce fintech innovations) would not reach such kind of agreements.[14]

In general, the critical profiles of the circulation of capital outside of banks do not refer to the quality of the assets, usually backed by credit rights (and therefore proportional to the creditworthiness of the debtor), but rather they refer to the high levels of *leverage* and the *opacity* of credit transformations.[15] In this context, the capacity to collect, store and circulate data would help, because the financial instruments will be able to circulate together with the information on their backing assets.[16] Hence, this capacity of fintech chains will reduce the failure of the ordinary prudential criteria (in relation to the objective of protecting the markets and investors), given that business analytics will enable the analysis of such data and measure the quality of the aforesaid assets, their volatility, correlation and value. Thus, it is possible to conclude—once again (Lemma, V. 2016a)—for the need of public intervention that sets the standard required to support the capacity of fintech tools to exchange and share information.

Indeed, a greater share of credit would produce a number of potential benefits, which are amplified by the nature of fintech activities. So, it can foster financial inclusion with respect to the possibility to entail investors to demand for financial products that are less correlated with the traditional banking and the opportunity to support borrowers in obtaining funding without the inefficiencies of traditional credit institutions.[17]

With respect to systemic and interconnected vulnerabilities due to both non-bank financial intermediation and fintech, both these phenomena are exposed to the negative effects of "correlated horizontal shocks" (and therefore, to the incidence of macro-systemic risk deriving from their contamination). Moreover, under conditions of uncertainty, the self-executing mechanisms would not be able to preserve the market, nor to ensure the maximization of social welfare (and, at the same time, unjustified individual extra profits), provided that they are not programmed to do so.[18]

According to the contemporary standards of public intervention, the focus on vulnerabilities and threats will show that the current rules are suited for the shadow banking system, but do not fit properly for fintech innovation. Indeed, in regulatory mechanisms, the centrality of the capital adequacy in the assessment of stability risks does not consider the effects of self-executing processes and any correlation due to the use of the same business analytics.[19]

In particular, it should be noted that the regulator, on the one side, focused its attention on the counterparty risks (born by banks) and the lack of liquidity (in the market), while on the other side, set forth rules aimed at balancing the negative effects of customers' non-performance (taking into account the strategic value of collateral and guarding against the domino effect made by their own funds). These safeguards have been considered to be sufficient to avoid the recurrence of the financial crisis of 2007, but nowadays they do not seem to be adequate enough to prevent any new turbulence due to the functioning of fintech tools (and in particular to the correlation in the decisions adopted by software, the aggregate amount of losses due to the high number of small value recurring inefficiencies, and the unexpected outcome from intelligent robotics, artificial deep neural networks, machine learning and meta-heuristics optimization).

That said, it is helpful to consider that fintech tools (aimed at creating chains through the execution of sequential market operations) deal with risks in a way radically distinct from the familiar notion of uncertainty. The coders should consider that risk refers only to non-measurable criticalities; uncertainty is based on the predictable and measurable negative events (the so-called expected losses) (Knight, F. H. 1921).

In this respect, it is not deniable that fintech requires principles able to drive the automatized analyses of risk factors, in order to consider both the subjects and the activities. This brings, therefore, into consideration the risks related to errors in the source code of the relevant software, as well as the negative effects of the programmed flow of operations. Note that, with respect to fintech chains, mistakes in programming the management of vulnerabilities, risks and uncertainties should undermine (continuously) both the economic performance (which must be in line with the expectations of those who have arranged the operations) and the financial performance (in connection with unbalances in the cash flows).[20]

Therefore, fintech affects the risk factors of market-based financing. This impact arises as non-fulfillment (by the counterparty) or as a non-execution (of the following stage of the process). Considering that such impact refers to risks that have a bilateral character (related to the assessment of the creditworthiness of the counterparty) and to those that have a multilateral character (bound to the completion of the circulation), it is necessary to regulate the behaviour of the parties from a dynamic perspective, as a new type of risk. Then, the pro-cyclical effects due to the correlation of business analytics' results should also be considered because these effects refer to both an undue amplification of the creditworthiness and an unsafe increase of the volumes.[21]

This suggests that the misuse of the information on a fluctuation of the economic cycle could lead to negative results that are more than proportional, due to the role of self-executing tools that are not supervised by a third party able to stop their functioning in the case that the decision-making process leads to an increase of the relevant systemic risk.

Undoubtedly—as it will be observed in the following chapters—the application of fintech to reserved activities could produce the same risks that have been reported in the analysis of the shadow banking system.[22] It is worth anticipating that the errors in the business analytics referred to capital adequacy (and, with it, the consistency of assets in comparison to the liabilities) should undermine the resilience of credit institutions, as well as inaccuracy in instructing the self-executing transaction orders will lead to a liquidity crisis.[23] However, it is clear that all the above threats and risks amplify themselves in the shadows, because of the limited knowledge of the environment that hosts the aforementioned shadow credit intermediation process.[24]

3.3   Public Intervention Between Economic Drivers and Innovations

The regulatory analysis of banking and finance moves from the general assumption that corporate governance is democratic, and authority over business belongs to the shareholder. Fintech jeopardizes this approach, because its innovations allow management to refer to software (developed by third parties) whose underlying code is unknown.

Considering specific examples of tools used these days, it is necessary to contemplate that managers rely on software for creditworthiness measurements and risk assessment, investment strategies, assets and liabilities management, the identification of the target market, and customer care. Currently, the regulator does not protect the managers from reliance on third-party software, nor from the overreliance on the data produced by the company, the shareholders or the stakeholders. Considering the need for the protection of savers, this set-up does not seem to comply with the general principles set forth by the most advanced democracies.

Surely, the first obligation of the regulator is to understand the nature of fintech. Policy-makers should claim their powers on this point and their familiarity with the accumulated experience of stories of the misuse of technology, and the legislator should not be too slow to anticipate certain negative effects.[25]

However, regulators need to bear in mind that each firm is a unique artefact, and each reserved activity has its own characteristics: a firm's most valuable asset is its individuality.[26] Indeed, the economic and organizational aspects of a firm are inextricably intertwined. It cannot be *operationally* free if it is enslaved organizationally.[27] Only a regulation that preserves this feature, and accordingly takes into account the essential differences among firms, can claim to be in accordance with democracies. Besides, evidence shows the weaknesses of the 'common firm' and that wealth grows through the initiative and ambition of uncommon firms.[28]

Moreover, economic freedom is illusory if the firm depends on its organizational and operational needs from third-party software. Indeed, it is impossible for a firm to be free and responsible for its business if another party is able to deny it the exercise of certain practices. And the firm's development, in both its organizational and operational aspects, cannot be directed by external forces (originating from the programmer of its software). On the contrary, the choices that govern its business would be—*tout court*—outsourced to other firms (whose business is the provision of fintech tools).[29]

So, in a wired environment and from a law and economics approach, the regulator should not allow that a supervised entity be regarded as a potential pawn of other firms (whether they be supervised or not), nor as a part of a general collectivity in which the individual features are not possible.

According to these results, it is understandable that public intervention over fintech should achieve the maximum amount of freedom for individual firms that are clients of fintech firms, because this is consistent with the maintenance of the financial order. Certainly, it has been a long time since scholars have agreed that the practice of market freedom requires the establishment of a legal order. However, this does not deny that a balance between individuality and the sharing of the same technology ideally exists. Nevertheless, it is clear that executing business analytics by means of only one software is in direct conflict with the plurality of competitive markets, which is a feature, above all, of limiting the power of certain operators, maximizing the outcome and redistributing the wealth.

Focusing on the deterrence of such widespread undesirable fintech mechanisms being able to homogenize the business of financial firms, the possibility of using monetary sanctions, the level of enforcement effort and the magnitude of their impact comes into consideration.[30] It is possible to assume that strict liability or fault-based liability would be the two basic forms for addressing the responsibility of harm a firm has caused.[31] However, the application of fintech shifts the choice of committing an act from managers to software; and, therefore, the supposed rationale of the convenience in committing an act if its expected benefit exceeds the expected sanction (from an individual perspective) or injury (from a social perspective) must be borne in mind (Pesic, V. and Mure, P. 2010). That is enough for supporting the opportunity to introduce specific backstops within the business analytics, in order to avoid that a rational approach will lead the firm to the mechanical abuse of customer rights. This does not imply that fintech tools must be risk-adverse,[32] but it will reduce the tendency to adopt speculative behaviour that can undermine the trust and confidence in banking and finance.

Furthermore, it is also necessary to consider fault-based liability for harm, because according to this rule, the firm is liable and bears a sanction if it causes damage by operating in a way that is undesirable.[33] Hence, regulators need information on both the likelihood and the benefit of the relevant operations, to determine the intervention of supervisors and the level of monetary sanctions. Therefore, it is possible to expect that an act-based liability rule would be more effective. Indeed, a fintech firm should be liable for the expected loss, regardless of whether such loss actually occurs. In fact, it is acknowledged that savers, borrowers and investors are used to adopting self-defensive strategies aimed at preventing the impact of a potentially harmful act of the counterparty. Consequently, public law enforcement in fintech and market-based financing would involve act-based sanctions in order to contrast behaviour that creates the risk of a loss.[34]

Actually, in this paragraph, the public intervention has been considered under the assumption of certain enforcement and of the optimal magnitude of sanctions (equal to the higher between the relevant loss and the gained benefit). Moreover, it has been useful to assume also that business analytics face sanctionable conduct according to a probability (to incur into sanctions), and that fintech tools are able to choose the most optimal behaviour to enact. Therefore, these findings suggest involving not only undeterrences, but also a structured system of supervision over the algorithms that underlie the fintech innovations in market-based financing.

The foregoing is meant to highlight the possibility of applying self-reporting of violations, by imposing the inclusion of supervisory algorithms in any fintech tool, business analytics or software used in banking and finance.[35] It is possible to rely on the capacity of tech-fuelled business models to disclose their own violations, not only because of the lowering of the sanctions (as it is generally provided by the current regulatory framework), but also because this duty is part of the general set-up of the relevant software (and so the self-executing tools cannot avoid such behaviour). However, considering self-reporting as socially advantageous, it lowers the costs of enforcement and reduces the delay in ascertaining the damages. [36]Nevertheless, a high probability of enforcement allows setting an adequate level of sanctions (to structure an optimal enforcement policy) and, therefore, avoiding consuming resources (that would be placed out of the market).

3.4   Fintech Business in Banking, Financial Services, Asset Management and Insurance

Once again, it is important to start with a few terms that will be defined precisely later. Indeed, the scope of this part of the analysis concerns the principles useful to set the rules for the 'fintechers', and their obligations or duties vis-à-vis the supervised entities. Next chapters will go deep into the meaning of the above definitions that give content to the application of financial technology to the affairs occurring in the capital market. Now, it is important to consider firstly that certain actions—even if performed in a high-tech environment, by means of tech-fuelled tools—offer the same outcome produced by the performance of traditional activities such as banking, financial services, asset management and insurance (or a combination of these).

Secondly, the focus goes to the use of such 'acts of fintech' by means of technology-enabled innovations in banking and finance. This will help us in understanding the rationale for regulating a combination of transactions that were previously organized by one entrepreneur (i.e. the bank) and that became organized by two or more firms (i.e. the fintechers) that rely on a platform or a software. This becomes unbundling when the latter involves a chain for actions that one organization previously carried out by itself.

Consequently, it is possible to conclude that non-bank financial intermediation expands—through the application of fintech—in either or both these two ways; then the whole of the fintech becomes tractable by the ordinary technique of economic analysis (Clarck, J. B. 1931).

To put this somehow differently, this investigation will be enhanced in a direct way as it is possible to consider the juridical difference between in-house providing and outsourcing, provided that the second model would require third-party providers and therefore would place certain responsibilities out of the subjective perimeter of the supervised entity that requires a contractual set-up (Ubertazzi, L. C. 1997). Hence, it is possible to suggest to update the current schemes provided by civil law, which—as shown in the following chapters—rely on a reality that is not virtual (and so cannot manage the possibility offered by digitalization with respect to sharing, common usage, duplicability, intermediation, etc.).[37]

As highlighted with respect to fintech firms, an extensive use of outsourcing policies in banking corporate governance can result in a 'depletion' of the supervised entity, even if it must comply with the European Union (EU) rules that set a minimum size for a credit institution (European Banking Federation 2018). Therefore, it is worth anticipating the role of contracts between the supervised entities and the fintechers (i.e. the fintech outsourcers that provide ancillary service undertakings), and that these contracts apply bank's fintech strategies in the provision of services. Thus, banks and non-banks should agree the duty, for the latter, to fulfill the duty of safe and sound management required by the financial regulation.

Keeping this topic in the current perspective (and referring the above to the next chapters), let me now sketch more of the argument about the regulation of technology-enabled innovations in banking.[38] In this respect, services provided to customers using cloud computing are currently based on a model for enabling ubiquitous, convenient, on-demand network access to a shared pool of configurable computing resources (e.g. networks, servers, storage, applications and services) that can be rapidly provisioned and released with minimal management effort or service provider interaction.[39] The current set-up of the banking regulation provides a substantial right to use cloud, both by direct management of such a model or by its outsourcing.

No scholars should be surprised that the analysis of cloud led to the extension of control. Regulators cannot be expected to neglect these huge aggregate amounts of data, as well as these third parties owning or managing data processing services, or similar activities that are ancillary to the principal activity of one or more credit institutions (Art. 4, paragraph 1, point 18, of EU Regulation no. 575/2013, as amended by EU Regulation no. 2019/876, and Art. 3, paragraph 1, point 17, of Directive 2013/36/EU).

In this respect, it is useful anticipating the possibility to extend this consideration to decentralized financial technologies, artificial intelligence, big data analytics, open banking and programming interfacing (APIs).[40]

Bearing in mind the above, the analysis focuses on the European Banking Authority (EBA) recommendations aimed at regulating the use of cloud and the aforesaid fintech tools by credit institutions and investment firms (as defined in Art. 4, paragraph 1, of Regulation EU No 575/2013), obviously according to the general principle of proportionality (with respect to the size, structure and operational environment of the institution, as well as the nature, scale and complexity of its activities).[41]

As expressly stated by EBA, the "materiality of cloud outsourcing determines whether an institution is required to adequately inform its competent authority about it" (EBA 2017). However, materiality is a *mere* convention on the importance or significance.[42] From a law and economics perspective, the recurring number of transactions in the market and the difficulties for the competent authority to measure their *numerousness* and *magnitude* suggest going beyond this selective approach, because (firstly) there is the risk that any minimum cloud introduces a leak in the bank, and (secondly) big data analytics will provide the authorities with the possibility to analyse all the information received on this topic.[43] Hence, it goes without saying that the cost-benefit analysis of this supervising activity results positive.

Specificities of cloud in banking and finance do not refer only to the security of the data and systems used (by means of physical defenses and encryption technologies for data in transit, data in memory and data at rest), but also to the risks associated with 'cloudy chains', where the cloud service provider subcontracts elements of the service to other providers, shares the aggregate information arising from its data, or sells other services based on such data. Indeed, it is difficult for auditors to control the use of information and data by these providers, and this uncontrolled use should not affect the symmetry of information among market operators.

Among diverse theories of cooperation—corresponding to the diverse meanings of cooperation among firms—a main dividing line is the one that divides the request of services to third parties as an unsafe state (and seek its treatment), and those that take outsourcing for granted and study the governance associated with it (Coase, R. H. 1988). Indeed, in recent years, the financial system is moving along the latter line towards a decentralized organization.[44] Thus, there should be a further divergence between chains due to rational or irrational relationships and operations. So, the application of fintech solutions can boost the decentralization of banking and finance, both because the business analytics support the rational decision making and the increasing possibilities for correct behaviour (in a contest-winning meaning) (Schelling, T. C. 1980).

But the main role of fintech in decentralization of financial services and development of financial chains refers to the reduction (in the role and the possibility of interventions) of one or more intermediaries that have traditionally been involved in the market-based financing. And this consideration is also applicable to the provision of services related to supervised activities (FSB 2019a).

This is one reason why, in some instances, such processes support risk-taking, and this evidence calls for a regulatory analysis.[45] Indeed, the focus goes to the possibility that in some cases it can also involve the decentralization of decision-making and record-keeping.

Recently, FSB concluded that "it is impossible to predict with certainty the future scope or degree of decentralization in the financial system" (FSB 2019a). This sounds like a call to action for policymakers, in order to agree along all three of these dimensions (risk-taking, decision-making and record-keeping), because the application of fintech to such practices has yet to achieve an economically significant scale (FSB 2019b). Providing—in the next chapters—examples of decentralization (in payments and settlement, capital markets, trade finance and lending) will help us in confirming this conclusion. However, it will also confirm the importance of agreements over both the right to audit (for the supervised entities' internal and external auditors) and the duty to provide 'own funds' to cover the expected losses (calculated on the basis of the relevant operational risks).[46]

There is no doubt that decentralization would lead to new areas of competition and diversity in the financial system, but this could also lead to the systemic importance of some service providers (with respect to cloud, business analytics and—as specified below—interface programming) and to the concentrations in the ownership of a few operators the key infrastructure and technology.[47] Moreover, the use of common approaches to decentralization could drive a greater degree of procyclicality (that should be regulated).[48]

That said, the key economic drivers underlying those innovations suggest to consider the delay of the regulator in setting forth the structure of legal liability and consumer protection, so that judges are dealing with the attempt to adapt the existing rules (on liability) to solve specific issues arising from these 'fintech chains' (Alpa, G. 2019).[49] However, recovery and resolution of decentralized structures may be more difficult, and specific rules have not yet been adopted. And this context seems to be a weak environment for hosting the growth of public trust in the innovated financial system.

Some analyses—mine included—have warned that the success of the shadow systems rests on unsafe foundations and that alternative financing will experience major problems when defaults arise. Adding the evolution made by the application of fintech, the perimeter of such analyses should be extended to the role of third parties (acting as innovation facilitators), the licensing and the perimeter of supervision, and the operational resilience of fintech tools (and cyber security). As in 2016, the previous researches aimed at understanding whether there was the need for checks and balances in the shadow banking system, the current analysis aims at verifying if the same need exists with respect to the fintech industry that supports banks and non-banks in performing their financial intermediation. This requires verifying the hypothesis that fintech firms are able to influence the performance of reserved activities. Obviously, this will take into account the effects of the recent evolution of EU supervision (due to the implementation of both the European System of Financial Supervision (ESFS) and the European Banking Union (EBU), with its single supervision and single resolution mechanisms).

3.5   Fintech, Circulation of Capital and Settlements

All of the above highlights the opportunities that new business models offer in the market-based financing and, in general, in non-bank financial intermediation. In particular, the previously mentioned evidence shows that the efficiency due to the application of technology-enabled innovation and the proliferation of innovative market chains can contribute positively to the circulation of capital, as well as to the velocity of settlements (EBA 2020b).[50] According to a previous study on the shadow credit intermediation processes, the analysis of the current evidence suggests that the operations supported by fintech are faster and safer in replicating the supply of banks and other supervised financial intermediaries.[51]

Therefore, it is worth investigating the development of web-based platforms as the infrastructure whereby parties engage the exchanges required for the circulation of capital (without the involvement of any intermediary).[52] It is also worth recalling the results of the 'new institutional economics' and, in particular, its line of analysis named 'transaction cost economics' (Williamson, O. E. 1985). Now, few applications of transaction cost reasoning show the potential benefits and risks of fintech for the growth of wealth and financial stability (FSB 2019a). Despite this, it is possible to approach the hypothesis that fintech application to the circulation of capital should be usefully examined in transaction cost terms, and the relevant outcome should drive the regulator in considering the mechanism design based on the conclusion of contracts (IOSCO 2015). Thus, it will lead us to confirm that the governance of this circulation is primarily effected through the institution of public ordering rather than through private agreements; hence the importance of both the alignment of incentives and the effectiveness of sanctions within a comprehensive system of regulation and control.[53]

Whereas the competitive model for introducing fintech in banking and finance industry has been (silently) approved by policymakers, the difficulties that show up in negotiating the provision of fintech services have been only recently perceived (in great part) because their relationship with the circulation of capital were aligned with the expansionary monetary policy (enacted by both European Central Bank (ECB) and Federal Reserve during the recent years).[54] Therefore, according to the aforesaid transaction perspective, it will be investigated whether the current private ordering approach to the circulation (of capital, money and financial assets) is able to apply bilateral contracts (and their regulation) as a form of market governance.[55] In this respect, the possibility to confirm such a hypothesis relies on the possibility of invoking the behavioural assumption of rationality and self-interest. However, it is easy to admit that this concession to 'human nature' would support the statement of the problem of organization in the non-human environment of fintech's artificial intelligence, smart contracts and big data analytics. And this seems to be (at the very least) apparently contradictory.

In emphasizing this point of view, it is possible now to assume another perspective bearing in mind that the current set-up of market-based financing is based on the role of contractual obligations as a substitute for the hierarchical power (that governs the functioning of supervised entities). As anticipated above, fintech boosts transactions, transactions rely on smart contracts and, therefore, fintech needs effective agreements to be efficient in promoting the circulation of capital. In this respect, representation and warranties are part of a general set-up enacted, at least at its early stages, by contractual men (Williamson, O. E. 1985), while the relevant contractual settlements would be part of a self-executing software (and should confirm the above-mentioned behavioural assumptions of rationality and self-interest).[56]

It should however be emphasized that programmers predetermine the level of rationality of fintech algorithms used for executing operations in the financial market.[57] Hence, if all of the relevant data are known, then an effective algorithm would be able to maximize the outcome of the transaction; if the algorithm is "intended to be rational, but only limitedly so" (Simon, H. 1945), then the economic consequences of assigning operations to business analytics are relatively disfavoured; if the flowchart of the algorithm is unclear, then risks rise. This leads us to the conclusion that the supervision must oversee the aforementioned algorithms, provided that financial stability requires their effectiveness (as do human decision processes require the professionalism of the managers responsible for the reserved activities to be carried out).

With respect to the self-interest orientation, the previously revealed fintech algorithms would be able to consider the outcome of a single transaction, as well as the final result of a fintech chain and any other operation enacted through fintech tools in the market.[58] The only constraint to such ability is the possibility of the relevant software to access the data and information on the whole circulation of capital.

Provided that the following chapters will assess the questions pertaining to the need for sharing knowledge, it is worth anticipating that these data and information support the business analytics applied to the orientation of a firm. Opportunism, self-interest seeking and obedience are the levels (of orientation) suggested by economists for analysing the behaviour of market players. These levels should help in analysing the aforesaid algorithms, in order to corroborate the idea that fintech solutions will pursue the maximization of social wealth and not individual profit at the cost of social losses, as well as the embezzlement of the surplus due to fintech efficiencies. In this context, ex ante and ex post opportunisms must be challenged by supervising authorities on the basis of the agreed conclusion on the topics of adverse selection and moral hazard, respectively.[59] Both of these conducts are criticized by scholars, and fintech will not be their 'trojan horse'.

Obviously, it is clear that an excess in supervision of algorithms limits their innovation, as well as it produces the risks of a sort of 'monolithic central plan' carried out by software that pursues imposed macrogoals (Lowe, A. 1965). Evidently, this is confirmed by the evidence that algorithms satisfy obedience requirements at zero social conditioning costs (within a limited range of responsiveness) (Williamson, O. E. 1985). However, this does not exclude the possibility of a 'public stewardship' in which self-interest will be aligned with the maximization of social wealth. According to the above, there would be relatively little scope for an unsupervised fintech decentralization in the circulation of capital. Indeed, even if comprehensive contracts have prevailed in the early evidence, it is expectable that policymakers and regulators will interfere with the application of fintech to avoid that financial stability be vulnerable to opportunism.

Hence, recalling the above on web-based platforms and cloud services, it is possible to highlight that decentralizing risk-taking involves the direct matching of creditors and debtors' rights (outside the assets of the intermediary), and decentralization of record-keeping moves data and records towards and across a broader consortia of users. This would enhance the relevance of the non-bank circulation of capital, but would also reduce its opacity and increase the effectiveness of settlements (FSB 2019c). Despite this, the regulation concerning the decentralization of decision-making will occur at a later stage because it involves a move away from a single trusted board of the supervised entities towards a software in which a broad set of decisions have been instructed by a programmer (and to the extent possible updated by the artificial intelligence) (EBA 2018).

In light of the above, it is possible to have a clear view of the conclusions of the FSB and the Bank for International Settlements on the role of fintech for the circulation of capital, which refers to the emergence of a new 'fintech credit market' within the shadow banking system, whose potential benefits are able to open access to alternative funding sources for the real economy.[60] These conclusions—together with all of the above—confirm the rationale for the regulation of fintech credit markets and requires to start looking at the applicable rules already provided by the current legal framework (to be shown in the following chapter). Preferences among alternatives in regulation may differ not because the effects of fintech are judged differently, but because policymakers will use different approaches in reaching an aggregate system of supervision (with respect to the introduction of a new authority or the increase of the functions of the existing authorities).

3.6   The Effects of the CSDR Mandatory Buy-Ins and the Incentive Towards New Technologies

At this stage of the analysis, it is useful to restate that fintech tools should reduce the costs of executing the operations required for raising capital and transferring securities. This helps in introducing that the securities settlement systems are of a systemic importance for the functioning of financial markets. As considered by the EU regulator in 2014, these systems are operated by central securities depositories (CSDs) and their proper functioning serve as an essential tool to control the integrity of an issue.[61]

As background, it is possible to consider that, in the last ten years, the FSB has called for more robust 'core market infrastructures',[62] and it has asked for the revision and enhancement of the existing regulatory standards for securities settlement systems (updated in April 2012 by the Committee on Payments and Settlement Systems (CPSS) of the Bank of International Settlements (BIS) and the International Organisation of Securities Commissions (IOSCO). Currently, Regulation (EU) no. 909/2014 (as amended by Regulation (EU) 2016/1033) and Regulation (EU) no. 1095/2010 ensure consistency among the standards established for this sector.

Bearing in mind the overall goal of maintaining investor confidence, it is clear that such systems are closely involved in securing collateral for both monetary policy operations and transactions between credit institutions.[63] Hence, as actors in the collateralization processes, these CSDs are involved in market-based financing, supporting the costs of the shadow credit intermediation process, and they are in a position to change towards a technological organization. This suggests considering those actors as potential recipients of regulatory intervention which would provide a set of common requirements for CSDs operating by means of fintech solutions and blockchain. Such an approach would lead to considering all market operators and CSDs as subjects of the same obligations, standards and rules.[64]

Assuming the cross-border nature of the market-based financing, EU institutions have preferred the means of the regulation (in order to prevent any diverging national rules and reduce the regulatory complexity for market operators and CSDs). However, the widespread use of fintech innovations throughout Europe is now requiring EU institutions to lay down—amending one of their regulations—additional uniform rules to be imposed on fintech firms to ensure the smooth operation of payment systems within the internal market.[65]

Regarding certain aspects of the settlement cycle and discipline, business analytics will ensure efficient and sound clearing and payments.[66] Therefore, the regulation of fintech will avoid hiding in the software a parallel set of rules, whose effect should prevent the operators from accessing the relevant information for their decision-making processes. One more time, the regulation of the fintech tools should not only ensure the safety of settlement, but also the ability to settle any obligation on the intended settlement date, currency and cost. [67]

There is no doubt that fintech speeds up such settlements, and short settlement periods for transactions in transferable securities reduce uncertainty and risk. Obviously, shifting performance of duty from human to computer, the application of fintech would reduce the different durations of settlement periods across CSDs or Member States, and it would easily manage the servicing related to complex operations composed of several transactions (such as securities repurchase or lending agreements). Indeed, this application would promote a standardized character, and it would probably be able to also regulate the transactions that are negotiated privately by the relevant parties, but executed on or reported to the regulated trading venues (mentioned in Directive 2014/65/EU and Regulation EU no. 600/2014).[68]

According to the above, the policymaker should consider that the relevant algorithms generally admit uniform rules concerning penalties and certain aspects of the buy-in transaction. And this avoids adversely impacting the liquidity and efficiency of securities markets, as well as the buy-in process (that should be initiated where the financial instruments are not delivered) (Saguato, P. 2017). Therefore, the main purpose of the regulator should be to provide a number of legal obligations that directly impose on programmers the duty to provide safeguards and backstops within the relevant software, and establish a form of day-to-day cooperation between the competent authority of the CSD and the other relevant authorities of the market operators. Those programmers are in the position to harmonize the settlement cycle and settlement discipline through the use of algorithms, and to promote a set of common requirements for CSDs operating securities settlement systems by means of blockchain technologies.[69] If such programmers were to play a pivotal role in creating post-trade harmonization, then this would help in increasing people's confidence in the capital market.

All the above suggests a clear level-playing field underlying the reports on internalized settlements.[70] In this respect, common knowledge refers to detailed information on the aggregated volume and value of settlement instructions settled by settlement internalisers outside securities settlement systems. Hence, fintech would support an objective and reliable system of methodologies able to facilitate data comparability across settlement internalisers, by means of a new logic, based on the full exploitation of computer capacity that is available in the market (as the immense potential of blockchain technology creates the possibility of a tamper-proof consolidated audit trail, of almost infinitesimal transaction cost, and increased transactional velocity).[71] Hence the question if the relevant legal framework has to adapt to this innovation (and, in the future, to *true* real-time clearing and settlement), or rather this innovation should comply with the traditional principles (of full transparency, responsibility and correctness).[72]

Therefore, there is the perspective of a review of the rules governing internalized settlement instruction, and a better regulation approach to specific transactions concerning the possibility of placing at the disposal of the recipient an amount of money or transferring the title to, or interest in, a security or securities by means of a book entry in a register, or otherwise, which is settled by the settlement internaliser in its own books and not through a securities settlement system.[73] Indeed, the reporting requirements—set out in the current regulatory framework—require significant changes in the mechanisms of communication and market testing, as well as adjustments to agreements with the institutions concerned and their customers.[74]

Concluding on this topic, the global nature of financial markets comes into consideration, and in this respect due regard should be given to the Principles for Financial Market Infrastructures, issued by the Committee on Payment and Settlement Systems and the International Organization of Securities Commissions ('CPSS-IOSCO Principles') in April 2012.[75] In light of the above, it seems that these principles still serve as a global benchmark, but it is worth investigating the ones applicable to those fintech mechanisms covering trade confirmation, settlement cycles and securities lending. Indeed, as remarked in the following chapters, fintech firms and operations are exploiting blockchain and other new technologies in a way that suggests the identification of new legal principles (or new rules based on traditional principles) able to guide this evolution towards the common goal of welfare.

3.7   The Approach of International Authorities

Complex systems are usually monitored from several points of view. Accordingly, monitoring financial market and the relevant fintech innovations has been the main task of several supervising authorities, central banks, and international bodies.[76] Hence, this paragraph points out the approaches of these subjects in order to highlight that the contents of fintech are endlessly varied. However, as shown better in the following chapters, the observation of this phenomenon displays that the main outcome of fintech application is the fostering of non-bank financial intermediation, and this allows us to reach some conclusions on the need for regulating it.[77]

The dominant view is that "technological innovation in the financial sector offers potentially huge benefits, not least in terms of efficiency and inclusiveness" (FSB 2019d). This view reminds us of—and probably it is influenced by—the results of the global monitoring on non-bank financial intermediation, published in 2019 by the FSB, and in particular the evidence that such financing is a valuable alternative to banking for many firms and households (whose main effect is fostering competition in the supply of capital, and positive externalities for real economic activities).[78]

In this respect, one interesting conclusion concerns the potential implications of new technologies in the decentralization of financial services.[79] For years, scholars instructed about the perspective of disintermediation of capital, and the growing size of firms (that were becoming *too big to*...[80]), but only the analysis of the new technology (concerning blockchain programming and distributed ledgers) suggested (or, rather, is going to suggest) that centralized processes (that have traditionally been involved in the provision of financial services) should be eliminated, and this could improve financial stability, as well as lead to greater competition and diversity in the financial system.[81] It is worth considering on this point that Systemically Important Financial Institutions (SIFIs) have an intrafirm complexity that could result more difficult to understand than the chains of transactions that occur in the market. Therefore, it is not possible to assume that SIFIs has lower negative consequences for the global economy than non-bank financial intermediation, as they present *non-cognizable* size, complexity and systemic interconnectedness.[82]

This research is not considering just the possibility of applying cryptography to legal tender (as contemplated in the following chapters) or blockchain to financial business (in order to enhance the official system of payments), but also the opportunity to extend such technologies to consumer and investor protection, anti-money laundering, countering the financing of terrorism, contingency and recovery plans, and other elements to be stopped or placed under scrutiny by the public authorities (Lothian, T. 2010).

Assessing vulnerabilities in the global financial system is at the core of the FSB's mandate and, as far as it is possible from a domestic perspective, of the state regulatory actions.[83] Hence, it is not surprising that the rapid progress of financial innovation is considered as a challenge from both global and national policymakers. However, harnessing benefits while covering risks, if considered as a goal, should prevent the policymakers from intervening in absence of an economic analysis of the phenomenon and the impact of the relevant public interventions.[84] Anyway, the regulation of fintech would be a part of the post-(next-)crisis reforms, as the monitoring of the anti-crisis (regulatory and monetary) measures shows the need for an open and resilient financial system (grounded in agreed upon international standards) and, recently, the Japanese G20 presidency concluded by submitting (to the FSB) the request to explore issues around market fragmentation and to consider tools to address these challenges.[85]

As noted, other entities broadened the inquiry and examined the implications of technological innovation. Having regard to the analysis developed by the International Money Fund and the World Bank, it is acknowledge of the assessment concerning the evolution of the markets for capital, whose concerns regard the balancing of competing policy priorities (given both the divergent tendencies of boosting emerging economies and raising new risks to the financial stability).[86] This research would not consider such evidence as an area of conflict between the poor underdeveloped countries and those of the G-20, but different preferences remain.

In this respect, it is useful to recall the IMF's identification of the key areas for international cooperation.[87] In particular, its conclusions seem to be in line with the foundations of the most common economic theories, provided that the focus on financial inclusion (as one of the areas where fintech solutions should be potentially transformative) refers to the possibility of addressing several areas of financial friction and, therefore, reducing transactional costs.[88]

Based on the evidence that many jurisdictions have set up a framework to monitor the emerging risks, the conclusion is that additional enhancements are desirable.

Both the extension of the scope beyond the present perimeter of the shadow banking system (up to and including the programmers and coders of fintech applications) and the implementation of an effective and balanced approach (to the capital requirements of any firm that operate in the non-banking financial industry) are more than desirable.[89] Taking into account that countries are taking different approaches in adapting their legal frameworks to business models using (rather, exploiting) new technologies or blockchain, the conclusion of an international treaty on fintech and the empowerment of global authorities would be even more desirable. However, such a conclusion is limited by the political set-up of global governance, which lacks public authorities able to exercise their power worldwide.[90]

Hence, it is easy to share the IMF conclusion about the widely acknowledged gaps in the legal framework to address fintech issues, and the subsequent need to modernize its framework. Consider now the linkages between public and private law, because currently the only frameworks in place are set because of contractual agreements among fintech firms, supervised entities and customers (as the case may involve them).

Therefore, there is the opportunity to highlight the centrality of legal solutions driven by the private sector, the emergence of common approaches set by market participants, and the substantial absence of a regulatory response.

With respect to the European approach, all of the above considered, there is the possibility that the ECB will publish continuous reviews of the guides to the assessments of license applications for banks and fintech credit institutions.[91] Indeed, as pointed out in the next chapter, ECB has explained its methodology for assessing the aspects of the supervisory assessment of license applications of banks with fintech business models; and in this way, it has revealed a strict adherence to the principle of reserving activities to licensed and supervised entities. There is no doubt that the ECB will be in a position to evaluate whether an entity complies with the licensing requirements set out in EU and national law, but this does not ensure that the assessment of such requirements will guarantee that the business algorithms will ensure the sound and safe management of the bank, provided that these algorithms are out of the scope of the supervision.

Postponing any other consideration, you will allow us that the European parliament aims at supporting the growth of any kind of technological innovation used to support or provide financial services,[92] and that this is not within the ECB mandate (whose primary objective is to maintain price stability, as laid down in the Treaty on the Functioning of the European Union, Article 127).[93]

Moving from Europe to the other side of the North-Atlantic Ocean, common opinion maintains that, in recent years, America needs to upgrade the financing tools at its disposal if it is to maintain its influence in the developing world.[94] Consequently, the Federal Reserve has shared its view on technology as a dynamic and increasingly important part of the financial system in the United States and throughout the world, and its idea that these opportunities will be able to expand and improve the way financial services are delivered (Tsai, G. 2017).

According to this approach, the structure of US financial regulation has been challenged by an industry that is growing within the broader framework of supervisors and not under the constraints of a single (comprehensive) fintech license or regulatory agency. Thus, fintech business and fintech applications to reserved activities can be both conducted by companies subject to a variety of regulators, at either the state or the federal level. Moreover, in the US domestic financial market, there is evidence that "not many fintech firms have opted to become or acquire banks, thus subjecting themselves to direct bank supervision, many banks and fintech firms … are partnering to offer financial services".[95]

It is worth emphasizing some of the fintech-related steps that US financial supervisors have taken since the beginning of the recovery. Indeed, the option for establishing programs similar to 'innovation hubs' is helping answer regulatory questions raised by new applications of technology, and then it is increasing the level of compliance of such fintech firms.[96] At first glance, these hubs do not seem like legal havens, but look like gatekeepers aimed at controlling that the channels through which fintech firms and traditional financial service firms interconnect will not transfer risk from one system to another (and therefore are aimed at managing the risk of contagion by a communication with the relevant supervisors).

Moreover, it must be noted that in the second place US regulators have also begun to consider licensing in the fintech industry. New York State's "BitLicense" program and its request for the licensing of companies engaged in cryptocurrency activities (started in 2014), whose framework includes consumer protection, anti-money laundering and cyber security rules for such activities, are worth mentioning.[97] This experience should have supported the 'Vision 2020' initiative of US Regulators, and in particular the goals to establish a common approach based on a '50-state integrated licensing and supervisory system'.[98]

It is useful to recall the aforesaid consideration on the need for supervising the fintech developers, and then consider the US measures enacted to address matters related to vendor or service-provider types of relationships between banks and third parties based on guidance on third-party lending arrangements[99] and a strengthened due diligence and risk assessment that national banks should take when they seek to obtain services from fintech firms.[100] All of the above relies on a wide and deep research programme on the incorporation of new technologies into the offerings of supervised entities, whose results should be able to support an analysis of impact that is—as anticipated above—often required by policymakers to intervene.

And that isn't *literally* half of the Anglo-Saxon approach to fintech. The Bank of England showed its interest in how technology is changing financial services, and started verifying the 'promise of fintech' with respect to both artificial intelligence and distributed ledger technology (DLT). While affirming the importance of being open to fintech, the British central bank exploited its approach in three directions: understanding how fintech developments may affect systemic stability; understanding how fintech developments may affect the safety and soundness of supervised entities; and applying fintech, where appropriate, to enhance its supervisory capabilities.[101]

However, the Bank of England has entitled supervising banks, building companies, credit unions, major investment firms and insurers, as well as financial market infrastructure (while acting also as settlement agent for payment systems); the Financial Conduct Authority regulates financial services, and the Payment Systems Regulator oversee the UK payment systems. Within this framework, the approach of the Bank of England (with respect to its mission) is seeking to understand "what fintech means for the stability of the financial system, the safety and soundness of financial firms, and its ability to perform its operational and regulatory roles".[102]

Anticipating the possibility of the randomization of promises and threats as a common feature of algorithms (that the following chapters will explore), there is a possibility to align the Anglo-Saxon approach (on both sides of the North-Atlantic Ocean) and to take into account the potential of unpredictable responses to unforeseen inputs, which jeopardize any analysis of fintech industry. Indeed, the use of randomization prevents algorithms to foresee other algorithms' responses, precludes any possibility that supervisors gain reliable predictions about supervised entities' own mode of conducting business, and protects the market from any telltale regularities of choices (that expectations can anticipate).[103] Therefore, regulators should also explore the possibility of having access to the algorithms used by supervised entities or their service providers (provided that the business analytics of the latter be able to mix conflict, individual interest and common wealth).

The key recommendations of the Reserve Bank of India Working Group on Fintech (established in 2016) confirms the above description. It suggested introducing an appropriate framework for a regulatory sandbox within a well-defined space and duration where the financial sector regulator would provide the requisite regulatory guidance, so as to increase efficiency, manage risks and create new opportunities for consumers. Thus, it is possible that such limited scale testing should enact a test for new products, services or business models, subject to certain safeguards and oversight (including the full knowledge of the flows underlying the algorithms and the relevant software).[104]

It is said that another approach to market-based financing has been in line with the 'administrative structure' of the eastern countries, being therefore ignorant of the overall situation of the widespread risks happening in the market.[105]

However, it must be contemplated that the possibility to "enable advancement through technology" relies on "a digitalized bank that offers an excellent user experience, rich scenarios, smooth online-offline coordination and innovative and flexible products, backed by efficient operations and management and intelligent risk control", by leveraging the current mobile banking channel and offering an integrated mobile financial portal. Such a portal would be available to customers to access whatever they need with a simple tap on their phones. At the same time, the opportunity to "drive development through innovation" refers to the capacity of accelerating innovation in technology, products and business. It appears that the leadership of the Bank of China could adopt innovative and groundbreaking initiatives, in order to become "a provider of high-quality financial services, a builder of connected platforms, a creator of data-driven value and a pioneer of intelligent services across the globe".[106]

Based on the FSA's "Strategic Directions and Priorities 2015–2016", Japan also has shown a new approach to the spreading fintech trends (considered in terms of applying the latest IT technologies in financial services), as confirmed by the launch of the FSA "Fintech Support Desk" (since December 2015). According to the provision concerning the possibility that such desk requests outline materials of the intended business scheme, it is possible to qualify such an initiative as a form of monitoring and knowledge sharing that usually anticipates the adoption of a form of control. It is worth recalling a recent speech given by the Japanese Deputy prime minister, in which he clarifies, "financial innovation is one of the G20 finance track priorities under Japan's Presidency" (Taro Aso 2019). Considering the possibility of future banking without banks, Japan's approach made explicit one of the concerns about the fintech revolution: «" regulators may no longer be able to rely on regulations of intermediary financial institutions to protect the public interest". This suggests that the presence of the intermediary in the market for capital and the current design of supervision are correlated, creating the need to explore a possible multistakeholder approach for the governance of a DLT-based financial system.

From a commercial perspective, this overview of the Association of Southeast Asian Nations (ASEAN) region will conclude with the evidence that Australian fintech firms are looking to broaden their client base or establish a geographic beachhead to the Indochinese peninsula because many ASEAN countries boast of strong GDP growth, deep smartphone penetration and broad online access to financial products and services. However, there are also high risks due to country-specific characteristics and the risk that these economies would not grow enough to overcome their status of being underdeveloped.

Concluding by focusing on the Italian approach, Bank of Italy, Consob and IVASS have based their actions on the analysis of this phenomenon, considering on a bi-univocal channel for sharing knowledge and receiving questions, also considering the useful input provided by scholars and operators. Hence, the high qualification of such authorities would probably confirm the conclusions that the fintech *revolution* invests both the business model of banking (launched by business analytics), and the existence of intermediaries (as the point of contact between supply and demand of capital). Both of these conclusions suggest an *evolution* of the supervisory practices, projected towards the need for oversight of the software used for banking, financial services and insurance. Hence further deduction on the extension of the subjective perimeter of the public intervention to the programmers and coders, to be considered as firms that adopt the (first and final) human decision on the design of the algorithms supporting fintech, and, therefore, the business analytics applied in the financial market.

These attractive views of fintech acknowledge that the level of technology and the accessibility to infrastructure are both important, as well as important were—at the beginning of the industrial revolution—capital and ownership. Rather the aforementioned approaches have gone beyond the monitoring of technology and infrastructure to include an examination of incentives, agreements, and governance. And since incentives, agreements and governance change from time to time, it is worth excluding that the study of fintech contemplates a *mere* production function formulation.

Concluding on this point, it is worth recalling the qualification of 'business lawyers' as 'transaction cost engineers' (Gilson, R. J. 1984), and then the value of the micro-analytic designing of transactions as a result of lawyering (Clark, R. C. 1981). These considerations lead us to the perspective that fintech tools would help market operators in contracting in its entirety, as well as in their exact enforcement. It is possible, then, that fintech will promote the use of contracts instead of organizations because of the reduction of their uncertainty and transaction costs.

Despite all of the above, backward integration in the fintech industry may occur in order to comply with the expectations of policymakers, and this will require a regulatory intervention. The need for a high level of cyber resilience should promote the high dimension of the relevant company, as well as the entering into the market of big-tech firms.[107] Indeed, the development of fintech activities within the shadow banking system poses new challenges for supervising and monetary authorities. Hence, these concluding remarks on the impact of fintech refer to the perspective of 'regtech' and 'suptech'. Regardless of the choice to postpone these topics until the following chapter on the evolution of supervision, it is worth highlighting now that the use of algorithms will boost the capacity of public authorities to develop a software to be used for compliance and reporting requirements, which are able to drive the business analytics of the supervised entity (the so-called regtech tools) and verify if this software has been properly installed and run by the supervised entity (the so-called suptech tools).

3.8   Fintech and Financial Stability

The previous paragraphs followed the assumption that the current regulatory framework will be able to avoid the recurrence of the events that, since the end of the 'short twentieth century', lead to the financial crisis (or rather to the recurrent arising of financial crisis, beginning with the one of the 'new economy' in 2001).[108] This allows analysing a simplified scenario in order to go deep into the key economic drivers of financial innovation, concluding that these would be able to boost market-based financing, but requires a regulatory intervention.[109] Thus, the doubt that the velocity of such innovation is faster than that of the experienced evolutions of banking and finance.[110]

This doubt suggests verifying whether the current regulatory framework is sufficient to prevent new turbulence due to the functioning of the market for capital.[111] Considering the need for protection and the goal of financial stability to deter the risks of fintech, public intervention should provide a new form of supervision over fintech mechanisms, to be applied in market-based financing, and in order to avoid asymmetries, to banks and other supervised entities. In line with this consideration, the provision of adequate prudential standards would promote a safe path for sustainable growth, and, at the same time, avoid the speculative appropriation of the surplus granted by the application of fintech.

According to the above analysis of the regulatory approach to fintech business models, it is foreseeable to conclude that the internal rules of any supervised entity should entitle the managers to override automatic tools and self-executing processes. This analysis also suggests that contingency plans and exit strategies should enable supervised entities to close fintech outsourcing without jeopardizing their business, so the supervisors will also verify the adequacy of the contractual and organizational arrangements among supervised entities and fintech providers.[112] At the same time, the regulator must extend the scope of supervision to programmer and software, in order to fight against unfair, opportunistic and speculative actions hidden behind business analytics and self-executing tools.

It is worth recalling the 'theory of interdependent decision', whose impact on 'game theories' has been shown by Schelling with respect to the 'element of conflicts' and the impact of such an element on mutual dependence (as part of the logical structure of collaboration or accommodation, tacit, if not explicit). There is no doubt that financial markets host both *games* in which the element of conflict provides dramatic interest, but there have also been *games* in which tough secrecy played a strategic role, and *games* in which "what a player *can* do to avert mutual damage affects what another player *will* do to avert it, so that it is not always an advantage to possess initiative, knowledge, or freedom of choice" (Schelling, T. C. 1980). In order to understand the impact of fintech on financial stability, the following should be agreed: the 'perceptual element' in the functioning of algorithms aimed at foreseeing the formation of mutually consistent expectations, some of the 'basic outcomes' of such algorithms (which may result in the actual application of decision-making processes related to market operations), the structural element of the flow that the outcomes depend on, and the capacity of communicating or preventing the communication (among business analytics). Therefore, the rational outcome of two parallel algorithms would not be able to achieve a mutual accommodation in the interest of the social welfare, nor exploit mutual dependence for the benefit of the financial stability.[113]

In light of the above, there is the option to confirm that fintech requires public intervention in order to identify the contents of the algorithms, the minimum inputs to be required by business analytics, and the duties and rights in case of their interdependence. This would drive programmers to develop flows sensitive to individual rights and the common welfare, but it would not be sufficient to ensure the proper functioning of market-based financing. In this respect, the *artificial* nature of the market and, therefore, its dependence on the choices of policymakers nowadays aimed at pursuing financial stability (or rather recovery in the context of financial stability) should be highlighted.

Hence, there are premises for verifying the need for the regulatory analysis of the descriptive contents of the algorithms and the need for understanding whether their codes act as norms. And this does not refer to one of the general theories of law because scholars agree that norms describe circumstances, natural events and human facts. Therefore, norms on algorithms should fix their requirements, their contents and the minimum characteristics to be qualified as such in the context of law (as other norms do with respect to contracts, firms, etc.) (Irti, N. 2004). Consequently, the regulator would probably create models and standardize, characterize, simplify and reduce the algorithms of fintech (and fintech itself), in order to highlight the features of subjects or objects requiring prescriptions to comply with the aforesaid pursuit of financial stability.

In this context, the analysis of the impact of the regulation concerning the functioning of algorithms with respect to financial stability moves from the evidence that circumstances and facts considered by any action (within a fintech process) enact in an *indirect* way (EBA 2019); they come into being by means of a (technologically enacted) flow that consists of (at least) two subsequent stages: programming the command and running the program. On the contrary, the functioning of human actions consists of one stage only: the (clearly complex) act of communicating one's will (without the predetermination of the internal process aimed at developing such will). This difference places fintech firms and human-driven ones on two different grounds because the regulator can act directly on the fintech process aimed at developing the will of acting (whilst on the human one, the regulator can only introduce elements of deterrence).

Hence, as well as making the rules of the game, the acts of the regulator on the fintech algorithms will make the next financial market. Thus the need for questioning the role of the state.[114]

Obviously, this conclusion is in line with the theories on that, which see in a rule the form of a process that is prescribed for an event (Pagliaro, A. 1952). However, there is the possibility that the regulation of algorithms and blockchain will establish a more comprehensive form of stability to the financial market related to the *constancy* of the decision-making processes and the *regularity* of the contents of the business analytics. Therefore, the regulation of fintech should be a structure made to support every market participant, but it is not appropriate for any of them (Gentile, G. 1916).

Focusing, then, on the need for regulation due to the potential impact of fintech on financial stability, it is not possible to rely on a comprehensive assessment of fintech applications and their latest effects on the resilience of the market participants. Currently, the research is still focused on the identification of the potential risks associated with the provision of new activities and the conclusion of agreements with non-supervised entities. It is important to highlight that the FSB has communicated its reliance on existing risk assessment frameworks for evaluating the systemic risks around banks, insurers and financial market infrastructure, as well as activities beyond the regulated sector. Its starting point was that "there is nothing new under the sun" (Carney, M. 2017).

Even if it has been shown above that there is a substantial difference between fintech firms and human-driven ones, and that this difference requires two specific regulatory approaches, it is agreeable that the financial market needs "consistent approaches" to activities that produce similar outcomes (in terms of financial supply and demand) within the financial market. Therefore, the confirmation of the previous conclusion that the programming of software (which is currently outside the regulatory perimeter) needs to be brought inside the scope of public supervision (because—it is worth repeating—the regulator can act directly on the fintech process aimed at developing the will of acting, whilst on the human process the regulator can only introduce elements of deterrence).

Notes

1. See FSB. 2019. "Global Monitoring Report on Non-Bank Financial Intermediation 2018" represents that on 22 October 2018, the FSB announced its decision to replace the term 'shadow banking' with the term 'non-bank financial intermediation' in future communications. According to FSB, this change in terminology is intended to emphasize the forward-looking aspect of the FSB's work to enhance the resilience of non-bank financial intermediation and clarify the use of the technical terms.

   In this respect, see Lemma, V. 2016. "The Shadow Banking System. Creating Transparency in the Financial Markets". London. p. 38, where it has been represented that "in analysing the economic determinants, however, it is still convenient to link them to the definition of a shadow banking system in which shadow does not necessarily mean dark and sinister." In that context it has been highlighted the presence of a system in which "a process takes place that can provide further (and additional) funding than that allowed by banking (subject to the constraints of prudential regulation); together with the possibility of increasing the resources available to meet the needs of the real economy (without undermining the global financial stability)".

See also FSB 2020. "Global Monitoring Report on Non-Bank Financial Intermediation 2019", 19 January; indeed, according to FSB, the change in terminology does not affect the substance or coverage of this phenomenon, nor the substance or coverage of the agreed monitoring framework and policy recommendations, which aim to address bank-like financial stability risks arising from non-bank financial intermediation (i.e. maturity/liquidity transformation, leverage and/or imperfect credit risk transfer).

It is worth recalling that—in response to the G20 Leaders' request to develop recommendations to strengthen oversight and regulation of shadow banking in November 2010—the FSB defined shadow banking as "credit intermediation involving entities and activities (fully or partly) outside of the regular banking system" and adopted a two-pronged strategy to address financial stability risks from shadow banking, including a system-wide oversight framework and the coordination and development of policies to address such risks.

2. See EBA. 2019. "The EBA 2020 Work Programme" highlights that "in line with the EBA's FinTech Roadmap, the EBA's work will focus on the following priority policy areas: (i) a regulatory perimeter and the Forum of European Innovation Facilitators; (ii) impacts on the business models, and risks and opportunities for financial institutions from FinTech; (iii) operational resilience; and (iv) regulatory obstacles for innovative technologies and business models".

3. In addition, it is worth considering that Committee on the Global Financial System and Financial Stability Board. 2017. "FinTech credit: Market structure, business models and financial stability implications" moves from the consideration that "FinTech credit—that is, credit activity facilitated by electronic platforms such as peer-to-peer lenders—has generated significant interest in financial markets, among policymakers and from the broader public. Yet there is significant uncertainty as to how FinTech credit markets will develop and how they will affect the nature of credit provision and the traditional banking sector".

4. The research relies on the data provided by Committee on the Global Financial System and Financial Stability Board. 2017. "FinTech credit: Market structure, business models and financial stability implications"

and by EBA 2020 "EBA Report on big data and advanced analytics", January.

5. It is worth considering also the conclusions of Buchak, G. and Matvos, G. and Piskorski, T. and Seru, A. 2017. "Fintech, Regulatory Arbitrage, and the Rise of Shadow Banks", *NBER Working Paper no 23288*, March.

6. It refers to Gourdel, R. and Maqui, M. and Sydow, M. 2019. "Investment funds under stress" that presents a model for stress testing investment funds, based on a broad worldwide sample of primary open-end equity and bond funds.

7. Let us recall Lemma, V. 2016. "The Shadow Banking System. Creating Transparency in the Financial Markets". London. Chapter 2, which considers the key economic drivers of shadow banking. This research begins by examining the efficiencies of this system that are the rationale for the bundling of activities that define as market-based financing. This chapter goes on to take into account the market failures amplified by the shadows, focusing on asymmetric information, lack of transparency, and market instability, aiming at clarifying that the current legal framework allows a lawful use of business freedom, but not a means of escape from banking supervision.

8. See FSB. 2019. "Global Monitoring Report on Non-Bank Financial Intermediation 2018", which moves from the consideration that "Non-bank financing is a valuable alternative to bank financing for many firms and households, fostering competition in the supply of financing and supporting economic activity. However, non-bank financing may also become a source of systemic risk, both directly and through its interconnectedness with the banking system, if it involves activities that are typically performed by banks, such as maturity/liquidity transformation and the creation of leverage".

9. This research moves from the approach suggested by Alpa, G. 1981. "Raccolta di informazioni, protezione dei dati e controllo degli elaboratori elettronici (in margine ad un progetto di convenzione del Consiglio d' Europa)" *Il foro italiano*, 1981, fasc. 2, pt. 5, p. 27 ff.

10. It is worth recalling Choi, B. 2019. "What is the Social Trade-off of Securitization? A Tale of Financial Innovation", *SSRN Research Paper no. 3440653*, where the author shows that securitization allows banks to increase the asset size while sacrificing the rate of return per unit of assets. The author also tries to demonstrate that the availability of securitization increases the resilience against banking sector breakdowns and increases the size of credit booms associated with a subsequent breakdown. Indeed, a calibrated version of the model illustrates that an optimal regulation on the incentives of securitization can make the availability of securitization socially beneficial.

11. See Gissler, S. and Narajabad, B. 2018. "Supply of Private Safe Assets: Interplay of Shadow and Traditional Banks" *SSRN Research Paper no. 3132058*; the authors show that the creation of private safe assets by shadow banks can crowd out traditional banks' supply of safe assets. In addition, these authors find out that "banks use FHLB borrowing as a perfect substitute for deposit financing" and that "the substitution of safe debt with FHLB borrowing does not go along with an overall increase in the balance sheet and therefore has no lending effect". So, if shadow banks create safe assets at the expense of traditional banks' deposits, then there will be a minimal effect on the total funding available for households and firms from banks and shadow banks.

See also Gebauer, S. and Mazelis, F. 2019. "Macroprudential Regulation and Leakage to the Shadow Banking Sector" *DIW Berlin Discussion Paper No. 1814*, which developed a DSGE model that differentiates between regulated, monopolistically competitive commercial banks and a shadow banking system that relies on funding in a perfectly competitive market for investments.

These authors, after estimating the model using euro area data from 1999 to 2014 including information on shadow banks, find out that "tighter capital requirements on commercial banks increase shadow bank lending, which may have adverse financial stability effects". Moreover, they show that "coordinating the macroprudential tightening with monetary easing can limit this leakage mechanism, while still bringing about the desired reduction in aggregate lending". It refers also to their discussion on regulators that either do or do not consider credit leakage to shadow banks, and how they set policy in response to macroeconomic shocks.

12. It is also worth recalling Geronimo, R. S. Q. 2017. "Why Long-Term Debt Instruments Cannot Be Deposit Substitutes" *Lexkhoj International Journal of Criminal Law*, Volume II, Issue II, because this paper situates the function of deposit substitutes within the context of shadow banking, where said instruments originated and are generally used. To show the incompatibility between a deposit substitute and a long-term debt instrument, the paper applies the fundamental theory of bond values.

13. In addition, see Gissler, S. and Ramcharan, R. and Yu, E. 2019. "The Effects of Competition in Consumer Credit Markets" *SSRN Research Paper no. 3170996*; the authors show that banks and non-banks respond differently to increased competition in consumer credit markets. According to the Authors, non-banks change their credit policy when faced with more competition and expand credit to riskier borrowers at the extensive margin, resulting in higher default rates.

14. See Tan, Y. 2017. "The Impacts of Competition and Shadow Banking on Profitability: Evidence from the Chinese Banking Industry" *North American Journal of Economics and Finance*, p. 89 ss., which tested the impacts of competition and shadow banking on bank profitability using a sample of 100 Chinese commercial banks over 2003–2013 with 417 and 395 observations.

15. See Buchak, G. and Matvos, G. and Piskorski, T. and Seru, A. 2018. "The Limits of Shadow Banks" *Columbia Business School Research Paper No. 18-75* on the types of activities that migrate to the shadow banking sector.

16. It is useful to recall Zaccaria, R. 1982 "Diritto all'informazione e riservatezza" *Il diritto delle radiodiffusioni e delle telecomunicazioni*, fasc. 3, p. 527 ff. that represents the role of self-regulation in the management of news and information.

17. FSB. 2017d. "FinTech credit. Market structure, business models and financial stability implications". Report prepared by a Working Group established by the Committee on the Global Financial System (CGFS) and the Financial Stability Board (FSB), 22 May.

18. It is worth considering Frame, W. S. and Wall, L. D. and White, L. J. 2018. "Technological Change and Financial Innovation in Banking: Some Implications for Fintech" *FRB Atlanta Working Paper No. 2018-11*, which described the role of the financial system in a modern economy and how technological change and financial innovation can affect social welfare.

    See also Gomber, P. and Kauffman, r. J. and Parker, C. and Weber, B. 2017. "On the Fintech Revolution: Interpreting the Forces of Innovation, Disruption and Transformation in Financial Services" *Journal of Management Information Systems*, which focused on the issues with respect to investments, financial markets, trading, risk management, robo-advisory and related services that are influenced by blockchain and fintech innovations.

19. See Chatterjee, S. and Jobst, A. A. 2019. "Market-Implied Systemic Risk and Shadow Capital Adequacy" *Bank of England Working Paper No. 823* on a forward-looking approach to measure systemic solvency risk using contingent claims analysis (CCA) as a theoretical foundation for determining an institution's default risk based on the uncertainty in its asset value relative to promised debt payments over time. Indeed, this market-implied valuation approach ('shadow capital adequacy') endogenizes bank solvency as a probabilistic concept based on the perceived default risk (in contrast to accounting-based prudential measures of capital adequacy).

20. In addition, we recall Packin, N. G. 2018 "Regtech, Compliance and Technology Judgment Rule" *Chicago-Kent Law Review* on the relevance

of the human error, whose consideration are extendable to the human error of programmers and coders.

21. See Zhu, S. H. and Pykhtin, M. 2007. "A Guide to Modeling Counterparty Credit Risk". *GARP Risk Review* with respect to a proposal for modelling credit exposure and pricing counter-party risk. They focus on two main topics: modelling credit exposure and pricing counter-party risk. It is important to recall they define credit exposure at contract and counter-party levels, introduce netting and margin agreements as risk management tools for reducing counter-party-level exposure and present a framework for modelling credit exposure. In the part devoted to pricing, they will define credit value adjustment (CVA) as the price of counter-party credit risk and discuss approaches to its calculation.

22. Let us recall Lemma, V. 2016. "The Shadow Banking System. Creating Transparency in the Financial Markets". London. Chapter 7 reviewed the risks of the shadow banking system and provided the background for understanding the different areas where the supervising authorities are planning to strengthen oversight and control.

    This is the background of that previous investigation, from a regulatory perspective, of the risks arising from the organizational structure of the operations, and the governance design of the non-bank firms. This suggested that the central banks and the supervisory authorities would have reduced the freedom of shadows in order to avoid future events like those that happened during the financial crisis.

23. It refers to the approach of McGuire, P. M. and von Peter, G. 2016. "The Resilience of Banks' International Operations" *BIS Quarterly Review March 2016* applied in documenting post-crisis changes in the structure of BIS reporting banks' global operations across bank nationalities.

24. See Garcia, J. A. 2012. "Who's Afraid of the Shadows?—EU Moves to Curb Emerging Threats from Shadow Banking" *Financial Regulation International*; the author highlighted that "regulators and policy makers are facing a daunting task of calibrating a set of rules that covers in a sensible fashion the various components of the shadow banking system. It is laudable that EU policy makers and regulators recognise the important role the shadow banking system performs in the wider financial system and that framing the appropriate response may turn out to be a long conquest".

25. See Committee on the Global Financial System and Financial Stability Board. 2017. "FinTech credit: Market structure, business models and financial stability implications", where a group of representatives from the membership of the Committee on the Global Financial System (CGFS) and the Financial Stability Board (FSB) Financial Innovation Network, together with the Secretariats of the CGFS and FSB, undertook this study

of FinTech credit. This paper draws on public sources and ongoing work in member institutions to analyse "the functioning of FinTech credit markets, including the size, growth and nature of activities". It also assesses "the potential microfinancial benefits and risks of these activities, and considers the possible implications for financial stability in the event that FinTech credit should grow to account for a significant share of overall credit".

26. See Coase, R. H. 1988. "The firm the market and the law" Chicago, p. 33 ff.; the authors highlighted that it is convenient first considering the economic system as it is normally treated by the economist, and then to discover why a firm emerges at all in a specialized exchange economy. Besides that, exchange transactions on a market and the same transaction organized within a firm are often treated differently by governments or other bodies with regulatory powers, and there are specific reasons for the emergence of a firm in a specialized exchange economy that this author examined.

27. See Beltratti, A. and Stulz, R. M. 2009. "Why Did Some Banks Perform Better during the Credit Crisis? A Cross-Country Study of the Impact of Governance and Regulation" *Fisher College of Business Working Paper No. 2009-03-012*, which investigated whether bank performance is related to bank-level governance, country-level governance, country-level regulation, and bank balance sheet and profitability characteristics before the crisis.

28. See Cave, J. 2016. "Regulation by and of Algorithms" *SSRN Research Paper no. 2757701*, which raised a set of challenges to regulation: "First, it suggests that detailed data aggregated and centralized may not provide adequate oversight over dispersed actors; indeed, modern data analytics is becoming decentralized and even less transparent as a result. Second, it means that 'incidental' aspects of communication and computation system performance (like latency or attenuation) may seriously interfere with the performance of automated sensing and decision systems, and that this in turn may change the intensity and pattern of communications through networks. Third, it means that regulatory relationships, by which individual actors are held responsible decisions or outcomes, may no longer provide effective governance". In brief, it is worth considering that this paper analysed the growing importance of interacting systems of algorithms for communications networks and, through them, for a set of domain-specific examples, and then it developed "proposals for structural or 'macro-prudential' monitoring and regulatory mechanisms to apply to algorithmic systems and identifies some principles that can usefully be developed when designing automated or algorithmic approaches to the regulation of human behavior".

29. Let us recall Bavoso, V. 2019. "The Promise and Perils of Alternative Market-Based Finance: The Case of P2P Lending in the UK" *Journal of Banking Regulation* leads "to critically evaluate the initiatives launched by the UK FCA, initially under the Innovation Hub, and more recently under the consultation for a new regulatory framework".

30. See Khalil, S. K. and Saffar, W. and Trabelsi, S. 2013. "Disclosure Standards, Auditing Infrastructure, and Bribery Mitigation" *Canadian Academic Accounting Association*; the authors investigate the impact of disclosure standards and auditing infrastructure on firm-level corruption, and find that firms are less likely to grant gift to secure a government contract in countries having more extensive financial reporting requirements and countries where audit firms face a higher litigation and sanction risk.

31. See DiLorenzo, V. 2009. "Mortgage Market Deregulation and Moral Hazard: Equity Stripping Under Sanction of Law" *St. John's Legal Studies Research Paper No. 09-0179*, which examines the failure of the current regulatory structure to adequately protect consumers against risks in a home mortgage lending market characterized by complexity and limited transparency. In particular, he explores "the reliance of bank regulators, particularly the Federal Reserve Board, on market discipline to control risks and the failure of market discipline" and "the Federal Reserve's view that market intervention is only justified based on net societal benefits". This is recalling a viewpoint that prevented regulatory intervention until the financial sector was in crisis, and a viewpoint that is at odds with the view of the Congress.

32. See Grody, A. D. 2018. "Can a Globally Endorsed Business Identity Code be the Answer to Risk Data Aggregation?" *Journal of Risk Management in Financial Institutions*, which describes the implications of new regulatory mandates on the technology and data management infrastructure underpinning risk management systems, within single financial enterprises and across multiple financial institutions and financial market utilities.

33. See Dempsey, M. J. 2000. "Ethical Finance: An Agenda for Consolidation or for Radical Change?" *Critical Perspectives on Accounting*, Vol. 11, p. 531 ff., on the possibility that corporate and financial ethics do not exist 'to do good', but rather to act reflexively to consolidate and sanction internal activity, with the consequence that the employee is called on to be ethical not on the individual's own terms, but on the profit-motivated terms of the institution. In the end, profit remains as the bottom line.

34. It is worth bearing in mind Moohr, G. S. 2003. "An Enron Lesson: The Modest Role of Criminal Law in Preventing Corporate Crime" *Florida Law Review*, Vol. 55, No. 4, 2003, which pointed out that the rational

choice model presumes that would-be criminals rationally calculate the risks and benefits of criminal conduct, which implies that increasing criminal sanctions is an effective prevention tool. But as the conduct at Enron shows, personal characteristics of executives, such as judgement biases and excessive optimism, can impair the capacity to calculate accurately the risk of punishment.

In this respect, the author shows that a "second model of law-abiding behavior posits that individuals obey the law because of unconscious instincts, based on social norms internalized at an early age. Although criminal punishment is not likely to create law-abiding norms, it can result in law-abiding behavior".

However, according to this author, a more effective method of controlling corporate misconduct utilizes the deterrent value of private remedial suits and government administrative actions, in addition to criminal enforcement. Unfortunately, the current system hamstrings civil plaintiffs and regulatory enforcement; hence, a three-part approach would deliver a single, consistent message to the corporate sector and reserve the power of criminal law as a last resort.

35. It is worth recalling the following studies on self-reporting: Walzl, M. and Feess, E. 2002 "Self-Reporting in Optimal Law Enforcement When There are Criminal Teams" *Aachen Micro Working Paper 02/02*; Bos, I. 2006 "Leniency and Cartel Size: A Note on How Self-Reporting Nurtures Collusion in Concentrated Markets" *Amsterdam Center for Law & Economics Working Paper No. 2006-03*; Berger, M. 2006. "Compelled Self-Reporting and the Principle Against Compelled Self-Incrimination: Some Comparative Perspectives" *European Human Rights Law Review*; Davidson, Bruce I. 2011. "The Effects of Reciprocity, Self-Awareness, and Individual Characteristics on Honesty in Managerial Reporting" *AAA 2011 Management Accounting Section (MAS) Meeting Paper*; Reimsbach, D. and Hahn, R. 2013 "The Effects of Negative Incidents in Sustainability Reporting on Investors' Judgments—An Experimental Study of Third-Party versus Self-Disclosure in the Realm of Sustainable Development" *Business Strategy and the Environment*;

36. See Kaplow, L. and Shavell, S. 1991. "Optimal Law Enforcement with Self-Reporting of Behavior" NBER Working Paper No. w3822, which considered self-reporting as "the reporting by parties of their own behavior to an enforcement authority" and point out that "it is a commonly observed aspect of law enforcement, as in the context of environmental and safety regulation". In this paper, the authors add self-reporting to the model of the control of harmful externalities through probabilistic law enforcement. The authors highlight that "optimal self-reporting schemes are characterized and are shown to offer two advantages over schemes

without self-reporting: enforcement resources are saved because individuals who are led to report harmful acts need not be identified; risk is reduced because individuals bear certain sanctions when they report their behavior, rather than face uncertain sanctions".

37. See Pollack, M. 2007. "A Listener's Free Speech, a Reader's Copyright" *Hofstra Law Review*, Vol. 35, p. 1457 ff., which highlights that, besides the US Supreme Court's continuing reluctance to burden speakers and authors for the benefit of listeners and readers, several existing doctrines offer possible routes to at least partial solutions. The A. summarized that "the Court still makes the analytical error ... That error is reinforced by a similar misstep in copyright theory. Nevertheless, with creativity, some media reform is possible". See also Barron, J. A. 1967 "Access to the Press—a New First Amendment Right", Harvard Law Review p. 1641 ff).

It is also useful to recall Levy, J. 2011. "Towards a Brighter Fourth Amendment: Privacy and Technological Change" *Virginia Journal of Law and Technology* about the problem of technological change eroding privacy by developing a framework of bright line US Fourth Amendment rules.

38. It is worth considering that the trajectory of compliance expenditures over the past several decades may be traced to a good corporate citizenship movement in the mid-1990s, when the government proposed a public-private sector partnership to combat corporate crime, market manipulation and moral hazards of the bankers. See Sepe, M. 2019. "Abusi di mercato" in *Manuale di diritto bancario e finanziario*, p. 792 ff.

See also Laufer, W. S. 2018. "A Very Special Regulatory Milestone" *University Pennsylvania Journal Business Law*, p. 391 ff., which argued that the government hoped to overcome the near-insurmountable challenge of getting evidence of corporate wrongdoing, while shifting as much of the burden and costs of policing to the regulated. Then companies continue to justify making compliance expenditures in reasonably defensive ways to levels that are now unprecedented. Moreover, the author highlights that those who rail against overcriminalization or corporate criminal liability, more generally, miss speaking out against a one-sided regulatory strategy of compliance cost shifting that brings us to this historic milestone. Indeed, the threat of unfair and burdensome costs was never with the very rare event of corporate criminal liability. Rather, the threat came from firms taking the government's bait that they needed to spend, and spend, and spend more.

39. EBA. 2017. "Final Report. Recommendations on outsourcing to cloud service providers" provides that "although general outsourcing guidelines have been in place since 2006 in the form of the Committee of European Banking Supervisors guidelines on outsourcing (CEBS guide-

lines), the outsourcing framework is constantly evolving. In recent years, there has been increasing interest on the part of institutions in using the services of cloud service providers. Although the CEBS guidelines remain applicable to general outsourcing by institutions, these recommendations provide additional guidance for the specific context of institutions that outsource to cloud service providers".

In recalling CEBS guidelines on outsourcing of 14 December 2006, the research would point out that the aforesaid recommendations apply to credit institutions and investment firms as defined in Article 4(1) of Regulation (EU) no. 575/2013. Hence, in view of the importance of contractually securing both the right to audit for institutions and competent authorities and the right of physical access to the business premises of cloud service providers, supervisory expectations for outsourcing institutions in these respects are further explained in the EBA's recommendations. However, the purpose of these EBA recommendations is to specify the supervisory requirements and processes that apply when institutions outsource to cloud service providers.

40. It is possible to consider this according to a past paradigm represented by Ferri, G. B. 1981. "Privacy e identità personale. nota a Pret. Roma 30 aprile 1981. Pret. Roma 11 maggio 1981" Rivista del diritto commerciale fasc. 7-12, pt. 2, p. 379 ff. on the need for procecting the use of individual data.

41. It is also worth considering that—compared with more traditional forms of outsourcing offering tailor-made solutions to clients—cloud outsourcing services are much more standardized, which allows the services to be provided to a larger number of different customers in a much more automated manner and on a larger scale. Although cloud services can offer a number of advantages, such as economies of scale, flexibility, operational efficiencies and cost-effectiveness, they also raise challenges in terms of data protection and location, security issues and concentration risk, not only from the point of view of individual institutions but also at industry level, as large suppliers of cloud services can become a single point of failure when many institutions rely on them. See EBA. 2017 "Final Report. Recommendations on outsourcing to cloud service providers", p. 5 ff.

42. Let us extend the above consideration to the whole sustainability of corporate; see Khan, M. and Serafeim, G. and Yoon, A. 2016 "Corporate Sustainability: First Evidence on Materiality" *The Accounting Review*, Vol. 91, no. 6, p. 1697 ff.

43. See Picker, R. C. 2008 "Competition and Privacy in Web 2.0 and the Cloud" *University of Chicago Law & Economics Working Paper No. 414*, which represented that "in the past, we have regulated intermediaries at

these transactional bottlenecks—banks, cable companies, phone companies and the like—and limited the ways in which they can use the information that they see. Presumably the same forces that animated those rules—fundamental concerns about customer privacy—need to be assessed for our new information intermediaries. In doing that, we need to be acutely aware of how our choices influence competition."

44. It recalls Mülbert, P. O. 2010. "Corporate Governance of Banks after the Financial Crisis—Theory, Evidence, Reforms" *ECGI – Law Working Paper No. 130/2009* on the links among risk management, board composition and executive remuneration.

45. See Bebchuk, L. A. and Spamann, H. 2010. "Regulating Bankers' Pay" *Georgetown Law Journal*, Vol. 98, No. 2, p. 247 ff., which show that "corporate governance reforms aimed at aligning the design of executive pay arrangements with the interests of banks' common shareholders—such as advisory shareholder votes on compensation arrangements, use of restricted stock awards, and increased director oversight and independence -cannot eliminate the identified problem. In fact, the interests of common shareholders could be served by more risk-taking than is socially desirable".

46. It is useful to recall Santos, J. A. C. 2000. "Bank Capital Regulation in Contemporary Banking Theory: A Review of the Literature" *BIS Working Paper No. 90*.

   See also Brescia Morra, C. 2019 "Le forme della vigilanza" in "Manuale di diritto bancario e finanziario", p. 136 ff.; Quagliariello, M. (ed.), 2009 "Stress Testing the Banking System: Methodologies and Applications", Cambridge on a comprehensive and updated discussion of the theoretical underpinnings as well as the practical aspects of the implementation of such exercises.

47. See Alpa, G. 1985. "Il diritto dei computers". *Informatica e diritto*, fasc. 1, p. 53 ff., which focused on the relevant interests of the regulators for such reality.

48. See Ivashina, V. and Becker, B. 2011. "Cyclicality of Credit Supply: Firm Level Evidence" *Harvard Business School Finance Working Paper No. 10-107*, which shows "close link between bank credit supply and the evolution of the business cycle" and the reason for its regulation.

49. See Verret, J. W. 2017. "A Dual Non-Banking System? Or a Non-Dual Non-Banking System? Considering the OCC's Proposal for a Non-Bank Special Purpose National Charter for Fintech Companies, against an Alternative Competitive Federalism System, for an Era of Fintech Banking" *George Mason Law & Economics Research Paper No. 17-05*, which contemplates the particular dynamics of the OCC's proposal in light of recent court decisions such as *Madden v. Midland Funding, LLC*

and CashCall that have called certain aspects of the fintech-bank partnership model (bank partnership model) historically favoured by fintech companies.

See also Ooi, V. and Soh, K. P. 2019. "Cryptocurrencies and Code Before the Courts", *SSRN Research Paper no. 3439306* highlights that '*B2C2 Ltd v Quoine Pte Ltd*' may serve as "a timely reminder of the importance of the legal principles supporting e-commerce and Fintech".

50. It refers to EBA 2020a. "Discussion Paper on the future changes to the EU-wide stress test", 22 January.

51. Let us recall Lemma, V. 2016, "The Shadow Banking System. Creating Transparency in the Financial Markets", London, on the alternatives provided by shadow banks.

See also Committee on the Global Financial System and Financial Stability Board. 2017. "FinTech credit: Market structure, business models and financial stability implications", where conduct and prudential regulatory policies in selected countries are also outlined.

52. See Lagarde, C. 2019. "Transcript of International Monetary Fund Managing Director Christine Lagarde's Opening Press Conference, 2019 Spring Meetings", Washington D.C. 11 April, which recalled the quote, "The sun is shining, fix the room", as an introduction to the consideration that "there are still many reforms that are outstanding and should be the focus of policymakers because it would help boost potential output to prevent disappointing long-term growth in advanced economies, and it would help developing countries catch up with their wealthier peers, which is a process that we see slowing down at the moment. ... And that means enhancing resilience by making smarter use of fiscal policy and by strengthening financial sector policies and discipline. ... create more space for when the next downturn comes up, and tackle issues that have a high potential to boost not only revenue but also growth and inclusion".

53. It recalls Alpa, G. 1998. "Aspetti della disciplina sui dati personali riguardanti gli enti e l'attività economica" *Rivista trimestrale di diritto e procedura civile*, 1998, fasc. 3, p. 713 ff., where the author delves into the aspect of the discipline concerning the processing of personal data (i.e. Italian Law 675/1996) which concerns the effects of the new discipline on "entities" and on the exercise of economic activities. The Italian legislator, in fact, has included in the protection also the "entities", both for profit and non-profit, both public and private, and economic operators, both public and private, individual entrepreneurs or collectives.

54. Let us recall the 'ECB Economic bulletin' as a general source of the raw data useful to support the above consideration. In any case, it refers also to ECB. 2019. "Annual Report" that refers to the fact that "In December, the Governing Council ... confirmed the need for continued significant

monetary policy stimulus to support the further build-up of domestic price pressures and headline inflation developments over the medium term".

With respect to progress made by non-euro area Member States towards achieving the criteria necessary for a country to adopt the euro and their monetary policies, see ECB. 2018. "Convergence Report", 23 May, which allows a more detailed examination of the sustainability of price developments in the country under review. In this connection, ECB paid attention to the orientation of monetary policy, in particular to whether the focus of the monetary authorities has been primarily on achieving and maintaining price stability, as well as to the contribution of other areas of economic policy to this objective. Moreover, the implications of the macroeconomic environment for the achievement of price stability are taken into account.

55. See Coffee, J. C. 2007. "Law and the Market: The Impact of Enforcement" *Columbia Law and Economics Working Paper No. 304*, which shows that the "variable of relative enforcement intensity explains the greater financial development of countries with common law origins or is instead the product of that differential in development remains open to question and depends on the direction of causality". In addition, the author examines several explanations and prefers the hypothesis that enforcement intensity is a product of the level of retail ownership in the jurisdiction, with a high level of retail ownership creating a political demand for greater enforcement.

It is useful to rely on the research of Haar, B. 2016. "Freedom of Contract and Financial Stability through the Lens of the Legal Theory of Finance" (LTF)—LTF Approaches to ABS, Pari Passu-Clauses, CCPs, and Basel III" *SAFE Working Paper No. 141*, on the influence of private law on financial markets.

A clear example is provided by Lu, L. 2018. "Shadow Banking for Cash-Strapped Entrepreneurs: A Study of Private Lending Agreements Under Chinese Contract Law" *Journal of Business Law* Issue 3, p. 216 ff., which shows one of the most popular commercial contracts in China: private lending agreement, and refers to moneylending arrangements between a business borrower and its debt investors.

More in general, see Lothian, T. 2010. "Law and Finance: A Theoretical Perspective" *Columbia Law and Economics Working Paper No. 388*. Also see Lothian, T. 2011. "Rethinking Finance Through Law: A Theoretical Perspective" *Columbia Law and Economics Working Paper No. 412*, which refers to a crucial test of every program of reform, whose success should be verified by considering its impact on forming the appropriate institutional vehicles for carrying its agenda forward. From this imperative arises the need to reinvent comparative law as a handmaiden of institutional innovation. The institutional details matter, and they exist only as law. Hence, a series of innovations in present institutions and practices can greatly enhance the usefulness of finance and mitigate its dangers. Regulation, as conventionally understood and practised, is not enough. Regulation, better oriented, can represent a first step towards institutional reorganization.

56. See Scholz, L. 2017. "Algorithmic Contracts" *Stanford Technology Law Review*, which explains that "algorithmic contracts are contracts in which an algorithm determines a party's obligations". In this respect, the author represents that some contracts are algorithmic because the parties used algorithms as negotiators before contract formation, choosing which terms to offer or accept. Other contracts are algorithmic because the parties agree that an algorithm to be run some time after the contract is formed will serve as a gap-filler. Such agreements are already common in high-speed trading of financial products and will soon spread to other contexts. It is worth considering that this author concludes that "contract law doctrine does not currently have a coherent approach to describing the creation and enforcement of algorithmic contracts".

57. Let us mention Kwon, O. and Tseng, K.C. and Bradley, J. and Tjung, L. C. 2010. "Forecasting Financial Stocks Using Data Mining" *SSRN Research Paper no. 1566268*, which presented a Business Intelligence (BI) approach to forecast daily changes in seven financial stocks' prices from 1 September 1998 to 30 April 2008, with 267 independent variables, with the purpose of comparing the performance of Ordinary Least Squares model and Neural Network model in order to see which model better predicts the changes in the stock prices and to identify critical predictors to forecast stock prices to increase forecasting accuracy for the professionals in the market.

58. It refers to Choi, B. 2019. "What is the Social Trade-off of Securitization? A Tale of Financial Innovation". Available at SSRN 3440653, this highlights that the economy with securitization option experiences less frequent financial recessions, but once a financial recession occurs, it is likely to be more severe. In the presence of the savings, the financial innovation of increasing the profitability of securitization can exacerbate an overinvestment in production. Therefore, under highly developed securitization, regulation may be needed to balance the social gains and the social losses from securitization.

59. Let us recall the results of Armour, J. and Hansmann, H. and Kraakman, R. H. 2009. "Agency Problems, Legal Strategies, and Enforcement" *Oxford Legal Studies Research Paper No. 21/2009*, which maps legal similarities and differences across jurisdictions. According to these authors,

some legal strategies are "regulatory" insofar as they directly constrain the actions of corporate actors: for example, a standard of behaviour such as a director's duty of loyalty and care. Other legal strategies are "governance-based" insofar as they channel the distribution of power and payoffs within companies to reduce opportunism. For example, the law may accord direct decision rights to a vulnerable corporate constituency, as when it requires shareholder approval of mergers. Alternatively, the law may assign appointment rights over top managers to a vulnerable constituency, as when it accords shareholders—or in some jurisdictions, employees—the power to select corporate directors. Then, it is useful to consider the relationship between different enforcement mechanisms—public agencies, private actors and gatekeeper control—and the basic legal strategies outlined. This helps in concluding that regulatory strategies require more extensive enforcement mechanisms—in the form of courts and procedural rules—to secure compliance than do governance strategies. However, governance strategies, for efficacy, require shareholders to be relatively concentrated so as to be able to exercise their decisional rights effectively.

60. See Committee on the Global Financial System and Financial Stability Board. 2017. "FinTech credit: Market structure, business models and financial stability implications". See also Annunziata F. 2018 "La disciplina delle trading venues nell'era delle rivoluzioni tecnologiche: dalle criptovalute alla distributed ledger technology" *Orizzonti del diritto commerciale*, 2018, fasc. 3, p. 40 ff.

61. See Recital 2, Regulation (EU) no. 909/2014.

62. It is worth to recall Pinna, A. and Ruttenberg, W. 2016. "Distributed Ledger Technologies in Securities Post-Trading Revolution or Evolution?" *ECB Occasional Paper No. 172*, with respect to the European approach.

63. It is useful to bear in mind Coffee, J. C. 2007. "Law and the Market: The Impact of Enforcement" Columbia Law and Economics Working Paper no. 304 for the regulatory background of the above considerations.

64. It refers to ESMA's open public consultations on the draft regulatory technical standards on which this regulation is based and the opinion of the Securities and Markets Stakeholder Group established in accordance with Art. 10 of Regulation (EU) no. 1095/2010.

65. It remarks the conclusions of the "Report on the outcome of the Committee of European Banking Supervisors call for evidence on custodian banks' internalization of settlement and Central Counterparties-like activities" of 17 April 2009.

66. In particular, the analysis refers to FSB. 2017a. "Artificial intelligence and machine learning in financial services. Market developments and financial

stability implications", 1 November, where it is highlighted that "new trading algorithms based on machine learning may be less predictable than current rule-based applications and may interact in unexpected ways. To the extent that firms using AI or machine learning techniques can generate higher returns or lower trading costs, it is likely that incentives for adoption will increase. In the absence of data on the extent of market-wide use, market movements may be ascribed to AI and machine learning models, and interpretation of market shocks may be hampered".

67. Reference is made to FSB. 2017. "FinTech credit. Market structure, business models and financial stability implications". Report prepared by a Working Group established by the Committee on the Global Financial System (CGFS) and the Financial Stability Board (FSB), 22 May.

68. See Cian M. 2019. "Le sedi di negoziazione diverse dai mercati regolamentati" *Studium iuris*, fasc. 4, p. 45 ff.; Annunziata F. 2018. "La disciplina delle trading venues nell'era delle rivoluzioni tecnologiche: dalle criptovalute alla distributed ledger technology" Orizzonti del diritto commerciale, 2018, fasc. 3, p. 40 ff.; Motti, C. 2009. "Tipologia e disciplina delle trading venues" *Diritto della banca e del mercato finanziario*, 2009, p. 177 ff.

69. In this respect, it is possible to recall the post-crisis approach to the topic mentioned above; see Corcoran, A. M., 2013. "International Standards for Central Counterparties and Replumbing the Financial System: Retrofitting Listed Derivatives Infrastructure for the Global OTC Derivatives Market" *Futures and Derivatives Law Report*; the author concluded his analysis by considering that as multiple national authorities are coping with bringing their settlement infrastructures into line with international benchmarks, national requirements and cross border measures based on equivalence, substituted compliance, deference and other criteria, the so-called Principles for Financial Markets Infrastructures are worthy of a second critical look. The author expressly refers to the fact that "both matters that were addressed and were not addressed by the international high-level look at market infrastructures have continuing importance". Hence, he questions whether more attention should be paid to differentiating the risk methodologies applicable to complex and structured products that are not amenable to being effectively 'futurized'.

70. See Mainelli, M. and Milne, A. K. L. 2016. "The Impact and Potential of Blockchain on the Securities Transaction Lifecycle". *SWIFT Institute Working Paper No. 2015-007*, which reports the outcome of a series of interviews and focus group meetings with professionals working in post-trade processing and the provision of mutual distributed ledger services, in order to document views on the current research hypotheses about the

potential impact of mutual distributed ledger technology on post-trade processing global securities markets.

Hence the possibility to highlight that the main questions refer to the appropriate access to mutual distributed ledger, the set-up of change as piecemeal or 'big bang', and the application of mutual distributed ledger in securities settlement. All these questions would require a regulatory response able to manage the major changes in business processes. This recalls the conclusions on litigation and settlement of Moffitt, M. L., 2009. "Three Things to Be Against ('Settlement' Not Included)—A Response to Owen Fiss" *Fordham Law Review* who recognize that settlement and litigation are no longer separate—in practice or in theory. According to the author, even if settlement and litigation are co-evolved symbiotic processes, to stand against one is to stand against the other.

71. See Caytas, J., 2016. "Developing Blockchain Real-Time Clearing and Settlement in the EU, U.S., and Globally" *Columbia Journal of European Law: Preliminary Reference.*

   See also Moffitt, Michael L. 2009. "Three Things to Be Against ('Settlement' Not Included)—A Response to Owen Fiss" *Fordham Law Review*; Bedell, F. 2015. "When Will Real-Time Clearing & Settlement Come?" *Global Finance*; Leander, T. 2015. "Harmony and Tempo: The Status of Real-Time Payments", *Global Finance.*

72. It is worth mentioning the ECB. 2016. "Programme Plan—T2S Migration Plan" with respect that, ECB suggests that, while it was not a CSD, T2S offers CSDs delivery versus payment in central bank funds across all European securities markets starting between June 2015 and September 2017.

73. This consideration is confirmed by the Association Française des Professionnels des Titres (AFTI). 2016. "AFTI response on CSDR Guidelines on Internalised", available at ESMA.europa.eu.

74. See Cerezetti, F. and Sumawong, A. and Shreyas, U. and Karimalis, E. 2017. "Market Liquidity, Closeout Procedures and Initial Margin for CCPs" *Bank of England Working Paper No. 643*, which "using the trade repository data available to the Bank (as a result of EMIR reporting) on over-the-counter interest rate swaps and ten years (i.e. 2005 to 2015) of information on related market risk factors, ... derives empirically an efficient hedging strategy that minimizes the CCP's risk exposure to a defaulting clearing member". Thus, the author highlights that endogenous trade-off structures between total risk (market risk plus funding needs) and transaction costs are also established, with marginal sensitivities to individual components of the hedging strategy determined.

75. All the above recalls the book published by ECB and FED Chicago on "The Role of Central Counterparties", published in July 2007, whose

contents refer to the issues related to central counterparty clearing discussed in the ECB-FED Chicago Conference of 3–4 April 2006 that began by assuming that "Central counterparties (CCPs) are structures that help facilitate the clearing and settlement process in financial markets". In the light of the above, this research investigates whether new technologies would provide new solutions to these processes, and the need for understanding the rules able to prevent any foreseeable market failure.

Let us recall also the conclusion of the G30 WORKING GROUP 2003. "Global Clearing and Settlement: A Plan of Action".

76. It is worth considering that supervisors reached the aforesaid conclusion, as confirmed by Barbagallo, C. 2019. "Fintech: ruolo dell'Autorità di Vigilanza in un mercato che cambia". *Bancaria*, fasc. 1, p. 10 ff.

77. It remarks FSB. 2017. "Financial Stability Implications from FinTech. Supervisory and Regulatory Issues that Merit Authorities' Attention", 27 June; highlights that, currently, any assessment of the financial stability implications of FinTech is challenging given the limited availability of official and privately disclosed data. So, the FSB qualified as important the materiality and risks in evaluating new areas. It will also be important to understand how business models of start-ups and incumbents, and the market structure, are changing.

78. In this respect, the available data suggests that, in aggregate, the shadow entities (the so-called Other-financial entities, OFIs) continue to be interconnected with banks, with funding channels operating in both directions, and that, in aggregate, OFIs sourced more funding from insurance corporations and from pension funds than from banks. FSB noted that the financial system interconnectedness varies substantially across jurisdictions, and the majority of jurisdictions reported higher OFI funding from banks than from insurance corporations or pension funds. See FSB. 2019 "Global Monitoring Report on Non-Bank Financial Intermediation 2018", 4 February.

79. It refers to the paradigm highlighted by Ahmad, J. K. and Devarajan, S. and Khemani, S. and Shah, S., 2005. "Decentralization and Service Delivery" World Bank Policy Research Working Paper No. 3603, which provided a model for analysing the relationships of accountability between different actors in the delivery chain.

80. It refers to Irresberger, F and Bierth, C. and Weiss, J.N.F. 2016. "Size Is Everything: Explaining SIFI Designations", *Review of Financial Economics*, the authors studied the determinants of the systemic importance of banks and insurers during the financial crisis. In particular, it is worth considering their investigation on the methodology of regulators to identify global systemically important financial institutions and find

that firm size is the only significant predictor of the decision of regulators to designate a financial institution as systemically important. Further, using a cross-sectional quantile regression approach, they found that Marginal Expected Shortfall and ΔCoVaR—as two common measures of systemic risk—produce inconclusive results concerning the systemic relevance of banks and insurers during the crisis.

See on this point Garret B.L., 2016b. "Too Big to Jail: How Prosecutors Compromise with Corporations", Harward; Simon, P. 2015. "Too Big to Ignore: The Business Case for Big Data", Hoboken; Sorkin, A. R. 2010. "Too Big to Fail: Inside the Battle to Save Wall Street", London.

It refers also to the study of Wilmarth, A. E., 2011. "The Dodd-Frank Act: A Flawed and Inadequate Response to the Too-Big-To-Fail Problem" *Oregon Law Review*, p. 951 ff., whose proposals would strip away many of the public subsidies currently exploited by financial conglomerates and would subject them to the same type of market discipline that investors have applied over the past three decades in breaking up inefficient commercial and industrial conglomerates.

See also—on this topic—Lemma, V. 2016. "Too big to escape". *Rivista trimestrale diritto dell'economia*, p. 45 ff; Lemma, V. 2015. "Too big to be popular". "La riforma delle banche popolari", Padova, p. 173 ff. and Brozzett., A. 2018. "'Ending of too big to fail' tra soft law e ordinamento bancario europeo. Dieci anni di riforme", Bari.

81. Let us recall again FSB. 2019. "Letter from the FSB Chair to G20 Leaders ahead of their Summit in Osaka". 25 June.

82. See Lumsdaine, R. L. and Rockmore, d. and Foti, N. and Leibon, G. and Farmer, J. D., 2016. "The *Intrafirm* Complexity of Systemically Important Financial Institutions" *SSRN Research Paper no. 2604166*, on the fact that "the failure of any one of them could have dramatic negative consequences for the global economy and is based on their size, complexity, and systemic interconnectedness".

It is worth mentioning also Roncalli, T. and Weisang, G. 2015. "Asset Management and Systemic Risk" *Finance Meeting EUROFIDAI—AFFI Research Paper*; Weber, R. H. and Arner, D. W. and Gibson, E. and Baumann, S. 2014 "Addressing Systemic Risk: Financial Regulatory Design" *Texas International Law Journal*; Packin, N. G. 2013 "The Case Against the Dodd-Frank Act's Living Wills: Contingency Planning Following the Financial Crisis" *Berkeley Business Law Journal*.

83. See Committee on the Global Financial System and Financial Stability Board. 2017. "FinTech credit: Market structure, business models and financial stability implications" which provides several key messages: "The nature of FinTech credit activity varies significantly across and within countries due to heterogeneity in the business models of FinTech credit

platforms. Although FinTech credit markets have expanded at a fast pace over recent years, they currently remain small in size relative to credit extended by traditional intermediaries. A bigger share of FinTech-facilitated credit in the financial system could have both financial stability benefits and risks in the future, including access to alternative funding sources in the economy and efficiency pressures on incumbent banks, but also the potential for weaker lending standards and more procyclical credit provision in the economy."

84. The analysis refers to Zaring, D. and Bignami, F. 2016. "Comparative Law and Regulation. Understanding the Global Regulatory Process". Northampton, MA, USA; the authors clarified that "Regulatory problems cross borders and therefore so too does the governance of these problems. Transnational, regional, and international bodies have proliferated. Deprived of the traditional police and revenue-raising powers of the nation state, these bodies govern primarily through rules and standards that both constrain and require regulatory action at the national level".

85. Reference is made to the 'Letter' from the FSB Chair to G20 Leaders ahead of their Summit in Osaka. 25 June 2019.

86. See Malpass, D. 2019. "Statement from World Bank Group President" *World Bank Group—International Monetary Fund Annual Meetings*, on challenges in the global economy: he remarked that "growth is slowing, investment is sluggish, manufacturing activity is soft, and trade is weakening. Climate change and fragility are making poor countries more vulnerable. But the good news is, broad-based growth is still possible".

87. See World Bank Group—International Monetary Fund, 2019. "Fintech: The Experience So Far" *IMF Policy Paper*, pp. 19–20 on the international cooperation efforts that are already underway. They noted "specific policy responses to fintech developments". In particular country authorities' have shared information with international financial institutions (IMF, WB, the Bank for International Settlements (BIS), etc.) or with other country authorities through international training and peer-learning programs.

88. Let us recall again World Bank Group—International Monetary Fund, 2019. "Fintech: The Experience So Far" IMF Policy Paper, p. 31 with respect to (a) cost barriers for delivering financial services—especially severe in remote rural locations and among marginalized groups such as women, the urban poor and migrants; (b) information asymmetries between service providers and consumers, especially among the unbanked who lack information needed to adequately assess risk; (c) lack of verifiable ID and difficulty in meeting CDD requirements; and (d) lack of suitable financial products for lower income segments.

89. It is worth mention the study of Behn, M. and Corrias, R. and Rola-Janicka, M. 2019. "On the interaction between different bank liquidity requirements," representing the discussion on the interaction of different regulatory metrics by empirically examining the interaction between the liquidity coverage ratio (LCR) and the net stable funding ratio (NSFR) for banks in the euro area. Their findings suggest that "the two liquidity requirements are complementary and constrain different types of banks in different ways, similarly to the risk-based and leverage ratio requirements in the capital framework".

90. It is acknowledged that such proposal is not in line with the international soft law tendance; however, sovereign authorities could be involved in a political exercise aimed at identifying the common principles for sharing innovations and applying its results to finance.

91. It is remarked by ECB. 2018. "Guide to assessments of fintech credit institution licence applications".

92. See European Parliament resolution of 17 May 2017 on "FinTech: the influence of technology on the future of the financial sector" (2016/2243(INI)), which calls on the Commission to draw up a comprehensive FinTech Action Plan in the framework of its Capital Markets Union (CMU) and Digital Single Market (DSM) strategies, which can contribute overall to achieving an efficient and competitive, deeper and more integrated and stable and sustainable European financial system, provide long-term benefits to the real economy and address the needs of consumer and investor protection and of regulatory certainty.

93. It is worth mentioning the Italian approach to such a problem by referring to Sepe, M. 2018. "Supervisione bancaria e risoluzione delle crisi: separatezza e contiguità" *Rivista Trimestrale di Diritto dell'Economia*, p. 302 ff.; Cuocolo, L. 2018. "Constitutional principles and the European banking union: what's gone wrong" *Diritto pubblico comparato ed europeo*, p. 1011 ff.; Capriglione, F. 2017 "La nuova finanza: operatività, supervisione, tutela giurisdizionale. Il caso "Italia". Considerazioni introduttive" *Contratto e impresa*, p. 75 ff.; Annunziata, F. 2017. "Chi ha paura della Banca Centrale Europea? Riflessioni a margine del caso Landeskreditbank c. BCE. Nota a TRIB. UE 16 maggio 2017 (causa T-122/15)" *Giurisprudenza commerciale*, 2017, fasc. 6, pt. 2, p. 917; D'Ambrosio, R. and Lamandini, M. 2017 "La "prima volta" del Tribunale dell'Unione europea in materia di Meccanismo di Vigilanza Unico. Nota a TRIB. UE sez. IV ampliata 16 maggio 2017 (causa T-122/15)" *Giurisprudenza commerciale*, 2017, p. 594 ff.; Rossano, D. 2014. "La crisi dell'Eurozona e la (dis)unione bancaria" *federalismi.it*, p. 31 ff.; Sarcinelli, M. 2012. "L'Unione bancaria europea. Intervento al "XII

Foro di dialogo italo-spagnolo", Madrid, 29–30 settembre 2012" *Banca impresa società*, p. 333 ff.

94. See the Editorial Board of the Financial Times, *US development finance needs urgent upgrading*, in FT.com, 26 September 2018.

95. Let us recall again Tsai, G. 2017. "Fintech and the U.S. Regulatory Response, Remarks at the 4th Bund Summit on Fintech Shanghai", July 9.

96. Sometimes, the contracts that underlie it can reflect the uncertainties and concerns arising from the instability of the capital market; however, it is not possible to admit agreements not adequate to support the challenges set by the changing taking place (and by the new centrality of banking compared to the recovery of the real economy); see Lemma, V. and Thorp, J. A. 2014. "Sharing Corporate Governance: The Role of Outsourcing Contracts in Banking" *Law and Economics Yearly Review*, Vol. 3, pt. 2, p. 357 ff.

97. It is worth mentioning that in August 2013 DFS announced its inquiry into the appropriate regulatory guidelines for virtual currencies. As part of an ongoing fact-finding effort informing that inquiry, the department held public hearings in January 2014. In March 2014, the department issued a public order announcing it will be considering formal proposals and applications for the establishment of regulated virtual currency exchanges operating in New York; see New York Department for Financial Services. 2014. "NY DFS releases proposed BitLicense regulatory framework for virtual currency firms" July 17 that has issued for public comment a proposed "BitLicense" regulatory framework for New York virtual currency businesses. This document proposed a regulatory framework—which is the product of a nearly year-long DFS inquiry, including public hearings that the department held in January 2014—that contains consumer protection, anti-money laundering compliance and cyber security rules tailored for virtual currency firms.

98. See CSBS 2019. "Conference of State Bank Supervisors, Vision 2020 for Fintech and Nonbank Regulation", which concludes: "Through Vision 2020, state regulators will transform the licensing process, harmonize supervision, engage fintech companies, assist state banking departments, make it easier for banks to provide services to non-banks, and make supervision more efficient for third parties."

99. See Office of the Comptroller of the Currency, 2017. "Third-Party Relationships: Frequently Asked Questions to Supplement OCC Bulletin 2013-29" on the relationships with financial technology (fintech) companies that involve some of these activities, including performing services or delivering products to a bank's customer base.

100. See Consumer Financial Protection Bureau (CFPB). 2017. "Supervisory Highlights" on the supervision over both bank and nonbank institutions

to help meet a consumer financial marketplace that is fair, transparent and competitive, and that works for all consumers.

101. See Financial Conduct Authority (FCA), 2017–2019. "Digital regulatory reporting" on the possible solutions to the increasing challenges financial institutions face in complying with their regulatory reporting obligations. See also "FinTech Sector Report", a report for the House of Commons Committee on Exiting the European Union following the motion passed at the Opposition Day debate on 1 November, which called on the government to provide the Committee with impact assessments arising from the sectoral analysis it has conducted with regards to the list of fifty-eight sectors referred to in the answer of 26 June 2017 to Q 239.

102. Reference is made to Bank of England, Quarterly Bulletin 2019 Q1, Embracing the promise of fintech.

103. In particular, Duflo, E. and Glennerster, R. and Kremer, M. R. 2006. "Using Randomization in Development Economics Research: A Toolkit" *MIT Department of Economics Working Paper No. 06-36* provided a practical guide (a toolkit) for researchers, students and practitioners wishing to introduce randomization as part of a research design in the field.

It is worth mention that this study, firstly, covers "the rationale for the use of randomization, as a solution to selection bias and a partial solution to publication biases". The paper also discusses (i) various ways in which randomization can be practically introduced in a field setting; (ii) design issues such as sample size requirements, stratification, level of randomization and data collection methods; (iii) discusses how to analyse data from randomized evaluations when there are departures from the basic framework.

It refers also to its suggestions on handling imperfect compliance and externalities, and on drawing general conclusions from randomized evaluations, including the necessary use of theory as a guide when designing evaluations and interpreting results.

104. Reference is made to Reserve Bank of India, Department of Banking Regulation, Banking Policy Division Draft Enabling Framework for Regulatory Sandbox, 8 February 2018.

105. It is worth recalling VV.AA. 2016. "Development of China's Financial Supervision and Regulation", Hu, Bin, Yin, Zhentao, Zheng, Liansheng (Eds.), on the current status, the development, and planned reform of the Chinese financial supervision and regulatory system in a systematic way.

106. See Development Strategies of Bank of China, 11 September 2019, available at boc.cn.

107. It is worth considering that the above is in line with the considerations of Argentati, A. 2018. "Le banche nel nuovo scenario competitivo. Fin-

Tech, il paradigma Open banking e la minaccia delle big tech companies" *Mercato concorrenza regole*, 2018, fasc. 3, p. 44 ff.

108. Let us recall Draghi, M. 2019 "Farewell Remarks", who recalled that "what the visionary leaders of that era saw, however, was that Europe had a powerful tool at its disposal to raise growth: to transform its common market into a single market. Removing existing barriers to trade and investment could reverse the decline in economic potential and bring more people back into work. Yet the Single Market was always about more than just this. It also aimed to protect people from some of the costs of the changes that would inevitably arise. Unlike the wider process of globalisation, it allowed Europe to impose its values on economic integration—to build a market that, to the extent possible, was free and just. Common rules would create trust between countries, give the weak recourse against the strong and provide safeguards for workers. The Single Market, in this sense, was a bold attempt at 'managed globalisation'. It combined competition with levels of consumer and social protection unseen in the rest of the world".

It also highlighted that "Freely floating currencies were therefore not an option, and fixed exchange rates would not work as capital became more mobile within Europe, as the ERM crisis in 1992-3 proved. The answer was to create a single currency: one market with one money. This construct has been largely successful: incomes across the continent have materially increased, integration and value chains have developed to an extent unimaginable 20 years ago, and the Single Market has survived intact through the worst crisis since the 1930s."

109. Let us recall Rodotà, S. 1991. "Protecting Informational Privacy. Trends and Problems", *Politica del diritto*, 1991, fasc. 4, p. 521 ff. for the beginning of a route towards a redefinition of the concept of privacy and data protection in the perspective of an 'open society', assessing conflicting rights and interests.

110. See Lagarde, C. 2019. "Transcript of International Monetary Fund Managing Director Christine Lagarde's Opening Press Conference, 2019 Spring Meetings", Washington D.C. 11 April, with respect to the fact that "We are looking at our Debt Sustainability Analysis. We are looking at our conditionalities. We are looking at improving our low-income country facilities. We are looking at a more comprehensive surveillance so that we can harness the benefits of technologies, best practices in all countries around the world, in order to provide the services that are expected by the membership".

111. It recalls Zaring, D. and Bignami, F. 2016. "Comparative Law and Regulation. Understanding the Global Regulatory Process". Northampton, MA, USA, who relies on the consideration that "as regu-

lation's domain has expanded, the processes by which it is mad across the world have come under scrutiny. The constitutional anomaly of a system of policymaking in which the *locus of power* rests neither with elected politicians nor with courts, but with public officials in specialized administrative agencies and transnational networks, has given rise to a number of legal innovations designed to foster public accountability".

112. Reference is made to Packin, N. G. 2013. "The Case Against the Dodd-Frank Act's Living Wills: Contingency Planning Following the Financial Crisis" *Berkeley Business Law Journal* on the functioning of comprehensive contingency plans for reorganization or resolution of their operations, whose goal is to mitigate risks to the financial stability of the US and encourage last-resort planning, which will allow for a rapid and efficient response in the event of an emergency.

113. See Ferran, E. 2004. "European Banking Union: Imperfect, But It Can Work" *University of Cambridge Faculty of Law Research Paper No. 30/2014* and in particular the consideration about an odd construction born of compromises and shaped to fit into legal territory bounded by EU Treaty constraints that cannot be adjusted in the current political environment, that can be repeated in the analysis of fintech.

114. This refers to Romano, S. 1909. "Lo Stato Moderno e la Sua Crisi", Pisa; it is worth recalling also Cassese S. 2011. "La prolusione romaniana sulla crisi dello Stato moderno e il suo tempo", Roma.

REFERENCES

Ahmad, J. K. and Devarajan, S. and Khemani, S. and Shah, S. 2005. "Decentralization and Service Delivery" World Bank Policy Research Working Paper No. 3603.

Alpa, G. 1981. "Raccolta di informazioni, protezione dei dati e controllo degli elaboratori elettronici (in margine ad un progetto di convenzione del Consiglio d' Europa)" Il foro italiano, 1981.

Alpa, G. 1985. "Il diritto dei computers", Informatica e diritto.

Alpa, G. 1998. "Aspetti della disciplina sui dati personali riguardanti gli enti e l'attività economica" Rivista trimestrale di diritto e procedura civile.

Alpa, G. 2019. "Fintech: un laboratorio per i giuristi" Contratto e impresa.

Annunziata F. 2018. "La disciplina delle trading venues nell'era delle rivoluzioni tecnologiche: dalle criptovalute alla distributed ledger technology", Orizzonti del diritto commerciale.

Annunziata, F. 2017. "Chi ha paura della Banca Centrale Europea? Riflessioni a margine del caso Landeskreditbank c. BCE. Nota a TRIB. UE 16 maggio 2017 (causa T-122/15)" Giurisprudenza commerciale.

Argentati, A. 2018. "Le banche nel nuovo scenario competitivo. Fin-Tech, il paradigma Open banking e la minaccia delle big tech companies", Mercato concorrenza regole.

Armour, J. and Hansmann, H. and Kraakman, R. H. 2009. "Agency Problems, Legal Strategies, and Enforcement" Oxford Legal Studies Research Paper No. 21/2009.

Association Française des Professionnels des Titres (AFTI). 2016. "AFTI response on CSDR Guidelines on Internalised", available at ESMA.europa.eu.

Bank of England. 2019. "Embracing the promise of fintech", Quarterly Bulletin 2019 Q1.

Barbagallo, C. 2019. "Fintech: ruolo dell'Autorità di Vigilanza in un mercato che cambia". Bancaria.

Barron, J. A. 1967. "Access to the Press – a New First Amendment Right", Harvard Law Review.

Bavoso, V. 2019. "The Promise and Perils of Alternative Market-Based Finance: The Case of P2P Lending in the UK" Journal of Banking Regulation.

Bebchuk, L. A. and Spamann, H. 2010. "Regulating Bankers' Pay" Georgetown Law Journal.

Bedell, F. 2015. "When Will Real-Time Clearing & Settlement Come?", Global Finance; Leander, T. 2015. "Harmony and Tempo: The Status of Real-Time Payments", Global Finance.

Behn, M. and Corrias, R. and Rola-Janicka, M. 2019. "On the interaction between different bank liquidity requirements".

Beltratti, A. and Stulz, R. M. 2009. "Why Did Some Banks Perform Better during the Credit Crisis? A Cross-Country Study of the Impact of Governance and Regulation" Fisher College of Business Working Paper No. 2009-03-012.

Berger, M. 2006. "Compelled Self-Reporting and the Principle Against Compelled Self-Incrimination: Some Comparative Perspectives" European Human Rights Law Review.

Bos, I. 2006. "Leniency and Cartel Size: A Note on How Self-Reporting Nurtures Collusion in Concentrated Markets" Amsterdam Center for Law & Economics Working Paper No. 2006-03.

Brescia Morra, C. 2019. "Le forme della vigilanza", Manuale di diritto bancario e finanziario.

Brozzett, A. 2018. "«Ending of too big to fail» tra soft law e ordinamento bancario europeo. Dieci anni di riforme", Bari.

Buchak, G. and Matvos, G. and Piskorski, T. and Seru, A. 2017. "Fintech, Regulatory Arbitrage, and the Rise of Shadow Banks", NBER Working Paper no 23288.

Buchak, G. and Matvos, G. and Piskorski, T. and Seru, A. 2018. "The Limits of Shadow Banks" Columbia Business School Research Paper No. 18-75.

Capriglione, F. 2017. "La nuova finanza: operatività, supervisione, tutela giuris-dizionale. Il caso "Italia". Considerazioni introduttive" Contratto e impresa.

Carney, M. 2017. "The Promise of FinTech – Something New Under the Sun? Speech given by the Bank of England Chair of the Financial Stability Board Deutsche Bundesbank G20 conference on Digitising finance, financial inclusion and financial literacy", Wiesbaden 25 January.

Cassese, S. 2011. "La prolusione romaniana sulla crisi dello Stato moderno e il suo tempo", Roma.

Cave, J. 2016. "Regulation by and of Algorithms" SSRN Research Paper no. 2757701.

Caytas, J. 2016. "Developing Blockchain Real-Time Clearing and Settlement in the EU, U.S., and Globally", Columbia Journal of European Law: Preliminary Reference.

Cerezetti, F. and Sumawong, A. and Shreyas, U. and Karimalis, E. 2017. "Market Liquidity, Closeout Procedures and Initial Margin for CCPs" Bank of England Working Paper No. 643.

Chatterjee, S. and Jobst, A. A. 2019. "Market-Implied Systemic Risk and Shadow Capital Adequacy" Bank of England Working Paper No. 823.

Choi, B. 2019. "What is the Social Trade-off of Securitization? A Tale of Financial Innovation", SSRN Working Paper No. 3440653.

Cian M. 2019. "Le sedi di negoziazione diverse dai mercati regolamentati", Studium iuris.

Clarck, J. B. 1931. "The distribution of wealth", New York.

Clark, R. C. 1981. "The Interdisciplinary Study of Legal Evolution", The Yale Law Journal.

Coase, R. H. 1988. "The firm the market and the law" Chicago.

Coffee, J. C. 2007a. "Law and the Market: The Impact of Enforcement" Columbia Law and Economics Working Paper No. 304.

Coffee, J. C. 2007b. "Law and the Market: The Impact of Enforcement" Columbia Law and Economics Working Paper No. 304 for the regulatory background of the above considerations.

Committee on the Global Financial System and Financial Stability Board. 2017. "FinTech credit: Market structure, business models and financial stability implications".

Consumer Financial Protection Bureau (CFPB). 2017. "Supervisory Highlights".

Corcoran, A. M. 2013. "International Standards for Central Counterparties and Replumbing the Financial System: Retrofitting Listed Derivatives Infrastructure for the Global OTC Derivatives Market", Futures and Derivatives Law Report.

CSBS. 2019. "Conference of State Bank Supervisors, Vision 2020 for Fintech and Nonbank Regulation".

Cuocolo, L. 2018. "Constitutional principles and the European banking union: what's gone wrong" Diritto pubblico comparato ed europeo.

D'Ambrosio, R. and Lamandini, M. 2017. "La "prima volta" del Tribunale dell'Unione europea in materia di Meccanismo di Vigilanza Unico. Nota a TRIB. UE sez. IV ampliata 16 maggio 2017 (causa T-122/15)" Giurisprudenza commerciale.

Davidson, Bruce I. 2011. "The Effects of Reciprocity, Self-Awareness, and Individual Characteristics on Honesty in Managerial Reporting" AAA 2011 Management Accounting Section (MAS) Meeting Paper.

Dempsey, M. J. 2000. "Ethical Finance: An Agenda for Consolidation or for Radical Change?" Critical Perspectives on Accounting.

Development Strategies of Bank of China, 11 September 2019. Available at boc.cn.

DiLorenzo, V. 2009. "Mortgage Market Deregulation and Moral Hazard: Equity Stripping Under Sanction of Law" St. John's Legal Studies Research Paper No. 09-0179.

Draghi, M. 2019. "Farewell Remarks".

Duflo, E. and Glennerster, R. and Kremer, M. R. 2006. "Using Randomization in Development Economics Research: A Toolkit" MIT Department of Economics Working Paper No. 06-36.

EBA. 2017. "Final Report. Recommendations on outsourcing to cloud service providers".

EBA. 2018. "The EBA's fintech roadmap. Conclusions from the consultation on the EBA's approach to financial technology (fintech)". 15 March.

EBA. 2019. "The EBA 2020 Work Programme".

EBA. 2020a "Discussion Paper on the future changes to the EU-wide stress test", 22 January.

EBA. 2020b "EBA Report on big data and advanced analytics", January.

ECB and FED Chicago. 2007. "The Role of Central Counterparties", July 2007.

ECB. 2016. "Programme Plan – T2S Migration Plan".

ECB. 2018a. "Convergence Report". 23 May.

ECB. 2018b. "Guide to assessments of fintech credit institution licence applications".

ECB. 2019. "Annual Report".

ESMA. 2020. "Guidelines on securitisation repository data completeness and consistency thresholds". 17 January.

ESRB. 2018. "EU shadow banking monitor", no. 3/September.

European Banking Federation. 2018. "The Future of the Banking Industry. Dialogue with the Banking Industry on ESCB Statistics", Frankfurt, 16 march.

European Parliament. 2017. "FinTech: the influence of technology on the future of the financial sector", resolution of 17 May 2017 (2016/2243(INI)).

Ferran, E. 2004. "European Banking Union: Imperfect, But It Can Work" University of Cambridge Faculty of Law Research Paper No. 30/2014.

Ferri, G. B. 1981. "Privacy e identità personale. nota a Pret. Roma 30 aprile 1981. Pret. Roma 11 maggio 1981" Rivista del diritto commerciale.

Financial Conduct Authority (FCA). 2017–2019. "Digital regulatory reporting" on the possible solutions to the increasing challenges financial institutions face in complying with their regulatory reporting obligations.

Frame, W. S. and Wall, L. D. and White, L. J. 2018. "Technological Change and Financial Innovation in Banking: Some Implications for Fintech" FRB Atlanta Working Paper No. 2018-11.

FSB. 2017a. "Artificial intelligence and machine learning in financial services. Market developments and financial stability implications", 1 November.

FSB. 2017b. "Chair's letter to G20 Finance Ministers and Central Bank Governors ahead of their Baden-Baden meeting", 17 March.

FSB. 2017c. "Financial Stability Implications from FinTech. Supervisory and Regulatory Issues that Merit Authorities' Attention", 27 June.

FSB. 2017d. "FinTech credit. Market structure, business models and financial stability implications". Report prepared by a Working Group established by the Committee on the Global Financial System (CGFS) and the Financial Stability Board (FSB), 22 May.

FSB. 2018. "Global Shadow Banking Monitoring Report 2017", March.

FSB. 2019a. "Decentralised financial technologies Report on financial stability, regulatory and governance implications", 6 June.

FSB. 2019b. "Fintech and market structure in financial services: Market developments and potential financial stability implications", February.

FSB. 2019c. "Global Monitoring Report on Non-Bank Financial Intermediation 2018", 4 February.

FSB. 2019d. Letter from the FSB Chair to G20 Leaders ahead of their Summit in Osaka, 25 June.

FSB 2020. "Global Monitoring Report on Non-Bank Financial Intermediation 2019", 19 Jannuary.

G30 WORKING GROUP. 2003. "Global Clearing and Settlement: A Plan of Action".

Garcia, J. A. 2012. "Who's Afraid of the Shadows? – EU Moves to Curb Emerging Threats from Shadow Banking" Financial Regulation International.

Garret B. L. 2016. "Too Big to Jail: How Prosecutors Compromise With Corporations", Harward.

Gebauer, S. and Mazelis, F. 2019. "Macroprudential Regulation and Leakage to the Shadow Banking Sector" DIW Berlin Discussion Paper No. 1814.

Gentile, G. 1916. "I fondamenti della filosofia del diritto", Firenze.

Geronimo, R. S. Q. 2017. Why Long-Term Debt Instruments Cannot Be Deposit Substitutes" Lexkhoj International Journal of Criminal Law.

Gilson, R. J. 1984. "Value creation by business lawyers: legal skills and asset pricing". The Yale Law Journal.

Gissler, S. and Narajabad, B. 2018. "Supply of Private Safe Assets: Interplay of Shadow and Traditional Banks" SSRN Research Paper no. 3132058.

Gissler, S. and Ramcharan, R. and Yu, E. 2019. "The Effects of Competition in Consumer Credit Markets", SSRN Research Paper no. 3170996.

Global Financial System and Financial Stability Board. 2017. "FinTech credit: Market structure, business models and financial stability implications".

Gomber, P. and Kauffman, r. J. and Parker, C. and Weber, B. 2017. "On the Fintech Revolution: Interpreting the Forces of Innovation, Disruption and Transformation in Financial Services" Journal of Management Information Systems.

Gourdel, R. and Maqui, M. and Sydow, M. 2019. "Investment funds under stress".

Grody, A. D. 2018. "Can a Globally Endorsed Business Identity Code be the Answer to Risk Data Aggregation?" Journal of Risk Management in Financial Institutions.

Haar, B. 2016. "Freedom of Contract and Financial Stability through the Lens of the Legal Theory of Finance" (LTF) – LTF Approaches to ABS, Pari Passu-Clauses, CCPs, and Basel III" SAFE Working Paper No. 141.

House of Commons Committee on Exiting the European Union. 2017. "FinTech Sector Report".

IOSCO. 2015. "Crowdfunding 2015 Survey Responses Report," December.

IOSCO. 2017. "IOSCO Research Report on Financial Technologies", February.

Irresberger, F and Bierth, C. and Weiss, J. N. F. 2016. "Size Is Everything: Explaining SIFI Designations", Review of Financial Economics.

Irti, N. 2004, "Ordine giuridico del mercato", Rome.

Ivashina, V. and Becker, B. 2011. "Cyclicality of Credit Supply: Firm Level Evidence" Harvard Business School Finance Working Paper No. 10-107.

Kaplow, L. and Shavell, S. 1991. "Optimal Law Enforcement with Self-Reporting of Behavior", NBER Working Paper No. w3822.

Khalil, S. K. and Saffar, W. and Trabelsi, S. 2013. "Disclosure Standards, Auditing Infrastructure, and Bribery Mitigation" Canadian Academic Accounting Association.

Khan, M. and Serafeim, G. and Yoon, A. 2016. "Corporate Sustainability: First Evidence on Materiality" The Accounting Review.

Knight, F. H. 1921. "Risk, Uncertainty and Profit". (2000 ed.).

Kwon, O. and Tseng, K. C. and Bradley, J. and Tjung, L. C. 2010. "Forecasting Financial Stocks Using Data Mining", SSRN Research Paper No. 1566268.

Lagarde, C. 2019. "Transcript of International Monetary Fund Managing Director Christine Lagarde's Opening Press Conference, 2019 Spring Meetings", Washington, DC, 11 April.

Laufer, W. S. 2018. "A Very Special Regulatory Milestone", University Pennsylvania Journal Business Law.

Lemma, V. 2015. "Too big to be popular". "La riforma delle banche popolari", Padova.

Lemma, V. 2016a, "The Shadow Banking System. Creating Transparency in the Financial Markets". London.

Lemma, V. 2016b. "Too big to escape". Rivista trimestrale diritto dell'economia.

Lemma, V. and Thorp, J. A. 2014, "Sharing Corporate Governance: The Role of Outsourcing Contracts in Banking" Law and Economics Yearly Review.

Levy, J. 2011. "Towards a Brighter Fourth Amendment: Privacy and Technological Change", Virginia Journal of Law and Technology.

Lothian, T. 2010. "Law and Finance: A Theoretical Perspective" Columbia Law and Economics Working Paper No. 388.

Lothian, T. 2011. "Rethinking Finance Through Law: A Theoretical Perspective" Columbia Law and Economics Working Paper No. 412.

Lowe, A. 1965. "On Economic Knowledge. Towards a Science of Political Economics", New York.

Lu, L. 2018. "Shadow Banking for Cash-Strapped Entrepreneurs: A Study of Private Lending Agreements Under Chinese Contract Law" Journal of Business Law Issue 3.

Lumsdaine, R. L. and Rockmore, d. and Foti, N. and Leibon, G. and Farmer, J. D. 2016. "The Intrafirm Complexity of Systemically Important Financial Institutions" SSRN Research paper No. 2604166.

Mainelli, M. and Milne, A. K. L. 2016. "The Impact and Potential of Blockchain on the Securities Transaction Lifecycle". SWIFT Institute Working Paper No. 2015-007.

Malpass, D. 2019. "Statement from World Bank Group President" World Bank Group – International Monetary Fund Annual Meetings.

McGuire, P. M. and von Peter, G. 2016. "The Resilience of Banks' International Operations" BIS Quarterly Review March 2016.

Moffitt, M. L. 2009. "Three Things to Be Against ('Settlement' Not Included) – A Response to Owen Fiss" Fordham Law Review.

Moohr, G. S. 2003. "An Enron Lesson: The Modest Role of Criminal Law in Preventing Corporate Crime" Florida Law Review.

Motti, C. 2009. "Tipologia e disciplina delle trading venues" Diritto della banca e del mercato finanziario.

Mülbert, P. O. 2010. "Corporate Governance of Banks after the Financial Crisis – Theory, Evidence, Reforms" ECGI – Law Working Paper No. 130/2009.

Office of the Comptroller of the Currency. 2017. "Third-Party Relationships: Frequently Asked Questions to Supplement OCC Bulletin 2013-29".

Ooi, V. and Soh, K. P. 2019. "Cryptocurrencies and Code Before the Courts", SSRN research Paper no. 3439306.

Packin, N. G. 2013. "The Case Against the Dodd-Frank Act's Living Wills: Contingency Planning Following the Financial Crisis" Berkeley Business Law Journal.

Packin, N. G. 2018. "Regtech, Compliance and Technology Judgment Rule" Chicago-Kent Law Review.

Pagliaro, A. 1952. "Necessità della forma", "Il segno vivente", Napoli.

Pesic, V. and Mure, P. 2010. "Are Sanctions Effective in Improving Bank Performance? A Study on Supervision and Administrative Sanctions Upon Italian Banks During the 1998–2009 Period" CAREFIN Research Paper No. 23/2010.

Picker, R. C. 2008. "Competition and Privacy in Web 2.0 and the Cloud" University of Chicago Law & Economics Working Paper No. 414.

Pinna, A. and Ruttenberg, W. 2016. "Distributed Ledger Technologies in Securities Post-Trading Revolution or Evolution?" ECB Occasional Paper No. 172.

Pollack, M. 2007. "A Listener's Free Speech, a Reader's Copyright" Hofstra Law Review.

Quagliariello, M. 2009. "Stress Testing the Banking System: Methodologies and Applications", Cambridge.

Reimsbach, D. and Hahn, R. 2013. "The Effects of Negative Incidents in Sustainability Reporting on Investors' Judgments – An Experimental Study of Third-Party versus Self-Disclosure in the Realm of Sustainable Development", Business Strategy and the Environment.

Rodotà, S. 1991. "Protecting Informational Privacy. Trends and Problems", Politica del Diritto.

Romano, S. 1909. "Lo Stato Moderno e la Sua Crisi", Pisa.

Roncalli, T. and Weisang, G. 2015. "Asset Management and Systemic Risk" Finance Meeting EUROFIDAI – AFFI Research Paper.

Rossano, D. 2014. "La crisi dell'Eurozona e la (dis)unione bancaria" federalismi.it.

Saguato, P. 2017. "The Liquidity Dilemma and the Repo Market: A Two-Step Policy Option to Address the Regulatory Void", Stanford Journal of Law, Business, and Finance.

Santos, J. A. C. 2000. "Bank Capital Regulation in Contemporary Banking Theory: A Review of the Literature" BIS Working Paper No. 90.

Sarcinelli, M. 2012. "L'Unione bancaria europea. Intervento al "XII Foro di dialogo italo-spagnolo", Madrid, 29–30 settembre 2012" Banca impresa società.

Schelling, T. C. 1980, "The strategy of conflict", Cambridge-London.

Scholz, L. 2017. "Algorithmic Contracts", Stanford Technology Law Review.

Sepe, M. 2018. "Supervisione bancaria e risoluzione delle crisi: separatezza e contiguità" Rivista Trimestrale di Diritto dell'Economia.

Sepe, M. 2019. "Abusi di mercato", Manuale di diritto bancario e finanziario.

Simon, H. 1945. "Administrative behaviour", London p. XXIV.

Simon, P. 2015. "Too Big to Ignore: The Business Case for Big Data", Hoboken.

Sorkin, A. R. 2010. "Too Big to Fail: Inside the Battle to Save Wall Street", London.

Taylor, R. C. and Wilson, C. and Holttinen, E. and Anastasiia M. 2020. "Institutional Arrangements for Fintech Regulation and Supervision", 10 January.

Tan, Y. 2017. "The Impacts of Competition and Shadow Banking on Profitability: Evidence from the Chinese Banking Industry" North American Journal of Economics and Finance.

Taro Aso. 2019. "Opening Remarks by Deputy Prime Minister Taro Aso at G20 High-level Seminar on Financial Innovation. Our Future in the Digital Age", 8 June.

The Editorial Board of the Financial Times. 2018. "US development finance needs urgent upgrading" in FT.com, 26 September.

Tsai, G. 2017. "Fintech and the U.S. Regulatory Response, Remarks at the 4th Bund Summit on Fintech Shanghai", July 9.

Ubertazzi, L. C. 1997. "Riservatezza informatica ed industria culturale" AIDA.

Van Loo, R. 2018. "Making Innovation More Competitive: The Case of Fintech" UCLA Law Review.

Verret, J. W. 2017. "A Dual Non-Banking System? Or a Non-Dual Non-Banking System? Considering the OCC's Proposal for a Non-Bank Special Purpose National Charter for Fintech Companies, against an Alternative Competitive Federalism System, for an Era of Fintech Banking" George Mason Law & Economics Research Paper No. 17-05.

VV.AA. 2016. "Development of China's Financial Supervision and Regulation", Hu, Bin, Yin, Zhentao, Zheng, Liansheng (Eds.).

Walzl, M. and Feess, E. 2002. "Self-Reporting in Optimal Law Enforcement When There are Criminal Teams" Aachen Micro Working Paper 02/02.

Weber, R. H. and Arner, D. W. and Gibson, E. and Baumann, S. 2014. "Addressing Systemic Risk: Financial Regulatory Design" Texas International Law Journal.

Williamson, O. E. 1985. "The Economic Istitutions of Capitalism", New York.

Wilmarth, A. E. 2011. "The Dodd-Frank Act: A Flawed and Inadequate Response to the Too-Big-To-Fail Problem" Oregon Law Review.

World Bank Group – International Monetary Fund. 2019. "Fintech: The Experience So Far" IMF Policy Paper.

Zaccaria, R. 1982. "Diritto all'informazione e riservatezza" Il diritto delle radio-diffusioni e delle telecomunicazioni.

Zaring, D. and Bignami, F. 2016. "Comparative Law and Regulation. Understanding the Global Regulatory Process". Northampton, MA, USA.

Zhu, S. H. and Pykhtin, M. 2007. "A Guide to Modeling Counterparty Credit Risk". GARP Risk Review.

CHAPTER 4

European Approaches to Fintech: The Role of Regulation and the Evolution of Supervision

This part of the research aims at clarifying the European approaches to financial innovation and the influences due to the common culture of freedom, welfare, and security. Accordingly, this chapter provides three sections in order to outline the common features of the regulatory methods across Europe, the interventions of the EU institutions and the importance of Switzerland. Focus on the current legal principles applicable to fintech will characterize the following pages.

As the underlying idea refers to a lawful use of technology, fintech will not be considered as an elusive way to escape from the standards set by the regulator. Hence, this idea led the Financial Stability Board (FSB) to monitoring of technologically enabled innovation in financial services, and helped policymakers in identifying the areas of financial markets that could be affected in the coming years by threats due to innovation. In this context, it is essential to outline that, apart from the efforts at the supranational level (i.e. the ones consolidated in the European Commission's (EC's) Action Plan on fintech, dated 8 March 2018), a uniform legal framework has not been established yet, neither in the European Union (EU) nor in the countries included in the Group of Twenty (G20).

However, the rules set forth by the EU regulator does not approach fintech as a new industry, so that the role of the European Central Bank will ensure that fintechers are properly authorized and have in place 'risk control frameworks' for anticipating, understanding and responding to the threats arising from executing their operations through tech-fuelled

© The Author(s) 2020
V. Lemma, *FinTech Regulation*,
https://doi.org/10.1007/978-3-030-42347-6_4

tools. Hence, an open approach to fintech firms that are willing to enter in the financial market by applying for a traditional license, even if they support the production and delivery of banking products and services with technology-enabled innovative business models.

From a regulatory perspective, evidence from Switzerland shows that an advanced democracy would be able to provide a secure environment for introducing the most advanced applications of financial innovation, able to support the world economy with a legal framework enacting the principles of freedom, independence and self-determination, and able to host fintechers in a wired but safe society.

Section I: In General

4.1   The Widespread Current Regulatory Approach

Questions raised by scholars about fintech have generally regarded the fundamental elements of such phenomenon, but—more and more often—are going to invest its definition and perimeter.[1] Obviously, questioners are not generally complaining about the definitions provided by the international bodies and sovereign authorities, but they seem to aim at promoting a debate on the possibility that the legal analysis of the financial technology will lead to a new form of supervision, in order to promote an increase in the efficiency of the market for capital.[2]

As shown in the previous chapter, the core idea refers to a lawful use of technology, and not to an application of high-tech tools to escape from supervision and other mechanisms enacted to drive any economic activity towards the social avail and individual benefit. Indeed, it can be assumed that the European approach to financial innovation would refer to the common culture of freedom, welfare and security (as well as the current legal principles underlying the regulation of traditional banking and finance activities). A clear formulation of the stated idea is not appropriate at the beginning of an analysis of the regulatory framework that frames fintech. After all, this is the starting point of the hypothesis that the policymakers have structured the supervisors by mirroring the organization of the credit institutions. As the main evidence shows, fintech is changing the governance of such institutions, and then it is expectable that the policymakers will innovate the supervisors.

In this context, it is essential to begin from the evidence that—apart from the efforts at the supranational level (i.e. the ones consolidated in the European Commission's Action Plan on fintech, dated 8 March 2018)—a uniform legal framework has not been established yet, neither in the European Union nor in the countries included in the Group of Twenty (G20). On the contrary, fintech business is growing faster and faster,[3] so threats due to innovation are rapidly increasing, and therefore the relevant risks can affect the stability of financial markets. It follows the need for investigating certain agreed regulatory principles that will protect the benefits of fintech and contain its risks (Verdegem, P. and Verhoest, P. 2009). So, the first areas of focus will be the role of third parties (acting as innovation facilitators), the operational resilience of fintech tools (and cybersecurity), the licensing and the perimeter of supervision (with respect to fintech firms), as well as the role of cryptocurrencies (that will be investigated in Chap. 7).

Nowadays, the regulators are assuming that fintech lies under the application of technological innovations to banking and finance, and that this phenomenon is improving the efficiency of the relevant business. Their goal is to reduce threats, but also to avoid asymmetries in the competition for raising savings, granting capital and providing financial services, and then to protect the safe and sound management of traditional banks and supervised entities.[4]

It is worth investigating whether the regulation of high-level technologies (and their application to improve the performance of supervised activities) relies on the same principle set forth for the employment of human resources to perform banking and finance (with respect to the need for protection of the investors and financial stability).[5] Hence, there is an opportunity for assessing the suitability of the European regulatory tradition with respect to the challenge arising from fintech, as this intensive use of algorithms questions the adequacy of public supervisory mechanisms structured for human decision-making processes.

First of all, it is useful to investigate what role will remain for people in the fintech environment, both as author and as target of new technologies (Rubinstein, I. S. 2013). This is not referring only to the protagonism of the programmers, but also to people who are at the beginning of the research for innovation, at the stage of application of the relevant findings (by developing algorithms and programming software) and at the end of the outcome due to this application (as investor, lender, borrower, insured, etc.), as well as those who are through the whole chain in the role of controllers.

In this respect, it is possible to look at any individual within the *prism* of fintech, in the light of his/her rights and duties. There is no doubt that technological innovations are changing personal behaviours and his/her social, constitutional and private dimension. And, several scholars have shown clear findings on the wired society, the network economy and the development of the personality in the digital age. Hence, there is an opportunity to focus on the fundamental rights, as the general framework for understanding the role of private law in regulating the impact of fintech on individuals (that will be developed in the following paragraphs) and on the performance of chain transactions (analysed in Chap. 4) or the organization of firms (stressed in Chap. 5).

In order to clarify the grounds for this analysis, it deserves considering the influence of the automatized networking on the relational dynamics among individuals as a qualifying characteristic of high-tech communities (Hacker, P. and Thomale, C. 2017). This is not a mere effect of the last industrial/digital revolution, but it arises from the continuous changes due to the frequency of the evolutionary economic cycles.[6] Therefore, the hypothesis of a new centrality of any individual with respect to each network he/she can access, provided that this run the risk to overexpose the content of the personality, by the fragmentation of the personal identity in a set of details, data and information shared among the lines of the global net.[7] And the possibility to collect and consolidate all of these will amplify the aforesaid risk.

According to the western approach to economics, since the first *liberal* instances, the policymakers considered access to the market a fundamental right of the individual.[8] Today, these instances concern access to the infrastructure, the technologies and—in brief—to the network. This leads to dwell on the digital device affair in the following paragraphs, and then to explore both the people's need to intertwine (as the business grows in the market) and the possibility to consider the connection as a prerequisite for substantial equality among citizens. This leads to the consideration that public intervention should extend its scope to 'IT literacy', website design and accessibility of the infrastructure, to ensure the standard of social cohesion required for the proper functioning of the market.

Moreover, substantial equality requires the protection of individuals from profiling, both as an abusive usage of personal data and as a behavioural analysis for the purpose of taking advantage of people.[9] This does not imply to question the usefulness of profiling in developing new products and services aimed at satisfying the needs of investors, lenders, borrowers or the insured (by ensuring also the financial stability of the relevant market).[10] However, the above challenges the risk of discrimination due to the use of stereotypes, the exploitation of inclinations and the advantage of asymmetries. Hence, there is the opportunity to regulate all of the applications of fintech, which are able to betray the aforesaid equality.

It should be easy to conclude by empathizing a mere a-synchrony between a (fast) society and a (slow) law,[11] but the development of this analysis requires to go deep into the need for regulating society in order to protect democracy (as we know it). Therefore, this investigation will bear in mind that the difficulties in the regulation of innovation cannot be reduced to a sort of 'time pressure', but these difficulties should be solved vis-à-vis the adoption of general rules aimed at regulating the main flow of this revolution, and not only the time-limited evidence of a global trend based on the predefinition of the decision-making process (incorporated by programmers in the algorithms).[12]

The European monitoring could not have been more chaotic. Hence, the strand of the following paragraphs aims at understanding if credit transformation processes would benefit from high-tech mechanisms (that can make the capital circulate from subjects in surplus to others in deficit according to different parameters from those established by the prudential supervision[13]). However, this would not mean that fintech should be outside the scope of public intervention aimed at minimizing the negative effects of market and technical failures. Rather, it recalls the need to move from the consideration that the current freedom in choosing fintech business models is the outcome of the deregulation process started in the twentieth century.

4.2   Regulation and Innovation in Banking and Finance

Following to the previous outline, it is possible to find out that the applications of fintech unveil by themselves the mechanisms behind their choices, even if codified within software and algorithms (and hidden to a naïve observer). In other words, business analytics and self-executing mechanisms have overridden human reasoning and instinctive choices that were embedded in the corporate governance paradigms, and therefore the leadership of the firms is not relying anymore on human decision-making processes, but on autonomous and preprogrammed flows able to collect inputs, move to the next stage and then produce an output. Hence, the attention goes to the programmers and coders before it goes to managers and employees of the supervised entities that run that software.[14]

In this respect, it is not possible to deny that the management bodies of any supervised entity can generally exclude the *autonomous guide* of the business, but this does not appear sufficient to deny the dominance of automation, whilst the human management and control seems to be limited. The relevant question refers to both the reliability of the current supervisors' organizational structures and action plans, and the need for clarifying the premises of the questions about the opportunity to adopt a new form of supervision able to control the algorithms and modify their essence by introducing self-executing constraints, limits, controls and security measures.

Bearing in mind the aforesaid considerations, this analysis considers diverse perspectives of innovation in banking and finance, corresponding to the diverse premises of such innovation (Wasserman, I. and Richmond-Abbott, M. 2005). There is a dividing line between the change due to a pathological state of the economy and the one corresponding to the success of research and development. According to the experience of the last few years, it is possible to take both changes for granted. Therefore, the policymakers must regulate them both (containing the transactional costs below the relevant benefit); whilst they are not generally called on to consider innovation in all its complexity or to focus on the more rational and effective characteristics of such phenomenon, they should be responsive to changes in the economic, social and technical conditions surrounding innovation (even if this task becomes more and more difficult because of rational or irrational interventions, conscious or unconscious behaviours, and conflicting or cooperative actions). Nevertheless, the monitoring of fintech is already producing effects on fintech, which suggests that regulation and fintech have developed a mutual and dynamic interface. Policymakers will influence the development of fintech, while the algorithms will try to predict the regulator and anticipate its constraints.

It is worth recalling that banks and financial institutions had traditionally been regulated with respect to investment portfolios, accounting practices, capital requirements (and other backstops against losses), as well as the limitation of the services which might be offered to customers (Draghi, M. 2019).[15] Obviously, these rules did not aim at promoting innovation, but were focused on controlling the money supply and ensuring smooth functioning of the economy because of efficient financial support.

Moving forward, it should be considered that information and communications technologies have forced alterations to financial operations at the national and international levels, and this has led to forum shipping, as well as to a wave of liberalization in this sector during the end of the twentieth century. At that time, several studies found productivity in US retail banking to be 30 per cent higher than in Germany or the UK, mainly due to the use of more innovative technologies and practices.[16] It is referring to the structural innovations and wider diffusion of new technologies in retail banking, and in particular to the elimination of the artificial segmentation of services which were offered by various types of banking institutions. Now, the improvement of these same technologies is supporting a new phenomenon (under the name of fintech), which is having implications for a revolution in banking and finance, because larger networks may be better able to exploit embryonic new products and services.[17]

Obviously, regulating financial innovations means correcting market failures and promoting universal access to networks, among other specific actions. Scholars agreed that, in the absence of government intervention, banking and finance would be characterized by excessive entry, unstable rates, inefficient services, costly duplication of facilities and inadequate investments in investor protection. Hence, the firms offering fintech solutions should be heavily regulated (or wholly or partly owned by governments) even if, in many cases, regulators have tended to hinder financial innovation.[18]

This is not denying the positive outcome of the mixture of privatization, deregulation and increased competition experienced by most of these sectors of the capital market, but it is questioning whether these results come also from certain technical changes whose application have stimulated further improvements. Scholars have agreed that policymakers, regulators and supervisors were often "inexperienced with new technologies, hostile to technical change and/or protective of domestic research efforts and nationally developed products and processes".[19]

Considering regulation and innovation as a whole, the forms of economic regulation intended to promote economic efficiency must be taken into account by ensuring that firms produce what customers most need (or rather, prefer), and sell it at the lowest possible prices. In this context, regulators should safeguard competition, prevent anticompetitive/non-inclusive behaviour and consent market accessibility. However, scholars have recorded trends of innovation in both concentrated market structures (which—according to Schumpeter—should support techno-logical progress mainly for reasons of static efficiency based on scale and scope economies) (Schumpeter, J. 1990) and competition among firms (which—according to Kenneth Arrow—have incentive to look for innova-tion capable of enabling control of the market) (Arrow, K. J. and Hahn, F. 1971).

In the end, the relevant question concerns the way to realize positive regulatory effects on fintech. The current freedom in selecting the busi-ness model and its analytics support allows entrepreneurs to rely on tech-fuelled tools and mechanisms able to supply cross-industry demands. This led to the conclusion that the current lack of regulation could allow an alternative to (human based) business conduct of traditionally supervised entities, whose trends could be driven by the self-orientation of algorithms and software. However, there is the threat that the application of fintech will first promote the innovation (of the business model, the organiza-tional structure and the way firms perform activities) and then it would inhibit corporate governance (and freeze the evolution of banks and the other financial intermediaries).

4.3   How Algorithms Think (in a Regulated Environment)

This analysis is going to focus on fintech innovations and their capability to set financial firms' demand, supply and production. It must be consid-ered that the European approach to fintech—as pointed out above—is based on the freedom of programming activities, arranging organizations and applying technology to the business models. This leads to the freedom of choosing software and algorithms that drive the decision-making processes.[20]

In this respect, it is possible now to contemplate that business analytics do not go straightforwardly, but rely on their programmers' experience, beliefs and unconscious fallacies or prejudice. This is considering that the activity of producing algorithms is confined by professional ethics, opin-ions and reviews, as well as limitations posed by technological, internal and external constraints. Hence, the development (or rather the self-development) of this algorithm is forward-looking and policy-based, it takes into account the predictable consequences of their outcome (in both the short and the long term, according to the availability of data and predictions). And this is not another form of ordinary practical reasoning.

From a mere regulatory perspective, these circumstances highlight the need for collecting essential information to develop a theory of automatized decision-making that takes into account the role of the programmers, the possibility to exclude human intervention and the political elements in the decision of business analytics.[21]

In light of these considerations, the assessment of the need for protection will focus on the reciprocal influence among programmers and the commercial and merchant banks that require algorithms. This would help in identifying the legal requirements able to apply an accurate control over risk taking and moral hazards.[22] Indeed, if there is not a 'rule of law', everything will be permitted to software and its programmers. However, public intervention exists, which means that both programmers and their customers (i.e. supervised entities) would be supervised and protected from an opportunist use of their abilities.

The key economic drivers and technological mechanisms of the banking and non-bank financial intermediation suggest that the efficiencies of fintech should be the rationale for the development of intermediation processes.[23] Indeed, there are many theories on algorithms functioning within fintech. All these theories feed into an approach that considers algorithms as the essential element of a chain that supports self-executing decision-making processes able to drive business analytics applied by fintech firms. This confirms the need for a specific legal analysis to support the forthcoming interventions, and verifies the possibility to set new standards for applying technology to finance.[24] According to the perspective mentioned in the paragraph above, it is expectable that the European regulator will be able to standardize the application of algorithms to the processes of financing and credit transformations in order to manage the allocation of risks and benefits among the tech-fuelled firms and their customers.[25]

In this respect, explanations about algorithms (and their outcomes) refer to the preferences that their programmers bring into the relevant flows. So the flows based on sequential stages are predicted to provide *disproportionate results*, due to the difficulties in ensuring the neutrality of the assumptions that originated such processes, from one side, and the absence of correctives applied to the weight of the preferences of the programmers, on the other. Whatever the method for determining an algorithm's *inclination* (and whatever the stage of the intermediation process that applies to such an algorithm), this inclination should explain much of

the correlation in the choices made by the software used for business analytics. And the higher the frequency of running algorithms and software
made by the same programmer, the greater explanatory power this (pref-
erential) constant has.

There is more: the outcome of an algorithm can be predicted by other
algorithms (that are subject to the aforesaid inclination). However, this is
not sufficient to conclude that all software and algorithms are best
explained as inclination motivated, just as the scope of fintech regulation
cannot refer only to the most recent applications of engineering to the
activities falling under the rules governing the techniques of banking and
finance.[26] However, the programmer who orients his/her algorithms and
software to his/her inclinations might be thought to be a target for public
intervention based on the principle of deterrence, which intensifies rather
than undermines the supervisors' choices. Those who regard public intervention as the most effective corrective for the market's failures should
welcome this possibility of intervention.

In this context, the legal scholars should be in the best position to propose that programmers must be forced to consider the effects of their
software's output on the market (and in particular on the maximization of
the wealth and the symmetry of its distributions). In other words, the current approach supposes that algorithms generally take into account the
reaction of the action driven by themselves and incorporate the result of
such action in their analysis. This would suggest applying the game theory
to sharpen the analysis of software and then to introduce new elements of
deterrence (to be caught by the algorithms). Hence the conclusion that
the software would be able to depart from the original output of its algorithms (as would be the outcome if it did not have to count the reaction
of the market to its output) and settle new results compatible with the
proper functioning of the market.

All of the above leads to a strategic-based conclusion, which is compatible with the presence of inclinations, as the first relay on the possibility
that the programmers tend to conform the outcome of their software to
the market trends, although they could care just about expressing an
unconditioned outcome. And this conclusion is compatible with any other
goal-oriented interpretation of a programmers motivation.

From another perspective, it should be considered that a programmer
could focus on 'small-group dynamics' (instead of considering the whole
market for capitals).[27] Due to this focus (on an industry, sector, practice,
group of firms or customers), this analysis would be able to go deep into

the preferences that would influence the aforesaid inclination (or rather the effects of the outcome on the wealth of a small group of market participants). In this respect, the presence of a panel of programmers (in lieu of a single programmer) should have an effect on the mitigation of this inclination for the well-being of 'small group', as the literature on polarization finds (Eagly, A. H. and Shelly, S. 1993). Thus, the option for a working group does not aim at increasing the production or the information, but at aligning the inclination of the algorithms to the interest of the people.

In any case, differences among panel programmers in the intensity of their inclinations and then of the preferences for a particular outcome lead to a sort of 'dissent aversion'. This is the consequence of the difficulties in collegiality while dealing with the coding of chains (based on flows), and this requires continuous efforts at minimizing the deviation from the original flow. Obviously, when inclinations and preferences are aligned, the collegiality would probably be slight and the diversity of such elements would lead to a wider distribution of benefits and costs (due to the outcome of the software).

All of the above does not cast doubt that a barely economic approach could model this situation as a hyper-rational environment, and a mere psychological analysis could consider it as the product of elementary illusions. However, it clarifies that the application of algorithms will be able to introduce cognitive consistency and instrumental rationality (driving flows to ends), and points out the need for supervising the software that substitutes human reasoning (and its programmers).

The focus goes deeper. A legal analysis of the programming of algorithms highlights the importance of preconceptions in modelling the software to be applied in the financial markets, as well as data limitations can explain its shortfalls. Indeed, the radical uncertainty that usually overwhelms managers in the most interesting and profitable operations must be borne in mind (which should make algorithms largely inapplicable to the relevant business decision-making in cases of rare and almost-unknown opportunities). Even if the economic theories generally treat the manager as a rationale, self-oriented, opportunistic maximizer, this analysis should also consider that he/she has personal behaviour that goes far beyond his/her 'utility function' (or rather the model that represents his/her preferences and inclinations).[28] Often, their personal behaviour is limited by an interplay of self-interests and a limitation of knowledge, but—at times—it helps managers in surmounting cognitive limitations and emotional forces (that shape behaviour along or against any rational calculation). Thus, this approach overlaps the organizational and pragmatic theories on human-driven business models and behaviour. At the same time, this recalls the intuition that agents and their principals have divergent interests, and the insight that an organizational structure is necessary for aligning such interests.

According to the previously mentioned hypothesis, business analytics would benefit from a regulatory intervention that would not extend the principles and the rules set forth by human behaviour, but considers the (conscious) outcome (of these algorithms) as it has been offered to the market.[29] So, it is possible to ask for a public intervention. Regulators should introduce the duty to internalize into the flow a sort of 'official constraints' considering that: such algorithms are not a mere syllogism, nor their product; their functioning does not refer to a decision of men, nor to an ideology; a normative functioning of software and algorithms cannot be determined by the law, nor by judgements. But the fact that business analytics follows precedent repeatedly does not undermine the need for protection (and does not mitigate the risk of correlation in the outcomes, examined in the previous pages with respect to the possibility of influencing the formation of fintech firms' supply and demand).

Therefore, the previously mentioned consideration should raise specific questions concerning the need for regulating the use of algorithms, and then this analysis would lead to demand the possibility to set new principles (or rather the opportunity to recast the current ones). Hence, software and algorithms do not jeopardize capital markets because of their mere application, but only because their use leads to asymmetries, market failures and sunk-costs. In this respect, as shown in the next paragraphs, it is desirable a strategic role for central banks, supervisory authorities, or any new private body able to regulate and control a reserve concerning the activity of 'high-tech service providers' operating in banking or financial markets (kept back to qualified and monitored firms).

4.4 THE ROLE OF PRIVATE LAW

It is worth investigating whether the 'new (dis)intermediation' would be able to reach an equilibrium able to sustain the wealth, the growth and the stability of the financial market, as well as to safeguard individual rights and the common welfare (Alpa, G. 2019). This means that the following consideration are going to develop and integrate what was anticipated above with respect to the impact of fintech on individuals, by looking at the prism spectrum of people's rights and duties that shine in the market (Witte, J. and Mannon, S. 2007).

If it has been asked what determines the current direction of this research, the answer will again be in the mixture of the interests for the stability of the market and the need to protect individuals.[30] From this perspective, it is acknowledged that the traditional models on transactions and the basic rules of private law do not consider the sustainability of development and financial stability as duties of the party. Moreover, the market fails to address a maintainable path for growth.[31] Fintech, nowadays, shows that the financial system is wider than its markets because—among other elements—of commons that are not traded (whose consideration is becoming more and more complicated, as shown while going deep into big data). Hence, it is not possible to deny that certain fintech applications are both tradeable goods or services (for the relevant buyer or seller) and commons, provided that—for example—their consumption (e.g. the download of a software or certain data) by one user does not preclude its consumption by another person (the so-called *rivalrousness*), and it is not possible (or rather very difficult) to prevent a user who has not paid for them from having access to them. In addition, in the latter case (the so-called *excludability*), it is clear that such prevention would result in losses (of efficiency) and an increase in the systemic risks (due to the action of a not-well-informed market-participant).

These losses and risks amplify their relevance in considering the externalities of private transactions also,[32] and the limited attitude of private law to force the internalization of them in the economic sphere of the parties. This does not allow this analysis to be limited within the boundaries of the market for capital, by only focusing on the role of the contract. These assumptions, in fact, help in understanding that the growth due to fintech is a 'deficit growth', and then if it may be able to *force* the market going into another systemic or monetary crisis.

Nowadays, a new phenomenon comes into consideration, whose size and features are quantitatively and qualitatively different from past-experienced (r)evolutions. Fintech recognizes specific value to certain attributes of the personality (that can also be shared or traded without being a direct and immediate burden for the person), and promotes both the 'objectivation' and the 'contractualization' of such attributes. Moreover, there are problems of the individuals' capacity to be in the position to negotiate them, to understand what they are negotiating and to withdraw from such negotiations (or the relevant agreements). So policy-makers are called to set up a system of safeguards and backstops able to protect the weak parties from such shortfalls as the exploitation of fintech tools, misconduct in managing personal data and abuse of power due to profiling.

In this situation, it is not possible to accept the thesis that reduces the relevant shortfalls to data limitations only, nor to the mere incapacity of analysing all the data collected.[33] It must be further investigated if the traditional mechanisms of private law are able to regulate fintech transactions or, instead, require new rules for multilateral transactions (based on sharing economies), to protect individual rights and to assess responsibilities.

And, in such situations markets do not clarify.

Uniform rules would represent a path of intervention, but policy analysers have shown that harmonization of all rules across countries is not efficient, given their different economies, judicial systems, social and cultural backgrounds.[34] However, at least, greater compatibility among the most important rules should be envisaged, in order to avoid the spiral of regulatory competition. These reflections imply that regulatory differences in private law (and its enforcement) can not only suggest a sort of 'forum shopping' (in choosing the jurisdiction and the law applicable to the contracts), but also delay technology diffusion as in the case of conflicting competition, financial and intellectual property laws. These elements create uncertainties and raise transactional costs, as market participants will invest in seeking the countries able to provide them with the most favourable regulatory environment.

Notwithstanding all of the above, individual can rely on private law to safeguard transparency, having regard to both the adoption of good faith in dealing and the banning of bargaining power. This would expand the role of private law, and would help in developing fintech business and its market, addressing the responsibility of individuals by means of contractual sanctions able to avoid that the outcomes of a single transaction do not jeopardize the common welfare. At this stage of the analysis, the definition of smart-contracts as 'programmable distributed applications that can trigger financial flows or changes of ownership if specific events occur' should be assessed (as defined by the FSB in 2017).[35]

Any economist can argue that parties are becoming fungible, as well as the objects of such contracts are.[36] But the point of all this is that, in regulating fintech, individuals matter. There are no clear evidences that undermine the original individualistic character of the legal framework (of private and public law) aimed at protecting the personality and the fundamental economic rights that refer to the interests contained in the market for capital. This leads to a harmonization between the private and the public approach to individual rights, and the role that private law should enact seems to be oriented towards the support of smart contracts and their predefined self-executing outcomes.

What makes the above different encourages this analysis to divert its path towards the role of a (smart-)contract in the wired society and the analysis of its bilateral regulation as the boundary of a new *social status*.[37] Indeed, the contract is one of the most analysed juridical forms in fintech. On the contrary, it is preferable to assume that private would be able to assess their own status, even if it is not possible to avoid recalling the previously mentioned consideration that fintech allows individuals to choose the software that will deal for them. This leads to questioning the applicability of traditional knowledge to the role of the physical person in the transaction, the contract and the market, while at the same time asking for new (social) studies on the status of people in an automatized environment (as a prerequisite for any comprehensive assessment of fintech transactions).

This does not undermine the enforcement of private law, but highlights it. Indeed, the alternative would drive individuals within a hierarchy with a regulation of the juridical relations of the groups based on pure orders and their executions. Instead, the principles set forth in a market democracy consider the individual as part of his/her social context, and then provides schemes for managing his/her multilateral relations (with others) as a bundle of conflictual or cooperative interests.[38]

A threat can be effective whether the policymakers would allow automatized limitations to the free construction of the individual's private sphere of interests, rights and duties.[39] Therefore, it is due to a regulatory intervention able to recognize and protect the inviolable rights of the person, in the markets where such sphere is assembled. Thus, there is the need for an institutional background able to support the status of any individual, the freedom in developing the personality and then the possibility of *resisting* against the influence due to profiling (and the subsequent power of fintech tools to influence the individual self-determination process). Obviously, status can be referred to as the notion of consumer, saver, investor, user and so on. However, in the fintech environment, the *status* of fintech user results also from the possibility to access the infrastructure, the software, and the data.[40] Hence, this *status* is not a personal desire, but a requirement for the exercise of individual rights in the new tech-fuelled market for capital.

Even in this perspective, the main paradox comes with the consideration that private law has supported the liberal-democracy and the free market, while now the former puts the latter at risk because of the unsustainability of the transactions compliant with the current rules.

4.5   THE APPROACH OF THE FINANCIAL STABILITY BOARD

The FSB expressly understands 'fintech' as technologically enabled innovation with an associated material effect on financial markets and institutions and the provision of financial services.[41] Indeed, the intuition that this phenomenon could influence the financial stability, because of both certain practical changes in business and new connections among market participants (that would reduce the safety space enacted in the last years to avoid any negative domino effect).[42] In an extremely clear and lucid synthesis, FSB's work opens to rational analysis of fintech-based financial markets. In these markets, the FSB's analysis goes beyond the monitoring it declares. It is an important contribution to understanding the conduct of the ambiguous path of innovators, considering also the opportunities due to cryptography and algorithms for the benefit of both regulators and supervisors (even if these last topics will be shown into Chap. 8).

As anticipated, the approach of the FSB emphasizes the possibility that "technological innovation in the financial sector offers potentially huge benefits, not least in terms of efficiency and inclusiveness" (Quarles, R. K. 2019). The focus goes to certain positive key elements, such as (1) greater access to and convenience of financial services, (2) greater efficiency of financial services and (3) a to push towards a more decentralized financial system, in which fintech firms may be disintermediating traditional financial institutions (even if this has led to the open question highlighted in Chap. 3). It follows the execution of their analysis within FSB's institutional mandate, and the clue of financial stability implications of trend towards a widespread adoption of fintech innovations. Besides a recommendation to any other body or authority to "be vigilant and … actively monitor the effects that fintech innovations have on specific products and services, as well as on incumbent financial institutions, financial markets, and the economy more broadly", the first conclusions lead to consider these innovations as a result of the post-crisis reforms.

Moreover—by questioning the possibility that fintech applications spring from their potential to unbundle banking into its core functions of settling payments, performing maturity transformation, sharing risk and allocating capital—FSB opened the debate on the possibility to override the role of banks as credit institutions. Then, scholars have been called to consider the risks of the competition among supervised entities (under prudential constrains) and incumbent firms (operating under market-based financings schemes), and policymakers have been called to ensure that fintech develops in a way that maximizes the opportunities and minimizes the risks for society.[43] The pervasiveness of such calls arises from two separate considerations. One mentioned in the first part of this chapter is that algorithmic bargaining requires an analytical model of finding a cooperative solution in the case that both regulators and supervised entities recognize that there is a wide range of rules preferable for the market participants over then no regulation at all. The second refers to the tacit agreements or implicit premises, which cannot be regulated by rules designed for explicit negotiations.

According to the above, it can easily be highlighted that the FSB did not move its analyses from the differences between the internal freedom of human-driven market participants and the external freedom of the fintech tools (which respond to input on the basis of an established outcome linked to a specific event). In this respect, the focus of the FSB on the 'fintech credit' has pointed out that credit activity can be facilitated by electronic platforms (such as peer-to-peer lenders), and that this opportunity has generated significant uncertainty as to how fintech credit markets will develop, how the software will boost the market-based intermediation chains and how they will affect the competition with the traditional banking sector.[44] Moreover, as a result of such detailed monitoring, scholars have developed the analysis on the 'shadow banking system' by considering that, because of the speed of fintech innovations, there is heterogeneity in the business models of the firms performing fintech credit activities (although they currently remain small in size relative to the credit extended by supervised entities).

At this stage of the market evolution, there is no need to investigate if a bigger share of fintech-facilitated credit could have financial stability benefits or risks. However, it is useful to point out that this trend is in line with the current expansionary monetary policies of both European Central Bank (ECB) and FED.[45]

It is worth considering that, since 2017, FSB has monitored that fintech was growing rapidly. In this respect, the collection of case studies has helped this board in highlighting three common and interrelated drivers of fintech innovation: (1) shifting customer expectations and other demand factors, (2) evolving technology, and (3) changes in market structure (FSB 2019).

From a regulatory perspective, this analysis can rely on this monitoring to suggest prioritizing the areas for intervention, having regard to the necessity that international bodies and national authorities should undertake regular assessments of cyber threats. There is no doubt that international cooperation is necessary for mitigating the risk of fragmentation or divergence in regulatory frameworks, which could lead to competition among national regulators (which limits the effectiveness of efforts to promote financial stability).

From the same perspective, whether the current evidence leads to the conclusion that, in general, financial stability is not often cited as an objective for recent or planned regulatory reforms, it would be possible to understand the approach of traditional authorities because of the policy objectives mentioned as the goals of their intervention: consumer and investor protection, market integrity, financial inclusion, and promoting innovation or competition (Bure, C. 2005). In fact, these authorities show their deep rooting in the environment of the entities they usually supervise. Indeed, this monitoring shows more what there is not than what there is: the intention to supervise operating system developers.[46]

Accordingly, many fintech activities would be covered within existing regulatory frameworks, by means of (planned or enacted) measures whose scope and scale of changes vary substantially (depending, among other things, on the relevant size and structure of domestic financial sectors as well as the flexibility and scope of existing frameworks). Indeed, evidence from such monitoring also shows that the majority of regulatory interventions refer to the areas of payments and capital raising, and to a lesser extent the sector of individual and collective portfolio management, insurance and market support.

Notwithstanding the above, the operational risks—due to the reliance on third-party service providers (such as the previously mentioned programmers and coders)—merit the authorities' attention and—as such—they become specific priorities for international cooperation.[47] In this respect, it is worth highlighting that these risks require a specific regulatory approach based on the technical knowledge of information technology, which is something different from the capabilities useful for mitigating micro-financial hazards or monitoring macro-financial threats.

Conversely, it is not possible to deny that the FSB concludes its analysis by summarizing that "fintech activities are also subject to similar micro-financial and macrofinancial risks. As such, authorities will continue to regulate for the same reasons they regulate traditional financial activities". Probably this conclusion is a regulatory starting point, but the impact that the fintech drivers are having on the provision of financial services suggests taking a look in another direction. The most recent monitoring activities show that in some jurisdictions large, well-established technology firms (the so-called Big-Tech) have recently entered the market for capital by providing financial services as part of the goods or services that they normally offer. They use a large quantity of their customer data to carry out risk assessments related to their provision of financing.[48]

This analysis is again forced back to consider the monitoring. In recent months, its result highlighted the role of decentralized financial technologies (such as those involving distributed ledgers and online peer-to-peer, or user-matching platforms). As anticipated, such technologies may reduce or eliminate the need for intermediaries, their assets and centralized processes that have traditionally been involved in the circulation of capital, because they unbundle banking, and then reorganize decision-making, risk-taking, and/or record-keeping. From a regulatory perspective, it is useful to consider the positive effects of such decentralization, and the fact that it this may lead to greater competition and diversity in the financial system. Besides this, the inefficiencies of an activity-based approach to regulation must be considered, as well as the newness of supervising activities that do not refer to the juridical sphere of an intermediary.

Even in this case, all the above confirms that as fintech continues to develop, it will be important to continue monitoring its financial stability implications.[49] However, all of the above suggests to begin regulating this phenomenon, having regard to both activities and entities, in order to avoid that the virtual will became the new shadows (FSB 2020).

4.6   The 'Digital Divide' Affair

'Digital divide' is an expression first used during the Clinton presidency (1993–2001) to point out the existing disparity in the access to information and communication technology.[50] It is possible to recall that, in 1998, Vice President Gore remarked, "five years ago, 3 million people were

connected to the Internet. Two years ago, 40 million people were connected. Last year, it was 100 million"[51]; In the 1980s, the entrepreneurs
of high-tech industry did not hide their objective to have a computer on
every desk and in every home.[52]

Nowadays, 'digital divide' refers to the specific difficulties and limits
related to the usage of the basic information and communication technology (ICT) tools, and the use of this expression reflects a common awareness in respect of the relevant problems. Hence, it is recalled to highlight
the possibility that fintech will determine asymmetries in financial markets.
These asymmetries refer to the generally recognized difficulties of aged
people in dealing with technology compared to the skills of young people:
indeed, these generations should collaborate to let capital circulate from
the old to the young (according to the traditional dynamics of saving and
investment). Hence, whether technology removes the elder generations
from the market, this should be considered as a loss (that cannot be com-
pensated by a mere increase in velocity, numerosity or effectiveness).
Moreover, the evidences gained from monitoring suggests other difficulties, due to various causes such as infrastructural deficits, educational
weakness and cognitive asymmetries (Zeng, F. 2011).

From the perspective of European policymakers, since 2000, innovation has been considered a support for inclusive growth. In other words,
their goal was to prepare for the transition to a knowledge-based economy
and an information society (by better policies for research and development), but also to step up the process of structural reform for competitiveness by completing the internal market.[53] Therefore, regulatory
intervention aimed at establishing a European area of research and innovation, and creating a friendly environment for starting up and developing
innovative businesses, especially SMEs. Indeed, the economic and social
determinants of this goal relied on the significant role played by research
and development in generating economic growth, employment and social
cohesion. Hence, the macroeconomic policy aimed at redirecting public
expenditure towards increasing the relative importance of capital accumulation—both physical and human—and supporting research and development, innovation and information technologies (Wyatt, S. et al. 2005).

All the above supported development that was unable to avoid the digital divide (Wei, L. and Hindman, D. 2011). And their further goal to
safeguard the proper functioning of an internal market indicated by the
distinction between those who have internet access and those who are
excluded from these services.[54]

From this perspective, it is clear that the digital divide keeps evolving and broadening with new technological developments. Indeed, it is not useful just taking into account the gap between individuals in the opportunities to access information and communication technologies (ICT) and their use of them (Scardovi, C. 2016) but referring to the gap among customers and firms, provided that the former can access tools for comparing the supply, while the latter can invest in fintech tools able to analyse the demand, profile the customer, influence the alternatives and—in the end—try to increase bargaining power.

In light of the above, in the fintech environment, the traditional analysis of the issues raised by the digital divide are not sufficient to reach the goals of this research, but it is useful to cast doubt that firms invest in fintech in order to change the equilibrium of the market in a way that reserves to them all the advantages of technological innovations. Herein lies one more consideration for supervising the software and the algorithms used in the financial market. All of the above also highlights the rights that protect the individuals, which refers to the individuality, as it has been constitutionalized, protected by public and private law, and now challenged by analytic behaviours of firms and institutions. These challenges have been experienced with regard to the qualitative changes owing to technological progress (more than just fintech alone); however, they seem to reflect the transformation of the relevant social and economic context,[55] as well as the integration of markets due to both the harmonization of the legal order and the interconnection of financial networks (within market-based financing schemes).[56]

In safeguarding individuality, the design of regulations can either hinder innovation or encourage it. Indeed, the problems related to the 'digital divide' should take into account the effects of the most advanced technologies and reflect the views of both producers and users, whilst a mere 'right of regressing' to analogic would raise the transactional costs (and therefore would not protect the 'under-digitally-evolved' individuals). Hence, it is worth recalling the conclusion on the need for regulatory approaches that are technology-friendly, rather than public intervention aimed at setting minimum standards (as in the case of the right to request a paper-printed copy of the contracts).[57]

However, it is not possible to deny that the digital divide matters require also an atomistic approach to defend individuals. This would not suggest coming back to the classic model that referred the protection of personality to a 'private and bilateral affaire', but it advocates applying the technique of full responsibility of the parties (even if this approach has been criticized because of the lack of protection against the abuse of wide-spread power, as it has been monitored in fintech).[58] This led to also propose adding (to this model of individual protection based on agreement and responsibility) specific procedural and organizational backstops, which would be able to rely on algorithms and fintech (so that they can be directly incorporated in the software that supports transactions).

Whether safeguards on the protection of individual rights can be defined in a private way is made more dubious, no less so by the increasingly versatile character of artificial intelligence. It is now widely recognized that there is a continuous gradation in the possible IT illiteracy that leads to digital divide, due to the lack of data, absence of capacity and/or time constraints. There seems to be consequently a return to the previously mentioned problems of the algorithmic management of transactions, which highlights the inescapability of the debate about the provision of preventive controls of the flows underlying the automatized decision processes.

In brief, digital divide requires an 'integrated juridical strategy'. It refers in particular to the simultaneous application of accountability, economic analysis of the impact of public intervention, regulation and control. Here is another reason for contemplating the idea of a supervisor in charge of the direct oversight over the programmers and coders of software, algorithms and flows.

SECTION II: THE APPROACHES WITHIN THE EUROPEAN UNION

4.7   SUPERVISORY PRACTICES OVER FINTECH APPLICATIONS: THE PROTAGONISM OF MONITORING

The emergence of innovation in the financial market always raises curiosity, suggests self-assessment and requires efforts in adapting the rules to the new business. So, it is not surprising that EU policymakers are making an allowance for the supervision of fintech within the scope of its mandate, nor that national regulators are going to require that fintechers will be properly authorized; and, they have in place risk control frameworks for anticipating, understanding and responding to the risks arising from the execution of technology-enabled innovative business models.

Considering that the first experience of fintech started on the edge of the last financial crisis, only in the last few years have the financial authorities begun to promote an evolution in the business model of supervised entities, suggesting a way to override the difficulties due to the reduction of interest margins. In this context, the copious production of studies shows the awareness for the current progression of technology, as well as the understanding of the relevant need for aptitude and capability in order to graduate the rules (to apply) with regard to the risk (to mitigate). Hence, the current analyses on fintech regulation cannot *lie* on the debate about the identification of the traditional rule applicable to new firms and operations. These analyses should verify if there is the need for setting new principles able to encourage (or rather, to push) the evolution of finance towards high levels of wealth production, stability and security, having regard to the possibility to establish new regulators, supervisors and controllers (adequate to the environment they will be overseeing) (Wyatt, S. et al. 2002). They should also verify when the aforesaid need must be satisfied, because only certain volumes are able to support the transactional costs of regulation.

In practice, this means that policymakers need to know (and understand) the applicability of a technology (and its effects), as well as they need to measure the benefit of a regulatory intervention aimed at promoting a preferred market equilibrium (Antonio, A. and Tuffley, D. 2014). Indeed, financial authorities are developing special projects in order to support the monitoring of fintech and the development of new tools for verifying the compliance of supervised entities.[59] Innovation hubs, regulatory sandbox and incubators pursue this purpose, and introduce new ways of structuring the supervision, by means of institutional meetings, derogation provided for fintech firms to explore certain innovations, partnerships and con-financing interventions.

This analysis is not going to go deep into the European treaties that established the Communities; the underlying reason does not refer to the lack of any reference to 'innovation', but because they were establishing a common background for a development based on innovation itself, driven towards peace and welfare. Henceforth, only in the 1990s the European policymakers started expressly referring to 'innovation' by providing that the Community and the Member States have to ensure that the conditions necessary for the competitiveness of the Community's industry exist, and then, for that purpose, "in accordance with a system of open and competitive markets, their action shall be aimed at ... fostering better exploitation of the industrial potential of policies of innovation, research and techno-logical development".[60] Nowadays, the EU Treaty has moved forward to the goal of "achieving balanced economic growth and price stability", set forth under the Declaration of Article 126 of the Treaty on the Functioning of the European Union. In this respect, EU rules can be interpreted in a way that supports economic reforms, innovation, competitiveness and the strengthening of private investment and consumption in phases of weak economic growth.

Starting from the action plan of the European Commission (EC), it comes into consideration its purpose to benefitting from financial innova-tion and providing firms and customers with the most suitable and acces-sible products, to guarantee a high level of protection for savers and investors and to ensure the resilience and integrity of the financial system. Indeed, the guidance role of the EC has supported the proposal that the European Supervisory Authorities should systematically consider fintech in the performance of all their institutional tasks, in order to provide a supervisory environment able to host an innovative business model that aims at reaching an EU scale through clear and consistent licensing requirements. In brief, it is clear that the EC has cast the doubt that diverging licensing requirements are affecting fintech firms and that this regulatory approach is not consistent with the smooth functioning of the financial markets. It follows the request for specific follow-up actions that (1) clarify the applicable EU legislative framework for services; (2)·assess the need for an EU framework to cover new innovative business models; and (3) provide guidance to national supervisors to ensure more conver-gence between national regulatory regimes.[61]

This also refers to the experience of the Financial Stability Board (FSB), the Basel Committee on Banking Supervision (BCBS), the European Banking Authority (EBA) and the European Securities and Market Authority (ESMA). In brief, as anticipated, the FSB focused on risks related to cybersecurity, to service providers and macro-prudential events; moreover, the BCBS stressed the effects of fintech on banking; the EBA promoted a 'Roadmap' for monitoring financial activities (according to Art. 9, para. 2, of its Statute).[62]

In this respect, it is worth repeating something that has been antici-pated before (i.e. the usefulness of a technology swift in the business mod-els exploited in capital markets) and then going to analyse deeply in the following pages by recalling again 'fintech' as 'technologically enabled financial innovation that could result in new business models, applications, processes or products with an associated material effect on financial markets and institutions and the provision of financial services'.[63] Indeed, the common goal of monitoring fintech (and its impact on both banking and shadow banking) precedes the option of regulatory intervention that seems to be oriented towards a *neutral* approach to the regulation and control of this phenomenon. By *Neutral* meaning that it would not support one of the developing technologies, although actively involved in promoting wealth, safe and sound management, as well as financial stability. Thus, the role of regulatory competition cannot be underestimated, considering the complexity due to the cross-border activities and the free circulation of capital.

The distortive effects due to different approaches by national governments, as well as their desire to attract fintechers (to be established in the relevant country) comes into consideration (Attewell, P. 2001). Anticipating that a country acting as a 'safe haven' for such operators would be useful for having physical control over them, this is not sufficient for justifying that certain democracies will not regulate fintech or will allow a free use of any innovation. Indeed, this does not place the conflict of interest between the *home* and the *host country* in any different terms from the traditional one, but it emphasizes its relevance because of the high-impact of fintech (with respect to its impact on the velocity of execution, the frequency of transactions and the length of processes).

From another perspective, it is contemplatable the result of the analysis on the evolution of application of technology to money in the past years, which argues against anticipating regulation and providing strict limits to the operators by considering that the costs of failures would be lower than the gains in development.[64] This does not lead to the discussion of the history of the use of technology in capital markets, but calls the attention to considering three distinct eras: firstly, beginning with the analogue and mechanical approach to the automation of human activities; secondly, the process of the digitalization of finance (begun with ATMs and which rapidly evolved in the last years of the twentieth century); thirdly, the rise of a new generation of market participants interested in establishing a new paradigm (known today as fintech).

On the basis of this evolutionary analysis, the monitoring should rely on a comprehensive topology of the relevant industry, and probably would approach the regulation of the capital market from different points of view, each of them mainly referred to one of the following topics: finance; collecting savings and investment activities; credit and risk management;

money, payments and infrastructure; data management and security; customer interface and the need for protection.

According to this approach, the main divergences monitored refer to the firms that use the technology to both supply or demand capital and offer service aimed at supporting the circulation of the latter (Arner, D. W. 2016). This leads to consider that there are firms that are going to enter into the capital market with limited or no pre-existing interaction with the supervising authorities, nor do they have an application for licensing. It would be easy to rely on the preconception that competition is not sufficient to promote the acquisition of financial expertise; however, this would not be adequate for assessing the presence of a 'compliance culture' (which supports the high level of safe and sound management or consumer protection required for dealing with other people's money).

Any further considerations about the exploration of specific options to set the scope of public supervision is postponed to the last chapter. Thereby, this analysis will take into account both the impact of the supervision on the competition among traditional supervised entities, fintech firms, innovation facilitators (as significant or ancillary service providers of regulated firms) and other market participants aimed at sharing, managing, covering and transferring money and risks within the new networks of the forthcoming wired economy.

4.8   Considerations of the EU Economic and Financial Affairs Council and the Basel Committee on Banking Supervision of the Bank for International Settlements

As the wind blows out the candle and fans the bonfire, the need for liquidity is increasing the research for substitute to money, and in particular, the development of *items* that offers an opportunity in terms of cheap and fast payments. This awakes the attention of the EU Economic and Financial Affairs Council (Ecofin), which approached fintech by recognizing that "technological innovation can produce great economic benefits for the financial sector, promoting competition and financial inclusion, broadening consumer choice, increasing efficiency and delivering cost savings for financial institutions and the economy at large".[65] Under this approach, the aim to introduce innovations and safeguarding financial stability leads Ecofin to highlight the multifaceted challenges and risks related to consumer protection, privacy, taxation, cybersecurity and operational resilience, money laundering, terrorism financing, market integrity, governance and legal certainty.[66]

Hence, the research for an *aquis comunitarie* of the innovations due to the application of high-tech mechanisms to banking and finance comes into consideration. In this perspective, the intervention of the EU regulators refers to the potential to reach a global scale, which amplifies any concern on the new potential risks to monetary sovereignty, monetary policy, the safety and efficiency of payment systems, financial stability and fair competition. It is clear that all the above suggested (to Ecofin) to focus on global cryptocurrency's projects, as an EU common understanding and coordinated approach to this topic have not been reached yet (and there is the possibility that a private successful initiative would be able to compete with the monetary monopoly in the European Union[67]).

Thus, the concerns of the EU institutions do not refer only to the evident need to ensure legal clarity about the status of fintech and its application to money, but also to the opportunity to defend the Euro and the banking industry (as it is today). In other words, it seems that the monitoring of the current projects is requesting for further information (on how precisely fintech firms intend to manage risks and operate their business) in order to both reaching a *definitive* conclusion on whether and how the existing EU regulatory framework applies, and conducting a predictive assessment on the effects of the rising of competition (between public and private) in the field of money.[68]

It is worth highlighting that the conclusion reached by the Ecofin clarifies the importance of continuous improvements to financial regulation, in order to meet market participants' expectations for efficient and effective transactions. Indeed, as remarked below, the central banks and national competent authorities are exploring further the ongoing digital transformation and, in particular, the consequences of initiatives such as cryptocurrencies; however, a coordinated global response cannot be the proper reaction, due to the fact that a country that qualifies as a 'safe haven' would be in the position for hosting fintech firms and their business (given their virtual nature and dimension). Thus, the need for considering a new legislation for a common EU approach to fintech and crypto-assets, which includes both the safeguard of the social-democratic principles and the evolution of the market (including the set-up of legal tender).

From another perspective, it is useful to consider also that Bank for International Settlements (BIS)—in order to complete its mission of serving central banks in their pursuit of monetary and financial stability (as well as fostering international cooperation in those areas and acting as a bank for central banks)—is monitoring fintech and its application in order to understand how central banks should assess the compliance of this phenomenon with the core principles for effective banking supervision.[69]

In this respect, agreeing with the BIS approach, the promotion of safety and soundness of banks and the banking system is the primary objective for banking supervision. Thus, it should be considered that its analysis documented that financial services have remained surprisingly expensive after the first applications of fintech innovations, which explains the emergence of new entrants (and is good evidence for supporting the results of the part of the current regulatory research dedicated to fintech firms, shown in Chap. 6). Indeed, this outcome is referred to in the context of the long-run evolution of the finance industry and its regulations after the crisis of 2007/2009. The underlying hypothesis was *somewhat* essential: fintech "can disrupt existing industry structures and blur industry boundaries, facilitate strategic disintermediation, revolutionize how existing firms create and deliver products and services, provide new gateways for entrepreneurship, democratize access to financial services, but also create significant privacy, regulatory and law-enforcement challenges".[70]

It is useful to recall the first cross-country empirical findings that show how financial innovation is necessary for fostering technological innovations and sustaining economic recovery.[71] Hence, the policymakers have been immediately challenged with the goal of providing the capital market with regulations that will not impede competition in the financial services industry, nor inhibit financial innovation (by slowing economic growth).

Moving towards the identification of the key elements of the envisaged financial regulatory architecture for fintech credit, the BIS focused on credit activity facilitated by electronic platforms.[72]

In this context, it seems to be a *support* for shadow credit intermediation processes, whose heavy digitalization of processes may lower transaction costs and provide convenience for end users; they may also increase the possibility of combining risks and returns and supply opportunities to borrowers and lenders.

The BIS has also shown that web-based platforms promote access to credit and investment for underserved segments of the population (provided that the digital divide is filled). Investor confidence and credit risk appetite should be unable to coexist, but several experiences present a range of benefits that suggest the significant possibility that platforms would intermediate a relevant share of overall credit. At the same time, these experiences awake the attention of the BIS itself, which concluded its first round of analysis by questioning "if fintech credit achieves a significant share of credit markets, it may give rise to systemic risk concerns".[73]

All the above is enough to understand the reason why the BIS pointed its attention towards fintech credit markets around the world.[74] As this institution detected that fintech credit had grown rapidly around the world in recent years, and its size still varies greatly across economies, the relevant research has focused on the concreteness of this alternative funding source (for businesses and consumers), and the regulatory intervention required for improving access to credit for underserved individuals (while ensuring adequate consumer and investor protection).

It should be acknowledged that some factors have had an impact on the growth of all forms of credit. These include the country's economic recovery, the expansionary monetary policies (and low interest rates) and the greater use of technological innovations in credit assessment. However, despite the newness of the fintech industry, the BIS has been able to highlight that—in principle—the use of new digital technologies and more granular customer data promises greater convenience, lower transaction costs and better credit risk assessments. This insight helps in developing a regulatory analysis aimed at verifying whether firms and operations would be able to maximize social wealth without jeopardizing individual rights (as the next chapters will summarize). Hence, this research relies also on the BIS conclusions about fintech, as it has in some cases helped improve credit access for financially underserved firms and individuals, while providing additional options to investors, but still rising credit losses in some jurisdictions suggest that these innovations need to be further tested over a full financial and economic cycle.[75]

Recently, the fast-growing adoption of financial technology has led the BIS to a deeper analysis of the implications of fintech developments for banks and bank supervisors.[76] In order to support this analysis, it is useful to rely on the finding that the emergence of fintech is only the latest wave of innovation to affect the banking industry, even if the first application of its innovation suggests the possibility of lowering barriers of entry to the financial services market and elevating the role of data as a key commodity, as well as driving the emergence of new business models.

Once again, new benefits and risks arise. This offers the possibility to intertwine this analysis with the BIS' historical research, analysis of current data, and examination of products, having a forward-looking perspective on fintech and its potential impact on the methodology of supervision. Therefore, this study will move away from the consideration that fintech innovations have the possibility to change traditional banking business models, structures and operations. Such changes require also policymakers to reconsider the current supervisory models, resources and organizations in order to continue the effective oversight of the market for capital.

Lastly, it is important to highlight the recent analysis of fintech developments in the insurance industry. It helps in understanding the premises of this part of the analysis (dedicated to insurtech), as well as the new challenges for both the insurance industry and its supervisors. Indeed, evidence from this industry shows emerging technologies and innovative business models that have the potential to transform the insurance business.[77] New technology start-ups are delivering a wide range of benefits (in terms of efficiency improvements, cost reductions and risk mitigation), even if one of the most relevant outcomes of the BIS analysis shows the expectation that competitiveness should decrease in the long term, assuming that innovation will create competitive advantages, possibly reducing the number of insurers that can adapt and then survive. Hence, a further challenge for policymakers arises: "to evaluate and, where appropriate, adjust their prudential regulation framework in order to capture new risks (such as the use of algorithms for underwriting purposes) and changes in corporate governance frameworks arising from third-party collaboration with insurtech companies".[78]

All of the above helps the analysis in considering also the current streamline regulations. As far as regulatory interventions place the burden of administrative fulfilments and transactional costs, there are no evidences able to negate that the efforts spent in dealing with public administration would be reduced by innovation. In this era of technical change, according to the transnational nature of this environment, a severe approach by policymakers would lead firms to a change of jurisdiction, as fintechers do not seem to tolerate duplicative and inefficient regulations. In brief, there is need for a comprehensive assessment of the costs and benefits of regulations, in order to support the development of a high-tech-fuelled environment to enhance the circulation of capital and minimize the relevant risks.

4.9   Fintech Within the Mandate of the European Central Bank

"Fintech for the people" has been used by a member of the Executive Board of the European Central Bank (ECB) in order to highlight the link between the two positive external consequences of innovation that generally policymakers are going to achieve: financial stability and financial inclusion (Cœuré, B. 2019).[79]

The ECB is now aiming towards fintech's potential for achieving greater access to the market for capital, and the clarification of the powers that central banks and other authorities need to help fulfil this potential (Verdegem, P. and Verhoest, P. 2009). Obviously, these powers require both a democratic legitimation and an organizational structure able to exercise them. Firstly, it is possible to clarify that the scope of its supervision concerns both the direct application of new technologies with monetary implications and the usage of high-tech tools by supervised entities (within the scope of the Single Supervisory Mechanism).

It is acknowledged that the contents of the sixth paragraph of Art. 127 have been stretched, and lengthened, and flexed, and extended. However, the current analysis is not warping this norm any more by including supervision over fintech within the "specific tasks ... concerning policies relating to the prudential supervision of credit institutions and other financial institutions" mentioned in this chapter.

It is also worth pointing out that, with respect to monetary policy, the ECB may submit opinions to the appropriate Union institutions, bodies, offices or agencies or to national authorities on matters in its fields of competence (according to Art. 127, para. 4, of the Treaty on the Functioning of the European Union). Thus, it is possible to propose a regulatory framework dedicated to cryptocurrencies (if they were to start influencing the maintenance of price stability), as well as the application of cryptography and other fintech solutions to legal tender (as investigated further in Chaps. 7 and 8), provided that the European Central Bank has the exclusive right to authorize the issue of euro banknotes within the Union (according to Art. 128 of the Treaty on the Functioning of the European Union).

As long as there is a regulatory framework that calls for an active role of the central banking in supervising the fintech industry, it would be easy to consider that the ECB would structure a team able to oversee algorithms and software; and it should be in the position to cooperate with any new authority in charge of controlling ICT innovation.[80]

It is useful to recall that in 2016 the ECB published a working paper showing that financing constraints lead firms to decrease production, but they may spur investment in innovation (R&D) (Malamud, S. and Zucchi, F. 2016). Indeed, in these years, a lot of constraints and innovations have been experienced. Hence, the focus is not going to be on the micro and macro implications of investments in innovation (to overcome business or regulatory constraints), nor on their outcomes in terms of economic growth (or financial stability). Beyond, the attention goes to the regulatory needs arising in the sectors that are benefitting most from fintech applications.

In this respect, monetary and supervisory interests converge towards the monitoring of the evolution that is occurring in the market for payments. High-tech is supporting new payment schemes not only to be able to increase access, but also to improve competition and drive down transaction costs (by relying on the use of technologies and contracts that are already in the hands of the final users, such as mobile devices).

In this context, the ECB has highlighted that any person needs to have the possibility of executing payments through conventional systems, in order to avoid that certain groups of people may look to unregulated arrangements (such as informal savings clubs, peer-to-peer platforms and cryptocurrencies). Indeed, such alternative solutions lack operational robustness, appropriate risk management, legal certainty and consumer protection; moreover, they could lead to the rise of 'shadow payments', which are inconsistent (from a monetary perspective) and dangerous (from a supervisory perspective, both at the micro- and the macro-prudential level). Moreover, the broadest access to payment services is becoming one of the first goals that central banks and is supervisors should accomplish in the fintech environment as a first step in the long journey towards truly universal financial integration and stability.[81]

Bearing in mind that policymakers have set up a regulatory framework able to provide customers with access to basic transaction accounts or a payment device by containing the costs of such services, the outcome of the ECB's analysis suggests investigating the possibility that payments are becoming a bank-free service whereby new technologies seem to be faster and cheaper than the ones that currently support the SEPA. Certainly, the most advanced tools offer transfers of funds in real time and around the clock across Europe. These tools may restrain the use of 'shadow payments'; however, their usefulness depends on both the financial inclusion of the people and the capacity of supervisors to control them. Hence, there is the need for providing regulation and control that is up to the challenges of fintech.[82]

All of the above leads to question whether the ECB has to identify a new task to fulfill its mandate: keeping the system safe in the age of fintech, at its core and its periphery. The same is true for the uncertainty that the traditional approach of supervision, being entity-based or activity-based, may not be effective in the digital age, due to unconventional, decentralized and integrated organizational forms that make it difficult to find a legal entity responsible for the activities performed through fintech chains. However, new technologies may make regulatory arbitrage an even more prominent concern which may also provide supervised entities incentive to migrate towards the aforesaid shadows (as less-regulated sectors of the financial system). Further evidence that international cooperation has to occur at the highest possible level.

Regarding the ECB mandate, it is not possible to deny that the current evolution of financial and monetary practices would suggest an extended interpretation to consider within the scope of the current supervision the new technology and how it is affecting the financial markets. This is now referring mainly to the 'distributed ledger technology' (DLT) and its potential to completely change the way the financial markets and banking work (and as a consequence the methodology of supervision itself).[83]

Dealing with DLT from a regulatory perspective, it is clear that its features suggest a classification equal to that of the database, which is spread across a network of many computers, rather than stored in a central register (creating problems of accessing, rather than issues of its property). Thus, it considers its capacity to develop a chain, protected by a complex defence (based on mathematical algorithms) and linked to a comprehensive record of all the transactions included in such a database. Potential advantages of this supervisory approach include the possibility to simplify (what can otherwise be very complex processes), to directly consider individuals (directly connected to the shared database) and to ensure that transactions can be made safely and efficiently across the euro area. And this is where the ECB comes into the picture.

This part of the analysis must consider that the ECB runs a number of mechanisms that help move money and assets around the internal market. Beside the prudence, there is no reason why the application of the most successful and safe fintech tools cannot be used by ECB itself. As a positive outcome, in addition to the improvement of ECB's efficiency—this application would also instruct and educate the supervisor in using services and products based on DLT (as long as the outcome of the controls demonstrates that DLT does not jeopardize the safe flow of transactions).

There was a joint research project of the European Central Bank and the Bank of Japan, whose goal was the clarification of the liquidity-saving mechanisms in a distributed ledger environment. From a regulatory perspective, this analysis leads to understand the individual rights *touched* by the set of tools for recording data, which allow a network of computers to verify and store updates without a single central management system. Indeed, the interests for market and price stability rely on the possibility that such tools facilitate safer, faster and cheaper financial transactions: the precedent condition for the utilization of DLT for financial market infrastructures.

Traffic and performance should be considered by the regulator as the parameters to fix, in order to ensure that the proper functioning of these tools will lead to a greater competition in the market for payments, as DLT performance is affected by network size and distance between nodes. Execution time, in this context, would be a constraint that could be provided by the regulator itself, but it would fix the number of nodes (provided the minimum number of nodes (quorum) required to achieve consensus were sufficiently close together and the effect of dispersion in the rest of the network on latency were limited).[84] Therefore, the supervising authority must oversee the issues concerning both the validating node failures and the incorrect data formats, as well as the certifying entities (whose role can undermine both the competition and the efficiencies of the exchanges).

All of the above recalls the first considerations of the role of the ECB at the beginning of the current wave of digitalization. While the general opinion was that scholars tend to overestimate the effect of a technology in the short run, and institutions tend to underestimate the effect in the long run, it is worth considering that the ECB raised specific questions relating to whether or not central banks should move money to DLT and whether there was a need for issuing central bank digital currency (Mersch, Y. 2016). This is not a matter of technicalities, but it raises specific doubts due to the results of the regulatory analysis of fintech applications.

In the ECB's considerations about DLT, it is easy to identify the underlying idea that any possible impact of DLT depends on how market players ultimately decide to embrace it, within the limits set forth by the regulators and governments. This should not suggest a scenario analysis, but should lead to focus on the general principles regulating the financial market mentioned in the first section of this chapter. Hence, the need for new rules aimed at taking advantage of technical innovation and meeting new user needs, while staying ahead of evolving operational and counterparty risks. And there is no doubt that this need will be satisfied with respect to the institutional mandate of the ECB from both a monetary and a supervisory perspective.[85]

It is clear—and often published[86]—that the ECB's approach to fintech and its tools was not conceived as a mere passive status of recipient of high-tech innovative pressure. On the contrary, its activities showed a clear path towards regulatory and supervising initiatives aimed at affecting the direction and speed of fintech applications, with consideration of the envisaged consequences implied for monetary policy, financial stability and savings. Indeed, allowing fintech to develop in an alternative and unregulated sector may also undermine financial stability (regardless of the attention of the supervisors). This does not deny that new technologies entail additional risks to the financial markets, but suggests that effective rules would help in selecting which exposure to risks is acceptable.

It is expectable that regulators and supervisors will approach fintech firms as part of the emerging network industries, provided that a technology-neutral approach should encourage the use of most efficient technologies. But this does not mean that regulators will not ignore the risks,[87] and—should regulatory loopholes emerge—they would need to intervene on the hardware, software and algorithms that underlay these technologies.

In conclusion, the ECB has been called to deal with fintech, regulatory arbitrage and the rise of shadow banking. The execution of this task should be supported by the consolidation of supervisory and monetary powers in the hands of one authority (i.e. the ECB), as it would facilitate an action plan able to oversee the shadow entities (and their operations), by means of the single supervisory mechanism.

All of the above confirms that the attention paid to the shadow credit intermediation process should now include fintech and its innovations too (because of the quantitative data generated from the use of the abovementioned technologies), hence the reference to non-bank intermediaries. Despite the scarcity of systematic evidence, the ECB has engaged in an intense debate about the possible consequences of fintech, ever since the first systematic examination of the evolution of shadow banking (and the economic forces that could explain the current drastic change in the nature of intermediation).[88]

4.10   THE EUROPEAN SECURITIES AND MARKET AUTHORITY FINDINGS WITHIN AND BEYOND CAPITAL MARKETS

Ten years ago, 'The High-Level Group of Financial Supervision in the EU', chaired by Jacques de Larosière, suggested including in the "main tasks of the Authorities ...(the)... adoption of binding technical decisions applicable to individual institutions".[89] However, it should be borne in mind that the first aim of the Lamfalussy report in 2000 was also to speed up the adoption of EU financial services law—providing a framework and mechanism for timely decision-making based on the technical expertise of the level 3 committees, open consultation, transparency and political accountability.[90] In this context, the Group of De Larosière concluded that, while the ample liquidity and low interest rates have been the major underlying factor behind the present crisis, "financial innovation amplified and accelerated the consequences of excess liquidity and rapid credit expansion".[91] At that time, the innovations referred to the evidence that those original investment products were "developing more and more innovative and complex instruments designed to offer improved yields, often combined with increased leverage".[92]

Anyway, this is in line with the original purpose of establishing an authority that "should take due account of the impact of its activities on competition and innovation within the internal market, on the Union's global competitiveness, on financial inclusion, and on the Union's new strategy for jobs and growth".[93] In fact, the relevant EU regulation provides that ESMA "shall establish, as an integral part of the Authority, a Committee on financial innovation, which brings together all relevant competent national supervisory authorities with a view to achieving a coordinated approach to the regulatory and supervisory treatment of new or innovative financial activities and providing advice for the Authority to present to the European Parliament, the Council and the Commission".[94] And, as shown below, the EU regulator replicated this option with respect to any of the ESAs.[95]

It is worth recalling one of the action points of the EC fintech Action plan, namely ESMA's mandate 'to map current authorising and licensing approaches for innovative fintech business models in Europe'. It is not possible to rely only on two surveys conducted by ESMA to gather evidence on the licensing regimes of fintech firms in their jurisdictions. However, as shown below with respect to the Italian and British approaches to public supervision over fintech, there has been the evidence of an evolution in the supervisory praxis. In particular, in January 2018, ESMA had identified potential gaps and issues in the existing EU regulatory framework. They assessed how the existing national regimes diverge and proposed recommendations to adapt the EU legislation to the emerging innovations. One year later, ESMA was able to identify the ways in which national competent authorities applied the principles of 'proportionality' and 'flexibility' when licensing fintech firms.[96]

In this respect, ESMA's approach pointed out a common feature of the above praxis: national authorities authorize a financial activity and not a technology. In other words, the regulatory framework does not catch the ICT system that supports the performance of a reserved activity, so it is not under the scrutiny of public controllers. However, this does not suggest to conclude that supervisors are indifferent to technology, but they seem to face only a specific stage of the ICT evolution or rather to consider that one software fits all the intermediaries (whose needs are technologically differentiated).

It should be obvious that the major findings of this research refer to the need for fostering an evolution in the supervisory practices, in order to keep programmers and coders at arm's length.

As highlighted above, new technologies are becoming wider and wider, spreading within and beyond capital markets (Maijoor, S. 2018). The ESMA's challenge is how to handle fintech and its major consequences (at least). This challenge refers to the thesis that regulators and supervisors are able to set rules and the praxis aimed at exploiting the potential to make capital markets work better and in a more inclusive way, provided that the latter is the goal of public intervention within the EU internal market. Henceforward, the strength of capital markets depends on the role of supervisors because new links between firms and investors involve complex decision-making and require trust. This is confirmed by ESMA's monitoring of a number of developments pioneered by fintech firms which are already having an impact on the way investment funds are distributed to clients.

Usually, at this stage of the analysis, scholars recall automated advice as a prominent example of the above.[97] They usually refer to the use of automated tools when investors are seeking recommendations prior to purchasing or selling financial products, prior to lending money or rather requesting services related to the circulation of capital.

On the contrary, from a regulatory perspective, it shall be considered that software is preprogrammed by someone; and the fact that this programmer is out of the scope of supervision shall be contemplated as a mere inadequacy of the regulation (as it is with respect to the choice of excluding financial journalists who write the articles used by financial advisors to support their communications to the customers). Indeed, this deficiency has been discussed, as remarked below, by the ESAs while monitoring fintech, considering the various ways in which customers can use automated tools (typically websites) to receive financial advice, without (or with very limited) human direct relations (provided that the human intervention is behind the algorithms of such tools).[98]

Consequently, the analysis will focus on financial inclusion because it is a worthy objective in its own right as it helps citizens meet their savings goals, manage their payments and reduce the effort needed when dealing with their personal finance. ESMA's approach concludes that fintech platforms can offer individual investors much better value for the money than their traditional counterparts (due to the benefit of the business and big data analytics) (Zeno-Zencovich, V. 2018).

Obviously, these platforms may also offer other services (as investigated in Chap. 6), as well as support the use of the most advanced technologies as is the case of AI-powered investment and trade execution strategies. In this respect, ESMA focused on the role of AI and machine learning tools used to detect subtle patterns in data to help predict price movements, by concluding that the current impact is limited in value (and then the risks for financial stability is low). However, one more time, it should be questioned whether the attention should also go to the activity of the programmers of such AI tools (in addition to focus on their current effects).

From a regulatory point of view, it seems that ESMA's major findings refer to the use of fintech to protect investors: "Algorithms can be used to help identify where people may be … acting on insider information or other bad conduct" (Maijoor, S. 2018). In this respect, there are no doubt that the mandate of the regulators concerns also the use of data analytics and pattern recognition systems to study trading behaviour and detect market abuse. This leads to suptech and regtech, which consider both AI-powered surveillance of market conduct and the use of new technology by supervised entities to meet their regulatory obligations (such as reporting and risk management). Hence the importance of ESMA's conclusion on common reporting standards—such as LEI, ISIN and ISO20022—that underpin the successful application of regtech.

From another perspective, ESMA's approach drives directly to innovation facilitators, as new market participants that play a central role in applying fintech. Their activity stands in an area where the legislation and licensing requirements need changes and adaptations because they provide the infrastructure (which supports the organization of fintech firms). So it is easy to highlight that their role has a direct link—and then interdependencies—with the innovations that the firms are going to apply to their business models. Hence, the conclusion suggests supervising their impact on the requirements provided by the licensing regime set forth for providing banking and financial services. Probably, this is proposing a *style* that is stricter than the one jointly published by ESMA, EBA and EIOPA.[99]

However, it is acknowledged that the ESAs are still operating within their mandate to oversee the subjects operating in the EU market for capital, and not changing their tasks to supervise the functions that market participants are operating. So, it would be expected that monitoring increases the knowledge of this phenomenon; such knowledge would point the attention towards the business analytics and the software that run the fintech firms; and then such attention will foster convergence in supervisory praxis.

In brief, evidence gathered from ESMA's monitoring supported the conclusion that, "most innovative business models can operate within the existing EU rules" which was easily predictable. Indeed, *if* the supervisor is neutral (with respect to technology) and does not perceive the difference between the human-driven business models (based on the ideas of the top managers) and the fintech ones (based on the ideas of programmers), *then* the conclusion cannot be different (and no further additional recommendations for changes in the EU regulation would be suggested). Nonetheless, it is possible to confirm the previous considerations on the need to reconsider the oversight over technology (and then—one more time—a reference to Chap. 8).

As a concluding remark, it is recallable that the current supervisory framework is based on the assumption that over-regulation should be avoided because it slows down financial innovation and thereby undermines economic growth in the wider economy.[100] However, challenging this assumption seems appropriate, because slowing down undesirable innovation is not avoiding a technological shift in the production possibilities, but rather it helps in managing the rising of new threats and gives time to implement risk management processes associated with both cybersecurity and fintech outsourcing. Therefore, it is possible to agree with the joint ESAs' advice on the need for legislative improvements relating to fintech business models, the applicable rules of conduct and the mandate of the supervisors (also considering the possibility of establishing a new supervisory authority in charge of operating system developers). Thus, this would lead to new costs, but also to comprehensive support for the resilience of market participants and infrastructure.

4.11   TOWARDS THE EUROPEAN BANKING AUTHORITY'S GUIDELINES: THE DIRECTIVE (EU) 2019/878

Having regard to the praxis of European authorities, besides ESMA's leading role on market-based financial intermediation, it is remarkable that in March 2018 the EBA published its 'Fintech Roadmap', setting out the priorities for further work on financial innovation, in which it describes the EBA's next steps and indicative milestones to execute the Commission's fintech Action Plan.[101] This confirms that the European regulator, while establishing the ESAs, considers innovation an important separate matter. It provided for the institution of a Committee as an integral part of these authorities (and, in addition to the ESMA's Committee, it also required the Committees of EBA and EIOPA, as stated in Art. 9, para. 4, of both Regulation (EU) no. 1093/2010 and no. 1094/2010).[102]

In this respect, it must be borne in mind that the EBA's tasks focus on the banking industry. Therefore, its analysis has to start with understanding the status of fintech firms and the perimeter of their activities which would help in understanding the meaning of the EBA's findings related to the application of the principles of proportionality and flexibility.

However, it is not possible to deny that the aforesaid point of view (related to the banking industry) has influenced their monitoring of national developments on the regulatory perimeter, the national regulatory status of fintech firms and the approaches followed by supervisors (when granting authorization under Directive 2013/36/EU, Directive (EU) 2015/2366, and Directive 2009/110/EC).[103] Hence, it is clear that the EBA's view at this stage is still limited to observing the outcome of the self-executing activities supplied in the banking sector. In this respect, the emphasis on the outcome does not help in understanding the importance of supervising the work that is behind the structuring of such self-execution, which is the reason for the lack of any action to put forward any specific recommendation. Thus, once again, there is the risk that supervisors will delay their intervention on the new, developing industry of software developers and device manufacturers.

Furthermore, the EBA's analysis of the national regulatory status of innovative business models or self-executing delivery mechanisms shows the extent of the scope of supervision with respect to payment initiation services and account information services (being generally subject to public oversight after the transposition of the second payment services directive into national law).[104] However, this also suggests that other high-tech activities and services (including the ones of an ancillary/non-financial nature) are not subject to any regulatory regime. In brief, the EBA's findings do not show a fully level-playing field in this area, which has uncovered the need to carry out specific amendments in the context of the mandate conferred by Directive (EU) 2019/878 amending the fourth Capital Requirements Directive, for the development of new guidelines to specify a common assessment methodology for granting authorizations all over Europe (Arnaboldi, F. 2019). There is the opportunity to use the regulatory technical standards developed by the EBA to foster the safe and sound application of fintech tools. Probably, these will be the sources of additional identification methodology for the programmers and coders of such tools, and this methodology could allow the recognition of the specificities of fintech firms within the context of the European supervisory and resolution mechanisms.

According to the above, only by considering a new form of supervision over programmers, it is possible to agree with the approaches that—under the current EU legal framework—suggest the application of the principles of proportionality and flexibility with respect to fintech banks (and not irrespective of whether the applicant presents a traditional or innovative business model and/or delivery mechanism).[105] Otherwise, there will be doubt about the efficiency and fairness of any special regime that would allow a lower initial capital or favourable calculations of prudential requirements for fintech banks themselves (with respect to Art. 12(4) od CRD IV).

All of the foregoing also raise the awareness on the potential prudential risks and opportunities that may arise from the application of mechanisms able to drive the supervised entities both towards the maximization of their outcome and away from the most dangerous operations. In this respect, it is worth considering the micro-prudential aspects of the application of fintech to existing financial processes, procedures and services (as the impact on the risk profile of supervised entities, according to the EBA's findings, could be highly dependent on the type of underlying technology and its implementation as well as the processes and business models adopted around it).[106]

Obviously, with respect to the prudential regulation, the EBA's interests concern the broader ongoing digital transformation across institutions' credit risk management functions, whereby the machine-learning techniques are being pursued by supervisory entities in order to improve their capabilities in both credit scoring and monitoring of quality of debtors (in order to register in due time any misperformance of the customers). In any case, this would result in a new operational risk (related to the capacity of software to operate the aforementioned analysis, also because the first-time application of these new technologies and banks are at the beginning of their learning curve) (Okafor, A. and Fadul, J. 2019),[107] as well as in a higher ICT risk (due to the combination of outsourcing risks and cybersecurity threats and digital fraud issues).[108] However, the results of the EBA's research do not suggest that further automation in credit decision processes and the use of new data sources involves third parties in the management of a bank (through the passive implementation of these extensive, wide and comprehensive credit analysis performed under these techniques), but highlights only that the fintech tools support quicker customer analysis, and then should enhance the overall credit risk management for institutions.

In this respect, the EBA's attention to the innovative use of data by supervised entities confirmed the close relationship between micro-prudential supervision and the protection of individual rights, which can be put at risk by a misuse of personal data by banks or their outsourcers.[109] Although any use of data is based on personal consensus and protective rules, there is no doubt that the development of new technological innovations are supporting big data analytics, artificial intelligence, and robo-advice to profile market participants, and then exploiting such profiling to force the banking business. Once again, the EBA's attention identified risks whose likelihood might vary. These considerations are referring to the absence of any backstop to inconsistency, irregularity and redundancy, as well as to the difficulties in gathering sufficient grounds for further industry-specific regulatory interventions. Hence, there are specific concerns regarding the potential lack of a level-playing field between banks and the new market participants that operate outside the scope of prudential supervision.

It is possible only to rely on 'best practices' regarding innovation facilitators, intended to provide indicative support for supervisors and to promote convergence in the design of the fintech tools and the operation of innovative mechanisms. However, at this stage of the analysis, it is not possible to assess whether the *mere* comparative analysis of the innovation facilitators would identify the premises required for establishing a level-playing field. Anyway, it should be expected that the current tendency to promoting 'innovation hubs' and 'regulatory sandboxes' will soon be overridden by the practices of regulating innovative financial products, advanced financial services and business analytics.[110]

Lastly, it is useful to consider the role of the EBA in drafting a single rulebook that supports the effective application of fintech innovations in a way that supports financial stability and protects the individual rights.[111] In this perspective, different threats and challenges arise depending on the actual fintech business models. In addition, a number of key rules need to be enacted relating to operation resilience, as well as new actions must support the safeguarding of recovery and wealth. Indeed, in terms of the level of implementation of innovative technologies, the EBA's monitoring registered that many institutions appear to mostly leverage third-party servicing with respect to cloud services and the development of digital/mobile tools, with an increase in outsourcing in the use of artificial intelligence, big data analytics and biometrics. This is not challenging that outsourcing speeds up the development of technology and the exploitation of new dynamics, but it arises the question whether the growing importance of a large supplier base may not necessarily fit the safe and sound management of a supervised entity.[112]

Concluding remarks on the role of the supranational authorities highlight both the usefulness of a wide view over fintech innovations and the limits of monitoring of their effects. Indeed, it seems necessary to consider the origins of financial innovation, the logic behind the algorithms and the software used by machine-learning processes, and naturally the human preferences that lie under this evolution. Even if the most recent reports have concluded that there is "no significant implementation of sophisticated technologies",[113] it is not possible to exclude that the current trends would lead to *dependencies* on fintech providers, such as device manufacturers, programmers and coders. This is another reason for promoting technological neutrality and sharing knowledge and experience in assessing fintech, provided that the actual supervisory practices over this phenomenon do not benefit from an effective governance structure aimed at supervising the developers of fintech tools.

4.12   THE EXPERIENCE OF BANCA D'ITALIA AND CONSOB

Italy has become a 'laboratory' where supervision is intertwined with the most creative part of policymakers' *utilitarianism*.[114] It is easy to observe that supervision is part of the Italian market for capital, and it involves the social totality of market participants, whose evolution from public towards private is still ongoing.[115] This evidence shows a way of working out the market- view, and not just from a once-a-quarter filing of information. Scholars, lawyers, consultants, technicians and politicians are preserving their attitude to participate in the processes of regulation and control (by means of specific consultations made by the supervising authorities before the adoption of new rules, according to law no. 262 of 2005).

In general terms, it is necessary to move away from a marked strong link between supervisory authorities and the supervised entities.[116] In order to best introduce the Italian experience regarding fintech, it is useful to refer to the approach of Banca d'Italia to sustainable development and climate risks, by highlighting its view on the relevant role of central banks.[117] There is no doubt that the financial industry plays a central role in the allocation of resources; then a strict regulation of the supply and demand could be an effective tool for influencing the scope, speed and smoothness of the transition to a sustainable economy. However, this requires the capacity of supervisors to oversee the investment decision-making processes, as well as control the actual directions of capital flows. In this context, regtech tools aimed at integrating the self-executing decision-making analytics (that supports the fintech mechanisms) would be able to influence supervised entities' risk management and investment strategies.[118]

It helps clarifying that this is not a deviation towards a critical research for a new task of central banks (that are no more in charge of the main responsibilities of the monetary policies and supervision over banks, as they are in the Eurozone). On the contrary, this is going straight to the need for supervising fintech by seeing the positive externalities of a super-vision that considers both the envisaged financial stability and the concrete market outcome, and then to verify whether the current institutions can play their part in assessing the main arising threats for human beings. First of all, with respect to the methodology, the current set-up of supervisors shows a growing interest for mixing economic knowledge, regulatory capabilities and technical skills, but it seems to be far from developing algorithms and moreover from incorporating them in self-executing tools (to be applied by supervisors), as will be shown in the last chapter of this book.

Obviously, the objective cannot be the awareness of the risks related to the sustainability factors, nor the understanding of the channels through which they are transmitted to the financial system. In the Italian legal order, the actual goal of supervision should be compliant with the role of law in pursuing the common welfare (as provided by the Art. 41 of the Italian Constitution), as well as the duty to protect savings (or rather, the future) and control the credit (according to Art. 47 of the Italian Constitution, provided that the government has to safeguard the natural landscape and the historical and artistic heritage of the Nation, as stated in Art. 9 of the Italian Constitution).

Hence, it is possible to identify and highlight the Italian approach to fintech, whose goal is to make financial intermediaries move from a backward-looking attitude to a forward-looking one, prompting them to foster cooperation and share the best practices (between the various stakeholders in the financial system).[119]

However, Italy's technological backwardness extends to the financial sector. Even if some progress is on track, evidence shows that Italian banks are not really growing their use of the most complex technologies (fintech), which are transforming the very structure of the financial industry. Italian banks are today expanding their online offering of traditional services; all of them allow payments to be made with mobile devices; more than half of them place savings products through digital channels; the number of intermediaries offering financing to families through portals is limited, but growing. This helps in a particular reference to the new methodologies for the management and analysis of large and complex data sets (big data), the use of artificial intelligence, automatic learning (machine learning) and the potential offered by the technologies of the "distributed ledgers" (Cœuré, B. 2018b).

Some surveys have demonstrated that half of the Italian banks have not yet started, nor are they planning experiments with these above-mentioned technologies, including tools for assessing creditworthiness.[120] Hence, a progressive erosion of Italian banks' market share is expectable.[121]

Thus, Italian banks are called to introduce innovations to collect large volumes of heterogeneous data and to analyse them with new methodologies (including those related to artificial intelligence and automatic learning) for a more innovative approach to their potential customers and a more accurate assessment of the creditworthiness of the current customers. These innovations would benefit the financing of companies operating in sectors and areas where intermediation is most risky, and these advantages tend to be greater for smaller banks, with customers consisting mainly of small businesses.[122]

In addition, the Banca d'Italia is committed to identifying how to promote particularly innovative (technological and organizational) solutions in the supervision of financial services.[123] In particular, the Italian supervisory authority has activated two specific channels of communication and dialogue with fintech operators.[124] Hence, the Italian approach to fintech is starting from a public intervention, and not from a legislative statement. Clearly, within the scope of the tasks assigned to the Italian authority, this intervention could be considered one of its institutional activities, and not a mere diversion to follow a generalist tendency to support innovation as such.

In this respect, any advanced approach to the authorization process is strictly related to the analysis of the key document provided by the applicants, that is, the 'programme' (of activities and operations).[125] This document takes on even greater significance in the fintech sector, where the evaluation of projects can be very complex because of the innovative nature of these projects, for which it is difficult, if not impossible, to find historical data, track records and reference operating practices.[126] In the attempt to overcome this issue, the ECB has published a guide in which it has provided indications to promote transparency and homogeneity on the criteria for granting the relative license to fintech initiatives.[127]

Through the aforesaid examination, the supervisory authority can verify the sustainability of the business model both in terms of compatibility with the traditional canons of sound and safe management and in relation to its future ability to ensure profits, such as to allow the firm to operate (and remain) in the market. An important additional element to include here refers to the information acquired at this stage: it is also very important afterwards, not only in terms of authorization, but in guiding all the ongoing supervisory activities.

The authorization provided by the Italian authorities over the last few years has demonstrated that great changes are emerging in the way credit is collected, and that these changes are related to financial technology too (Barbagallo, C. 2019). In addition to the increase in authorizations for lending-based crowdfunding projects, it is possible to observe authorization requests in relation to new technological platforms used for the purchase and sale of assets that are not compatible with the current requirements of capital adequacy (and in particular, the sale of non-performing exposure from the banks to speculative investors). The same is true for the platforms that distribute insurance products.[128] Nowadays, many platforms receive the demand of both retail and institutional investors, increasing the financial inclusion and reducing the transactional costs for circulating capital. Obviously this technique reduces the difficulties in entering into capital markets, as well as it allows retail investors to rely on the analysis of the professional ones (and then copying their strategies).[129]

From another perspective, it is useful to highlight the attention of Consob with respect to the *transition* from banking to market-based credit intermediation.[130] This transition can be significantly facilitated by those platforms, which through the development of crowd-businesses reduces the traditional barriers to access to capital raising (as the aforesaid demand goes on the same marketplace) (Ciocca, P. 2019).

In the following stage of this analysis, Consob contributions to the study of fintech will be taken into account, because their contents refer also to fintech operations, considering the digitalization of financial activities as the next evolutionary stage of financial industry, whose outcome would be a change in the relevant market.[131] Moreover, this institution supported legal analyses on civil and criminal aspects of data management within the fintech environment,[132] on the financial data aggregation, account information services,[133] and on marketplace lending.[134]

All of the above suggests to anticipate to the consideration that supervising authorities feel the need for understanding this phenomenon, for acquiring new methodologies to control it and—in brief—for setting common strategies in regulating its evolutionary path. However, what needs to be assessed is the suitability of the current supervision with respect to the organization of the fintech firms and their third-party providers. In other words, the Italian experience confirms the risk that the supervisory approach would not include in its scope the activity of software developers and device manufacturers.[135]

At the same time, it is possible to consider that—as technological progress advances further—the question of the Italian digital divide is not free of economic consequences (in terms of opportunities and changes for the qualitative profiles of labor demand and services supply).[136] However, this highlights that the attention of policymakers is at its highest, and it refers to an open dialogue with all stakeholders, and then to the need to take prompt measures on fintech innovations, because the activities that produce that same outcome (or outcomes that are perfect substitutes) must be subject to the same regulatory safeguards.

4.13   FCA (Despite Brexit)

The strategic approach of the UK to the challenges of these years has yielded important insights and critics. However, the regulatory analysis has not yet reached a shareable outcome on the strategy of action where mutual dependence is mixed with conflict (Rosa, H. 2003). And in the UK, because of Brexit, conflict arises.

The analysis of the British approach to fintech is developed in between the reference to the economic relevance of financial operators based in the UK, and the conflicting environment due to the decision to leave the European Union. Provided that British policymakers are not entirely distracted by the debate on Brexit, the UK would verify the possibility to qualify as a 'safe haven' outside the EU internal market, rather than being its *favourite* Member State for hosting the financial industry. Obviously, in modern history, there are situations in which the element of conflict provides mutual dependence and mutual accommodation, at least to prevent a common disaster. Brexit could be one of these situations, or rather one in which what one party *can* do (to avoid a disaster) affects what the other party *will* do (to close the deal). So, nowadays, British markets are the best environment to observe the influence of *uncertainty* over market participants, as timing is a useful data for the actuarial calculations, but the computation of the relevant costs is more complex.[137]

However, before Brexit, UK authorities started looking into innovations, namely the Financial Conduct Authority (FCA) started Project Innovate in October 2014, and now have a team working across all innovation services. This remarks the significant data for exploring the British methodology for encouraging innovation in the interest of consumers.

Firstly, it comes into consideration the experience of the 'regulatory sandbox', structured as an environment that allows businesses to test innovative test products and service propositions in a controlled environment (that replicates the market), with real consumers. Such experience shows that firms can reduce time-to-market, by containing the magnitude of the risk related to unforeseen harms, as well as lower the cost to apply (fast) consumer protection safeguards (in case harms occur).

Moreover, considering the scholars' approach to bargaining power, the access to such a sandbox invokes trust in firms' future actions, not merely in the present supplying. However, FCA oversees tests using a customized regulatory environment for each test, so that regulations should enforce promises given in a sandbox. Hence, it seems that the use of such a sandbox would help in understanding what fintech supply should be enforceable at law, and what should be the remedy for fintech breaching its promises. In this respect, evidences show that FCA works closely with fintech firms to ensure that sufficient safeguards would mitigate risks during and after testing, being these safeguards were modified to each test (including extra capital requirements, systems penetration testing and secondary review of robo-advice by a qualified financial adviser, among others).[138]

It is worth recalling the criticism to the bargaining theory, due to the fact that fintech tools should provide the person with what they want, whilst it is actually providing the best outcome according to their algorithms; so, the sandbox seems to be both over inclusive (in arguing for the enforceability of innovations that ought not to be applied) and under-inclusive (in not arguing for the full compliance to the current level-playing field) (Cooter, R and Ulen, T. 2008).

In this perspective, it is possible to highlight that—despite Brexit—the UK launched the 'Global Financial Innovation Network' (GFIN) in January 2019, which intertwines an international group of financial regulators and related organizations to create a global sandbox. Committed to supporting financial innovation in the interests of consumers, this group aims to create a new framework for co-operation between regulators in order to provide a more efficient way for supervisors to oversee fintech firms and their activities (while the latter *navigate* among countries by exploiting innovative products, services or business models across more than one jurisdiction).[139]

Probably, such experience would clarify whether the sandbox—as a regulatory tool—is an inclusive and farther-reaching global mechanism for assessing the suitability of fintech innovations with respect to the individual rights and financial stability. In this respect, the development of this approach would lead to the intensification of firms accessing a sandbox, as well as an increase in the number of sandboxes.[140] However, it is clear that such a sandbox would provide a new *territory* between the current status and the next stage of the financial market: the future is reached by ways of the middle-earth *territories*.

It is clear that the British approach to fintech refers to the envisaged outcome to support firms in innovating. Thus, no one should be surprised that FCA—considering itself a forward-looking regulator—stated that it is constantly evolving its approach, in order to help fintech firms tackle regulatory barriers to innovation, and to give them space to innovate in the interest of their customers.[141]

Concluding remarks have to highlight the FCA programmes to help face the fintech challenges. Indeed, the goal to create machine-readable versions of the FCA Handbook throws this supervisor to the next stage of public intervention in the market, whereby the production of algorithms would allow the use of devices for both being compliant and controlling the compliance. Indeed, the British approach is exploring the use of semantics and triples (a statement in subject/predicate/object form) in order to map and translate multiple internal and external data ontologies from different predicative rules into a universal format (suitable for self-executing processes).[142]

In this respect, integration (of the ICT systems) and standardizing (the model for expressing data and processes) would be the task for the regulators, provided that British policymakers have started a path straight to the combination of predictability, learnability and simplification of regulatory technology.[143] So, here again, this analysis is dealing with a future that may or may not bring about a new financial crisis or new economic growth, and whose outcome will not be under the complete control of supervisors. To share such increase in uncertainty, fintech and regtech may provide firms and authorities an overpowering incentive to lay off many of the traditional business. The newest is yet to come.

Section III: The Importance of Switzerland in the Fintech Environment

4.14   Overview

From a regulatory perspective, evidence from Switzerland suggests that a secure and advanced country can provide a fertile environment for hosting fintech firms and the most advanced financial innovations.[144] Then, the analysis is now going to question whether fintech industry requires an international harmonized legal framework securing the principles of freedom, independence and self-determination for fintech or a country to be a 'safe haven' for the digital flows between market participants all around the world.[145]

It goes without saying that the latter option relies on the decision of a single country to develop a specific economic policy, aimed at setting up a digital haven, while it requires an agreement among several countries (to be consolidated in a piece of supranational law and then enacted in relevant jurisdictions). Hence, there is no doubt that the first country that will offer safety and effective hosting will seize the advantage to attract fintech firms, and the evidence shows that Switzerland is one of the 'first movers' in this direction.

In these situations, the outcome is socially ideal for two reasons: programmers and coders tend to establish a 'software house' in a safe haven, and their level of interconnections tends to be even higher than optimal. A country acting as a safe haven is also desirable from a regulatory point of view. One way of seeing this is to note that it raises the wellbeing of the relevant community, as there is a lower expenditure to understand the relevant legal framework and a higher probability of complying with it.

In this respect, a regulatory analysis would welcome public intervention aimed at further improving the prerequisites so that a country can offer the opportunity to host digitalization, as a leading, innovative and sustainable location for fintechers. It comes into consideration that the Swiss Federal Council "wants to create the best possible framework conditions so that Switzerland can establish itself and evolve as a leading, innovative and sustainable location for fintech and blockchain companies—and innovative companies in general".[146]

Considering that the main route through which fintech applications benefit society is the reduction of transactional costs and increasing efficiencies, there would be economic reasons for the introduction of regulatory incentives.[147] As it is explained in this section, if there are gains in efficiency, the regulation of digital ledger technology and blockchain should be encouraged, and, in the end, this would benefit the market functioning.[148] Besides this, the calculation of the net social desirability of an alternative to supervised banking and finance involves an overview of both the regulatory policy and the supervisory praxis.

However, it should be noted as well that Switzerland has identified a legal framework aimed at being socially optimal.[149] The national legislator seems to be interested in protecting fintech firms against the risk of the reclassification of their business (as a reserved activity) and in setting an effective incentive to take optimal care while designing potentially promising developments in digitalization.

To put the point differently, in other countries where such clarification is lacking, using fintech would bring legal risks (and might require excessive care) and users would be just as unprotected. In this respect, it is worth considering that Switzerland has expressed its intention to ensure that the "innovative potential of blockchain technology is maintained and that the associated risks, particularly in the fight against money laundering and terrorist financing, are addressed in a coordinated manner".[150]

4.15   THE SURVIVAL
OF TWENTIETH-CENTURY PRINCIPLES

In a sharing-based environment (where the possibility to copy and reuse does not cancel out the rights of the original owners), any question about the applicability of the principles developed in the tradition of civil law cannot be discarded. Above and beyond, the body of these principles has been created and applied considering the technical features of the pre-globalization, pre-financialization and pre-digitalization of the economics.[151] Therefore, the laws of property, contracts, torts and the relevant remedial or ancillary provisions (such as damages, restitutions and injunctions) are going to be the object of a dynamic analysis, in which the time dimension would drive the assessment of the relevant adjustments due to the evolution of technology.

Suppose that, in the fintech environment, all property rights over shareable innovations have been abolished (or rather are not protected).[152] A programmer develops his/her own code, and then—when the relevant algorithm or software is useable—another firm will exploit it for providing banking and financial services. As the programmer has no remedy against the firm's conduct (because this sharing does not prevent the latter from using such software too, provided that ownership only implies the legal right to exclude others from using it), there is no incentive to develop the software, nor any safeguards to stop such activity from being abandoned and the industry shifting to business models that involve less preparatory investments. All of these consequences are undesirable, and they can be avoided if the programmer will be able to charge any firm for the use of the code (even if incorporated within someone else's algorithm or software).

The role of private law in setting these rights concerns the identification of the entity that can determine the use and economic exploitation of data (or big data). In this respect, it should also be noted that in Switzerland the current regulation does not provide for a general right of ownership of data. Apart from copyright law and other intellectual property rights, competition law provides a certain degree of protection, and it seems possible to rely on an ownership-like legal status (under certain conditions) (Thouvenin, F. and Weber, R. H. 2017). However, the concept of data ownership is currently the subject of intense academic debate (Thouvenin, F. et al 2017). Even if it seems that the applicable law (currently in force), under certain conditions, conveys sufficient protection,[153] it must be noted that advancing digitalization will follow a path that the Swiss legal system does not cover: the continued existence of data after the firm has ceased to exist (and then the possibility of the introduction of a right to restitution or deletion of big data, as well as other rules for the treatment of such data in the event of bankruptcy or in case of the sale of assets).[154]

In this respect, the need for moving codes and data from less to more valuable uses reflects the importance of a voluntary exchange or sharing of the fintech mechanisms or tools. Hence, there are calls for regulators to remove the various obstacles to value-maximizing transactions. So, the economic roles of contracts and contract law are evident. As has been shown, these roles involve five distinct economic functions: "(1) to prevent opportunism; (2) to interpolate efficient terms either on a wholesale or a retail basis; (3) to punish avoidable mistakes in the contracting process; (4) to allocate risk to the superior risk bearer; and (5) to reduce the costs of resolving contract disputes" (Posner, R. 2007).

The survival of twentieth-century principles reflects the condition of the current wired society, still based on consumerist behaviour and the need to protect people. Because of this, contemporary democracies can make progress by means of ordinary political decisions to regulate the application of innovations in consideration of the results that they achieve.

Focusing on the experience under consideration, the Swiss regulatory approach to blockchain and distributed ledger technology (DLT) shows that a generally technology-neutral intervention does not mean neglecting any consideration of the status of the technology that supports the business of banking and finance, but refers to a principle-based and technology-neutral legislative activity. According to the current time dimension of policymakers, the legislative process should not be concerned with the individual technologies, but to the activity resulting from their application, which should be subject to the same safeguards, limits and requirements set forth for the traditional equally risky activities. So, the quality and the certainty of the legal framework should support the positioning of a country as an attractive location for fintechers, as tolerating any fraudulent or abusive conduct cannot be accepted in a wired economy (because of the possibility for other countries to intervene in the international electronically enabled cash flows).

In this context, certain innovations require proper definition, and then the intervention of the policymaker to identify the applicable rules. This refers to the case of the tokens, which exist digitally (as a token merely constitutes an entry in a decentralized register), but cannot be handed over, in the true sense of the phrase. So, ownership does not apply to them because of the lack of physical materiality. However, a token becomes relevant when values or rights are linked to such an entry in a digital register, and this is a bilateral contractual relationship, whose object is the usability of the token within a network, under the conditions provided by the relevant platform.

Aware of this consideration, the Swiss Financial Market Supervisory Authority, FINMA, classified tokens as falling under financial market law and then supervised their initial offerings.[155] In order to classify tokens under civil law, it is vital to choose which legal relationship prevails in consideration of the tokens, and this means that the circumstances of the individual use influence their definition itself.[156] Hence, the Swiss approach has a specific starting point: the principle of freedom of contract, and in particular the freedom of the terms of the contract (which may be freely determined within the limits of the law, including those aimed at protecting savers and maintaining financial stability).

In conclusion, it is necessary to question whether—at a supranational level—governments should discuss the current, proven and balanced legal framework, which supports a consumeristic capitalism that is exploiting the earth's resources without considering the constraints of sustainability. Obviously, this question would drive to the above consideration on the need for a global legal framework that covers fintech transactions. However, considering the timing of such a solution, the option for a leading country (aimed at setting the standards for regulating fintech) seems to be the most valuable solution to the current asymmetries between supervised entities and fintech firms.

4.16   FINMA, INNOVATION AREAS AND SANDBOXES

An eclectic group of fintechers could design their own social structure, and then pretend that it would support the circulation of capital. In this respect, it is possible to bear in mind that any legal order provides a certain specific and mandatory leeway for individual structuring of company forms, in light of the fact that, in general, it is not permissible to create a hitherto unknown form of membership.[157]

According to the above, the policymaker should consider that the current set of principles requires new corollaries with respect to the embodiment of rights *in rem* through ownership and the separation of ownership and direct possession. The Swiss experience shows the need to consider the framework of private autonomy and the limits to freedom of contract. Nevertheless, it is useful to recall the economic theory that suggests possible ways of limiting the effects of such corollaries, as the danger of collusion among fintechers (including the use of software to collude) is higher when there is an effective quality and responsiveness of the network, and the supervisors are not exploiting the relevant innovations (as is the case in the international fintech environment).

It is worth mentioning that FINMA set up its fintech desk at end-2015, which bundled all enquiries relating to innovation in banking and finance. Thus, a channel was established: fintech firms have been asked to deal with the supervisor and the supervisor cannot ignore such approaches.[158] The capital stock of questions and answers is the joint product of that channel, and this led to specific guidelines that indicated the points of contact between ICOs and applicable financial market law, as well as the possibility to consider tech-fuelled activities as reserved (if that was the case). This might seem an oddly informal process but several decisions have come out of it.

Another factor to highlight in the experience of Switzerland is that the relevant approach to fintech activities starts from the assumption that the acceptance of deposits from the public is subject to the Federal Law on Banks and Savings Banks (namely Banking Act or BankA) and requires in all cases an authorization from FINMA. So the licensing applies in particular to certain blockchain and DLT-based business models, which come under the scope of public supervision.[159] In particular, such a scope does not refer to mere traditional banking businesses but also to innovative business models that may entail a high risk from the point of view of protecting customers and maintaining financial stability (with respect to the time limit transformation, the short-term deposits and the granting of long-term loans), as banking regulation aims to minimize the risks of liquidity and rates.

An important qualification to these matters is suggested by two inter-related key issues regarding blockchain and DLT-based business models (that have been expressly highlighted by the Swiss experience): the newly created authorization category (fintech authorization), which entered into force at the start of 2019, as well as the fintech innovation area (sandbox) and the extension of the exemption for settlement accounts.[160] This calls to contemplate that, in some cases, it may be best for the regulator to insist on low requirements for the enforcement of supervision, and not to allow an alternative way for exchanging capitals.

In promoting innovation, Art. 1b of BankA defined a scope that may include fintechers accepting the deposit of third-party money, and the Federal Department of Finance (FDF) established previously that the acceptance of Bitcoins might constitute a public deposit.[161] As mutually beneficial completely specified contracts, this kind of deposit is regulated by a provision for each and every contingency. As this may be a simplifying assumption (rather than a qualification), a smart contract would also self-execute each possible outcome at the same level of legal cost; therefore, any contract would state whether or not a party will execute it.

Besides that, the treatment of crypto-assets in the context of capital adequacy should be analysed in order to set out new rules for the case of customers entrusting their cryptocurrencies to a fintech bank for safekeeping. In general, such assets absorb own funds, and are not stored in a vault but invested in this kind of bank. However, this does not deny the possibility of considering that a certain exemption would apply in connection with the application of tech-fuelled business models and the provision of a sandbox for innovation in banking.

Hence, no authorization would be necessary if public deposits are accepted on a non-professional basis, and—according to the legislation in force—to remain in such an innovation area, the accepted public deposits must not amount to more than CHF 1 million in total, and there must be no interest operations.[162] In any case, the depositor must be aware that he/she is operating outside the scope of public supervision and monetary backstops or deposit insurance (being notified prior to acceptance of the deposit).[163]

An innovation area, however, should not be a riskier environment. As was earlier noted, it is imaginable that the format of the innovation area would not result in a *mere* trade-off between the overall economic benefit and the risks with respect to financial stability and client protection. On the contrary, this is an environment where new forms of supervision can be experienced that exploit technological developments from digital evolution, while beginning some kind of control over programmers and coders.

4.17   REGULATING SWISS FINTECHERS AS USUAL EXPORTERS: THE RELEVANT MARKET AND THE PROPER RIGHTS

Swiss banking law includes a new authorization category: 'fintech authorization'. As mentioned above, fintech firms do not always enter into a bilateral contract having the effect of transferring resources from the customers' ownership to the firms' assets, or involving credit enhancement, maturity transformation or leveraging, and thus nobody incurs the related risks. Under this framework, the need for licensing refers to a social evaluation of affairs consisting of two elements: the individual rights and financial stability.[164]

There are no doubts that the aforesaid fintech authorization project steers fintech firms towards the domestic market, as it gives firms the possibility to accept public deposits of up to CHF 100 million on a professional basis, whereby any higher amount requires a full authorization. Even if it is envisaged that the Federal Council may amend this limit, it is possible to suggest that fintech banks should apply for a full authorization, provided that the supervisory team would remain the one specialized in the dynamic development of the fintech sector and in particular of blockchain- and DLT-based business models. Indeed, this approach will project the authorized firms outside the border of the domestic market, towards cross-border activities that contemplate the full exploitation of the World Wide Web and the globalized economy.[165]

According to the above, the impact of the new fintech authorization requires careful oversight. It is acknowledged that the protection of the individual rights of a customer are an indicator of market functioning, whether such a market supports a person's utility and his/her well-being. It is clear, then, how suitable and attractive this new authorization category is for fintech firms, due to the fact that the framework conditions of the fintech authorization seem to take sufficient account of the needs of this arising industry.

In this respect, an envisaged market progress would refer to the opportunity that Switzerland will qualify more and more as a safe haven, and there is a possibility that any additional regulations would be a clear indication of the development of relevant business models. It is important to note too that where there is certainty about the current and the future legal framework, the capacity to attract foreign investors increases. As all the above suggests, this implies that Switzerland will host more fintech firms than the ones required by its internal market, and that a group of Swiss fintechers will qualify as usual exporters.

Affording to such a regulatory framework, the social evaluation of the Swiss fintech environment should be based on the possibility of an amalgamation of banks' and non-banks' utilities (in some way).[166] In particular, it depends positively on each and every banks' and non-banks' costs and benefits, and does not depend on factors apart from their compliance with the relevant set of rules. Hence, the need for considering a vast multitude of ways of aggregating and raising capital from the market, and no single way is endorsed under the current regulatory and supervisory policies, provided that credit institutions are obliged to hold a minimum amount of own funds for the assets they hold.

Considerations about equity and debt in the banking industry will drive away from the core issues surrounding fintech. However, it should be remembered that in Switzerland there are not yet any capital requirements specifically for cryptocurrencies. Accordingly, FINMA determines only the concrete requirements in each individual case, with respect of each kind of token (e.g. market risks and operational risks) and according to a conservative risk weighting (that seems appropriate for tokens regarded as private duties).[167]

In this respect, the assumption that the size of the own funds depends only on factors apart from technology cannot be accepted.[168] Indeed, a tech-based measure of capital adequacy would be able to differentiate a fintech bank from a traditional one. Probably this is introducing a subjective notion of fintech applications; however, there are numerous conceptions of what technology would imply to be correct, fair, just or moral. These conceptions would segregate, on the one side, the new business models that apply fintech to the credit transformation process and, on the other, the traditional models that depend on basic ICT solutions and third-party software.

Considering their offering to the worldwide-globalized economy, Swiss fintech firms are in the position of acting most of the time as a third-country intermediary in another host state.[169] This would suggest that compliance with the Federal Act on Financial Market Infrastructures and Market Conduct in Securities and Derivatives Trading (Financial Market Infrastructure Act, FMIA) would refer to a traditional picture of a centrally structured firm, which can result in unanswered questions when a fintech firm is a primarily decentralized organization.[170]

From another perspective, in regulating fintechers, Swiss policymaker and authorities refer to some concepts of innovation and finance that are concerned with whether or which tokens fall under the definition of 'security' or 'derivative', and then whether the relevant regulation (in their current form) supports the safe and smooth circulation of these new financial instruments enhanced by means of cryptography. Questioning whether any token that is standardized and suitable for mass trading would be considered to be a security (or a derivative, as the case may be) would lead into the legal implications of such a classification.[171]

In particular, it is necessary to bear in mind that provisions about trading venues are only relevant for securities. In the case of tokens, it is not possible to deny that they offer an applicable solution for incorporating rights into intangibles, and for facilitating the circulation of such rights (and then they may be classified as uncertificated securities, derivatives or, under certain circumstances, as intermediated securities).

In this respect, as FINMA indicated in its guidelines, there are differing opinions in legal studies; nevertheless, the Swiss approach would suggest that a technological-neutral approach leads to classifying tokens as securities (if the first presents the characteristics provided in the definition of the second).[172] Hence, the flows leaving Switzerland towards foreign economies are referring to a kind of tool (i.e. the token) that cannot be classified in a uniform manner under financial market law in all circumstances, and, under certain conditions, such classification may result in a cumulative application of the corresponding requirements under financial market law and payment service regulation.

Provided all the above, the need for considering the time dimension again rises. Depending on the fintech business model, the collection of capital would take place by issuing tokens or any other crypto-assets, rather than exchanging them for sovereign currencies. As a result, such a collection relies on the current financial market infrastructure and the relevant regulation, which have not been designed for widespread international operability based upon a considerable flexibility due to the content-related design of tokens, nor the possibility that these tokens would self-execute certain changes in their structure or contents. Then, further developments are expected, aimed at implementing a clear choice of accepting or rejecting a scheme that would guarantee to make any party's rights less vulnerable.[173]

4.18   The Conscience of a Legal Order: Combating Money Laundering and Terrorist Financing

For the purpose of being at least somewhat prepared for crises and unforeseen turmoil, there is the possibility to institute some flexible standby arrangements for understanding the sources of any flow of capital, as well as its final destination. In particular, the Swiss will to play a new role in global capitalism is a good argument for overbuilding a system of inspections and controls relative to fintech and the use of its innovations. Having the capacity to enlarge and intensify this system, Switzerland would qualify as a safe haven and a conscientious environment, and may have a good success in hosting fintechers looking for a competitive and certain legal order..

In this respect, it should be considered that FMIA is governing the operation of financial market infrastructures and the obligations in trade with securities and derivatives with the goal of ensuring smoothly operating financial markets. It is acknowledged that fintech is making it possible to standardize, automate and accelerate the various steps in processing a securities transaction (trade, clearing, settlement and reporting), and that fintech firms require such speedy infrastructures. This is not going to question if trading institutions will continue to be of fundamental importance (in matching supply and demand) after the full application of cryptography and distributed ledger technology, but it is agreeable that there will still be the need for ensuring the safety of the exchanges (that now rely on the resilience of the central counterparties).

Moreover, it is likely that Switzerland will be one of the first movers through the comprehensive supervision of programmers, and that this country will lead a public international intervention aimed at considering the reliability and usefulness of software in terms of trust (while recognizing that regulation may arise when there is a powerful crash of market-based financing, provided that there will be enough time to set up an ad hoc supervisory system).

It is also true that a comprehensive approach would lead to the provision of licensing requirements for platforms, whether they are exchanges (among private cryptocurrencies and sovereign currencies) or trading venues (for cryptocurrencies or crypto-assets), provided that such an authorization would be technologically neutral, and would also apply to decentralized platforms.[174] In brief, the use of DLT would not place such activities out of the scope of the current supervision. Given this background, it is possible to expect the creation of a new set of intermediaries, aimed at managing platforms, rather than a mere extension of today's rules for trading venues.

In accordance with the current legal situation, the users of a platform—provided that they have an agreement with the relevant manager—must fulfil a duty of disclosure necessary for the transparency of securities market trading, as well as for the purpose of combating money laundering and terrorist financing. Behind the new capacity of record-keeping and reporting duties provided by cryptography and the self-executing algorithms, there is the opportunity to track any cash flow and make gatekeeping more efficient. And the same is true with respect to the clearing and settlement of payment obligations that would not only be based on uniform rules and procedures, but also on algorithms, cryptography and smart contracts, provided that FMIA regulation of payment systems is not restricted to legal tender.[175]

All the above leads to deal with the risks of money laundering and terrorist financing presented by crypto-based assets and ICOs in the Swiss environment.[176] In going deep into the question raised by fintech, it is useful to assume that the existing legal basis reflects the international legal standards, and its enforcement is in line with the most advanced democracies' attitude. However, this is not sufficient to ensure the applicability of such a legal basis to activities involving crypto-assets (and, to some extent, ICOs).[177]

There is no doubt that the grounds for this control refers to the due diligence duties of the person that is receiving or transferring any assets or money in execution of an order of his/her counterparty. Indeed, the execution of such duties leads to the understanding of the economic reason for the transaction, and—in the event of a suspicion reason—to reporting of the suspicions to the Money Laundering Reporting Office Switzerland immediately. Thus, this seems to be an international standard, and the technology that supports the aforesaid transaction is neutral. So, the digital evolution of the Swiss financial industry would not interact with this reality.

However, it is predictable that these controls would benefit from fintech innovations, as well as algorithms, software, cryptography and DLT, because they would help supervised entities in submitting an adequate report whenever they suspected a business relationship related to money laundering or terrorist financing.[178] As shown in the last chapter, the threat associated with cryptocurrencies and fintech transactions is real and proven. It affects all countries, and Switzerland is not unusual in this. Hence, the regulator should not focus only on the use of cryptocurrencies to add complexity to the paths used for money laundering, but must also take into account that such assets (and their underlying technology) pose a new threat. And this is due to the inconsistency of the value and the anonymity of the owner (or rather, the difficulties for supervisors to collect and analyse the data needed to identify the beneficial owner of certain assets). Then, it is possible that Swiss policymakers will lead the development of algorithms able to catch any sum that is going to be transferred from one electronic account to another in a matter of seconds (without anyone knowing who is initiating the transaction) (Fluhmann, D. and Hsu, P. 2019). Indeed, such algorithms would be the basis for promoting a regulatory intervention aimed at safeguarding the transmission of wallets online to third parties (together with their keys). So that there will be a supervisory mechanism able to deal with the combination of anonymity, speed and mobility that characterize the chain transactions of fintech.

As the vulnerabilities of all countries with an advanced economy are considerable in respect to the need for protecting the economy from the misuse of the outcome of illicit actions, it is desirable that the results achieved by Swiss regulators and supervisors will become a *standard* for other developed countries. So, if the same principles (developed in banking and financial markets) apply (to the fintech industry), then the use of technology will support supervisors in controlling programmers, platforms and service providers involved in the circulation of such assets.

Concluding remarks aim at pointing out the limits of the application of the principle of neutrality, when all the above suggests that global policymakers should provide an optimal regulation contributing to innovation, and not set the prevailing technologies. Besides the asymmetry in the timing of regulation and technical developments, policymakers must safeguard the proven and balanced legal framework designed for banking and finance, and then—as a corollary of the traditional principles—make only targeted changes as a consequence of fintech innovations.[179] Then, the focus goes to the evidence from Switzerland, which converges towards a point where Swiss authorities are positioning themselves as open innovators, and highlight the concrete dialogue between industry's representatives and policymakers, as the latter are promoting rules designed for unifying banking and shadow banking under the scope of an *advanced* supervision.

Indeed, all the above shows that the fintech industry is ready for a principle-based and technology-neutral legislative regulatory approach, as its operators are challenging a tech-fuelled competition environment, whereby the lack of regulation is not neutral but risky.[180] In this respect, it is possible to appreciate that Switzerland is aiming to make itself an attractive location vis-à-vis fintech firms, and this aim has been pursued by means of legal certainty and efficient regulation (in which the misuse of innovative technologies for fraudulent or abusive acts or to circumvent the regulatory framework cannot be tolerated). So, this shows the *intention* of the policymakers, as a new political agenda aimed at promoting changes in domestic policies, at re-establishing a truly, viral, competitive market for capital. Because in the end, in the current regulatory perspective, a comprehensive and inclusive market is what being a regulator is mainly about.

NOTES

1. In addition, it is worth referring to Merton, R. C. 2018. "Observations on the Digital Revolution: Financial Innovation and FinTech" Speech at 17th International Conference on Credit, Venice, which addressed four challenges for the successful and wide-scope adoption of FinTech: (1) Trust—fundamental to financial services; technology by itself is not sufficient to create it; (2) Credit risk—what's worse than being uninsured? Believing you are insured when you are not; (3) Innovation risk—implementation of innovation mismatched to the infrastructure to support it; (4) Regulation—supports trust; government is ultimately responsible for system failures.

   See also Vulkan, N. and Astebro, T. and Sierra M. F., 2016. "Equity crowdfunding: A new phenomena(opens in new window)" *Journal of Business Venturing Insights*; Wang, W. and Mahmood, A. and Sismeiro, C. and Vulkand, N. 2019. "The evolution of equity crowdfunding: Insights from co-investments of angels and the crowd" *Research Policy*, which found evidence of information flows in crowdfunding platforms between angels, and from angels to the crowd. These authors showed that angels play an important role in funding of large ventures, whereas the crowd not only fill the funding gaps for such large ventures but also play a pivotal role in the funding of small ones. The complementarity between angels and crowd investors seems to increase the overall efficiency in an otherwise highly asymmetric and uncertain market, confirming that digitization can indeed bring important benefits to venture investment.

2. This analysis is moving from the consideration on the 'ongoing changes' to the current business models of fintech firms; see Lemma, V. 2018. "Fintech regulation: the need for a research" *Open review of management, banking and finance*; see also Engst, A. and Lemma, V. 2018. "Insurtech and interoperability of Fintech firms" *Open review of management, banking and finance*, para. 2, where it is highlighted that 'regulatory issues are related to the algorithms supporting the partially automated activities in insurance undertaking (and other advanced technique of risk mitigation)'.

3. Market players data shows that increasing consumer and SME awareness of, and engagement with, FinTech is driving concrete growth in adoption rates; see Hwa, G. and Lloyd, J. and Hatch, M. 2019. "Eight ways FinTech adoption remains on the rise" and "EY third biennial FinTech adoption trends survey".

4. Thus, the need for a clarification of the scope of this research with regard to the role of the public in this sector; see Cassese, S. 2000. "Quattro paradossi sui rapporti tra poteri pubblici ed autonomie private" *Rivista trimestrale diritto pubblico*, p. 390 ss.

   See also Capriglione, F. 2018. "Considerazioni a margine del volume: il tramonto della banca universale?" *Rivista Trimestrale di Diritto dell'Economia*, p. 22 ff.

5. Nowadays, several researches cast doubt that ICT service providers are able to produce the same output of banking and finance, as well as that the shadow banking system satisfies the needs of several firms and savers (in the market for capital and investments); see Gorton, G. B. and Metrick, A. 2010. "Regulating the Shadow Banking System" *SSRN Research Paper no. 1676947*; Ricks, M. 2010. "Shadow Banking and Financial Regulation" *Columbia Law and Economics Working Paper No. 370*; Jagtiani, J. and Lemieux, C. 2018. "The Roles of Alternative Data and Machine Learning in Fintech Lending: Evidence from the Lendingclub Consumer Platform" *FRB of Philadelphia Working Paper No. 18-15*.

   Therefore, it aims at clarifying that such alternatives (to banking and finance) are able to execute also activities that have been reserved to banks and financial firms, provide that there are no specific limitations to place their supply and demand within the market for capitals. Indeed, it is necessary to understand whether there are rights to protect, and then the role of the international bodies, national governments and central banks in the oversight of the financial innovation (i.e. new tools and instruments provided by the evolution of personal devices, network infrastructures and software).

6. On this point, see Begley, T. A. and Srinivasan, K. 2019 "Small Bank Lending in the Era of Fintech and Shadow Banking: A Sideshow?" *Northeastern U. D'Amore-McKim School of Business Research Paper No. 3317672*, which found that cross-sectional variation in consumer preferences for traditional banks and institutional features of the mortgage market play important roles in explaining these findings, and whose results highlight the continued importance of small banks despite the rise of shadow banks and financial technology disruption.

7. In addition, this analysis refers to the conclusions of Simoncini, A. 2016. "The Constitutional Dimension of the Internet: Some Research Paths" *EUI Working Paper Law 2016/16*; Messina, D. 2018. "Il Regolamento (EU) 2016/679 in materia di protezione dei dati personali alla luce della vicenda Cambridge Analytica", *Federalismi.it*.

8. For the purposes of this analysis, it is worth starting from the approach suggested by Coase, R. H. 1988. "The firm the market and the law" Chicago.

9. See Zuiderveen Borgesius, F. 2014. "Behavioural Sciences and the Regulation of Privacy on the Internet" *Institute for Information Law Research Paper No. 2014-02*, which examines the policy implications of behavioural sciences insights for the regulation of privacy on the Internet, by focusing in particular on behavioural targeting.

   See also Baker, H. K. and Ricciardi, V. 2015. "Understanding Behavioral Aspects of Financial Planning and Investing" *Journal of Financial Planning*, which pointed out that understanding fundamental human tendencies can help financial planners and advisers recognize behaviours that may interfere with clients achieving their long-term goals; see also Ricciardi, V. and Simon, H. K. 2000. "What is Behavioral Finance?" *Business, Education & Technology Journal*, which investigates the cognitive factors and emotional issues that impact the decision-making process of individuals, groups, and organizations.

10. See Zuiderveen Borgesius, F. 2013. "Behavioral Targeting, A European Legal Perspective" *IEEE Security & Privacy*, p. 82 ff.; Davies, G. B. 2017 "New Vistas in Risk Profiling" *CFA Institute Research Foundation*, which suggests the usefulness of analytics aimed at controlling the crucial elements of (a) risk tolerance, (b) behavioural risk attitudes and (c) risk capacity.

11. In this regulatory context, it is not possible to deny that—if compared—the technical enhancement of velocity, frequency and size of financial dealing seems greater; and the legal order seems to have little possibility of orienting social behaviours. In the wired society, relations are direct (or

rather dis-intermediate); the institutions of democracies seem to be un-resilient, nor are they able to conform the reality to the principles set forth—to safeguard freedom, justice and welfare; see Canalini, V. 2019 "Il FinTech e le nuove frontiere dell'innovazione finanziaria", "Manuale di diritto bancario e finanziario", Padova.

12. Let us recall Cassese, S. 2009. "Il diritto globale" Torino; Carcaterra, G. 1979. "La forza costitutiva delle norme. L'uomo e la società", Roma; Carcaterra, G. 2014. "Le norme costitutive", Torino on the 'performa-tive utterances', which aim to look for and interpret traces in legal experi-ence, from constituent judgements to rights and powers, then going back to the rules of structure and the fundamental rule, and finally looking at the totality of the system.

13. See Olkova, A. 2018. "Portfolio Performance Measurement: Traditional vs Utility-Based Approaches" *1st International Management, Quality and Marketing Conference Research Paper* on the role of traditional and utility-based approaches in constructing risk-adjusted performance mea-sures. This paper suggests the possibility to facilitate investor profiling and portfolio assessment by a piecewise-linear utility framework. To model an investor profile, and proposed an approximation to the possibly non-linear utility curve, under the assumption of discretely changing marginal utility.

14. In this respect, the analysis may rely on the considerations of Zillien, N. and Hargittai, E. 2009. "Digital Distinction: Status-Specific Internet uses". *Social Science Quarterly*, p. 274 ff.

15. In particular, this has been summarized by Draghi, M. 2019. "Farewell Remarks". See also de Guindos, L. 2019. "Welcome Remarks at the third ECB Forum on Banking Supervision", Frankfurt am Main, 6 November. In general on this point, see Capriglione, F. 2019. "Un secolo di rego-lazione" "Manuale di diritto bancario e finanziario", Padova.

16. It refers to McKinsey Global Institute 1992, "Service Sector Productivity", Washington, DC.

17. See Zhang, t. "Balancing Fintech Opportunities and Risks. Remarks by IMF Deputy Managing Director" Vilnius, who stated that "Fintech can support productivity and growth by strengthening financial develop-ment, inclusion, and efficiency, but may pose risks to consumers and investors and, more broadly, to financial stability and integrity."

18. See OECD 2019 "Regulatory effectiveness in the era of digitalisation", Paris, which assumed that governments and regulators play a major role in encouraging digital innovation and in incentivizing the development of these technologies for the benefit of society.

19. It refers to the document of OCSE, "Regulatory Reform and Innovation", which recalls BAILY, M. N. 1993. "Competition, Regulation and Efficiency in Service Industries" *Brookings Papers in Microeconomics*.

20. See Bruckner, M. A. 2018. "Regulating Fintech Lending" *Banking & Financial Services Policy Report*; Runshan, F. and Yan, H. and Param Vir, S. 2019. "Crowds, Lending, Machines, and Bias" *SSRN Research Paper no. 3206027*.

    See also Borselli, A. 2018. "Insurance by Algorithm" *European Insurance Law Review* on an example of algorithmic systems that have the potential to transform large sectors of the economy.

21. It is worth recalling the efforts of the regulatory analysis on the legal reasoning, see Posner, R. 2008. "How judges think", Harvard and Vandevelde, K. J. 2011. "Thinking like a lawyer", Boulder, 2011.

22. See Engst and Lemma, *Insurtech and interoperability of Fintech firms*, in *Open review of management, banking and finance*, 2018, para. 2 on the absence of significant changes of the national legislative framework, which 'should suggest a complete freedom in starting up a fintech firm that would support the business of insurance companies or distributors'.

23. See Banca d'Italia, 2017. "FinTech In Italia. Indagine conoscitiva sull'adozione delle innova-zioni tecnologiche applicate ai servizi finanzi-ari, Roma; Panetta, F. 2017. "L'innovazione digitale nell'industria finanziaria italiana", Milano, 26 september; Bofondi, M. 2017. "Il lending-based crowdfunding: opportunità e rischi", *Questioni di Economia e Finanza*, Roma, p. 7.

24. This would refer also to the outcome of Warschauer, M. 2009. "Demystifying the Digital Divide" *Elsevier*, p. 191 ff.

25. In particular, it refers to Warschauer, M. 2003. "Technology and Social Inclusion: Rethinking the Digital Divide", Cambridge. See also Capriglione, F. 2004. "Etica della finanza mercato globalizzazione", Bari, Chapter V; Lastra, R. 2013. "The Globalization Paradox: Review of Dani Rodrik, The Globalization Paradox: Democracy and the Future of the World Economy", *International Journal of Constitutional Law*, p. 809 ff.

26. Let us recall Engst, A. and Lemma, V. "Insurtech and interoperability of Fintech firms" *Open review of management, banking and finance*, 2018, para. 2 with respect to both the consideration that "the current legislative path for the adoption of a EU directive would not be timely for driving the innovation in this industry, anyway new rules should be able to set common standards (in order to ensure a fair competition in this market)" and the doubt "that new technologies and different business models are spreading in the insurance business, so the monitoring of outsourcing

(and then the perspective of certain developments in licensing the ancillary service provided to traditional insurance companies) should allow the starting of new form of supervision without jeopardizing the market for servicing".

27. See Jackson, G. and Deeg, R. 2006. "How Many Varieties of Capitalism? Comparing the Comparative Institutional Analyses of Capitalist Diversity" *MPIfG Discussion Paper No. 06/2* on the distinct institutional configurations that generate a particular systemic "logic" of economic action.

28. See Grant, S. H. and Van Zandt, T. 2007. "Expected Utility Theory" *INSEAD Business School Research Paper No. 2007/71/EPS*, which present the mathematical structure of additive and linear utility representations and their axiomatizations, in the context of abstract choice theory and using intertemporal choice as a source of examples.

   See also Campbell, J. Y. and Cochrane, J. H., 1998. "By Force of Habit: A Consumption-Based Explanation of Plantation of Aggregate Stock Market Behavior" *Center for Research in Security Prices Working Paper No. 412* for a model that adds a slow-moving external habit to the standard power utility function. See also Chang, H. F. 1999. "A Liberal Theory of Social Welfare: Fairness, Utility, and the Pareto Principle" *University of Pennsylvania Law School, Institute for Law and Economics, Working Paper No. 272*, which give weight to considerations other than the overall utility level of each individual.

29. In this respect, regulator should consider that the firms and other types of organizations are feverishly exploring ways of taking advantage of the big data phenomenon; see Galbraith, J. R. 2014. "Organizational Design Challenges Resulting from Big Data" *Journal of Organization Design*, p. 2 ff.

   See also Ezrachi, A. 2018. "EU Competition Law Goals and the Digital Economy" *Oxford Legal Studies Research Paper No. 17/2018;* Wachter, S. and Mittelstadt, B. 2018. "A Right to Reasonable Inferences: Re-Thinking Data Protection Law in the Age of Big Data and AI" *Columbia Business Law Review.*

30. Let us recall Rodotà, S. 1973. "Elaboratori elettronici e controllo sociale", Bologna; in addition, see D'Acquisto, G. and Naldi, M. 2017. "Big data e privacy by design", Torino; Pollicino, O. and Frosini, T. and Apa, E. 2017. "Diritti e libertà in Internet", Milano.

31. See Goanta, C. 2018. "How Technology Disrupts Private Law: An Exploratory Study of California and Switzerland as Innovative Jurisdictions" Stanford-Vienna TTLF Working Paper No. 38/2018.

32. See Remolina, N. 2019. "Open Banking: Regulatory Challenges for a New Form of Financial Intermediation in a Data-Driven World" *SMU Centre for AI & Data Governance Research Paper No. 2019/05* on the

consideration that open banking—as a service—is emerging as a new form of intermediation that portraits positive and negative externalities for the financial system. See also Belleflamme, P. and Lambert, T. and Schwienbacher, A. "Crowdfunding Dynamics" *CESifo Working Paper No. 7797*, which pointed out various forms of social learning and network effects that are at work on crowdfunding platforms, giving rise to informational and payoff externalities.

33. In general, it is worth recalling Cirillo, P. and Taleb, N. 2015. "Expected Shortfall Estimation for Apparently Infinite-Mean Models of Operational Risk" *Quantitative Finance*, whose research showed that statistical analyses on actual data depict operational risk as an extremely heavy-tailed phenomenon, able to generate losses so extreme as to suggest the use of infinite-mean models. However, these authors concluded that no loss can actually destroy more than the entire value of a bank or of a company, and this upper bound should be considered when dealing with tail-risk assessment.

Hence, the need for a deeper analysis of a sort of multipurpose data-driven optimization heuristic capable to deal efficiently with a variety of risk functions and practical constraints on the positions in the portfolio, as suggested by Gilli, M. and Këllezi, E. and Hysi, H. 2006. "A Data-Driven Optimization Heuristic for Downside Risk Minimization" *Swiss Finance Institute Research Paper No. 06-2.*

34. This refers to OCSE, "Regulatory Reform and Innovation". In this respect, see also Lehmann, M. 2019. "Global Rules for a Global Market Place? – The Regulation and Supervision of FinTech Providers" *Boston University International Law Journal*; and—with respect to EU—Zetzsche, D. A. and Preiner, C. 2017. "Cross-Border Crowdfunding – Towards a Single Crowdfunding Market for "*European Banking Institute Working Paper Series 2017*, which—in contrast to the European Commission's Capital Market Action Plan—takes the view that national limitations on crowd investing and crowd lending de facto are the result of limits de jure.

35. This part of the analysis specifically recalls FSB, 2017. "Financial stability implications from fintech", 27 June.

36. See Berlingò, V. 2017. "Il fenomeno della datafication e la sua giuridicizzazione", *Rivista Trimestrale di Diritto Pubblico*, p. 3 ff.; Wachter, S. 2018. "Normative challenges of identification in the Internet of Things: Privacy, profiling, discrimination, and the GDPR", *Computer law & security Review*.

37. See Status, R. 1971. "Contract and the Welfare State" *Stanford Law Review*, 1971, p. 941 ff. Recently, Stylianou, T. 2018. "An Investigation into the Utility and Potential Regulation of Initial Coin Offerings and Smart Contracts in Selected Industries and Jurisdictions" *King's College*

London Law School Research Paper No. 19-8 sought to give an answer whether regulatory bodies are required to make more steps into creating a regulatory framework for the utilities of blockchain technology.

See also Zetzsche, D. A. and Buckley, R. P. and Arner, D. W. and Barberis, J. N., 2017. "Regulating a Revolution: From Regulatory Sandboxes to Smart Regulation" *Fordham Journal of Corporate and Financial Law.*

38. Moreover, see Hansmann, H. and Kraakman, R. H. 2004. "What is Corporate Law?" *Yale Law & Economics Research Paper No. 300,* on the details of the economic importance of the corporate form's features: legal personality, limited liability, transferable shares, delegated management and investor ownership.

    This recalls Armour, J. and Hansmann, H. and Kraakman, R. H. "The Essential Elements of Corporate Law" *Oxford Legal Studies Research Paper No. 20/2009,* which represented that whilst the 'core' features of corporate law are present in all—or almost all—legal systems, different systems have made different choices regarding the form and content of many other aspects of their corporate laws.

39. See Carcaterra, G. 2014. "Le norme costitutive", Torino on the 'performative utterances', which moves on a theoretical-logical research level, and it is with this in mind that he investigates the possibility of using constitutive propositions in regulation as reconstructive models of standardisation activity.

40. Henceforth, freedom depends not only on the mere absence of public limitations, but also on an infrastructure; see Balkin, J. M. 2008. "The Future of Free Expression in a Digital Age" *Pepperdine Law Review.*

41. It remarks the conclusion of FSB 2019. "Fintech and market structure in financial services: Market developments and potential financial stability implications", which is a part of the FSB's ongoing work to monitor FinTech market developments and their potential implications for financial stability.

42. It may be noted that Thakor, A. V. 2019, "Fintech and Banking: What Do We Know?" *Journal of Financial Intermediation,* provided a definition of fintech and examined some statistics and stylized facts, and then the author reviewed the relevant theoretical and empirical literature.

43. Furthermore, these considerations reflect the conclusion of Dell'Ariccia, G. and Marquez, R. 2006. "Competition among regulators and credit market integration" *Journal of Financial Economics.* Let us recall also Berle A. A. and Means G. C. 1932. "The Modern Corporation and Private Property"; Engineer, M. 1990. "Brennan and Buchanan's Leviathan models" *The Social Science Journal;* and—with respect to fintech—Lehmann, M. 2019. "Global Rules for a Global Market Place? The

Regulation and Supervision of FinTech Providers" *Boston University International Law Journal*

44. In this respect, reference is made to Bennett, S. and Maton, K. and Kervin, L. 2008. "The 'Digital Natives' Debate: A Critical Review of the Evidence" *British Journal of Educational Technology*, p. 775 ff.

45. In particular, see De Polis, A. and Pietrunti, M. 2019. "Exchange Rate Dynamics and Unconventional Monetary Policies: It's All in the Shadows" *Bank of Italy Temi di Discussione (Working Paper) No. 1231.*; Cohen-Setton, J. and Vallée, S. 2018. "Federalizing a Central Bank: A Comparative Study of the Early Years of the FED and the ECB" "Lessons for EU Integration from US History. Report to the European Commission"

    See also Orphanides, A. 2014. "European Headwind: ECB Policy and Fed Normalization" *MIT Sloan Research Paper No. 5119-14*; Cukierman, A. 2014. "Euro-Area and US Banks Behavior, and ECB-Fed Monetary Policies During the Global Financial Crisis: A Comparison" CEPR Discussion Paper No. DP10289. With regard to the beginning of this century, see also Wray, L. R. and Sardoni, C. 2005 "Monetary Policy Strategies of the European Central Bank and the Federal Reserve Bank of U.S." *Levy Economics Institute Working Paper No. 431*; Savona, P. 2002. "Politica economica e new economy", Milano; Savona, P. 2008. "I momenti d'oro dell'economia visti da Paolo Savona", Roma.

46. See FSB 2019. "Resolution Report: Mind the Gap. Eighth Report on the Implementation of Resolution Reforms", which pointed out that an important lesson of the global financial crisis was that it is insufficient for authorities to rely entirely on policies aimed at reducing the probability of individual financial firms failing.

47. According to the FSB, "The fact that many third party providers may fall outside the regulatory perimeter places increased emphasis on the importance of managing related operational risks, which could ultimately undermine financial stability"; see FSB. 2017. "Financial Stability Implications from FinTech. Supervisory and Regulatory Issues that Merit Authorities' Attention", 27 June.

48. Consequently, it has been easy for the FSB to add a new consideration concerning the risk that the entry of BigTech firms could expedite or amplify the alternative market-based financing (through these firms' existing wide customer base, trusted customer relationships, strong capital positions, easy access to external funding and potentially different business focus).

49. Hereafter, there is the opportunity to take into account the further efforts that are ongoing in the Basel Committee on Banking Supervision (BCBS) and the International Organization of Securities Commissions (IOSCO),

considering that the relevant market structure is characterized by such factors as the number and size of market participants, barriers to entry and exit, and accessibility of information and technology to all participants.

50. The above consideration refers to Clinton, B. 2000 "From Digital Divide to Digital Opportunity", Washington D.C., February 2.

51. It worth notice that all the above refers to THE WHITE HOUSE, Office of the vice president, Remarks by Vice President Al Gore "Digital Divide Event", April 28, 1998.

52. In particular, this part of the research refers to Negreiro, M. 2015. "Briefing at EPRS | European Parliamentary Research Service. Bridging the digital divide in the EU", Bruxelles; see also the foundations of the research conducted by Abu-Shanab, E. and Al-Jamal, N. 2015 "Exploring the Gender Digital Divide in Jordan", *Gender, Technology and Development*, p. 91 ff.

53. It is worth noting that "Presidency Conclusions" at Lisbon European Council 23 and 24 March 2000; see also Piazolo, D. 2001. "The Digital Divide" *CESifo Forum*, p. 29 ff.

54. By referring to this asymmetry with respect to the objective of bridging the digital divide in the EU, the European Parliament refers to the fact that about half of the less-educated and the elderly in the population do not use it regularly, and about 58 million EU citizens (aged 16–74 years old) have never used it at all; see UNEVOC – UNESCO 2014 "Digital divide" *Resources and Services*.

55. Let us recall Rodotà, S. 2012. "Il diritto di avere diritti", Roma-Bari; Rodotà, S. 2006. "La vita e le regole. Tra diritto e non diritto", Milano; Rodotà, S. 2004. "Tecnopolitica. La democrazia e le nuove tecnologie della comunicazione", Rodotà, S. 1995. "Tecnologie e diritti", Bologna, Rodotà, S., 2004. "Diritto, scienza, tecnologia: modelli e scelte di regolamentazione", "Scienza e diritto nel prisma del diritto comparato", p. 397 ss.

56. See Hertig, G. and McCahery, J. A. 2003. "Company and Takeover Law Reforms in Europe: Misguided Harmonization Efforts or Regulatory Competition?" *ECGI – Law Working Paper No. 12/2003*, which suggested that harmonization is likely to be ineffective or to promote bureaucratic uniformity rather than enable market-driven diversity.

57. See Maume, P. 2018. "Reducing Legal Uncertainty and Regulatory Arbitrage for Robo-Advice" *European Company and Financial Law Review*, which argued that robo-advisers provide investment advice within the meaning of the Second Markets in Financial Instruments Directive.

58. It is worth considering Rodotà, S. 1973. "Elaboratori elettronici e controllo sociale", Bologna, p. 183 ss. and the literature about 'small claims';

see Stone, K. 2004. "Alternative Dispute Resolution" *Encyclopedia of Legal History*, Oxford; Wissler, E. 1997. "The Effects of Mandatory Mediation: Empirical Research on the Experience of Small Claims and Common Pleas Courts" *Willamette Law Review*.

59. See European Commission's Action Plan on how to harness the opportunities presented by technology-enabled innovation in financial services (FinTech), 8 march 2018.

60. It refers to Art. 130, Treaty of European Union, signed at Maastricht on 7 February 1992.

61. It is worth adding a reference to European Commission 2018, *European Commission's Action Plan on how to harness the opportunities presented by technology-enabled innovation in financial services (FinTech)*, 8 march.

62. It refers to EBA 2018. "The EBA's fintech roadmap. Conclusions from the consultation on the EBA's approach to financial technology (fintech)". 15 March.

63. It remarks that FSB. 2019. "FinTech and market structure in financial services: Market developments and potential financial stability implications". 14 February, recalls the EBA has published its results on the application of new high-tech business models by credit institutions, and the new risks and opportunities for financial operators from which it then developed a 'Fintech Knowledge Hub'; see EBA 2019, Report on crypto-assets, available at www.eba.europa.eu.

64. In addition to the considerations above, it is worth to include a reference to Arner, D. W. and Barberis, Janos Nathan and Buckley, Ross P., The Evolution of Fintech: A New Post-Crisis Paradigm? (October 1, 2015). University of Hong Kong Faculty of Law Research Paper No. 2015/047. See also Barrantes, R. 2007. "Analysis of ICT Demand: What is Digital Poverty and how to Measure it?" "Digital poverty: Latin American and Caribbean perspectives" Ottawa.

65. The analysis recalls Ecofin (2019) "Draft Joint Statement by the Council and the Commission on Stablecoins" Brussels, 6 November 2".

66. See, on this point, the general critique of Bonfadelli, H. 2002. "The Internet and Knowledge Gaps – A Theoretical and Empirical Investigation" *European Journal of Communication*, p. 65 ff. See also Solove, D. J. 2002. "Conceptualizing Privacy" *California Law Review*; Longo, E. and Lorenzini, L. 2017. "Ict e parlamenti: oltre la mera diffusione dei contenuti", "Studi Pisani sul Parlamento VII. La crisi del Parlamento nelle regole sulla sua percezione" Pisa.

67. It is sufficient to recall Pellegrini, M. 2003. "Banca Centrale Nazionale e Unione Monetaria Europea. Il caso italiano", Padova, with respect to central banking and monetary policy.

68. In view of the above, the Council and the Commission state that no global stablecoin arrangement should begin operation in the European

Union until the legal, regulatory and oversight challenges and risks have been adequately identified and addressed; see Ecofin (2019) "Draft Joint Statement by the Council and the Commission on Stablecoins" Brussels, 6 November. Hence, whether this statement is covered by the EU Treaties or not is the rising doubt.

69. It refers to Basel Committee on Banking Supervision (BCBS) 2012. "Core principles for effective banking supervision", Basel.

70. In addition, see Philippon, T. 2017. "The FinTech Opportunity", *BIS Working Papers No 655*. However, the current market trends suggest that nowadays the regulatory interventions have made the financial sector safer, and it is possible that the scope of supervision will include fintech, even if this approach would increase political economy and coordination costs (as certain analysis shows).

71. Moreover, see Laeven, L. and Levine, R. and Michalopoulos, S. 2015. "Financial innovation and endogenous growth", *Journal of Financial Intermediation*, p. 1 ff., with respect to the consideration that, sometimes, the contracts underlying fintech can reflect the uncertainties and concerns arising from the instability of the capital market; however, it is not possible to admit agreements not adequate to support the challenges set by the changes taking place (and by the new centrality of banking compared to the recovery of the real economy); see Lemma, outsourcing.

72. This suggested making a distinction between the platforms aimed at supporting bank's supply and those able to sustain alternative forms of market-based financing (as—e.g.—invoice trading). Indeed, the latter would require specific rules, their being a sort of marketplace that usually involves borrowers being matched directly with investors (although some platforms use the balance sheet of their managing company to lend). Even if the BIS declares a limited availability of official data on fintech credit, it is possible to rely on its summaries (most of them based on non-official sector surveys and financial disclosures of platforms); see Working Group established by the Committee on the Global Financial System (CGFS) and the Financial Stability Board (FSB) 2017. "FinTech credit. Market structure, business models and financial stability implications".

73. It refers to Working Group established by the Committee on the Global Financial System (CGFS) and the Financial Stability Board (FSB) 2017. "FinTech credit. Market structure, business models and financial stability implications".

74. In this respect, the BIS shared available data showing that fintech credit activity has expanded rapidly in many countries over recent years, albeit from a very low base (and that estimates from the CCAF indicate that $284 billion in such credit was extended globally in 2016, up from $11 billion in 2013); see Claessens, S. and Frost, J. and Turner, G. and Zhu,

F. 2018 "Fintech credit markets around the world: size, drivers and policy issues" *BIS Quarterly Review*.

75. Let us recall again Claessens, S. and Frost, J. and Turner, G. and Zhu, F. 2018. "Fintech credit markets around the world: size, drivers and policy issues" *BIS Quarterly Review*.

76. It recalls the Basel Committee on Banking Supervision (BCBS) 2018. "Sound Practices Implications of fintech developments for banks and bank supervisors", February.

77. Bank for International Settlements (BIS) and Financial Stability Institute (FSI) 2019. "Fintech developments in the insurance industry", which describes fintech innovations that are relevant to the insurance industry and presents an overview of their potential impacts on the insurance sector and supervisory approaches.

78. In particular, see BIS-FSI 2019. "Fintech developments in the insurance industry" with respect to the possibility that the insurance value chain becomes fragmented as new technology-enabled players enter the market, and so the traditional customer relationship weakens.

79. In particular, it recalls Cœuré, B. 2019 "Fintech for the people. Keynote speech by the chair of the CPMI and Member of the Executive Board of the ECB, at the 14th BCBS-FSI high-level meeting for Africa on strengthening financial sector supervision and current regulatory priorities", Cape Town, 31 January. In addition, see also Cœuré, B. 2018, "A Euro Cyber Resilience Board for pan-European Financial Infrastructures", introductory remarks at the first meeting of the Euro Cyber Resilience Board for pan-European Financial Infrastructures, Frankfurt, 9 March.

80. This is considering the general outcome of Barzilai-Nahon, K. 2006. "Gaps and Bits: Conceptualizing Measurements for Digital Divide/s", *The Information Society*, p. 269 ff.

81. It is worth highlighting the consideration that Central banks and other authorities should recognize this. Moreover, they should be explicit in their commitment to expand payments access. This needs to make it known to the industry and the public alike that we, as authorities, are putting the emphasis on inclusion for everyone; See Cœuré, B. 2019. "Fintech for the people. Keynote speech by the chair of the CPMI and Member of the Executive Board of the ECB, at the 14th BCBS-FSI high-level meeting for Africa on strengthening financial sector supervision and current regulatory priorities", Cape Town, 31 January.

82. It refers to the conclusion of FSB 2017. "Financial stability implications from FinTech", 27 June. See also CPMI 2017, "Distributed ledger technology in payment, clearing and settlement", February; European Commission 2018. "FinTech action plan: For a more competitive and innovative European financial sector", 8 March.

See also ECB and Bank of Japan 2017, "Payment systems: liquidity saving mechanisms in a distributed ledger environment", a joint research project of the European Central Bank and the Bank of Japan—STELLA, September.

83. It is worth recalling ECB Advisory Group on Market Infrastructures for Securities and Collateral 2017. "The potential impact of DLTs on securities post-trading harmonization and on the wider EU financial market integration", which highlighted that some distributed ledgers do not use double-entry bookkeeping but single-entry bookkeeping with cryptographic linkages. This calls into question the role of an issuance or distribution account. Hence, in the case of DLT adoption, it is possible that DLTs would be used as "niche" solution for the issuance of specific products that currently takes place in an inefficient way; transfer instructions and enrichment to trade data would flow in near-real time.

84. See also ECB and Bank of Japan 2017, "Payment systems: liquidity saving mechanisms in a distributed ledger environment", a joint research project of the European Central Bank and the Bank of Japan—STELLA, September.

85. Indeed, there is no doubt that there was persistent, directional change in the regulation adopted to prevent further degeneration of the financial markets and to avoid the experienced pro-cyclical effects.

86. All of the above complies with the assumption that opening up market access to fintech companies will help increase competition, lower costs and be incentive for further innovation.; see Cœuré, B. 2018a. "Financial regulation and innovation: a two-way street. Introductory remarks by the member of the Executive Board of the ECB, at a roundtable organised by FinLeap", Berlin, 14 March 2018.

87. See Nabilou, H., 2019. "Central Bank Digital Currencies: Preliminary Legal Observations". *Journal of Banking Regulation*.

See also Walch, A. 2015. "The Bitcoin Blockchain as Financial Market Infrastructure: A Consideration of Operational Risk" *NYU Journal of Legislation and Public Policy*, which highlights the importance of functioning financial market infrastructure to global financial stability, and describes relevant principles that global financial regulators have adopted to help maintain this stability, focusing particularly on governance, risk management and operational risk.

88. See Buchak, G. and Matvos, G. and Piskorski, T. and Seru, A. 2017. "Fintech, Regulatory Arbitrage, and the Rise of Shadow Banks", Columbia Business School Research Paper No. 17-39, which showed how two forces, regulatory differences and technological advantages, contributed to the growth of fintech.

89. 'The High-Level Group of Financial Supervision in the EU', chaired by Jacques de Larosière, "Report", 25 February 2009, p. 57. See Venturi, E. 2009. "Globalizzazione, interconnessione dei mercati e crisi finanziaria. Identificazione di possibili interventi correttivi" *Banca borsa titoli di credito* I, p. 84.; Pellegrini, M. 2012 "L'architettura di vertice dell'ordinamento finanziario europeo: funzioni e limiti della supervisione" *Rivista trimestrale di diritto dell'economia*, I, p. 54.; Guarracino, F. 2012 "Supervisione bancaria europea (Sistema delle fonti e modelli teorici)" Padova.

90. The Lamfalussy process did not deal with strengthening prudential oversight—but the report warned: "While the committee strongly believes that large deep, liquid and innovative financial markets will result in substantial efficiency gains and will therefore bring individual benefits to European citizens; it also believes that greater efficiency does not necessarily go hand in hand with enhanced financial stability"; see Troiano, V. 2012 "Interactions Between EU and National Authorities in the New Structure of EU Financial System Supervision" *Law and Economics Yearly Review*, p. 104 ff.

91. See 'The High-Level Group of Financial Supervision in the EU', chaired by Jacques de Larosière, "Report", 25 February 2009, p. 7.

92. Obviously, in this period, the meaning of 'technical' itself improved, and therefore this group highlighted that "given the speed at which financial markets evolve, it is important to maintain a consistent set of technical rules applying to all financial firms"; see 'The High-Level Group of Financial Supervision in the EU', chaired by Jacques de Larosière, "Report", 25 February 2009, p. 58.

93. See REGULATION (EU) No 1095/2010, Recital 15.

94. See REGULATION (EU) No 1095/2010, Art. 9, para. 4.

95. In addition, it is worth referring to Recine, F. and Teixeira, P. G. 2009 "The New Financial Stability Architecture in the EU" *Paolo Baffi Centre Research Paper No. 2009-62* on the need to reinforce significantly—ten years after the introduction of the euro—the financial stability architecture at the EU level.

96. It refers to ESMA Report. Licensing of FinTech business models, of 12 July 2019 | ESMA50-164-2430.

97. See on this Lener, R. and Parrillo, G. 2018 "Quali regole per fintech?" ""Fintech: diritto tecnologia e finanza" Roma, p. 7 ff.

98. See ESMA, EBA, EIOPA, Joint Committee Discussion Paper on automation in financial advice, JC 2015 080, 4 December 2015.

99. This refers to ESAs Report on FinTech: Regulatory Sandboxes and Innovation Hubs, January 2019.

100. It is worth recalling again to 'The High-Level Group of Financial Supervision in the EU', chaired by Jacques de Larosière, "Report", 25 February 2009, p. 13.

101. See EBA. 2018. "The EBA's fintech roadmap. Conclusions from the consultation on the EBA's approach to financial technology (fintech)". 15 March.

102. It is worth recalling that innovation was consider also at the time of the Basel III review; see Delimatsis, P. 2012. "Financial Innovation and Prudential Regulation – The New Basel III Rules" *TILEC Discussion Paper No. 2012-016*.

103. In general, this topic refers also to the digital divide, see Brandtzæg, P. B. and Heim, J. and Karahasanovic, A. 2011. "Understanding the new digital divide—A typology of Internet users in Europe" *International Journal of Human-Computer Studies*, p. 123 ff.

104. See Keidar, R. and Blemus, S. "Cryptocurrencies and Market Abuse Risks: It's Time for Self-Regulation" *Lexology*, which highlighted that market abuse risks have not been eliminated by distributed ledger technology (DLT), and, given the nature of unregulated ICOs or cryptocurrencies investments, such risks are, in many ways, far greater.

105. See Ellis, E. 1999. "The principle of proportionality in the laws of Europe" Oxford, and in particular Tribimas, T. 1999. "Proportionality in community law: searching for the appropriate standard of scrutiny", which moves to a specific reference to the appropriateness and the relevant objectives.

106. It refers to EBA 2018. "Report on the prudential risks and opportunities arising for institutions from fintech", 3 July p. 4.

107. It recalls, in particular, Okafor, A. and Fadul, J. 2019. "Bank Risks, Regulatory Interventions and Deconstructing the Focus on Credit Risk" *Research Journal of Finance and Accounting*. See also de Fontnouvelle, P. and Jordan, J. S. and Rosengren, E. S. 2005 "Implication of alternative operational risk modeling techniques" *National Bureau of Economic Research*; Ebnöther, S. and Vanini, P. and McNeil, A. and Antolinez-Fehr, P. 2003. "Modelling Operational Risk" *Journal of Risk* p. 1 ff.

108. It is worth considering the possibility to exploit a board-level technology committee; see Harrast, S. and Swaney, A. 2019. "What Is the Role of the Board-Level Technology Committee?" *SSRN Research Paper no. 3456770*.

109. See EBA Report on innovative uses of consumer data by financial institutions, 28 June 2017.

110. See EBA, Fintech: Regulatory Sandboxes and Innovation Hubs, JC 2018 74, p. 10.

111. On the arduous process of completing the single regulatory rulebook for the European Union; see Ferran, E. and Babis, V. 2013. "The European Single Supervisory Mechanism" *University of Cambridge Faculty of Law Research Paper No. 10/2013.*

   See Wymeersch, E. 2012. "The European Banking Union. A first Analysis", *Financial Law Institute Working Paper Series WP 2012-07*; Capriglione, F. "L'unione bancaria europea", Torino, 2013; Ibrido, R. 2017. "L'unione bancaria europea. Profili costituzionali" Roma, 2017.

   See also Babis, B. 2014. "Single Rulebook for Prudential Regulation of Banks: Mission Accomplished?" *European Business Law Review.*

112. It is worth recalling the EBA 2019. "EBA report on the impact of fintech on payment institutions' and e-money institutions' business models", July.

113. See EBA 2018. "EBA Report on the prudential risks and opportunities arising for institutions from fintech", 3 July, p. 54.

114. This assumption refers to the latest public intervention on the banking industry, aimed at overriding specific problems, with respect to the resolution of certain banks, the management of their crises, the reform of the cooperative banking (i.e. popular and mutual banks). Indeed, Italian market has recorded a remarkable activism by the policy-makers, legislators and supervisors; see Troiano, V. 2019, "Le Banche" "Manuale di diritto Bancario e Finanziario", Padova, p. 350 ff.

   See also Capriglione, F. 1995, "Cooperazione di credito e testo unico bancario" *Quaderni di ricerca giuridica della Consulenza Legale della Banca d'Italia,* Roma; Oppo, G. 1997, "Mutualità e integrazione cooperativa", Rivista di diritto civile, 1997, I, p. 357 ss.; Capriglione, F. Banche popolari. Metamorfosi di un modello, Bari, 2001; Saccomanni, F. 2010, "La sfida per le banche popolari nel nuovo scenario regolamentare" Verona, 26 febbraio; VV.AA. 2015, "La riforma delle banche popolari", Padova; VV.AA. 2018, "Per un'ipotesi ricostruttiva della riforma delle BCC", *Rivista Trimestrale di Diritto dell'economia*; Bonfatti, S. 2017, "La responsabilità degli "enti ponte" (e delle banche incorporanti) per le pretese risarcitorie nei confronti delle "quattro banche" (vantate dagli azionisti "risolti", e non solo)", dirittobancario.it, 2017.

115. Let us recall on this topic the considerations of De Vecchis, P. 1982. "Spunti per una rinnovata riflessione sulla nozione di banca", *Banca borsa titoli di credito,* p. 754 ss.

116. Indeed, this refers not only to the praxis of empowering the public authorities with the duty to supervise the resolution of the crisis of a supervised entity, but also to the continued interventions of the supervisors' employees in carrying out lectures at the university, and interaction with writers in academic collective productions. The result is a constant supervisory update, due to the continuous sharing of common knowl-

edge; see D'Ambrosio, R. 2015, "The ECB and NCA liability within the Single Supervisory Mechanism" *Quaderni di Ricerca Giuridica della Consulenza Legale della Banca d'Italia*, Roma; Lamandini, M. and Muñoz, D. R. and Álvarez, J. S. 2015, "Depicting the limits to the SSM's supervisory powers: The Role of Constitutional Mandates and of Fundamental Rights' Protection" *Quaderni di Ricerca Giuridica della Consulenza Legale della Banca d'Italia*, Roma.

See also Cassese, S. 2014, "La nuova architettura finanziaria europea" and Costi, R. 2014, "Il Testo Unico Bancario, oggi" and Capolino, O. 2014, "Il Testo unico bancario e il diritto dell'Unione Europea" and Perassi, M. 2014 "Brevi conclusioni" "Dal Testo unico bancario all'Unione bancaria: tecniche normative e allocazione di poteri" *Quaderni di Ricerca Giuridica della Consulenza Legale della Banca d'Italia*, Roma.

117. See Visco, I. 2019. "Sustainable development and climate risks: the role of central banks. Speech by the Governor of the Bank of Italy at the 18th International Conference for Credit Risk Evaluation "Assessing and Managing Climate Change Risk: Opportunities for Financial Institutions" Venice, 26 September.

Whereby Ignazio Visco started by noting that "the issue of the compatibility between natural resources and the development goals of nations has been studied since at least the end of the eighteenth century, with the works of Thomas Malthus on food supply and population growth. It has then re-emerged a number of times in the public debate".

118. See Barbagallo, C. 2019. "Fintech: Ruolo dell'Autorità di Vigilanza in un mercato che cambia" Napoli, 8 February, which recalls on this point "Global Monitoring Report on Non-Bank Financial Intermediation 2018", published by the Financial Stability Board and highlights that the range of applications of regtech is very wide: policy, management of regulatory updates, reporting, processing and exploitation of corporate information. The most qualifying aspect concerns the tendency to use innovation not only in a passive logic of respect for the rules but in an active perspective of exploitation of the regulatory framework to develop competitive capacity, especially through the increase of efficiency of the organizational infrastructure.

119. It is worth adding a reference to VV.AA., 2018 "Intelligenza artificiale, protezione dati personali e regolazione", Milano.

120. It recalls Visco, I. 2019. "Lezione Giorgio Fuà 2019. Centenario della nascita", which pointed out that policy-makers must dwell also with the delay accumulated over the last thirty years in the spread of innovation in the economic and financial system and in the skills of adults and students. See also Visco, I. 2019. Speech at Associazione Bancaria Italiana – Assemblea degli Associati. Milan, July 12.

121. It refers to Wong, Y. C. and Law, C. K. and Fung, J. Y. C. and Lee, V. W. P. 2010. "Digital divide and social inclusion: policy challenge for social development in Hong Kong and South Korea'" *Journal of Asian Public Policy*, p. 37 ff.

122. In addition, it may be considered the conclusion of Jagtiani, J, and Lemieux, C. 2018. "Do Fintech Lenders Penetrate Areas that are Underserved by Traditional Banks?" *FRB of Philadelphia Working Paper No. 18-13* on the role of innovation in shaping financial and banking landscapes.

123. See Visco, I. 2019. *Considerazioni finali del Governatore. Relazione annuale*. Roma, May 31, with regard to the use of artificial intelligence, which should not be limited to the search for improvements in the forecasting of economic and financial variables. To this end, the Italian central bank actively participates in the work of international committees and bodies to define a framework of harmonized rules aimed at supporting the virtuous development of financial innovation.

124. The first is the "fintech channel"; the second is represented by a 'unit' set up with the aim of dealing with the authorizations process of new entities intending to enter the financial perimeter, in which a special "fintech sector" has recently been established.

125. It is worth recalling the approach used in the 1990s to understand the need for a comprehensive assessment of the rules governing the authorizations to operate in the capital market; in this respect, see Amorosino, S. 1994. "L'autorizzazione all'attività creditizia nel nuovo T.U. delle leggi bancarie" *Diritto della banca e del mercato finanziario*, 1994, p. 149 ff.

126. This suggests that the high-tech nature of the business model cannot influence the duty to have an authorization (or not). Indeed, any market operator has to meet the safety standards necessary for the proper functioning of financial transactions and work to ensure savers' confidence and prevent any abuse (regardless of the level of technology applied by those who carry out such activities). And the same is true for the protection of monetary stability, whereby the introduction of non-sovereign cryptocurrencies may entail risks of a different nature from those directly linked to technological innovation.; see Cœuré, B. and Loh, J. 2018, "Bitcoin not the answer to a cashless society", opinion piece in the Financial Times, 12 March.

127. See ECB 2018 "Guide to assessments of fintech credit institution licence applications", which pointed out that the ECB and NCAs will assess whether the applicant can demonstrate that it is able to hold in reserve sufficient capital to cover start-up losses in the first three years of activity and, where applicable, the costs associated with the possible execution of an exit plan. This is why this document requires that the business plan

should precisely describe the forecast start-up losses in the first three years of activity and should include financial forecasts for the period up to the break-even point.

128. IVASS is currently challenging the need for supervising the software that trade and share risks among undertakers, insurance and reinsurance companies. However, at this stage, supervisors have not begun to run towards the control of the innovations that are influencing the insurance sector, nor extending the scope of their intervention to the tools able to contain the threats and dangers that would arise in risks (and then supports the market for insurance policies); see Rossi, S. 2018. Speech at the Conference 'FinTech e InsurTech: tecnologie digitali, banche, assicurazioni, nell'ambito dell'iniziativa "Incontri con la Banca d'Italia". September 10.

129. The benefit of these developments can easily be seen in Italy, where the trends of the market depends predominantly on the banking system.; see Visco, I. 2019. Speech at Associazione Bancaria Italiana – Assemblea degli Associati. Milan, July 12.

130. Hence, it is possible to highlight the current effort of Consob, which— rather than monitoring fintech applications only—is going to "outline the broad direction of this process of digitalisation of the financial system and the structural changes prompted by competition in intermediaries' business models; highlight the main open issues, with a view to preserving the smooth running of the financial market, preventing risks to investors, but also to safeguarding the innovation capability of operators (and potential new comers); predesign the viable public policy (wide-ranging) actions, where deemed useful"; see Savona, P. 2019. "Incontro annuale con il mercato finanziario Discorso del Presidente" Milano, 14 June.

131. See Schena, C. and Tanda, A. and Arlotta, C. and Potenza, G. 2018. "The development of FinTech. Opportunities and risks for the financial industry in the digital age", Quaderno FinTech n. 1 – marzo 2018.

132. All the above considers the preliminary evidences shown by Palmerini, E. and Aiello, G. and Cappelli, V. and Morgante, G. and Amore, N. and Di Vetta, G. and Fiorinelli, G. and Galli, M. 2018. "Il FinTech e l'economia dei dati. Considerazioni su alcuni profili civilistici e penalistici. Le soluzioni del diritto vigente ai rischi per la clientela e gli operatori", Quaderno FinTech n. 2 – December.

133. In this respect, it goes beyond the approach used by Burchi, A. and Mezzacapo, S. and Musile Tanzi, P. and Troiano, V. 2019. "Financial Data Aggregation e Account Information Services. Questioni regolamentari e profili di business", Quaderno FinTech n. 4, March.

134. It is worth adding also a reference to the research of Sciarrone Alibrandi, A. and Borello, G. and Ferretti, R. and Lenoci, F. and Macchiavello,

E. and Mattassoglio, F. and Panisi, F. 2019. "Marketplace lending, Verso nuove forme di intermediazione finanziaria?", Quaderno FinTech n. 5, July.

135. This is not the case, but there is the risk that while the wise intermediaries point at programmers and coders, and the supervisors still examine the intermediaries; see in this rexpect Burchi, A. and Mezzacapo, S. and Musile Tanzi, P. and Troiano, V. 2019. "Financial Data Aggregation e Account Information Services. Questioni regolamentari e profili di business", Quaderno FinTech n. 4, March

136. It is worth considering that "supporting technological innovation, and its efficient diffusion throughout the economy is key to obtaining sustained increases in productivity in the longer term, and to safeguarding the living standards of future generations, as well as the sustainability of our countries' social security systems and public finances"; see Visco, I. 2019. "Remarks at the Event to Commemorate Thirty Years of Banca d'Italia in Japan. Speech by the Governor of the Bank of Italy. Thirty Years of Banca d'Italia in Japan: Anniversary Celebration" Tokyo, 11 June.

137. It is worth recalling Amorosino, S. and Lemma, V. 2016. "Administrative and Transaction Costs Arising from Brexit. A Regulatory Challenge" *Law and economics yearly review*; see also Capriglione F. and Ibrido, R. 2017. "La Brexit tra finanza e politica", Milano.

138. It refers to FCA Regulatory sandbox lessons learned report, October 2017.

139. See FCA, Global Financial Innovation Network (GFIN), 09/08/2019. Nowadays, GFIN provides cross-border testing applications for creating an environment that allowed firms to simultaneously trial and scale new technologies in multiple jurisdictions, gaining real-time insight into how a product or service might operate in the market.

140. See GFIN, The global financial innovation network on its first year, June 2019.

141. See Innovating for the future: the next phase of Project Innovate, Speech by Christopher Woolard, Executive Director of Strategy and Competition at the FCA, delivered at the Innovate Finance Global Summit., 10/04/2017.

142. Furthermore, it also investigates the possibility of using blockchain technology for automating regulation and compliance. It would be expectable that reporting requirements, compliance procedures, databases and standards will flow together into a universal machine-readable format, and then will run into a smart device; see FCA 2019, "Blockchain Technology for Algorithmic Regulation and Compliance (BARAC)", University College London, 11 September 2019.

143. See FCA, Digital regulatory reporting, 13 March 2019.

144. This starts from the content of the "Legal framework for distributed ledger technology and blockchain in Switzerland An overview with a focus on the financial sector", *Federal Council* report, Bern, 14 December 2018.

145. It refers to a previous analysis that, before the current fintech wave, reviewed the historical reasons behind the success of Swiss private banks and discussed whether they possess the attributes necessary to be successful in the future. The authors suggested that, although at that time Swiss banquiers were positioned to retain their global supremacy, they needed to make important strategic decisions concerning the way they manage their businesses and the relevant technological support; see Shojai, S. and Feiger, G. 2002. "Les Banquiers Suisses: Can They Remain Leaders in Private Banking?". *Journal of Financial Transformation*, p. 65 ff.

146. It refers to "Legal framework for distributed ledger technology and blockchain in Switzerland. An overview with a focus on the financial sector", *Federal Council report*, Bern, 14 December 2018, whose content aims to provide an overview of the relevant legal framework and to clarify the need for action. In addition, the report should send a signal and show (1) that Switzerland is open to technological developments such as DLT and blockchain, (2) that the Swiss legal framework is already suitable for dealing with business models based on DLT and blockchain, (3) that Switzerland wants to further improve the innovation-friendly framework conditions and (4) that the Swiss authorities are determined to rigorously combat abuses.

147. See Bartlett, R. P. and Morse, A. and Stanton, R. H. and Wallace, N. E. 2019. "Consumer-Lending Discrimination in the Fintech Era" *NBER Working Paper No. w25943* with respect to provide a workable interpretation of the courts' legitimate-business-necessity defense of statistical discrimination.

148. In addition, see Chen, Y and Bellavitis, C. 2019. "Blockchain Disruption and Decentralized Finance: The Rise of Decentralized Business Models" *Journal of Business Venturing Insights*, which assessed the benefits of decentralized finance, identify existing business models and evaluate potential challenges and limits.

149. It is worth recalling the analysis of Whitacre, B. and Mills, B. 2007. "Infrastructure and the rural-urban divide in high-speed residential internet access" *International Regional Science Review*, p. 249 ff.

150. It recalls the "Legal framework for distributed ledger technology and blockchain in Switzerland. An overview with a focus on the financial sector", *Federal Council report*, Bern, 14 December 2018, p. 42.

151. It refers to the foundation of the analysis provided by Willis, S., & Tranter, B. 2006 "Beyond the 'digital divide'. Internet diffusion and inequality in Australia", *Journal of Sociology*, p. 43 ff.

152. This risk adds to Buckley, R. P. and Arner, D. W. and Zetzsche, D. A. and Selga, E. 2019. "The Dark Side of Digital Financial Transformation: The New Risks of FinTech and the Rise of TechRisk" *University of Luxembourg Law Working Paper 2019-009*, which highlighted that the digitization and datafication combined with new technologies are taking place in developed global markets and at times even faster in emerging and developing markets.

153. See Weber, R. H. and Thouvenin, F. 2018. "Dateneigentum und Datenzugangsrechte – Bausteine der Informationsgesellschaft?" *ZSR* p. 60 ff. See also the press release by the Federal Council of 9 May 2018 on measures for a future-oriented data policy in Switzerland ("benchmarks").

154. It is worth to recall Art. 16 D-FADP (Draft of the Federal Act on Total Revision of the Federal Act on Data Protection and amendment of other enactments on data protection, BBl 2017 7193, 7213); Art. 20 Regulation (EU) 2016/679 of the European Parliament and of the Council of 27 April 2016 on the protection of natural persons with regard to the processing of personal data and on the free movement of such data, and repealing Directive 95/46/EC (GDPR); and Parliamentary initiative Dobler 17.410 of 7 March 2017.

155. In particular, see Swiss Financial Market Supervisory Authority FINMA, ICO. Guidelines for enquiries regarding the regulatory framework for initial coin offerings (ICOs), updated 16 February 2018.

156. Moreover, see Hacker, P. and Thomale, C., "Crypto-Securities Regulation: ICOs, Token Sales and Cryptocurrencies under EU Financial Law" *European Company and Financial Law Review* p. 645 ff., which close their research by offering two policy proposals to mitigate legal uncertainty concerning token sales.

157. On this topic, see the outcome of Grey, R. and Dharmapalan, J. 2017. "The Macroeconomic Policy Implications of Digital Fiat Currency" "The Case for Digital Legal Tender", which articulated a vision for how widespread adoption of Digital Fiat Currency may affect the macroeconomic levers a nation has at its disposal to steady economic growth.

158. This refers to the process related to the enhancement of the regulatory framework to facilitate client onboarding via digital channels made by FINMA, see "Asset management: technology-neutral FINMA regulations", 1 July 2016; "FINMA reduces obstacles to FinTech", 17 March 106; "Due diligence requirements for client onboarding via digital channels (Valid until 31.07.2018)", 3 March 2016.

159. See Federal Department of Finance FDF, 2017. "Report on amendments to the Banking Ordinance (Fintech), Explanations", p. 11 ff. See in general Reiser, N (2018). "Ist der Bankbegriff im Lichte aktueller technolo-

gischer Entwicklungen noch zeitgemäss?" *AJP*, p. 811 ff. See also Swiss Financial Market Supervisory Authority FINMA, Fact sheet: "Virtual Currencies", updated 30 August 2018.

160. See again "Legal framework for distributed ledger technology and block-chain in Switzerland. An overview with a focus on the financial sector", *Federal Council report*, Bern, 14 December 2018, p. 85.

161. See "Federal Council report of 25 June 2014 on virtual currencies in response to the Schwaab (13.3687) and Weibel (13.4070) postulates", p. 12 ff.

   See also "Swiss National Bank: Survey on payment methods 2017, Survey on payment methods and use of cash in Switzerland", May 2018.

162. See Art. 6 para. 3 BankO as amended on 1 January 2019.

163. See Art. 6 para. 2 let. c BankO.

164. It is worth considering also the digital divide, as mentioned above; in this respect, see Verdegem, P. and Verhoest, P. 2009 "Profiling the Non-user: Rethinking Policy Initiatives Stimulating ICT Acceptance" *Telecommunications Policy*, p. 642 ff.

165. Furthermore, see again Zetzsche, D. A. and Preiner, C. 2017 "Cross-Border Crowdfunding – Towards a Single Crowdfunding Market for "European Banking Institute Working Paper Series 2017.

166. It recalls the conclusions of Stulz, R, M. 2019 "FinTech, BigTech, and the Future of Banks". *Fisher College of Business Working Paper No. 2019-03-020.*

167. It is worth considering again "Legal framework for distributed ledger technology and blockchain in Switzerland. An overview with a focus on the financial sector", *Federal Council report*, Bern, 14 December 2018, p. 92.

168. All the above recalls the research of Barth, J. R. and Caprio, G. and Levine, R. E. 1999. "Banking Systems Around the Globe: Do Regulation and Ownership Affect Performance and Stability?" *World Bank Policy Research Working Paper No. 2325.*

169. In this respect, this is considering that Ganchev, A. 2018. "The Swiss National Bank – a Central Bank or a Hedge Fund?" *Zlaten vestnik.* Tavex questions certain foundations of banking and central banking.

170. See "Legal framework for distributed ledger technology and blockchain in Switzerland. An overview with a focus on the financial sector", Federal Council report, Bern, 14 December 2018, p. 92.

171. It refers to art. 2 let. c FMIA no. 2; Art. 94 para. 3 FMIA; Art. 2 para. 3 FMIO; and Art. 80 FMIO; see in this respect Favre, O. and Kramer, S.2017 "Art. 2 FinfraG". "Kommentar zum Finanzmarktinfrastrukturgesetz FinfraG". Zurich.

172. See FINMA 2018a: section 3.2.

173. This is considering that "Legal framework for distributed ledger technology and blockchain in Switzerland. An overview with a focus on the financial sector", *Federal Council report*, Bern, 14 December 2018, p. 96, provides that this kind of approach would primarily entail risks: risks in the areas of investor protection and the reputation of the Swiss financial market; risks relating to the equivalence of Swiss financial market law provisions to foreign requirements; the risk of being treated unequally without good reason compared with financial market players that do not use blockchain technology; and opportunities for regulatory arbitrage via the use of blockchain technologies.

  It is worth recalling on this point Allenspach, N. and Monnin, P., 2006. "International integration, common exposures and systemic risk in the banking sector: An empirical investigation". Working paper, Swiss National Bank; Avgouleas, E. and Kiayias, A., 2018. "The Promise of Blockchain Technology for Global Securities and Derivatives Markets: The New Financial Ecosystem and the 'Holy Grail' of Systemic Risk Containment". Edinburgh School of Law Research Paper No. 2018/43; ESMA. 2017. "ESMA alerts investors to the high risks of Initial Coin Offerings (ICOs)".

174. See Chen, Y and Bellavitis, C. 2019. "Blockchain Disruption and Decentralized Finance: The Rise of Decentralized Business Models" *Journal of Business Venturing Insights*, which highlighted how—as a new area of financial technology—decentralized finance may reshape the structure of modern finance and create a new landscape for entrepreneurship and innovation, showcasing the promises and challenges of decentralized business models.

175. See Art. 81 FMIA. See also Bärtschi, H. and MEISSER, C. 2015. "Virtuelle Währungen aus finanzmarkt- und zivilrechtlicher Sicht". "Rechtliche Herausforderungen durch webbasierte und mobile Zahlungssysteme. Zurich: Schulthess" p. 115 ff.

176. In addition, see Baker, F. J. 2018. "The Concept of Cybercrime: Applying the General Part to Limit Offending via Cyber Means" *People's Procuratorial Semimonthly*; de Boyrie, M. E. and Pak, S. J. and Zdanowicz, J. S. 2001 "The Impact of Switzerland's Money Laundering Law on Capital Flows Through Abnormal Pricing in International Trade" *EFMA 2001 Lugano Meetings; CIBER Working Paper.*

177. See Laskowski, M. and Kim, H. M. and Zargham, M. and Barlin, M. and Kabanov, D. 2019. "Token Economics in Real-Life: Cryptocurrency and Incentives Design for Insolar's Blockchain Network" *SSRN Research Paper no. 3465085* about systems and simulation combined with cryptocurrency expertise that are able to design a mechanism to incentivize enterprises and individual users—and in particular through the use of

subsidy pools, application developers—to help adoption of their new public blockchain network.

178. It recalls Yu, G. and Zhang, J. 2017. *"A Revisit to Capital Control Policies When Bitcoin Is in Town" 31st Australasian Finance and Banking Conference 2018* on the magnitude and statistical properties of triangle arbitrage gains.

179. It refers to the Italian approach to the juridical system, provided that traditional banks and fintech serve the same needs of the society. Hence the importance of the legal studies on the *unity* of the legal order, and the coherence of its principles and norms.

In fact, legal orders are dynamic systems, the meaning of which shows that individual legal propositions, although they can also be considered in themselves, in their abstractness, tend to be interpreted as part of a system. The result is the possibility of a systemic interpretation, understood as a form of interpretation of a system that is justified on the assumption that some rules constitute an ordered totality. Therefore, the legislator must tend to derive all the rules from certain general principles, considered in the same way as the postulates of a scientific system.

In particular, the system will have to be completed with an inductive procedure, that is, starting from the content of the individual technical solutions in order to constitute increasingly general concepts, as Bobbio suggested; see Bobbio, N. 1992 "Teoria generale del diritto", Torino, p. 201 ff.

180. See FINMA 2019. "Partial revision of the Circular 2008/3 'Public deposits with non-banks'" with respect to the fact that investing and paying interest on deposits received is no longer prohibited within the sandbox, but merely operating the so-called interest rate differential business, which remains the privilege of the banks.

References

Abu-Shanab, E. and Al-Jamal, N. 2015. 'Exploring the Gender Digital Divide in Jordan', *Gender, Technology and Development.*

Allenspach, N. and Monnin, P., 2006. "International integration, common exposures and systemic risk in the banking sector: An empirical investigation". Working paper, Swiss National Bank;

Alpa, G. 2019. "Fintech: un laboratorio per i giuristi" *Contratto e impresa*, 2019.

Amorosino, S. and Lemma, V., 2016. "Administrative and Transaction Costs Arising from Brexit. A Regulatory Challenge" *Law and economics yearly review.*

Amorosino, S., 1994. "L'autorizzazione all'attività creditizia nel nuovo T.U. delle leggi bancarie" *Diritto della banca e del mercato finanziario.*

Antonio, A. and Tuffley, D. 2014. "The gender digital divide in developing countries" *Future Internet.*

Armour, J. and Hansmann, H. and Kraakman, R. H. 2009. "The Essential Elements of Corporate Law" *Oxford Legal Studies Research Paper No. 20/2009.*

Arnaboldi, F. 2019. "Progress on the First Two Pillars of the Banking Union" "Risk and Regulation in Euro Area Banks", London.

Arner, D. W. and Barberis, J. N. and Buckley, R. P., 2016. "FinTech, RegTech and the Reconceptualization of Financial Regulation". *University of Hong Kong Faculty of Law Research Paper No. 2016/035.*

Arner, D. W. and Barberis, J. N. and Buckley, Ross P. 2015 "The Evolution of Fintech: A New Post-Crisis Paradigm?" *University of Hong Kong Faculty of Law Research Paper No. 2015/047.*

Arrow, K. J. and Hahn, F. 1971 "General Competitive Analysis", San Francisco.

Attewell, P. 2001. "The First and the Second Digital Divides" *Sociology of Education.*

Avgouleas, E. and Kiayias, A., 2018. "The Promise of Blockchain Technology for Global Securities and Derivatives Markets: The New Financial Ecosystem and the 'Holy Grail' of Systemic Risk Containment". *Edinburgh School of Law Research Paper No. 2018/43.*

Babis, B., 2014. "Single Rulebook for Prudential Regulation of Banks: Mission Accomplished?" *European Business Law Review.*

Baily, M. N., 1993. "Competition, Regulation and Efficiency in Service Industries" *Brookings Papers in Microeconomics.*

Baker, F. J., 2018. "The Concept of Cybercrime: Applying the General Part to Limit Offending via Cyber Means" *People's Procuratorial Semimonthly.*

Baker, H. K. and Ricciardi, V., 2015. "Understanding Behavioral Aspects of Financial Planning and Investing" *Journal of Financial Planning.*

Balkin, J. M. 2008. "The Future of Free Expression in a Digital Age" *Pepperdine Law Review*

Banca d'Italia, 2017. "FinTech In Italia. Indagine conoscitiva sull'adozione delle innova-zioni tecnologiche applicate ai servizi finanziari, Roma.

Bank for International Settlements (BIS) and Financial Stability Institute (FSI), 2019. "Fintech developments in the insurance industry".

Barbagallo, C., 2019. "Fintech: Ruolo dell'Autorità di Vigilanza in un mercato che cambia" Napoli, 8 February.

Barrantes, R. 2007. "Analysis of ICT Demand: What is Digital Poverty and how to Measure it?" "Digital poverty: Latin American and Caribbean perspectives" Ottawa.

Barth, J. R. and Caprio, G. and Levine, R. E., 1999. "Banking Systems Around the Globe: Do Regulation and Ownership Affect Performance and Stability?" *World Bank Policy Research Working Paper No. 2325.*

Bartlett, R. P. and Morse, A. and Stanton, R. H. and Wallace, N. E., 2019. "Consumer-Lending Discrimination in the Fintech Era" *NBER Working Paper No. w25943.*

Bärtschi, H. and Meisser, C., 2015. "Virtuelle Währungen aus finanzmarkt- und zivilrechtlicher Sicht". "Rechtliche Herausforderungen durch webbasierte und mobile Zahlungssysteme. Zurich: Schulthess".

Barzilai-Nahon, K. 2006 "Gaps and Bits: Conceptualizing Measurements for Digital Divide/s", *The Information Society*.

Basel Committee on Banking Supervision (BCBS), 2012. "Core principles for effective banking supervision", Basel.

Basel Committee on Banking Supervision (BCBS), 2018. "Sound Practices Implications of fintech developments for banks and bank supervisors", February.

Begley, T. A. and Srinivasan, K., 2019. "Small Bank Lending in the Era of Fintech and Shadow Banking: A Sideshow?" *Northeastern U. D'Amore-McKim School of Business Research Paper No. 3317672.*

Belleflamme, P. and Lambert, T. and Schwienbacher, A. "Crowdfunding Dynamics" *CESifo Working Paper No. 7797.*

Bennett, S. and Maton, K. and Kervin, L. 2008. "The 'Digital Natives' Debate: A Critical Review of the Evidence" *British Journal of Educational Technology*.

Berle A. A. and Means G. C. 1932. "The Modern Corporation and Private Property";

Berlingò, V. 2017. "Il fenomeno della datafication e la sua giuridicizzazione", *Rivista Trimestrale di Diritto Pubblico.*

BIS-FSI, 2019. "Fintech developments in the insurance industry".

Bobbio, N., 1992. "Teoria generale del diritto", Torino.

Bofondi, M., 2017. ""Il lending-based crowdfunding: opportunità e rischi", *Questioni di Economia e Finanza*, Roma.

Bonfadelli, H. 2002. "The Internet and Knowledge Gaps – A Theoretical and Empirical Investigation" *European Journal of Communication*.

Bonfatti, S., 2017. "La responsabilità degli "enti ponte" (e delle banche incorporanti) per le pretese risarcitorie nei confronti delle "quattro banche" (vantate dagli azionisti "risolti", e non solo)", dirittobancario.it, 2017.

Borselli, A. 2018 "Insurance by Algorithm" *European Insurance Law Review.*

Brandtzæg, P. B. and Heim, J. and Karahasanovic, A. 2011. "Understanding the new digital divide—A typology of Internet users in Europe" *International Journal of Human-Computer Studies.*

Bruckner, M. A. 2018 "Regulating Fintech Lending" *Banking & Financial Services Policy Report*. Runshan, F. and Yan, H. and Param Vir, S. 2019 "Crowds, Lending, Machines, and Bias" *SSRN Research Paper no. 3206027.*

Buchak, G. and Matvos, G. and Piskorski, T. and Seru, A. 2017 "Fintech, Regulatory Arbitrage, and the Rise of Shadow Banks", Columbia Business School Research Paper No. 17–39.

Buckley, R. P. and Arner, D. W. and Zetzsche, D. A. and Selga, E., 2019. "The Dark Side of Digital Financial Transformation: The New Risks of FinTech and the Rise of TechRisk" *University of Luxembourg Law Working Paper 2019-009.*

Burchi, A. and Mezzacapo, S. and Musile Tanzi, P. and Troiano, V. 2019. "Financial Data Aggregation e Account Information Services. Questioni regolamentari e profili di business", *Quaderno FinTech n. 4*, March.

Bure, C. 2005. 'Digital Inclusion without Social Inclusion: The Consumption of Information and Communication Technologies (ICTs) within Homeless Subculture in Scotland', *The Journal of Community Informatics*.

Campbell, J. Y. and Cochrane, J. H., 1998. "By Force of Habit: A Consumption-Based Explanation of Plantation of Aggregate Stock Market Behavior" *Center for Research in Security Prices Working Paper No. 412.*

Canalini, V., 2019. "Il FinTech e le nuove frontiere dell'innovazione finanziaria", *Manuale di diritto bancario e finanziario*, Padova.

Capolino, O., 2014. "Il Testo unico bancario e il diritto dell'Unione Europea"

Capriglione F. and Ibrido, R., 2017. "La Brexit tra finanza e politica", Milano.

Capriglione, F. 1995 "Cooperazione di credito e testo unico bancario" *Quaderni di ricerca giuridica della Consulenza Legale della Banca d'Italia*, Roma.

Capriglione, F. 2001. "Banche popolari. Metamorfosi di un modello", Bari.

Capriglione, F. 2004. "Etica della finanza mercato globalizzazione", Bari.

Capriglione, F. 2013. "L'unione bancaria europea", Torino.

Capriglione, F. 2018. "Considerazioni a margine del volume: il tramonto della banca universale?" *Rivista Trimestrale di Diritto dell'Economia.*

Capriglione, F. 2019. "Un secolo di regolazione" "Manuale di diritto bancario e finanziario", Padova.

Carcaterra, G. 2014. "Le norme costitutive", Torino.

Cassese, S., 2000 "*Quattro paradossi sui rapporti tra poteri pubblici ed autonomie private*" *Rivista trimestrale diritto pubblico.*

Cassese, S., 2009. "Il diritto globale" Torino; Carcaterra, G. 1979 "La forza costitutiva delle norme. L'uomo e la società".

Cassese, S., 2014. "La nuova architettura finanziaria europea".

Chang, H. F. 1999. "A Liberal Theory of Social Welfare: Fairness, Utility, and the Pareto Principle" *University of Pennsylvania Law School, Institute for Law and Economics, Working Paper No. 272.*

Chen, Y. and Bellavitis, C. 2019 "Blockchain Disruption and Decentralized Finance: The Rise of Decentralized Business Models" *Journal of Business Venturing Insights.*

Christopher, Woolard, 2017. "Innovating for the future: the next phase of Project Innovate" Speech by the Executive Director of Strategy and Competition at the FCA, delivered at the Innovate Finance Global Summit., April.

Ciocca, P., 2019 "Il tempo è adesso – FinTech: mercato, regolazione, futuro".

Cirillo, P. and Taleb, N. 2015. "Expected Shortfall Estimation for Apparently Infinite-Mean Models of Operational Risk" *Quantitative Finance.*

Claessens, S. and Frost, J. and Turner, G. and Zhu, F. 2018. "Fintech credit markets around the world: size, drivers and policy issues" *BIS Quarterly Review.*

Clinton, B. 2000. "From Digital Divide to Digital Opportunity", Washington D.C., February 2.

Coase, R. H., 1988. "The firm the market and the law" Chicago.

Cœuré, B. 2018a "Financial regulation and innovation: a two-way street. Introductory remarks by the member of the Executive Board of the ECB, at a roundtable organised by FinLeap", Berlin, 14 MarcH.

Cœuré, B. 2018b, "A Euro Cyber Resilience Board for pan-European Financial Infrastructures", introductory remarks at the first meeting of the Euro Cyber Resilience Board for pan-European Financial Infrastructures, Frankfurt, 9 March.

Cœuré, B. 2019 "Fintech for the people. Keynote speech by the chair of the CPMI and Member of the Executive Board of the ECB, at the 14th BCBS-FSI high-level meeting for Africa on strengthening financial sector supervision and current regulatory priorities", Cape Town, 31 January

Cœuré, B. and Loh, J., 2018. "Bitcoin not the answer to a cashless society", opinion piece in the Financial Times, 12 March.

Cohen-Setton, J. and Vallée, S. 2018. "Federalizing a Central Bank: A Comparative Study of the Early Years of the FED and the ECB".

Cooter, R and Ulen, T., 2008. "Law and Economics", Boston.

Costi, R., 2014. "Il Testo Unico Bancario, oggi. Quaderni di Ricerca Giuridica della Banca d'Italia". Roma

CPMI 2017, "Distributed ledger technology in payment, clearing and settlement", February.

Cukierman, A. 2014. "Euro-Area and US Banks Behavior, and ECB-Fed Monetary Policies During the Global Financial Crisis: A Comparison" CEPR Discussion Paper No. DP10289.

D'Acquisto, G. and Naldi, M. 2017. "Big data e privacy by design", Torino.

D'Ambrosio, R., 2015. "The ECB and NCA liability within the Single Supervisory Mechanism" *Quaderni di Ricerca Giuridica della Consulenza Legale della Banca d'Italia*, Roma.

Davies, G. B., 2017. "New Vistas in Risk Profiling" *CFA Institute Research Foundation.*

de Boyrie, M. E. and Pak, S. J. and Zdanowicz, J. S., 2001. "The Impact of Switzerland's Money Laundering Law on Capital Flows Through Abnormal Pricing in International Trade" *EFMA 2001 Lugano Meetings; CIBER Working Paper.*

de Fontnouvelle, P. and Jordan, J. S. and Rosengren, E. S. 2005. "Implication of alternative operational risk modeling techniques" *National Bureau of Economic Research;* Ebnöther, S. and Vanini, P. and McNeil, A. and Antolinez-Fehr, P. 2003 "Modelling Operational Risk" *Journal of Risk.*

de Guindos, L., 2019. "Welcome Remarks at the third ECB Forum on Banking Supervision", Frankfurt am Main, 6 November.

De Polis, A. and Pietrunti, M. 2019. "Exchange Rate Dynamics and Unconventional Monetary Policies: It's All in the Shadows" *Bank of Italy Temi di Discussione (Working Paper) No. 1231.*

De Vecchis, P., 1982. "Spunti per una rinnovata riflessione sulla nozione di banca", *Banca borsa titoli di credito.*

Delimatsis, P. 2012. "Financial Innovation and Prudential Regulation – The New Basel III Rules" *TILEC Discussion Paper No. 2012-016.*

Dell'Ariccia, G. and Marquez, R. 2006. "Competition among regulators and credit market integration" *Journal of Financial Economics.*

Draghi, M. 2019. "Farewell Remarks".

Eagly, A. H. and Shelly, S. 1993 "The psychology of attitudes".

EBA 2017. "Report on innovative uses of consumer data by financial institutions", 28 June.

EBA 2018a. "EBA Report on the prudential risks and opportunities arising for institutions from fintech", 3 July.

EBA 2018b. "Fintech: Regulatory Sandboxes And Innovation Hubs", JC 2018 74.

EBA 2018c. "Report on the prudential risks and opportunities arising for institutions from fintech", 3 July.

EBA 2018d. "The EBA's fintech roadmap. Conclusions from the consultation on the EBA's approach to financial technology (fintech)". 15 March.

EBA 2019a "Report on crypto-assets", available at www.eba.europa.eu.

EBA 2019b. "EBA report on the impact of fintech on payment institutions' and e-money institutions' business models", July

ECB Advisory Group on Market Infrastructures for Securities and Collateral 2017 "The potential impact of DLTs on securities post-trading harmonization and on the wider EU financial market integration".

ECB and Bank of Japan 2017, "Payment systems: liquidity saving mechanisms in a distributed ledger environment", a joint research project of the European Central Bank and the Bank of Japan – STELLA, September.

ECB, 2018. "Guide to assessments of fintech credit institution licence applications".

Ecofin, 2019. "Draft Joint Statement by the Council and the Commission on Stablecoins" Brussels, 6 November 2.

Ellis, E. 1999. "The principle of proportionality in the laws of Europe" Oxford.

Engineer, M. 1990. "Brennan and Buchanan's Leviathan models" *The Social Science Journa.*

Engst, A. and Lemma V., 2018. "Insurtech and interoperability of Fintech firms", in *Open review of management, banking and finance.*

ESAs 2019. "Report on FinTech: Regulatory Sandboxes and Innovation Hubs", January.

ESMA 2017. "ESMA alerts investors to the high risks of Initial Coin Offerings (ICOs)".

ESMA 2019 "Report. Licensing of FinTech business models", 12 July.

ESMA, EBA, EIOPA Joint Committee 2015 "Discussion Paper on automation in financial advice", JC 2015 080, 4 December.

European Commission 2018a "European Commission's Action Plan on how to harness the opportunities presented by technology-enabled innovation in financial services (FinTech), 8 March.

European Commission 2018b, "FinTech action plan: For a more competitive and innovative European financial sector", 8 March.

Ezrachi, A. 2018. "EU Competition Law Goals and the Digital Economy" *Oxford Legal Studies Research Paper No. 17/2018;*

Favre, O. and Kramer, S., 2017. "Art. 2 FinfraG". "Kommentarzum Finanzmarktinfrastrukturgesetz FinfraG", Zurich.

FCA 2019a. "Blockchain Technology for Algorithmic Regulation and Compliance (BARAC)", University College London, 11 September.

FCA 2019b. "Digital regulatory reporting", 13 March.

FCA 2019c. "Global Financial Innovation Network (GFIN)" 9 August.

FCA Regulatory sandbox lessons learned report, October 2017.

Federal Department of Finance FDF, 2017. "Report on amendments to the Banking Ordinance (Fintech), Explanations".

Ferran, E. and Babis, V. 2013. "The European Single Supervisory Mechanism" *University of Cambridge Faculty of Law Research Paper No. 10/2013.*

FINMA, 2016a. "Asset management: technology-neutral FINMA regulations", 1 July.

FINMA, 2016b. "Due diligence requirements for client onboarding via digital channels (Valid until 31.07.2018)", 3 March.

FINMA, 2016c. "FINMA reduces obstacles to FinTech", 17 March.

FINMA, 2019. "Partial revision of the Circular 2008/3 "Public deposits with non-banks".

Fluhmann, D. and Hsu, P., 2019. "Switzerland: Fintech 2019".

FSB 2019a "Regulatory issues of stablecoins".

FSB 2019b. "Fintech and market structure in financial services: Market developments and potential financial stability implications".

FSB 2019c. "Resolution Report: Mind the Gap. Eighth Report on the Implementation of Resolution Reforms".

FSB. 2017. "Financial Stability Implications from FinTech. Supervisory and Regulatory Issues that Merit Authorities' Attention", 27 June.

FSB 2020. "Global Monitoring Report on Non-Bank Financial Intermediation 2019", 19 January.

Galbraith, J. R. 2014. "Organizational Design Challenges Resulting from Big Data" *Journal of Organization Design.*

Ganchev, A., 2018. "The Swiss National Bank – a Central Bank or a Hedge Fund?" *Zlaten vestnik.* Tavex questions certain foundations of banking and central banking.

GFIN, The global financial innovation network on its first year, June 2019.

Gilli, M. and Këllezi, E. and Hysi, H. 2006. "A Data-Driven Optimization Heuristic for Downside Risk Minimization" *Swiss Finance Institute Research Paper No. 06-2.*

Goanta, C. 2018. "How Technology Disrupts Private Law: An Exploratory Study of California and Switzerland as Innovative Jurisdictions" *TTLF Working Paper No. 38/2018*

Gore, A. A. Jr. 1998 "Digital Divide Event", April 28, 1998

Gorton, G. B. and Metrick, A., 2010. "Regulating the Shadow Banking System" *SSRN Research Paper no. 1676947.*

Grant, S. H. and Van Zandt, T. 2007. "Expected Utility Theory" *INSEAD Business School Research Paper No. 2007/71/EPS.*

Grey, R. and Dharmapalan, J., 2017. "The Macroeconomic Policy Implications of Digital Fiat Currency" "The Case for Digital Legal Tender".

Guarracino, F. 2012. "Supervisione bancaria europea (Sistema delle fonti e modelli teorici)" Padova.

Hacker, P. and Thomale, C., 2017. "Crypto-Securities Regulation: ICOs, Token Sales and Cryptocurrencies under EU Financial Law" *European Company and Financial Law Review.*

Hacker, P. and Thomale, C., 2018. "Crypto-Securities Regulation: ICOs, Token Sales and Cryptocurrencies under EU Financial Law" *European Company and Financial Law Review.*

Hansmann, H. and Kraakman, R. H. 2004. "What is Corporate Law?" *Yale Law & Economics Research Paper No. 300.*

Harrast, S. and Swaney, A. 2019 "What Is the Role of the Board-Level Technology Committee?" *SSRN Research Paper no. 3456770.*

Hertig, G. and McCahery, J. A. 2003. "Company and Takeover Law Reforms in Europe: Misguided Harmonization Efforts or Regulatory Competition?" *ECGI – Law Working Paper No. 12/2003.*

Hwa, G. and Lloyd, J. and Hatch, M. 2019. "Eight ways FinTech adoption remains on the rise" and "EY third biennial FinTech adoption trends survey"

Ibrido, R., 2017. "L'unione bancaria europea. Profili costituzionali" Roma.

Jackson, G. and Deeg, R. 2006. "How Many Varieties of Capitalism? Comparing the Comparative Institutional Analyses of Capitalist Diversity" *MPIfG Discussion Paper No. 06/2.*

Jagtiani, J, and Lemieux, C., 2018a. "Do Fintech Lenders Penetrate Areas that are Underserved by Traditional Banks?" *FRB of Philadelphia Working Paper No. 18-13.*

Jagtiani, J. and Lemieux, C., 2018b. "The Roles of Alternative Data and Machine Learning in Fintech Lending: Evidence from the Lendingclub Consumer Platform" *FRB of Philadelphia Working Paper No. 18-15.*

Keidar, R. and Blemus, S., 2018. "Cryptocurrencies and Market Abuse Risks: It's Time for Self-Regulation" *Lexology*.

Laeven, L. and Levine, R. and Michalopoulos, S. 2015, "Financial innovation and endogenous growth", *Journal of Financial Intermediation*.

Lamandini, M. and Muñoz, D. R. and Álvarez, J. S., 2015. "Depicting the limits to the SSM's supervisory powers: The Role of Constitutional Mandates and of Fundamental Rights' Protection" *Quaderni di Ricerca Giuridica della Consulenza Legale della Banca d'Italia*, Roma.

Laskowski, M. and Kim, H. M. and Zargham, M. and Barlin, M. and Kabanov, D., 2019. "Token Economics in Real-Life: Cryptocurrency and Incentives Design for Insolar's Blockchain Network" *SSRN Research Paper no. 3465085*.

Lastra, R., 2013. "*The Globalization Paradox: Review of Dani Rodrik, The Globalization Paradox: Democracy and the Future of the World Economy*", *International Journal of Constitutional Law*.

Lehmann, M. 2019. "Global Rules for a Global Market Place? – The Regulation and Supervision of FinTech Providers" *Boston University International Law Journal*.

Lemma, V., 2018. "Fintech regulation: the need for a research" *Open review of management, banking and finance*.

Lener, R. and Parrillo, G. 2018. "Quali regole per fintech?", *Fintech: diritto tecnologia e finanza*, Roma.

Longo, E. and Lorenzini, L. 2017. "Ict e parlamenti: oltre la mera diffusione dei contenuti", "Studi Pisani sul Parlamento VII. La crisi del Parlamento nelle regole sulla sua percezione", Pisa.

Maijoor, S. 2018 "New technologies within and beyond capital markets" ESMA71-99-1036.

Malamud, S. and Zucchi, F. 2016 "Liquidity, innovation, and endogenous growth" No 1919.

Maume, P. 2018. "Reducing Legal Uncertainty and Regulatory Arbitrage for Robo-Advice" *European Company and Financial Law Review*.

McKinsey Global Institute, 1992. "Service Sector Productivity", Washington, DC.

Mersch, Y. 2016 "Distributed Ledger Technology: role and relevance of the ECB. Speech by the member of the Executive Board of the ECB, 22nd Handelsblatt Annual Conference Banken-Technologie", 6 December.

Merton, R. C., 2018. "Observations on the Digital Revolution: Financial Innovation and FinTech" Speech at 17th International Conference on Credit, Venice.

Messina, D., 2018. "Il Regolamento (EU) 2016/679 in materia di protezione dei dati personali alla luce della vicenda Cambridge Analytica", Federalismi.it.

Nabilou, H., 2019. "Central Bank Digital Currencies: Preliminary Legal Observations". *Journal of Banking Regulation*.

Negreiro, M. 2015. "Briefing at EPRS | European Parliamentary Research Service. Bridging the digital divide in the EU", Bruxelles;

OCSE, 1996 "Regulatory Reform and Innovation".

OECD, 2019. "Regulatory effectiveness in the era of digitalisation", Paris.

Okafor, A. and Fadul, J. 2019. "Bank Risks, Regulatory Interventions and Deconstructing the Focus on Credit Risk" *Research Journal of Finance and Accounting*

Olivieri, G. and Falce, V., 2016. "Smart cities e diritto dell'innovazione" Milano.

Olkova, A., 2018. "Portfolio Performance Measurement: Traditional vs Utility-Based Approaches" *1st International Management, Quality and Marketing Conference Research Paper.*

Oppo, G., 1997. "Mutualità e integrazione cooperativa", Rivista di diritto civile, 1997.

Orphanides, A. 2014. "European Headwind: ECB Policy and Fed Normalization" *MIT Sloan Research Paper No. 5119-14.*

Palmerini, E. and Aiello, G. and Cappelli, V. and Morgante, G. and Amore, N. and Di Vetta, G. and Fiorinelli, G. and Galli, M., 2018. "Il FinTech e l'economia dei dati. Considerazioni su alcuni profili civilistici e penalistici. Le soluzioni del diritto vigente ai rischi per la clientela e gli operatori", *Quaderno FinTech n. 2*, December.

Panetta, F., 2017. "L'innovazione digitale nell'industria finanziaria italiana", Milano, 26 september.

Pellegrini, M. 2003. "Banca Centrale Nazionale e Unione Monetaria Europea. Il caso italiano", Padova.

Pellegrini, M. 2012. "L'architettura di vertice dell'ordinamento finanziario europeo: funzioni e limiti della supervisione" *Rivista trimestrale di diritto dell'economia.*

Perassi, M., 2014. "Brevi conclusioni" "Dal Testo unico bancario all'Unione bancaria: tecniche normative e allocazione di poteri" *Quaderni di Ricerca Giuridica della Consulenza Legale della Banca d'Italia*, Roma.

Philippon, T. 2017 "The FinTech Opportunity", *BIS Working Papers No 655.*

Pollicino, O. and Frosini, T. and Apa, E. 2017. "Diritti e libertà in Internet", Milano.

Posner, R. 2007. "Economic Analysis of Law", New York.

Posner, R. 2008 "How judges think", Harvard.

Quarles, R. K. 2019. "FSB Letter from the FSB Chair to G20 Leaders ahead of their Summit in Osaka", 25 June Vehovar, V., Sicherl P., Hüsing T. and Dolnicar, V. 2006 "Methodological Challenges of Digital Divide Measurements", *The Information Society.*

Recine, F. and Teixeira, P. G. 2009 "The New Financial Stability Architecture in the EU" *Paolo Baffi Centre Research Paper No. 2009-62.*

Reiser, N, 2018. "Ist der Bankbegriff im Lichte aktueller technologischer Entwicklungen noch zeitgemäss?" *AJP*, Swiss Financial Market Supervisory Authority FINMA, 2018. Fact sheet: "Virtual Currencies", updated 30 August.

Remolina, N. 2019. "Open Banking: Regulatory Challenges for a New Form of Financial Intermediation in a Data-Driven World" *SMU Centre for AI & Data Governance Research Paper No. 2019/05*

Ricciardi, V. and Simon, H. K., 2000. "What is Behavioral Finance?" *Business, Education & Technology Journal.*

Ricks, M., 2010. "Shadow Banking and Financial Regulation" *Columbia Law and Economics Working Paper No. 370.*

Rodotà, S. 1973a. "Elaboratori elettronici e controllo sociale", Bologna.

Rodotà, S. 1973b. "Elaboratori elettronici e controllo sociale", Bologna, p. 183 ss. and the litterature about 'small claims';

Rodotà, S. 1995. "Tecnologie e diritti", Bologna,

Rodotà, S. 2004a. "Tecnopolitica. La democrazia e le nuove tecnologie della comunicazione",

Rodotà, S. 2006. "La vita e le regole. Tra diritto e non diritto", Milano;

Rodotà, S. 2012. "Il diritto di avere diritti", Roma-Bari;

Rodotà, S., 2004b. "Diritto, scienza, tecnologia: modelli e scelte di regolamentazione", "Scienza e diritto nel prisma del diritto comparato".

Rosa, H., 2003. "Social acceleration: ethical and political consequences of a desynchronized high-speed society", *Constellations.*

Rossi, S., 2018. Speech at the Conference '*FinTech e InsurTech: tecnologie digitali, banche, assicurazioni, nell'ambito dell'iniziativa "Incontri con la Banca d'Italia*". September 10.

Rubinstein, I. S., 2013. "Big Data: The End of Privacy or a New Beginning?" *International Data Privacy Law.*

Saccomanni, F., 2010. "La sfida per le banche popolari nel nuovo scenario regolamentare" Verona, 26 febbraio.

Savona, P. 2002. "Politica economica e new economy", Milano;

Savona, P. 2008. "I momenti d'oro dell'economia visti da Paolo Savona", Roma.

Savona, P. 2019 "Incontro annuale con il mercato finanziario Discorso del Presidente" Milano, 14 June.

Scardovi, C. 2016. "Restructuring and Innovation in Banking", London

Schena, C. and Tanda, A. and Arlotta, C. and Potenza, G., 2018. "The development of FinTech. Opportunities and risks for the financial industry in the digital age", *Quaderno FinTech n. 1*, march.

Schumpeter, J., 1990. "Storia dell'analisi economica", Torino.

Sciarrone Alibrandi, A. and Borello, G. and Ferretti, R. and Lenoci, F. and Macchiavello, E. and Mattassoglio, F. and Panisi, F. 2019. "Marketplace lending, Verso nuove forme di intermediazione finanziaria?", *Quaderno FinTech n. 5*, July.

Shojai, S. and Feiger, G., 2002. "Les Banquiers Suisses: Can They Remain Leaders in Private Banking?". *Journal of Financial Transformation.*

Simoncini, A., 2016. "The Constitutional Dimension ofthe Internet: Some Research Paths" EUI Working Paper Law 2016/16.

SNB. 2018. "Swiss National Bank: Survey on payment methods 2017, Survey on payment methods and use of cash in Switzerland", May.

Solove, D. J. 2002. "Conceptualizing Privacy" *California Law Review.*

Status, R. 1971. "Contract and the Welfare State" *Stanford Law Review.*

Stone, K. 2004. "Alternative Dispute Resolution" *Encyclopedia of Legal History,* Oxford;

Stulz, R. M., 2019. "FinTech, BigTech, and the Future of Banks". *Fisher College of Business Working Paper No. 2019-03-020.*

Stylianou, T. 2018. "An Investigation into the Utility and Potential Regulation of Initial Coin Offerings and Smart Contracts in Selected Industries and Jurisdictions" *King's College London Law School Research Paper No. 19-8.*

Swiss Financial Market Supervisory Authority FINMA, ICO. 2018. "Guidelines for enquiries regarding the regulatory framework for initial coin offerings (ICOs)", updated 16 February.

Thakor, A. V. 2019. "Fintech and Banking: What Do We Know?" *Journal of Financial Intermediation*

Thouvenin, F. and Früh, A. and Lombard, A., 2017, "Eigentum an Sachdaten: Eine Standortbestimmung" *SZW 2017/1.*

Thouvenin, F. and Weber, R. H., 2017 "Zum Bedarf nach einem Dateneigentum", *Jusletter IT* of 11 December 2017

Tribimas, T. 1999. "Proportionality in community law: searching for the appropriate standard of scrutiny".

Troiano, V. 2012. "Interactions Between EU and National Authorities in the New Structure of EU Financial System Supervision" *Law and Economics Yearly Review.*

Troiano, V., 2019. "Le Banche" "Manuale di diritto Bancario e Finanziario", Padova.

UNEVOC - UNESCO 2014. "Digital divide" *Resources and Services.*

Vandevelde, K. J. 2011 "Thinking like a lawyer", Boulder.

Venturi, E. 2009. "Globalizzazione, interconnessione dei mercati e crisi finanziaria. Identificazione di possibili interventi correttivi" *Banca borsa titoli di credito.*

Verdegem, P. and Verhoest, P. 2009 "Profiling the Non-user: Rethinking Policy Initiatives Stimulating ICT Acceptance" *Telecommunications Policy.*

Visco, I. 2019a. Speech at Associazione Bancaria Italiana – Assemblea degli Associati. Milan, July 12.

Visco, I., 2019b. "Lezione Giorgio Fuà 2019. Centenario della nascita".

Visco, I., 2019c. "Remarks at the Event to Commemorate Thirty Years of Banca d'Italia in Japan. Speech by the Governor of the Bank of Italy. Thirty Years of Banca d'Italia in Japan: Anniversary Celebration" Tokyo, 11 June.

Visco, I., 2019d. "Sustainable development and climate risks:the role of central banks. Speech by the Governor of the Bank of Italy at the 18th International Conference for Credit Risk Evaluation "Assessing and Managing Climate Change Risk: Opportunities for Financial Institutions" Venice, 26 September.

Visco, I., 2019e. *Considerazioni finali del Governatore. Relazione annuale.* Roma, May 31.

Vulkan, N. and Astebro, T. and Sierra M. F., 2016. "Equity crowdfunding: A new phenomena (opens in new window)", *Journal of Business Venturing Insights.*

VV.AA. 2015. "La riforma delle banche popolari", Padova.

VV.AA. 2018a. "Intelligenza artificiale, protezione dati personali e regolazione", Milano.

VV.AA. 2018b. "Per un'ipotesi ricostruttiva della riforma delle BCC", *Rivista Trimestrale di Diritto dell'economia.*

VV.AA., 'The High-Level Group of Financial Supervision in the EU', chaired by Jacques de Larosière, "Report", 25 February 2009.

Wachter, S. 2018. "Normative challenges of identification in the Internet of Things: Privacy, profiling, discrimination, and the GDPR", *Computer law & security Review*

Wachter, S. and Mittelstadt, B. 2018. "A Right to Reasonable Inferences: Re-Thinking Data Protection Law in the Age of Big Data and AI" *Columbia Business Law Review.*

Walch, A. 2015 "The Bitcoin Blockchain as Financial Market Infrastructure: A Consideration of Operational Risk" *NYU Journal of Legislation and Public Policy.*

Wang, W. and Mahmood, A. and Sismeiro, C. and Vulkand, N., 2019 "The evolution of equity crowdfunding: Insights from co-investments of angels and the crowd" *Research Policy.*

Warschauer, M., 2003. "Technology and Social Inclusion: Rethinking the Digital Divide", Cambridge.

Warschauer, M., 2009. "Demystifying the Digital Divide" *Elsevier.*

Wasserman, I and Richmond-Abbott, M., 2005 "Gender and the Internet: Causes of Variation in Access, Level, and Scope of Use" *Social Science Quarterly.*

Weber, R. H. and Thouvenin, F., 2018. "Dateneigentum und Datenzugangsrechte – Bausteine der Informationsgesellschaft?" *ZSR.*

Wei, L. and Hindman, D. 2011. "Does the Digital Divide Matter more? Comparing the Effects of New Media and Old Media Use on the Education-Based Knowledge Gap" *Mass Communication and Society.*

Whitacre, B. and Mills, B., 2007. "Infrastructure and the rural-urban divide in high-speed residential internet access" *International Regional Science Review.*

Willis, S. and Tranter, B., 2006. "Beyond the 'digital divide'. Internet diffusion and inequality in Australia", *Journal of Sociology*.

Wissler, E. 1997. "The Effects of Mandatory Mediation: Empirical Research on the Experience of Small Claims and Common Pleas Courts" *Willamette Law Review*.

Witte, J. and Mannon, S. 2007. "The Internet and Social Inequalities" New York

Wong, Y. C. and Law, C. K. and Fung, J. Y. C. and Lee, V. W. P., 2010. "Digital divide and social inclusion: policy challenge for social development in Hong Kong and South Korea'" *Journal of Asian Public Policy*.

Working Group established by the Committee on the Global Financial System (CGFS) and the Financial Stability Board (FSB), 2017. "FinTech credit. Market structure, business models and financial stability implications".

Wray, L. R. and Sardoni, C. 2005. "Monetary Policy Strategies of the European Central Bank and the Federal Reserve Bank of U.S." *Levy Economics Institute Working Paper No. 431*.

Wyatt, S. and Henwood, F. and Hart, A. and Smith, J. 2005. "The digital divide, health information and everyday life', *New Media and Society*.

Wyatt, S. and Thomas, G. and Terranova, T. 2002. "They Came, they Surfed, they Went Back to the Beach: Conceptualising Use and Non-Use of the Internet" "Virtual Society? Technology, Cyperbole and Reality", Oxford.

Wymeersch, E., 2012. "The European Banking Union. A first Analysis", *Financial Law Institute Working Paper Series WP 2012-07*.

Yu, G. and Zhang, J., 2017. "A Revisit to Capital Control Policies When Bitcoin Is in Town" *31st Australasian Finance and Banking Conference 2018*.

Zeng, F. 2011. 'College students' perception of the second-level digital divide: An empirical analysis', *Asian social science*.

Zeno-Zencovich, V. 2018 "Dati, grandi dati, dati granulari e la nuova epistemologia del giurista", *Media Laws, Rivista di diritto dei media*, 2/2018.

Zetzsche, D. A. and Buckley, R. P. and Arner, D. W. and Barberis, J. N., 2017. "Regulating a Revolution: From Regulatory Sandboxes to Smart Regulation" *Fordham Journal of Corporate and Financial Law*.

Zetzsche, D. A. and Preiner, C. 2017 "Cross-Border Crowdfunding – Towards a Single Crowdfunding Market for *"European Banking Institute Working Paper Series 2017*

Zhang, T. 2019 "Balancing Fintech Opportunities and Risks. Remarks by IMF Deputy Managing Director" Vilnius.

Zillien, N. and Hargittai, E., 2009. "Digital Distinction: Status-Specific Internet uses". *Social Science Quarterly*.

Zuiderveen Borgesius, F., 2013. "Behavioral Targeting, A European Legal Perspective" *IEEE Security & Privacy*.

Zuiderveen Borgesius, F., 2014. "Behavioural Sciences and the Regulation of Privacy on the Internet" *Institute for Information Law Research Paper No. 2014-02*.

CHAPTER 5

Fintech, Chain Transactions and Open Banking

At this stage of the analysis, fintech should appear as wide as the horizon appears to any researcher. However, it is acknowledged that networks allow the wide-spreading of both big data and technology, and this allows the transactions to cross any jurisdiction all around the world. Furthermore, the unbundling of banking into chains of transactions allows market participants to apply fintech innovations to activities that are outside the scope of supervision.

In this context the most recent rules governing banking, financial services, asset management and insurance set forth an environment where any technology-enabled innovation cannot result in new activities (outside of the scope of the above rules), but the definition of the relevant reserved activities still include any innovative business models based on applications, processes or products that go beyond the operative standards of traditional banks and intermediaries.

Hence, the analysis is going to investigate the reason why the levels and the types of technology do not appear to be regulatory-neutral. The focus on big data shows that the application of high-tech mechanisms to the processes of financing and credit transformations will influence the allocation of risks and benefits between the lender and the borrower. As this evidence calls policymakers to regulate the relevant bargain power, this chapter highlights that big data awareness helps us in understanding that it is not just a big amount of data, but a set of information that self-executes, self-updates, self-assesses, self-corrects and then self-executes

© The Author(s) 2020
V. Lemma, *FinTech Regulation*,
https://doi.org/10.1007/978-3-030-42347-6_5

again. In other words, fintech operations, big data and artificial intelligence call regulators to act in order to set incentives and limits which are compliant with the individual rights and the financial stability that qualify the current democracies.

This part of the research will identify a flow of open innovation in banking, or rather a new open form of banking. This flow requires both incentives to pursue social wealth and constraints to limit risk-taking in complex situations that can repeat themselves for an indefinite number of cycles (in a specific sequence, which goes from lending or financing to asset management, risk mitigation, credit enhancement and maturity transformation). Accordingly, this chapter begins investigating the 'acts of fintech' and the responsibility of individuals in developing chain transactions and networks of operations, taking the need to avoid that their outcomes undermine the common welfare. Consequently, the analysis will go deep into the current need for transparency with regard to both the circulation of financial information in the market and the bargaining power in bilateral transactions.

5.1   The 'Acts of Fintech'

The application of a high-tech mechanism to the provision of financial services and credit intermediation provides outcomes different from those experienced under the use of the traditional human-driven governance of banks and other financial firms or intermediaries (ECB 2018).[1] This assumption suggests keeping an eye on any financial transaction that occurs by means of a high-tech device, as the device should be studied to determine whether the intended executor of the transaction understands the benefit being transmitted to him/her and whether changes to the format, delivery and/or content of such transaction would be better for protecting the customer (as borrower, saver or investor, as the case may be) (Iannarone, N. G. 2017).

However, the interfaces (which show only the results) hide the *astronomical numbers* and the *continuity* of the proliferation of data, users, operations, services and chains involved in the execution of any market-based transaction by means of fintech mechanisms. Henceforth, in order to introduce a regulatory focus on the activities supported by fintech, it is useful to highlight the core juridical elements of the aforementioned chains: the information and data (widespread in the social environment), the algorithms and software (applied by firms) and the input and output (of fintech chains). These elements are intertwined by means of a bundle of rights and relations made on the basis of the private law.[2]

As a preliminary remark, information and data are under investigation as both 'raw material' and 'finished goods' of the information and communication technology (ICT) industry, so this part of the analysis is going to ponder whether the current rules are able to drive the high-tech mechanisms of collection and production of information and data towards the best outcome for the common welfare.[3] Hence, this chapter begins with the examination of big data. Indeed, it is necessary to understand if and how the aforesaid rules are suitable for the proper functioning of algorithms and software as cognitive functions of artificial intelligence, it can be noted that currently the safeguards are showing their limits in protecting personal spheres of privacy and interests. However, the way big data and artificial intelligence combine should be governed by rules set forth by humans, or rather by regulatory and supervised processes designed in accordance with principles set forth by humans, but developed by machines (both able to execute automatic programmed processes and develop them).

Algorithms and software, on the contrary, are going to be investigated as a part of the 'black box' that transforms input into output. And—as shown in the previous chapters—the more the firm is fintech(ed) in nature, the less this black box remains to humans employed by the firm itself.[4] Hence, as this analysis is willing to clarify, fintech does not remove humans from banking and finance, but it transfers them to the previous (different) stage of programming and coding firms.

In this context, it is necessary to begin by identifying the underlying principles of the current EU approach to chain transactions (and cleared trades), because certain rules seem to jeopardize the current market equilibriums.[5] Therefore, at this stage of the analysis, there is the need to investigate not only the legal framework set forth by fintech activities, but also the most recent rules governing the 'open market operations'. Hence, the focus goes to the role of private law, in order to understand the responsibility of individuals in setting the market trends, taking into account the possibility that bilateral incentives and sanctions could drive the outcomes of fintech activities towards the maximization of individual wealth while augmenting also the common welfare.

Concentrating on the activities then, the analysis is going to move from the evidence that fintech is supporting the unbundling of banking into its core functions of settling payments, performing maturity transformation, sharing risk and allocating capital. As the Financial Stability Board (FSB) pointed out (FSB 2020), new firms are driving this possibility: payment service providers, aggregators and robo-advisors, peer-to-peer lenders, and innovative trading platforms. Indeed, these firms are becoming part of the shadow credit intermediation process that is benefitting from the adoption of new technologies, economies of scale and scope.[6] Hence, the following analysis will also consider the regulation applicable to the new infrastructure (that could reduce costs, increase efficiency, affect credit quality and even improve market functioning or develop macroeconomic dynamics). Definitely, this is accelerating the overriding of traditional banking (which is still combining operations of the customer relationship, retail and commercial deposits and lending, and a wide range of activities in wholesale money and capital markets) by open-market operations.[7] Hence, there is an interest for the European Union (EU) regulation of financial markets (MiFID II–MiFIR) and its capacity to supervise fintech transactions (and to contemplate their effects).[8]

In brief, this chapter—it is worth spoiling—will assess the current need for transparency, with regard to the imperative for rules that promote the circulation of financial information and ban the use of bargaining power by one firm to exert influence over others. This analysis begins by questioning which fintech activities are currently reserved to supervised entities; which automatized process must support the safety and soundness of these entities (particularly those judged to be systemic); what are the aggregate potential outcomes, risks and changes to macroeconomic and macrofinancial dynamics.

These questions will help us to understand the capacity of the current rules in supporting the new high-tech mechanisms applied to structuring the trading venues and executing the relevant operations.

5.2   Big Data Awareness

It is worth beginning this topic by questioning whether what traditional banks and financial intermediaries are doing with information today has changed or not. Probably, most of the market participants and supervisors understand that there is just more data and information, as well as opportunities and threats.[9] On the contrary, what fintechers and their algorithms are doing is quite different (FSB 2017).[10] Indeed, certain market participants understand that 'Big Data' is not only a bigger amount of data, nor a better set of news, nor a wiser selection of information.[11]

Hence, the notion of 'big data' as a term that is largely misunderstood and difficult to explain should now be addressed, above all because of the lack of a defining provision. One more time, the policymakers are called to act in this respect—to provide a basic and effective tool for constructing a network of rules and duties capable of driving innovation in the direction of the general welfare (by protecting individual rights).[12]

Introducing big data by referring to the 'numerousity adaptation effect'[13] leads to observe policymakers perceiving this phenomenon in numerical cognition when they refer broadly to it in order to describe the storage and analysis of large and/or complicated data sets using a variety of techniques, including artificial intelligence (FSB 2017).[14] Indeed, this reference shows a sort of non-symbolic numerical intuition, and exemplifies how the numerical precepts can impose themselves upon the human brain automatically, instead of presenting the new features of these sets (which can update and expand automatically) (Grossman, R. and Siegel, K. 2014). Thus, under a juridical analysis, this phenomenon cannot be simply explained in terms of size, density or contrast; it requires a supervising methodology that applies technical evaluations able to ensure the financial stability (EBA 2020).

It is possible to refer to numerical cognition, to distinguish the use of data by human and software, in order to highlight that the current regulation is closely related to other aspects of human thought—particularly spatial cognition (Hubbard, E. M. et al. 2005). Hence, it can be questioned whether (and how) policymakers should start thinking like a *coder*, and then develop human constraints for programmers (employed by software houses to produce software) and algorithms for software (exploited by fintech firms to perform fintech activities) (Anderson, C. 2008).

Above all the technicalities, a jurist must take into account that the economic institutions of capitalism refer to human mental processes such as "attention, language use, memory, perception, problem solving, creativity, and thinking".[15] Nowadays, the fintech perspective suggests that organizational innovation (as a result of technological innovation) sets and keeps the engine in motion (as Schumpeter suggested in 1942 with respect to new consumers).[16] And the same is true with respect to what Arrow observed in 1971 with respect to man's innovations, among which the use of organization to accomplish his ends is among both his greatest and his earliest.[17] In this respect, it should be borne in mind that Williamsons pointed out in 1985 that innovators may prefer to bury their mistakes than have them recorded.[18] But at that time Garry Kasparov won with a perfect score of 32-0 his Kasparov Simul versus 32 Micros (Hamburg 6 June 1985).

So, nowadays, recording successes and failures helps programmers to make such (positive and negative) outcomes predictable, and this brings the attention to the meaningful capacity of data. Although contract law scholars have demonstrated that contracts are not enforced literally (Posner, R. 2008),[19] and in the absence of an agreement on an alternative theory of contract, recent evidence shows that fintech is ordering the flows of transactions, which were usually provided by contracts, because algorithms fulfill contractual obligations in a linear way. And this emphasizes the need for big data awareness. Hence, from a regulatory perspective, it is possible to consider that the aforesaid technical skills have become a powerful tool for analyzing a wide number of legal issues related to the use of big data, with respect to rationale choices, evaluations, bi- and multilateral transactions or fulfillment of duties.

First of all, big data supports the rational choice in an environment where resources and information are limited in relation to human needs.[20] From a regulatory perspective, as a preliminary remark, big data qualifies as goods able to support certain behaviour that could undermine the competition (Benos, E and Sagade, S. 2012). In particular, the usage of them in order to support the sharing of the basic elements allows fintech firms to foresee the commercial actions that will prevent or restrict competition; and this is due also to the usage of algorithms that would provide the same outcome (when provided the same data), including the setting of the same prices (or differentiated prices on the basis of the profiling of customers).[21] Hence, there is a perspective of fintechers gaining commercial power as a 'group of firms sharing the same tools and data' and then exploiting it to dominate the relevant markets, and any restriction on the usability of big data would erect barriers to entry (due to the relevance of such data for the dealing among software).

According to the current evidence, the policymakers do not suggest (only) to monitor the development of big data itself, but (also) to investigate the relationships between big data and fintech activities[22]; thus, it is possible to raise in new terms an old syllogism: "If transactions differ in their attributes, if governance structures are aligned to the needs of transactions in a discriminating way, and if private ordering can be used in combination rather than separately, then the study of contracts will benefit from an effort to identify the mix of private and public structures that best serve the purpose of the parties" (Williamson, O. E. 1985).[23] However, in the fintech environment, a bilateral transaction can be regulated by something different from a *mere* contract, one which is not an *agreement* of the parties to set their reciprocal interests, but one which is a sort of *affair* that two fintech tools develop while interacting (besides both fintech tools verify the preprogrammed premises and then execute the preprogrammed actions) (Simon, P. 2015). Henceforth, there is a need to introduce the principle of 'recta ratio' into the software that governs the previously mentioned relations (between big data and fintech activities) as a principle which programmers should respect as they develop the relevant algorithms (and then the *identities* of their fintech tools).[24]

In this respect, big data cannot be ubiquitous.[25] Otherwise, policymakers, regulators and supervisors would continue to approach this regardless of its content. This is not only a call for action to scholars, to pursue further research goals and eliminate ambiguity, but the grounds for considering how a concrete definition would support and foster development of regtech and suptech (Davenport, T 2014). It is acknowledged that such a definition should be able to consider both data storage and data analysis as features of big data; however, it is useful to recognize how big data management is *notably* different from conventional data processing techniques, and that this difference requires a specific regulatory intervention.

It is worth considering the threefold characteristics encompassing big data's volume, velocity and variety, remarked on by the scholars who focused upon the increasing size of data, the increasing rate at which it is produced, and the increasing range of formats and representations employed.[26] In this respect, it should also include *veracity*, as a matter of trust and uncertainty of the relevant data and the outcome of analysis of that data.[27] Obviously, this approach does not contemplate that big data can be self-updating or self-executing (and then to autonomously develop third-party relations); hence, there are difficulties in classifying it as something different from a mere database (for regulatory purposes). Thus, there is the possibility to postpone any further considerations to the later paragraphs on the dynamic nature of big data.

As a boundary of this analysis, it is possible to conclude by considering the privacy regulation, provided that the protection of natural persons in relation to the processing of personal data has been recognized as a fundamental right by the EU (as stated in the first recital of the Regulation EU no. 2016/679). However, it is known that the processing of persons' personal data should be considered in relation to its function in society, and therefore the relevant rights have to be balanced against other fundamental rights, in accordance with the principle of proportionality.

Moreover, the scale of the collection and sharing of personal data has increased significantly because of the rapid technological developments and globalization, and the regulator has challenged the rising threats coming from this with strict constraints based on the explicit agreement of the persons themselves (Einav L. and Levin J. D. 2013). Unfortunately, people's awareness is not yet aligned with this level of protection, so it is not difficult to assume that usually anyone easily provides his/her permission-consensus to the use, sharing and reuse of this personal data for the purposes of analytics.[28]

5.3   Big Data Sets are Never Complete: The Dynamic Nature of Big Data as a Regulatory Matter

From a regulatory perspective, it is useful to assume that big data merits an autonomous approach because of its capacity to influence the market by developing self-standing relationships (which can influence cognitive capacity, information completeness, the establishment of operations and the chain that such operations will follow to complete a transaction).[29] Hence, it is possible to consider that big data is the evolution of the traditional relational database and business decision-making analytics, augmented with a new capacity to exploit the sources of unstructured data and execute automatic operations in cases when the new data satisfies pre-programmed conditions.

As such, it is possible to state that any set of big data is never complete.

Therefore, augmenting existing operations is one of the characteristics that presents structural issues that should be resolved without having regard to the content of the set of big data (Flood, M. et al. 2014). So, this suggests that from a legal perspective there is no need to quantify the experiences to develop a juridical strategy aimed at managing its impact on individual rights, financial stability and the common welfare. However, it is necessary to bear in mind that, as any other software or fintech tool, big data has a logical-syntactical structure; hence, it is necessary to understand the nature of its structure (as prescriptive) and the relevant classification for regulatory purposes (Mullainathan, S. 2014). Notably, and perhaps unsurprisingly, this is focusing upon the relevant infrastructure of the set itself (Paech, P. 2016). In fact, it is worth considering big data as a set of information and technologies (regardless of the types) in order to present both a definition (of big data) and a regulation (for big data).

It is clear that the study of big data (for regulatory purposes) does not deny other methodologies for considering fintech tools and big data analytics. If the analysis pursues understanding the convenience for public intervention over such phenomena, then the object of this research cannot be not limited to definitions, but extents to contents (which refers to the operations that will affect the people and the market).[30] Hence, the study of the form of big data would not be a formalistic study of it. This is why it is worth considering big data with respect to technologies such as machine learning and artificial intelligence (by supporting the concept of 'set' itself, also being involved with data-related tools that are a key element of the aforesaid definition), and several examples provide evidence which suggests that there is a growing set of technologies frequently involved in big data analytics.[31] Thus, it is possible to rely on such complexity to develop both a holistic definition and comprehensive regulation of the fintech environment (as a whole).

However, at this stage of the analysis, the preconception that big data is challenging the current paradigms and practices cannot be limited to data mining, nor data analytics. It involves the fintech activities based upon big data, and the strategy developed by their programmers.

In view of the banking activities that can exploit big data, it is possible to consider a sequence of fintech applications that would call for the legal rules to evolve with respect to collecting savings and lending money.[32] Indeed, big data gives the management of any bank, its shareholders, and its stakeholders (who have access to such data) the basis for a full view of the business: big data is the raw material for an analysis which can be easily shared with these subjects,[33] and then any of them is in position to exploit information on a wide range of features of the banking business (from customer behaviour patterns to internal process efficiency, to even broader market trends).

All the above means that anyone will be able to reach the position of a well-informed market participant, by using software and business analytics to gain information from big data and assume data-driven decisions. Hence, there is need to protect the end users (of the software able to read and interpret such data). In other words, it is useful to assume that market participants cannot directly understand big data, and so the aforesaid subjects are exposed to the risks arising from the exploitation of algorithms and the software that are able to *deal* with them.[34]

In this respect, it is worth also considering that one of the most relevant fintech activities in banking and finance relies on big data to streamline their internal processes. It refers to the practices of assessing the *practices* of the bank, and then to simplify, rationalize and optimize them. This is the background for the renewal of the organizational structure of the bank in order to apply machine learning and artificial intelligence. As a result, the automation of the bank's procedures will lead to the increase of the amount of data collected, boosting the databases to be more dynamic, and the need for a general and common use of algorithms. Hence, the operational risk related to the alignment of the ICT infrastructure (and the stability of the bank's entire system) and the processing capacity required for taking advantage of big data (Simon, P. 2015).

It is not possible to discard that scholars generally agree that operations cannot rely on big data during periods of increased heterogeneity, market fragmentation and sudden turns in economic activity.[35] According to them—under such conditions—it is difficult for policymakers to understand and assess the most effective regulations for managing the underlying forces driving the use of big data analytics in unsolicited marketing and other relevant areas (such as pricing, underwriting, claims management sales and/or risk measurement), which require a safe and sound approach, in order to analyse the benefits of the innovation and potential risks related to any unfair treatment of customers.

Concluding on this point, it is useful to summarize that big data is both a database and a software, or rather is the *derivative* of the integration between database and software able to self-update, self-assess, self-correct and self-execute. Henceforth, there is the need to regulate big data as a set of information, as a result of the activity of collecting the information into a framework, as a result of the activity of programming its self-capacities, and as a tool to be used by firms in providing activities in the banking and financial industry. So, there is another reason for promoting the establishment of supervisory tasks aimed at controlling the collectors and the programmers of this data, in addition to the oversight provided for the firms that are exploiting them.

5.4 High-Tech Market Intermediation Processes and the Randomization of Promises and Threats

The application of fintech innovations to the circulation of capital would lead to high-tech mechanisms (to support the supply and demand of credit and investment), as well as to one or more chains that unbundle the credit intermediation or provision of financial services into several subsequential stages of activities that involve a multitude of affairs connected together by specific purposes (i.e. credit enhancement and maturity transformation). Obviously, self-executing algorithms, machine learning and (other forms of) artificial intelligence can manage these chains, as well as humans did in the intermediation processes provided for the past market-based financing. Hence, it is necessary to understand whether and how these activities could pose risks different from those managed under the traditional business of banks and other financial firms or intermediaries, but close to the one experienced in the shadow banking system (Lemma, V. 2016).[36]

From a legal perspective, it should be clear that fintech activities help market participants in managing the various stages of the intermediation process that occurs in the market (i.e. outside the juridical sphere of an intermediary). This evidence confirms that savings and credit cannot be regulated as the assets and liabilities of a sole entity, and that—also in the fintech environment—market financing diverges from traditional banking (in which all the acts required for matching supply and demand of capital are realized within a single entity). To this feature it is corollary that, on the one hand, the assets will be subject to the activity of credit transformation (carried out at each stage of the process), and, on the other hand, these assets are the "initial-final products" to be produced in order to remunerate all the market participants who have executed these (sort of shadow) operations (De Fiore, F. and Uhlig, H. 2005).

It comes into consideration the dynamic and sequential nature of the 'shadow credit intermediation process' (highlighted by the analysis of several international authorities). In this respect, the adoption of self-executing algorithms and big data corresponds to a legal framework in which the provision of credit (in the beginning) and the supply of financial instruments (at the end) could be considered both as raw materials for financial intermediation and as their product.[37] This will be observed with regard to any operation and to any process, mainly in light of the proliferation of several chains of market based operations. Because of this, it is possible to identify the need for controlling the fintech tools aimed at supporting the non-bank intermediation that can influence the financial stability. Henceforth, supervision must take into account the whole 'shadow credit intermediation process' as a preprogrammed process, rather than just check (and face) the negative consequences of certain operations or transactions (resulting in a measurable loss for the relevant market or its participants).[38]

In brief, the results of the analysis are suggesting to pay specific attention to the fintech activity that could increase the systemic risk, considering that the financial system suffers the application of self-executing programmes that correlate their results to each other.[39] Thus, regulation could be able to manage the (negative) externalities produced by fintech activities (through interconnections with the capital market). And, again it appears necessary to continue with an analysis of the current legal framework applicable to the aforesaid activities, because the balancing of these externalities cannot be considered as an individual task (of the supervised entity) nor a bilateral agreement (when dealing with the relevant counterparty). Hence the perspective of an extension of the goal of supervision aimed at promoting collective behaviours and actions to reach the maximization of social welfare.

At this stage of the analysis, it is possible to highlight the systemic and interconnected vulnerabilities of fintech applications to the intermediation processes. This is referring to the incidence of macro-systemic risk deriving from the contamination ability of cross-industry transactions (among banking, finance, asset management and insurance), because this jeopardizes the wealth–risk–revenue circuit at the basis of the supervised dynamics of capital markets.

According to the current regulation of the banking industry, the focus on risks implies the need to understand if the traditional rules suit the high tech-market transactions, as well as the whole application of financial technology to the chain transactions. It is acknowledged that, considering fintech firms, the capital adequacy has no central role in the assessment of their stability, nor does the professionalism of their structure support safe and sound management. So, it is likely that the regulation of fintech will not just consider the duty to structure a significant system of guarantees preordained to balance the negative effects of algorithms and software. Then, this research would not rely on the strategic value of collaterals, but it envisages a set of rules designed to identify the elements of the chains to be regulated in order to reduce the burden of the cyber risks on capital.[40]

Besides this envisaged legal framework, it is possible that the applications of fintech will improve the market's ability to absorb shocks arising from the cycle or pathological stress, whatever the source is. At the same time, it is acknowledged that insufficient sets of data or levels of transparency put at risk the functioning of fintech tools, which leads to 'uncertainty' and deviates from the competitive equilibrium necessary to increase the common welfare (and, at the same time, prevent unjustified individual extra profits).[41]

Therefore, this part of the research has been divided into two phases: the first dedicated to the activities, and the second to the firms. This therefore brings into consideration the risks related to errors in programming the software, as well as to opportunistic behaviour of the firms.[42] Accordingly, the monitoring of fintech has shown that these risks undermine financial stability (with respect to the balancing of cash flows), the capital adequacy (and, with it, the consistency of assets in comparison to the liabilities within the vehicle used for supporting market-based processes) and the effective performance of chain transactions.[43]

Henceforward, it is possible to confirm that all the above requires a new type of supervision over fintech operations, which should be able to take into account the risks that do not arise in a bank but do in the non-bank financial intermediation. Once again, also from this perspective, it is necessary to question whether the existing supervisory system is able to manage the risks due to new high-tech intermediation techniques. Thus, there are further doubts that the resilience of the capital market cannot depend upon the sustainability of the algorithms and software applied by market participants only.[44]

5.5   OPEN BANKING ACTIVITIES

Opening banks means both authorizing these intermediaries to update their organizational structure (acknowledging to competitors' inputs) and sharing their knowledge with any other market participant.[45] In this respect, in order to open their knowledge, banks have to collect the consensus of their shareholders and stakeholders. It is not worth repeating the aforesaid conclusion on the propensity of the people to consent to this kind of sharing; however, the safety of savings would also consider the possibility to strengthen the data protection with public intervention that increases the role of the supervising authorities.[46]

It is worth considering that this *opening* requires the performance of specific tasks related to the redesign of the internal procedures, in order to perform activities based on rationale and sequential processes, which can be executed by means of algorithms, software and big data. This leads to contemplate that the use of them can increase the value of the firm, since the latter is using them as *input* for their internal development. Since a long time, specific evidence shows that banks are applying fintech innovations to certain activities in order to gain advantages in the supplying or demanding capital to or from the market (Gorton, G. B. and Metrick, A. 2010).

Customer development comes into consideration with respect to the activities aimed at personalizing the customers' experience with a more individualized, tailored advisory.[47] This is not referring (only) to the positive correlation between the ability to offer the client what they need and the increase in the annual revenues, but also to the fulfilment to provide adequate and suitable products to the client (in respect of the current MiFID II–MiFIR provisions[48]).[49] However, the regulator should expect that banks will not use big data only to know their customers better (and as a result, to find new ways to satisfy them), but will exploit fintech activities and chains to connect with them in a more extensive way.[50] As a result, the bank can also take preventive actions, and then gain more value. This suggests that technology will drive both the business and its supervision because of the efforts required for controlling the information of a relational database and the strings of a software.

Focusing on distribution activity, fintech is a great opportunity to not only save expenses in identifying client needs, but also generating additional revenue through highly targeted marketing strategies. Banks, financial intermediaries and insurance companies should maintain, operate and review a process in order to ensure that the supply meets the demand of the target market. Fintech activities can automatize the process applied for identifying a target market for each product or service that the aforesaid firms intend to offer, so that algorithms and big data would be called to verify if all relevant risks to such identified target markets are assessed, and if the intended distribution strategy is consistent with the relevant customers, and take reasonable steps to ensure that the distribution is coherent with the identified target market. Furthermore, the aforesaid process should ensure that the intermediaries take all appropriate safeguards to identify and manage the conflicts of interest between themselves and their customers or between one customer and another (especially in cases of managing peer-to-peer platforms).[51]

Big data would also be able to gain information from such distribution, and then the relevant fintech activity could provide feedback able to support the renovation of the offering itself (by means of a modification of the products or services' features). However, the policymaker should consider the effect of such 'social listening' in banking and finance because of the relevance of the individual rights (related to savings), and then regulate the set of actionable insights that can be collected from user activity.[52]

All of the above leads to question whether banks may reduce the risk of misconduct and non-compliance by eliminating the human factor from some critical processes. Obviously, it is acknowledged that such programmes will both increase the capacity of reviewing documents and decrease the human error associated with loan-servicing, but there are no evidences to deny that fintech activities will transfer these risks to the providers of business analytics (Barone, E. and Masera, R. 2000), as well as to the programmers of the software that is run to optimize some of the processes (including algorithmic trading, commercial loan agreement interpretation, and machine learning).[53] However, the fintech activities of banks and their providers can transfer the business models from the professionalisms of directors and employees, to real-time machine learning and predictive modelling able to analyse big data and pinpoint fraudulent behaviour, to minimize financial risk and then perform banking.

With respect to 'open banking' as the performance of bank's activities relying on the knowledge that market participants put in common, it is worth considering the following: it must be considered that collaborative experience among market participants relies on contractual models that regulate the *platform* used to pursue the relevant common goals.[54]

Henceforth, from a regulatory perspective, specific agreements lay below any open virtual platform used firstly for accessing it, and then for sharing knowledge, workplace, client data and base. These agreements can be negotiated or unilaterally drafted by the manager of the platform; however—in any case—private law plays an important role in setting up the relations among the users of the platform and its manager, as well as among users themselves. In any case, it is not possible to assume either that there are no agreements or that a platform relies on the status of their participants (instead of contracts).[55]

Focusing on the agreement for accessing the platform to rely on its infrastructure and benefit from the data stored in it, and the services provided by its manager, there are specific difficulties related to the definition of the financial agreements.[56] Obviously, this agreement can be easily configured as bilateral, whereby the undertakings of the users refer to the payment of fees and the provision of data (that the manager of the platform can use or resell). In this context, the undertakings of the manager should consider the maintenance of the infrastructure, the protection from cyber-risks and the management of conflicts of interests. This part of the analysis is not going deep into the need for establishing specific limits to private dealing, because the bargaining power stands with the party that better exploits its data and technology. Hence, it is possible to explain the difficulties in a sort of '*ex-ante* regulatory interventions' aimed at prefiguring the contents of such an agreement.[57]

From another perspective, the agreements between the users of the platform come into consideration because of their effects on the possibility to set up a sort of open banking (whose characteristics allow users to exchange information directly, data and knowledge, or rather money, financial instruments and thus banking services).[58] In this context, these kinds of exchanges imply bilateral or multilateral transactions, executed directly or through the intervention of a central counterparty or intermediary.[59] Hence, it is possible to consider the conclusion of specific agreements, whose terms and conditions can be decided directly by the software used to explore (and take advantage of) the opportunities placed in these platforms. So, the will to enter into this agreement can be communicated at the time of such a conclusion or it can be conveyed at the time of running the software. Thus, it is necessary to investigate if it is possible to rely on the discipline of the mandate, the provision of services or another kind of contract based on the features of a wired environment characterized by modern liquidity of rights and duties.

5.6   CROWD-BUSINESS: FUNDING AND LENDING WITH THE PEOPLE

Suppose a crowd of unregulated entities and people collectively enters into the affairs of banking and finance, by meeting in a physical place. If this occurred, nowadays, it is possible to record a *mere* breach of the rules that reserve banking and finance to supervised entities.[60] Therefore, it is not possible to admit that a crowd that enters into those affairs by a remote connection sets the activities of funding or lending and remains out of the scope of the supervision.

It should be borne in mind that the early economic analysis of banking and finance focused on the efficiency benefits of defining an intermediary over previously unregulated firms. In particular, the argument was that unless an intermediary had a legally protected interest in funding and lending from the people, there would be diminished incentive to invest in developing the organizational structure required for assessing the credit-worthiness and managing the relevant risks, under the benefit of the economies of scale and scope.[61] Moreover, users who have access to commonly owned resources, typically tend to misuse them,[62] hence—as represented in the 'tragedy of the commons'—the decision to place the ownership of the responsibility of funding and lending over to an intermediary (which would then have the appropriate incentive to set up the safe and sound management and to exclude the crowd to challenge for them) and to devise an enforceable and effective method of restricting access to the business of banking and finance (by setting capital and professional requirements). [63]

However, it should also be considered that supervised intermediaries, because of a strict approach to lending, are endowed with the right to exclude potential borrowers from their resources, and no one has an effective use of such capital (which would be deposited in central banks). In this respect, because of algorithms and platforms, private interests can be so finely divided as to impose a significant unbundling of banking into a more valuable *whole* of segregated activities of borrowing and lending. Therefore, according to the foundations of the economic analysis, the problems of the commons and of the anti-commons suggests that there are efficiency issues in 'propertization' of resources and affairs (Hardin, G. 1968).

In particular, a climate of uncertainty has emerged in the market for capital, accompanied by negative repercussions on the relations between the banks and their customers.[64] Indeed, borrowers are looking for alternative paths to support their economic-financial development, given the substantial stalemate that still characterizes the ordinary mechanisms of banking. So that, market participants are facing a restriction of the supply of loans and, therefore, a widespread lack of liquidity (which amplifies the risk of a recessionary phase and, at the same time, slows the recovery).[65]

In this context, fintech provides new mechanisms capable of effectively channelling resources towards the entrepreneurial system, favouring the creation of alternative financing channels to the traditional banking system; and this is justified with respect to the shadow banking system.[66] Hence, the firms are creating particular forms of capital raising supported by software and algorithms, and the customers will experience their effects in terms of returns and risks. This is not going to question whether fintech would facilitate the circulation of money,[67] but if the economic development of innovative investment projects would be emphasized by the use of new technologies or rather by the escape from the capital adequacy requirements. Hence, the crowdfunding lies in the epicentre of the fintech phenomenon, as a technique useful for the acquisition of monetary funds (whereby the essential nature of the bank's intermediary function is lost and the presence of a direct relationship between the supplier and the demanders is welcomed) (Moritz, A. and Block, J. H. 2013). It is understood that the subjects among whom the financial relationship is carried out both assume a primary role in this *crowdy* operational meeting (which, obviously, will have to be self-executing and outside the conventional logic of credit intermediation).

On the basis of this technique, the users actively finance a project of a specific company through the provision of monetary contributions of different entities in exchange for a promise (concerning the envisaged returns). Thus, this results in a sort of mixture of the interests that, in banking, the various intermediaries ordinarily bear by themselves.

It follows that the subjects participating in the financing (conveyed through computer platforms) assume the dual role of lender and potential customer of the borrower; and this gives rise to the emergence of a particular form of individual 'professional consumer', a term with which reference is made to the aggregation by a single operator of the needs—usually opposed to each other—of the professional supplier of capital and the private consumer of the outcome (Hazen, T. L. 2012).

According to the above, the connections *intertwine* more and more. Then, both new competition for financing the real economy (between banks and direct lending prosumers) and specific advantages deriving from this net (as a result of an increasingly interconnected financial system) would be foreseeable.[68] Moreover, this could help to fill the gap resulting from the crisis of traditional forms of credit intermediation (Fahlenbrach, R. et al. 2016).

From now on, it must be considered that crowd-businesses have the common feature of matching the opposite interests of an indefinite number of people that accedes to a single network node. As a multilateral phenomenon, the relevant contractual structure can regulate both the access to that node and the matching of the interests. This would lead to a triparty agreement, whereby one party would offer the services and the other two would offer, respectively, the money and the promise to pay the money back (as debt or capital).[69] Hence the simultaneous presence of platform managers, lenders and borrowers (or rather fintechers, entrepreneurs and investors).

From an operational point of view, the potential benefits that firms (especially if small) could obtain from the application of such a financing mechanism are evident; in particular, the cost savings refer to the exploitation of a direct interaction with the lender/investor, as well as the *simplifications* that fintech tools allow in such an environment.[70] Henceforth, in a logical-systematic way, it is possible to conclude what a concrete evaluation of the effectiveness of such a platform would enact.

A careful evaluation of the reasons that may have led fintechers to develop such crowd-businesses suggests to observe both the intention to pursue, through the application of standardized procedures by potential users of the platforms, and the objective of increasing their revenues by offering an alternative to the supervised markets. Hence the prospect of a possible extension of the traditional supervisory backstops and safeguards, perhaps intended to satisfy the needs of small and medium-sized enterprises that cannot match the requirements set forth for the creditworthiness' assessments of banks and financial institutions.[71]

It is worth considering that the growing degree of computer literacy is certainly affecting the development of crowd-businesses; as already mentioned, the latter are based on the use of the self-executing algorithms aimed at taking advantage of the information, ideas and content shared on the web.[72] This is considering not only that the new communication technologies have given rise to the removal of barriers that sometimes hindered the interaction between subjects physically to transform the economic-social reality into a virtually reduced space, but the whole impact of big data on the possibility to develop further chain transactions.[73]

Moreover, it should be noted that the crowdfunding operations manage to combine criteria of economic and financial convenience with personal preferences. Among the latter, the concept of a wired society is certainly exalted, in which investors would benefit from a direct and immediate return due to the *mere* participation in (the financing of) the project.

From a technical point of view, funding (and lending) would make use of the support of different types of platforms and agreements, generally classifiable in the categories of reward-based, donation or pre-selling.[74] Henceforth, the opportunities offered by the implementation of crowd-based techniques should not be underestimated, and the relevant agreements should not be deferred to the sole private autonomy.[75] As already mentioned, the distinctive features of the fintech mechanisms are offering to individuals a solution for participating in a business programme (through debt or equity); however, the arising of a class of 'cybernetic investors', who even though through small sums play the role of a crowd, poses new problems, in terms of both corporate governance and minority shareholders' rights.[76]

Concluding on this topic by questioning whether these platforms are simply confronting inequality would not help to reverse the asymmetries in the capital market. Henceforth, the reason to supervise the crowd-businesses is the straightforward matter of financial stability. Beyond, however, there is the damage that extreme inequality does to the financial environment, to the society, and—in the end—to the democracy.

5.7   Network of Operations: The Need for Transparencies

This analysis—it is worth recalling—is assessing the current need for transparency, required by innovation, competition and sustainability. According to the results shown in the previous chapter, policymakers seem to be able to affect the direction and speed of innovation in the financial sector, and they may prevent fintech firms from challenging the standards set forth by fair antagonism, safe production and harmless risk-taking that can boost the economic growth.[77]

In this context, it is possible to point out the operations involving both fintech firms and traditional financial intermediaries, and to recognize the networks intertwining the relevant relationships that give contents to the agreements among market participants. This would help in understanding whether there are functional, practical and technological connections able to satisfy users' needs faultlessly. Indeed, new entrants in these networks may rise to cause specific concerns, such as the risk that the *winning* technology takes all the customers, service and products, which would lead to the abuse of this *win*. This is not a reason to deny that—in the fintech environment—regulators are in charge of designing networks and the relevant market structure, but it seems that they have to *standardize* the technology (and then the operators that develop its functioning) which is *regulating* the access to the networks of operations used for market-based financing.[78] It is worth mentioning a clever intuition about the possibility that the application of distributed ledger technology to the trading infrastructure could lead to a new form of trading venue.[79] However, it is convenient to save for the last chapter any further consideration on the impact of such innovation on the intertwining of new networks within the forthcoming wired economy based on algorithms and big data analytics.

That said, the analysis is now focusing on the role of contracts in establishing the relationships among several market participants aimed at sharing, managing, covering and transferring money and risks (and other uncertain exposures). Such contracts regulate both the acquisition of the productive factors that are used in performing the core activities of fintech firms and the provision of services that come out from such activity. Hence, it is not useful to deny that private law performs a proper role, even if these contracts arise from the *virtual* meeting of the individuals' willingness, and they rely on standards and other forms developed in market practices (with respect to arrangements that had not ever been codified in the last century) (Haldane, A. 2013).

Scholars must ask themselves, then, whether market practices exploit the master agreement schemes, for both servicing and licensing. It is not necessary to go deeply into the analysis of such contractual structure to appreciate the need for a public intervention, provided that its terms and conditions—as well as the exhibits attached hereto or subsequently entered into by and between the parties—set forth the licensing of software products and the provision of services, which are often jointly offered by fintech firms to their customers. In this respect, this structure may also regulate any further agreement related to additional software or services (by executing a mere form). It also supports the exchange of information and data under the regulation set forth by the parties themselves. However, according to the current regulatory framework on data protection, any big data based upon the other party's confidential information must be protected and managed in accordance with the permission or restriction agreed upon for the basic information.

From a law and economics perspective, such structure creates a permanent connection, which also is the basis for developing a flow (of financial products, personal data and money) that is able to *swell* (as occurs in cases that any other entity adheres to the relevant agreement, as a party or a third-party beneficiary). There is no doubt that such a feature could lead to the sharing of the relevant transactional costs (among a higher number of parties); however, there is the risk of bonding links that share more than the expected, are difficult to dissolve and—in the end—create a path for dependence that reduces competition.

It should also be considered that such networks also share additional services (usually included in relevant web-based platforms) for no additional fees, so the question whether their price has been included in the base amount or rather the price for these services is the usage of the services themselves (and then the collection of the relevant data) (Paech, P. 2016). Hence the opportunity for public assessment over the resources responsible for all the installation, deployment and configuration of the data integration and management platforms, provided that it affects competition, stability and efficiency.

On the contrary, certain additional services would support the implementation of the main platform, and such services could be out of the scope of the original agreement,[80] so that the parties should mutually agree on additional fees. In this respect, reference is not made to the *possibility* to exploit the network, but to the *risk* that the provider may require further tasks or rather the *uncertainty* to accomplish additional objectives, including development, entry into production, operation and maintenance of a particular business case (because of the variability of the relevant costs).

In other words, with platforms come possibilities, risks and uncertainties. This requires continuous activity of consulting and analytics, as well as workflow management and model development, which are fintech activities themselves. The same is true with respect to big data and, then, to the capacity of building in a data asset.

This particular hypothesis leads to question whether the notion of 'product' applies to the object of such platforms. It is acknowledged that fintech allows the circulation of rights and obligations in patterns different from the traditional ones, and according to a paradigm based on the assumption that proprietary commercial software, big data and algorithms are provided in connection with a platform (or rather by means of a network) supported by a set of helpers, models, algorithms, extensions, plug-ins and add-ons. Hence, programmers—directly or indirectly—create the configuration, and the policymakers should assess the relevant duties and responsibilities (even if the programmers believe in the neutrality of the technology with respect to the regulatory options).[81]

Notwithstanding the foregoing, from a regulatory perspective, this analysis is focusing on the possibility that the 'product' refers only to the service provided or the right exchanged (and the relevant payments) through the network, and not the software or the big data that each of the parties develops independently as a result of the networking, nor any other 'material' that the parties have agreed to specifically author or develop for such purposes.

Concluding on this point, it is expectable that such an approach would promote the use of the externalities arising from any network, and it would not prevent any third party from implementing the network's platform (if it were possible and profitable) by creating, developing, building, authoring or using software that partially overlaps the previous platform for any purpose compatible with the individual rights and the master agreement scheme.

5.8   Regulatory Evidences from Insurtech

Considering the reason why policymakers allow voluntary application (or disapplication) of artificial intelligence and big data analytics in the insurance business (Hacker, P. et al. 2018),[82] it should be necessary to point out specific evidences on the role of technological innovation in finance and, in particular, to identify specific applications able to mitigate risks and develop opportunities (EIOPA 2019).[83] Indeed, firms aim at preventing fraud, mitigating threats and managing risk even if the regulator has not set minimum technological requirements able to increase the efficiency in this sector. In this respect, it is worth considering that European regulation on the solvency of insurance undertakings was approved in the first years of the crisis (on 25 November 2009), while the new rules on the insurance distribution are not so old (being this directive enacted on 20 January 2016).[84]

However, none of these directives considers the application of technology as a way to reduce transactional costs, and then encourage customers to undertake insurance policies to cover the risk they bear (Jagtiani, J. A. and Lemieux, C. 2017). Currently, in fact, the EU regulatory framework does not push insurance companies and supervisors to act jointly for developing automated mechanisms (that are able to enhance the accessibility and quality of both data and algorithms) (Susskind, R. and Susskind,

D. 2015), nor to make it compulsory to provide customers with this type of bundling (insurance and data-recording machine or security automation mechanism). Instead, only the relevant industry is promoting the expansion of the automated and semi-automated data recording tools to manage the risk considered in the insurance business. However, notwithstanding the above, high tech is rapidly expanding in use, along with artificial intelligence tools that protect people and goods (and therefore reduce the probability and economic relevance of events covered by the relevant insurance policies).[85] Hence, there is the expectation that a clever public intervention may drive 'client risk-profiling algorithms' (and knowledge of client habits/characteristics) to an adequate classification of the clients and the assignment of an accurate risk profile, together with the possibility to provide customers with a suitable supply of insurance products they really need at the exact price they can pay.[86]

This perspective goes far beyond the current tools for online comparisons of insurance products.[87] It drives to the (almost) full reliance on the aforesaid capacity of big data to self-execute, self-update, self-assess, self-correct and self-execute again. It also involves the management of litigation, whereby the disputes concerning certain risks and events do not involve the outcome of significant negotiations, but the automatic acceptance of standard agreements used to manage certain claims automatically.[88] Moreover, policymakers are not taking into account certain doubts on the current regulatory foundations of the duty of care, data protection and treatment parity. And there is not enough evidence that insurance companies are using technologies and data to reach the aforesaid goals, nor adopting new internal controls aimed at improving the quality of the insurance undertaking. Hence, the need for reshaping the insurance directives with respect to the rules concerning the business conduct, solvency requirements and insurance products distribution.

It is worth mentioning the recital 33 of the Directive (EU) 2016/97, which expressly considers intermediaries and undertakings that advise on, or sell, insurance-based investment products to retail customers.[89] In such cases, these firms need to possess an appropriate level of knowledge and competence in relation to the products offered, and that the relevant employees will be able to share such knowledge with their customers. Indeed, the continuous innovation in the design of insurance products increases the need for understanding their function (as coverage or as an investment or both). The increasing level of complexity requires continuous effort; hence, the customers should be able to rely on the information and quality of distributed services provided.

Indeed, sometimes specific doubts casted the logical admissibility of the automatisms provided for by the algorithms and it seemed to be appropriated to qualify the obligation of the programmers to act with caution; however, it is useful to contemplate that the previously mentioned directive provided that employees should be given adequate time and resources to be able to provide all relevant information to customers about the products that they provide, and it does not regulate the use of comparison tools or rather that the whole process of distribution could be delegated to insurtech mechanisms. Moreover, the regulation does not consider that such mechanisms should influence the quality of service and then the effectiveness of consumer protection (as such, influence is not yet regulated). It refers, in particular, to the risk that more than one intermediary or insurance company applies the same software (and big data analytics), so—as a result—the *agent* would not be able to operate freely in offering its services to the customers (because of the application of automatic and aligned practices that undermine the competition and hinders the proper functioning of the relevant portion of the internal market).[90]

In this context, it is difficult to envisage how the general principle provided under Art. 17 of the Directive (EU) 2016/97 would be restated to cover the insurtech business. However, there is no doubt that insurance distributors that apply high-tech mechanisms must act honestly, fairly and professionally in accordance with the best interests of their customers. So, it is predictable that the programmers of such mechanisms are not remunerated (or do not remunerate or assess the performance of their employees) in a way that conflicts with their duty to act in accordance with the best interests of the customers of their customers.

It follows the matters of conflicts of interest and transparency in a market for 'risks and coverages'. If big data always says the truth, then not anyone would have to inform the insurance company in order to the optimal level of coverage.[91] However, the evidence shows that (big data sets are never complete and) predictive software and artificial intelligence know (or rather, have been programmed to consider that) a harmful truth would be helpful and a harmless lie cannot. Hence, the policymaker should extend all the current safeguards and backstops up to programmers, and then the scope of supervision will include all the firms that participate in the chains aimed at structuring the insurance product and at distributing it.[92] This would suggest updating the regulations based on the target market and the product governance testing, and then setting up a system of analytics aimed at matching the need of the customers with the solvency of the insurance undertakers.

That said, it refers to the duty of care in insurtech, especially when it is supported by smart contracts and tech-filled business models, provided that this duty today relies on the rules provided for the human-based insurance distributing activities.[93] Therefore, the need for regulating new duties goes beyond fair advice, and up to the care of the insurance customer by the application of safe and all-encompassing innovation.

All of the above leads to conclude that fintech is exploiting ideas that are external to banking, finance and insurance to develop the way able to support the circulation of capital and the development of wealth. In this respect, it has been highlighted that the innovation processes are distributed through chain transactions that *open* the aforesaid reserved activities.[94] Therefore, in this perspective, fintech does not pertain only to research and developments, but promote external paths to the capital markets. In the transition to new lifestyles, regulation of insurance companies can play a key role in developing more inclusive and sustainable financial dynamics. There is no doubt that technology can support risk measurement, threat reduction and, ultimately, the flexibility of products offered in the market. Therefore, insurtech qualifies as an opportunity, which the policymakers can regulate to promote new models of sustainable growth, made possible by the proper and generalized application of technology innovations.

NOTES

1. In particular, the analysis refers to ECB. 2018. "Guide to assessments of fintech credit institution licence applications".
2. In addition, see the consideration of Marcacci, A. 2017. "Digitally-provided Financial Services under EU Law: Overcoming the Current Patchwork of Europeanized Private International Law and Sectorially-harmonized National Private Laws" *Studi sull'integrazione europea*; the author begins his analysis from the forward-looking idea of a pan-European private law code merging national legal traditions—both civil and common—and, eventually, replacing them (horizontal approach).
3. Obviously, the role of private law is preeminent; see Paech, P. 2016. "The Governance of Blockchain Financial Networks" *Modern Law Review* p. 1073 ff.

4. See Buchak, G. and Matvos, G. and Piskorski, T. and Seru, A. 2017. "Fintech, Regulatory Arbitrage, and the Rise of Shadow Banks", *NBER Working Paper no 23288*; the authors studied how two forces, regulatory differences and technological advantages, contributed to this growth.

5. See European Commission's Action Plan on how to harness the opportunities presented by technology-enabled innovation in financial services (FinTech), 8 march 2018.

   See also Vezzoso, S. 2018. "Fintech, Access to Data, and the Role of Competition Policy" "Competition and Innovation", São Paulo, on the revised EU Directive on payment services in the internal market (PSD2) that entered into application on 13 January 2018 and introduced a sector-specific data portability rule dubbed access to account, or XS2A.

6. It is remarked by "The Promise of FinTech – Something New Under the Sun?", speech given by Mark Carney, Governor of the Bank of England, Chair of the Financial Stability Board Deutsche Bundesbank G20 conference on "Digitising finance, financial inclusion and financial literacy", Wiesbaden, 25 January 2017.

7. In particular, see Capriglione F. and Sacco Ginevri, A. "Metamorfosi della governance bancaria" Milano, 2019 on the issues in banking and the management of its risks.

8. See Maume, P. 2018. "Reducing Legal Uncertainty and Regulatory Arbitrage for Robo-Advice" *European Company and Financial Law Review*, which argues that robo-advisers provide investment advice within the meaning provided by MiFiDII. Hence, they are subject to authorization by the national regulator and ongoing conduct requirements. It might be tempting to introduce regulatory sandboxes to address the persisting legal uncertainties in practice, but such a regulatory change does not seem likely in the near future. Instead, regulatory arbitrage should be reduced by a uniform application of the MiFiDII framework throughout the EU to the fintech business also.

9. Moreover, see Varian, H. R. 2014. "Big Data: New tricks for econometrics" *Journal of Economic Perspectives*. P. 3 ff.; the author began his analysis by describing how computers are now involved in many economic transactions and can capture data associated with these transactions, which can then be manipulated and analysed. The author also described a few of these tools for manipulating and analysing big data.

10. It refers specifically to FSB 2017, "Artificial intelligence and machine learning in financial services," November, on the need of technological applications to *deal* with big data and greater computing power.

11. Furthermore, see Bholat, D. 2015. "Big data and central banks" *Big Data & Society*, which recalled one standard definition of Big Data: "It is data displaying one or more of the following characteristics: (a) These data are

of high volume, often because data are reported on a granular basis, that is, item-by-item, for example, loan-by-loan or security-by-security; (b) these data are of high velocity, because these data are frequently updated and, at the limit, collected and analysed in real-time; (c) these data are qualitatively various, meaning they are either non-numeric, such as text or video, or they are extracted from novel sources, such as social media, Internet search records or biometric sensors."

12. Moreover, see Cœuré, B. 2017. "Policy analysis with big data. Speech by the member of the Executive Board of the ECB, at the conference on Economic and Financial Regulation in the Era of Big Data", Banque de France, Paris, 24 November who recalls Tissot, B. 2017. "Big data and central banking", IFC Bulletin No 44; indeed, big data usually refers to unstructured data resulting from non-statistical activity and/or structured data that create operational challenges owing to their size or complexity; see for example, Nymand-Andersen, P. 2015. "Big data: the hunt for timely insights and decision certainty: Central banking reflections on the use of big data for policy purposes", IFC Working Paper No 14.

13. It is worth considering the authors that went deep into this issue; see Dehaene, S. 2009 "Origins of Mathematical Intuitions: The Case of Arithmetic". *Annals of the New York Academy of Sciences*, p. 1156; Burr, D. and Ross, J. 2008 "A Visual Sense of Number" *Current Biology* p. 425 ff.; Izard, V. and Dehaene, S. 2008. "Calibrating the mental number line" *Cognition* p. 1221 ff.; Burr, D. and Ross, J. 2008 "Response: Visual number" *Current Biology* p. 18 f.; Durgin, F. H 2008 "Texture density adaptation and visual number revisited". *Current Biology*.

14. It recalls FSB 2017. "Artificial intelligence and machine learning in financial services. Market developments and financial stability implications", p. 4 ff. In addition, see Ward, J. S. and Barker, A. 2013 "Undefined By Data: A Survey of Big Data Definitions" Cornell University research paper no. arXiv:1309.5821.

15. It refers to American Psychological Association 2013 "Glossary of psychological terms". Apa.org. Retrieved 2014-08-13.

16. In particular, it recalls Schumpeter, J. 1942, "Capitalism, socialism and democracy, (ed. 1994, Abingdon-on-Thames, p. 83.

17. See Arrow, K. J. 1971, "Essays in theory of risk bearing", Chicago, p. 224.
    See, on this topic, Savelyev, A. 2016 "Contract Law 2.0: 'Smart' Contracts As the Beginning of the End of Classic Contract Law" *Higher School of Economics Research Paper No. WP BRP 71/LAW/2016*, about the issues in aligning the powers of the government with distributed technologies.

18. See Williamson, O.E. 1985 "The economic institution of capitalisms", London, p. 404.

19. It refers to Posner, R. 2008 "How Judges think", Harvard, p. 230. See also Hermalin, B. E. and Katz, A. W. and Craswell, R. 2006 "The Law and Economics of Contracts" *Columbia Law and Economics Working Paper No. 296*, in respect of four topic areas that correspond to the major doctrinal divisions of the law of contracts. These areas include freedom of contract (i.e., the scope of private power to create binding obligations), formation of contracts (both the procedural mechanics of exchange and the rules that govern pre-contractual behaviour), contract interpretation (what consequences follow when agreements are ambiguous or incomplete) and enforcement of contractual obligations.

    This refers also to Boschetti, B. 2016. "Soft law e normatività: un'analisi comparata" *Rivista della Regolazione dei mercati*, p. 32 ff.; the author's analysis highlights the variety of phenomena that fall into the soft law category and the many roles played by soft law at different levels (including the interinstitutional one). This author pointed out that it is precisely in this wider context that the regulative and regulatory functions of soft law come to light. In all of the legal systems examined, soft law shows itself to be an extraordinary instrument, playing a key role in ensuring and guaranteeing the effectiveness, balance and dynamicity of the legal system itself. Furthermore, the author refers to these multiple roles that are strengthened and underpinned by legislators, who implement mechanisms that not only permit soft law to accede to the field of normativity, but also encourage compliance with it by increasing the costs of non-compliance by the imposition of duties, such as the duty to report non-compliance, to give reasons for non-compliance, to disclose the names of those who are not in compliance with soft law, thereby ensuring the effectiveness of soft law and, ultimately, the regulatory process itself.

20. It recalls Bank of England 2014 "Strategic plan: Background information".
21. "Big data is the term increasingly used to describe the process of applying serious computing power—the latest in machine learning and artificial intelligence—to seriously massive and of- ten highly complex sets of information", see "The Big Bang: How the Big Data Explosion Is Changing the World – Microsoft UK Enterprise Insights Blog – Site Home – MSDN Blogs".
22. See Wibisono, O. and Ari, H. D. and Widjanarti, A. and Andhika Zulen, A. and Tissot, B. "The use of big data analytics and artificial intelligence in central banking" *IFC Bulletin no. 50*, which analysed the various aspects related to the use of big data (associated techniques by central banks), and covered three main aspects: (1) an assessment of the main big data sources and associated analytical techniques that are relevant for central banks; (2) the insights provided by big data for economic policy, with an overview of concrete central bank projects aiming at improving statistical information,

macroeconomic analysis and forecasting, financial market monitoring and financial risk assessment; and (3) the use of big data in crafting central bank policies, including organisational aspects and related challenges.

23. See Williamson, O. E. 1985. "The economic institution of capitalisms", London, p. 399, which recalls Kronman, A. T. 1985, "Contract law and the state of nature" *Journal of law, economics and organization*

24. It recalls Bholat, D 2013. "The future of central bank data". *Journal of Banking Regulation* p. 185 ff.; see also Buzzi, F. 2005, "La teologia per il diritto dell'uomo e dei popoli" *Iustitia* p. 269 ff., and Bianco Alberto, A. 1981, "La grazia perfeziona la natura. Il fondamento scritturistico del diritto naturale" *Studi cattolici*, p. 266 ff.

25. This remarks the conclusions of Edwards, l. 2016. "Privacy, Security and Data Protection in Smart Cities: A Critical EU Law Perspective" *European Data Protection Law Review*, which argues that smart cities combine the three greatest current threats to personal privacy, with which regulation has so far failed to deal effectively; the Internet of Things (IoT) or "ubiquitous computing"; "Big Data"; and the Cloud. He seeks solutions both from legal institutions such as data protection law and from "code", proposing in particular from the ethos of Privacy by Design, a new "social impact assessment" and new human: computer interactions to promote user autonomy in ambient environments.

26. It includes a reference to Diebold, F. X. 2012. "On the Origin(s) and Development of the Term 'Big Data'" *PIER Working Paper No. 12-037*, which highlighted that the first significant academic references (independent of each other and of Silicon Graphics) appear to be Weiss and Indurkhya (1998) in computer science and Diebold (2000) in statistics/econometrics. Douglas Laney of Gartner also produced insightful work (again unpublished and non-academic) slightly later. According to this author, the term is now firmly entrenched, but the phenomenon continues unabated, and the discipline is still emerging.

27. See Kache, F. 2015. "Dealing with digital information richness in supply chain management. A review and a big data analytics approach" Kassel, who questioned what are the implication of these analytics on information usage at corporate level.

  See also Beyer, M. A. and Laney, D. 2012. "The importance of big data: A definition". Stamford, CT: Gartner.

28. Therefore, this part of the research will not go deeply into the analysis of the regulation provided for the protection of the above rights, due to the current pro-sharing behaviour of people.

  On this point, see Tene, O. and Polonetsky, J. 2013. "Big Data for All: Privacy and User Control in the Age of Analytics" *Northwestern Journal of Technology and Intellectual Property*, which highlighted that data are now available for analysis in raw form, escaping the confines of structured databases and enhancing researchers' abilities to identify correlations and conceive of new, unanticipated uses for existing information. In addition, the increasing number of people, devices and sensors that are now connected by digital networks has revolutionized the ability to generate, communicate, share and access data.

See also Rubinstein, I. 2012. "Big Data: The End of Privacy or a New Beginning?" *NYU School of Law, Public Law Research Paper No. 12-56*; Wachter, S. and Mittelstadt, B. 2018. "A Right to Reasonable Inferences: Re-Thinking Data Protection Law in the Age of Big Data and AI" *Columbia Business Law Review*, which argued that a new data protection right, the 'right to reasonable inferences', is needed to help close the accountability gap currently posed by 'high risk inferences', meaning inferences drawn from big data analytics that damage privacy or reputation, or have low verifiability in the sense of being predictive or opinion-based while being used in important decisions.

It is worth mention that—according to these authors—this right would require ex-ante justification to be given by the data controller to establish whether an inference is reasonable. Hence, this disclosure would address (1) why certain data form a normatively acceptable basis from which to draw inferences; (2) why these inferences are relevant and normatively acceptable for the chosen processing purpose or type of automated decision; and (3) whether the data and methods used to draw the inferences are accurate and statistically reliable. However, the ex ante justification is bolstered by an additional ex post mechanism enabling unreasonable inferences to be challenged.

29. In addition, it is worth considering the analysis of Dijcks, J. P. 2012. "Oracle: Big data for the enterprise". *Oracle White Paper*

30. In addition, it recalls the considerations of Taylor, L. and Schroeder, R. and Meyer, E. 2014. "Emerging practices and perspectives on Big Data analysis in economics: Bigger and better or more of the same?" *Big Data & Society*

31. Reference is made to Google, 2013. "Google Trends for Big Data". It is worth considering also Tene, O. 2007, "What Google Knows: Privacy and Internet Search Engines" *Utah Law Review*; Preis, T. and Moat, H. S. and Stanley, H. E. 2013, "Quantifying Trading Behavior in Financial Markets Using Google Trends" *Scientific Reports* p. 1684 ff.; Newman, N. 2014, "Search, Antitrust and the Economics of the Control of User Data" *Yale Journal on Regulation* and their focus on the control of personal data by corporations, which can entrench monopoly power in an economy shaped increasingly by the power of big data.

32. In particular, it can be noted that Cohen, J. E. 2012 "What Privacy Is For" *Harvard Law Review*, considered that the efforts to repackage pervasive

surveillance as innovation—under the moniker "Big Data"—are better understood as efforts to enshrine the methods and values of the modulated society at the heart of the system of knowledge production. In short, privacy incursions harm individuals, but not only individuals. Privacy incursions in the name of progress, innovation and ordered liberty jeopardize the continuing vitality of the political and intellectual culture.

33. See Banterle, F. 2018, "Data Ownership in the Data Economy: A European Dilemma" *EU Internet Law in the digital era*, whose analysis refers to the question arising where a multitude of actors interact in the elaboration of data: Who owns the data? Indeed, according to this author, while organized data sets can be subject to intellectual property rights, and the use of personal data is regulated by data protection laws, this question particularly applies to raw (machine-generated) data, which are increasing their value as a source of precious insights and fall outside the scope of classical ownership/property schemes.

34. See Grossman, R. and Siegel, K. 2014. "Organizational Models for Big Data and Analytics" *Journal of Organization Design*, p. 20 ff.

See also Kitchin, R. 2014, "Thinking Critically About and Researching Algorithms" *The Programmable City Working Paper 5*, which starts from the consideration that the era of ubiquitous computing and big data is now firmly established, with more and more aspects of the everyday lives being mediated, augmented, produced and regulated by digital devices and networked systems powered by software.

35. It refers to Cœuré, B. 2017. "Policy analysis with big data. Speech by the Member of the Executive Board of the ECB, at the conference on Economic and Financial Regulation in the Era of Big Data", Banque de France, Paris, 24 November 2017.

36. It recalls also Maume, P. 2018. "Reducing Legal Uncertainty and Regulatory Arbitrage for Robo-Advice" *European Company and Financial Law Review*, which highlighted that regulators and courts should also be aware that software replacing human advisers diverges from the basic idea of human interaction that forms the basis of contract law. Indeed, it seemed that investment firms were able to use new technology in the services they provide. However, as this means introducing new risks for investors, the investment firm should be subject to a strict liability regime for failures of the respective technology (e.g. the unavailability of the service).

37. Moreover, see Gebauer, S. and Mazelis, F. 2019. "Macroprudential Regulation and Leakage to the Shadow Banking Sector" *DIW Berlin Discussion Paper No. 1814*, which developed a model that differentiates between regulated, monopolistically competitive commercial banks and a shadow banking system that relies on funding in a perfectly competitive market for investments.

38. It is worth referring to the research of Barth, J. R. and Caprio, G. and Levine, R. E. 2001. "The Regulation and Supervision of Banks Around the World: A New Database" *World Bank Policy Research Working Paper No. 2588* for a comprehensive analysis of the following aspects of banking: entry requirements, ownership restrictions, capital requirements, activity restrictions, external auditing requirements, characteristics of deposit insurance schemes, loan classification and provisioning requirements, accounting and disclosure requirements, troubled bank resolution actions, and (uniquely) the quality of supervisory personnel and their actions.

39. Furthermore, see Ait-Sahalia, Y. and Karaman, M. and Mancini, L. 2018. "The Term Structure of Variance Swaps and Risk Premia" *Swiss Finance Institute Research Paper No. 18-37* about a model-free analysis that reveals a significant price jump component in variance swap rates.

40. It recalls Tene, O. and Polonetsky, J. 2013. "Big Data for All: Privacy and User Control in the Age of Analytics" *Northwestern Journal of Technology and Intellectual Property*, which pointed out that data creates enormous value for the world economy, driving innovation, productivity, efficiency and growth. At the same time, the 'data deluge' presents privacy concerns which could stir a regulatory backlash dampening the data economy and stifling innovation. In order to craft a balance between beneficial uses of data and in individual privacy, policymakers must address some of the most fundamental concepts of privacy law, including the definition of 'personally identifiable information', the role of individual control, and the principles of data minimization and purpose limitation.

   These authors emphasized the importance of providing individuals with access to their data in usable format, in order to conclude that this will let individuals share the wealth created by their information and incentivize developers to offer user-side features and applications harnessing the value of big data. Hence, where individual access to data is impracticable, data are likely to be deidentified to an extent sufficient to diminish privacy concerns. This research shows, in addition, that organizations should be required to disclose their decisional criteria, since in a big data world it is often not the data but rather the inferences drawn from them that give cause for concern.

41. It refers to uncertainty "in a sense radically distinct from the familiar notion of risk", hence the option to report the first term only to non-measurable criticalities, and the second to the predictable and measurable negative events (the so-called expected losses). See Knight, F. 1921 "Risk, Uncertainty, and Profit", (Ed. 2009) Cambridge, where it is highlighted that "the difficulties ... arisen from a confusion of ideas which goes deep down into the foundations of our thinking."

42. In particular, it can be recalled Morellec, E. and Wang, N. 2004. "Capital Structure, Investment, and Private Benefits of Control" *Simon Business School Working Paper No. FR04-17*, which examined the impact of the opportunistic behaviour of the controlling shareholder on investment and financing decisions.

43. These considerations recall Buchak, G. and Matvos, G. and Piskorski, T. and Seru, A. 2017. "Fintech, Regulatory Arbitrage, and the Rise of Shadow Banks", NBER Working Paper no 23288, with respect to the conclusion that a difference—in difference tests exploiting geographical heterogeneity—induced by four specific increases in regulatory burden—capital requirements, mortgage servicing rights, mortgage-related lawsuits, and the movement of supervision to Office of Comptroller and Currency following closure of the Office of Thrift Supervision—reveals that traditional banks contracted in markets where they faced more regulatory constraints; shadow banks partially filled these gaps.

44. It is worth adding that Brito, J. and Shadab, H. B. and Castillo O'Sullivan, A. 2014. "Bitcoin Financial Regulation: Securities, Derivatives, Prediction Markets, and Gambling" *Columbia Science and Technology Law Review* suggested that—to the extent regulation and enforcement becomes more costly than its benefits—policymakers should consider and pursue strategies consistent with that new reality, such as efforts to encourage resilience and adaptation.

45. In addition, see Chesbrough, H. and Bogers, M. 2014. "Explicating Open Innovation: Clarifying an Emerging Paradigm for Understanding Innovation" "New Frontiers in Open Innovation", Oxford who clarify and develop the conceptualization of open innovation, which can be defined as a distributed innovation process based on purposively managed knowledge flows across organizational boundaries, using pecuniary and non-pecuniary mechanisms in line with the organization's business model.

    See also Sandulli, F. D. and Chesbrough, H. 2009. "The Two Sides of Open Business Models" *SSRN research paper no. 1325682* about the role of key resources, and how they can be aggregated into open business models.

46. It includes the conclusion of Arner, D. W. and Barberis, J. N. and Buckley, R. P. 2016. "FinTech, RegTech and the Reconceptualization of Financial Regulation" *University of Hong Kong Faculty of Law Research Paper No. 2016/035*, which argued that, whilst the principal regulatory objectives (e.g. financial stability, prudential safety and soundness, consumer protection and market integrity, and market competition and development) remain, their means of application are increasingly becoming inadequate. Regtech developments are leading towards a paradigm shift necessitating the reconceptualization of financial regulation.

47. It is remarkable that Maume, P. 2018, "Regulating Robo-Advisory" *Texas International Law Journal*, referred to them as internet-based advisory services that use algorithms to create investment recommendations with no human input. The author argues that robo-advisory is essentially different from traditional financial advice. Nevertheless, it demonstrates that current regulation, in particular the European Union framework for financial intermediaries, is able to address most of the resulting issues. The core conclusion is that, in applying the existing rules to robo-advisors, the rules should not be interpreted to create a level-playing field for all market participants.

    See also Maume, P. 2018. "Reducing Legal Uncertainty and Regulatory Arbitrage for Robo-Advice" European Company and Financial Law Review, which pointed out that the nature of the interaction between client and machine raises many legal questions under the applicable EU regulation.

48. The analysis may include also a reference to Sanz Bayón, P. and Vega, L. G. 2018. "Automated Investment Advice: Legal Challenges and Regulatory Questions" *Banking & Financial Services Policy Report*, which examined the basics of the automated investment advice (Robo-Advisory), attempted a definition and a taxonomy, lays the necessary groundwork for analysing this phenomenon, and offered a broad framework to allow a better understanding of the current legal situation of Robo-Advisory.

49. See, on this point, Gomber, P. and Kauffman, R. J. and Parker, C. and Weber, B. 2017. " On the Fintech Revolution: Interpreting the Forces of Innovation, Disruption and Transformation in Financial Services" *Journal of Management Information Systems*, p. 220 ff.; the authors discuss: (1) operations management in financial services, and the changes that are occurring there; (2) technology innovations that have begun to leverage the execution and stakeholder value associated with payments settlement, cryptocurrencies, blockchain technologies and cross-border payment services; (3) multiple fintech innovations that have impacted lending and deposit services, peer-to-peer (P2P) lending and the use of social media; (4) issues with respect to investments, financial markets, trading, risk management, robo-advisory and related services that are influenced by blockchain and fintech innovations.

50. It recalls Maume, P. 2017. "In Unchartered Territory – Banking Supervision Meets Fintech" *Corporate Finance* p. 373 ff., which lays out the current German legal framework, considering that, in the EU credit institutions and financial service providers, including outsourcing, are regulated under EU laws, most notably Directive 2014/65/EU ('MiFiD2'), Directive 2013/36/EU ('CRD IV') and Regulation (EU) 575/2013 ('CRR'). Within this framework, the author discusses the trend towards

cooperation between banks and fintechers, the applicable legal framework, potential banking license requirements and the obstacles of outsourcing of banking functions to fintechers under the current framework.

51. See Zirpoli, F. and Becker, M. C. 2008. "Organizing Complex Product Development: Outsourcing, Performance Integration and the Role of Product Architecture" *SSRN research paper no. 1087236*, which questions the key micro-organizational decisions for seizing the benefits of a networked innovation strategy. The authors show that managers can greatly benefit from focusing their attention on the organizational aspects of leveraging external sources of innovation and adjusting their innovation strategy, including 'make or buy' choices, accordingly. Hence, they propose to consider strategic and micro-organizational decisions as tightly coupled and mutually influencing in the context of complex product development.

52. It remarks the findings of Ban, G. Y. and Rudin, C. 2018. "The Big Data Newsvendor: Practical Insights from Machine Learning" *Operations Research 67* who investigated the data-driven newsvendor problem when one has n observations of p features related to the demand as well as historical demand data. The authors proposed solving the 'Big Data' newsvendor problem via single-step machine learning algorithms. Specifically, they refer to algorithms based on the Empirical Risk Minimization (ERM) principle, with and without regularization, and an algorithm based on Kernel-weights Optimization (KO).

53. See Marcacci, A. 2017. "Digitally-provided Financial Services under EU Law: Overcoming the Current Patchwork of Europeanized Private International Law and Sectorially-harmonized National Private Laws" *Studi sull'integrazione europea.*

54. See Torresetti, R. and Nordio, C., 2014. "Scaling Operational Loss Data and Its Systemic Risk Implications" *SSRN Research paper no. 2360483.*

It is worth considering Jacobsen, S. F. and Tschoegl, A. E. 1997. "The Norwegian Banks in the Nordic Consortia: A Case of International Strategic Alliances in Banking" *SSRN research paper no 52068*. On this topic, see also Mainelli, M. and Smith, M. 2015. "Sharing Ledgers for Sharing Economies: An Exploration of Mutual Distributed Ledgers (Aka Blockchain Technology)" *Journal of Financial Perspectives.*

55. It is worth considering the conclusions of Maine, H. J. S. 1861. "Ancient law" (ed. 2005) p. 170.

56. Let us recall Greco, P. 1930. "Le operazioni di banca", Padova on the tendence to form special kind of agreement to regulate the operations of banking and finance, who admitted that looking for the essential element in the economic function and the corresponding legal structure of bank contracts, bringing them back and framing them in the general system of

legal acts, are among the most difficult tasks, but also the most attractive for the lawyer.

57. See Lobel, O. 2016. "The Law of the Platform" *Minnesota Law Review*, which assumed that *unsurprisingly* the platform economy defies conventional regulatory theory. Indeed, the author poses a foundational inquiry: Do the regulations carry over to the platform economy?

58. See, in this respect, Jagtiani, J. A. and Lemieux, C. 2017. "Fintech Lending: Financial Inclusion, Risk Pricing, and Alternative Information" *FRB of Philadelphia Working Paper No. 17-17*, whose conclusions highlighted that Fintech has been playing an increasing role in shaping financial and banking landscapes.

59. In addition, see Van Loo, R. 2018. "Making Innovation More Competitive: The Case of Fintech" *UCLA Law Review*, which highlighted that innovation has raised the stakes for fixing this structural flaw. However, the author suggests that if allowed to compete fully, financial technology challengers could bring large consumer welfare advances and reduce the size of "Too Big To Fail" banks, thereby lessening the chances of a financial crisis. Furthermore, if allowed to grow unchecked, either fintech start-ups or the big banks acquiring them may reach the size of technology giants, thereby increasing systemic risk. Hence, the author concludes that if the goal is to benefit consumers, strengthen markets, or prevent crises, a reallocation of competition authority would better position regulators to navigate the future of innovation.

60. Let us recall the Italian experience on the unlawful banking in absence of the relevant authorization; see Severino, P. 2000. "Le disposizioni integrative e correttive del Testo Unico delle leggi in materia bancaria e creditizia. Il quadro sanzionatorio: innovazioni nelle fattispecie e nella procedura applicativa" *Diritto della banca e del mercato finanziario*; Capriglione, F. 1997. "La problematica della "banca di fatto" dopo il d.lg. 385/1993" *La nuova giurisprudenza civile commentata*; Cantone, R. 1996. "L'abusivismo finanziario: esperienze da un'indagine giudiziaria. Nota a Cass. sez. V pen. 6 ottobre 1995" *Cassazione penale*, p. 3122 ff.; Criscuolo, L. "L'esercizio abusivo di attività finanziaria: profili giuridici e strumenti di contrasto" *Cassazione penale*, 1996, p. 1334.

61. Moreover, see Capriglione, F. and Masera, R. 2016. "Bank Corporate Governance: A New Paradigm" *Open Review of Management, Banking and Finance*. See also Canova, T. A. 2009. "Financial Market Failure as a Crisis in the Rule of Law: From Market Fundamentalism to a New Keynesian Regulatory Model" *Harvard Law & Policy Review*; Gadinis, S. 2013. "From Independence to Politics in Financial Regulation" UC Berkeley Public Law Research Paper No. 2137215.

62. It refers to Kumar, A. and Jacobson, S. H. 1998. "Optimal and Near-Optimal Decisions for Procurement and Allocation of a Critical Resource with a Stochastic Consumption Rate" University of Michigan Business School Working Paper No. 98019, which—using the illustration of a periodic-review, stochastic-demand, fixed-route, centralized, multi-echelon distribution system—proposed a non-ranking allocation policy that is faster than those existing in the literature and also develop an optimal replenishment algorithm that is independent of the allocation assumption.

63. See Zetzsche, D. A. and Preiner, C. 2017. "Cross-Border Crowdfunding – Towards a Single Crowdfunding Market for Europe" *University of Luxembourg Law Working Paper No. 2017/002*; the authors—in contrast to the European Commission's Capital Market Action Plan—take the view that national limitations on crowd investing and crowd lending de facto are the result of limits de jure.

   In particular, the authors detailed how European regulators could facilitate a Single European Crowdfunding Market while limiting both the risks for investors and the regulatory burden for crowdfunding platforms and recipients. In light of the regulatory experience with other financial products and the segregating effect of product-based approaches, many of which exist in the EU/EEA Member States, they believed that existing product regulation is insufficient to enable a European cross-border crowdfunding market. Instead, regulation based on the 'MiFID light' framework could function as basis for a cross-border crowdfunding manager passport, given the minimum protection it affords both investors and the financial system, and the low costs it imposes on the platform.

64. Furthermore, see Scott, K. E. 2009. "Lessons from the Crisis" *Stanford Law and Economics Olin Working Paper No. 385*, which provided a simplified approach based on three stages: first, a look at the key factors that led to the increasing riskiness of US home mortgages; second, how those risks were transmitted as securities from US housing lenders to institutional investors around the globe; and third, how those risks led to huge losses and created a credit crunch that moved the impact from the financial economy to the real economy and produced a severe recession. Then there is a factual foundation for deriving the lessons that ought to be taken away from this very expensive experience.

   See also Masera, R. 2013. "US Basel III Final Rule on Banks' Capital Requirements: A Different-Size-Fits-All Approach" PSL Quarterly Review; Popov, A. A. and Udell, G. F. 2010. "Cross-Border Banking and the International Transmission of Financial Distress During the Crisis of 2007-2008" *ECB Working Paper No. 1203*; Chan-Lau, J. A. and Chen, Z. 1998. "Financial Crisis and Credit Crunch as a Result of Inefficient

Financial Intermediation—With Reference to the Asian Financial Crisis" *IMF Working Paper No. 98/127.*

65. In the light of the financial constraints that the operators have had to face, some phenomena of small entity (which, in a different socio-economic context, would not have aroused any interest in the market) end up taking on importance. It is referring to activities to which it is certainly not possible to attribute significance on the level of their concrete contribution to the processes of economic development; see Mollick, E. R. 2013. "The Dynamics of Crowdfunding: An Exploratory Study" *Journal of Business Venturing.*

66. It raises a reference to Glinavos, I. 2010. "Regulation and the Role of Law in Economic Crisis" *European Business Law Review,* which offers a discussion on the relationship of deregulation to financial crisis, arguing that there is a direct link between the receding reach of the state and market instability, drawing analogies with previous instances of market failure, like the Great Depression. On the basis of this connection, a theoretical portrayal of perceptions of the role of law in modern capitalism is attempted, where the main message is that dominant modern perceptions of the state market relationship allow a role for regulation but still do not recognize the state as the legitimate author of such regulation, showing a preference for market-led solutions.

67. In this respect, it brings up the conclusions of Jagtiani, J. A. and Lemieux, C. 2017. "Fintech Lending: Financial Inclusion, Risk Pricing, and Alternative Information" *FRB of Philadelphia Working Paper No. 17-17,* which find that Lending Club's consumer-lending activities have penetrated areas that could benefit from additional credit supply, such as areas that lose bank branches and those in highly concentrated banking markets. Moreover, the authors find a high correlation with interest rate spreads, Lending Club rating grades, and loan performance.

68. It refers also to Bernstein, S. and Korteweg, A. G. and Laws, K. 2015. "Attracting Early Stage Investors: Evidence from a Randomized Field Experiment" *Stanford University Graduate School of Business Research Paper No. 14-17,* which used a randomized field experiment to identify which start-up characteristics are most important to investors in early stage firms.

69. It is worth considering the options of the Italian legislator, who has regulated the crowd-businesses, in the wake of what has already been achieved in the United States with the introduction of the JOBS Act (Jumpstart Our Business Startups Act) of April 2012. This refers in particular to Legislative Decree no. 179 of 18 October 2012, called 'Crescita Bis' and converted with amendments by Law no. 221 of 17 December 2012, which introduced the regulation of equity crowdfunding (as well as its application to

financing processes for the so-called innovative start-ups) as part of specific measures aimed at boosting competition, the development of national infrastructures and the competitiveness of the internal market.

70. See again Zetzsche, D. A. and Preiner, C. 2017. "Cross-Border Crowdfunding – Towards a Single Crowdfunding Market for Europe" University of Luxembourg Law Working Paper No. 2017/002, which— following the (1) too-small-to-care, (2) too-large-to-ignore, and (3) too-big-to-fail development path of FinTech business models—suggested adding a relevance threshold of €250,000 in transaction volume to the MiFID light framework and imposing regulation to address systemic risk concerns for very large crowdfunding platforms that may arise in the future.

71. It is worth considering also Kaminski, J. and Hopp, C. and Tykvova, T. 2019. "New Technology Assessment in Entrepreneurial Financing – Can Crowdfunding Predict Venture Capital Investments?" *Technological Forecasting and Social Change* whose *cointegration* tests suggest a long-run relationship between crowdfunding and venture capital investments, while impulse response functions indicate a positive effect running from crowd-funding to venture capital within two to six months.

72. See Haldane, A. and Shanbhogue, R. and Attanasio, O. and Besley, T. J. and Lindert, P. H. and Piketty, T. and Ventura, K. 2015. "Capital in the 21st Century" *Bank of England Quarterly Bulletin 2015 Q1*, which presented research on various issues relating to inequality, including: access to education; wealth and taxation policy; and the role of governance and institutions.

See also Upadhyay, V. 2015. "Can Capitalism Survive High Degree of Automation? A Comparison with Thomas Piketty's Argument" *SSRN Research Paper no. 2558989*; Magness, P. and Murphy, R. P. 2014. "Challenging the Empirical Contribution of Thomas Piketty's Capital in the 21st Century" *Journal of Private Enterprise*

73. In this way, the availability of various forms of network has allowed the dissemination of multiple business projects, underlying the development of innovative ideas (especially in the fields of art, music, film, as well as dona-tions to solidarity and social utility).

74. In a nutshell, there is a modus operandi that involves a review of the fees of the credit intermediation activity; this is because, against the disburse-ment made by the saver, the appointed mechanisms of financing do not provide for an immediate counter-value (monetary and/or material) to be allocated to the latter. In addition, there are the operational peculiarities found in online social lending platforms, aimed at satisfying the credit needs of private individuals (sometimes the ones falling into the categories of 'non-bankable' individuals), who interact with each other through direct meeting mechanisms (in the so-called peer-to-peer mode) resulting

in the creation of alternative financing channels to those provided by banking intermediaries.

75. In addition, see Cumming, D. J. and Johan, S. A. and Zhang, Y. 2019. "The Role of Due Diligence in Crowdfunding Platforms" *Journal of Banking and Finance*, which pointed out that that due diligence is related to legislation requirement, platform size and type or complexity of crowdfunding campaigns.

76. See Omarova, S. T. 2019 "New Tech v. New Deal: Fintech As A Systemic Phenomenon" *Yale Journal on Regulation* on *how* and *why* specific fintech applications—cryptocurrencies, distributed ledger technologies, digital crowdfunding and robo-advising—are poised to amplify the effect of these destabilizing mechanisms, and thus potentially exacerbate the tensions and imbalances in today's financial markets and the broader economy. It is this potential that renders fintech a public policy challenge of the highest order. The author introduced the concept of the New Deal settlement in finance: a fundamental political arrangement, in force for nearly a century, pursuant to which profit-seeking private actors retain control over allocating capital and generating financial risks, while the sovereign public bears responsibility for maintaining systemic financial stability. Moreover, He presented an alternative account of fintech as a systemic, macro-level phenomenon: grounding his analysis of evolving fintech trends in a broader institutional context, exposes the normative and political significance of the current fintech moment. It argues that the arrival of fintech enables a potentially decisive shift in the underlying public–private balance of powers, competencies and roles in the financial system.

77. See Masera, R. 2011. "Taking the Moral Hazard Out of Banking: The Next Fundamental Step in Financial Reform" *PSL Quarterly Review*, which highlighted that the path between financial meltdown and moral hazard in banking is, at best, narrow and impervious. Moreover, the author pointed out that, during the financial crisis, public support became the standard response to save the banks in difficulty, heightening and broadening the moral hazard issue: subordinated/senior debt holders and large depositors were bailed out and equity holders were partially sheltered. In the Eurozone, the implicit promise to bail out governments in difficulty has encouraged SIFIs and other financial operators to speculate on the yield differential between sovereigns and the ECB money market interest rates. The policy framework proposed here is two-pronged: the EFSF should evolve to permit more flexible and wide-ranging interventions, and be able to manage sovereign debt restructuring; with respect to SIFIs, very early corporate, market and supervisory responses are suggested. Intervention of supervisory authorities with mandatory (special) powers

would occur before the threshold of non-viability and, on a gone-concern basis, in terms of a European resolution procedure.

See also Rifkin, J. 2014 "The Zero Marginal Cost Society: The Internet of Things, the Collaborative Commons, and the Eclipse of Capitalism". New York

78. Moreover, see Buchak, G. and Matvos, G. and Piskorski, T. and Seru, A. 2017. "Fintech, Regulatory Arbitrage, and the Rise of Shadow Banks", NBER Working Paper no 23288, which pointed out that fintech lenders appear to offer a higher-quality product and charge a premium of 14–16 basis points. Relative to other lenders, they seem to use different information to set interest rates. A quantitative model of mortgage lending suggests that regulation accounts for roughly 60% of shadow bank growth, while technology accounts for roughly 30%.

79. In addition, it is worth considering that the above is in line with the first attempts made to clarify the contents of this phenomena; see Lucantoni, P. 2019. "Distributed ledger techonology e infrastrutture di negoziazione e post-trading", in VV.AA., "Fintech: diritto, tecnologia e finanza", Roma, p. 97 ff.

80. Furtheromore, see Maume, P. 2018. "Reducing Legal Uncertainty and Regulatory Arbitrage for Robo-Advice" *European Company and Financial Law Review* who pointed out that the nature of the interaction between client and machine raises many legal questions under the applicable EU regulation. See also Maume, P. 2018. "Regulating Robo-Advisory" *Texas International Law Journal*.

81. Obviously, this refers also to any format, including any improvements, modifications, derivative works, patches, updates and upgrades thereto.

82. In particular, it refers to Hacker, P. and Lianos, I. and Dimitropoulos, G. and Eich, E. 2018. "Regulating Blockchain: Techno-Social and Legal Challenges" "Regulating Blockchain. Techno-Social and Legal Challenges", Oxford; see also—on this point—the considerations of Powell, L. 2017. "Big Data and Regulation in the Insurance Industry" *SSRN Research Paper no. 2951306.*

83. See Malhotra, Y. 2016. "Beyond Model Risk Management to Model Risk Arbitrage for FinTech Era: How to Navigate 'Uncertainty'...When 'Models' Are 'Wrong'...And Knowledge'...'Imperfect'! Knight Reconsidered Again: Risk, Uncertainty, & Profit Beyond ZIRP & NIRP! *Research Presentation at: 2016 Princeton Quant Trading Conference,* which presented certain basis for understanding emerging Cyber Finance practices at the intersection of leading-edge developments in both finance- and cybersecurity-related risk and uncertainty management. In addition, it also developed computational quantitative finance modelling foundations for industrywide insurance practices.

84. It recalls Eling, M. and Schmeiser, H. and Schmit, J. T. 2006. "The Solvency II Process: Overview and Critical Analysis" *Risk Management and Insurance Review*; Vaughan, T. M. 2009. "The Implications of Solvency II for U.S. Insurance Regulation" *Networks Financial Institute Policy Brief No. 2009-PB-03*; Filipovic, D. and Kremslehner, R. and Muermann, A. 2013. "Optimal Investment and Premium Policies under Risk Shifting and Solvency Regulation" *Swiss Finance Institute Research Paper No. 11-11*.

    Furthermore, Colaert, V. A. 2015. "European Banking, Insurance and Investment Services Law: Cutting Through Sectoral Lines?" *Common Market Law Review* questioned: (1) what is the adequate level and model of financial supervision in the EU, and (2) what is the adequate level and model of financial legislation in the EU.

    See also Scalise M. and Fichera F. 2017. "Solvency II: impatti del nuovo regime sui profili pubblicistici della vigilanza assicurativa" *Diritto del mercato assicurativo e finanziario*, p. 119 ff.; Sartori, F. 2017. "Disciplina dell'impresa e statuto contrattuale: il criterio della sana e prudente gestione" *Banca borsa e titoli di credito*, p. 131 ff.

    It is worth recalling Argentati, A. 2018. "Polizze assicurative abbinate al credito e tutela del cliente: analisi critica dei più recenti sviluppi normativi" *Rivista Trimestrale di Diritto dell'Economia*, 2018, p. 271; Corrias, P. 2018. "Profili generali della nuova disciplina recata dalla Direttiva 2016/97/EU" *Rivista Trimestrale di Diritto dell'Economia*, 2018, p. 158 ff.; Landini, S. 2018. "Distribuzione assicurativa da IDD al decreto attuativo passando per EIOPA e IVASS" *Diritto del mercato assicurativo e finanziario*, p. 183 ff.

85. See Lamberton, C. and Brigo, D. and Hoy, D. 2017. "Impact of Robotics, RPA and AI on the Insurance Industry: Challenges and Opportunities" *Journal of Financial Perspectives*; the authors consider the current challenges and opportunities in applications of Robotics to financial services and to insurance, and then discuss advanced Artificial Intelligence (AI) applications, arguing that such applications depend on the general advancements of AI, where human-level interaction is not yet available.

    It is also worth recalling on this point Prince, A. and Schwarcz, D. B. 2019. "Proxy Discrimination in the Age of Artificial Intelligence and Big Data" *Iowa Law Review* on proxy discrimination, considered as a particularly pernicious subset of disparate impact. Like all forms of disparate impact, it involves a facially-neutral practice that disproportionately harms members of a protected class. But a practice producing a disparate impact only amounts to proxy discrimination when the usefulness to the discriminator of the facially neutral practice derives, at least in part, from the very fact that it produces a disparate impact.

86. Regulatory studies have to understand the multifaceted implications of algorithm accountability on the expectations that individuals may have thereof with respect to automated decision-making, by considering that the rationales can only be served if controllers cannot hide behind algorithms for automated individual decision-making; see Moerel, E.M.L. and Storm, M. 2019. "Automated Decisions Based on Profiling: Information, Explanation or Justification – That Is The Question!" *Autonomous Systems and the Law*, Oxford.

87. See Peters, G. and Shevchenko, P. V. and Cohen, R. 2018. "Understanding Cyber-Risk and Cyber-Insurance" *Macquarie University Faculty of Business & Economics Research Paper*, the authors discuss the emerging market of cyber risk insurance and the challenges faced by this market resulting from the diversity of insurance coverage on uncertainty relating to potential exposures and vulnerabilities associated with this risk class.

88. See Yeung, K. 2016. "Hypernudge: Big Data as a Mode of Regulation by Design" *Information, Communication & Society*, which argued that concerns about the legitimacy of these techniques are not satisfactorily resolved through reliance on individual notice and consent, touching upon the troubling implications for democracy and human flourishing if big data analytic techniques driven by commercial self-interest continue their onward march unchecked by effective and legitimate constraints. See also Marcacci, A. 2017. "Digitally-provided Financial Services under EU Law: Overcoming the Current Patchwork of Europeanized Private International Law and Sectorially-harmonized National Private Laws" *Studi sull'integrazione europea*.

89. It is worth recalling that the nature of the interaction between client and machine raises many legal questions under the applicable EU regulation; see Maume, P. 2018. "Reducing Legal Uncertainty and Regulatory Arbitrage for Robo-Advice" *European Company and Financial Law Review*.

90. See El Khoury, A. 2018. "Personal Data, Algorithms and Profiling in the EU: Overcoming the Binary Notion of Personal Data through Quantum Mechanics" *Erasmus Law Review*, which proposed to analyse the binary notion of personal data and highlight its limits, in order to propose a different conception of personal data.

    See also Ben-Shahar, O. and Logue, K. D. 2012. "Outsourcing Regulation: How Insurance Reduces Moral Hazard" *Michigan Law Review*; Verhoef, P. C. and Donkers, N. 2001. "Predicting Customer Potential Value: An Application in the Insurance Industry" *ERIM Report Series Reference No. ERS-2001-01-MKT*; Skeel, D. A. 1999. "The Market Revolution in Bank and Insurance Firm Governance: Its Logic and Limits" *Washington University Law Quarterly*.

91. See Swedloff, R. 2014. "Risk Classification's Big Data (R)evolution" *Connecticut Insurance Law Journal* on the promise that the algorithms driving big data will offer greater predictive accuracy than traditional statistical analysis alone.

      It recalls also the analysis of Gaver, J. J. and Paterson, J. S. 1998. "The Association between External Monitoring and Earnings Management in the Property-Casualty Insurance Industry" *SSRN Research Paper no. 144419*, which examined the association between external monitoring and earnings management by property-casualty insurers.

92. It is worth considering Kerber, W. and Frank, J. 2017. "Data Governance Regimes in the Digital Economy: The Example of Connected Cars" *SSRN Research Paper no. 3064794*, which reviewed the issues of privacy, data ownership and data access from a specific point of view. In this perspective, the authors applied their analytical framework to the complex problem of data governance in connected cars (with its different stakeholders car manufacturers, car owners, car component suppliers, repair service providers, insurance companies and other service providers), and identifies several potential market failure problems in regard to this specific data governance problem (especially competition problems, information/behavioral and privacy problems).

93. It is worth recalling the analysis of Raskin, M. 2017. "The Law and Legality of Smart Contracts" *Georgetown Law Technology Review*, p. 305 ss.; Kôlvart, M. and Poola, M. and Rull, A. 2016 "Smart Contracts" "The Future of Law and eTechnologies", London, p. 133 ss.; Mik, E. 2017 "Smart Contracts: Terminology, Technical Limitations and Real World Complexity", *Law, Innovation & Technology*, p. 269 ff.

94. It is worth considering the conclusions of Helveston, M. 2016. "Consumer Protection in the Age of Big Data" *Washington University Law Review*, which, in describing the potential problems raised by insurers' uses of data and constructing a regulatory framework for addressing these issues, raised as many questions about the factors that should determine whether a certain type of coverage falls within the consumer regulatory scheme or not. Hence, the need for a regulatory intervention aimed at choosing the trade-offs between actuarial fairness and other goals (as stability, inclusion, wealth) that cannot be resolved through analytic reasoning, but are inherent to normative matters.

REFERENCES

"The Big Bang: How the Big Data Explosion Is Changing the World" – Microsoft UK Enterprise Insights Blog – Site Home – MSDN Blogs.

Ait-Sahalia, Y. and Karaman, M. and Mancini, L. 2018. "The Term Structure of Variance Swaps and Risk Premia", *Swiss Finance Institute Research Paper No. 18-37.*

American Psychological Association, 2013. "Glossary of psychological terms", Apa.org.

Anderson, C. 2008. "The end of theory: The data deluge makes the scientific method obsolete", *Wired Magazine.*

Argentati, A. 2018. "Polizze assicurative abbinate al credito e tutela del cliente: analisi critica dei più recenti sviluppi normativi", *Rivista Trimestrale di Diritto dell'Economia.*

Arner, D. W. and Barberis, J. N. and Buckley, R. P. 2016. "FinTech, RegTech and the Reconceptualization of Financial Regulation" *University of Hong Kong Faculty of Law Research Paper No. 2016/035.*

Arrow, K. J. 1971. "Essays in theory of risk bearing", Chicago.

Ban, G. Y. and Rudin, C. 2018. "The Big Data Newsvendor: Practical Insights from Machine Learning", *Operations Research 67.*

Bank of England, 2014. "Strategic plan: Background information".

Banterle, F. 2018. "Data Ownership in the Data Economy: A European Dilemma" *EU Internet Law in the digital era.*

Barone, E. and Masera, R. 2000. "Capital Requirements, Capital Adequacy and Risk Management", *SSRN research paper no. 2574336.*

Barth, J. R. and Caprio, G. and Levine, R. E. 2001. "The Regulation and Supervision of Banks Around the World: A New Database" *World Bank Policy Research Working Paper No. 2588.*

Benos, E., and Sagade, S. 2012. "High frequency trading behaviour and its impact on market quality: Evidence from theUK equity market", *Bank of England Working Paper 469.*

Ben-Shahar, O. and Logue, K. D. 2012. "Outsourcing Regulation: How Insurance Reduces Moral Hazard", *Michigan Law Review.*

Bernstein, S and Korteweg, A. G. and Laws, K. 2015. "Attracting Early Stage Investors: Evidence from a Randomized Field Experiment", *Stanford University Graduate School of Business Research Paper No. 14-17.*

Beyer, M. A. and Laney, D. 2012. "The importance of big data: A definition". Stamford, CT: Gartner.

Bholat, D. 2013. "The future of central bank data". *Journal of Banking Regulation.*

Bholat, D. 2015. "Big data and central banks" *Big Data & Society.*

Bianco Alberto, A. 1981. "La grazia perfeziona la natura. Il fondamento scritturistico del diritto naturale" *Studi cattolici.*

Boschetti, B. 2016. "Soft law e normatività: un'analisi comparata", *Rivista della Regolazione dei mercati.*

Brito, J. and Shadab, H. B. and Castillo O'Sullivan, A. 2014. "Bitcoin Financial Regulation: Securities, Derivatives, Prediction Markets, and Gambling", *Columbia Science and Technology Law Review.*

Buchak, G. and Matvos, G. and Piskorski, T. and Seru, A. 2017. "Fintech, Regulatory Arbitrage, and the Rise of Shadow Banks", *NBER Working Paper No 23288.*

Burr, D. and Ross, J. 2008a. "A Visual Sense of Number" *Current Biology.*

Burr, D. and Ross, J. 2008b. "Response: Visual number" *Current Biology.*

Buzzi, F. 2005. "La teologia per il diritto dell'uomo e dei popoli", *Iustitia.*

Canova, T. A. 2009. "Financial Market Failure as a Crisis in the Rule of Law: From Market Fundamentalism to a New Keynesian Regulatory Model" *Harvard Law & Policy Review.*

Cantone, R. 1996. "L'abusivismo finanziario: esperienze da un'indagine giudiziaria. Nota a Cass. sez. V pen. 6 ottobre 1995", *Cassazione penale.*

Capriglione, F. 1997. "La problematica della "banca di fatto" dopo il d.lg. 385/1993", *La nuova giurisprudenza civile commentata.*

Capriglione, F. and Masera, R. 2016. "Bank Corporate Governance: A New Paradigm", *Open Review of Management, Banking and Finance.*

Capriglione, F. and Sacco Ginevri, A. 2019. "Metamorfosi della governance bancaria", Milano.

Carney, M. 2017 "The Promise of FinTech – Something New Under the Sun? Speech given by the Governor of the Bank of England Chair of the Financial Stability BoardDeutsche Bundesbank G20 conference on Digitising finance, financial inclusion and financial literacy", Wiesbaden, 25 January.

Chan-Lau, J. A. and Chen, Z. 1998 "Financial Crisis and Credit Crunch as a Result of Inefficient Financial Intermediation--With Reference to the Asian Financial Crisis" *IMF Working Paper No. 98/127.*

Chesbrough, H. and Bogers, M. 2014. "Explicating Open Innovation: Clarifying an Emerging Paradigm for Understanding Innovation", *New Frontiers in Open Innovation*, Oxford.

Cœuré, B. 2017. "Policy analysis with big data. Speech by the member of the Executive Board of the ECB, at the conference on Economic and Financial Regulation in the Era of Big Data", Banque de France, Paris, 24 November.

Cohen, J. E. 2012. "What Privacy Is For" *Harvard Law Review.*

Colaert, V. A. 2015. "European Banking, Insurance and Investment Services Law: Cutting Through Sectoral Lines?", *Common Market Law Review.*

Corrias, P. 2018. "Profili generali della nuova disciplina recata dalla Direttiva 2016/97/EU", *Rivista Trimestrale di Diritto dell'Economia.*

Criscuolo, L. 1996. "L'esercizio abusivo di attività finanziaria: profili giuridici e strumenti di contrasto" *Cassazione penale.*

Cumming, D. J. and Johan, S. A. and Zhang, Y. 2019. "The Role of Due Diligence in Crowdfunding Platforms" *Journal of Banking and Finance*.

Davenport, T. 2014. "Big Data at Work: Dispelling the Myths, Uncovering the Opportunities", *Harvard Business Review*.

De Fiore, F. and Uhlig, H. 2005. "Bank Finance Versus Bond Finance: What Explains the Differences between Us and Europe?", *ECB Working Paper No. 547*.

Dehaene, S. 2009. "Origins of Mathematical Intuitions The Case of Arithmetic". *Annals of the New York Academy of Sciences*.

Diebold, F. X. 2012. "On the Origin(s) and Development of the Term 'Big Data'", *PIER Working Paper No. 12-037*.

Dijcks, J. P. 2012. "Oracle: Big data for the enterprise", *Oracle White Paper*.

Durgin, F. H. 2008. "Texture density adaptation and visual number revisited", *Current Biology*.

EBA 2020 "EBA Report on big data and advanced analytics", January.

ECB. 2018. "Guide to assessments of fintech credit institution licence applications".

ECB 2020, "Central bank group to assess potential cases for central bank digital currencies", Bruxelles, 21 January.

Edwards, l. 2016. "Privacy, Security and Data Protection in Smart Cities: A Critical EU Law Perspective", *European Data Protection Law Review*.

Einav L. and Levin J. D. 2013. "The data revolution and economic analysis". *NBER Working Paper Series No. 19035*.

EIOPA 2019. "Report on best practices on licencing requirements, peer-to-peer insurance and the principle of proportionality in an insurtech context", 27 March.

El Khoury, A. 2018. "Personal Data, Algorithms and Profiling in the EU: Overcoming the Binary Notion of Personal Data through Quantum Mechanics", *Erasmus Law Review*.

Eling, M. and Schmeiser, H. and Schmit, J. T. 2006. "The Solvency II Process: Overview and Critical Analysis" *Risk Management and Insurance Review*.

Fahlenbrach, R. and Prilmeier, R. and Stulz, R. M. 2016. "Why Does Fast Loan Growth Predict Poor Performance for Banks?", *Swiss Finance Institute Research Paper No. 16-24*.

Filipovic, D. and Kremslehner, R. and Muermann, A. 2013. "Optimal Investment and Premium Policies under Risk Shifting and Solvency Regulation", *Swiss Finance Institute Research Paper No. 11-11*.

Flood, M. et al. 2014. "The application of visual analytics to financial stability monitoring", *OFR Working Paper 14*.

FSB. 2017. "Artificial intelligence and machine learning in financial services. Market developments and financial stability implications".

FSB 2020. "Global Monitoring Report on Non-Bank Financial Intermediation 2019", 19 January.

Gadinis, S. 2013. "From Independence to Politics in Financial Regulation" *UC Berkeley Public Law Research Paper No. 2137215*.

Gaver, J. J. and Paterson, J. S. 1998. "The Association between External Monitoring and Earnings Management in the Property-Casualty Insurance Industry", *SSRN Research Paper No. 144419.*

Gebauer, S. and Mazelis, F. 2019. "Macroprudential Regulation and Leakage to the Shadow Banking Sector", *DIW Berlin Discussion Paper No. 1814.*

Glinavos, I. 2010 "Regulation and the Role of Law in Economic Crisis" *European Business Law Review.*

Gomber, P. and Kauffman, R. J. and Parker, C. and Weber, B. 2017. "On the Fintech Revolution: Interpreting the Forces of Innovation, Disruption and Transformation in Financial Services" *Journal of Management Information Systems.*

Google, 2013. "Google Trends for Big Data".

Gorton, G. B. and Metrick, A. 2010. "Securitized Banking and the Run on Repo" *Yale ICF Working Paper No. 09-14.*

Greco, P. 1930. "Le operazioni di banca", Padova.

Grossman, R. and Siegel, K. 2014. "Organizational Models for Big Data and Analytics" *Journal of Organization Design.*

Hacker, P. and Lianos, I. and Dimitropoulos, G. and Eich, E. 2018. "Regulating Blockchain: Techno-Social and Legal Challenges", Oxford

Haldane, A. 2013. "Why institutions matter (more than ever)". *Speech delivered at the Centre for Research on SocioCultural Change Annual Conference, School of Oriental and African Studies, London.*

Haldane, A. and Shanbhogue, R. and Attanasio, O. and Besley, T. J. and Lindert, P. H. and Piketty, T. and Ventura, K. 2015. "Capital in the 21st Century", *Bank of England Quarterly Bulletin 2015 Q1.*

Hardin, G. 1968. "The Tragedy of The Commons", *Science.*

Hazen, T. L. 2012. "Crowdfunding or Fraudfunding? Social Networks and the Securities Laws – Why the Specially Tailored Exemption Must be Conditioned on Meaningful Disclosure", *North Carolina Law Review.*

Helveston, M. 2016. "Consumer Protection in the Age of Big Data", *Washington University Law Review.*

Hermalin, B. E. and Katz, A. W. and Craswell, R. 2006. "The Law and Economics of Contracts", *Columbia Law and Economics Working Paper No. 296.*

Hubbard, E. M. and Piazza, M.; Pinel, P. and Dehaene, S. 2005. "Interactions between number and space in parietal cortex", *Nature Reviews Neuroscience.*

Iannarone, N. G. 2017. "Computer As Confidant: Digital Investment Advice and the Fiduciary Standard" *Chicago-Kent Law Review.*

Izard, V. and Dehaene, S. 2008. "Calibrating the mental number line" *Cognition.*

Jacobsen, S. F. and Tschoegl, A. E. 1997. "The Norwegian Banks in the Nordic Consortia: A Case of International Strategic Alliances in Banking", *SSRN research paper no 52068.*

Jagtiani, J. A. and Lemieux, C. 2017. "Fintech Lending: Financial Inclusion, Risk Pricing, and Alternative Information", *FRB of Philadelphia Working Paper No. 17-17*.

Kache, F. 2015. "Dealing with digital information richness in supply chain management. A review and a big data analytics approach", Kassel.

Kaminski, J. and Hopp, C. and Tykvova, T. 2019. "New Technology Assessment in Entrepreneurial Financing – Can Crowdfunding Predict Venture Capital Investments?" *Technological Forecasting and Social Change*.

Kerber, W. and Frank, J. 2017. "Data Governance Regimes in the Digital Economy: The Example of Connected Cars", *SSRN Research Paper No. 3064794*.

Kitchin, R. 2014. "Thinking Critically About and Researching Algorithms", *The Programmable City Working Paper 5*.

Knight, F. 1921. "Risk, Uncertainty, and Profit", (Ed. 2009) Cambridge.

Kôlvart, M. and Poola, M. and Rull, A. 2016. "Smart Contracts", *The Future of Law and eTechnologies*, London.

Kronman, A. T. 1985. "Contract law and the state of nature" *Journal of law, economics and organization*.

Kumar, A. and Jacobson, S. H. 1998. "Optimal and Near-Optimal Decisions for Procurement and Allocation of a Critical Resource with a Stochastic Consumption Rate", *University of Michigan Business School Working Paper No. 98019*.

Lamberton, C. and Brigo, D. and Hoy, D. 2017. "Impact of Robotics, RPA and AI on the Insurance Industry: Challenges and Opportunities", *Journal of Financial Perspectives*.

Landini, S. 2018. "Distribuzione assicurativa da IDD al decreto attuativo passando per EIOPA e IVASS", *Diritto del mercato assicurativo e finanziario*.

Lemma, V. 2016. "The Shadow Banking System. Creating Transparency in the Financial Markets". London.

Lobel, O. 2016. "The Law of the Platform", *Minnesota Law Review*.

Lucantoni, P. 2019. "Distributed ledger techonology e infrastrutture di negoziazione e post-trading", on VV.AA., *Fintech: diritto, tecnologia e finanza*, Roma.

Magness, P. and Murphy, R. P. 2014. "Challenging the Empirical Contribution of Thomas Piketty's Capital in the 21st Century", *Journal of Private Enterprise*.

Maine, H. J. S. 1861. "Ancient law" (ed. 2005).

Mainelli, M. and Smith, M. 2015. "Sharing Ledgers for Sharing Economies: An Exploration of Mutual Distributed Ledgers (Aka Blockchain Technology)", *Journal of Financial Perspectives*.

Malhotra, Y. 2016. "Beyond Model Risk Management to Model Risk Arbitrage for FinTech Era: How to Navigate 'Uncertainty'...When 'Models' Are 'Wrong'...And Knowledge'...'Imperfect'! Knight Reconsidered Again: Risk, Uncertainty, & Profit Beyond ZIRP & NIRP!", *Research Presentation at: 2016 Princeton Quant Trading Conference*.

Marcacci, A. 2017. "Digitally-provided Financial Services under EU Law: Overcoming the Current Patchwork of Europeanized Private International Law and Sectorially-harmonized National Private Laws" *Studi sull'integrazione europea.*

Masera, R. 2011. "Taking the Moral Hazard Out of Banking: The Next Fundamental Step in Financial Reform", *PSL Quarterly Review.*

Masera, R. 2013. "US Basel III Final Rule on Banks' Capital Requirements: A Different-Size-Fits-All Approach", *PSL Quarterly Review.*

Maume, P. 2017. "In Unchartered Territory – Banking Supervision Meets Fintech", *Corporate Finance.*

Maume, P. 2018a. "Reducing Legal Uncertainty and Regulatory Arbitrage for Robo-Advice" *European Company and Financial Law Review.*

Maume, P. 2018b. "Regulating Robo-Advisory" *Texas International Law Journal.*

Mik, E. 2017. "Smart Contracts: Terminology, Technical Limitations and Real World Complexity", *Law, Innovation & Technology.*

Moerel, E.M.L. and Storm, M. 2019 "Automated Decisions Based on Profiling: Information, Explanation or Justification – That Is The Question!" *Autonomous Systems and the Law*, Oxford.

Mollick, E. R. 2013 "The Dynamics of Crowdfunding: An Exploratory Study", *Journal of Business Venturing.*

Morellec, E. and Wang, N. 2004. "Capital Structure, Investment, and Private Benefits of Control" *Simon Business School Working Paper No. FR04-17.*

Moritz, A. and Block, J. H. 2013. "Crowdfunding und Crowdinvesting: State-of-the-Art der wissenschaftlichen Literatur", *Zeitschrift für KMU und Entrepreneurship.*

Mullainathan, S. 2014. "Big data and the inductive method to theory testing: A framework with applications", *Hahn lecture delivered at the Royal Economics Society Annual Conference, University of Manchester*, Manchester.

Newman, N. 2014. "Search, Antitrust and the Economics of the Control of User Data", *Yale Journal on Regulation.*

Nymand-Andersen, P. 2015. "Big data: the hunt for timely insights and decision certainty: Central banking reflections on the use of big data for policy purposes", *IFC Working Paper No 14.*

Omarova, S. T. 2019. "New Tech v. New Deal: Fintech As A Systemic Phenomenon" *Yale Journal on Regulation.*

Paech, P. 2016. "The Governance of Blockchain Financial Networks" *Modern Law Review.*

Peters, G. and Shevchenko, P. V. and Cohen, R. 2018. "Understanding Cyber-Risk and Cyber-Insurance", *Macquarie University Faculty of Business & Economics Research Paper.*

Popov, A. A. and Udell, G. F. 2010 "Cross-Border Banking and the International Transmission of Financial Distress During the Crisis of 2007-2008" *ECB Working Paper No. 1203.*

Posner, R. 2008. "How Judges think", Harvard.

Powell, L. 2017. "Big Data and Regulation in the Insurance Industry", *SSRN Research Paper No. 2951306*.

Preis, T. and Moat, H. S. and Stanley, H. E. 2013. "Quantifying Trading Behavior in Financial Markets Using Google Trends", *Scientific Reports*.

Prince, A. and Schwarcz, D. B. 2019. "Proxy Discrimination in the Age of Artificial Intelligence and Big Data", *Iowa Law Review*.

Raskin, M. 2017. "The Law and Legality of Smart Contracts", *Georgetown Law Technology Review*.

Rifkin, J. 2014 "The Zero Marginal Cost Society: The Internet of Things, the Collaborative Commons, and the Eclipse of Capitalism". New York.

Rubinstein, I. 2012. "Big Data: The End of Privacy or a New Beginning?", *NYU School of Law, Public Law Research Paper No. 12-56*.

Sandulli, F. D. and Chesbrough, H. 2009. "The Two Sides of Open Business Models", *SSRN research paper No. 1325682*.

Sanz Bayón, P. and Vega, L. G. 2018. "Automated Investment Advice: Legal Challenges and Regulatory Questions" *Banking & Financial Services Policy Report*.

Sartori, F. 2017. "Disciplina dell'impresa e statuto contrattuale: il criterio della sana e prudente gestione", *Banca borsa e titoli di credito*.

Savelyev, A. 2016. "Contract Law 2.0: «Smart» Contracts As the Beginning of the End of Classic Contract Law" *Higher School of Economics Research Paper No. WP BRP 71/LAW/2016*.

Scalise M. and Fichera F. 2017. "Solvency II: impatti del nuovo regime sui profili pubblicistici della vigilanza assicurativa", *Diritto del mercato assicurativo e finanziario*.

Schumpeter, J. 1942. "Capitalism, socialism and democracy", (ed. 1994, Abingdon-on-Thames.

Scott, K. E. 2009. "Lessons from the Crisis", *Stanford Law and Economics Olin Working Paper No. 385*.

Severino, P. 2000. "Le disposizioni integrative e correttive del Testo Unico delle leggi in materia bancaria e creditizia. Il quadro sanzionatorio: innovazioni nelle fattispecie e nella procedura applicativa", *Diritto della banca e del mercato finanziario*.

Simon, P. 2015. "Too Big to Ignore: The Business Case for Big Data", Hoboken.

Skeel, D. A. 1999. "The Market Revolution in Bank and Insurance Firm Governance: Its Logic and Limits", *Washington University Law Quarterly*.

Susskind, R. and Susskind, D. 2015 "Future of the Professions: How Technology will Transform the Work of Human Experts", Oxford.

Swedloff, R. 2014. "Risk Classification's Big Data (R)evolution", *Connecticut Insurance Law Journal*.

Taylor, L. and Schroeder, R. and Meyer, E. 2014. "Emerging practices and perspectives on Big Data analysis in economics: Bigger and better or more of the same?", *Big Data & Society*.

Tene, O. 2007. "What Google Knows: Privacy and Internet Search Engines", *Utah Law Review*.

Tene, O. and Polonetsky, J. 2013 "Big Data for All: Privacy and User Control in the Age of Analytics" *Northwestern Journal of Technology and Intellectual Property*.

Tissot, B. 2017. "Big data and central banking", *IFC Bulletin No 44*.

Torresetti, R. and Nordio, C., 2014. "Scaling Operational Loss Data and Its Systemic Risk Implications" *SSRN Research paper no. 2360483*.

Upadhyay, V. 2015. "Can Capitalism Survive High Degree of Automation? A Comparison with Thomas Piketty's Argument", *SSRN Research Paper No. 2558989*.

Van Loo, R. 2018. "Making Innovation More Competitive: The Case of Fintech" *UCLA Law Review*.

Varian, H. R. 2014. "Big Data: New tricks for econometrics" *Journal of Economic Perspectives*.

Vaughan, T. M. 2009 "The Implications of Solvency II for U.S. Insurance Regulation", *Networks Financial Institute Policy Brief No. 2009-PB-03*.

Verhoef, P. C. and Donkers, N. 2001. "Predicting Customer Potential Value: An Application in the Insurance Industry", *ERIM Report Series Reference No. ERS-2001-01-MKT*.

Vezzoso, S. 2018. "Fintech, Access to Data, and the Role of Competition Policy" "Competition and Innovation", São Paulo.

Wachter, S. and Mittelstadt, B. 2018. "A Right to Reasonable Inferences: Re-Thinking Data Protection Law in the Age of Big Data and AI", *Columbia Business Law Review*.

Ward, J. S. and Barker, A. 2013. "Undefined By Data: A Survey of Big Data Definitions" *Cornell University Research Paper No. arXiv:1309.5821*.

Wibisono, O. and Ari, H. D. and Widjanarti, A. and Andhika Zulen, A. and Tissot, B. 2019 "The use of big data analytics and artificial intelligence in central banking" *IFC Bulletin no. 50*.

Williamson, O. E. 1985. "The economic institution of capitalisms", London.

Yeung, K. 2016. "Hypernudge: Big Data as a Mode of Regulation by Design", *Information, Communication & Society*.

Zetzsche, D. A. and Preiner, C. 2017. "Cross-Border Crowdfunding – Towards a Single Crowdfunding Market for Europe", *University of Luxembourg Law Working Paper No. 2017/002*.

Zirpoli, F. and Becker, M. C. 2008. "Organizing Complex Product Development: Outsourcing, Performance Integration and the Role of Product Architecture", *SSRN research paper no. 1087236*.

CHAPTER 6

Fintech Firms

The Financial Stability Board provided a definition of a 'fintech institution' that is the starting point for the analysis of the characteristics of a firm that operates in the fintech environment and provides products or services that interact with the regular course of financial markets. Hence, this part of the research will take into account both the supply of business analytics to supervised entities and unbundling banking, considered as the scope of the entities that offer alternative solutions for savers, lenders, borrowers or investors. The goal is to verify if such firms require the application of a special regime to protect individual rights, financial stability and market wealth.

In the previous chapters, it has been doubted that fintech innovations affect the need for protection, and the application of new high-tech mechanisms at several stages of capital circulation influences the way of supervising these firms and their operations. Consequently, fintech firms would fall within the scope of the current supervision. Indeed, it is foreseeable that if policymakers want to avoid asymmetries in the market for capital, then public intervention will require the regulation of both the firms that provide high-tech services to supervised entities and their programmers or coders (i.e. the ones who create the relevant software). The same is true for the firms that offer products or services that substitute banking and finance (such as the management of web-based platforms supporting individuals in trading credits or sharing financial opportunities).

© The Author(s) 2020
V. Lemma, *FinTech Regulation*,
https://doi.org/10.1007/978-3-030-42347-6_6

In order to reach this conclusion, this part of the research will go deep into the analysis of the corporate governance of fintech firms to understand whether there is the need for recasting the current rules, provided that the criterion of the safe and sound management of 'other people's money' be applied to any resolution, even if it comes from automatized decision-making processes. This chapter will also review the risks arising from the business of fintech credit institutions, and will provide the background for understanding the option for strengthening oversight and control over their relevant ancillary service undertakers (included, but not limited to the aforementioned programmers and coders). This should not cast doubt that the relationships between supervised fintech firms and supervised entities jeopardize the market for capital. However, this suggests that supervisory authorities would be soon in the position to require an authorization for high-tech service providers that deal with supervised entities.

All the above is enough to start questioning the policymakers' attitude to structure supervisors by mirroring the supervised.

6.1   THE 'FINTECHERS'

As a preliminary remark it is worth highlighting that fintech can affect the supply to banks and financial intermediaries or their traditional customers or both. This helps in understanding that the fintech firms are in a position to affect the individual's rights, the management of supervised entities and the financial market functioning both indirectly (by influencing the running of the aforesaid entities) and directly (by dealing with the aforesaid customers) (FSB 2017d).[1] Hence, this chapter investigates, firstly, fintechers as a new category of firms, then the fintech firms as new market participants (having regard to their regulation, the management of platforms and their interoperable capacity), and in conclusion, as new service providers for supervised entities (focusing on the outsourcing in banking).

That said, it is necessary to take into account that, at the top of the fintech chain, there are software houses, programmers and coders, as well as the authors of the set of rules that will lead to an outcome by means of automatism and self-executing mechanisms.[2] Being aware that algorithms have to be described, implemented and written in a code (that is usable by the personal devices), its need of being continuously updated and verified, and then updated again should be considered.[3] While this awareness helps in providing the awareness of the innumerable stages, the following analysis will move from the evidence that the technological innovations are the premises of fintech (as shown before), and that humans are still the ones who produce such innovations.

In this respect, it is worth considering that any person could be in the position of carrying out the activity of designing algorithms dedicated to fintech and programming the relevant software, as well as being able to produce devices capable of supporting their execution. Indeed, in the past, banking was linked to territories more than the bank vaults. Nowadays, capital flows freely, and it is not permanently contained within the boundaries of any country. But this lets the aforesaid person to be free to choose the country of incorporation of the firm used to carry out the aforesaid activity; moreover, this does not provide any direction as to the orientation of its supply, and neither any certainty that the relevant activities refer to a market whereby the circulation of capital leads to the maximization of the common welfare, within the limits of individual rights and financial stability.

Nowadays, in fintech chaos, the rule and order is the exception. This leads the analysis to consider humans running fintech firms as businesspersons who are exploiting opportunities without being subject to the strict supervision provided for banking and finance, even if algorithms suggest the idea of an order that is *monotone*, regular, repetitive and predictable.[4] From this perspective, this research will refer to them as 'fintechers' in order to highlight the difference between them and those people in charge of the responsibilities of supplying and demanding capital without jeopardizing the economy by means of non-bank financial intermediation.

According to the relevance of the innovation due to the business of certain non-bank intermediaries (or rather shadow banks[5]), the fintechers could be driven by the expectation that the success of their *idea* and its application will provide *plenty* of revenues, a *series* of third-party offerings, and other ways to *monetize* their fintech innovations.[6] Among others, these aim at buying the assets of the fintech firm, licensing its products, and participating in its equity by acquiring the relevant shares.[7] The last option requires a specific stipulation in the agreements among the founders of the firm, because the exit of a fintecher could create such discontinuity capable of jeopardizing the future of the business itself.[8] It should be bore in mind that this risk of discontinuity could be managed if the fintechers were not entitled to sell or otherwise transfer to any third-party their own shares (in whole or in part) and there were no sale of the assets or licensing of the know-how until a certain period after the date of the beginning of the business (the so-called lock-up period).[9] Then upon the expiration of such a lock-up period, any of the shareholders (be he/she one of the founders, or one of the investors) would have the right to buy the assets, to license the know-how, or to acquire all the interest in the equity. Such a right could rely on the traditional mechanism set forth in the international praxis of mergers and acquisitions, rather than for a price calculated based on specific algorithms.[10]

The mechanism for selling and notifying the exercise of this right (and the relevant price) would ensure a smooth transaction for the benefit of the fintech firm itself. However, under private agreements, any fintecher runs the risk that one of his/her partners could force the fintecher him/herself to transfer his/her own shares to the envisaged buyer who aims at acquiring the whole fintech firm.[11] Hence, the provision of a drag-along right would cause the sale to a third-party to be at the same price and on the same terms and conditions as the first would have bought the firm. Furthermore, there are no evidences to deny that the by-laws of a fintech firm should also provide that—after the lock-up period—the fintechers would only be entitled to sell their shares to a third-party that (irrespective of the offered purchase price) undertakes to further acquire all the shares of the fintech firms subscribed by all the fintechers (at the same terms and conditions offered for the shares of the first seller, by means of a sort of tag-along right).

In view of the foregoing, fintechers would be in a position of having divergent interests soon after the incorporation of their firm, and that these interests could also diverge from the ones of the firm itself.[12] Consequently, the regulatory analysis would confirm the need for supervising both the humans that are at the top of the chain and the humans that apply fintech innovation. These humans find themselves in an individualized, privatized, uncertain, flexible, vulnerable modern world, and—as it will be shown—national governments are showing their difficulties in supervising them. According to the above, the policymakers' attitude to structuring supervisors by mirroring the supervised would now suggest structuring public authorities being able to develop algorithms and software by themselves, and that these tools should be widespread for controlling and correcting the functioning of fintech tools used by fintech firms and supervised entities.

6.2   THE REGULATION OF FINTECH FIRMS AND THEIR ROLE IN MARKET-BASED CHAINS

All the above suggests recalling the role of private law in order to understand the responsibility of individuals in organizing fintech firms, taking into account that—as anticipated—such organizations will result in performing activities that supply and demand capital (while managing risks, because of their interoperability), support the circulation of money (in the case of the management of platforms), and cooperate for the execution of reserved activities (in the case of servicing supervised entities).[13] Indeed, all the above matters to the extent that the trust in the system supports financial stability and the rights of individuals, and it should also be protected by the government (Shackelford, J. and Myers, S. 2017).[14]

In the absence of strict rules on the organizational structure of fintech firms, fintechers are called to set the relevant social structure, governance and ideology, provided that supervisors have to open up the 'black box' of the fintech firm and explore its contents.[15]

This places fintech firms within the 'shadow banking system', and then suggests to consider them as market participants that contribute to the realization of the market-based alternative process, regardless of the type of relationship (contractual or participatory) that supports the exchange of financial instruments, money or risks. Recalling that fintech firms (as shadow entities) are—in principle—excluded from direct access to the liquidity injections (and, in particular, to the so-called FED's discount window or to the ECB's operations) helps in distinguishing such firms from the 'fintech banks' (which will be explored a few lines below) (Lemma, V. 2016).

Indeed, this brings the analysis to the current topic. It is useful to bear in mind that the 'shadow credit intermediation process' is based on the presence of one or more special purpose vehicles (SPVs), in the legal form of companies, designed for the acquisition of assets (i.e. the credits arising from the loans) and for the offering of financial instruments (i.e. ABCP, ABS, and CDO).[16] Thus, from a regulatory perspective, the vehicles used to start the securitization will be the 'initial creditor' (of the debtors who signed the loan contracts, originated or received through a credit assignment agreement), while the (other) vehicles used to proceed in the offering of the CDOs will be the 'final debtor' (towards the investors, the market and the public supervision authorities) (ESMA 2020).

In this context, fintech affects the roles of many operators involved in the aforesaid process. From a mere economic perspective, this gets close to reality by considering that the application of the same fintech tools leads to the full alignment of all the aforesaid operators, and this is outstanding evidence—in the market-based financial intermediation— that suggests considering them as a whole, and then as a sort of 'shadow bank' (FSB 2017b and FSB 2020).[17]

Obviously, in principle, any single operator or company can operate as a free and independent firm (by performing only one phase of the CDO production cycle and providing intermediate goods and services), but the widespread application of the same business analytics (that are fully intertwined) shows that fintech firms act under the direction and coordination of high-tech mechanisms that are becoming responsible for the whole organization of the relevant market-based financing (Grossman, R. and Siegel, K. 2014).

From another perspective, it is useful to recall the recent ECB explanations concerning the application process and licensing requirements for banks in general and for 'fintech credit institutions'. In fact, the latter have been qualified as supervised entities, and not as 'shadow banks' (and then as a firm performing fund raising and lending by acting (i) outside the areas of public supervision, and (ii) without direct relations with the monetary authorities). On the contrary, ECB has adopted a forward-looking approach by considering the specific nature of "banks with fintech business models". Hence, fintechers have to take into account that the more their innovations replicate banking, the more they have to ensure that their firm is properly authorized and has in place risk-control frameworks that enable them to anticipate, understand and respond to the risks arising in their fields of operation.[18]

Needless to say, the above approach tries to ensure a regulatory level playing field,[19] because European fintech banks must be held to the same standards as other banks. However, this backstop is not sufficient, because of the aforesaid lightness of the financial markets that allows fintechers to establish their firms in any jurisdiction, and at the same time to present their offering in Europe by means of connections that intertwine the wired-society (Global Financial System and Financial Stability Board 2017).

However, the monitoring of fintech firms is confirming the usefulness of marking a perimeter in banking.[20] Indeed, the following paragraphs will show that the principles set by the European regulation appear to be designed to prevent that platforms expose individuals to excessive risks, and that outsourcing translates into an 'escape from responsibility' or into a speculative use of the model Originated to Distribute (i.e. becomes an operating technique that ends up reducing the dimensions of the credit institution to minimum measures, not compatible with the stability requirements that qualify the current banking industry).

Nevertheless, it is worth anticipating that the baseline of this research shows a substantial compatibility with the main fintech policies regarding individual rights related to savings, inclusions and stability.[21]

Whether or not the impact of fintech on the integrity of the banking business refers to the compliance of the practices with the fundamental rights, it is possible to anticipate the need to intensify the controls on the fintech firms that operate the essential stages of credit assessment and decision-making processes (both as market participants, platforms or outsourcers). Hence, it is likely that the ESFS, the ECB and the national authorities will move towards a proper configuration of supervisory practices on the application of fintech in order to control that individuals will be able to take advantage of this progress without putting wealth at risk.[22] Therefore, the goals of this regulatory analysis reflect the need to understand how (and to what extent) the disclosure of frameworks supporting big data analytics is relevant to supporting the trust, and then to a 'long-standing finance' (EBA 2020).

6.3   The Interoperability of Fintech Firms

Nowadays, European authorities aim at regulating and supervising any business model used in the market for capital, including the ones based on an intensive use of financial innovation and big data analytics.[23] Moreover, national governments are showing their interest in improving a more systematic control regime over start-ups, and—at the same time—in adapting their legal order to host new 'national champions' able to lead the digital transformation in the financial industry.

However, no one is currently arguing for the need to protect both individuals and markets, although the rights of the first and the features of the second are changing. This suggests assuming that a new supervising approach has not come yet, but a new standard for the application of the principle of proportionality may be closer; however, the policymakers agree that the current level playing field does not equally support all market participants within the financial industry.[24]

It refers to the last chapter with respect to any consideration on the exploration of specific options to update the scope of public supervision, taking into account both the impact of tech-fueled innovations on the traditional insurance business, the role of innovation facilitators (as significant or ancillary service providers of regulated firms), and the perspective of new networks of market participants aimed at sharing, managing, covering, or transferring money or risks (and other uncertain exposures). However, it should also be considered that professionally those firms collect and use financially related data, and therefore, their supervision should protect both the savings and the individual rights related to the privacy of the person, as well as the integrity of the private juridical sphere from the systematical collection and use of individual relevant information.[25]

All of the above suggests to challenge the interoperability of fintech firms as a qualifying feature of the entrepreneurs who operate in this industry. It refers mainly to the customary tendency to perform more than one financial, banking and/or insurance activity at the same time, and then being able to provide more than one service that substitutes those provided by banks, financial intermediary or insurance companies, as well as other services that satisfy the individual needs of savers, borrowers, investors or insured. In this respect, however, all the above does not deny that fintech firms seem to rely on advanced tools for assessing the suitability of credit worthiness, structuring financial products and setting up insurance policies, also at a level of freedom that has not been experienced since the first banking acts of the last century. Moreover, fintech firms are also providing automated advice for banking and financial products.

The common approach to automated advice is based on the application of machine learning, and there are specific algorithms for the classification of data (and linear regression), which have regard to the statistical inference (as it provides the foundation for most of the methods covered).[26] Obviously, the regulation of these algorithms considers both the onboarding of the customers and the setting up of the subsequent relationships with the firms (to update their profile), which must comply with the current protectionary framework.[27]

Indeed, the Joint Committee Report of the ESAs in its conclusions on the results of the monitoring exercise on 'automation in financial advice' (in 2018) highlighted the emergence of ongoing changes to the current business models of fintech firms.[28] There is the first evidence of new activities based on an intraoperative business model, whereby business analytics make continuous decisions while executing any transaction, with the possibility to combine all the aspects of the traditionally reserved activities (that the current regulatory framework shared among several different types of intermediaries): banking, financial services, asset management, insurance, and so on.

It is important considering there seem to have been very few studies that have directly examined the cognitive skills underlying business decision making during operations (under a law and economic perspective), probably because in traditional business models the power to decide is fragmented in the organizational structure of the supervised entities, and so any immediate action is confined within the boundaries of the powers held by the relevant employee (and the most relevant operations are managed directly by the board of directors).[29] On the contrary, there is a specific need for investigating the intraoperative decisions in fintech firms because of the role of algorithms that are able to instantly activate any part of the decision process while it is supporting a transaction.

In this context, a regulatory point of view shows the absence of any significant change to the relevant legislative framework that supports this interoperability, nor the option for complete freedom in starting up a fintech firm.

In other words, the results of the current analysis can be summarized in the question concerning the duty to respect the current regulatory reserves, provided there is not an exception that allows the automation of the relative business to put the fintechers outside the actual scope of the regulation or supervision. Indeed, it is not possible to agree that a *freedom* arises from the absence of human actions when an automated tool executes the reserved activities (and, then, an algorithm chooses both what type of services and how it should be provided to customers) (Blemus, S. 2017). And this dissenting opinion is based on the fact that—on the top of the chain—there are humans that programmed these algorithms to choose 'what and how' from amongst a set of combinations (set by such programmers), so that there is full responsibility of the humans for setting up both the algorithm and information. And then there is a specific need for traditional supervision also, aimed at regulating and controlling programmers and coders.

Following the perspective arising from the aforesaid regulatory point of view, it should be borne in mind that banking and banks are both regulated. And the same is true for asset management and managers, finance and financial firms, insurance and insurance undertakings. This projects the (part of the) analysis (dedicated to the fintech firms) to the conclusion that regulators would not be able to make any distinction between automatic and human-driven firms that provide the same services (Schrepel, T. 2018). Therefore, both need to meet the same high-quality standards and duty of care in order to satisfy the need to protect individual rights and market stability. Hence, the interoperability of fintech firms seems to be an effect of the current lack of supervision over fintech, provided that, in principle, any supervised entity can extend its business in such a direction (by implementing its organizational structure and resources). There was a time when universal banking included financial services, direct investments and other services related to risk and money (and the policy-makers did refuse such a configuration of banking after the crisis of the 1929).[30]

6.4   The *Role* of Web-based Platforms in a *Tragedy* of the Commons

In the past few years, capital circulation has expanded beyond the dynamics experienced during the twentieth century, whereby website technology has been used for designing a virtual shared-resource system where individual users, acting independently according to their own self-interests, behave by offering or demanding money or risks. Indeed, technological evolution has made possible the circulation of money through new types of systems (such as a website), based on the possession of a compatible electronic instrument (a device), the use of a computer program (an application), and the access to an interconnection network (even immaterial). In other words, through technological solutions, these websites host platforms that allow the execution of exchanges (or the provision of services) that in the past were exclusively related to the performance of reserved activities (by credit institutions, brokerage firms, asset managers, insurance companies, etc.) (FSB 2017d).[31]

A specific role is played by the infrastructure (digital or traditional) behind the website, through which customers can exercise their negotiations; an infrastructure that must be taken into consideration by the regulator in order to ensure the compliance of the relevant platform to the disciplinary framework. The same is true for the firms running the website, programming the algorithms of the platform, and managing the data of the customers.[32] From this perspective, all these kinds of firms will be considered as fintech firms, and as such have to be regulated and controlled.

A useful starting point for verifying the above consideration is the diffusion of the platforms, whose wide (subjective and objective) scope must be taken into account in assessing the need for supervising the fintech industry. This takes the research beyond the assumptions made during the twentieth century, when the circulation of capital was achieved through the intervention of an intermediary or the direct access to trading venues, in an juridical order that requires full compliance with specific rules of conduct, transparency and protection of the weak contractor.[33]

That said, the analysis is going to highlight that, in general, fintech platforms support the matching of the supply and demand formulated by subjects in surplus with that of others in deficit. So, their operating offers a common alternative to the services that are carried out through the intermediation of a traditional matrix (i.e. the exercise of the lending or the provision of activities and financial services by supervised subjects, as well as the management of the trading venues).

It is worth noting that, before the advent of the 2000s new economy, the capital market was characterized by a static content (of activities and services) and a minimum of interactivity (between firms and customers), even if there had been some relevant innovation due to the application of technology (Demers, E. A. et al. 2002).[34] Only in recent times, in fact, have operators started using—in a systematic manner—ICT tools for the management of the contents of the relative relationship (from new infrastructures, to new devices, to new block programming). In addition, in the same short period, the orientation towards the integration of mechanisms able to auto-operate the activity and the service provided to customers has been observed. The same is true for the accessing of firms to significant aggregations of information (so-called big data) and the application of new software architectures (including blockchain technology), with the effect of overcoming the standardization that has characterized the 'mass market'. Nowadays, in fact, the relationship between companies/intermediaries and customers are projected beyond this type of market (and in the end, they take as a reference a "mass of markets").[35]

Here it is a confirmation of the *forthcoming* central importance of the platforms in the financial sector. Hence, the need for understanding whether they should be considered as 'new commons' (or rather, as shown below, a new form of market).

This is not denying, in the context of general application of ICT tools and the affirmation of a 'digital single market', the increases in competition (and the new types of incentives that suggest the intermediaries to evolve), nor the possibility that platforms will induce market participants to overcome the concentration of relationships (credit and debt) in the assets of a bank. The outcome of the analysis is simply introducing that firms managing platforms are also involved in the current trend of automation of the business processes and innovation of the systems. Moreover, the use of platforms improves the conditions of performing reserved activities, and supervised entities are now starting to be commonly and widely used 'fintech solutions' that apply digital identification, mobile applications, cloud computing, big data analysis, artificial intelligence, blockchain and distributed ledger technologies (FSB 2017a).[36]

It is also worth anticipating the importance of the speed of the application of the results of scientific research to the forms and methods of exercising reserved activities; speed that is accelerated by the improvement of personal devices and by the affirmation of new needs (of resources and performance) expressed by an integrated society (so-called wired society). Devices and needs are, therefore, elements that—as a result of technological innovation—determine innovative ways to reach an agreement (including through access to platforms that frequently impose lower costs than those that characterize traditional negotiations). Thus, there is evidence of activities (i) alternative to the banking system (so called non-bank financial intermediation), (ii) instrumental (aimed at improving the use of traditional services, e.g. websites comparing the offer), or (iii) other similar activity (and the need for a special authorization, e.g. FinTech Banks).[37]

Central, in such an investigative perspective, is the interference between the provision of services (for the circulation of risks, assets and money) and the management of the infrastructure supporting these services[38]; both are integrated in a computerized system that gives content to a 'platform'. This, obviously, occurs in a context that today still needs the safeguards provided for the protection of savings, price stability and the promotion of competition.

With regard to what has been outlined so far, it is useful to dwell on the first regulatory directions concerning the innovations that the technological evolution has brought regarding the reserved activities that are carried out. This aspect comes into consideration with respect to the safe and sound management (of the supervised entity), the transparency of information, the correctness (of business relations), and the financial stability (of economic systems) (ECB 2018).[39] Hence, there is a double path for developing this investigation: on the one hand, towards the verification of the contents of the activities supported by the platforms, and on the other hand, towards the failures in which such activities may incur (if carried out in the absence of appropriate corrective measures).

It should also be borne in mind that the Financial Stability Board, in its analysis, has considered the application of 'technology-enabled innovation in financial services' to be useful in order to formulate indications aimed at guiding the regulator towards the adoption of a complex disciplinary system that takes into account the peculiarities of such an "ecosystem".[40]

Therefore the FSB's discussion on global and regional financial vulnerabilities highlighted the need to monitor these innovations (FSB 2019b).[41] In particular, the suggestion of a supervisory mechanism refers to a limited space (the so-called regulatory sand-box), with the goal of gaining experience to adapt the current regulation to the supervision of firms that make widespread use of technology to operate across intangible networks (when they intervene in the movement of capital or in the provision of an activity with similar content or effects to those of reserved activities) (FSB 2017c).[42]

In light of the above, it is possible to agree with the decision to turn attention to platforms that—being 'self-standing'[43]—exploit new ways of supplying and demanding capital (and consequently, to support the option of extending the supervision beyond the cases in which an intermediary merely applies a platform in the provision of its services).[44] In fact, both the management of this kind of 'supporting infrastructures' and the relevant provision of services (alternative, instrumental or in any case connected to the circulation of capital) must be taken into account. And with respect to these elements, it becomes possible to observe that the supply and the demand (matched by means of the platforms) realizes *mere* composition of reciprocal interests (to give and to have).[45] This composition in turn justifies the transferring of information and orders, to be regulated then through settlements and deliveries (anchored to the systems provided for by the legal framework applicable to the financial product or the money that is the object of the exchange).

Regardless of the analyses formulated by the FSB with reference to cryptocurrencies (mentioned in the following chapter), it is necessary to consider the conclusions reached with regard to the possible systemic implications of the most recent developments of fintech. Indeed, conditions of greater competition and diversification (in the granting of financing, collection of savings, provision of payment services, etc.) could lead to a more resilient financial system. However, there is a real danger that such a system will be characterized by high levels of competitive pressure, hence there is the threat that this may induce intermediaries to take risks of a new kind. In addition, the risk of an abuse of the power held by their ICT service providers (and in particular, by the large companies that are technologically more advanced, the so-called BigTech) must also be taken into account.[46]

All of the above challenges the reliance of platforms themselves.

That said, it is necessary to have regard to the approach proposed by the European Commission (through the 'Financial Technology Action Plan' COM_2018, 109). A common EU regulatory goal is identified in the adoption of a European framework capable of enabling companies operating in the EU single market to benefit from financial innovation and to provide their customers with services that are appropriate (to new needs) and accessible (electronically).[47] This approach also aims at encouraging the spread of new types of financial activities (allowed by the technological innovation process), under a legal order able to avoid asymmetries within the capital market (between traditional operators and platforms), because any asymmetry could undermine trade security and system stability (in the absence of self-executing tools able to block operations able to undermine the welfare).

This explains the EU proposal for a complex set of rules that would enable operators to expand throughout the internal market only if harmonized, clear and consistent authorization requirements were met (enacting—to this end—a common regime for all bodies, i.e. regardless of whether traditional or innovative tools are used to support the circulation of capital).[48] Therefore, it is possible to rely on a clear regulatory trend aimed at applying the mutual recognition principle also to platforms and activities that use the most advanced technological innovations to allow or support the circulation of capital (Lothian, T. 2010 and Lothian, T. 2011). Thus, a first conclusion can be summarized with regard to the prospective of a remodelling of the European system aimed at ensuring the neutrality of the business model of reference (traditional or fintech).

This suggests to convene that the platforms cannot be considered as mere commons. However, even continuing to assume such an interpretation (of platforms as commons), the policymakers cannot support their deregulation (as it is in the case of commons). This conclusion is supported by the generally accepted theory that "ruin is the destination toward which all men rush, each pursuing his own best interest in a society that believes in the freedom of the commons. Freedom in a commons brings ruin to all" (Hardin, G. 1968) However, this theory does not consider the possibility that a 'regtech tool' would be able to avoid that the algorithms will pursue the individual interest of a market participant by damaging the common welfare, because of a 'string' that would stop a transaction that produces a social negative result or that will not be inclusive or sustainable in the long run. Obviously, if such possibility exists, the policymaker should decide to limit the private actions by means of self-executing controls aimed at leading the private affairs to the social utility.

6.5   The Possibility to Regulate a Platform as 'Market Operator'

From a regulatory standpoint, in the capital market, technological platforms perform a dual function: referring the former to the provision of services (alternative or instrumental to the exercise of reserved activities) and the latter to the circulation of capital (and so, to the meeting of supply and demand).[49] Moreover, the firms running platforms operate the decision necessary for the functioning of this business itself.[50] In this respect, it can also be noted that platforms operate as multilateral systems that bring together or facilitate the bringing together of multiple third-party supplying and demanding interests in a way that results in a contract among these third-parties.

The result is an apparent dualism between the functions of providing service and those of managing the market, so that the activity of a platform does not exhaust its value in the bilateral relationship (related to servicing), but extends itself to influence the generalized dynamics of this web-based environment. Hence, the first reason for supporting a public intervention aimed at controlling these platforms and avoiding asymmetries or failures (which, as is well known, distance the exchanges from optimal results) (FSB 2017c and FSB 2019a).

It seems now appropriate to start from the general rule that the operation of the platforms must comply with the rules laid down for the exercise of reserved activities to which they refer.[51] According to this rule, the fintech firms managing platforms used by supervised entities must be also subject to specific regulatory assessments (able to evaluate the benefit of regulating the management of the infrastructure, and when appropriate, of reserving its exercise to qualified entities) (Scherer, M. U. 2015). This explains the orientation (of the supervisory authorities) that brings the exercise of the aforesaid activities (similar to the traditional ones) within the scope of traditional supervision (as it will be possible to specify with reference to the ECB approach to the so-called Fintech Banks).

There is no doubt that the regulation of the EU capital market has always sought to direct the effects of technological innovation towards the traditional aims pursued by public intervention in the real economy and financial market (with regard to Articles 41 and 47 of the Italian Constitution, as well as Article 127 of the Treaty on European Union). One more time, it is worth recalling that many scholars, over time, have analysed the choices of the legislator on the diffusion of the most relevant technological innovations, by highlighting the generalized recourse to measures aimed at supporting the evolution of the reserved activities (electronic money, distance offering, etc.).[52]

With specific regard to banking regulation, it seems possible to believe that the application, by a credit institution, of the fintech innovations interacts with its business model, and therefore, such interaction requires a self-assessment process concerning the activities to be performed and the related organizational structure. This also requires identifying the types of risks (including operational risks, with regard to the principles set forth by CRD V–CRR II) that could arise because of the innovations made possible by the technology of a platform.[53] It is obvious that, in such a case, the policymakers ought to ensure that the benefits (due to the application of these innovations to the banking business models) will not jeopardize the overall financial stability or the common welfare.[54]

In this context, it should be borne in mind that—if the aforesaid conditions are met—the current rules on internal organization and outsourcing may apply. Significant at this point are the rules concerning outsourcing, included—as it will be shown in the paragraphs below—in the perimeter of the supervision (and in particular with regard to art. 3, paragraph 1, point 17, of the Directive 2013/36/EU and art. 4, paragraph 1, point 18, of the EU Regulation no. 575/2013, where it is expressly refers to an outsourcer as "an undertaking the principal activity of which consists of owning or managing property, managing data-processing services, or a similar activity which is ancillary to the principal activity of one or more institutions").[55]

The same attention should be paid to the role of platforms in connection with collective portfolio management because of the growing importance of the fintech firms' running these platforms, and through the provision of varied services, supporting asset managers to implement the investment policies of their investment funds (through one or more systems that allow the matching of supply and demand of goods included in the scope of the funds themselves).[56] It goes without saying that the business model of an asset manager can be influenced by the configuration of such platforms (and then, by the content of the agreements concluded between the fintech firms and the asset manager). This leads to the obvious consequence of evaluating innovations with regard to the discipline of outsourcing essential or important operational functions, as well as services (an example is provided by art. 50 et seq., Joint Regulation of the Bank of Italy—Consob on the organization and procedures of intermediaries). Hence, this analysis is going to verify—considering the concrete aspects of the functioning of these platforms—whether the relations among fintech firms and asset managers involve a sort of outsourcing (whereas, in the affirmative, public intervention applies).

Trying to summarize an interim conclusion, it is useful to point out a regulatory framework aimed at monitoring the relationships that may exist between supervised entities and platforms, as well as the adoption of specific rules to govern the innovation of the operating model of traditional operators.

However, as will be seen in the following paragraphs, the rules on outsourcing appear inadequate to reach the aforesaid goals, so it is possible to suggest that the firms running platforms should obtain an authorization (as it is provided for the exercise of similar activities managing the multilateral systems that bring interests together).[57] Indeed, it is difficult to justify that the activities that are carried out through the application of these technological innovations are not going under the scrutiny of any authority. On the contrary, it is clear that the platforms are a 'perfect substitute' for those activities that banks perform, in a low-tech environment, to support the capital circulation that their customers need.

Otherwise (i.e., by bringing the management of the platforms back among the non-reserved activities), there would be an asymmetry (in terms of costs and safeguards) that is difficult to justify with reference to the effectiveness (of the individual rights) and the efficiency (of the financial market). Consequently, it is not possible to *reduce* the platforms themselves as a 'peculiarity' of the banking business model (and not as an operational innovation, which determines the exercise of activities outside the scope of supervision).

Infrastructure, devices and programming are the elements that the regulator may consider in order to set up a public intervention that makes irrelevant the level of technology used by an operator to provide services related to the matching of supply and demand in the capital market. Rather, an intervention that supports the safe application of innovation to the circulation of capital is what is desired.

From a law and economics perspective, in fact, there is no suitable justification to allow fintech firms, solely because of their mere use of technological innovation, to seize new opportunities without following a safe process (similar to that provided to take possession of the authorization to carry out one of the reserved activities that these firms intended to replace, supplement or improve).[58] The European Central Bank's "Guide to assessments of fintech credit institution licence applications" also provides evidence in this respect. In re-calling the fintech definition of the FSB, the ECB also refers to banks that adopt "a business model in which the production and delivery of banking products and services are based on technology-enabled innovation", considering them to be subject to control. It refers in particular to: (i) new firms owned by existing entities (authorized to carry out banking activities); (ii) newly created entities (entering the market and adopting technological innovation to compete with established banks along the entire value chain); (iii) existing financial services providers (payment institutions, investment firms, electronic money institutions, etc.); (iv) new entities (entering the market and adopting technological innovation to compete with established banks along the entire value chain), or (v) existing financial services providers (payment institutions, investment firms, electronic money institutions, etc.) that extend their mission to banking (and for this reason need to be authorized to do so).

It seems clear now that this stage of the analysis supports a holistic approach to platforms. Accordingly, it is necessary to verify compliance with the regulatory principles of the mechanisms used for organizing and running the platforms. While awaiting a review of the relevant regulatory framework, what remain to be regulated are the requirements and the constraints related to the running of platforms that substitute banking.[59] With particular reference to the business of credit institutions, in fact, it is necessary to consider whether the collection of savings between the public and the exercise of credit should *always* be achieved through the interposition of the supervised entities' own funds (which internalize credits and debts in their own juridical spheres). On the contrary, a dissenting opinion would consider banking also in cases of the performance of such collection and lending by supporting the direct dealing of subjects in surplus and in deficit (remaining—the firm—extraneous to the relative debtor/creditor relationships, and keeping these subjects behind the platform).[60]

In the end, looking at the evolution of business models, specific doubts arise as to the possibility that firms running platforms can operate without any form of supervision. This would be in opposition to the general principle that attributes a kind of neutrality (*rectius*: indifference) to the technology of the mechanism used with respect to the purposes that the parties intended to achieve. At the present time, clear attention of the supervisory authorities towards the evolution of banking is outlined, as well as the intention of the European regulator to reduce the freedom in exercising activities alternative to those regulated within the perimeter of the Single Supervisory Mechanism and the European System of Financial Supervision (as highlighted in the previous chapters). Hence, this stage of the analysis provides another reason for supporting an assessment of the current regulatory framework and the supervising practices, by taking into account the necessity of an intervention capable of preserving (but controlling) the variegated opportunities arising from the application of technology to capital markets.

6.6   Fintech Firms as Outsourcers of Banks and Other Supervised Entities

It is worth investigating the role of fintech firms as outsourcers of supervised entities, provided that the current set up of market regulation aims at ensuring that the latter provide a safer and sounder environment for savers and borrowers. Nowadays, more than a decade later, the general outsourcing guidelines provided in 2006 by the Committee of European Banking Supervisors (CEBS guidelines) are showing their limits. As anticipated in the previous chapters, outsourcing tendencies are more and more evolving (in their contents and relationships), and the supervising authorities are providing additional guidance for specific contexts.[61]

Indeed, it is possible to verify the assumption that the role of fintech-outsourcers be designed to respect the general principles set forth for the relationship between supervised entities and third-parties (and, as specified below, there can be conditions for maximizing the wealth, and yet the market becomes more unstable and riskier).[62] On the contrary, there would be concrete justification for the asymmetries that would support the option for an unregulated environment for fintechers. The goal of supervision, in fact, is to avoid jeopardizing both competition (in banking and finance) and the effectiveness of public interventions over management.[63]

Thus, it is useful to remember the conclusion of the previous chapter to share the preliminary assumption that software and big data analytics models are driving transformation across the market of capital by providing its operators with the capability of conducting extensive analytics rapidly.[64] Hence, it is acknowledged that the applications of both software and big data analytics are becoming more prevalent in the functioning of supervised entities and their customers, as a basis for both the decision-making processes (including the adoption of the resolution of the governance bodies) and the direct provision of services to customers (across the full range of the supply chain, including lending, investment and insurance). However, the complexity and opacity of decision-making software and big data analytics do not manage to dispel the *lingering* doubts concerning the possibility that market participants are not *fully* in control of their decision-making processes (that remains constrained by certain undisclosed predetermined software's automatisms).[65] And this possibility elevates uncertainty.

This is not only referring to the fact that many algorithms are intrinsically difficult to audit (more difficult than humans are), nor to the time constraints that limit the possibility of assessing the benefits and desirability of the concrete results that—according to the analyses run through these software—the firm should operate at the provided price risk (Alpa, G. 2013). The results of the analysis are pointing out also the possibility that the programmers choose to fix certain outcomes (that cannot be changed by any intervention of the managers of the customer that runs the software).

It is useful discussing about banks as companies that outsource certain stage of their business process to optimize the way they accede to the financial market.[66] This places a direct relationship between the supply provided by the outsourcer and the way the banks match the demand for and the supply of capital, by originating risks with a direct impact on their equity.[67] Indeed, the essence of their role is in connection with the possibility to satisfy the needs of people who have resources in surplus with others that are willing to remunerate a temporary leasing of money, without the need for a direct relationship between these people (who would be connected through the bank itself). This activity implies overcoming the barriers that hamper the meeting of demand and supply with obstacles which are referable to the asynchrony of deadlines, the asymmetry of risk profiles, and the existence of geopolitical difficulties.[68] Hence, policymakers—in deciding if and how regulate to fintech outsourcers—cannot discard that banks are under public supervision because of both the relevance of the interests involved in their activities and the effect of this business on monetary policies.

It is worth considering that the success of fintechers as service providers of banks may be one of the effects of the 'outsourcing wave' going on in the banking sector. The results of this analysis will clarify the need for regulating the limits to the organizational structure required to perform the credit intermediation activities by means of fintech tools, in order to apply the principles underlying the rules provided by Directive no. 2013/36/EU in the technological environment currently hosting the banking industry. In particular, it is required to understand the *ifs* and *hows* that the 'outsourcing agreements' between banks and fintech firms affect the mechanisms, processes, and relationships by which banks are directed (having regard to the circulation of information, the evaluation of creditworthiness, and the internal controls). This requires also investigating whether these agreements jeopardize competition or the safe and sound management of banks.[69]

Sometimes, outsourcing is not an option but the direct consequence of certain market conditions (Grote, M. H. and Taube, F. A. 2007). This is referred to in the results of the integrated analyses of horizontal and vertical links to operators acting within and outside the firm's perimeter. Even if these analyses show qualitative evidence (from interviews with investment bank analysts), there is the need to consider that the option of outsourcing (of certain stages of business processes and offshoring parts of the value chain) to providers placed in low-wage countries is possible only if the relevant processes can be linked to the departments which remain in the bank. This is more evident in the case of the UK industry, where the world-wide English language helps the banks approach the emerging countries (of the commonwealth and, in particular, India).[70] However, British authorities have always been aware that international outsourcing (to lower-wage countries) can best be understood through models that explain the vertical organization of credit intermediation.[71]

At this stage of the analysis, it is worth considering the 'research and development' department and highlighting that it had been the origin of numerous choices that have contributed to the spread and the triggering of the recent financial crises (Martinez, M. and Sorrentino, M. 2000). The outsourcing of such departments risks amplifying shocks (endogenous or exogenous), due to the strict interconnection of fintech outsourcers, the possibility of a correlation in choices, and the reduction of the 'spaces' that should prevent the domino effect.

Provided that banking refers to a specific way of collecting savings and granting credit (by involving the assets and liabilities of a credit institution), it is likely that fintech would be able to offer the possibility to reduce the circulation of capital to a set of contracts, whose function would refer to deposit and lending without the participation of a credit institution. According to this expectation, it is foreseeable that certain banks may choose not to provide banking, but to support the circulation of capital only (via fintech). This would imply the minimization of the organizational structure of these banks below a certain size by relying on fintech (and its outsourcers) to execute all the activities required to collect savings, arrange the maturity transformation process, provide loans, and manage risks.[72]

In this respect, the primary role attributed by the legal system of trust within the financial industry has to be highlighted. Therefore, any policy of outsourcing must be compatible with prerogatives of the open market (Alpa, G. 2013).

Hence the need for humans to guide the use of fintech outsourcers, software, and any other tool useful for providing banking. In this context, it is worth considering some interventions that were made to this business by the European regulator, in an attempt to rebalance the role and powers of the 'ancillary services undertakings', which supply *services* (to the intermediaries) according to the outsourcing model, being independent (from senior management) but responsible (for the externalization).[73] Thus we will be better able to understand which limits must be applied to fintech firms, and if there is any need for additional constraint.

It is acknowledged that the European regulation links the banking execution modalities to the structural profiles of credit institutions (and to specific corporate governance and internal control measures, from the view of the proper functioning of any bank).[74] Moreover, there is no doubt that the attention paid by the EU policymakers to the organizational structure does not rely on the mere verification of the mathematical models, nor on the relationships between the resources and the capital adequacy requirements.

Here and now, there is the need to analyze the supervisory mechanisms in order to understand which of these are able to verify the *adequacy* of the company's business analytics (due to the application of fintech tools), along with the need for an efficient delivery of banking. This would lead to the conclusion that public intervention can predetermine (or at least limit) the cases in which a bank will outsource certain processes by which it performs its own banking activity.[75] However, it is necessary to identify the backstops required to ensure that the processes based on algorithms are able to combine the banks' need for solidity with the growing levels of efficiency and profitability (set as objectives by ownership and supervisors).[76]

This approach helps in understanding how the definition of a minimum size (of a bank's internal organization) should be considered as a supervisory action that aims at identifying a rational balance between the tendency to take advantage of innovation and the need to avoid that banks not have any people (employees) becoming vehicles and no-longer business entities.[77] Therefore, there is the need to update the contents of Directive 2013/36/EU, which sets the regulation for credit institutions, in addressing the definition of art. 4, paragraph 1, point 1, of the (EU) Regulation no. 575/2013. This directive defines a bank according to its activity (lending) and its structure (which must present adequate levels of professionalism), but does not take care of the relevant ICT architecture.[78]

Bearing in mind the aforesaid conclusion on fintech operations, it is doubtful that the contracts (agreed between the bank and the fintech firms) implement the rules required to apply the strategies of outsourcing chosen by the management bodies (of the bank). It is also useful to take into account these contracts because they are particularly significant in the analysis of fintech processes and the control of the activity of fintech firms (especially while operating as outsourcers of the banks).[79] Indeed, once fintech firms are chosen to entrust some stages of the bank's production cycle, the establishment of contractual regulations cannot limit the supply (by third-parties) and the use (by the bank) of the activities (outsourced), but must define the fintechers, their software and the big data as part of an organizational structure that must be compliant with the indications contained in the authorization provided by the supervisory authority.

Clearly, in 'fintech-ing' one or more business units, the outsourcing must not only consist in the agreement between two parties (who wish to establish and regulate their legal relationship), but it must also consist in a smart-tool that extends its economic function to areas of public oversight compliance (Scherer, M. U. 2015). In the application of fintech by means of outsourcing strategies, the bank should consider the limits that the supervisory system imposes on the exercise of its enterprise, in order to compose the interests that qualify the present case, and to reach a voluntary collaboration that is in line with the quantum authorized by the supervisory authority.

Consequently, in these agreements, the *stare pactis* extends its efficacy beyond the legal sphere of the contracting parties, as the rules that they have voluntarily established influence the stability of the intermediary, and the correct movement of capital (entrusted to it by the market).[80] So, the consensus and the formation of any contract supporting fintech servicing must follow not only the pursuit of the interests of the parties (cost reduction or efficiency of procedures, and the maximizing of profit) but also an economic balance that preserves the more general interest of the safe and sound management of the banking industry.

In this context, it is easy to understand the reason why the contents of these agreements must continue to be under examination by the supervisory authority. It is a duty of loyalty and transparency that is one of the prerequisites for the smooth operation of the internal market (advocated by recital no. 6 of Directive 2013/36/EU), which "requires not only legal rules but also close and regular cooperation and significantly enhanced convergence of regulatory and supervisory practices between the competent authorities of the Member States".[81]

The object of the (outsourcing) contract and that of the (fintech) obligation are, therefore, the pillars of a private legal background that allows (a bank) to carry out certain functions outside the supervised entity's juridical sphere, for reasons of convenience (or managerial politics) attributable to the ideas of the management or the ownership. This suggests that the proper definition of contractual settlement (and the obligation resulting from it) is essential to limiting the risks. Otherwise, the option for fintech may be considered noncompliant with the supervisory requirements, and the relevant contract may be considered null, and under certain circumstances, its obligations may be considered settled.[82]

Beyond that, it will be necessary to evaluate the incidence of banking regulation on the effects of contracts with regard to third-parties. As well as the bank benefits of fintech tools, the fintech firm gains information and data from the bank and its customers or suppliers. In following the traditional criterion of the interests (and not those of participation in the formation of the contract), in fact, doubts are raised about the 'relativity of contracts' (i.e. the identification of those who remain essentially external to the contract and those who are invested in terms of direct effects, reflections, or consequences). And these doubts become observable when referring to the outsourcing of customer management, credit assessment, or automatic trading.

All of the foregoing highlights that the fintech providers must take into account the *quantum* of business authorized to the bank, and therefore, the contents of the aforesaid contract (more than being smart) must reflect the 'program of initial operations'. Otherwise there would be a contrast that could not be considered to be free of juridical consequences.[83] In this regard, the provision of art. 65, dir. 2013/36/EU concerning the supervising tasks to collect the information necessary for this purpose, as well as the opportunity to intervene (through surveys or inspections) on third-parties to whom credit institutions "have outsourced operational functions or activities" must also be taken into account.

In other words, the language of the agreements between banks and fintech firms must show a correspondence to the correctness of the negotiation phase and the responsibility of the provision of safe fintech tools (compliant with professional standards and disclosure requirements provided for the banking industry), considering also the economics of blockchain (and in particular two key costs affected by the technology: the cost of verification and the cost of networking.).[84] Only such correspondence can place fintech between 'service' and 'contract', with duties of conduct (to be borne by the fintechers) that reflects the complexity of the contributions owed by these special kind of service providers.

6.7 The Relevant European Regulatory Framework for 'Management' and 'Ancillary Services Undertaking'

The EU regulations place one or more "management bodies"—including 'the persons who effectively direct the business of the institution'—at the center of the banking governance; these bodies are entrusted (by the statutory by-laws) with the power to define the strategies of the bank and to supervise senior management. This clarifies the European regulator's will to allocate the persons who are in charge of the management of the power in a single assembly, according to an effectiveness criterion that will promote the transparency of the organization, its supervision, and consequently, the imputation of certain responsibilities (art. 3, para 1, points 7–8, Dir. 2013/36/EU). Evidently, this regulatory set up does not comply with the perspective of business analytics whereby the bank can be driven by (the reliance on) software, self-executing business models, high-tech devices and automatic trading.[85]

At the operational level, the use of software supports the managers in pursuing the integrity of the accounting and financial reporting systems, together with the monitoring of the process of (internal and external) communication. But it does not mean that they remain in the hands of the bank's managers. On the contrary, the activity of the fintech firms outlines a network of functions and information (linked to the bodies responsible for corporate governance, even if) extended towards the external providers (who may use the information contained therein for the achievement of their own institutional purposes). This leads to worries that cannot be squelched by considering that this network is subject to controls by the competent authorities (and to complying with Directive 2013/36/EU and Regulation (EU) No. 575/2013).[86]

The focus goes to the outsourcing of banking-relevant functions to fintech firms. Obviously, the alternative between 'originated to hold' or 'originated to distribute' business model influences the outsourcing strategies and the use of fintech tools. Indeed, an algorithm can manage the following option: keeping (within the assets of the current bank) or transferring (to third parties) the credits originating from lending.[87] In the first case, fintech tools relate to the asset management (sometimes owned by outsourcers), whose function is outsourced (in whole or in part). In the second case, the ancillary activity of fintech firms concern the financial products and on the contracts used for the sale of the assets, as well as on the application of the most advanced techniques of credit enhancement or maturity transformation (developed by specialized outsourcers).[88]

Hence, the possibility that programmers (instead of managers) will drive the choice for a holding or a distributing business model. This possibility, at first glance, appears oriented towards entrusting fintechers with the responsibility of the 'production function' (or rather: intermediation formula) of the serviced bank. However, it should be noted that these possibilities raise specific problems in terms of the allocation of managerial decisions (and of commoditization of the banking business, as is now happening in the Italian mutual banks after the structuring of two groups whose hundreds of banks are served by the same outsourcers[89]). In fact, the use—approved by the management body—of an algorithm or a software owned by third-parties involves specific organizational consequences, both for the dependence of the fintecher providing it, and for the outsourcing of tasks that qualify the essence of the banker.[90]

It is acknowledged that the option for the 'origin to distribute' model places the bank on the border of the 'shadow banking system', becoming the provider of assets to be used in its chains. This suggests the need to identify the rules for controlling the cases in which a fintecher, after being the service provider for banks, will be the firm that provides support to securitizations (originated by the aforesaid banks). It is understood that the intervention of a fintech firm should not place some stages of the movement of capital outside the scope of the supervision, but must support an efficient system of trading. Therefore, banks must adopt certain internal rules to avoid that outsourcing to fintech firms will lead to a significant proliferation of the risks (in compliance with art. 98, paragraph 3, dir. 2013/36/EU).

Reaching a first conclusion on this point, it can be said that fintech firms should produce easily measurable quantitative improvements in banking (in terms of cost reduction or increase of the output). However, the intervention of such firms as outsourcer (which produces one or more phases of the tasks necessary for the conduct of banking) follows contractual rules (predetermined at the time of the commitment) that are not attributable to traditional forms of a business relationship. It is clear that this relationship (between the management bodies of the bank and the fintechers) will have an equal—bilateral character, having to conform its provisions to the will of the supervisory authorities (Annunziata, F. 2018 and Merusi, F. 2014).

In brief, it is worth questioning the provision according to which "the competent authorities shall grant authorization to commence the activity of a credit institution only where at least two persons effectively direct the business of the applicant credit institution" (art. 13, dir. 2013/36/EU). If on the one hand the minimal number identified (two people) overcomes the longstanding problem of the monocratic direction of a company, on the other it stands at a level very contained, whose capacity to ensure that the banks operate relies on software and outsourcers.[91] It is not possible to deny that the European regulator refers to an essential core of individuals that, being the head of governance, must necessarily be supported by a community (of individuals), which supports the intermediation activities that characterize the business purpose of the institution in question (Harris, A. et al. 1998). However, after the fintech (r)evolution, these rules legalize an intensive and extensive reliance on fintech tools. Anyway, private self-regulation sets the organization, which must be arranged within the limits specified by the technical standards developed by the EBA and approved by the Commission, as well as by the conditions laid down by the Member States (art. 8, dir. 2013/36/EU).

Provided that bankers will rely on fintechers, it is possible to understand the way to show such reliance within the 'program of activities' (which accompanies the application for a bank's authorization), whose contents must indicate both the type of operations provided and the organizational structure of the credit institution (art. 8, dir. 2013/36/EU).[92]It is now appropriate to analyse the role of a fintech firm as potential "ancillary services undertaking", as nowadays the European institutions consider it. Indeed, it is expected that the clarification of the problems underlying these services will allow the evaluation of the parameters that a credit institution must use in order to adapt its business to the new challenges arising in a high-tech environment.

Indeed, fintech firms operating as outsourcers of banks may be considered as "ancillary to the principal activity of one or more institutions" (art. 4, paragraph 1, point 18, of EU Regulation no. 575/2013 and art. 3, paragraph 1, point 17, of Directive 2013/36/EU). This does not mean that all the high-tech providers are banks' outsourcers, nor that all the bank suppliers can be subject to a special regime (if their activity does not refer to a service essential for banking core functions). However, this definition seems to be drafted for comprehending a wide range of subjects, taking into account the type of work performed and its "ancillary" character in relation to banking.[93] Furthermore, the qualification as ancillary leads to the subjection of the fintech business to supervision (accordingly to art. 118 of Directive 2013/36/EU), even when these are not *subjective proliferations* linked to the banking group. In fewer words, the legislation clarifies that public supervision extends itself to these firms because of the servicing relationship that connects them with banks.[94]

Recalling EU Regulation n. 575 of 2013 (art. 4, point 27, and 15) helps in considering an ancillary business undertaking to be included within the financial consolidation of a credit institution as a "financial sector entity", with obvious consequences on the application of the supervision requirements. Significant, in this matter, is that the intention to avoid the outsourcing of business functions has an impact on the calculation of the elements of the Common Equity Tier 1 (which will therefore have to deduct any contingent liability towards ancillary companies that would otherwise be consolidated), and the calculation of the minimum core capital (in which one has to consider: the full value of the holdings, the subordinated credits, and other instruments relating to these companies). This justifies the need for monitoring the capital and the funding sources of all the companies included in the banking group, identified by the European Regulator, which comes to impose the adoption of specific internal controls to the EU investment firms (art. 15, paragraph 1, last paragraph of the EU Regulation n. 575/2013). However, it should be highlighted that the legislation does not exclude the possibility of a proportional consolidation (even through the use of the so-called equity method), where this is not an obstacle for the effective protection of the savings collected by the intermediary (art. 18, EU regulation 575/2013).[95]

In other words, the regulation regarding the capital requirements for credit risk reaches the objective of preventing that fintech allows an arbitrage in the application of the capital adequacy rules. What is significant, in this regard, is that institutions may choose to treat equity exposures to ancillary services undertakings in accordance with the treatment of 'other non-credit obligation assets' (art. 155, EU regulation n. 575/2013).

6.8   The Need for Supervising Fintech Firms Servicing Banks

The doubt that the outsourcing of banking functions to fintech firms may affect the organizational structure of the bank seems to be clarified; hence the importance of the authorization (originally provided by the supervisory authorities), which marks the perimeter of the internal organization and the use of tech-fueled tools to boost banking performance (Maugeri, M. 2010). Therefore, it is possible conclude that the discipline concerning "management bodies" and "senior management" appears to be only partially adequate to avoid the pursuit of *unbridled* outsourcing policies (Capriglione F. and Sacco Ginevri, A. 2019) in addition to the threat that fintech *empties* the company structure of the bank. Indeed, there is a new challenge for the policymaker—that of identifying a balance point in the relationship between "banking business", "organization," and "individual".[96]

According to the European legal framework, a bank that applies fintech tools must ensure its safe and sound management. Then the main components of internal governance come into consideration: strategies, models, and rational decision-making processes.

In general, policymakers had called for the promotion of an organizational structure in which the operational guidelines and responsibilities were well defined, transparent, and consistent. In particular, effective processes were required (for identification, management, monitoring and risk reporting), as well as adequate structures (for the execution of administrative and accounting tasks, together with the internal audit) (Ray, B. K. et al. 2013). All of the above had been subject to public supervision (from the request for the authorization to pursue banking operations), and consequently, presented to the competent authority—from the early stages of the authorizing procedure—in complete and proportionate (to the nature, scale and complexity of the risks that characterize the plan indicated in the "activity program") modalities. The regulator has been dealing with this issue for long time, in relation to the senior management and to the danger that certain strategies (weighted on short-term volumes or measurements) could undermine the bank's solidity.

Clearly, it is necessary to consider that the current art. 74 of Directive 2013/36/EU is oriented in this way. This article relates organization to the "remuneration policies and practices" in order to ensure that corporate decisions promote sound and effective risk management. However, there are new questions with respect to the fintech phenomenon. Indeed, after a control on the internal personnel (exercising important tasks for the bank) remuneration policies, the principles contained in directive 2013/36/EU (together with the EBA orientations and the principles announced by the Commission[97]) should be extended until they condition the prices for the fintech tools (i.e. the calculation methods for the money owed by the bank to the fintech firms).[98] Hence, there is the need for rules to allow the establishment of a price (for the "service" in question) which would adequately remunerate the programmers providing the algorithms, software and big data analytics, even if their activities are done outside the bank's subjective perimeter.[99]

From a regulatory point of view, the responsibilities of the body appointed to the strategic supervision of the bank come to mind. It is not possible to exclude that a bank that fully applies the fintech tools must consider taking the remuneration of the fintech providers to the "remuneration committee" (set in art. 95 of Directive 2013/36/EU).[100] Obviously, in this regard, the relevant information should also be transmitted to the competent public authorities that, as stated by art. 75 of Directive 2013/36/EU, collect data on the operating procedures of the credit institution to ensure a complete observation of the "trends" in the industry.

On this matter, it is useful to consider the practice of using predictive software to develop policies and strategies (that should be the responsibility of the management bodies of the credit institution). In these cases, the approach to this particular consulting activity leads to conflicting interpretations: for this reason, there is the risk that the bank would apply a standard algorithm without developing a personal operating profile (able to produce a competitive advantage for the credit institution itself), and it would perform a standard business. And if many banks perform a standard business, the supply and the demand will align (leading to a deterioration in competition). Hence, one more reason to consider that fintech falls under a 'reserved activity paradigm', and to prevent that the decision-making process (in which a bank's strategies and business plans are elaborated) is entrusted to a non-supervised entity.[101]

From another perspective, it is clear that the regulation imposes on the management body specific tasks for the organization and the mitigating of "risks the institution is or might be exposed to, including those posed by the macroeconomic environment in which it operates in relation to the status of the business cycle" (art. 76, Dir. 2013/36/EU). In this context, this body must verify that the fintech firm complies with the European standard set forth for the exercise of outsourced functions. With particular reference to the use of software and algorithms to support the internal controls, it seems possible to argue that the organization will have to ensure that these tools: (i) are independent from the software used by the business units; and (ii) have the necessary access to information and data (in compliance with art. 92, dir. 2013/36/EU).

In the light of above, it is clear that any firm that exploits fintech qualifies as a cross-border provider of banking and payment services, as mentioned in the previous chapters with respect to the Swiss evidences and to non-bank nature of that form of financial intermediation. This means that these firms are able to reach any consumers not only across Member States in accordance with EU treaty provisions, but also worldwide. However, the body of EU and international law is structured in a manner that ensures that risks to financial stability and market integrity are mitigated and that consumers are adequately protected, as EBA recently pointed out (EBA 2019a).[102] However, such a body has been designed for an industry based on intermediaries that are centralized and physically established in a territory. Thus, the eligibility of these rules for regulating the non-bank financial intermediation requires their capability to regulate distributed ledger technology and digitalized processes that occurs in the market for supplying and demand capital (in a way that is alternative to banking).

In order to verify the aforesaid capability, it is necessary consider that EU law has been considered highly or less prescriptive, with respect to "the means by which outcomes are to be achieved", depending on the specific product or services, provided that Member States and competent authorities have discretion to bring forward such measures as they consider proportionate. Besides the need for setting new rules aimed at establishing who crosses the borders (the firm or the customer),[103] potential issues refer to the fact that the rules provided for guiding human activities do not always suit digital solutions that enable fintechers to reach a wider population of customers.

Generally speaking, it should be noted that the application of fintech innovations should be oriented towards effective management of the bank, having regard also for the efficiencies in the business (Huges, S. R. 2013). There is no doubt, in fact, that the software represents one of the highest degrees of independence between the functioning of the task and the organizational structure of the bank. However, it is not possible to appreciate the current regulatory set up, which preserves the overall responsibility in the hands of the management body (which is, therefore, also responsible for the approval and monitoring of the implementation of the strategic objectives), and it does not yet involve fintech firms in the responsibilities for providing fintech tools for banking.

6.9   A Focus on the Perspective
of the European Supervisors

In these times of crisis, many banks have suffered competitive pressure due to the need to conquer new market share, to meet the growing expectations of customers, and to maximize shareholders' value. And banks are still exploring fintech tools as a way to mitigate this pressure. Similarly, it must be said in regard to the need to comply with a wavering and increasingly stringent regulation. Since both the theorists and supervisors expect further developments in this field, the possibility that fintech innovations will promote a greater international outsourcing wave (that can also increase the thickness of markets and reduce the transactional costs, given the enforceability of the contracts in foreign countries) must be taken into account. This means that the supervising authorities will focus on the choice of a bank's organizational form.[104] This also explains the reason for the prevalence of firms choosing different organizational forms, rather than focusing on the traditional organizational model.

The previously mentioned pressure spurred the management to research innovative solutions in the fintech market. As shown in the previous chapters, these solutions are not only able to reduce costs but also to take advantage of the experience and the economies (of scale) that allow all outsourcers to deliver 'tailored services' to quickly respond to market challenges.

This shows an industry in which the fintech perspective can promote a homogenization of services (according to the 'one size fits all' theory) (Masera, R. 2014), even when the bank asks for a new software, an algorithm (e.g. contract centre or mortgage operation), or a customer solution (i.e. a full end-to-end business process). Thus, the evolution of the banking sector—from the prevalence of the 'in-house service provision' model to another centred on the intervention of a 'specialist third party provider'—questions the regulator and the supervisory authorities about their capability of evaluating the holistic framework of this new banking system.[105]

In this context, the industry of fintech cannot escape the controls of the new European system of financial supervision, since—according to the deductions of the De La Rosiere Report—the inadequate configuration of banking corporate governance is one of the causes that has contributed to the worsening of the financial crisis. Hence, there is the need to understand the role of the ESRB and the EBA, together with the tasks of the ECB and other competent authorities with respect to the fintech industry itself. Many, in fact, are the intervention profiles necessary to protect the general interests that, in this case, are affected by the solutions provided by fintech firms; this analysis will take into account not only the protection of savings and price stability (from macro and micro-prudential risks) but also consumer rights (i.e. transparency, disclosure and privacy).

It is worth mentioning that the ESRB has prompted the need to examine "the systemic implications of so-called misconduct risk in the banking sector, i.e. the risk that banks are subject to fines and other sanctions due to the violation of good conduct rules". These risks are related to rare events, in relation to which the growing level of sanctions creates "uncertainty about the business model, solvency and profitability of banks". In fact, these risks tend to produce systemic effects (for their inter-subjective, pro-cyclical character and anti-market confidence).[106] It follows the intent

to analyse the definition (together with the EBA) of "a minimum methodology for banks to apply when calculating potential misconduct costs
under stress".[107]

As background, it is useful to bear in mind the contents of the *Guidelines
on Outsourcing*, written before the beginning of the last crisis (and published on the 14 December 2006, by CEBS, and updated on 25 February
2019, by EBA) on the basis of the best practices in the industry.[108] Despite
the problems caused by the absence of 'harmonisation at the EU level in
the area of outsourcing undertaken by credit institutions', it is not surprising that—in 2006—the "different supervisory approaches ... developed
across the EU to address the potential risks arising from this practice" was
already perceived.[109] Overall, according to EBA's explicit statement, the
guidelines have been reviewed to provide better differentiation between
the requirements for the outsourcing of critical and important functions,
to which a stricter framework applies, and for other, non-material,
outsourcing.[110]

However, the "EBA Guidelines on Internal Governance" must be
taken into account, and in particular the fact that they deal with the outsourcing issue together with the regulation of the "management body". It
is easy to extend—one more time—such consideration to fintech firms:
the aforesaid body has to "approve and regularly review the outsourcing
policy of an institution", as the same impacts on the activities and on the
risks that a bank must face (such as operational, reputational and concentration risk) (EBA 2017 and EBA 2011).[111] According to the Eurosystem's regulatory framework, a bank that outsources is responsible for
the effects that the activities carried out produce (in the relationships with
customers or with supervisory authorities), and this (also) applies to cases
of outsourcing to fintech firms.

In this regard, it is useful to rely on the orientation of the ECB, which—
considering the impact of fintech outsourcing to the banking structure—
claims that "bank supervisors seem to deal with outsourcing risk by
encouraging precautionary measures on the part of banks and service providers, and some convergence of supervisory approaches and practices in
relation to outsourcing is under way" (ECB 2004).[112] Concluding on this
point it can be said that—in the last decade—the European supervisory
system has moved towards the management of the outsourcing phenomenon that—as was anticipated in 2005 by the "Basel Committee on
Banking Supervision"—"is increasingly used as a means of both reducing
costs and achieving strategic aims".[113]

And this can encourage the analysis in continuing to assess any feature of fintech from a regulatory perspective.

NOTES

1. In particular, it refers to FSB 2017d. "FinTech credit. Market structure, business models and financial stability implications". Report prepared by a working group established by the Committee on the Global Financial System (CGFS) and the Financial Stability Board (FSB), 22 May.
2. In addition, see Wachter, S. and Mittelstadt, B. and Floridi, L., 2017. "Why a Right to Explanation of Automated Decision-Making Does Not Exist in the General Data Protection Regulation" *International Data Privacy Law* about the circumstance that the right to explanation is viewed as "an ideal mechanism to enhance the accountability and transparency of automated decision-making".
3. Moreover, see Scherer, M. U. 2015. "Regulating Artificial Intelligence Systems: Risks, Challenges, Competencies, and Strategies" *Harvard Journal of Law & Technology*, who highlights "growing chorus of commentators, scientists, and entrepreneurs has expressed alarm regarding the increasing role that autonomous machines are playing in society, with some suggesting that government regulation may be necessary to reduce the public risks that AI will pose", and then explores "the public risks associated with AI and the competencies of government institutions in managing those risks" to conclude with "a proposal for an indirect form of AI regulation based on differential tort liability".
4. Furthermore, see Schrepel, T. 2018. "Is Blockchain the Death of Antitrust Law? The Blockchain Antitrust Paradox" *Georgetown Law Technology Review*, who describes the challenges that blockchain presents for analyses of unilateral anticompetitive practices and proposes some changes to antitrust law and regulations that address those challenges.
5. Let us recall Lemma, V. 2016. "The Shadow Banking System. Creating Transparency in the Financial Markets". London, p. 67 ff. where it has been clarified that "The words 'shadow bank' suggest that, in the system under observation, there is a subject performing fund raising and lending by acting (i) outside the areas of public supervision, and (ii) in the absence of direct relations with the monetary authorities. ... On the contrary, in the shadow banking system, more companies are observed dealing together to lend money, create securities, and collect capitals on the financial markets. Currently there is a binomial formula that summarizes the economical function of the shadow credit intermediation process, unifying in a single 'black box' a reality that, in legal terms, involves different subjects and scope in the process that goes from the organization

of any shadow banking operation to the satisfaction of (credit) demand and supply (of CDO securities)".

6. This is not dwelling with the effects of patents on the starting up of a firm; see Graham, S.J.H. and Merges, R. P. and Samuelson, P. and Sichelman, T. M., 2008. "High Technology Entrepreneurs and the Patent System: Results of the 2008 Berkeley Patent Survey" *Berkeley Technology Law Journal*, p. 255 ff.

7. It recalls Haddad, C. and Hornuf, L. 2016. "The Emergence of the Global Fintech Market: Economic and Technological Determinants" *CESifo Working Paper Series No. 6131* on the economic and technological determinants inducing entrepreneurs to establish ventures with the purpose of reinventing financial technology.

8. It remarks Boudreau, K. 2018. "Notes on Designing Your Company" *Harvard Business School Strategy Unit Working Paper No. 16-131* with respect to a series of steps required for designing a company and how it will create, deliver, and capture economic value—whether it is an established enterprise or entrepreneurial start-up.

9. It can be noted that Bygrave, W. D. and Lange, J. and Mollov, A. and Pearlmutter, M. and Singh, S. 2008. "Pre-Startup Formal Business Plans and Post-Startup Performance: A Study of 116 New Ventures" *Venture Capital Journal*, p. 1 ff. detected no difference between the performance of new businesses launched with or without written business plans; indeed, their findings suggest that unless a would-be entrepreneur needs to raise substantial start-up capital from institutional investors or business angels, there is no compelling reason to write a detailed business plan before opening a new business.

10. It includes the conclusions to Van Loo, R. 2018. "Making Innovation More Competitive: The Case of Fintech" *UCLA Law Review*, who pointed out that "the Department of Justice (DOJ), hindered by statutes and knowledge gaps, devotes significantly fewer resources to banking than to other industries in merger review".

11. It is worth considering Salamzadeh, A. and Kawamorita Kesim, H. 2015. "Startup Companies: Life Cycle and Challenges" *Speech at 4th International Conference on Employment, Education and Entrepreneurship*, Belgrade who recognize the challenges *start-up* might face, and—after reviewing the life cycle and the challenges—conclude by recalling that these kind of firms normally begin with one founder and/or some cofounders: "as time goes by, founder needs more experts to develop the prototype, MVP, etc. Then, he/she has to negotiate with people, make team and finally hire employees. This process is so critical to succeed and if the founder lacks enough knowledge of the field, the startup might fail due to human resource management issues".

12. In addition, see Moenninghoff, S. C. and Wieandt, A. 2013. "The Future of Peer-to-Peer Finance" *Zeitschrift für Betriebswirtschaftliche Forschung*, p. 466 ff. who indicate a gradual movement towards funded risk management, transforming peer-to-peer platforms into institution-to-peer platforms.

13. It recalls Zetzsche, D. A. and Buckley, R. P. and Arner, D. W. and Barberis, J. N. 2017. "From FinTech to TechFin: The Regulatory Challenges of Data-Driven Finance" *New York University Journal of Law and Business* whose considerations points out two trends: "the first is the speed of change driven by the commoditization of technology, Big Data analytics, machine learning and artificial intelligence. The second is the increasing number and variety of new entrants into the financial sector, including pre-existing technology and e-commerce companies".

14. See also Wachter, S. and Mittelstadt, B. and Floridi, L., 2017. "Why a Right to Explanation of Automated Decision-Making Does Not Exist in the General Data Protection Regulation" International Data Privacy Law.

15. It refers to Zaring, D. and Bignami, F. 2016. "Comparative Law and Regulation. Understanding the Global Regulatory Process". Northampton, MA, USA, who recalled that "legal procedures [may] result in regulation in the public interest or agency capture by interest groups", hence the debate on "what combination of legal tools and regulatory strategies will produce successful enforcement and industry compliance, and how elected officials can use the law to control regulators".

16. This remarks the conclusion of Gebauer, S. and Mazelis, F. 2019. "Macroprudential Regulation and Leakage to the Shadow Banking Sector" *DIW Berlin Discussion Paper No. 1814* with respect to a model that differentiates between regulated, monopolistically competitive commercial banks and a shadow banking system that relies on funding in a perfectly competitive market for investments.

17. It refers to FSB 2017b. "Chair's letter to G20 Finance Ministers and Central Bank Governors ahead of their Baden-Baden meeting", 17 March and to FSB 2020. "Global Monitoring Report on Non-Bank Financial Intermediation 2019", 19 January.

Let us recall again Lemma, V. 2016. "The Shadow Banking System. Creating Transparency in the Financial Markets". London, p. 27 on the importance of the institutional features of the so-called shadow banks, to which is given a central economic role in relation to the dynamics of the circulation of relevant cash flows. Hence, the boundaries of the shadow banking system include all the "sources of funding for credit by converting opaque, risky, long-term assets into money-like, short-term liabilities," being understood that "credit creation through maturity, credit, and liquidity transformation can significantly reduce the cost of credit relative to direct lending"; see See Pozsar, Z., Adrian, T., Ashcraft, A. B. and Boesky, H., 2013. "Federal Reserve Bank of New York Staff Reports—Shadow Banking", p. 1, where it is affirmed that "shadow banks conduct credit, maturity and liquidity transformation similar to traditional banks. However, what distinguishes shadow banks from traditional banks is their lack of access to public sources of liquidity such as the Federal Reserve's discount window, or public sources of insurance such as Federal Deposit Insurance".

18. It has been remarked by Draghi, Mario. 2018. "Monetary policy in the euro area", Speech by the President of the ECB, ECB Forum on Central Banking, Sintra, 19 June 2018, whereby the author highlights that "We have set out three conditions that must be in place for our net asset purchases to end. We need to see the convergence of inflation towards our aim over the medium term; we need to have sufficient confidence that this convergence will be realised; and the inflation path needs to show resilience and be self-sustaining without additional net purchases. Assessing these conditions is a forward-looking exercise, because the full effects of monetary policy are felt only after long lags. We have to rely on our projections, the probability distributions surrounding them, and the extent to which they are dependent on our own monetary policy actions."

19. It is worth recalling Enriques, L. 2005. "Company Law Harmonization Reconsidered: What Role for the EC?" *ECGI—Law Working Paper No. 53/2005* on the possibility that a uniform law also rules out the possibility that divergent expectations and preferences at the national level are taken into account.

20. In addition, see Mülbert, P. O. 2010. "Corporate Governance of Banks after the Financial Crisis—Theory, Evidence, Reforms" *ECGI—Law Working Paper No. 130/2009* on the evidence that, whereas banking regulation/supervision acts as a functional substitute for debt governance, equity governance benefits less from such regulation/intervention.

21. In particular, it includes a reference to Hannig, A. and Jansen, S. 2010. "Financial Inclusion and Financial Stability: Current Policy Issues" *ADBI Working Paper No. 259* who argued that greater financial inclusion presents opportunities to enhance financial stability by considering that financial inclusion poses risks at the institutional level, but these are hardly systemic in nature, as well as the evidences that suggest that low-income savers and borrowers tend to maintain solid financial behaviour throughout financial crises, keeping deposits in a safe place and paying back their loans.

22. It can be noted that it is in line with the conclusions of Demirgüç-Kunt, A. and Klapper, L. F. 2012. "Measuring Financial Inclusion: The Global

Findex Database" *World Bank Policy Research Working Paper No. 6025* on the *barriers* that might be addressed by public policy.

23. In this respect, see Cortina Lorente, J. J. and Schmukler, S. 2018. "The Fintech Revolution: A Threat to Global Banking?" World Bank Research and Policy Briefs No. 125038 that—although the new players are ramping up competition—highlighted that "the period since the global financial crisis of 2008 has been characterized by the emergence of a broad set of tech-driven financial companies … acting in parallel with traditional banking services."

24. Moreover, see Zetzsche, D. A. and Buckley, R. P. and Arner, D. W. and Barberis, J. N. 2017. "From FinTech to TechFin: The Regulatory Challenges of Data-Driven Finance" *New York University Journal of Law and Business* about the firms hereby termed 'TechFins' that may be characterized by their capacity to leverage the data gathered in their primary business into financial services. In other words, according to the authors, TechFins represent a shift from financial intermediary (FinTech) to data intermediary (TechFin), which raises implications for incumbent financial services firms and regulators.

25. In particular, it is worth recalling the Committee on the Global Financial System and Financial Stability Board. 2017. "FinTech credit: Market structure, business models and financial stability implications" which highlights that the nature of FinTech credit activity varies significantly across and within countries due to heterogeneity in the business models of fintech credit platforms, as shown in the following paragraph.

26. It is useful recalling Appleby, G. J. and Brennan, S. and Lynch, A., 2018. "Keep Calm and Carry on: Why the Increasing Automation of Legal Services Should Deepen and Not Diminish Legal Education", *The Future of Australian Legal Education,* whose approach highlights that "the more drastic changes are those that threaten to displace or rival the provision of those services themselves by the introduction of Artificial Intelligence and the development of platforms for cheap and easily obtainable automated legal advice".

See also Simshaw, D. 2018 "Ethical Issues in Robo-Lawyering: The Need for Guidance on Developing and Using Artificial Intelligence in the Practice of Law".

27. In addition, see De Fiore, F. and Uhlig, H. 2005. "Bank Finance Versus Bond Finance: What Explains the Differences between Us and Europe?" *ECB Working Paper No. 547* who present a dynamic general equilibrium model with agency costs, where heterogeneous firms choose among two alternative instruments of external finance—corporate bonds and bank loans.

28. It refers to Joint Committee of the European Supervisory Authorities. 2018 "Joint Committee Report on the results of the monitoring exercise on 'automation in financial advice'.

29. Moreover, Bharadwaj, A. and El Sawy, O. A. and Pavlou, P. A. and Venkatraman, N. V. 2013. "Digital Business Strategy: Toward a Next Generation of Insights" *MIS Quarterly* argued that the time is right to rethink the role of IT strategy, from that of a functional-level strategy—aligned but essentially always subordinate to business strategy—to one that reflects a fusion between IT strategy and business strategy. This fusion is herein termed digital business strategy.

    See also Martinsons, M. G. 2001. "Comparing the Decision Styles of American, Chinese and Japanese Business Leaders" *Best Paper Proceedings of Academy of Management Meetings, Washington, DC, August 2001* that used the Decision Styles Inventory to compare the decision making.

30. Under an Italian perspective, it is remarkable to recall Sciarrone Alibrandi, A. 2017. "Il Problema". "Il tramonto della banca universale", Napoli; Capriglione, F. 2018b. "Considerazioni a margine del volume Il tramonto della banca universale?" *Rivista Trimestrale di Diritto dell'Economia*, p. 1 ff.

    Let us consider also the path followed by an Italian Author: Minervini, G. 1984. "La legge bancaria verso il tramonto?" *Politica ed economia*, p. 6 ff.; Minervini, G. 1988. "Impresa bancaria e Costituzione", *Banca borsa e titoli di credito*, p. 657 ff.; Minervini G. 1991. "Banca universale e gruppo polifunzionale", *Il diritto fallimentare e delle società commerciali*, p. 601 ff.; Minervini, G. 1992 "I poteri della capogruppo nei gruppi bancari polifunzionali" *Banca borsa e titoli di credito*, p. 461 ff.

31. It refers—in particular—to FSB 2017d. "FinTech credit. Market structure, business models and financial stability implications". Report prepared by a working group established by the Committee on the Global Financial System (CGFS) and the Financial Stability Board (FSB), 22 May, where it is highlighted that "Most platforms encourage investors to invest in multiple loan applications to spread their risk … Most platforms offer free early loan repayment options to borrowers, often without prepayment penalties. Moreover, as long as loan repayments are regularly made as agreed upon, no additional risk monitoring is carried out after the provision of funds. As such, some borrowers may have discretion to use funds for a different purpose than that for which they were solicited. Platforms generally advise borrowers to get in contact with them early in case they risk missing a repayment. If payments are sufficiently late, platforms tend to collaborate with debt collection agencies to recover the loan. This may result in higher fees to investors when collection of the loan is executed."

32. In particular, it has been pointed out that the resulting digital market-places allow participants to make joint investments in shared infrastructure and digital public utilities without assigning market power to a platform operator, and are characterized by increased competition, lower barriers to entry, and a lower privacy risk; see Catalini, C. and Gans, J. S. 2019. "Some Simple Economics of the Blockchain" *Rotman School of Management Working Paper No. 2874598.*

    See also Davidson, S. and De Filippi, P. and Potts, J. 2016 "Economics of Blockchain" *SSRN Research Paper no. 2744751* on the evidence that it facilitates new types of economic organization and governance based on creating spontaneous organizations.

33. In addition, it is worth including a reference to Scholz, L. 2017. "Algorithmic Contracts" *Stanford Technology Law Review*, who highlighted that "the algorithmic contracts that present the most significant problems for contract law are those that involve 'black box' algorithmic agents, whose decision-making is not functionally understandable ex ante—or sometimes even not human-intelligible at all".

    He considered also that "there is only a tenuous case for their enforceability under currently accepted approaches to contract law. The Uniform Electronic Transactions Act (UETA) was written and widely adopted nearly twenty years ago to make sure that contracts made electronically using basic automation techniques would be recognized as enforceable". However, the A. showed that the language of the UETA may be read to treat all putative contracts made with algorithms as properly formed, simply because they happen to be electronic. So, unintended consequences of this approach include opportunities for fraud, market manipulation, and a general lack of algorithmic accountability.

34. It recalls Demers, E. A. and Shackell, M. B. and Widener, S. K. 2002. "Complementarities in Organizational Design: Empirical Evidence from the New Economy" *Simon School of Business Working Paper No. FR 03-01.*

    In addition, see Frehen, R. and Goetzmann, W. N. and Rouwenhorst, K. G. 2013. "New Evidence on the First Financial Bubble" *Journal of Financial Economics*, who suggested that, since the crises of the eighteenth century, innovation was a key driver of bubble expectations and presented evidence in contrast with the currently prevailing debt-for-equity conversion hypothesis and related stock returns to innovations in Atlantic trade and insurance.

    See also Posner, R. A., 2000. "Antitrust in the New Economy" *U Chicago Law & Economics* who addressed the application of the antitrust laws to computer software and related "new economy" industries.

35. It is worth mentioning Hakansson, H. and Snehota, I. 1995 "Developing relationships in business networks", London and Demers, E. A. and

Shackell, M. B. and Widener, S. K. 2002 "Complementarities in Organizational Design: Empirical Evidence from the New Economy" Simon School of Business Working Paper No. FR 03-01. They suggest the complementarities between the various components of a firm's organizational design, and provide evidence on the role of knowledge specificity, firm strategy, span of control, and various ownership and governance characteristics in the design of the firm's organizational architecture.

36. It refers to FSB 2017a. "Artificial intelligence and machine learning in financial services. Market developments and financial stability implications", 1 November.

37. It is worth adding that Buchak, G. and Matvos, G. and Piskorski, T. and Seru, A. 2017. "Fintech, Regulatory Arbitrage, and the Rise of Shadow Banks", *NBER Working Paper no 23288*, March showed how shadow bank market share in residential mortgage origination nearly doubled from 2007 to 2015.

38. It includes a reference to Meucci, A. 2010. "Factors on Demand: Building a Platform for Portfolio Managers, Risk Managers and Traders" *Risk* who provided a framework that rests on the conditional link between flexible bottom-up estimation factor models and flexible top-down attribution factor models, and that attains a useful explanatory power in respect of specific goals.

39. In particular, it refers to ECB 2018. "Guide to assessments of fintech credit institution licence applications"; EU Commission 2018. "Commission action plan on financing sustainable growth"; EBA 2019b. "Report on regulatory perimeter, regulatory status and authorisation approaches in relation to FinTech activities" whose joint reading suggests the duty to map current authorizing and licensing approaches for innovative FinTech business models and to provide regulatory solutions to the day-by-day activities of fintech firms.

40. There is no doubt, in fact, that the innovation made possible by technology, in banking and financial services, can give rise to business models, applications, processes or new products, with an associated significant effect on the supply of capital and services.

41. Reference is made to FSB 2019. "FSB Americas group discusses regional vulnerabilities, non-bank financial intermediation, stablecoins and cyber incidents", 31 October, about the FSB's ongoing work to develop effective practices for cyber incident response and recovery, on which the FSB will consult in early 2020. In that event, members expressed concern at the increased frequency and sophistication of cyberattacks, discussed supervisors' and firms' actions to strengthen resilience in the region and stressed the need for coordination and communication.

42. It refers to FSB 2017c. "Financial Stability Implications from FinTech. Supervisory and Regulatory Issues that Merit Authorities' Attention", 27 June.

43. See O'Reilly, T. 2007. "What is Web 2.0: Design Patterns and Business Models for the Next Generation of Software". *Communications & Strategies* who shows the network as platform, spanning all connected devices as the basic to be considered for regulating this phenomenon.

44. See FSB 2019. "Decentralised financial technologies. Report on financial stability, regulatory and governance implications", 6 June.

45. Moreover, see Trautman, L. J. 2016. "Is Disruptive Blockchain Technology the Future of Financial Services?" *The Consumer Finance Law Quarterly Report 232* who discusses recent developments that provide a validation of blockchain application to financial services markets and the regulatory challenges to the adoption of this new technology.

46. Furthermore, see Frost, J. and Gambacorta, L. and Huang, Y. and Shin, H. S. and Zbinden, P. 2019. "BigTech and the Changing Structure of Financial Intermediation" *BIS Working Paper No. 779* on the drivers and implications of the growth of "BigTech" in finance—that is, the financial services offerings made by technology companies with established presence in the market for digital services.

 See also Stulz, R, M. 2019. "FinTech, BigTech, and the Future of Banks". *Fisher College of Business Working Paper No. 2019-03-020* on the evidence that fintechers and BigTech firms are contributing to a secular trend of banks losing their comparative advantage as they have less access to unique information about parties seeking credit.

47. It raises a call to the considerations of De Fiore, F. and Uhlig, H. 2005. "Bank Finance Versus Bond Finance: What Explains the Differences between Us and Europe?" *ECB Working Paper No. 547* that characterize the financing choice of firms and the endogenous financial structure of the economy.

48. It refers to EU 2018. "FinTech action plan: For a more competitive and innovative European financial sector" 8 March; FISMA DG 2018 "Opening remarks by Vice-President Dombrovskis on the Action Plans on Sustainable Finance, FinTech and a proposal for a Regulation on Crowdfunding" Brussels, 8 March, who considered to incorporate sustainability into prudential requirements.

49. It refers to the outcome of the analysis made by Evans, D. S. and Schmalensee, R. and Noel, M. D. and Chang, H. H. and Garcia-Swartz, D. D. 2011. "Platform Economics: Essays on Multi-Sided Businesses" *Competition Policy International*, who explain how platforms create value by providing products that enable two or more different types of customers to get together, find each other and exchange value.

50. In addition, see Bharadwaj, A. and El Sawy, O. A. and Pavlou, P. A. and Venkatraman, N. V. 2013. "Digital Business Strategy: Toward a Next Generation of Insights" *MIS Quarterly*, who refer to the fact that the business infrastructure has become digital with increased interconnections among products, processes and services. These authors highlighted that across many firms spanning different industries and sectors, digital technologies (viewed as combinations of information, computing, communication and connectivity technologies) are fundamentally transforming business strategies, business processes, firm capabilities, products and services and key interfirm relationships in extended business networks.

51. It is worth recalling the conclusions of the previous chapter. In general, it is useful to consider Eisenmann, T. R. and Parker, G. and Van Alstyne, M. W. 2008. "Opening Platforms: How, When and Why?" *Harvard Business School Entrepreneurial Management Working Paper No. 09-030*, whose contents suggest that market forces tend to push both proprietary and shared platforms toward hybrid governance models characterized by centralized control over platform technology (i.e., closed sponsorship) and shared responsibility for serving users (i.e., an open provider role).

52. See Arner, D. W. and Barberis, J. N. and Buckley, R. P., 2016. "FinTech, RegTech and the Reconceptualization of Financial Regulation" *Northwestern Journal of International Law & Business*; Arner, D. W. and Barberis, J. N. and Buckley, R. P., 2015 "The Evolution of Fintech: A New Post-Crisis Paradigm?" *University of Hong Kong Faculty of Law Research Paper No. 2015/047*, referring to a new era of FinTech, which has emerged in both the developed and developing world. This era is defined not by the financial products or services delivered but by who delivers them and the application of rapidly developing technology at the retail and wholesale levels. This latest evolution of FinTech, led by start-ups, poses challenges for regulators and market participants alike, particularly in balancing the potential benefits of innovation with the possible risks of new approaches.

53. This remembers the Masera, R. 2014 "CRR/CRD IV: The Trees and the Forest" *PSL Quarterly Review, vol. 67 n. 271* who offers a review of the new CRR/CRD IV capital regulatory framework for banks in the EU (that represented the transposition into European law of the Basel III standard). In fact, the A. examined the major shortcomings of the Second Capital Accord, and the repair work is assessed in the light of the recognized need to amend the flaws. In this chapter, it is argued that the necessary adjustments must be evaluated in the holistic framework provided by the Banking Union approach, and that the main features of the new system are reviewed as components of an interconnected, complex network. The author highlights the significant improvements with respect to the

Basel II standard, but it also brings to the fore the weaknesses which continue to characterize the new capital regulatory framework.

54. See Arner, D. W. and Barberis, J. N. and Buckley, R. P., 2016 "FinTech, RegTech and the Reconceptualization of Financial Regulation" *Northwestern Journal of International Law & Business*, who argued that the transformative nature of technology will only be captured by a new approach that sits at the nexus between data, digital identity and regulation. These authors expose the inadequacy and lack of ambition of simply digitizing analogue processes in a digital financial world. Hence, they propose a foundation for a practical understanding of regtech and propose sequenced reforms that could benefit regulators, industry and entrepreneurs alike in the financial sector and other industries.

55. It is useful to represent, in this regard, that—in the current legal system—activities connected with banking may be reserved to qualified subjects (in the case of the provision of investment services, payment services, issuance of electronic money, etc.); see Maume, P. 2017 "In Unchartered Territory—Banking Supervision Meets Fintech" *Corporate Finance 2017*, p. 373 ff. on the fact that there is uncertainty among financial markets participants as to how to apply the traditional banking regulation to fintechs.

56. In addition, see Dao, T. L., 2018. "Systematic Asset Management" *SSRN Research Paper no. 3208574* who recalls that, back in the 1980s, the first attempts to combine applied mathematics, numerical algorithms with high-performance computers in trading and portfolio construction gave birth to a new trend of asset management "systematic asset management" and shows that the last evolutions allowed more and more opportunities for fintech to improve the systematic asset management.

57. It refers to Bellardini, L. and Del Gaudio, B. Belinda Laura and Previtali, D. and Verdoliva, V. 2019. "How Do Banks Invest in Fintech? Empirical Evidences Around the World" *SSRN Research Paper no. 3467024* who investigated how banks react to digital transformation outsourcing innovative activities.

58. It is worth considering Mülbert, P. O. 2010. "Corporate Governance of Banks after the Financial Crisis—Theory, Evidence, Reforms" *ECGI—Law Working Paper No. 130/2009* on the fact that poor corporate governance of banks has increasingly been acknowledged as an important cause of the recent financial crisis.

59. Moreover, see Lin, T. C. W. 2016. "Compliance, Technology, and Modern Finance" *Temple University Legal Studies Research Paper No. 2017-06*, who highlights that the rise of new technology has dramatically altered many of the key functions and functionaries of modern finance, as well as the way to assess the compliance.

See also Packin, N. G. 2017. "Regtech, Compliance and Technology Judgment Rule" *Chicago-Kent Law Review* that refers to the possibility that fintech helps entities cut costs, promotes good corporate practice in compliance management and enhances desired regulatory compliance outcomes. In particular, regtech does this by enabling businesses to automate ordinary compliance tasks, reduce operational risks associated with compliance obligations, enable compliance functions to make informed risk choices based on data provided insight, and create cost-effectives solutions to problems.

60. It refers to Admati, A. R. and DeMarzo, P. M. and Hellwig, M. F. and Pfleiderer, P. C., 2013. "Fallacies, Irrelevant Facts, and Myths in the Discussion of Capital Regulation: Why Bank Equity is Not Socially Expensive" *Max Planck Institute for Research on Collective Goods 2013/23* and in particular the conclusion that better capitalized banks suffer fewer distortions in lending decisions and would perform better, and that banks choosing high leverage does not imply that this is socially optimal.

61. This is referred, on this point, to the conclusions of Lemma, V. and Thorp, J. A. 2014. "Sharing Corporate Governance: The Role of Outsourcing Contracts in Banking" Law and Economics Yearly Review, Vol. 3, Part 2, p. 357 ff.

62. A research assessed the potential impact of the outsourcing as an ongoing phenomenon of services offshoring, with impact on the occupational structure of the labour market; see Bardhan, A. and Kroll, C. A. 2003. "The New Wave of Outsourcing" *Fisher Center for Real Estate & Urban Economics Research Report Series No. 1103.*

63. Reference is made to European Banking Federation, 2018. "The Future of the Banking Industry. Dialogue with the Banking Industry on ESCB Statistics", Frankfurt, 16 March.

64. It recalls the analysis of Maugeri, M. 2016. "Proxy Advisors, esercizio del voto e doveri fiduciari del gestore" *Orizzonti del diritto commerciale,* p. 16 ff. who suggested that the relationship between the PA and the institutional investor should be governed by the provisions relating to the outsourcing of essential or important business operations, services or activities.

65. See Montaseb, M. M. and Ragheb, M. A. and Ragab, A. A. and Elsamadicy, A. M, 2018. "The Factors Affecting of SMEs' Outsourcing Decision Making" *Business and Management Review* about a conceptual framework for firms' outsourcing decision making which highlights that the risk factors of outsourcing are hidden costs, loss of core competence, less flexibility, loss of knowledge, supplier problems and low morale.

66. See Geis, G. S. 2006 "Business Outsourcing and the Agency Cost Problem" *Notre Dame Law Review* who argued that business outsourc-

ing has thrived in recent years not only because globalization has unlocked inexpensive production markets but also because it is becoming easier for firms to monitor and prevent the agency costs of outsourcing.

67. Furthermore, see Hon, W. K. and Millard, C. 2016. "Use by Banks of Cloud Computing: An Empirical Study" *Queen Mary School of Law Legal Studies Research Paper No. 245/2016* who concluded that, while some barriers are internal and some external, cloud is still misunderstood, and further educational efforts are needed to ensure regulatory approaches and guidance are sufficiently cloud-aware to strike the appropriate balance between risk management and efficiency/innovation across the European Economic Area. However, these authors highlighted certain barriers arising from banking regulatory rules on outsourcing, critical or material, and the contentious issue of contractual audit rights for regulators.

68. In addition, see Gerding, E. F. 2009. "The Outsourcing of Financial Regulation to Risk Models and the Global Financial Crisis: Code, Crash, and Open Source" *Washington Law Review* who considered that regulators should promote "open source" in code used to market consumer financial products, price securitizations and derivatives, and manage financial institution risk.

69. At the end of this investigation, the analysis will aim at assessing the impact of fintech on the corporate governance of a bank, bearing in mind that the services provided by the fintechers also refer to the functioning of the board of directors and the board of auditors.

70. See Amiti, M. and Wei, S. J. 2004. "Fear of service outsourcing: is it justified?", *IMF Working Paper* 04/186 who pointed out that although service outsourcing has been steadily increasing, it is still very low, and that in the United States and many other industrial countries "insourcing" is greater than outsourcing. Using the United Kingdom as a case study, the authors found that job growth at a sectoral level is not negatively related to service outsourcing.

    See also Ravi, S. P. and Rivers, T. and Ravi, C. and Jain, K. and Sharma, P. h. 2011. "An Analysis Of Business Process Outsourcing Strategies Of Public And Private Sector Banks In India", *International Business & Economics Research Journal*, p. 1 ff. on the recent trends of Business Process Outsourcing (BPO) strategies and practices among banking institutions in India.

71. In particular, Wang, Y and Niu, B. and Guo, P. 2014. "The Comparison of Two Vertical Outsourcing Structures under Push and Pull Contracts" *Production and operations management*, p. 610 ff. where the authors compare the two outsourcing structures under a push contract (whereby orders are placed before demand is realized) and a pull contract (whereby

orders are placed after demand is realized), finding out that the equilibrium production quantity is higher under control than under delegation for the push contract whereas the reverse holds for the pull contract. Both the OEM and the CM prefer control over delegation under the push contract.

72. It is worth considering that Scholz, L. 2017. "Algorithmic Contracts" *Stanford Technology Law Review* looks to the common law of agency for inspiration. Some algorithms commonly used in contract formation have been delegated a level of responsibility that justifies the use of agency principles. The A. provides that "algorithms should be considered constructive agents for the purpose of contract formation".

Indeed, according to this A., the company consenting to the contract can be said to have authorized or ratified the contract formed on its behalf by the algorithm. This approach explains easy cases while also showing why algorithmic contracts, even many black box algorithmic contracts, are enforceable. Furthermore, he concluded that "establishing a doctrinally robust connection between the actions of the algorithm and the intent of the contracting party promotes algorithmic accountability".

See also Lemma, V. 2018, "Commento sub art. 13 d. lgs. 385 del 1993", *Commentario al testo unico delle leggi in materia bancaria e creditizia*, Padova, p. 172 on the function of the bank's register provided by European regulation since art. 3, Directive no. 77/780/EC.

73. See Hon, W. K. and Millard, C. 2016. "Use by Banks of Cloud Computing: An Empirical Study" Queen Mary School of Law Legal Studies Research Paper No. 245/2016 who analysed legal and practical issues such as risk assessments, security, business continuity including exit plans, concentration risk and bank resolution, continuing regulatory oversight, banking secrecy laws, barriers under data protection law, including personal data export restrictions, problems arising from layered service models where SaaS services are built on another provider's IaaS/PaaS service, and commonly negotiated contractual provisions regarding termination, service changes and liability.

74. It is worth recalling Capriglione, F. 2018a "Commento sub art. 10 d. lgs. 385 del 1993", *Commentario al testo unico delle leggi in materia bancaria e creditizia*, Padova, p. 111 ff.

75. In addition, see Aubert, B.A. and Patry, M. and Rivard, S. 2003. "A tale of two outsourcing contracts. An agency-theoretical perspective" *Wirtschaftsinformatik*, p. 181 ff. for a study on the management of the relationships.

76. See Feng, B. and Yao, T. and Jiang, B. 2013. "Analysis of the Market-Based Adjustable Outsourcing Contract under Uncertainties" *Production and operations management*, p. 178 ff. for an analysis of the market-based

adjustable contracts for customized goods or services that have emerged in outsourcing practices.

77. On the role of incentives, see Osei Bryson, K.M. and Ngwenyam, O. 2006. "Managing risks in information systems outsourcing: An approach to analyzing outsourcing risks and structuring incentive contracts", *European Journal of Operational Research*, p. 245 ff.

78. As shown in the following chapters, this provision must be related to the analysis on the relation between the government body and the outsourcers (having regard to the agreed contracts); see Spencer, B.J. 2005 "International outsourcing and incomplete contracts" *Canadian Journal of Economics*, p. 1107.

79. See Seshasai, S. and Gupta, A. 2004. "Global Outsourcing of Professional Services" *MIT Sloan Working Paper No. 4456-04* about the effects of such long-term ramifications on business and society.

80. See Bradshaw, S. and Millard, C. and Walden, I. 2010. "Contracts for Clouds: Comparison and Analysis of the Terms and Conditions of Cloud Computing Services" *Queen Mary School of Law Legal Studies Research Paper No. 63/2010*, who highlights that the greater flexibility of a cloud computing service as compared with a traditional outsourcing contract is balanced by less certainty for the customer in terms of the location of data placed into the Cloud and the legal foundations of any contract with the provider.

On this point, see also Alpa, G. 2018. "Diritti, libertà fondamentali e disciplina del contratto: modelli a confronto" *Giustizia civile*, 2018, p. 5 ff.

81. See the following authors in order to highlight the Italian approach to this topic: Capriglione, F. 2018b. "Considerazioni a margine del volume Il tramonto della banca universale?" *Rivista Trimestrale di Diritto dell'Economia*, p. 1 ff.; Pellegrini, M. 2018. "Piani di risanamento e misure di early intervention" *federalismi.it*, p. 13 ff.

See also Mirone, A. 2017. "Regole di governo societario e assetti statutari delle banche tra diritto speciale e diritto generale" *Banca impresa società*, p. 33 ff.; Sacco Ginevri, A. 2017 "Il problema dell'interesse sociale nelle banche" *La Nuova giurisprudenza civile commentata*, 2017, p. 1550 ff.; Portale G. B., 2016. "La "corporate governance" delle società bancarie" *Rivista delle società*, 2016, p. 48 ff.

82. All the disputes (between the bank and the outsourcer), in fact, have effects on the validity of the requirements at the base of the authorization to exercise banking and then on the levels of responsibility of the leaders of the credit institution. Hence, this identifies the need to provide special form and content requirements in order to allow the formation of the consensus and the establishment of an agreement resulting in a 'synal-

lagmatic contract', brought to the attention of the supervisory authorities and appropriate to clearly define the obligation of the other (non-banking) party.

Therefore, this is a complex set of rules in which the subjection of the contract to the control of the judicial authority—conceivable in cases of dispute between the parties—raises specific concerns. This applies, in particular, to the possibility to ensure that the favour for equal relations between private individuals (for example, in the presence of an obligation to contract, unfair competition or abuse of position) will not be subordinated to other interests (i.e. the protection of savings, credit control, the preservation of monetary policies and, ultimately, price and market stability).

83. This is not referring (only) to the Italian provision of art. 1418 civil code but (also) to the specific indications on prudential supervision, contained in art. 64, dir. 2013/36/EU, where it is established that "competent authorities shall be given all supervisory powers to intervene in the activity of institutions that are necessary for the exercise of their function, including in particular the right to withdraw an authorization".

84. See Catalini, C. and Gans, J. S. 2019. "Some Simple Economics of the Blockchain" *Rotman School of Management Working Paper No. 2874598* on a discussion about how blockchain technology can shape innovation and competition in digital platforms.

85. It is worth recalling that the UK Banking act of 2009 shows a regulatory approach that reflects the findings of most-advanced organization theories, given that the outsourcing policies open up powerful ways of business. They have helped managers to analyse complicated situations and discover the effective means of dealing with the challenges placed by the capital markets. While, in banking, the high level of regulation can suggest that there is only one approach to the relation with the service providers, in fact there are many organization settings and they do not always fit neatly together. Scholars often justify this diversity by pointing out the complexity of any business organization and the different techniques of dealing with an outsourcing agreement. This means that, in the common law context, the analysis encountered a large and complex phenomenon, with perceptual equipment that suggests supervising it in a holistic way.

See Hatch, J. 1997. "Organization theory", London, p. 7. See also Li, X. 2014 "Relational Contracts, Growth Options, and Heterogeneous Beliefs: A Game-Theoretic Perspective on Information Technology Outsourcing", *Journal of Management Information Systems*, p. 319 ff. where the author suggests that, because salient forms of relational bonuses are often not adopted, relational incentive provision is likely more pervasive than what it is possible to observe.

86. It is worth mentioning again the study of Behn, M. and Corrias, R. and Rola-Janicka, M. 2019 "On the interaction between different bank liquidity requirements" that—according to the authors—"dispels claims that the LCR and the NSFR are redundant and underlines the need for a faithful and consistent implementation of both measures (and the entire Basel III package more broadly) across all major jurisdictions, to maintain a level playing field at the global level and to ensure that the post-crisis regulatory framework delivers on its objectives".

87. See Rosen, R. J. "The Impact of the Originate-to-Distribute Model on Banks Before and During the Financial Crisis" *24th Australasian Finance and Banking Conference 2011 Paper.*

    See also Wilmarth, A. E. 2009. "The Dark Side of Universal Banking: Financial Conglomerates and the Origins of the Subprime Financial Crisis" *Connecticut Law Review*, for a review of universal banks that pursued an "originate to distribute" (OTD) strategy, which included (i) originating consumer and corporate loans, (ii) packaging loans into ABS and CDOs, (iii) creating OTC derivatives whose values were derived from loans, and (iv) distributing the resulting securities and other financial instruments to investors, including off-balance-sheet conduits.

88. See Committee on the Global Financial System and Financial Stability Board 2017. "FinTech credit: Market structure, business models and financial stability implications", which pointed out that "a bigger share of FinTech-facilitated credit in the financial system could have both financial stability benefits and risks in the future, including access to alternative funding sources in the economy and efficiency pressures on incumbent banks, but also the potential for weaker lending standards and more pro-cyclical credit provision in the economy".

89. See the research presented at the Conference "Per un'ipotesi ricostruttiva della riforma delle BCC", held at Università "Parthenope" in Naples and published in *Rivista Trimestrale di diritto dell'economia*, 2018.

90. See Ezrachi, A. 2018. "EU Competition Law Goals and the Digital Economy" *Oxford Legal Studies Research Paper No. 17/2018.*

91. Following this approach, it is also possible to understand the reasons for the option to include within a single category, called "senior management", the individuals with executive functions and who are responsible for the daily management of the institution, reporting to the management body (art. 3, para 1, dir. 2013/36/EU). It goes without saying that the explicit reference to individuals suggests that the same are placed in a direct employment relationship with the bank, having to exclude that these functions could be outsourced outside of the bank's economy.

92. Therefore, the latter is the document in which the subjects that request authorization must clearly indicate the activities that they intend to carry

out within the company and those which, instead, will be outsourced. In this program, the levels of disclosure of the outsourcing contracts (and of the characteristics of the service providers) appear to be of central importance; that is, the information that the individuals are required to provide to the supervisory authority, which may take elements (from these) in order to evaluate which controls fall within its powers (i.e. belong to the safe and sound management); see Amorosino, S. 2018, 'Commento sub art. 14 d. lgs. 385 del 1993', in *Commentario al testo unico delle leggi in materia bancaria e creditizia*, Padova, p. 180 ff.

See also Popoli, P. 2017. "The Role of the Outsourcing Contract From a Partnership-based Perspective" *Chinese Business Review* about the relational contents which outsourcer and outsourcee arrange and formalize inside a contract.

93. It goes without saying that these ancillary activities can be reserved (in the case of the provision of payment services, electronic money issuance and, in some ways, credit rating evaluations). But, in this regard it should be noted that the interpretation key is the position of a real estate fund responsible for the ownership and the management (through the fund manager) of the bank's ancillary properties, given the difficulty to include this subject within the juridical definition of business identified in EU Regulation n. 575/2013; see.); see Maume, P. 2017. "In Unchartered Territory—Banking Supervision Meets Fintech" Corporate Finance 2017, p. 373 ff.

94. This interpretation is also confirmed in art. 124 of Directive 2013/36/EU, where it is stated that "in the case of financial holding companies, mixed financial holding companies, financial institutions or ancillary services undertakings, the collection or possession of information shall not imply that the competent authorities are required to play a supervisory role in relation to those institutions or undertakings standing alone"; see Honess, S. 1996. "Outsourcing—A legal perspective on contract critical success factors" *Information security technical report*, p. 57 ff.

95. Hence, the justification for the extension of the legislation in question also to the cases in which the exercise of consolidated supervision appeared appropriate because of the relative importance of the single activities in the various countries (and, therefore, applies the principles of art. 111, Dir. 2013/36/EU).

Similarly, this also applies to the option, of the competent authorities, to exclude an undertaking from the consolidation in the cases where: (i) "it is situated in a third country where there are legal impediments to the transfer of the necessary information"; (ii) "it is of negligible interest only with respect to the objectives of monitoring credit institutions"; (iii) "the consolidation of the financial situation … would be inappropriate or misleading as far as the objectives of the supervision of credit institutions are concerned", on the understanding that, in case of the involvement of several undertakings, "collectively they are of non-negligible interest with respect to the specified objectives" (art. 19, EU regulation n. 575/2013).

96. In order to protect the stability of credit institutions, this balancing may ensure that the exercise of intermediation activities refers to an *agere* able to connect the efficiency levels (of the business) to a minimum size of the organizational social structure (adequate to ensure the bank's solidity); see Mülbert, P. O. 2010. "Corporate Governance of Banks after the Financial Crisis—Theory, Evidence, Reforms" *ECGI—Law Working Paper No. 130/2009*; Hopt, K. J. and Leyens, P. C. 2004. "Board Models in Europe—Recent Developments of Internal Corporate Governance Structures in Germany, the United Kingdom, France, and Italy" *ECGI—Law Working Paper No. 18/2004*; Ciancanelli, P. and Reyes-Gonzalez, J. A. 2000 "Corporate Governance in Banking: A Conceptual Framework" *SSRN Research Paper no. 253714.*

97. It refers to Recommendation 2009/384/EC of the Commission, of 30 April 2009, on the retribution policies in the financial services sector.

98. It is worth considering Berríos, M. R. 2013. "The Relationship between Bank Credit Risk and Profitability and Liquidity" *The International Journal of Business and Finance Research*, p. 105 ff. who focuses on the concept of prudent lending by public state commercial banks, insider ownership, and chief executive officer compensation and tenure, which are governance-related bank characteristics.

See also Ayyagari, M. and Demirgüç-Kunt, A. and Maksimovic, V. 2008 "Formal versus Informal Finance: Evidence from China" *World Bank Policy Research Working Paper Series*; Kenyon, C. 2005 "Optimal price design for variable capacity outsourcing contracts" *Journal of Revenue and Pricing Management*, p. 124 ff. where a solution method is proposed. The resulting linear (and quadratic) mixed integer optimizations can be solved numerically using standard software. According to the author's interpretation, the solution yields Pareto-efficient outcomes with respect to the provider and the client. The frontier of Pareto-optimal designs serves as an appropriate space for practical contract negotiation.

99. Therefore, the criteria used to determine this price may promote a sound and prudent risk management, avoiding the encouragement to recruit risks exceeding the level tolerated by the credit institution, also in order to avoid conflicts of interests and other hazards that may occur in the long term. This, even with regard for every distinction between fixed base remuneration (that should reflect, in this case, the standing and the guarantees given by the ancillary business) and the variable remuneration (due for services that go beyond the minimum concluded in the contract); see art. 92 and art. 94 Directive 2013/36/EU.

100. According to the article cited in the text, this allows the latter to detect (and, where appropriate, report) any differences between the functions that cooperate (from the inside to the outside) for the conduct of banking.

101. This statement is in line with the standard approach of Mifid Directive, where the investment advices have been regulated; see Sciarrone Alibrandi, A. 2010. "Il servizio di consulenza in materia di investimenti: profili ricostruttivi di una nuova fattispecie" *Scritti in onore di Francesco Capriglione. Le regole del mercato finanziario*, Padova, p. 597 ff.

102. It specifically refers to EBA 2019a. "EBA report on potential impediments to the cross-border provision of banking and payment services", p. 4.

103. EBA highlights the need for the European Commission to update its 1997 Communication in order to promote greater convergence of practices in determining when business is to be regarded as being provided cross-border under the freedom to provide services, taking particular account of technological developments; see Commission interpretative communication: Freedom to provide services and the interests of the general good in the Second Banking Directive (97/C 209/04).

104. It recalls Berríos, M. R. 2013. "The Relationship between Bank Credit Risk and Profitability and Liquidity" *The International Journal of Business and Finance Research* showed a negative relationship between less prudent lending, which may be interpreted as a positive effect of more prudent lending.

105. See Ellul, A. 2015. "The Role of Risk Management in Corporate Governance" *Kelley School of Business Research Paper No. 15-81* discussed risk management's responsibilities and relevance for a value-maximizing bank, and argued that conventional governance structures alone may be unable to restrain risk-taking in banks and thus the presence of a strong and independent risk-management function becomes necessary to monitor and control enterprise-wide risk exposures.

106. In addition, see Draghi, M. 2014. "*Hearing before the Committee on Economic and Monetary Affairs of the European Parliament—Introductory statement*", Brussels, 17 November 2014, who—as Chair of the ESRB—said that "The systemic nature of this risk derives from a number of factors. In many cases, misconduct issues arise across markets and also at systemically important banks. The costs typically rise in times of crisis and as such have a procyclical impact. Finally, misconduct can damage confidence in financial markets and institutions, which is vital for the proper functioning of the financial system".

107. It is worth considering also that Draghi, M. 2014. "*Hearing before the Committee on Economic and Monetary Affairs of the European Parliament—Introductory statement*", Brussels, 17 November 2014 on the perspective of a "a robust, rigorous and comparable assessment across banks and a consistent approach and appropriate contingency planning

across jurisdictions. Misconduct risks should also be adequately captured in future EU-wide stress tests".

108. Current practices and common elements of policy had been chosen, by CEBS, to promote an appropriate level of convergence in the internal market about the "authorised entity's use of a third party ... to perform activities that would normally be undertaken by the authorised entity", see CEBS 2006, *Guidelines on Outsourcing*, 14 December 2006, p. 2.

109. See CEBS, 2006. *Guidelines on Outsourcing*, 14 December 2006, pp. 1–2; if, on the one hand, some Member States had, at that time, adopted 'formal outsourcing regimes', others remitted this subject only to private enterprise (with obvious negative effects on the consistency of national legal frameworks).

   In this respect, the result of the analysis on fintech recalls the consideration that the "outsourcing institution's senior management" is of central importance. Indeed, it was explicitly stated that "outsourcing arrangements can never result in the delegation of senior management's responsibility" (Guidelines 2–3). At the operational level, the possibility that "an authorised entity may not outsource services and activities concerning the acceptance of deposits or to lending", unless the service provider was authorized by the supervisor (Guideline 4), resulted to have been precluded. An appendix to these rules stated that it was the duty to avoid that outsourcing strategies undermine the functioning of the bank or its management bodies. Following this approach, the CEBS suggested that "the outsourcing institution should have a policy on its approach to outsourcing, including contingency plans and exit strategies" to manage the risks related to the service entrusted (Guidelines 6–7).

   The above construction also notes the establishment of a "formal and comprehensive contract" and of a "written agreement on the responsibilities of both parties and a quality description" configured as "a mixture of quantitative and qualitative performance targets, to enable an outsourcing institution to assess the adequacy of service provision" (Guideline 8–9). The same has to be said for the relationships with supervisory authorities, which should have "access to relevant data held by the outsourcing service provider, and where provided for by the national law, the right ... to conduct onsite inspections at an outsourcing service provider's premises" (Guideline 11).

110. See Lu, Y. and Ng, T. and Tao, Z. 2012. "Outsourcing, Product Quality, and Contract Enforcement" *Journal of Economics & Management Strategy*, p. 1 ff. where the authors question if outsourcing compromises product quality or sound contract enforcement alleviates this concern. They also offer a simple model to illustrate how outsourcing leads to lower product quality and how contract enforcement helps mitigate this problem.

It is worth recalling Enriques E. and Zetsche, D. A. 2015 "Quack Corporate Governance, Round III? Bank board regulation under the new European capital requirement directive" *Theoretical Inquiries in law*, p. 218 ff.; Angelici, C. 2012 "Principi e problemi". "Trattato di diritto civile e commerciale" Milano; Masera, R. 2006. "La corporate governance nelle banche" *Bologna*.

111. See specifically, EBA 2017 "Final Report. Guidelines on internal governance under Directive 2013/36/EU", 26 September; and this confirms EBA 2011, "EBA Guidelines on Internal Governance", London, 27 September 2011, p. 31.

112. It refers to ECB 2004, "Report on EU Banking Structure", November, p. 27 ff. and p. 31.

113. See Basel Committee on Banking Supervision 2005, "The Joint Forum— Outsourcing in Financial Services", February, p. 1.

REFERENCES

Admati, A. R. and DeMarzo, P. M. and Hellwig, M. F. and Pfleiderer, P. C., 2013. "Fallacies, Irrelevant Facts, and Myths in the Discussion of Capital Regulation: Why Bank Equity is Not Socially Expensive", *Max Planck Institute for Research on Collective Goods 2013/23*.

Alpa, G. 2013. "Presentazione", *Banche e etica*, Padova.

Alpa, G. 2018. "Diritti, libertà fondamentali e disciplina del contratto: modelli a confronto", *Giustizia civile*.

Amiti, M. and Wei, S. J. 2004. "Fear of service outsourcing: is it justified?", *IMF Working Paper* 04/186.

Amorosino, S. 2018. "Commento sub art. 14 d. lgs. 385 del 1993", *Commentario al testo unico delle leggi in materia bancaria e creditizia*, Padova.

Angelici, C. 2012. "Principi e problemi", *Trattato di diritto civile e commerciale*, Milano.

Annunziata, F. 2018. "I "postumi" del caso Landesbank "vs." BCE. Nota a TRIB. UE sez. IV ampliata 16 maggio 2017 (causa T-122/15)", *Analisi giuridica dell'economia*.

Appleby, G. J. and Brennan, S. and Lynch, A., 2018. "Keep Calm and Carry on: Why the Increasing Automation of Legal Services Should Deepen and Not Diminish Legal Education" *The Future of Australian Legal Education*.

Arner, D. W. and Barberis, J. N. and Buckley, R. P. 2016. "FinTech, RegTech and the Reconceptualization of Financial Regulation", *Northwestern Journal of International Law & Business*.

Arner, D. W. and Barberis, J. N. and Buckley, R. P., 2015. "The Evolution of Fintech: A New Post-Crisis Paradigm?", *University of Hong Kong Faculty of Law Research Paper No. 2015/047*.

Aubert, B.A. and Patry, M. and Rivard, S. 2003. "A tale of two outsourcing contracts. An agency-theoretical perspective", *Wirtschaftsinformatik.*

Ayyagari, M. and Demirgüç-Kunt, A. and Maksimovic, V. 2008. "Formal versus Informal Finance: Evidence from China", *World Bank Policy Research Working Paper Series.*

Bardhan, A. and Kroll, C. A. 2003. "The New Wave of Outsourcing", *Fisher Center for Real Estate & Urban Economics Research Report Series No. 1103.*

Basel Committee on Banking Supervision. 2005. "The Joint Forum – Outsourcing in Financial Services", February.

Behn, M. and Corrias, R. and Rola-Janicka, M. 2019. "On the interaction between different bank liquidity requirements".

Bellardini, L. and Del Gaudio, B. Belinda Laura and Previtali, D. and Verdoliva, V. 2019. "How Do Banks Invest in Fintech? Empirical Evidences Around the World", *SSRN Research Paper no. 3467024.*

Berríos, M. R. 2013. "The Relationship between Bank Credit Risk and Profitability and Liquidity" *The International Journal of Business and Finance Research.*

Bharadwaj, A. and El Sawy, O. A. and Pavlou, P. A. and Venkatraman, N. V. 2013. "Digital Business Strategy: Toward a Next Generation of Insights" *MIS Quarterly.*

Blemus, S. 2017. "Law and Blockchain: A Legal Perspective on Current Regulatory Trends Worldwide" *Revue Trimestrielle de Droit Financier.*

Boudreau, K. 2018. "Notes on Designing Your Company" *Harvard Business School Strategy Unit Working Paper No. 16-131.*

Bradshaw, S. and Millard, C. and Walden, I. 2010. "Contracts for Clouds: Comparison and Analysis of the Terms and Conditions of Cloud Computing Services", *Queen Mary School of Law Legal Studies Research Paper No. 63/2010.*

Buchak, G. and Matvos, G. and Piskorski, T. and Seru, A. 2017. "Fintech, Regulatory Arbitrage, and the Rise of Shadow Banks", *NBER Working Paper no 23288.*

Bygrave, W. D. and Lange, J. and Mollov, A. and Pearlmutter, M. and Singh, S. 2008. "Pre-Startup Formal Business Plans and Post-Startup Performance: A Study of 116 New Ventures" *Venture Capital Journal.*

Capriglione F. and Sacco Ginevri, A. 2019. "Metamorfosi della Governance Bancaria" Milano.

Capriglione, F. 2018a "Commento sub art. 10 d. lgs. 385 del 1993", *Commentario al testo unico delle leggi in materia bancaria e creditizia*, Padova.

Capriglione, F. 2018b. "Considerazioni a margine del volume Il tramonto della banca universale?", *Rivista Trimestrale di Diritto dell'Economia.*

Catalini, C. and Gans, J. S. 2019. "Some Simple Economics of the Blockchain" *Rotman School of Management Working Paper No. 2874598.*

CEBS. 2006. *Guidelines on Outsourcing*, 14 December.

Ciancanelli, P. and Reyes-Gonzalez, J. A. 2000 "Corporate Governance in Banking: A Conceptual Framework", *SSRN Research Paper no. 253714.*

Committee on the Global Financial System and Financial Stability Board. 2017. "FinTech credit: Market structure, business models and financial stability implications".

Cortina Lorente, J. J. and Schmukler, S. 2018. "The Fintech Revolution: A Threat to Global Banking?" *World Bank Research and Policy Briefs No. 125038.*

Dao, T. L. 2018. "Systematic Asset Management", *SSRN Research Paper no. 3208574.*

Davidson, S. and De Filippi, P. and Potts, J. 2016. "Economics of Blockchain" *SSRN Research Paper no. 2744751.*

De Fiore, F. and Uhlig, H. 2005. "Bank Finance Versus Bond Finance: What Explains the Differences between Us and Europe?" *ECB Working Paper No. 547.*

Demers, E. A. and Shackell, M. B. and Widener, S. K. 2002 "Complementarities in Organizational Design: Empirical Evidence from the New Economy" *Simon School of Business Working Paper No. FR 03-01.*

Demirgüç-Kunt, A. and Klapper, L. F. 2012. "Measuring Financial Inclusion: The Global Findex Database" *World Bank Policy Research Working Paper No. 6025.*

Draghi, M. 2014. *"Hearing before the Committee on Economic and Monetary Affairs of the European Parliament – Introductory statement"*, Brussels, 17 November.

Draghi, Mario. 2018. "Monetary policy in the euro area", Speech by the President of the ECB, ECB Forum on Central Banking, Sintra, 19 June 2018.

EBA. 2011. "EBA Guidelines on Internal Governance", London, 27 September.

EBA. 2017. "Final Report. Guidelines on internal governance under Directive 2013/36/EU", 26 September.

EBA, 2019a. "EBA report on potential impediments to the cross-border provision of banking and payment services".

EBA. 2019b. "Report on regulatory perimeter, regulatory status and authorisation approaches in relation to FinTech activities".

EBA 2020 "EBA Report on big data and advanced analytics", January.

ECB. 2004. "Report on EU Banking Structure", November.

ECB. 2018. "Guide to assessments of fintech credit institution licence applications".

Eisenmann, T. R. and Parker, G. and Van Alstyne, M. W. 2008. "Opening Platforms: How, When and Why?", *Harvard Business School Entrepreneurial Management Working Paper No. 09-030.*

Ellul, A. 2015. "The Role of Risk Management in Corporate Governance", *Kelley School of Business Research Paper No. 15-81.*

Enriques E. and Zetsche, D. A. 2015. "Quack Corporate Governance, Round III? Bank board regulation under the new European capital requirement directive", *Theoretical Inquiries in law.*

Enriques, L. 2005. "Company Law Harmonization Reconsidered: What Role for the EC?" *ECGI – Law Working Paper No. 53/2005.*

ESMA 2020. "Guidelines on securitisation repository data completeness and consistency thresholds". 17 January.

EU 2018. "FinTech action plan: For a more competitive and innovative European financial sector" 8 March.

EU Commission. 2018. "Commission action plan on financing sustainable growth"

European Banking Federation, 2018. "The Future of the Banking Industry. Dialogue with the Banking Industry on ESCB Statistics", Frankfurt, 16 march.

Evans, D. S. and Schmalensee, R. and Noel, M. D. and Chang, H. H. and Garcia-Swartz, D. D. 2011. "Platform Economics: Essays on Multi-Sided Businesses", *Competition Policy International.*

Ezrachi, A. 2018. "EU Competition Law Goals and the Digital Economy", *Oxford Legal Studies Research Paper No. 17/2018.*

Feng, B. and Yao, T. and Jiang, B. 2013. "Analysis of the Market-Based Adjustable Outsourcing Contract under Uncertainties", *Production and operations management.*

FISMA DG. 2018. "Opening remarks by Vice-President Dombrovskis on the Action Plans on Sustainable Finance, FinTech and a proposal for a Regulation on Crowdfunding" Brussels, 8 March.

Frehen, R. and Goetzmann, W. N. and Rouwenhorst, K. G. 2013. "New Evidence on the First Financial Bubble" *Journal of Financial Economics.*

Frost, J. and Gambacorta, L. and Huang, Y. and Shin, H. S. and Zbinden, P. 2019. "BigTech and the Changing Structure of Financial Intermediation" *BIS Working Paper No. 779.*

FSB 2017a. "Artificial intelligence and machine learning in financial services. Market developments and financial stability implications", 1 November.

FSB 2017b. "Chair's letter to G20 Finance Ministers and Central Bank Governors ahead of their Baden-Baden meeting", 17 March.

FSB 2017c. "Financial Stability Implications from FinTech. Supervisory and Regulatory Issues that Merit Authorities' Attention", 27 June.

FSB 2017d. "FinTech credit. Market structure, business models and financial stability implications". Report prepared by a Working Group established by the Committee on the Global Financial System (CGFS) and the Financial Stability Board (FSB), 22 May.

FSB 2019a. "Decentralised financial technologies. Report on financial stability, regulatory and governance implications", 6 June.

FSB 2019b. "FSB Americas group discusses regional vulnerabilities, non-bank financial intermediation, stablecoins and cyber incidents", 31st October.

FSB 2020. "Global Monitoring Report on Non-Bank Financial Intermediation 2019", 19 January.

Gebauer, S. and Mazelis, F. 2019. "Macroprudential Regulation and Leakage to the Shadow Banking Sector" *DIW Berlin Discussion Paper No. 1814.*

Geis, G. S. 2006. "Business Outsourcing and the Agency Cost Problem", *Notre Dame Law Review.*

Gerding, E. F. 2009. "The Outsourcing of Financial Regulation to Risk Models and the Global Financial Crisis: Code, Crash, and Open Source", *Washington Law Review.*

Global Financial System and Financial Stability Board. 2017. "FinTech credit: Market structure, business models and financial stability implications".

Graham, S.J.H. and Merges, R. P. and Samuelson, P. and Sichelman, T. M., 2008. "High Technology Entrepreneurs and the Patent System: Results of the 2008 Berkeley Patent Survey" *Berkeley Technology Law Journal.*

Grossman, R. and Siegel, K. 2014. "Organizational Models for Big Data and Analytics" *Journal of Organization Design.*

Grote, M. H. and Taube, F. A. 2007. "When outsourcing is not an option: International relocation of investment bank research – Or isn't it?", *Journal of International Management.*

Haddad, C. and Hornuf, L. 2016. "The Emergence of the Global Fintech Market: Economic and Technological Determinants" *CESifo Working Paper Series No. 6131.*

Hakansson, H. and Snehota, I. 1995. "Developing relationships in business networks", London.

Hannig, A. and Jansen, S. 2010. "Financial Inclusion and Financial Stability: Current Policy Issues" *ADBI Working Paper No. 259.*

Hardin, G. 1968 "The Tragedy of the Commons", *Science, New Series.*

Harris, A. and Giunipero, L. C. and Hult, G. T. M. 1998. "Impact of Organizational and Contract Flexibility on Outsourcing Contracts", *Industrial Marketing Management.*

Hatch, J. 1997. "Organization theory", London, p. 7.

Hon, W. K. and Millard, C. 2016. "Use by Banks of Cloud Computing: An Empirical Study", *Queen Mary School of Law Legal Studies Research Paper No. 245/2016.*

Honess, S. 1996. "Outsourcing – A legal perspective on contract critical success factors", *Information security technical report.*

Hopt, K. J. and Leyens, P. C. 2004. "Board Models in Europe – Recent Developments of Internal Corporate Governance Structures in Germany, the United Kingdom, France, and Italy", *ECGI – Law Working Paper No. 18/2004.*

Huges, S. R. 2013. "Outsourcing and Contract Services" *Journal of Laboratory Automation.*

Joint Committee of the European Supervisory Authorities. 2018. "Joint Committee Report on the results of the monitoring exercise on 'automation in financial advice'.

Kenyon, C. 2005 "Optimal price design for variable capacity outsourcing contracts", *Journal of Revenue and Pricing Management.*

Lemma, V. 2016. "The Shadow Banking System. Creating Transparency in the Financial Markets". London.

Lemma, V. 2018, "Commento sub art. 13 d. lgs. 385 del 1993", *Commentario al testo unico delle leggi in materia bancaria e creditizia,* Padova.

Lemma, V. and Thorp, J. A. 2014. "Sharing Corporate Governance: The Role of Outsourcing Contracts in Banking", *Law and Economics Yearly Review.*

Li, X. 2014. Relational Contracts, Growth Options, and Heterogeneous Beliefs: A Game-Theoretic Perspective on Information Technology Outsourcing. *Journal of Management Information Systems,* 31(2), 319–350.

Lin, T. C. W. 2016. "Compliance, Technology, and Modern Finance", *Temple University Legal Studies Research Paper No. 2017–06.*

Lothian, T. 2010. "Law and Finance: A Theoretical Perspective", *Columbia Law and Economics Working Paper No. 388.*

Lothian, T. 2011. "Rethinking Finance Through Law: A Theoretical Perspective", *Columbia Law and Economics Working Paper No. 412.*

Lu, Y. and Ng, T. and Tao, Z. 2012. "Outsourcing, Product Quality, and Contract Enforcement" *Journal of Economics & Management Strategy.*

Martinez, M. and Sorrentino, M. 2000. "The Outsourcing of IT Services in Banking: Beyond the Transaction Cost Framework", *BIT Banking and Information Technology.*

Martinsons, M. G. 2001. "Comparing the Decision Styles of American, Chinese and Japanese Business Leaders" *Best Paper Proceedings of Academy of Management Meetings,* Washington, DC.

Masera, R. 2006. "La corporate governance nelle banche", Bologna.

Masera, R. 2014. "CRR/CRD IV: the Trees and the Forest'", *Does one size fit all,* Bologna.

Maugeri, M. 2010. "Esternalizzazione di funzioni aziendali e "integrità" organizzativa nelle imprese di investimento", *Banca borsa e titoli di credito.*

Maugeri, M. 2016. "Proxy Advisors, esercizio del voto e doveri fiduciari del gestore", *Orizzonti del diritto commerciale.*

Maume, P. 2017. "In Unchartered Territory – Banking Supervision Meets Fintech", *Corporate Finance 2017.*

Merusi, F. 2014. "Impresa pubblica e Costituzione economica", *Lo Stato.*

Meucci, A. 2010. "Factors on Demand: Building a Platform for Portfolio Managers, Risk Managers and Traders", *Risk.*

Minervini G. 1991. "Banca universale e gruppo polifunzionale", *Il diritto fallimentare e delle società commerciali.*

Minervini, G. 1984. "La legge bancaria verso il tramonto?" *Politica ed economia.*

Minervini, G. 1988. "Impresa bancaria e Costituzione", *Banca borsa e titoli di credito.*

Minervini, G. 1992. "I poteri della capogruppo nei gruppi bancari polifunzionali", *Banca borsa e titoli di credito.*

Mirone, A. 2017. "Regole di governo societario e assetti statutari delle banche tra diritto speciale e diritto generale", *Banca impresa società.*

Moenninghoff, S. C. and Wieandt, A. 2013. "The Future of Peer-to-Peer Finance" *Zeitschrift für Betriebswirtschaftliche Forschung.*

Montaseb, M. M. and Ragheb, M. A. and Ragab, A. A. and Elsamadicy, A. M., 2018. "The Factors Affecting of SMEs' Outsourcing Decision Making", *Business and Management Review.*

Mülbert, P. O. 2010. "Corporate Governance of Banks after the Financial Crisis – Theory, Evidence, Reforms", *ECGI – Law Working Paper No. 130/2009.*

O'Reilly, T. 2007. "What is Web 2.0: Design Patterns and Business Models for the Next Generation of Software". *Communications & Strategies.*

Osei Bryson, K.M. and Ngwenyam, O. 2006. "Managing risks in information systems outsourcing: An approach to analyzing outsourcing risks and structuring incentive contracts", *European Journal of Operational Research.*

Packin, N. G. 2017. "Regtech, Compliance and Technology Judgment Rule", *Chicago-Kent Law Review.*

Pellegrini, M. 2018. "Piani di risanamento e misure di early intervention", *federalismi.it.*

Popoli, P. 2017. "The Role of the Outsourcing Contract From a Partnership-based Perspective", *Chinese Business Review.*

Portale G. B., 2016. "La "corporate governance" delle società bancarie", *Rivista delle società*, 2016.

Posner, R. A., 2000. "Antitrust in the New Economy" *U Chicago Law & Economics.*

Pozsar, Z., Adrian, T., Ashcraft, A. B. and Boesky, H., 2013. "Federal Reserve Bank of New York Staff Reports – Shadow Banking".

Ravi, S. P. and Rivers, T. and Ravi, C. and Jain, K. and Sharma, P. h. 2011. "An Analysis Of Business Process Outsourcing Strategies Of Public And Private Sector Banks In India", *International Business & Economics Research Journal.*

Ray, B. K. and Tao, S. and Olkhovets, A. and Subramanian, D. 2013. "A decision analysis approach to financial risk management in strategic outsourcing contracts", *EURO J Decis Process.*

Rosen, R. J. "The Impact of the Originate-to-Distribute Model on Banks Before and During the Financial Crisis", *24th Australasian Finance and Banking Conference 2011 Paper.*

Sacco Ginevri, A. 2017. "Il problema dell'interesse sociale nelle banche", *La Nuova giurisprudenza civile commentata.*

Salamzadeh, A. and Kawamorita Kesim, H. 2015. "Startup Companies: Life Cycle and Challenges" *Speech at 4th International Conference on Employment, Education and Entrepreneurship.*

Scherer, M. U. 2015. "Regulating Artificial Intelligence Systems: Risks, Challenges, Competencies, and Strategies", *Harvard Journal of Law & Technology*.

Scholz, L. 2017. "Algorithmic Contracts", *Stanford Technology Law Review*.

Schrepel, T. 2018. "Is Blockchain the Death of Antitrust Law? The Blockchain Antitrust Paradox" *Georgetown Law Technology Review*.

Sciarrone Alibrandi, A. 2010. "Il servizio di consulenza in materia di investimenti: profili ricostruttivi di una nuova fattispecie", *Scritti in onore di Francesco Capriglione. Le regole del mercato finanziario*, Padova.

Sciarrone Alibrandi, A. 2017. "Il Problema". "Il tramonto della banca universale", Napoli.

Seshasai, S. and Gupta, A. 2004. "Global Outsourcing of Professional Services", *MIT Sloan Working Paper No. 4456-04*.

Shackelford, J. and Myers, S. 2017. "Block-by-block: Leveraging the power of blockchain technology to build trust and promote cyber peace" *Yale Journal of Law and Technology*.

Simshaw, D. 2018 "Ethical Issues in Robo-Lawyering: The Need for Guidance on Developing and Using Artificial Intelligence in the Practice of Law".

Spencer, B.J. 2005. "International outsourcing and incomplete contracts", *Canadian Journal of Economics*.

Stulz, R. M. 2019. "FinTech, BigTech, and the Future of Banks". *Fisher College of Business Working Paper No. 2019-03-020*.

Trautman, L. J. 2016. "Is Disruptive Blockchain Technology the Future of Financial Services?" *The Consumer Finance Law Quarterly Report 232*.

Van Loo, R. 2018. "Making Innovation More Competitive: The Case of Fintech" *UCLA Law Review*.

Wachter, S. and Mittelstadt, B. and Floridi, L., 2017. "Why a Right to Explanation of Automated Decision-Making Does Not Exist in the General Data Protection Regulation", *International Data Privacy Law*.

Wang, Y and Niu, B. and Guo, P. 2014. "The Comparison of Two Vertical Outsourcing Structures under Push and Pull Contracts", *Production and operations management*.

Wilmarth, A. E. 2009. "The Dark Side of Universal Banking: Financial Conglomerates and the Origins of the Subprime Financial Crisis" *Connecticut Law Review*.

Zaring, D. and Bignami, F. 2016. "Comparative Law and Regulation. Understanding the Global Regulatory Process". Northampton, MA, USA.

Zetzsche, D. A. and Buckley, R. P. and Arner, D. W. and Barberis, J. N. 2017. "From FinTech to TechFin: The Regulatory Challenges of Data-Driven Finance", *New York University Journal of Law and Business*.

CHAPTER 7

Fintech and Money

This chapter shows the impact of the evolution of financial technology on the market for money, in order to understand the role of fintech with respect to the effects on monetary trends, by considering the development of tech-fuelled instruments used as an alternative to sovereign money. Hence, this would imply a specific regulatory analysis of the current tolerance of non-sovereign cryptocurrencies by policymakers and central banks.

In this context, this chapter assesses the opportunities related to the regulation of the cryptocurrencies and, in particular, the current set-up of supervising initial coin offerings to the market. It moves from the hypothesis that the protection of savings invested in such 'crypto-instruments' refers to individual rights; therefore, the analysis aims at understanding the convenience to set specific safeguards able to guarantee their capacity to preserve their value and support payments, along with further backstops for avoiding thefts, plagiarisms and frauds.

Next chapter analyses the legal analysis of the new opportunities in preventing and combating money laundering and terrorism financing, whereas in this chapter the focus goes to the current application of cryptography and distributed ledger technology to substitute money. Hence, the analysis will take into account the possibility of a supervisory intervention over private cryptocurrencies and the prospects of applying the cryptography's innovation to the activity of issuing sovereign money performed by central banks, currently based on a central sequential ledger (and a serial number) and the 'feel, look and tilt' method for verification. Finally,

© The Author(s) 2020
V. Lemma, *FinTech Regulation*,
https://doi.org/10.1007/978-3-030-42347-6_7

it discusses the possibility of sovereign cryptocurrencies referring to the economies of the most developed countries, as this would represent a safe alternative to banknotes, electronic money and payment services developed in the twentieth century.

Section I: The Path Towards the Regulation of Money-tech

7.1   Money and Tech-Fuelled Instruments

Over the last years, the use of tech-fuelled instruments alternative to the currencies issued by central banks has grown.[1] Observing this phenomenon, the common denomination of cryptocurrencies highlights the use of such instruments as a substitute for money, as well as the reliance of their users on cryptography. As it is going to be shown in this chapter, the regulatory analysis moves from the results of the first examinations made by international authorities, which led to understand the benefits of the innovations herein applied with respect to the speed, cost efficiency and protection from hacking.[2]

Indeed, a first use of a combination of 'fintech and money' refers to the development of new technological tools able to provide specific characteristics to digital instruments and, in particular, the possibility to provide an assertion,[3] such is the indication of the source of such instruments, as well as ensuring that they are transferrable.[4] This combination leads people to the assumption of deeming digital instruments to be reliable even if they do not refer to sovereign money and do not entitle the owner with the right to request for the conversion of these instruments into sovereign money (as provided for the issue of electronic money).[5] Obviously, governments or any other public authorities do not guarantee for the value of such instruments and the entire life of the latter ones relies on the agreements reached by their users.

In this context, it is useful to begin by considering the risk of confusing the use of non-sovereign money with the use of cryptography and distributed ledger technologies.[6]

Both are facts due to financial innovations.[7] However, the former refers to the need of protection (required to increase market efficiency and to succeed in reaching social fairness), whereas the latter brings up the opportunity for the public intervention to reach its goals with fewer resources (thus, to increase its efficiency by leveraging the improvements in technology).

Both facts require a regulatory intervention, in order to reduce the risk of market failures. In the former case, this is due to their microeconomic relevance and interactions with the welfare of any user, and to the perspective of a macroeconomic impact (of these) on the interest rates and asset markets, as it appears by considering the relations highlighted by Hicks[8] and Hansen[9] in their IS-LM model.

Certainly, despite the above, the common line of attack on these instruments has unfolded from a holistic approach, so that their origins (as non-sovereign instruments) and their high level of technology are regarded as indissoluble components of a new phenomenon.[10]

Conversely, first, it is useful to consider that the ambition of private entities to issue instruments alternative to money is a long-standing story. There is a tendency to forget old stories, yet they remain the same over time (and then they must be studied again within the context of a market at odds with itself).

It is easy to recall the Italian Civil Code of 1942, whose Art. 1278 stated that a debt denominated in a currency that is not endowed with legal tender in the state can be fulfilled by the debtor with the sovereign money (provided that such obligations be converted at the exchange rate set forth at the date and place set forth for the payment). Analogous rule was also in the previous Italian Commercial Code of 1882, under Art. 39. This helps in highlighting that the Italian policymaker had known the use of alternative sources of liquidity in private transactions and that the legislator has chosen a specific rule to discipline the *dominance* of the sovereign money (as legal tender issued by the competent public authority) over any other currency, as the former is the ultimate instrument able to satisfy any obligation of payment.

Secondly, the public intervention on the market for money has referred to the definition and implementation of monetary policy, the execution of foreign-exchange operations (between national and foreign currencies), the holding and management of reserves (able to back the value of money) and—over the recent years—fostering the smooth functioning of payment systems.[11] In this respect, central banking action has benefitted from any development of technology that was able to increase its effectiveness and efficiency, and regulation supported the implementation of innovations (in both the organizational structure and the activities). Hence, the opportunity to investigate the rules required to promote the application of the technology used in cryptocurrencies to central banking and to sovereign money.

In accordance with the above, the need for investigating this use of alternative instruments concerns whether (and how) governments should oversee the cryptocurrencies and the action required for starting any further intervention in order to ensure the protection of individuals and the proper functioning of the monetary mechanisms.[12]

However, on a regular basis, cryptocurrencies should enter into circulation via retail trade: therefore, by means of a sale-and-purchase agreement (in exchange of money) or a barter (in exchange of goods or services), it is not possible to exclude that these could support lending activities or the reimbursement of savings (or the execution of any other activity reserved to supervised firms) (Lemma, V. 2018).

In this context, the end user of cryptocurrencies should qualify as consumer of such goods (if their acquisition aims at having an instrument able to complete payments) or as saver (if considered as a store of value). Furthermore, certain market trends showed the tendency of financial operators to regard cryptocurrencies as investment targets, both as an opportunity of allocating financial resources and a store of value, being possible to retrieve and exchange them at a later time. In addition, certain authorities have approached this phenomenon under the principles set forth for the provision of financial services, asset management and admission of securities to trading.[13]

Hence, the above qualifications (as either consumer or savers highlight the need for protection of such end users. This justifies the following analysis, aimed at understanding the regulatory principles presiding over the fairness of the regulation of the shared record-keeping and processing system or the large global ledger account (as a form of public intervention aimed at reducing the regulatory asymmetries in the capital markets). This also leads to improving the backstops provided in the anti-money-laundering regime, which can leverage the digital tracks of cryptocurrencies or, rather, impose the rule of leaving tracks of every digital currency transaction that occurs (kept safe by means of cryptography).[14]

In short, it is expectable that technology would improve the resilience of the financial system and the advantages due to the implementation of a payment flows that will not send money from one party to another (through the intervention of a supervised intermediary) but rather will write the exchange down in a ledger (even if there is not a central authority or official body assigned with the task of updating a central ledger and keeping track of all the transactions). This leads to uncentralized ways of payment and, therefore, sharing of a set of information among an indefinite number of private operators. Thus, public intervention requires the use of additional tools able to monitoring these multiple ledgers and their synchrony, taking into account the market networks (so that any transaction can be recorded by all the operators, making the ledgers verifiable).[15]

Therefore, public authorities must be able to oversight a peer-to-peer network, being maintained in terms of strict protocols and multiple copies of the same ledgers. This will lead to discuss the role of supervisors as manufacturers of the infrastructures, as well as the latter ones' auditors (by means of software to support the transactions and control their execution).

7.2 The Rise of Cryptocurrencies

As a result of the above initial considerations, a regulatory approach to (public or private) currencies must consider blockchain technology and cryptography as a whole and, thus, as the core elements of one of the innovations arisen in capital markets. Hence, this analysis is going to verify whether the current rules may be able to ensure that this innovation will not put savings at risk or jeopardize the transmission of monetary policy. Of course, it is going to start from the externalities of such innovation, and then to the (positive or negative) effects on the velocity of circulation, as well as on the overall amount of liquidity.

It is worth considering that monetary policy is benefitting from the development of fintech. As of today, no authority in charge of the latter might ignore the existence of non-sovereign currencies and their disruptive impact not only on the traditional channels of conveying central banks' impulses, but on the business models of several financial institutions as well. There is no doubt that technology is rightfully deemed to be the most relevant driver of the rise of cryptocurrencies. However, the discussion should turn on whether such phenomenon may be faced by regarding cryptocurrencies as money, for such an assertion is far from achieving any consensus.[16]

As anticipated in the first chapter, it has been chosen to take into account that individuals could use these cryptocurrencies with the expectation to store value or enact payments, even if (generally) they are not backed by any public authority,[17] are not supported by the legal duty to accept them as form of payment, and are volatile as any other speculative asset. Now, in light of their relevant proprieties, it is useful to recall what is potentially regarded as money: namely, whatever is a medium of exchange, a unit of account and a store of value at the same time, ending up with the conclusion that money is what money does.[18]

Furthermore, what actually legitimizes the difference between 'money' and 'currency' consists in the tool having legal tender.[19] This feature cannot rely upon the characteristics commonly certified by the public—that is, all the subjects connected with the usage of money—but needs a superior acknowledgement, which the highest monetary and political authority is entrusted of. At present-day, as the international monetary system becomes growingly integrated at an institutional level, the fourth 'pillar' of money is hard to disentangle from the other three.[20]

In order to understand the consequences of allowing cryptocurrencies to be subjected to the same rules as official coins, minted by sovereign states, it is necessary to recall the historical evolution of the international monetary system and its future prospects. With a glance at what lies ahead, it is possible to detect the phenomenon that scholars already defined as the denationalization of money: that is, abandoning traditional exchange rate regimes to establish a framework of a few solid, worldwide-accepted monies, ultimately converging to a universal standard in a way which would have narrowed the space for governments' intervention and central banks' discretionary policies (Hayek, F.A. 1976, 1978). Thanks to cryptocurrencies, this path is fairly unfolding before our sight; nevertheless, many have underlined the theoretical difficulties that it will ineluctably encounter.[21] The substantial failure to regulate the monetary novelties at a global level, and even the polarization of supervisory approaches to cryptocurrencies (either a near-complete ban or no discipline at all), seemingly certify that the previously mentioned intuition—however fascinating it was—still copes with a grandly complicated reality. Hence, it needs to point out the effects of 'cryptizing' with respect to the relevance of individual rights involved in the exchange of money, rather than the possibility that these would influence the effectiveness of transactions or the effects of monetary policy.

It is worth considering that, until the end of the Second World War, the international monetary system had been far from integrated. And after such war, the developed countries began configuring central banking as it is today (except for the European Central Bank (ECB)). Many of the largest economies had kept the gold standard in charge, ensuring that circulating banknotes were backed by sufficient amount of gold reserves. Hence, the so-called fiat or 'paper' money—whose spread had de facto mirrored the advance of industrialization—was often able to prevent inflationary bubbles or substantive damage to the financial system (Grey, R. and Dharmapalan, J., 2017). This held even in times when a certain misallocation of resources gave rise to significant economic slowdown: for example, in the United States, the 1873 Great Depression. Most importantly, the institutional drawbacks of the separation between distinct central banks—who had not yet constituted the modern 'System'—was somehow counterbalanced by the gold standard. For long time, the dollar was not the centre of the international monetary order, a role that the pound sterling played instead. Conversely, US public finances remained substantially sound, whereas the banking system was characterized by a legislation aimed at keeping lenders small and, thus, intrinsically unable to stir relevant monetary effects.

In this respect, it is possible to take into account that all the above has been considered as the basis for protecting savings and for controlling credit (as the functioning of most advanced economies requires). In 1913, the Federal Reserve System was created not only to fulfil its monetary tasks, nor was its scope circumscribed to influencing the effectiveness of sovereign monetary policy. Conversely, the Fed should also have taken care of people's individual rights and overall market stability. The relationship between Fed policies and the onset of the 1929 crisis has been widely investigated, especially from a libertarian standpoint opposed to the centralization of monetary functions (Rothbard, M.N. 1963). Economic historians have often regarded the industrial effort in war production, along with the 'Keynesian consensus' based on public investments in the aftermath of the conflict, as the major contributors to overcoming the depression of the 1930s.

However, the monetary overhaul ignited at the 1944 Bretton Woods conference should not be understated. Henceforth, it is worth recalling a lesson from the past before going deep into the regulatory analysis of the newest currencies: in fact, said conference gave rise to a system wherein national monies were pegged to the US dollar, which was convertible into gold too. Moreover, the International Monetary Fund (IMF) was established; also, it was empowered with the faculty of managing its currency reserves for the sake of keeping exchange rates within reasonable floating boundaries. For this purpose, in 1969, a reference unit of account—namely, the Special Drawing Rights (SDR)—was introduced by the IMF. Between 1971 and 1973, given that the rising oil price had deeply aggravated the US trade deficit, the need to devalue the currency with a view to boosting exports led the American government to suspend the dollar's convertibility into gold, first, ultimately withdrawing it. Hence, there have been more than 40 years in which exchange rates have been widely free to float, apart from what happened in Europe with the progressive construction of a monetary union. As for the East, traditionally dominated by the yen (which is a very relevant currency for derivatives transactions, too), the renminbi was added to the SDR basket in 2016, yet this did not prevent the United States from engaging in a harsh trade war with China, pursued in an attempt to weaken the dollar by pressuring the Fed to lower interest rates.[22]

All the above leads to one preliminary conclusion. Governments cannot delay more in having regard to the rights of end users of cryptocurrencies and in verifying whether their use can rely on the same rights that people exercise when dealing with monies endowed with legal tender.

7.3   Economic Criticisms Supporting Regulation: An Overview

As far as the academic debate on cryptocurrencies is concerned, it is useful to bear in mind the theories advanced by leading scholars in either the Austrian or the monetarist school, as it is foreseeable that such theories support the possibility that technology applied to cryptocurrencies would be useful for increasing the financial system's resilience.[23]

In this perspective, it is worth beginning by considering that Hayek stated the following: "I have now no doubt whatever that private enterprise, if it had not been prevented by government, could and would long ago have provided the public with a choice of currencies, and those that prevailed in the competition would have been essentially stable in value and would have prevented both excessive stimulation of investment and the consequent periods of contraction" (Hayek, F.A. 1976, 1978). On the other side of the anti-Keynesian and pro-market thinking, other scholars basically shared Hayek's view of spontaneous market forces eventually driving the monetary system toward an equilibrium (Friedman, M. and Schwartz, A.J. 1987). Hence, the possibility to move from the economic conclusion that the Federal Reserve system should have been put to an end,[24] given the negative role that it had played across the US monetary history, considering the libertarian analysis on the roots of the 1929 crisis

(Rothbard, M.N. 1963). In practice, this laid the foundations of modern cryptocurrencies.

Notwithstanding the above, it is possible to spot that cryptocurrencies are not generally welcomed in market practices, but rather deemed to constitute something more akin to a speculative bubble.[25] Such statement came at a time in which it was not an obvious one, at all, for there were several other asset classes whose unusually high prices should have alarmed investors. Obviously, it referred to the capacity of the current cryptocurrencies to store value, and—in this respect—it seems that public intervention can control both the peer-to-peer network and the capacity to convert these assets into sovereign money at an "honest" value (Bianca, C.M. 1999).

Goals of the public intervention, until the financial environment is still characterized by extremely low interest rates, should consider that any rise in the relevant prices remains difficult to explain based on macrofundamentals, and actually seems to be unrelated with many of its traditionally acknowledged determinants.[26] While admitting this, and even noting that cryptocurrencies prices might have been suffering from a similar deviation from their econometrically justifiable level, it has been denounced that cryptocurrencies show the most astonishing departure from fundamental value.

From a regulatory perspective, it can be noticed that end users (who rely on software to invest their savings) may not be captured by irrationality, which is commonly regarded as the main propellant of any bubble. Hence, as this research is going to point out in its final remarks, the analysis refers to the fact that even more companies are attaching the term 'blockchain' to their names, in an attempt to become more appealing to investors and ostensibly achieving the goal of propping their valuation up (FSB 2017b).[27] To the aforesaid scholars, this was another proof of the impossibility to observe something like a fully rational Homo oeconomicus in everyday life; moreover, it constituted an alarming situation closely mirroring those periods in history which have shortly preceded the outbreak of dramatic financial crises (e.g. the 1987 'Black Monday' and the dot-com bubble, burst at the beginning of the Millennium).[28] Therefore, once again it can be highlighted that there should be a way to regulate the use of the term 'fintech', 'blockchain' or 'crypto-', as it is provided for the term 'bank' in several regulatory frameworks.

This is not simply recalling the warnings against the risks associated with letting cryptocurrencies proliferate; indeed, it refers to a much more severe economic judgement that can support a call to banning cryptocurrencies. With respect to the studies on the role of information asymmetries, it is worth considering Joseph Stiglitz's thought and his concerns with the current macroeconomic dynamics, at neither an international nor a domestic level.[29] In fact, this prevented an efficient oversight from being exerted over such opaque and usually illiquid instruments.

In practice, however distant from the Monetarist school any academic may be, the research resulted in a broader defence of the current international monetary system, where circulating fiat currencies do not enjoy any collateralization ultimately provided by central banks, not even a partial one. In brief, this is one of the main economic grounds to investigate with respect to the additional regulatory task of monitoring these cryptocurrencies, their multiple ledgers and synchrony.

Not all of the above suggests that the risk arising from the lack of safeguards refers to the digital nature of the environment where the currency transaction occurs, but to the political aspects of cryptocurrencies (as Paul Krugman has recently highlighted; given that their 'ideological' roots may be traced back to the US libertarian movement, which upheld the reinstatement of the gold standard and even the abolition of central banking, Krugman launched a harsh attack on what he saw as something more similar to a belief than to a well-grounded economic theory).[30]

Henceforth, it is possible to consider such criticism as the result of the fact that cryptocurrencies do not show any material trait, as they are made just of code strings (nothing but a digital record stored on computers). In this view, all the above marks a substantial, irredeemable difference vis-à-vis all other assets. Even the fact that the record itself is not centralized in a single physical location, but rather distributed across many places, was regarded as a negative aspect, for it originates the absence of any formally sanctioned ownership and, thus, makes it impossible to find out who the proprietors are.

Hence, it is likely that now policymakers will be able to understand the need for an improvement in the anti-money-laundering regime of fintech firms, by exploiting the regulation of the records made by every digital currency transaction that occurs. [31]

Besides, and coming back to the possibility of storing value, the vision of several scholars is apodictic: bitcoin has no intrinsic value at all, remarking that such lack of tether was complemented by a very limited circulation.[32] However, this approach confirms the need for protection, and it suggests that crypto-assets raise several broader issues that require a public intervention in order to ensure (along with consumer and investor protection) strong market integrity protocols, incentives for tracking their circulation and international measures to prevent tax evasion or forum shopping.

This would suggest to conclude on this point by considering the opinion of Robert Shiller.[33] In light of this, the actual realization that the market was far from stable and profitable—maybe ending up in a sudden crash—might have come too late, preventing investors from detecting the underlying danger. Despite this, scholars generally agree on the need for warnings against the bubble steadily growing, up to the point at which its bursting would have been impossible to avoid and extremely pernicious upon its occurrence (Baily, M. N. et al. 2011).

In other words, scholars that are monitoring the cryptocurrencies clearly reflected some convictions that are widely spread, even across economists inspired by a different way of thinking than the new-keynesian one. In this respect, it is useful to bear in mind the consideration on the 'efficient market hypothesis'—was particularly concerned with crypto-assets' volatility (Baily, M. N. et al. 2013).[34]

It is convenient to mention a different approach that can be taken by considering that Bengt Holmström provided a valuable theoretical basis to the so-called use of debt (i.e. that can be automatically settled via the blockchain infrastructure) (Holmstrom, B. 2015). Indeed, it is expectable that policymakers would rely on such approach because of the meaningful criticism in respect of the idea of centralized cryptocurrencies supported by smart contracts. In this respect, such approach would be particularly pernicious in the event of a crisis that would entail algorithms to block any run, the latter being forced to stop. Ultimately, these contracts could proceed with a liquidity injection (from one of the parties), therefore starting a process whose result might be disruptive from a financial stability standpoint.[35]

7.4 WHAT CRYPTOCURRENCIES ARE: THE NEED FOR REGULATORY BOUNDARIES

It is worth clarifying that in the following paragraphs the analysis would not repeat the difficulties in considering cryptocurrencies as "money" (Mersch, Y. 2018) or, rather, "private money". On the contrary, it is going to assume that people believe in their capacity to store value and enact payments, and then it would look for the regulatory boundaries required to protect the legal tender (provided that public authorities will only defend sovereign money, to the extent it is possible).

However, it is also worth recalling the definition of cryptocurrency as a digital coin, created with blockchain technology (Tiwari, N. 2018). In turn, from a legal perspective blockchain consists in a mere instrumental attribute of a new (generally) accepted way to fulfil obligations by means of a device and an infrastructure laying down certain decentralized databases, maintained by distributed networks of computers (Wright, A. and De Filippi, P. 2018).[36] In the launch of the first digital assets, the 'unknown father' of bitcoin identified an electronic coin with a chain of digital signatures.[37] Further definitions have tried to overcome such vagueness, focusing on the possibility to consider cryptocurrencies as money. From a purely economic point of view, they have represented one of the most popular assets to be included in investors' portfolios: in this sense, regulation is indirectly exerted upon them by means of the supervised entities involved in either their minting or their transactions.

Put in a geopolitical and historical perspective, the origins of bitcoin seem to trace back to Asia, where one of the igniting events occurred during the 1997 financial crisis, due to the use of stress testing and a direct involvement by international organizations. At that time, Asian people pioneered cryptocurrencies and blockchain a decade before Satoshi Nakamoto.[38] In addition, it is worth anticipating that central banks can improve sovereign virtual currencies in the context of their traditional activity. Hence, nowadays, it is not possible to exclude that national central banks will issue 'public crypto-currencies'.

Anyway, this part of the analysis is interested in assessing whether they can be treated as cash and, thus, whether governmental monopoly over their issuance be a legitimate answer or not. In modern times, a commonly agreed idea is that governments should not allow private entities to take decisions regarding the minting of coins, albeit central banking has not always coexisted with the idea that money supply should be regulated and, instead, cannot be treated as something merely spontaneous. In fact, some rough hints of what is nowadays known as the 'quantity theory of money' well precede its formal statement, generally attributed to Hume.[39]

From a juridical perspective, it can be observed that the shift in power over coin minting from a political body to a technical one is a further step that the United States has taken only at the end of a very harsh debate, which the Supreme Court did not restrain from entering by providing an interpretation of the Constitution's meaning.[40] This is referring to the traditional analysis that intended the fundamental law of the United States as entrusting the government with the duty to harmonize money circulation in the whole of the country. As mentioned above, such power was ultimately transferred onto the Federal Reserve System. Regardless of the latter's independence from the legislative and executive branches (which is far from complete, unlike many European countries), there are no evidences to deny that, pursuant to the current legal order, the monopoly on money may be exerted upon cryptocurrencies too in order to prevent new risks from arising (for the twofold purposes of protecting individual rights and preserving financial stability). This is particularly relevant in light of some contemporary issues and trends: on the one hand, the most common instrument in that asset class (namely, bitcoin) has a limited supply by design; on the other, a large private company (namely, Facebook) has recently declared its intention to start minting a new cryptocurrency, to be used in commercial relationships with clients (but whose future is still difficult to predict).

Indeed, actually, the need for regulatory boundaries refers—once again—to the relevance of individual rights involved in the exchange of cryptocurrencies, rather than the possibility that these would influence the effects of monetary policies.[41] Thus, the possibility of questioning—in the next section of this chapter—the role of public intervention provided that an effective market should allocate the relevant resources in an efficient way.

7.5   Safe Asset and Money Dualism in the Regulatory Approaches to Blockchain

As anticipated, the ground for the supervisory intervention is understanding whether cryptocurrencies fulfil—by means of the blockchain and distributed ledger technology[42]—the three functions of money, or rather if such functions, other than just existing, actually need a formal legal acknowledgement to be enforced. In this respect, the classification of non-sovereign cryptocurrencies as a substitute of money would help in assessing the need for a public intervention aimed to protect the effectiveness of public intervention over monetary policies, provided that any increase in using substitutes for legal tender would expand the quantitative base of money itself.

According to the above, it should first be considered that, even in very recent times, cryptocurrencies lack that process of 'material' origination which is associated with minting traditional monies. It refers to the appraisal of such assets for being 'money-like' in the sense that it is based upon trust, with private platforms playing the same role as central banks, as these two are elements which turn coin users' 'ignorance' into a source of knowledge of its possibilities.[43] Hence, users are enabled to use coins by neglecting their 'representative' value and, thus, unknowing what is represented by them. Actually, it would be useful to recall the possibility that, notwithstanding the 'promises' of cryptography, the 'moneyness' of its current applications is yet to be confirmed by further studies, and, most importantly, it remains linked to speculative assets far from being regarded as safe or backed by the sovereign authority (Nabilou, H., Prüm, A. 2018).

A risk-adverse person would probably consider the above enough for siding with legal tender, but this fails to highlight any significant difference vis-à-vis fiat money (Haney, B. S. 2019), whose value is generally very distant from an allegedly 'intrinsic' one. In fact, if the real problem associated with money was its acceptance by the public (and the backing of a state), the minting process should be regarded as secondary. Even if this were not considered a convincing argument, the physical inputs used to produce cryptocurrencies (e.g. a particularly massive and stable power supply, to keep large and expensive servers working) cannot be ignored.[44] Conversely, some have argued that cryptocurrencies and their infrastructure may serve as the fulfilment of the project ignited by the establishment of the previously mentioned SDR (Lo, S. and Wang, J. 2014).

Considering a monetary policy in which the social goal is to maximize the sum of the people's utilities, it would be optimal for a cryptocurrency to be minted if (and only if) its utility to the user and its external effect for the people were, on net, positive. This leads to discuss the possibility of regarding cryptocurrencies as commodities.

In particular, several studies have focused on analysing similarities and differences between these kinds of assets, on the one hand, and gold, on the other. They refer to the consideration that such an asset has its own peculiarities (Baur, D. G. et al. 2018), which pose it far from both gold and the legal tender, and—in an attempt to provide a final answer to the long-standing question of whether it is a gold-like store of value or an investment asset—scholars noted that the volatility of bitcoin is decisively higher than, and substantially uncorrelated with, that of assets comparable to it. In spite of this, different studies—conducted with regard to other financial instruments, over different time horizons—seemingly conclude that the divergence between bitcoin and a safe asset is not so wide.[45]

Even the ECB's scholars acknowledged that, since the beginning of 2018, not only certain cryptocurrencies have been little volatile compared to other assets endowed with similar investment properties, but that the crypto-asset world is actually moving toward greater stability vis-à-vis its past experience (Bullmann, D. et al. 2018). This is mainly the case of the so-called stablecoins, which achieve their goals by claiming to exhibit a stable value through a flexible coin supply (i.e. algorithmic money) or backing the crypto-asset with collateral (i.e. collateralized stablecoins). As a matter of fact, the stablecoins fail to fall within the definition of assets and, also, are mainly used for hedging purposes, as they try to 'fine-tune' the adequate level of volatility needed to balance their portfolios and, thus, be protected against unexpected market movements. However, the contractual structure of such collateralization requires both an agreement and a third party able to support the promise of a guarantee. In this respect, private law (and an efficient judicial system) would ensure that an optimal behaviour might involve not the cessation of mining unsafe digital coins, but the amelioration of the harm through the exercise of the aforesaid precaution.[46] Although such characteristic would drive these coins out of the scope of 'money' and rather strengthen their classification as mere securities, it would nonetheless support the classification of cryptocurrencies as instruments fulfilling the 'store of value' function of money. In fact, no scholar would ever doubt that a traditional currency fails to fulfil the definition of money just because of actions aimed at containing its fluctuations, or because of the issuers owns silver or gold to back the circulating notes.

Obviously, this is not promoting the use of a common resource to back non-sovereign cryptocurrencies, even if it could be socially desirable when the benefit exceeds its cost. That said, it is not possible to deny that the use of a common resource could back a futuristic sovereign cryptocurrency.

The relevance of confidence comes into consideration, which underlies the circulation of both traditional currencies and digital ones, and its effects cannot be managed through bargaining among the involved parties.[47] This analysis would not examine the costs of spreading confidence in the market for cryptocurrencies, nor the obstacles to it; however, it is necessary to consider the contrast to negative spillovers by means of the implementation of a coherent regulatory framework.[48] This rises a debate on the necessity of a fractional reserve, cryptocurrency denominated, as well as for fiat monies. The substantial difference, as remarked the economists, is that—unlike official currencies—growth supply is usually limited by a properly designed algorithm. Indeed, mining reflects a decreasing policy that does not take into account the maximization of social welfare.

In this way, the possibility for credit institutions to multiply the amount of coins in the system due to growing demand, in spite of minting being limited, would stir negative consequences for financial stability. Moreover, this would weaken the efficacy of monetary policy targeting the inflation rate, as rising prices would not be easily controlled. All the above amplifies by considering that the fintech environment supports a sort of frictionless bargaining.

All the above leads to a safe asset versus money dualism, which reflects itself in the nature of cryptocurrencies. Provided that frictionless bargaining does not necessary lead to a maximization of social welfare (regardless of wealth being widespread or not), reference goes to the findings that show how cryptocurrencies may be successfully used for risk management purposes and, in particular, to serve the financial needs of risk-averse investors.[49] Such findings show that such assets possess intermediate characteristics—also from a purely investment standpoint—between gold and the legal tender, dismissing many concerns related to the volatility of cryptocurrencies. However, it was also noted that, with regard to trading, the frequency of transactions "may be higher for bitcoin as trading and reactions to market sentiment are quick", as well as volatility appears to be as persistent as for gold, showing good forecasting power too. In addition, certain cryptocurrencies have ultimately been considered as a relatively safe asset, whose financial properties are similar to that of gold and—in accordance with the findings of previous research—may be used to pursue successful hedging strategies against a sovereign currency (Tully, E. and Lucey, B. 2007).

At this stage of the analysis, the scope of the previously mentioned studies has not shown any limitation to the use of cryptography by central banks legally entitled to issue banknotes. Hence, the next section will highlight the need for investigating the operators that digitally issue and withdraw cryptocurrencies (as well as any one that pretends to issue money outside the traditional monetary systems). This would lead to understand whether (and how) governments can (or must) oversee cryptocurrencies and their minting. It follows from the preceding debate that confidence toward this market segment requires an effective public intervention aimed at ensuring the proper functioning of the monetary mechanisms.

Indeed, this does not deny the possibility that cryptocurrencies would enter into circulation via retail trade, lending or any other activity reserved to supervised firms. On the contrary, it allows considering that such currencies may follow a specific path across banking and finance, as well as the real economy. Even if such entering into circulation does not result in a social welfare optimum, yet it may improve the liquidity and the availability of means able to satisfy payments.

All the above suggests that public authorities should oversee the network that uses cryptocurrencies, in order to ensure that it is being maintained in terms of strict protocols and multiple copies of the same ledgers, as well as fair rules for mining. As a result, the conclusion of this first section can point out that blockchain technology and cryptography are, in the context of fintech, part of the foundational innovations underlying the development of the new ways able to let capital and wealth circulate. Hence, the need for supervision should be verified, and, furthermore, whether the current organization of supervising authorities is able to ensure that crypto-currencies will not reduce transparency, security and efficiency (of any transaction that occurs in the capital market).

SECTION II: REGULATORY AND SUPERVISING CONSISTENCIES

7.6 THE STATE OF REGULATION

A deeper analysis starts from the state of the current regulation of the shared record-keeping and processing system or the large global ledger account. According to the preeminent role of private law, it is not possible to avoid investigating the need for a regulatory intervention aimed at reducing the asymmetries in such sector. It is worth anticipating that the goal is the understanding of possibility of enacting specific mechanisms related to the regulation of the cryptography or the programmers that apply such cryptography in order to develop new assets.[50]

As anticipated above, policymakers seem to be very far behind in regulating cryptocurrencies as either a product (with respect to a minimum quality) or its circulation (having regard to the safety of the exchanges). The same is true for miners, in light of this definition referred to the producers of any piece of cryptocurrency (according to the process set up by the relevant programmers), as they are also responsible of verifying transactions and rewarding those who perform such activity.[51]

In the next section of this chapter, the analysis will go deep into the functions of these miners, as well as the role of the managers of the platforms used for trading such cryptocurrencies or exchange them into sovereign ones, and the tasks of the other service providers. Thus, it is worth anticipating the regulatory convenience to set specific safeguards able to guarantee the capacity of these cryptocurrencies to preserve their value, together with the need for further backstops for avoiding thefts, plagiarisms and frauds, safeguards that would bear on the aforesaid subjects (i.e. miners, traders, exchangers, platform managers and the programmers of their business analytics).[52]

Nevertheless, some scholars have focused on issues that are similar to those of traditional securities and their trading, such as transparency. At the same time, it is necessary to also consider that cryptocurrencies have the capacity to produce monetary effects, so their analysis cannot rely only on the principles used for asset management per se, but rather deals with monetary aspects too.

From a law and economics perspective, a very concerning aspect of cryptocurrencies is concentration, as the majority of transactions is settled in euro and a very few subjects hold a particularly large portion of all circulating cryptocurrencies (in respect of each kind or denomination). As a consequence of this, regulating platforms as central counterparties would manage the risk of a market collapse; even if the current volume of such currencies suggests a difficulty in transmitting the consequence of default to a systemic level, it is likely that it would impose severe losses (onto users).

It is worth considering the possibility of the 'tethering' of cryptocurrencies in respect of traditional monies or, more, broadly about the relationship of cryptocurrencies vis-à-vis existing monetary structures. In this industry, in fact, miners act as either a central bank, a stock exchange operator and a clearing house (Chohan, U.W. 2018). The real case study showing this relationship is provided by Tether, a cryptocurrency allegedly backed by $1 per each coin minted. At the time of the relevant studies, the absence of external auditors raising concerns over security and oversight has been noted. In fact, theft is not quite uncommon in the crypto-world, and Tether itself had been stolen of assets just a few weeks before it suspended its relationship with the external auditor. Thus, once again, the importance of exploiting the mechanisms for blocking the circulation of a stolen asset and regulating this feature.

Furthermore, it is worth regulating also the evidence that a cryptocurrency is actually backed by fiat currency or any other asset. This leads, also, to specific conflict of interests, whose management can be considered within the tasks of the regulators.[53]

Also, it is a matter of fact that miners are not a credit institution and, thus, did not hold any reserve at any central bank. It is sufficient to recall the European Union (EU) regulation on banks to verify that credit institutions can only perform banking business considered as taking deposits or other repayable funds from the public and extending credit on their own account (as stated in Directive 2013/36/EU and Regulation EU no. 575/2013). Therefore, much of the alleged safety of transactions based upon the purported similarity to real currencies was not actually enforced or could not be carefully proven. Certain miners and users were de facto experiencing an information asymmetry, and this was not limited to that specific cryptocurrency.[54]

From a technical standpoint, it seems to share many features of privately issued cryptocurrencies. However, since the government controls it and, thus, is aware of its circulation and use, such cryptocurrency may be easily subjected to taxation too and to any other effect of sovereignty. Obviously, in such a case, the national legislator would be in the best position to deny the possibility that such crypto-sovereign-currencies will refer to specific anti-money-laundering provisions (but it cannot avoid the limits of international sanctions levied on trade, as well as an international backstop to such new sovereign assets). Notwithstanding the above, it is expectable that other countries—especially within BRICS (Brazil, Russia, India, China and South Africa)—are supposedly planning to enter the cryptocurrency market, because of the positive externalities in terms of financial inclusions (highlighted in the previous chapters).[55]

More in general, the application of cryptography to the legal tender does not require private mining, as it has been experienced in non-sovereign cryptocurrencies.[56] There would be many other benefits from governments mining cryptocurrencies, but several threats as well. First, transaction costs would be lower and, thus, foster many payment and investment services currently provided under the traditional systems based on legal tender. As well as other fintech activities and akin to the spread of cryptocurrencies in general, this would significantly impair the market share of traditional intermediaries by substantially curbing their revenues.

However, it is clear that sovereign cryptocurrencies would have a wider and deeper impact (than private ones). This is not referring only to the material evidence that the sole use of a sovereign state's official acknowledgement would prompt the general public to prefer this kind of cryptocurrencies over decentralized ones, but also to their backing (with the resources of the public finance). Hence, their coexistence in the market would not lead to a competition between sovereign and private cryptocurrencies, but to a new playing field as it is currently into force with sovereign and private bonds in the capital markets. So, in such a case, this industry would benefit from the use of law enforcement public power to support the circulation of cryptocurrencies (endowed with the government's own imprimatur).

In light of this, it is useful to bear in mind the idea of a global cryptocurrency (named iCurrency), which would doubtlessly solve many of the issues associated with digitalism, especially with regard to transparency and informational concerns (Kakushadze, Z. and Liew, J. K. S., 2018).

Coming to the present regulation of decentralized cryptocurrencies, it should immediately be noted that the most common approach entails a severe restriction of their use, close to a full ban.[57] India has been an example in this regard, as underlined by several economists: it has been noted that the Indian law—though of Anglo-Saxon origin and, thus, strongly protective of contractual rights—allows government interference into private practices when monetary issues are concerned, for financial stability purposes (Hussain, H. 2017). Hence, the discussion focuses on whether private cryptocurrencies can be subjected to taxation: if they are proper money, they should be exempted from any fiscal burden (except for certain gains in trading); if their nature of securities prevails, they can provide revenues to their owner. Obviously, this yields the problem of setting the incorporation of a gain or a revenue within a jurisdiction, and then the right to tax it; such problem being particularly concerning in a dematerialized and cross-border environment, where a government might not intervene with certainty.

7.7   The Effects of a 'Passive' Regulation

Elsewhere in the world, the regulatory approach is not going in the direction of a complete deregulation, but a transferral of powers and competences is taking place from a general hard law to a specific set of orders to the credit institutions. The latter, however, should not be necessarily intended as exerted by regulatory authorities. In fact, in the United States, the Congress has been particularly active in conducting hearings and enquiries, promoting symposia too.[58]

First of all, the question is no more whether private cryptocurrencies can be treated as legal tender, but whether cryptography can be applied to legal tender. And then, the following question would be whether sovereign cryptocurrencies would lead to an 'optimal currency area'.

Far from answering with certainty, economists have just tried to weigh pros and cons of abandoning pre-existing national monies in favour of the euro within the theoretical framework of optimal currency areas (pioneered by Mundell 1961).[59] It is no doubt that, if the Eurozone actually enjoyed such 'optimality', the circulation of parallel currencies (particularly cryptized ones) would pose additional challenges that might eventually put monetary union to an end.[60]

The same threat is exerted within each area adopting a single official currency, including nation states, but in many of them the alternative to legal tender may be too small to represent a serious menace. It is also worth recalling the experience of countries that are using other countries' sovereign money (so called dollarization), and the one of countries (like the United States, the United Kingdom and Japan) that have their currencies exchanged worldwide, both for monetary purposes (by central banks and supranational authorities) and to settle contracts involving various financial instruments (particularly derivatives).

While resorting to the euro area, different outcomes should be envisaged. First, the supervisory architecture has been built—and is expected to be completed over the near future—as if the area were an optimal one. Many pieces of EU legislation, in fact, follow a one-size-fits-all approach, mirrored from that taken by cross-country bodies devoted to disciplining the financial realm (e.g. the Basel Committee of Banking Supervision, even if it has been harshly criticized by many recipients of regulation and even external observers). Second, the freedom of providing services and making capitals flow across the whole internal market of the European Union may theoretically boost the circulation of any cryptocurrency (both as a means of payment and as a financial asset) and, thus, subjected to the regulatory framework wherein money circulates and securities are exchanged.

It is worth also considering that the ECB's scholars assessed that the risks posed by 'crypto-assets' to the stability of the monetary union are limited and/or manageable on the basis of the existing regulatory and oversight frameworks (Bullmann, D. et al. 2018); nevertheless, they stated the ECB's commitment to monitor crypto-assets, raise awareness and develop preparedness. Said commitment refers to a direct, harsh attack on the function of crypto-assets, defined as something not entailing any financial claims towards any 'identifiable entity' and—most significantly—being characterized by high volatility, as well as the absence of an identifiable fundamental value, and a speculative nature exposing to potentially high losses (ECB 2020).[61] Therefore, the supervisory reaction to an environment that is benefitting from a passive regulatory approach is clear; however, the ECB may seem to be ignoring such phenomenon as long as it remains of a circumscribe ( )d size (and then is not producing any material monetary effect). This is the ground for the consideration that crypto-assets do not currently pose an immediate threat to the financial stability of the euro area. Besides, quoting the findings by a member of its Executive Board, the authority in charge of the European System of Central Banks denied that cryptocurrencies fulfil the functions of money (Mersch, Y. 2019).

It is not surprising that the assessment of the ECB on the role of crypto-assets in post-trade services concluded that cryptocurrencies requires an (IMF) intervention to preserve stability at a global level, and that such conclusion refers to the sake of the whole exchange industry, including the operations carried out by central counterparties (CCPs)[62] and central securities depositories (CSDs).[63]

What it is necessary to take into account for a regulatory purpose is that the ECB deems the entire market infrastructure to be particularly sensitive to what happens to the circulation of crypto-assets, and the possibility that such correlation will soon increase is acknowledged too. Moreover, in its responsibility of driving the Single Supervisory Mechanism, ECB warned about not hampering the systemic resilience to shocks originated by crypto-assets, something which would occur if the EU Member States addressed the issue on their own, without duly participating a common effort and, thus, potentially triggering regulatory arbitrage.

The results of this analysis may suggest that the ECB, while monitoring crypto-assets, relies (to a great extent) on publicly available third-party aggregated data.[64] Now note that there are multiple sources of such kind of data, diverging by nature and accessibility (i.e. publicly vs. privately available), their content (prices, volumes, estimates), the degree of completeness of their coverage, and the possibility to access underlying raw information. Furthermore, working on those data is no trivial activity: even if data were particularly granular, their quality should be carefully checked, with substantive time devoted to it. Before amplifying this point, it seems useful to reconsider the ECB's approach with respect to its guide on how to collect, aggregate and elaborate data from various sources. A plea to exert continuous monitoring—similarly to what occurs in other fields where financial innovation be driven by technological progress, like high-frequency trading—is also encompassed by the above-mentioned document. Given this monitoring, a higher need for regulation would be recorded.

One implication of the preference of the ECB for the lawfulness of the current use of alternative currencies and assets (based on cryptography) is directly connected with the possibility that the real economy would benefit from an increasingly intertwining. It has been seen that such intertwining is forecast to grow along with time, especially if the role played by platforms were to expand. However, it should also be considered that the lack of regulation would allow the investment in basket including both crypto-assets and some derivatives written on cryptocurrencies, similarly to what occurred to other commodity ETFs in the past.[65]

Of course, at this stage, the analysis light on the often-debated regulatory question of whether the authority in charge of minting euros fears that cryptocurrencies may be mined in an unregulated manner, utterly different from the cautious decisions taken by sovereign authorities. In fact, it reports the attention to the initial coin offerings (ICOs), regarded as the processes made by entities creating money supply as for cryptocurrencies.[66] To understand and reply to the previous question, ICOs come into consideration, as well as their substantial growth over 2018, in terms of both number of operations and amounts raised.

Although these processes could be considered as regulated (as public offerings of something that should be considered as a financial instrument), the fact that they are becoming increasingly common is a possible alert on cryptocurrencies, as they would grow up to interfering with the functioning of the traditional monetary system. Given, then, the assumption that their market-based circulation—where allowed—is (almost by definition) free and unconstrained, it is possible to highlight that its 'real' effects started being undisputed and rather gained a certain literature consensus (approximately, with the oil crises in the 1970s).

As for the informational realm, the ECB lamented a great deal of confusion, as long as there are hardly any suitable public data sources that allow the use of crypto-assets as substitutes for money to be measured and monitored and, in particular, statistics on the number and value of payments received by merchants in crypto-assets are not publicly available. A scholar may be inclined to think that even more common types of data are either fragmented and un-vetted (or dimly indicative of the actual economic phenomenon), such that this creates difficulties in correctly addressing risk management issues, provided that the inducement of reliance is necessarily a requirement in such a market.

More in general, a full consideration of the aforesaid phenomenon would also take into account the European Banking Authority's (EBA's) proposal to take a conservative approach to regulating this industry, in light of the absence of any best practice recognized at a supranational level. A full consideration of the passive regulatory approach would suggest to adopt the point of view of the intermediaries involved in minting and transacting cryptocurrencies, as they should entail Pillar 1 requirements (i.e. for the sake of internal capital adequacy), supplemented by Pillar 2 ones (related to external supervisory control). However, no Pillar 3 obligation has been enforced, however useful and adequate it might have been; nor has the EBA pushed itself to suggest a role for 'market discipline' in addressing certain issues which are very likely to continue being lightly regulated.

Unfortunately, nowadays, regulations are expected to remain passive, and this market to be opaque. Conversely, since the first analysis of this phenomenon, the traceability has been considered as a driver for the development of this instrument. In particular, considering that anonymity properties of electronic cash pose several law enforcement problems (because they[67] prevent withdrawals and deposits from being linked to each other), and these problems prevent detection of cryptocurrencies. From a technical perspective, there are several options: (i) one way to minimize these concerns without tracking all the transaction is to require large transactions or large numbers of transactions in a given time period to be perceptible to human scrutiny; (ii) another way is to provide a mechanism to restore traceability under certain conditions, such as a court order.

Both of these options require a choice, provided that once the traceability is restorable, then market operators would be in the position to override anonymousity.[68] Provided that ability to restore traceability does not detect forged coins, it is not possible to exclude a distinctive use of cryptocurrencies (by naming any coin, user and transaction). Hence, this calls for an action of the policymakers, whose intervention to regulate payment schemes that currently provide user anonymity and payment untraceability in order to save their efficient mechanisms and to apply the latter within a regulated environment (Law, L. 1997).

7.8   EVIDENCES FROM THE ACCOUNTING CLASSIFICATION AND THE CAPITAL ADEQUACY REGULATION OF CRYPTO-ASSETS

What effects have laws on the cryptocurrencies can be verified by looking at their accounting classification. Yet this is no easy task, at all.

Under such perspective, there is the need to understand how the management of the firm considers such cryptocurrencies, provided that the current reports of any firm aim at showing the current state of the business and the envisaged path of the affairs. Hence, this is not questioning whether managers would invest more cautiously, check platforms more diligently and analyse algorithms more deeply because they were required to account for these assets (Manaa, M. et al. 2019).

As a preliminary remark, their accounting would lead to a new asset class or to a new object that can be considered within an existent asset class. However, it is important to point out that regardless of whether cryptocurrencies had been treated as cash, foreign exchange positions or commodities, they should be considered as prudentially deductible (albeit to different extents, because their non-sovereign nature).

The fact that the relevant boards started questioning which feature of the cryptized assets would drive in accounting confirms that such perspective helps in understanding how their users perceive them (Venter, H. 2016). And the reference to cash, cash equivalents, financial assets (other than cash), intangible assets or inventories teaches a lot about the functions that market participants recognize to them.[69]

In order to go ahead with this in-depth regulatory analysis of fintech, the synthesis on this topic would be directed towards the clarification of the building blocks of the current legal system aimed at regulating credit institutions, namely capital adequacy, risk mitigation and governance. In the light of this goal, it is useful to move from the ECB consideration that, under the aforesaid uncertainty surrounding the Pillar 1 treatment, Pillar 2 obligations acquire even greater relevance. Abiding by different rules set forth by the Basel Committee for Banking Supervision (BCBS) would not be easier, nor would it achieve larger consensus among standard setters. In fact, a risk management framework built around the execution of the Internal Capital Adequacy Assessment Process (ICAAP), exerted not upon cryptocurrencies themselves but rather upon the subjects that use them, would probably fail to gauge all the nuanced consequences for an entity in investing in this kind of money-like assets. Hence, the importance of considering both the trustworthiness of cryptocurrencies (i.e. the possibility of exchanging them into currency endowed with legal tender, in the future, or the possibility of using them to fulfil payment obligations) and the relevant counterparty risks (i.e. the possibility that the programmers, or the platform manager or any other third-party provider that has a fundamental role in the circulation of the relevant cryptocurrencies will not perform its undertakings).

Dealing with liquidity would bring no larger certainty, as crypto-assets are not included in the list of eligible instruments for the liquidity coverage ratio (LCR) liquidity buffer. It is worth considering that this is because the criteria to be met in order to allow the inclusion would entail, first, a low price volatility; and, in light of their features, transactions in crypto-assets are treated as derivatives for regulatory purposes related to liquidity, including the computation of the Net Stable Funding Ratio (NSFR).

Furthermore, crypto-assets are most likely to be subject to a 100% stable funding requirement, regardless of how they are treated as for the composition of capital. Several comments should be made about the monetary effect of a 'fair' ponderation, yet it can be considered as another assessment of their intrinsically low degree of liquidity and trustworthiness (as this rule is usually provided for assets that are difficult to be monetized by means of a sale, or—alternatively—to be used as collateral in secured borrowing transactions). The truth of such claim does not come as a surprise. Suppose that fair ponderation should be provided for both sovereign money and sovereign bonds, and that all the credit institutions prefer to dismiss national currencies when a certain type of difficulties arise. From a regulatory perspective, if such preference is marked, then regulating ponderation would influence the market trends.

According to the above, wherever independent weight be given to the role of algorithms under the supervisory set-up, then in some situations the utility of cryptography will be lowered as a result of advancing that measure of safeness which is required for protecting both individual rights and financial stability. Hence, provided that the investment-related nature of cryptized assets and currencies is highly valorized by the regulator (in the euro area), this part of the analysis should have regard to the risks that might arise.

That said, it is useful to bear in mind that other ECB concerns were raised with respect to the regulated market infrastructure, where the use of cryptocurrencies is severely restricted: for instance, the latter cannot be used by CSDs, as they do not qualify as transferable securities. Also, regulation of the segregation of businesses related to cryptography and fintech is invoked to prevent that, even if they are excluded from being part of the official market infrastructure, their failure might yield negative spillovers and, thus, generate turmoil at a systemic level.[70]

Most of the current regulations concerning the reporting of cryptocurrencies challenges the functioning of the payment systems. With respect to the ECB's analysis of 'TARGET2', it should be considered that this is one of the most EU-wide topics in the entire realm of financial markets.[71] However, the regulatory burden charged upon payment system providers dealing with cryptocurrencies remains very light: as acknowledged by the ECB itself, it bears noting though that any segregation requirements emanating from TARGET2 would only apply to its direct participants, whereas the clients of participants' banks would be out of scope. As a matter of fact, since scholars and institutions have not yet reconciled monetary flows with the underlying transactions, the settlement of crypto-related payments within the TARGET2 system cannot be fully avoided.[72]

In other words, the EU regulatory system has been structured in a way that substantially fails to enforce the ECB's wishful thinking. To possibly close such regulatory loophole, the regulator should provide new rules or the supervisors would apply practical solutions, entailing the scenario wherein central counterparties (CCPs) may in the future undertake clearing of crypto-asset based products, provided that (i) they are authorized to do so and (ii) regulatory requirements can be satisfied.

Nowadays, it would be somewhat a (r)evolution.

In fact, products based upon digitalization and cryptography would have to be regarded as financial instruments per se, that is, pursuant to the EU legislation outstanding: mainly EMIR, such that they would become eligible for use by CCPs, as long as an amount of funds be mobilized to face the losses incurred in providing the service.[73]

Unfortunately, the EU regulator has already created other barriers that could anyway prevent cryptocurrencies from being used by CCPs as collateral in EMIR transactions. Despite the possibility that the use of cryptocurrencies under EMIR would mean that the former ones have started being regarded as a sort of non-cash securities, it is not convenient to look for the conclusion that their magnitude and characteristics are pulling them away from the scope of the definition of money. In fact, the Commission Delegated Regulation (EU) 2016/2251 has excluded crypto-assets from the list of eligible collateral for EMIR-compliant transactions. Such exclusion is plainly understandable with regard to their risk profile.[74] Hence, it would not be very easy to achieve—particularly from a political standpoint—the aforesaid inclusion, under the current set-up of non-sovereign cryptocurrencies. On the contrary, by acknowledging that technology has definitely changed the financial environment, it should be expected that spread of cryptocurrencies would be halted, and then that a comprehensive and effective discipline would be required for the proper functioning of the internal market. However, it might result in an increase in systemic turmoil, potentially yielding negative spillovers onto the real economy, a fortiori with respect to an issue—namely, derivatives and their clearing—which is among the most pivotal ones from a regulatory standpoint.

Concluding on this topic, it is necessary to highlight the aforesaid evidences from the accounting classification and the capital adequacy regulation. They give rise to the need for considering the risks associated with cryptocurrencies, and the possibility that the effects of such risks will exceed the importance of individuals' utilities in having a sort of 'smart-money' instead of legal tender (whether the utility differences between these two are small enough).

7.9   The Perspective of Controlling the Exchangers' Role

Suppose that the exploitation of cryptocurrencies grow and the ECB misperceive the level of due care that market participants apply in dealing with cryptocurrencies, and—because of underestimating it—this phenomenon starts being highly concerned with the current situation, in which the advance of cryptocurrencies is not matched by a tantamount regulatory effort.[75] Then, it is possible to assume that said authority would take the level of care that it believes to constitute the due care in respect of its goals (of price stability), unless this exceeds its mandate so much that it would seem to be convenient acting in a 'soft way', as shown before. However, whether ECB overestimates the effect of an alternative to legal tender, it would be expectable that this supervisor will take either more care or optimal care.[76]

That said, it seems possible that the ECB would consider the effects of the cryptocurrencies in respect of their alignment with its monetary policy, so that—at the time of quantitative easing—any 'object' with expansionary effects could be welcomed or rather tolerated. This possibility explains the reason why the proposal coming from Frankfurt is a very simple one: since crypto-assets are not financial instruments in the current sense provided for by the EU law, but they nonetheless play an increasingly significant role in financial markets where instruments are exchanged, supervision should be exerted on the intersection between the traditional, regulated realm and the cryptized, unregulated one (FSB 2020).[77]

This mainly refers to the supervision of the service providers that buy or sell cryptocurrencies in exchange for sovereign money, as well as the intermediaries that professionally invest 'other people's money' in them within the context of individual or collective portfolio management services. Moreover, such point has been identified with respect to 'gatekeeping services', including crypto-assets custody too (not merely trading/exchange services), and then it would regulate the risk of insider trading and market manipulation.[78]

In this respect, however, it should be considered that—consisting of custodian wallet providers, trading platforms and exchanges—gatekeepers participate in the networks where crypto-asset transactions are instructed and validated to hold, buy and sell crypto-assets on behalf of their clients (Bullmann, D. et al. 2018). Also, it is worth considering that the market structure is designed by 'decentralized' networks, run and intertwined by software rather than by any identifiable entity, so that there is not an entity to supervise other than the programmers setting up such networks and software. So, regulators may be uncertain about the level of care of the programmers, yet should not abstain from performing some unavoidable checks, referred to a set of very clear principles.[79]

Nevertheless, this would entail a relevant supervisory obtrusion onto services and activities that—being excluded from the scope of application of most of the major EU pieces of financial legislation—have hitherto been mostly carried out by a crowd of unregulated entities. Besides, it could prevent supervision from effectively unfolding. It should also be noted that the ECB itself acknowledges that there might be unintended consequences, such as the undermining of the monetary level-playing field supposed for the internal market, and even a remarkable shift of activities from centrally supervised intermediaries to decentralized gatekeeping, in an attempt to flee a stronger supervision to experience a weaker one.[80]

With respect to the above, the interpretation of the point under discussion in this type of situation is that if the ECB's underestimation of future monetary effects is correct, policymakers will have appropriate motives for protecting individual rights only (and then continuing allowing such

activities of cryptocurrencies' exchange having regard to its bilateral profiles and the need to protect the weak party of the affair). There would be
no need for regulators to determine what market's losses turn out being.

On the contrary, it is worth recalling the concerns shown by those
European Supervisory Authorities that have devoted their attention to
cryptzing: namely, the European Banking Authority and the European
Securities Markets Authority.[81] Both of them are pushing for an EU-wide
review of supervisory actions to be accomplished soon. Hence, the need
for considering that currently crypto-assets and the business of them are
now circulating as tech-fuelled and unregulated. Such characteristics avoid
any sort of 'regularization', any limitation of an improper discipline of
gatekeeping circumscribed to supervise exchanges. Therefore, once again,
it might be socially desirable to encompass programmers and coders within
the scope of ECB supervision, as an alternative approach would make
monetary responsibilities entail the duty to approximate the effects of
cryptocurrencies, and adjust monetary policies accordingly.

Obviously, the extension of the scope of the supervision is also supported by the evidences arising from the approach published by the
Federal Reserve. In recalling the exemplification made by clever scholars,
this part of the analysis would reach the position for asserting that it is
probably the most open and direct one with respect to how supranational
institutions are dealing with the issue of cryptocurrencies. The Fed does
not provide any narrow definition of money and, thus, explicitly defines
cryptocurrencies as money (Lo, S. and Wang, J. 2014).

In addition to the above, it is worth remarking that the Fed shows
strong awareness of the potential regulatory arbitrage which might arise if
a proper cross-country coordination of regulatory practices were not soon
put in place. It is not possible to deny that the Fed has been considered as
a supervisor highly concerned with volatility; hence, it is predictable that
such institution would consider also this feature in supervising cryptocurrencies. In fact, there exists the risk that the current level of volatility
would offset any benefits associated with using cryptography (as highlighted by scholars who affirmed that the practice of expressing retail
prices by using the latter ones is still very rare, and extremely far from
becoming a standard for any market).[82] Hence the risk that individuals
would perceive such currencies useful and valuable as traditional ones:
neither is their volatility any serious counterindication against using them
as a means of payment, nor are the costs associated with operating the
underlying infrastructure deemed to be unbearable. In this sense, the

regulatory debate would focus on the way to avoid such misperception and to satisfy the need of protecting the individual that buys such cryptocurrencies from miners, as well as on the opportunity to strengthen their everyday use, provided that the statement concerning that non-sovereign cryptocurrencies simply closely mirror electronic money is far from building any consensus, especially at the highest decision-making level.[83]

Under this point of view, limitations should not be found in the inner digital and private nature of cryptocurrencies—for there is no practical difference in the function they perform vis-à-vis traditional currencies—but rather in the functioning of the area they populate.

All the above does not question whether such area is a portion of the regulated markets, alternative trading venues or a new unregulated system instead. However, on average, it shows more frictions and higher costs compared to that based upon monies endowed with legal tender. Some legal commentators favour the reliance over the emphasis—put by the World Bank—on the rise of cryptocurrencies as part of the fintech revolution, whose main driver should be identified with the users progressively losing confidence towards the traditional financial players. In this sense, the issues connected with that phenomenon are political at their core, much more than economic, for innovation—regardless of the field to which it applies—should always be addressed from a systemic perspective.

In particular, it is possible to conclude on this point by deeming cryptocurrencies and blockchain technologies to deserve regulatory scrutiny with regard to three major aspects: (a) financial oversight, in a broader sense relating to consumer protection and tax collection too; (b) power supply, in order to support activities requiring large amounts of electricity and, thus, a proper physical infrastructure; (c) the delivery of services to the public, as long as the technological progress has not yet made administrative bodies more efficient.[84]

7.10 The Need for Regulatory Requirements

Still on the 'moneyness', in order to stress the need for regulatory requirements that guide the supervision towards certain subjects performing certain functions, it is possible to understand whether, or how much, algorithms and cryptography influence the level of reliance over cryptocurrencies. Such influence would be optimal if it maximized the expected joint value of the miners, intermediaries and final users involved in the circulation of non-sovereign cryptocurrencies and provided the full respect of individual rights.[85]

This is not questioning the difficulties in applying the Quantity Equation of Money, especially because of the hard feasibility of estimating its components.[86] In fact, the latter is subject to a tremendous degree of uncertainty (Lo, S. and Wang, J. 2014). This would refer, instead, to the issue related to the velocity of circulation: in fact, it remains particularly difficult to assess, for large amounts of cryptocurrencies, how often they are stored up.[87] Unfortunately, this is not the sole concern: previous research—among which the World Bank credits Ofek & Richardson[88]— had clearly shown the possibility that assets be seriously overvalued when two characteristics are shown at the same time: the agents hold widely heterogeneous views, on the one hand; and short-selling is legally restricted, on the other. This results in the market price reflecting mainly the opinion of optimists and, thus, being too inflated compared to the 'fundamental value' of the asset. Moreover, pricing remains difficult due to the narrowness of futures and derivatives markets whereby instruments written upon cryptocurrencies are exchanged: they are actually growing, of course, yet still remain distant from any minimum desirable size.

The aforesaid concerns extend, also, to any virtual aspect of the realm of cryptocurrencies. Inter alia, the statement that transactions are basically free is harshly questioned (Lo, S. and Wang, J. 2014). This claim—according to the World Bank[89]—considers only the explicit out-of-pocket expense faced by users (as required by the protocol, substantially ignoring the 'implicit' costs which are related to the functioning of the underlying platform, and especially with regard to the process of minting), which rewards the first 'miner' who solves the 'hash' function (i.e. the one required to validate the transaction).

According to the above, it is possible to conclude that this is tantamount of 'classical' money creation, and, since it is endowed with the same potential of devaluing existing currency by means of inflation, it may be viewed as a form of negative externality. Moreover, as long as there is the power of impairing the value of money, further asymmetries and abuses would be possible. Furthermore, in this context, fees have hitherto been particularly high if the analysis computes their incidence over a transaction, as this seems to be the result of them being de facto fixed by software (or big data analytics[90]). This incidence is expected to rise in the future, as long as the minting of new assets of one kind can be limited by design through the use of cryptography.

This does not allow to deny the positive aspects of private minting, as well as those due to the use of cryptography and distributed ledger technologies. Hence, it should be acknowledged that data seems to suggest that the everyday use of cryptocurrencies for commercial transactions has actually grown much more than the use of that same asset for investment speculative purposes. And such use can be more efficient than electronic money or payment systems.[91]

Henceforth, it would be possible to conclude this section by highlighting that an expenditure on reliance over cryptized assets and currencies is optimal only if its expected benefit exceeds the costs of controls. Whilst market participants are concluding contracts, the role of private law should refer to the possibility of stipulating mutually optimal and completely specified agreements, such that the role of public regulation would concern the maximization of social welfare in a context of financial stability and economic growth. Considering now the possibility to assume that contracts are incomplete and supervisors limited, the arising question discusses the remedies for increasing the level of care and the effectiveness of reliance.

It is worth considering that, whether the public should contain the tendency towards low care and excessive reliance, market participants should not expect that the regulatory intervention will lead to obtain more in case of underperformance, because any solution to preserve the position reachable by performance is limited by the difficulties in ascribing the responsibilities to an entity. Hence, the need for identifying the hubs of the networks and the firms responsible for their existence, maintenance and functioning (with respect to both hardware and software profiles).

Several additional remarks about the need for regulatory requirements linked to cryptocurrencies refer to sophisticated damage measures, provided that policymakers, regulators and supervisors do not confirm to have access to enough information to determine the optimal intervention. Provided that the monitoring of fintech and its application (also, to money) has been run, this cannot cast the doubt that the analysts are observing the final part of the chain only, and not chainers that intertwined the networks, managed the platforms and codified the algorithms supporting all of this.

SECTION III: MINING, TRADING AND
EXCHANGING CRYPTOCURRENCIES

7.11   MINING, MINTING OR
ISSUING CRYPTOCURRENCIES?

In this chapter, the possibility of regulating and supervising the entities producing cryptocurrencies (and providing related services) has not been deeply investigated yet. As anticipated, however, certain kinds of business and activities should be regulated and reserved respectively. Hence, it is useful assuming that supervision will take place costly, unless otherwise mentioned that the comprehensive economic effect would be positive if its costs are lower than the burden of the market failures.

The following has been hardly questioned; nevertheless, it should be considered that mining is a multifaceted activity, for it relates to something which has been separately produced and, thus, potentially entails a production process that would be reignited from the beginning. There are evidences that capital, energy and labour are exploited to supply cryptocurrencies. Relying on such evidences, it is possible to anticipate that the process ending up with minting cryptocurrencies may be regarded as a proper production that transforms inputs into outputs by means of a chain that anyway occurs within an entity, or involving several market participants (i.e. by means of a chain). Hence, it is worth considering that the scope of such process is not circumscribed to mere coinage, issuing or offering, but extends to the validation of such cryptized output instead (i.e. mining).[92]

Starting by summarizing the nature of market participants, it is clear that any cryptocurrency user can enter a direct or indirect agreement with miners (who participates in validating transactions on the blockchain by solving a cryptographic puzzle), exchanges (which offer exchange services usually against payment of a certain fee), trading platforms (as market places bringing together different users that are looking to either buy or sell coins, providing them with a network on which they can directly trade with each other), wallet providers (that provide tools used for holding, storing and transferring coins), programmers (acting as coin inventors who have developed the technical foundations of a cryptocurrency and set the initial rules for its use) and coin offerors (who offer coins upon the coin's initial release, either against payment or at no charge) (Houben, R. and Snyers, A. 2018).

Henceforth, it is likely that the regulator will consider that multiple players create a new 'block' of data, which can contain all sort of information and supports different kinds of operations, as well as that any new block is then encrypted and broadcast to every party in the network. Thus the need for investigating the possibility for promoting common standards for private parties involved in such transaction (and for a minimum content of a cryptocurrency to be compatible with the economic order), as well as exploiting such fintech innovations with respect to legal tender.

It is clear that the public supervision over capital markets cannot tolerate the anonymity that currently qualifies certain participants, as well as it has to deal with an environment that does not refer to a single entity (i.e. an intermediary) to be responsible for specific tasks (the identification, the collateralization, etc.). At the same time, public intervention should extend its scope to cybersecurity, data protection and privacy[93]; so, this would require new regulatory standards (based on the functioning of the blockchain itself).

Hence, what is worth investigating refers to the regulation of platforms, the way of preserving cryptocurrencies value and, in brief, the possibility that such innovation will support increase in the efficiency of the financial stability without jeopardizing its stability, and then support the economic growth. With regard to this, it is likely that the technology of blockchain and distributed ledger (exploited by miners, traders, exchangers and programmers) is something more than an overly complex and expensive method of sending information, whose sole actual benefit lies in operating outside the scope of the supervision and the intervention of monetary backstops (Haney, B. S. 2019).

7.12 The Regulation of Platforms and Trading Venues

The nature of the platforms where cryptocurrencies are traded is another relevant issue, as they combine the characteristics of regulated, traditional venues operating by means of an automatic matching of orders such as the Electronic Communication Networks (ECNs), on the one hand, with customized services provided by brokers and dealers, on the other.[94] Obviously, in the former case, the human decision-making process stands with the programmers, whereas in the latter it is in the management of the aforesaid providers. All of this belongs to a network of affairs, interests and agreements that are intertwined by both human decision and algorithms, and requires an intervention of the policymakers to drive the public oversight.[95]

Under such environment, counterparties are required to hold accounts denominated in cryptocurrencies and, thus, confirmation procedures are substantially speeded up compared to the deposit of sovereign ones by means of electronic money or payment services.[96] Given the assumption that the access to a platform will take place whenever the mutually desirable outcome (expected by the manager and the relevant user) would occur, it is essentially a tautology that a network is always online. Hence, it is worth starting from the World Bank consideration on the presence of drawbacks too: in fact, should an exchange fall short in matching users' orders (and, thus, safeguarding their accounts), the latter ones can experience severe losses. In this respect, it is useful to consider also that the presence of intermediaries—and, of course, the intermediation activity itself—is as important in the networks of non-sovereign currencies as it is in the standard banking system, even with respect to the monetary implications of such activity.

Given the current situation, this calls policymakers to refine the supervision that they exert, for loopholes may still be found and, thus, counterparties of digital transactions are still too exposed to potential losses, due both to the lack of controls over the firms and to the absence of common standards in the negotiation (Lothian, T. 2011). It is clear, in fact, that the safety of individual exchange users is essential to the future spread of such cryptized technologies, products and activities.

In this respect, it is worth considering the verification of digital transactions in cryptocurrencies as another issue worth of a tighter regulatory oversight compared to the one currently exerted. Indeed, at present day, said activity keeps being performed within traditional market infrastructure, where clearing houses play a fundamental role. Given the characteristics of these transactions, this is practically a purely bookkeeping task, which is a form of information processing. Moreover, policymakers should consider whether there exist relevant economies of scale, such that this activity may be delegated to a small number of intermediaries, so that the most efficient decision to be taken would be the introduction of size limits (as experienced for the Italian case of one kind of mutual/cooperative banks named 'popolari'[97]). Moreover, there is the need to consider also that, in the past, this finding seemed not to depend upon the type of securities exchanged but, rather, constitute a characteristic inherent to such task (Diamond, D.W. 1984).

Specific evidences suggest that there are still too many individual miners, informally delegated by market participants of verifying transactions; nonetheless, consolidation is progressing. According to the Federal Reserve, mining will become more concentrated in the future as individual miners gradually exit or join a coalition (Lo, S. and Wang, J. 2014). The dark side of this likely process is that certain anti-competitive behaviours might ultimately emerge, giving rise to collusive practices. Unfortunately, the mining industry seems to suffer from high fragmentation, such market structure being clearly detrimental to the business that they conduct. Hence, in terms of 'social efficiency', the regulator has also called to intervene because this current state of mining is a suboptimal one.

Of course, this calls for stronger regulatory actions, extended to antitrust safeguards.[98] It is reasonable to argue that, should one of the GAFA—namely, Google, Apple, Facebook and Amazon—or Microsoft ever effectively enter the cryptocurrency field, they would exploit any one of their competitive advantages, due to their remarkable involvement with big data, and even rely upon the information collected by observing the reaction of monetary authorities to private cryptocurrencies.

That said, it is necessary to regard the need for regulation with respect to the infrastructure's safety. As a matter of fact, given that cryptocurrencies are still at a very early stage, safeness is one of the major drivers of investment for business purpose: safer (perceived) exchanges will generally attract a higher number of transactions.

Such 'freedom' of moving trades from a platform to another has not always been guaranteed in the recent history of financial markets: in the European Community, for instance, legislation pre-existing to MiFID I had enacted the so-called concentration rule, entailing that the owners of a security admitted to the regulated market was banned from trading it across multiple exchanges or alternative trading venues. [99]

Since this principle was repealed by the EU regulator, it witnessed a clear surge in the degree of competition among European platforms: this has benefitted their competitiveness too. However, it should be stressed that EU regulator did not deregulate it but rather enacted a new principle, based on the authorization and supervision of trading venues, being them (strictly)-regulated markets, non-(strictly)-regulated markets, multilateral or organized trading facilities.[100]

Considering that the access to trading occurs when it is mutually desirable (and the cost is less than the gain), if such principle applies to cryptocurrencies, it follows even greater benefits from having the possibility to choose where a security or an asset will be traded, as long as the decision is mainly (but not exclusively) economic. Transaction fees play one of the most relevant roles, but in certain asset classes—particularly those encompassing the opaquest securities—the material configuration of the exchange is highly valorized as well. As noted by the World Bank, this overlaps with the issue of what specific kind of crypto-asset a hypothetical investor might be interested in.[101]

Specifically, it can be shown that, given any of the above principles, a change in the public approach to platforms and trading venues will rely on the Organization for Economic Cooperation and Development (OECD)'s investigation on cryptocurrencies in connection with the System of National Accounts (SNA), the core question being whether these platforms are trading an asset or not.

In order for such question to be answered, it should be considered that, whenever an exchange results in a simple update of a ledger where the platforms store a mere information, the intangibility prevails over the digital nature of cryptocurrencies and the exchange occurs because of a bilateral agreement concluded by the buyer and the seller (even if based on a form provided by the platform itself).

Being the possibility that cryptocurrencies should be owned by some unit and the owner should be able to derive economic benefits by holding them over a period of time,[102] it is useful to focus on the regulatory requirements that should be provided for managing platforms with respect to the evidences that property over cryptocurrencies may be easily defined (for anyone possessing the private keys associated with a given cryptocurrency account have the ability to use them as much as they would use cash). And, in this respect, blockchain technology provides the tools required for a clear definition and an easy proof of property rights.

However, the legal and practical clarity about ownership, albeit necessary, is not sufficient at all.

In regulating the trading venues supported by such platforms, it should be provided if there should be a guarantor for the minimum float, as well as for the right to redeem the investment in traded crypto-assets. As the latter ones should be eligible for carrying forward value between accounting periods, it should be avoided any market failure due to moral hazard of miners, traders or exchangers. This does not suggest to conclude that the issuers' liability will be the optimal solution, yet it is expectable that the regulation of the platforms as trading venues would not reduce the risk if it laid down on the duty of transparency, best execution or extract settlements only.

This dates back to the origins of modern finance and, more directly, to the function attributed to interest rates as long as they were used to devise securities: in practice, as well as for cash, the question is whether cryptocurrencies may be used to transfer value onwards in time, by allowing the holder to renounce consumption today to gain fruits from retaining such asset and, thus, getting higher consumption in the future. Of course, this inherently requires that the marked-to-market price of an asset be stable over time, exactly with the same mechanism by which inflation threatens not only the store-of-value function of money, but the role of interest rates in allocating capital and achieving the equilibrium in the market for funds too.

Perhaps surprisingly, the OECD assesses that from the above, it is clear that cryptocurrencies meet the asset boundary, yet a problem remains unsolved: What kind of asset do they exactly represent, that is, whether of financial or non-financial nature? In order for an asset to be generally regarded as financial, the SNA highlighted the need for a corresponding claim on another institutional unit to exist, as well as it being structured in a manner that entitles the holder to receive an agreed sum at an agreed date.[103] And this confirms that, although platforms achieve performance when that is mutually desirable regardless of the level of transparency and the quality of the services, remedies for breach of information duties, best execution rights and settlement requirements exert a relevant influence on reliance and also on the allocation of risks. That is preferable from a regulatory standpoint.

7.13   Cryptocurrencies' Corresponding Liability

As anticipated, the existence of a corresponding liability is not inherent to cryptocurrencies in general; conversely, it may be observed just in case of assets issued or authorized by central banks or a government, backed by sovereignty as for traditional legal tender.[104] As discussed before, this is something that might probably be envisaged for sovereign cryptocurrencies, but has not been hitherto experienced by private ones to any sizeable worldwide extent.

Moving from the consideration that actually cryptocurrencies are not backed, it should be noted that the inherent definition of cryptocurrencies should exclude them from the scope of the SNA definition of financial assets, as long as there is no contractual obligation for an economic agent to provide a payment or series of payments upon the redemption of a given coin unit.[105]

One might consider that there are several occasions in which currencies are backed by 'physical' assets (regardless of their modern dematerialization), such as in the repurchase agreements ('repo') or other open-market operations conducted by central banks for the purpose of creating monetary base (e.g. by 'quantitative easing' programmes). Such occasions are becoming increasingly common, yet they do not constitute the sole means by which central banks fulfil their monetary tasks.[106]

Therefore, it seems easy to understand the reason why the OECD comments in favour of cryptocurrencies being regarded as currency under the SNA framework, as the restrictions existing to their use and circulation are not enough to overcome their inner nature, and within its mandate the trading by means of fintech innovations (namely, cryptography and distributed ledger technologies) seems to be costless and operates successfully, even if the remedies for market failures remain relevant. Anyway, if all the above-mentioned reasons were deemed not to suffice in order for cryptocurrencies to be regarded as 'produced assets' with substantial liabilities, a different classification would entail that they should be regarded as the result of other changes in assets accounts.

In fact, it should be questioned whether the unmatching of the official definitions prevents cryptocurrencies from neither being endowed with 'moneyness' nor being excluded from the scope of financial instruments, or rather it should suggest to update the aforesaid definitions. Apart from more technical and detailed considerations, it is hardly questionable that—for the state being—private currencies are far safer and more commonly accepted than sovereign ones (which, however provided with legal tender they may be, actually show huge weaknesses and cannot be reliably used neither in financial markets nor for everyday commercial transactions[107]).

In order to go deep into the analysis of the fintech trading venues, it might also be questioned whether cryptocurrencies are able to circulate as equity or equity-like instruments. According to the OECD, one might possibly consider a cryptocurrency as a form of a collectively owned entity in which coin holdings represent a stake in its value. It is also possible to remark that, once acquired private currencies, the owners of the cryptocurrencies are exposed at a full risk vis-à-vis the miners (and, to a certain extent, to traders and exchangers as well). However, this would entail attributing to those owners a specific claim upon the residual value of that 'entity', which is clearly not the usually provided in the agreements set forth by the issuers, which are mainly oriented towards the full segregation of their responsibilities. Indeed, this characteristic is a good indicator of the level of trust which cryptocurrencies are endowed of, thus legitimizing their treatment as a means of payment (usable as currency too).

In brief, a very 'practical' approach to the issue of the 'moneyness' of cryptocurrencies would lead to consider their corresponding liabilities, which in turn results in a very open attitude towards recognizing them as akin to traditional currencies. However, it is worth regulating the organizational and operational standards related to such entities and activities, considering the possibility that the policymaker would establish whether these objects are 'produced' or rather 'non-produced', in a juridical sense. Thus, even if their issuing is costless and operates successfully with respect to the goal of increasing the liquidity of capital markets, as well as of speeding up the circulation of wealth.

As mentioned above, there are evidences that capital, energy and labour are exploited to supply cryptocurrencies. Therefore, whether the process ending up with minting cryptocurrencies may be regarded as a proper 'production' one, transforming inputs into outputs by means of a process that anyway occurs by the direct use or the support of material tools, inside one entity or rather through a market-based chain.

Hence, it is necessary to recall that the scope of such process is not circumscribed to mere coinage, issuing or offering, but rather extends to the validation of such cryptized output (i.e. the mining). Yet, if mining were ultimately regarded as production, it should be required to explain what kind of output it yields and the level of public intervention it requires in order to avoid any market failures.

On the one hand, it should be observed that as long as mining might be regarded as a potential financial service, its analysis could be influenced by traditional knowledge and, thus, by questioning whether the application of current levels of transparency and correctness to cryptized environment is enough to avoid the aforesaid failures. On the other, it is not possible to deny that the provision of financial and payment services is coessential to mining and these services cannot be disjointed from it.

Hence, it could not be treated in the same way as the above-mentioned services, which had faced no problem in being unbundled from the mere functioning of an exchange: in fact, the latter ones can be easily regarded as a different component of the 'value chain' of financial transactions. On the basis of the monitoring of cryptocurrencies made by the international authorities, it is not possible to rely on any evidence that can apply to mining (which is often assimilated to the activity of unearthing gold, silver or any other precious metal which was used to produce and back currencies yesteryear). However, without validating transactions, cryptocurrencies would not properly exist, and in this respect both blockchain and distributed ledger technology are valuable innovations due to fintech (that would apply also to legal tender, as elsewhere it has been proposed).[108]

Concluding on this point, it should be considered that cryptocurrencies may not have any corresponding liability or backing, even if they can enjoy certain existing activities: from warehousing to securitization, from collateralization to derivatization (ESMA 2020). In trying to evaluate the output of mining with respect to the liabilities used in the market for transforming certain compounds into cryptocurrencies (the mining's derivative), it is worth assuming a 'sum of cost' approach. Hence, it should be taken into account all the liabilities—in terms of the opportunity cost of running servers—and the raw material that have been needed for mining (from both a financial and an economic perspective).

In other words, all the above suggests to consider a completely different method in regulating and supervising both cryptocurrencies and their related entities (i.e. miners, traders, exchangers and programmers): rather than banning mining or confining it within an unregulated area, they should promote the application of fintech innovations to the traditional reserved activities (or rather impose on supervised entities the obligation to apply tech-fuelled mechanisms within their organizational structure). Obviously, this would require the analysis of the relevant 'sunk' costs—that are fixed, implicitly incurred and unrecoverable—focusing on its 'variable' nature too. The outcome of applying the two methods would be substantially different, leaving apart the issue of how to manage the costs associated with unsuccessful applications, which might be quite relevant and, thus, impossible to ignore without incurring in substantial mistakes.

7.14   THE IMF CONCERNS AND THE SWISS PERSPECTIVE

Relatively clear concerns arise from the perspective of establishing a comprehensive definition of cryptocurrencies and crypto-assets, and the possibility to regulate the use of cryptography to incorporate a right into a digital element. Indeed, it is worth highlighting that—from a juridical perspective—the use of tech-fuelled instruments (in lieu of the paper) does not affect the principles underlying the protection of individuals, the safeguard of competition and the preservation of the financial stability. Once again, it is worth considering the possibility that regulating fintech would not lead to establish new principles, but to apply the current ones by means of new rules and practices, able to manage the technical advancements made in the field of algorithms, software and hardware.

In this respect, it is useful to bear in mind that the International Monetary Fund (IMF) has categorized the current cryptocurrencies as a subset of private virtual currencies, defined as digital representations of value, issued by private developers and denominated in their own unit of account (IMF 2016).

However, as the concept of virtuality may cover a wider array of currencies, particular relevance should be attributed to the financial technologies (such as those supporting digitalization) that are 'shaking' the system of payments, and then continuing referring to cryptocurrencies only.[109] It should be highlighted that such concerns upraised shortly after the first rumours over big-tech's Libra had started circulating and the major global banks were trying to address the fintech realm by means of particularly aggressive strategies, including ones of integration with firms operating in that innovative industry.[110]

According to the previous analysis, the growing connections between supervised entities and firms involved in fintech business (or, more in general, in the non-bank financial intermediation) is per se a source of greater systemic risk, mainly because of the 'operational' component. All the above called the global institutions to become more attentive to 'tech-companies' trespassing the boundaries of their commercial activity to become involved in the banking, financial or insurance business.

In this sense, the IMF seemed not to depart from the classical way of shaping financial oversight: that is, on subjects and activities much more than objects (i.e. cryptocurrencies). Henceforth, it is not convenient to think through the limits of such an approach, but the analysis would rather focus on its boundaries: it seems unavoidable the regulation of the 'moneyness' of non-sovereign cryptocurrencies, instead of actually driving the exercise of supervision in measuring the risk related to the use of such currencies in financial transactions, and in the duty to fund a reserve for covering the relevant risks (in the balance sheets of the supervised entities).

Going to go deep into that this topic with respect to those countries where cryptocurrencies and the blockchain technology are spreading the most, the focus goes to Switzerland again, in order to show how policy-makers may embrace innovation to welcome the firms that wants to offer new products to the market or to modernize their business model. This implies that the national regulator has to face the issue without any ideo-logical prejudice on fintechers, still remaining aware of all the matter's opaqueness and, thus, the caution to be applied to protect individual rights and financial stability.

Focusing on cryptocurrencies only, in the Helvetic Confederation—as anticipated—the rise of the first banks specialized in cryptized assets and currencies, has been an evidence.[111] Hence, once again, whether this rise becomes material, the legislator has to regulate the entrepreneurial envi-ronment evolved around cryptocurrencies or, on the contrary, deregulate the monetary matters. There are no doubts that the latter alternative is not viable, according to the conclusion reached by the relevant scholars on the need for sovereignty to ensure an economic order based on the stability of prices.[112]

It is worth remarking that provisional banking and securities dealer licences support their business, and they are projected to become full-fledged banks.

From a law and economics perspective, it is necessary to consider the general structure of the relevant regulation, as the supervisory recognition could represent a global milestone.[113] From the juridical standpoint, Switzerland is updating its financial legislation to address the numerous and quick changes that are occurring in the realm of cryptocurrencies. However, the Swiss regulator expressly tends to doubt that these players be innocuous to systemic stability, as this conclusion would entail that the integration between the 'old' world and the 'new' one occurs without creating too much market turmoil. Hence, the need for considering the timing of the public intervention provided that it is the primary dimension of any means of controlling the conduct of business (Shavell, S. 2004).

In this respect, a vote has confirmed that Switzerland would not defend itself by coming back to outdated positions (namely the 'Vollgeld-initiative' in 2018). Hence, as market structure is changing well along with business models, the Helvetic Confederation environment seems to be safe and efficient, and then able to start reasoning on the regulation of cryptogra-phy and distributed ledger technologies. In this respect, the path will require the understanding of the use of the latter, and then the verification that is a new form of securitization (that incorporates rights into a 'string' an 'array data structure of bytes'). Thus, the need for considering the role of private in performing such activities, and the choice to structure a public intervention able to set up a legal order able to host the relevant firms and, at the same time, serve the global community by supervising this industry.

What cannot be regarded with too much scepticism, actually, is the spread of distributed ledger technology, with numerous applications that actually ensure a higher degree of safety and speed. However, any improvement in the public intervention over cryptocurrencies should involve a portion of international law, as a detailed regulation would consider that supervisors have to commit multiple acts. In such a perspective, at the domestic level, the rules should be more detailed and, at the international level, a treaty should link the developed democracy in managing these new instruments (the latter being considered as currencies or assets).

Nevertheless, the path undertook by the relevant authorities is a very remarkable one yet. It is worth recalling that the first report on the issue dates back to 2014, in line with the first enquiries conducted by the Federal Reserve. At that time, however, the Swiss Federal Council took a strict position, as both moneyness and the possible categorization under the label of assets were denied.[114] Of course, relevant changes have occurred since the publication of that report: at present day, the most significant threats connected with the use of cryptocurrencies is due to their private nature (i.e. the lack of sovereign backing), but they have been supervised with respect to different areas of control: the unacceptable economic behaviours (i.e. money laundering, terrorism financing, performance of illicit activities, etc.) and the unstable financial practices (i.e. the anonymous issuing, the unregulated trading, the unsettled transactions, etc.).

All the above suggests that the aforesaid innovations would benefit of the outcome provided by the 'Blockchain/ICO working group' set up to study how to properly regulate the financial applications of said technology by the Swiss State Secretariat for International Financial Matter.[115]

Moreover, it should be noted again that the Switzerland pioneered the regulation of initial coin offerings (ICOs). This effort is helping in understanding the regulatory differences between payment tokens (i.e. cryptocurrencies stricto sensu), utility tokens (which allow to access an application or process by means of a blockchain infrastructure) and asset tokens (which are a debt or equity instrument, thus encompassing a claim against the issuer; hence, they are quite distant from the crypto-realm and much closer to the securities one).[116] Moreover, this is the background for increasing legal certainty, enabling innovation and safeguarding the integrity of the financial centre in this sector.[117]

According to these results, it is easy to accomplish that any country has to evaluate its legal framework with respect to the specific applications of cryptography and distributed ledger technology, due to the fact that such innovations substitute the traditional instruments used for the financial sector-specific applications, but do not affect the foundations of the social-democratic character of their form of government and political systems (and then the relevant regulatory principles). In addition, it is also possible to conclude that the closer a cryptized instrument is to a security, the more similar the treatment will be to that of 'common' financial assets, such as those regulated pursuant to the EU legislation applying across the whole EEA (e.g. MiFID II, EMIR and UCITS V) and, thus, tradable as either 'mass market product'—that is, potentially purchased by collective investment schemes—or potential object of customized services provided to clients on an individual basis.

7.15   PRESERVING CRYPTOCURRENCIES VALUE

Another dimension of the public intervention refers to the need of preserving the value of cryptocurrencies, whose feasibility is probably more complex than the storing or depositing of traditional monies. The form of storage may involve services for preventing their usage, whereas other concerns refer to the safety of platforms that provide the storage service, notwithstanding the reassuring properties of blockchain technology (which is specifically designed to prevent any fraud).

These issues are inherently connected with the absence of any intermediary providing payment services, whose intervention would clearly mean that the counterparties have been identified, and then they are known not only to the intermediary itself but to supervisors too. In turn, this would help contain the 'counterparty risk' in terms of the other side's solvency and viability and the 'legal' one (by avoiding performing anonymous transactions and, thus, being sued for that).

Nevertheless, storing cryptocurrencies entails some 'operational' concerns that cannot be restrained from presenting. These concerns date back to Nakamoto's (2008) White Paper: inter alia, regarding the attempt to avoid duplication in transaction data recording, something which would have significant consequences—unduly widening money supply and undermining individual rights over any piece of cryptocurrencies—in case electronic assets be spent twice.

Nakamoto himself thought of the solution as being based on an electronic payment system based on cryptographic proof instead of trust: that is, the blockchain technology programmed in order to comply with such basic principle (of single storage and single expenditure of each coin). Obviously, this means that the possibility to share the content of a coin does not allow users to copy or use it twice (which is a basic feature of banknotes). In this respect, whether it would concern on the initiation of legal intervention, the decision of private parties to apply this principle by means of blockchain mechanisms of enforcement is a good starting point. It is worth recalling the foundations of economic analysis of law to confirm that the use of a legal system may be instigated when a private party ask for that to occur (Shavell, S. 2004).

However, as noted above, the common interpretation of blockchain requires a legal remark: private parties are free to rely upon a system that ensures a very good degree of safety from an 'operational' standpoint, yet such set-up cannot be regarded as if private parties were acting as a sort of central bank (and the governments were allowing money being created outside of both the use of sovereign powers and the scope of monetary supervision). At this stage of the evolution of cryptocurrencies, it would be useful to reduce the 'material' notion of trustworthiness to technically securing the functioning of those mechanisms used to mint and store cryptocurrency, leaving apart any other reasons for believing in their present or future value.[118]

From a legal standpoint, it is not possible to deny that this entire subject is deeply influenced by a sort of 'technological utopianism' (i.e. the misplaced conviction that progress will steadily advance with no interruption, even in an exponential manner).[119] However, the focus goes to the legal aspects of operational risk, which relate to the possibility of substantial reliance upon the use of cryptocurrencies as an alternative to the payment services and legal-tender electronic money (in fact, the financial realm has recently shown some examples of failures in which either human error in applying technological tools or the malfunctioning of ICT infrastructure leads to sudden drops in market indexes and, thus, imposes severe losses on investors).[120]

Anyway, it is necessary to consider that the blockchain infrastructure underlying cryptocurrency transactions differs from trading venues and central counterparties. In particular, it is useful to refer to the presence of clearing houses for risk mitigation and, to a lesser extent, of systematic internalizers and market makers for liquidity creation; furthermore, certain traditional asset classes are mandatorily subjected to clearing (e.g. pursuant to EU law, derivatives traded over the counter).[121] Of course, the rationale of cryptocurrency transactions is utterly different, as the relevant chains supporting their circulation were primarily structured for serving the execution of payments. This marks a substantial hiatus in the fintech environment, as long as the most recently developed, advanced technologies may be used for two diverging purposes: either to foster intermediation by making it quicker and more effective when leaving expenditure intact (or even increasing it, for an even better level of service), or to eradicate it and curb the related costs. Hence, the possibility that this factor would bear on the socially optimal tool for regulatory intervention.

As a general matter, the consequences of adopting blockchain are widely discussed from a regulatory model standpoint too. Considering the results of the latest economic analysis, it would be possible to argue that these developments will be highly disruptive to every user, yet it should be noted that they will probably fail to spread wide and rapidly because of the relevance of entry barriers: therefore, achieving simplicity—that is, the full application of blockchain by credit institutions and financial firms—should be one of the major goals to be pursued in the near future (Shackelford, J. and Myers, S. 2017). In particular, this would be the most direct and reliable way throughout which decentralization may be accomplished, albeit the latter's very functioning is currently threatened by a phenomenon of recentralization of economic power and authority from the Federal Government to technologically elite companies with massive amounts of computing power (Haney, B. S. 2019). In this respect, it appears that the worst scenario envisages that knowledge possessed by the supervisors about the dangerousness of the platforms be limited; hence, there would be no possibility to verify and measure the safeness of their storages, trading and fulfilments.

Other authors have pointed out that, as for the relationship between people and cryptocurrencies, the latter ones have been largely unsuccessful in gaining the public's confidence and, thus, being used worldwide for different kinds of everyday transactions. If people knew relatively little about the harmfulness of the use of alternatives to legal tender (and even less about the functioning of platforms and the resilience of their managers), then public intervention would be appealing.

Hence, from a regulatory perspective, it is expectable that new projects bring relevant novelties to the issue of decentralization and to the way of satisfying the need for preserving the value of cryptocurrencies. And the safer (*rectius*, designed to be perceived as such) these novelties, the more big-tech would enter the market.[122] It is possible to envisage that the set-up of the market would prompt private parties to reach an agreement for denying participants the possibility to mint new assets, regardless of the actual composition of such 'issuing base' (often made of financial institutions, which are the only subjects able to overcome the entry barriers). Conversely, the aforesaid structure suggests that market participants would exploit their bargaining power to structure a fully centralized framework, in which a market leader would develop algorithms and software aimed to connect a group of subjects and, by exploiting such network, validate transactions.

Therefore, rather than private parties benefitting from asymmetries in these kinds of networks, it is governments that perceive their monetary powers and prerogatives to be undermined. The proposed advent of high-standing miners and traders cannot but be met with open hostility from political institutions (and even supervised entities). Such conclusion is strengthened by the consideration that big techs are in the position not only to store their cryptocurrencies, but also to exchange them for online services (in order to preserve their value by linking it to the value of the services provided, as a sort of collateralization). This marks a substantial difference vis-à-vis bitcoin and other cryptocurrencies, which were not commonly backed by a store of value (i.e. the value of providing services). The effectiveness of such sort of collateralization depends on both the quality of the relevant contract and the likelihood that people be interested in demanding the aforesaid services.[123] Once again, private elements are used as a substitute for sovereign power to force any entity to accept the legal tender as a means for fulfilling the duties.

In light of the above, it is possible to remark the role of private law in supporting both the agreements related to cryptocurrency and the environment generate by the aforesaid platforms, whose ultimate goal is to provide services to a wide array of unbanked subjects, exploiting those network externalities that the so-called wired society has helped to spread. Many concerns have been raised over the economic feasibility of these new projects, regardless of whether, and such concerns only relate to costs (which can be higher than the profits) or rather extend to the sustainability of this alternative being endowed with legal tender. [124]

The phenomenon of addressing the needs (or rather the desires) of unbanked individuals and households cannot be ignored, for it yields relevant socioeconomic consequences even in Western countries, particularly the United States.[125] Hence, the need for applying new safeguards aimed at pursuing the traditional goal of protecting the weak parties. As well as social networks have actually drawn on psychological, interpersonal mechanisms (which had existed long prior to the creation of the Internet), public intervention should extend its scope to consider that alternative currencies—consisting of the most disparate materials—have always existed over different times in history. Hence, any initiative based on a new use of fintech applications is certainly not the first to exploit remarkable economies as of the knowledge necessary to establish the infrastructure and ensure it work.

Although deprived with those peer-to-peer mechanisms which are typical of current communities, and not relying upon that distributed ledger technology, it is possible that cryptocurrencies issued by a group of qualified entities (rather than an open community) be able to preserve their value as far as the regulatory framework allows that such coins are de facto backed by the assets—rectius, the possibility of positive financial results and cash flows in an unyielding going-concern perspective—of a very large, well-capitalized, liquid and profitable multinational enterprise. This implies both a significant advantage over any other kind of peer-to-peer cryptocurrencies and a specific need for legal requirements structured in terms of representations, undertakings and responsibilities of the parties, rather than the technical capabilities on which platforms are based in order to ensure the correctness of transactions.

7.16   Concluding Remarks

Over the previous paragraphs, the analysis has reviewed the issues arising from the use of cryptocurrencies from the regulatory aspect of their monetary effects (to which the whole scope of this chapter is mainly devoted). Nowadays, an extensive strand of research on this topic is focusing on the arguments in favour and against the need for regulating the 'moneyness' of cryptocurrencies. The debate is particularly harsh, as the substantial opaqueness of the cryptocurrency realm does not help economists in assessing whether cryptocurrencies may be intended as a store of value, or to what extent they are used as a means of payment or a unit of account.

In light of the above, this regulatory analysis leads to rely on the principles set forth for the shadow banking system, as this seems to be perceived as an alternative to legal tender. Hence, the investigation on the possibility of defining cryptocurrencies as financial instruments and, thus, subjecting them to the whole of the legislation on securities. Besides, in case they were classifiable as such, it should be assessed whether they are the object or the subject of financial services' agreements. Hence, the inner nature of these instruments is far from clear, and no consensus has been reached over the last years. In this context, different national regulators pursue different policies, which are going to structure said sector by mirroring the domestic financial system (and, with regard to the use of currencies, of payment services and consumption behaviours).

Far from attempting to say any final word on this, all the above just highlights that the clearest definition of what works as a currency—money is what money does—has allowed very awkward physical goods to serve as monies over the centuries and across the globe; hence, there should be no practical reason from a priori preventing an immaterial string of code, stored on computers not concentrated in a single place, whose proprietors are unknown but whose ownership rights are particularly protected thanks to the safety ensured by blockchain. As pointed out by economists, issuing cryptocurrencies requires capital and labour anyway, and this marks the need to gain profit from them (indeed, the fact that cryptocurrencies are largely immaterial, however controversial, should not suffice to deny certain burden of them).

Hence, in regulating such business in order to protect individual rights, the question of whether they are money, or an asset, or any tertium genus, should probably lay on the background.[126] Had this feature not been at the centre of the debate, probably a regulatory model would have already extended the safeguards introduced for protecting consumers and savers, and other existing oversight models would have been exploited in addressing such a disruptive novelty.

Up to now, policymakers have put too little effort in this field, proportionally to the small size of this phenomenon in comparison with the global dimension of sovereign legal tenders: in fact, they are polarized between either a full ban or a complete liberalization.

Addressing this issue cannot be postponed. In fact, various figures suggest that cryptizing is spreading worldwide: even in countries which, although having hitherto failed to record any significant activity in the financial industry, nonetheless are seemingly exploiting the new opportunities brought forth by technological progress. And this goes under the 'umbrella' purpose of financial inclusion.[127]). However, volatility is a matter of fact, yet there is no agreement on where the 'fair price' should be: in fact, the latter is that whereby an equilibrium between supply and demand may be obtained.

This, however, de facto fails to suggest that the absence of a legal framework will always prevent the cryptocurrencies' moneyness from reaching the same level as official currencies. Accepting this view would entail that the question will remain unsolved until governments—that is, central banks, regardless of how independent the monetary authority is from the political one—will have definitely stepped in the market, commencing the issuance of sovereign cryptocurrencies. However, the global trend does not point to that direction. Many economists, based on both anecdotal and empirical evidence, are particularly concerned with the potential drawbacks of this kind of interventions.

Nevertheless, supervisors should not give up exerting due control and regulation over the transactions that mix cryptized assets and currencies with financial instruments and money, for much is at stake in terms of systemic stability. Moreover, the phenomenon needs to be preserved due to its valuable economic purpose, yet it is not possible to avoid fearing the intensive use of cryptocurrencies for illicit activities of any kind, which has hitherto represented one of the aspects addressed with the greatest emphasis by regulators. So, cryptocurrencies should also be controlled for the uses and the users that they are intended to serve.

Also, it is useful to point out the conclusion that this topic refer to a system that were ultimately endowed with a proper, well-designed regulatory framework (based on the rules set forth by the programmers of the relevant algorithms and networks) and, thus, put on a sort of 'level playing field' where competition with supervised entities may unfold their business models (and that the latter are going to be reshaped because of the rise of newcomers. Conversely, for the moment being, supervision is mainly exerted upon the subjects involved in transactions de quo.

Unfortunately, as underlined above, scholars usually refer to infrastructure as being designed in a way which prevents the exact identification of counterparties; however, it seems preferable to consider that the current agreements (based on private law) do not set forth the identification of the parties, but the blockchain technology can do it (as any node within a blockchain network can propose the addition of new information to the blockchain) (Houben, R. and Snyers, A. 2018). Therefore, a mere public intervention would lead to the identification of any user and any transaction, in a way that is more effective than the control of banknotes.[128]

A solution, apparently, cannot be the 'conventional' one. Instead, it is worth concluding by requiring a supervision over the objects: that is, cryptocurrencies themselves. The know-how should be acknowledged: to which extent they circulate, how they interact with monetary aggregates (for transactions might be settled in traditional currencies, or entail the exchange of monetary assets), how and wherefore the encounter between counterparties occur, what underlies the flows, and so on. And this would be possible by means of big data and its analytics (as shown in previous chapters).[129]

It is acknowledged, in fact, that traditional prudential supervision—which envisages that overseen entities provide the controlling authority with the requested data—is based upon schemes and methodologies that would be neither appropriate nor sufficient to regulate this new, vast sector.[130]

Finally, it is worth coming back where this analysis started: namely, how cryptocurrencies should be treated within the international monetary system.[131] Actually, what should not be forlorn is the possibility to provide cryptocurrencies with a proper backing, even in absence of systems designed around the mandatory convertibility of fiat currencies into commodities (e.g. gold), the power of sovereignty and national economies, or the bargaining power of certain firms (as the forthcoming initiatives suggest).[132] This suggests that the value of private cryptocurrencies, while remaining free from governments' control, would be measured pursuant to clear exchange rate rules.

However, thanks to higher confidence, the issue will be inherently political: promoting private currencies requires that central banks should give up a little part of their sovereignty because of the computation of such aggregate for the sake of greater stability within the international monetary system (and then regulate their supply accordingly).[133]

As far as the boundaries of the alternative to legal tender are not defined, the need for a regulatory intervention is remarkable. As expected, the above-mentioned researches have not tested the actual resilience of the financial system against fintech solutions being applied to money, the latter being regarded as the major expression of sovereignty. This consideration has not expressly mentioned the possibility that all the above does not stand within the shadow banking system, but it is going to breach one of the several reserves provided by the current regulatory framework (as well as there is not the conclusion that using cryptocurrencies is not only sharing files from one party to another, nor just writing the exchange down in a ledger).

Conversely, it has been shown that the current functioning leads to an undistributed system of organized information shared among an indefinite number of market participants requiring both prevention schemes and sanctions, on the one hand, and the need for supervising these platforms along with the provision of services thereof, on the other. Anyway, this should take into account the risks lingering upon individual rights, financial stability, social utility and common welfare.

NOTES

1. It is worth considering that the current debate on any solution to provide an alternative to the sovereign currencies in executing the payments implies a direct consequence on the sovereign power of the governments, as the monetary policies are one of the most important outcomes of the politicians aimed at influencing the trends of the economy. Focusing on the current topic, we have to refer to ECB 2019. "Crypto-assets—trends and implications", Bruxelles where is stated that "ECB actually first started to explore trends in crypto-assets back in 2011 and published its first report on virtual currency schemes in 2012, followed by a second one in 2015. In the light of the recent increase in market interest, the ECB set up an internal task force to develop a common understanding of crypto-assets and assess their potential impact on some of its core areas of responsibility: monetary policy, financial stability, payments and market infrastructures".

   It is worth also considering Houben, R. and Snyers, A. 2018. "Cryptocurrencies and blockchain. Legal context and implications for financial crime, money laundering and tax evasion", European Parliament—Policy Department for Economic, Scientific and Quality of Life Policies—Directorate-General for Internal Policies, p. 11.

2. In addition, see Law, L. and Sabet, S. and Solinas, J. 1997. "How to make a mint. The cryptography of anonymous electronic cash" *American University Law Review*, p. 1131 ff., which pointed out, among the most important uses of the technologies, electronic commerce, qualified as "performing financial transactions via electronic information exchanged over telecommunications lines". They move from such evidence to highlight that "a key requirement for electronic commerce is the development of secure and efficient electronic payment systems". In particular this essay focused on electronic cash: "as the name implies, electronic cash is

an attempt to construct an electronic payment system modelled after our paper money system. Paper money has such features as: portability (easily carried); recognizability (as legal tender), and thus readily acceptable; transferability (without involvement of the financial network); untraceability (no record of where money is spent); anonymity (no record of who spent the money); and the ability to make 'change.' The designers of electronic cash focused on preserving the features of untraceability and anonymity. Thus, electronic cash is defined to be an electronic payment system that provides, in addition to the above security features, the properties of user anonymity and payment untraceability".

It is worth recalling also Dam, K. W. and Lin, H. S. 1996. "Cryptography's Role In Securing The Information Society" Danvers. p. 49; Chaum, D. 1985. "Security Without Identification: Transactions to Make Big Brother Obsolete" *Computing Machinery*, p. 1030 ff.; Chaum, D. and Pedersen, T.D. 1992b. "Wallet Databases With Observers" *Advances In Cryptology--Crypto '92, Lecture Notes In Computer* p. 93 ff.; Chaum, D. et al. 1988. "Untraceable Electronic Cash" *Advances in Cryptology-crypto '88, lecture notes in computer science,* p. 319 ff.; these articles provide the background for the current regulatory analysis (that follows the success of the main applications, and the passive regulatory behaviour of the policymakers in the last years).

More in general, see Lothian, T. 2010. "Law and Finance: A Theoretical Perspective" *Columbia Law and Economics Working Paper No. 388*; Capriglione, F. 1975. "I surrogati della moneta nella vigente normativa del T.U. n. 204 del 1910 sugli Istituti di emissione", *Banca borsa titoli di credito*, p. 365 ff.

3. It refers also to Sabett, R. V. 1996. "International Harmonization In Electronic Commerce And Electronic Data Interchange: A Proposed First Step Toward Signing On The Digital Dotted" *American University Law Review*, p. 512 ss.; the author questioned that "The law's ability to respond to changes in technology, most notably the Internet, remains in doubt."

It seems hard to justify more than 20 years of delay, but it is sufficient to recall the choice to regulate the effects of tech-fuelled innovations according to the principle of proportionality. Indeed, the policymakers have chosen to regulate the material effects of these innovations, and not to drive the path of technical evolutions. According to the above, the delay refers to a political choice, which seems to be inadequate to ensure a level-playing field that is not jeopardized by the perspective of an unregulated alternative to the activities reserved to supervised firms.

4. In this respect, see both Brands, S. 1993. "Untraceable Off-line Cash in Wallets with Observers", *Advances In Cryptology-Crypto '93, Lecture*

Notes In Computer Science. p. 302 and Okamoto, T. and Ohta, K. 1991. "Universal Electronic Cash" *Advances in Cryptology-Crypto '91, Lecture Notes in Computer Science p. 324.*

5. In particular, see Fullenkamp, C. and Nsouli, S. M., 2004. "Six Puzzles in Electronic Money and Banking" *IMF Working Paper,* the authors identified the main issues raised by e-money and e-banking and built a framework for analysing the effects of e-money and e-banking, and for choosing the appropriate approach to regulating electronic money and banking.

On this topic, see also Rogers, J. S., 2005. "The New Old Law of Electronic Money" *SMU Law Review,* p. 1253 ff.; Georgescu, M. and Georgescu, I. E. 2004 "The Emergence of Electronic Payment Systems for the Growth of E-Business". *International Symposium Economics and Management of Transformation.*

It is worth considering the Italian approach to this topic as a background of the above considerations, see Costi, R. 1993. "Servizi di pagamento: il controllo sugli enti produttori", *Banca borsa titoli di credito,* p. 129 ff.; Antonucci, A. 1994. "Gli intermediari finanziari 'residuali' dalla legge antiriciclaggio al Testo unico delle leggi in materia bancaria e creditizia", Rassegna economica, p. 245 ff.; Olivieri, G. 2001. "Appunti sulla moneta elettronica. Brevi note in margine alla direttiva 2000/46/CE riguardante gli istituti di moneta elettronica", *Banca borsa titoli di credito,* p. 809 ff. Troiano, V. 2001. "Gli istituti di moneta elettronica", *Quaderni di ricerca giuridica della Consu-lenza Legale. Banca d'Italia,* n. 53, Roma, p. 16 ff. Criscuolo, L. 2003. "Gli intermediari finanziari non bancari", Bari, p. 110 ff.; Clarich, M. 2010. "L'armonizzazione europea dei servizi di pagamento: l'attuazione della direttiva 2007/64/CE", in *Scritti in onore di Francesco Capriglione,* Padova, p. 459 ff.; Basso, R. 2011. "Informazioni relative alle operazioni di pagamento e ai contanti", *La nuova disciplina dei servizi di pagamento,* Torino, p. 537 ff.; Lemma, V. 2017. "Commento sub articolo 126 quinquies del d. lgs. 385 del 1993" "Codice commentato dei contratti", Padova; Burchi, A. et al., 2019. "Financial Data Aggregation e Account Information Services", *Consob, Quaderni FinTech,* n. 4; Troiano, V. 2019. "Gli istituti di moneta elettronica". "Manuale di diritto bancario e finanziario. Padova.

6. Indeed, the former refers to the issuing of money out of the activities of central banks, the latter to the opportunities led by the application of fintech (and, also, to legal tender).

7. Moreover, see Bollen, R. A. 2013. "The Legal Status of Online Currencies: Are Bitcoins the Future?" *Journal of Banking and Finance Law and Practice* with respect to the evidence that, being a decentralized system, there is no central issuer, authority or register-keeper in cryptocurrencies.

8. See Hicks, J.R. 1937. "Mr. Keynes and the "classics"; a suggested interpretation", *Econometrica. Journal of the Econometric Society*, 5(2), p. 147 ff.

9. See Hansen, A.H. 1953. "A Guide to Keynes", New York.

10. It is worth recalling Haar, B. 2016. "Freedom of Contract and Financial Stability through the Lens of the Legal Theory of Finance" (LTF)—LTF Approaches to ABS, Pari Passu-Clauses, CCPs, and Basel III" SAFE Working Paper No. 141, on the example of the private creation of money by structured finance products. This paper also shows further implications referring to pari passu clauses and collective action clauses, which both exhibit a differential application of these legal rules according to the hierarchical status of the respective market participant, and can therefore endanger sovereign debt restructurings. Legal instruments to avoid this are briefly explored. An example of another key role of the law in crisis that is the task to resolve the tension between market discipline and financial stability is exemplified by the regulation of the OTC derivatives market and proposals of effective loss-sharing among CCPs. Related questions about the significance of legal rules to ensure financial stability are raised in the analysis of minimum capital requirements under Basel III.

11. Furthermore, see Draghi, M. 2018. "Monetary policy in the euro area", *Speech by the President of the ECB, ECB Forum on Central Banking*, Sintra, 19 June 2018, whereby the author restated ECB's recent decisions on policy instruments: "First, our anticipated ending of asset purchases in December this year is subject to incoming data confirming the medium-term inflation outlook. Moreover, the APP can always be used in case contingencies materialise that we do not currently foresee. Second, we announced that we intend to maintain our policy of reinvesting the principal payments from maturing securities purchased under the asset purchase programme (APP) for an extended time after the end of net purchases, and in any case for as long as necessary to maintain favourable liquidity conditions and an ample degree of monetary accommodation. Third, we conveyed our expectation that the key ECB interest rates will remain at their present levels at least through the summer of 2019, and in any case for as long as necessary to ensure that the evolution of inflation remains aligned with our current expectations of a sustained adjustment path. This enhanced forward guidance clearly signals that will remain patient in determining the timing of the first rate rise and will take a gradual approach to adjusting policy thereafter. The path of very short-term interest rates that is implicit in the term structure of today's money market interest rates broadly reflects these principles."

12. Note Zaring, D. and Bignami, F. 2016. "Comparative Law and Regulation. Understanding the Global Regulatory Process".

Northampton, MA, USA, which represented a "extensive scholarly inquiry on how to further liberal democratic ideals in an age of regulatory governance", and this refers to "the instrumental ambition of controlling private market and social activity to suit public purpose [that] has provoked debate on the types of legal procedures, rules, and sanctions that are most likely to produce effective regulation".

13. It is worth mentioning US SEC. 2019 "SEC Orders Blockchain Company to Pay $24 Million Penalty for Unregistered ICO", Sept. 30.

    See also ESMA 2017b. "ESMA alerts firms involved in Initial Coin Offerings (ICOs) to the need to meet relevant regulatory requirements" and ESMA 2017a. "ESMA alerts investors to the high risks of Initial Coin Offerings (ICOs)"; Financial Consumer Authority (FCA) 2017. "Consumer warning about the risks of Initial Coin Offerings ('ICOs')"; Commission de Surveillance du Secteur Financier (CSSF) 2018. "Warning On Initial Coin Offerings ("Icos") And Tokens"; Consob 2019. "Le offerte iniziali e gli scambi di cripto-attività. Documento per la Discussione".

14. It includes a reference to Alpa, G. 1997. "La normativa sui dati personali. Modelli di lettura e problemi esegetici". *Il diritto dell'informazione e dell'informatica*, fasc. 4–5, p. 70 ff. on the political-institutional reading of the protection of the person; the legal-formalist reading of drafting techniques and of the normative plot; and the legal-realist reading of the interests at stake and of the juridical construction of the individual identity.

15. It recalls Finck, M. 2017. "Blockchains and Data Protection in the European Union" *Max Planck Institute for Innovation & Competition Research Paper No. 18-01*, which examines the consequences flowing from that state of affairs and suggest that in interpreting the GDPR with respect to blockchain, fundamental rights protection and the promotion of innovation must be reconciled.

16. However far progress may go, only a few long-standing and largely accepted properties will ultimately decide upon 'moneyness'.

17. *Inter alia*, see: Hicks, J.R. 1967. "Critical Essays in Monetary Theory", Oxford; Harrod, R. F. 1969 "Money", London; Scitovsky, T. 1969. "Money and the balance of payments", *The Economic Journal*, 79(316), p. 904 ff.

    In 1787, during the debates on adopting the US Constitution, James Madison stated that *[t]he circulation of confidence is better than the circulation of money*. It means that the founding father chose to use public trust in money as the yardstick for trust in public institutions, for money and trust are as inextricably intertwined as money and the state. Money is an *indispensable social convention* that can only work if the public trusts in its stability and acceptability and, no less importantly, if the public has confidence in the resolve of its issuing authorities to stand behind it, in bad times as well as in good. Madison's eighteenth-century remark on the link between money and trust has lost none of its relevance in the twenty-first century. The issue of trust in money has resurfaced in the public debate on privately issued, stateless currencies, such as bitcoin, and their promise to serve as reliable substitutes for public money.

18. In earlier times, when credit activities did not enjoy the same diffusion as today and money supply was largely made of cash (with metal coins circulating in high amounts too), Jevons had used to discern between *standard of value*, which encompasses the modern notion of value stability over time, and *store of value*, which related to the physical storability and transportability of coins. See Jevons, W.S. 1875. "Money and the Mechanism of Exchange", New York.

19. In this regard, *tender* has the same meaning as *course*, but the latter's root may still be found in the form which said expression takes in many Romance languages (e.g. 'corso legale' in Italian).

20. For instance, consider the case of Montenegro. In this young Balkan republic, the euro circulates with the same ease and bounty as in the nineteen countries which have officially joined the monetary union: yet is not endowed with legal tender, for the country is not an EU Member State and, thus, cannot participate in the single currency. Hence, Montenegro does not experience the effects associated with a membership of the euro area: for instance, it is not an ECB counterpart. In turn, this yields "real" economic effects. Assessing whether it would be better for Montenegro to join the EU and officially adopt the euro is not one of this chapter's goals, for it would require a completely separated analysis, yet it enables to say that the evolution of the legal status of cryptocurrencies could not lay on the background. In fact, the decision to let a money-like instrument to become an official currency ultimately impacts the wealth of any subject who would use that instrument regardless of it having legal tender or not. In turn, this "micro-" consequences affect the monetary system as a whole: for instance, via payment services.

21. The most significant contribution traces back to Friedman, M. and Schwartz, A.J. 1987. "Money in Historical Perspective", Chicago.

22. A wide and fair account of the issue is provided in Davies, G. 2019. "How China dodged a trade war recession", appeared on *Financial Times*, 15 September 2019.

23. This recalls the exemplification made by Friedrich August von Hayek and Milton Friedman, respectively; both of them received the Nobel Prize in Economics: the former in 1974, the latter two years later.

24. Hence, by vigorously upholding the disintermediation of transactions, in a 1999 interview he declared that the one thing that's missing, but that will soon be developed, is a reliable e-cash, a method whereby on the Internet you can transfer funds from A to B, without A knowing B or B knowing A.; see Cawrey, D. 2014, "How Economist Milton Friedman Predicted Bitcoin".

25. Among those who have recently spoken against cryptocurrencies, Richard Thaler declared that bitcoin and its brethren were the markets most resembling a bubble; see ECO Portuguese Economy 2018. "Economics Nobel prize winner, Richard Thaler: The market that looks most like a bubble to me is Bitcoin and its brethren".

26. In addition, see Zeno Zencovich, V. 1983. "Telematica e tutela del diritto all'identità personale" *Politica del diritto*, fasc. 2, p. 345 ff., whose conclusion highlighted that to the general problems related to the protection of confidentiality in relation to the collection of information by databases (prohibition to collect information on very personal aspects of the individual, right of the individual to access data from others held on his behalf, right of rectification of inaccurate data by the person concerned), the introduction of interactive devices will add a wide set of rights to be protected, resulting from the "involuntary" concentration of data so far necessarily dispersed.

27. It refers to FSB 2017a. "Chair's letter to G20 Finance Ministers and Central Bank Governors ahead of their Baden-Baden meeting", 17 March.

28. In addition, see Garonna, P. 2019. "Ethics from Within: A Paradigm Shift for Financial Ethics"; the author stated that "even though the ethical dimension figures prominently in many specific questions of financial innovation (i.e. cryptocurrencies, … etc.), there should not be a specific ethical problem "inherent" in finance, and there should not be a special financial branch or model that can be considered "ethical" as distinct from—or opposed to—the rest of finance.

29. It refers to Stiglitz, J. E. 2017. "Where Modern Macroeconomics Went Wrong" *NBER Working Paper No. w23795.* The author argues that at the heart of the failure were the wrong micro-foundations, which failed to incorporate key aspects of economic behavior, for example incorporating insights from information economics and behavioral economics. Inadequate modelling of the financial sector meant they were ill-suited for predicting or responding to a financial crisis; and a reliance on representative agent models meant they were ill-suited for analysing either the role of distribution in fluctuations and crises or the consequences of fluctuations on inequality.

This analysis will take into account the alternative benchmark models that this author proposes, which may be useful both in understanding deep downturns and responding to them by means of a regulatory intervention.

30. All the above would not lay down on Krugman' statement that it's a bubble wrapped in techno-mysticism inside a cocoon of libertarian ideology, as he wrote in an op-ed during those days in which bitcoin stationed around its historical high. However, this cannot deny that such approach opened the current debate by proposing a direct comparison between the situation of that digital coin, on the one hand, and the 'tulip mania' experienced in the Netherlands during the seventeenth century, allegedly propelled by the establishment of markets which at that very time were—upon their "invention"—seen as particularly opaque (e.g. futures ones); see Krugman, P.R. 2018. "Bubble, Bubble, Fraud and Trouble, appeared on *The New York Times*, 29 January.

31. Questioning the actual usability of bitcoin as a means of payment may seem a defence; however, "there's really no reason to use bitcoin in transactions—unless you don't want any-one to see either what you're buying or what you're selling, which is why much actual bitcoin use seems to involve drugs, sex and other black-market goods". Hence, the consideration that the ultimate backing behind the dollar is actually the fact that the US government will accept it, in fact demands it, in payment for taxes, whereas a solid and well-reputed institution like the Federal Reserve intervenes to stabilize its power; see Krugman, P.R. 2018. "Bubble, Bubble, Fraud and Trouble, appeared on The New York Times, 29 January.

32. In addition to this (and to confirm it), Krugman noted that bitcoin's volatility over the six weeks preceding his article would have meant something like an 8000% inflation rate, had that asset been regarded as a currency. Furthermore, the author saw a wandering price as allowing larger room for manipulation, as some relevant cases had already occurred. Also, he mentioned the fact that certain reports allege the possibility that foreign powers might have hidden behind some episodes of that kind, for the purpose of financing themselves in breach of existing international agreements; see Krugman, P.R. 2018. "Bubble, Bubble, Fraud and Trouble, appeared on *The New York Times*, 29 January.

33. It is worth recalling Shiller, R. J., 2014. "Speculative Asset Prices (Nobel Prize Lecture)" *Cowles Foundation Discussion Paper No. 1936* about the role of rationality in the formation of the *prices* and the growing trend towards behavioural finance and, more broadly, behavioural economics, the growing acceptance of the importance of alternative psychological, sociological and epidemiological factors as affecting prices.

However, the relevant background refers to Shiller, R. J. 2013. "Reflections on Finance and the Good Society" *Cowles Foundation*

Discussion Paper No. 1894, where the author appreciated the important role of professional organizations in moderating the tendencies towards aggression and hoarding, which no financial institutions and codes of ethics can eliminate. Then, he acknowledged the important principle of reciprocity, and when this principle is made part of financial education a better public acceptance of the important role that finance plays in the society can be expected.

34. Moreover, see Hansen L. P. 2019. "Reflection on MFR's conference on Cryptocurrencies and Blockchains"; the author concluded that "market evolution happened because a good idea was coupled with capable technology and mutual commercial interest with enough time to catch on and gain traction".

35. Furthermore, see Nabilou, H. and Prum, A. 2018 "Ignorance, Debt and Cryptocurrencies: The Old and the New in the Law and Economics of Concurrent Currencies" *Journal of Financial Regulation*, which draw parallels between the information economics of money and quasi-money creation within the current central banking, commercial banking and shadow banking systems with that of the cryptocurrency ecosystem.

36. Let us Wright, A. and De Filippi, P. 2018. "Blockchain and the Law: The Rule of Code", Harvard Cambridge (MS).

37. It is worth recalling Nakamoto, S. 2008. "Bitcoin: A peer-to-peer electronic cash system", available at *www.bitcoin.org/bitcoin.pdf*.

38. Namely, B-money by Wei Dai and Bit gold by Nick Szabo.

39. It refers to the classic Hume, D. 1748. "Of Interest", in *"Essays Moral and Political"*, A. Millar, London. See, on this topic, Dow, S. C. 2009. "David Hume and Modern Economics" *Capitalism and Society*, Paganelli M. P. 2006. "Endogenous Money and David Hume" *Eastern Economic Journal*, about the possibility to consider the effects of 'more' money on the markets that record less trade.

40. See Norman v. Baltimore & O.R. Co., 24 U.S. 421, 4451 (1884).

41. As ECB highlighted, private cryptocurrencies have little or no prospect of establishing themselves as viable alternatives to centrally issued money that is accepted as legal tender; see Mersch, Y. 2019, "Money and private currencies. Reflections on Libra. Speech by Member of the Executive Board of the ECB", at the ESCB Legal Conference, Frankfurt am Main, 2 September.

42. See the conclusion of Niels, F. 1993. "Single Term Off-line Coins" *Advances In Cryptology-Eurocrypt '93*; Chaum D. and Pedersen T. P. 1992a "Transferred Cash Grows in Size" *Advances In Cryptology-Eurocrypt '92*; Eng, T. and Okamoto T. 1994. "Single-Term Divisib Electronic Coins" *Advances In Cryptology-Eurocrypt '94*; Okamoto T. 1995. "An Efficient Divisible Electronic Cash Scheme" *Advances In Cryptology-Crypto '95*.

43. In addition, it refers to Pasquini, N. 1983. "Identità personale e lesione della reputazione: appunti in margine ad alcune recenti sentenze. Nota a Trib. Roma 10 marzo 1982" *Giurisprudenza italiana*, fasc. 3, pt. 1B, p. 189 ff. on the problems of the misinformation.

44. See on this point the classic work of Minsky, H.P. 1986. "Stabilizing an Unstable Economy", New York.

45. For instance, Nelson observed that digital currency investments entail low leverage and, thus, are not particularly dangerous from a systemic stability standpoint. See Nelson, B. 2018. Financial stability and monetary policy issues associated with digital currencies, *Journal of Economics and Business*, 100, 76–78.

   However, Shiller had already warned on the likelihood that technology propagates bubbles, as those times were witnessing with regard to the stock price of dotcoms; see Shiller, R.J. 2000, "Irrational Exuberance", Princeton.

46. It is worth recalling the conclusions of both Kaplow, L. and Shavell, S. 1991. "Optimal Law Enforcement with Self-Reporting of Behavior" NBER Working Paper No. w3822; and Shavell, S. 2003. "Economic Analysis of the General Structure of the Law" *Harvard Law and Economics Discussion Paper No. 408.*

47. It should be noted that even Nakamoto (op. cit.), with regard to the fact that bitcoin erased the necessity of a transaction being financially intermediated, acknowledged that such cryptocurrency relied upon *no trusted third party.*

48. It is worth considering Holmström, B. R. 1989. "Agency Costs and Innovation"). *Journal of Economic Behavior & Organization* on the forces that supports and reduce the innovation.

49. See Dyhrberg, A.H. 2016. Bitcoin, gold and the dollar—a GARCH volatility analysis, *Finance Research Letters*, 16, 85–92, which found something different from the literature consensus.

50. See Fenwick, M, and Kaal, W. A. and Vermeulen, E. P.M., 2017. "Regulation Tomorrow: What Happens When Technology is Faster than the Law?" American University Business Law Review, Vol. 6, No. 3, where it is pointed out that "In an age of constant, complex and disruptive technological innovation, knowing what, when, and how to structure regulatory interventions has become more difficult". The authors propose the following solution and questions: "lawmaking and regulatory design needs to become more proactive, dynamic, and responsive. So how can regulators actually achieve these goals? What can regulators do to promote innovation and offer better opportunities to people wanting to build a new business around a disruptive technology or simply enjoy the benefits of a disruptive new technology as a consumer?"

51. See Draghi, M. 2019. "Farewell Remarks", also highlighted that "Freely floating currencies were therefore not an option, and fixed exchange rates would not work as capital became more mobile within Europe, as the ERM crisis in 1992–3 proved. The answer was to create a single currency: one market with one money. This construct has been largely successful: incomes across the continent have materially increased, integration and value chains have developed to an extent unimaginable 20 years ago, and the Single Market has survived intact through the worst crisis since the 1930s."

52. In addition, see Sciarrone Alibrandi, A. 2008. "L'adempimento dell'obbligazione pecuniaria tra diritto vivente e portata regolatoria indiretta della Payment services directive 2007/64/CE", "Il nuovo quadro normativo comunitario dei servizi di pagamento. Prime riflessioni", *Quaderni di Ricerca Giuridica della Banca d'Italia*, n. 63; Barillà, G. 2015. "Il trasferimento dei servizi di pagamento", *Le Nuove leggi civili commentate*, p. 1031 ff.; Libertini, M. 2011. "Brevi note su concorrenza e servizi di pagamento" *Banca borsa e titoli di credito*, p. 181 ff.

    See also EUCJ, sect. III 11 September 2014, C-382/12 P, *Il Foro italiano*, 2015, pt. 4, c. 38 ss. and the comment of Granieri, M. "Diritto europeo. Pagamento tramite carte di credito: rispetto del regime della concorrenza ed applicazione di commissioni interbancarie multilaterali".

    With respect to the Italian regulation, See Lucantoni, P. 2018. "Commento sub art. 126 octies" and Ferretti, R. 2018. "Commento sub art. 126 decies", both in "Commentario al testo unico delle leggi n materia bancaria e creditizia", Padova.

53. It is worth recalling also that the Bank of Canada, the Bank of England, the Bank of Japan, the European Central Bank, the Sveriges Riksbank and the Swiss National Bank are liaising together with the Bank for International Settlements (BIS), and they have created a group to share experiences as they assess the potential cases for central bank digital currency (CBDC) in their home jurisdictions; see Bank of England 2020, "Central Bank group to assess potential cases for central bank digital currencies", 22 January.

54. But there is another side of the moon: namely, cryptocurrencies minted by sovereign states, whose characteristics concerns from both a monetary standpoint and, more broadly, a financial stability one. This may be the case of CryptoRuble, whose coinage has been recently envisaged by Russia; see Kakushadze, Z. and Liew, J. K. S., 2018. "CryptoRuble: From Russia with Love" *World Economics* p. 165 ff.

55. See Gupta, S. and Roy, A. K., 2011. "BRICS at the Gate: Modern International Monetary System in Conditions of Balanced Uncertainty" *Journal of Emerging Knowledge on Emerging Markets*; the authors repre-

sented that "Looking ahead, a 21st century international monetary order that is entirely de-anchored from gold and rests merely on the full faith and credit of its fiat money trustees will necessitate that its mechanisms of international coordination and adjustment to restore balance be ratcheted-upwards equivalently."

56. Since mining requires large amount of computational—and, thus, electric—power, its absence would clearly overcome one of the tallest barriers to such market.

57. In particular, see Ganguly, M. and Delaney, M. 2018. "Unregulated Financial Markets and the Shadow Banking Narrative: China, India and the United States" *Market Express*, provided that, as well as highlighting recent initiatives being undertaken by government regulators such as the CFTC and SEC, to regulate virtual currencies such as the cryptocurrency markets, this paper highlights why the need to address unregulated financial markets—with particular focus on shadow banking activities, presents ever-growing concerns—not just for investors and regulators, but also in respect of their interconnectedness with other financial sectors.

58. Neither federal nor state regulation has ever gone beyond, until the US government was involved in discussing issues regarding Facebook-backed cryptocurrency—namely, Libra—at the 2019 G7 summit in Biarritz, mainly at the initiative of France. The same is true for the euro area, where the relevant authorities are monitoring this phenomenon; see G7. 2019. "Biarritz Strategy for an Open, Free and Secure Digital Transformation" for the results of a discussion on the best strategies to promote an open, free and secure digital transformation, and reiterated the determination to protect it from current challenges.

59. It refers to Mundell, R.A. 1961. "A theory of optimum currency areas", *The American Economic Review*, p. 657 ff.

60. The above reflects the considerations of Consob. 2018. "Lo sviluppo del FinTech. Opportunità e rischi per l'industria finanziaria nell'era digitale", 1 March.

61. Obviously, it refers to the content of such instruments and not to the applicability of Directive 2014/65/EU (MiFID II) and Regulation (EU) 600/2014 (MiFIR) to the relevant financial services.

62. It refers to CCPs as entities that preside over clearing in a multilateral way, that is, taking long positions towards all sellers and short ones towards all purchasers in an exchange.

63. It refers to CSDs as entities entrusted with the duty to store the securities involved in a transaction, albeit in a dematerialized, electronic format.

64. It is worth considering that Gambaro, A. 1981. "Falsa luce agli occhi del pubblico" Rivista di diritto civile, 1981, fasc. 1, pt. 1, p. 84 ff. addressed this question with respect to the 'false light in the public eye' paradigma.

65. In this sense, crypto-assets are treated as if they were akin to commodities more than to money, fuelling the idea that their categorization is far from certain.

66. It recalls the study of Marchetti, P. 1981. "Le offerte pubbliche di sottoscrizione e la legge 216" *Rivista delle società*, fasc. 6, pp. 1137 ff. on the duty of privacy in case of offerings.

67. It is worth recalling Nou, J. and Stiglitz, E., 2019. "Regulatory Bundling", *Yale Law Journal* on the ability of administrative agencies to aggregate and disaggregate rules.

68. It is worth considering Dang, T. V. and Gorton, G. B. and Holmström, B. R. and Ordoñez, G. 2014. "Banks as Secret Keepers" *NBER Working Paper No. w20255*, which pointed out that banks are optimally opaque institutions: they produce debt for use as a transaction medium (bank money), which requires that information about the backing assets—loans—not be revealed, so that bank money does not fluctuate in value, reducing the efficiency of trade. The same is not true form markets, so the oxymora to be regulated in this sector.

69. In particular, see IFRS 2018. *IASB update January 2018*, available at *www.ifrs.org* IFRS 2016, *Summary Note of the Accounting Standard Advisory Forum*; FASB 2017. *Report of the Chairman*; EY 2018, *IFRS (#). Accounting for Crypto-Assets*, available at *www.ey.com*.

70. In addition to this, it can be noted that a trade involving the settlement of a transferable security against cryptocurrencies could nevertheless be executed in the form of a free-of-payment security transfer by the CSD, whereas the crypto-asset leg would have to be settled separately. This is due to the rise of principal risk—that is, the component of the counterparty risk which is related to the other side failing to comply with its obligations—and, thus, due to the possibility of facing significant legal expenses.

71. Moreover, see Cecchetti, S. G. and McCauley, R. N. and McGuire, P. M. 2012. "Interpreting TARGET2 Balances" *BIS Working Paper No. 393*, on the evidence for the current account financing interpretation. It is useful to consider that BIS international banking data points to the importance of TARGET2 balances as a symptom of a reduction by core European banks of credit previously extended to borrowers in peripheral Europe.

72. Furthermore, Hristov, N. and Hülsewig, O. and Wollmershäuser, T. 2019. "Capital Flows in the Euro Area and TARGET2 balances" *Deutsche Bundesbank Discussion Paper No. 24/2019*, whose results suggest that the built-up of TARGET2 balances was mainly driven by capital flow shocks while being barely responsive to other aggregate shocks.

See also Minenna, M. 2019. "The New Eurozone Risk Morphology" *SSRN Research Paper no. 3341540.*

73. In addition, it refers to Avgouleas, E. and Kiayias, A., 2018. "The Promise of Blockchain Technology for Global Securities and Derivatives Markets: The New Financial Ecosystem and the 'Holy Grail' of Systemic Risk Containment". *Edinburgh School of Law Research Paper No. 2018/43*, with respect to the utility of complex FMI comprising long custodial chains and large global Central Counterparties (CCPs) for the operation of modern markets seems undisputable. The authors highlighted that "a shift in the technology paradigm with the introduction of DLT systems for securities and derivatives FMI, could, however, increase investor control, the efficiency of systemic risk distribution, and create a more diverse and resilient financial ecosystem".

74. Actually, only very safe assets are allowed to be used by CCPs to clear transactions executed pursuant to EMIR: namely, debt instruments issued or explicitly guaranteed by a government, a central bank, a multilateral development bank, the European Financial Stability Facility or the European Stability Mechanism. In this respect, see Peters, G. and Vishnia, G. 2016b. "Overview of Emerging Blockchain Architectures and Platforms for Electronic Trading Exchanges" *SSRN: Research Paper no. 2867344*, which provided an overview of the new exchange regulations appearing in different jurisdictions around the world, including EMIR, Dodd Frank, MiFID I/II, MiFIR, REMIT, Reg NMS and T2S.

    See also Peters, G. and Vishnia, G. 2016a. "Blockchain Architectures for Electronic Exchange Reporting Requirements: EMIR, Dodd Frank, MiFID I/II, MiFIR, REMIT, Reg NMS and T2S" *SSRN Research Paper no. 2832604* in regard to transparency reporting and trade/transaction reporting requirements under the regulations mentioned above.

75. See Committee on the Global Financial System and Financial Stability Board 2017. "FinTech credit: Market structure, business models and financial stability implications", whose conclusions provide that "the emergence of FinTech credit markets poses challenges for policymakers in monitoring and regulating such activity. Having good-quality data will be key as these markets develop".

76. It is worth mentioning the study of Consolo, G. 1975. "Informazione, riservatezza e calcolatori elettronici. aspetti sociologici e giuridici" Amministrazione e politica, fasc. 2–3, p. 240 ff.

77. In addition, it is worth recalling also the FSB 2017b. "FinTech credit. Market structure, business models and financial stability implications". Report prepared by a Working Group established by the Committee on the Global Financial System (CGFS) and the Financial Stability Board (FSB), 22 May.

78. See Flick, G. M. 1991. "Insider trading: una tappa significativa—anche se controversa—della lunga marcia verso la trasparenza". *Rivista delle società*, fasc. 4, p. 957 ff. on the difficulties of the repression of the insider trading, in the perspective of the damage, and thus his conclusion on the alternative of protection of the "par condicio", by shifting from abuse to violation of the obligation to abstain (with regard to the emblematic, educational and ethical meaning of repression).

79. They should include (i) *technological integrity, meaning, inter alia, no back doors/loopholes or hidden functionalities, no white listing of malware, no fraudulent collusion, responsible cryptographic key management, and the pursuit of the state of the art;* (ii) *algorithms/protocol service performance and transparency so as to ensure the correct performance of the service and facilitate any necessary audit;* (iii) *stress-tested operational security and cyber-resilience;* (iv) *regulatory compliance intended as audibility by users and supervisors in line with the regulatory obligations/requirements that may be triggered by participation in or use of the network.*

80. It is worth recall a brief analysis provided by Minto, A. 2017. "FinTech and the Hunting Technique": How to Hit a Moving Target", *Open Review of Management, Banking and Finance*; see also Rispoli Farina, M. 2015. "Informazione e servizi di pagamento", *Analisi giuridica dell'economia*, p. 175 ff.

81. In particular, it refers to EBA 2019. *Report on crypto-assets*, available at *www.eba.europa.eu* and to ESMA 2019, *Advice on initial coin offerings and crypto-assets*, available at *www.esma.europa.eu.*

82. In fact, prices are often denominated in dollars, and their equivalent figures in bitcoins are updated along with the USD/BTC floating exchange rate, such that vendors manage to collect the desired amount of dollars. Actually, since the value of bitcoin—as well as any other cryptocurrency—is marked-to-market, whereas retail prices inevitably show a certain degree of "stickiness", figures expressed in USD and BTC cannot be but (slightly) different. See again Lo, S. and Wang, J. 2014. "Bitcoin as Money?" published by Federal Reserve Bank of Boston.

83. As clearly descends from the above, in this case it refers to the same "dignity" to either of the two major functions, as cryptocurrencies are acknowledged to create money without central banks and facilitate payments without financial institutions; see World Bank 2018, "Cryptocurrencies and blockchain", available at *www.documents.worldbank.org.*

84. See again the World Bank 2018, "Cryptocurrencies and blockchain", available at www.documents.worldbank.org.

85. It refers to Zeno-Zencovich V. and Zoppini A. 1992. "La disciplina dei servizi telematici nel quadro delle proposte comunitarie di tutela dei dati

personali" *Il diritto dell'informazione e dell'informatica*, fasc. 3, p. 755 ff. on the certain relevant aspects for telematic services: information privacy, marketing, commercial information; the authors analysed the SYN 288 Directive with respect to its guidelines and elements of *aporia* and identified the provisions applicable to ICT services.

86. It recalls World Bank 2018. "Cryptocurrencies and blockchain", available at www.documents.worldbank.org.

87. With regard to this, strong empirical evidence backs the commonly shared idea that digital coins are mainly intended as a store of value: for instance, by analysing data up to May 2012, it has been pointed out that about half of bitcoin stock was not spent within at least three months after having been received (World Bank, *op. cit.*); see Shamir, A. 2013. "Quantitative analysis of the full bitcoin transaction graph" "Financial Cryptography and Data Security" Berlin-Heidelberg.

88. It refers, in particular to Ofek, E. and Richardson, M. 2003. "Dotcom mania: The rise and fall of internet stock prices" *The Journal of Finance*, p. 1113 ff.

89. See World Bank 2018. "Cryptocurrencies and blockchain", available at www.documents.worldbank.org.

90. It is worth considering Markesinis, B and Alpa, G. 1997. "Il diritto alla "privacy" nell'esperienza di "common law" e nell'esperienza italiana" *Rivista trimestrale di diritto e procedura civile*, fasc. 2, p. 417 ff. in which the authors refer to the experience of English and American common law, in the field of the right to "privacy", and to the German system, also with reference to concrete cases on which the jurisprudence has been pronounced. Particular attention is paid to the criteria followed by the German jurisprudence in determining the damage and to the other recognized remedies of protection (publication of a statement to the contrary, of a defeat or of a correction).

91. The fact that trading is concentrated in a few exchanges worldwide should not be regarded as something negative, for the situation is not much different from that of equities in the United States before the Securities and Exchange Commission (SEC) adopted an ad hoc regulation, back in 2005, to increase competition. In fact, there exists a positive association between the number of trades and the degree of liquidity, such that having a small number of venues where transactions be executed (thus, with greater "intensity" of trades) is doubtlessly beneficial from a liquidity standpoint.

92. Also, upon its first-ever minting, bitcoin was so illiquid that it debuted with a price very close to zero, and it basically took nine years to experience a bubble situation in which its price substantially diverged from fundamental value; see Kristoufek, L. 2015. "What are the main drivers of

the Bitcoin price? Evidence from wavelet coherence analysis" *PLoS One*; Phillips, R.C. and Gorse, D. 2017. "Predicting cryptocurrency price bubbles using social media data and epidemic modelling", *IEEE Symposium Series on Computational Intelligence (SSCI)*.

93. It is worth recalling the conclusions of Bessone, M. 1978 "L'esperienza francese del diritto alla intimità della vita privata". *Politica del diritto*, fasc. 3, p. 335 ff.

94. See Zaring, D. and Bignami, F. 2016. "Comparative Law and Regulation. Understanding the Global Regulatory Process". Northampton, MA, USA, considers that "dissatisfaction with some of the more classic forms of rulemaking and enforcement has given rise to calls for more flexible arrangements that rely more heavily on soft law and private initiative in crafting the standards and control mechanisms designed to discipline the market and society".

95. In particular, see Clarich, M. 1996. "Diritto d'accesso e tutela della riservatezza: regole sostanziali e tutela processuale" Diritto processuale amministrativo, 1996, fasc. 3, p. 430 ff. with respect to the objective and subjective scope of the right of access and the relationship between the right of access and administrative secrecy, who focused on the need to reconcile the right of access with the right of confidentiality of third parties.

96. It refers to EUCJ, Sec. V, 4 October 2018, n. 191, C-191/17, published in *Giurisprudenza commerciale*, 2019, with the comment of Greco, G. "Il conto che non opera con terzi non è un conto di pagamento. Note critiche alla sentenza C-191/17 della Corte di Giustizia dell'Unione Europea".

97. It is worth recalling the considerations of Lemma, V. 2015 "Too big to be popular", "La riforma delle banche popolari" Padova, p. 173 ff.

98. In addition, see Van Loo, R. 2018. "Making Innovation More Competitive: The Case of Fintech" *UCLA Law Review*, which highlights that "Competition authority—including antitrust and the extension of business licenses—is spread across at least five regulators. Each is focused on other missions or industries. The Federal Reserve and other prudential regulators prioritize financial stability, which conflicts with their competition mandate. The Department of Justice (DOJ), hindered by statutes and knowledge gaps, devotes significantly fewer resources to banking than to other industries in merger review. No regulator has the right authority, motivation, and expertise to promote competition in consumer finance".

99. It is worth mention Ferrarini, G. 2000. "Osservazioni in merito alla disciplina della concentrazione degli scambi azionari" *Banca impresa società*, p. 281 ff.

100. See Di Maggio, M. and Egan, M. and Franzoni, F. A. 2019. "The Value of Intermediation in the Stock Market" *CEPR Discussion Paper No. DP13936*, which used an empirical model to investigate the unbundling of equity research and execution services related to the MiFID II regulations.

    See also Burilov, V., 2019. "Regulation of Crypto Tokens and Initial Coin Offerings in the EU" *European Journal of Comparative Law and Governance* p. 146 ff.; the author argued that EU regulators should first ensure legal certainty by defining the scope of *tokenised* financial instruments subject to MiFID.

101. In fact, although bitcoin keeps the first-mover advantage, its competitors—collectively known as "altcoins"—are advertising their differences vis-à-vis the dominant cryptocurrency, and the level of safety is one of the characteristics that are likely to be more appealing.

102. It refers to OECD 2018. "How to deal with Bitcoin and other cryptocurrencies in the System of National Accounts?" *Meeting of the Working Party on Financial Statistics*, 5 November.

103. It is crystal-clear that such definition might theoretically throw shares outside of the scope of financial assets, but the OECD (*ibidem*) notes that the 'claim' is that on the residual value of a corporation in case it being wound up, something which is explicitly encompassed by the legal agreement underlying the share purchase, regardless of the timing of liquidation. Instead, the SNA acknowledged "monetary gold" as the sole exception to the definition above.

104. However, this should not be taken literally: in *fact*, fiat currencies are generally not backed by any commodity such that coins may be physically redeemed.

105. See OECD 2018. "How to deal with Bitcoin and other cryptocurrencies in the System of National Accounts?" Meeting of the Working Party on Financial Statistics, 5 November.

106. Especially in the past, "helicopter money" was much more common: that is, new currency was just "printed", without incurring any direct expense apart from printing itself. This is a practice that many countries—particularly underdeveloped or emerging ones—still refuse to completely rule out, as it may easily end up stirring inflationary spirals.

107. For instance, the Venezuelan bolívar and the Zimbabwean dollar, both suffering from hyperinflation; see Zalduendo, J., 2006. "Determinants of Venezuela's Equilibrium Real Exchange Rate" *IMF Working Paper*; Miller, S. M. and Ndhlela, T. 2019. "Money Demand and Seignorage Maximization before the End of the Zimbabwean Dollar" *Mercatus Research Paper* no. *3329378*.

108. See Manaa, M. et others. 2019. "Crypto-Assets: Implications for Financial Stability, Monetary Policy, and Payments and Market Infrastructures" *ECB Occasional Paper No. 223*, which summarizes the outcomes of the analysis of the ECB Crypto-Assets Task Force.

109. Moreover, see Zaring, D. and Bignami, F. 2016. "Comparative Law and Regulation. Understanding the Global Regulatory Process". Northampton, MA, USA, offered the evidence that "the variation of the legal powers, procedures and standards that bind regulators ... provides crucial context or the understanding and evaluation of a global phenomenon".

110. See again the clear statement of Mersch, Y. 2019, "Money and private currencies: Reflections on Libra. Speech by Member of the Executive Board of the ECB", at the ESCB Legal Conference, Frankfurt am Main, 2 September.

111. Namely, Sygnum and Seba: see Allen, M. 2019, "World's first crypto banks seen as game changer for Switzerland", appeared on *Swissinfo.ch* on 27 August 2019.

112. It refers to Ciocca, P. 1973, "Note sulla politica monetaria italiana". "Lo sviluppo economico italiano". Bari, p. 241; Savona, P. 1974. "La sovranità monetaria", Rome; Carli, G. and Capriglione, F. 1981 "Inflazione e ordinamento giuridico". Milano, p. 33 ff.

113. Also, these intermediaries committed themselves to blazing the trail for the rise of a new generation of credit institutions fully devoted to the 'crypto-'economy, based on managing and transacting crypto-assets thanks to the benefits provided by blockchain-based frameworks.

114. It refers to Swiss Federal Council, *Federal Council report on virtual currencies in response to the Schwaab (13.3687) and Weibel (13.4070) postulates,* 25 June 2014.

115. In its response to the Béglé motion on 15 November 2017, the Federal Council promised that State Secretariat for International Financial Matters (SIF) would set up such a working group because blockchain technology gives rise to fundamental legal issues concerning both financial market law and general pieces of legislation (Code of Obligations, Swiss Civil Code, etc.); see State Secretariat for International Financial Matters (SIF) 2018 "Blockchain/ICO working group established". Bern, 18 January.

116. In addition, see Confederazione Svizzera—Working Group Blockchain / ICO (2018) "Consultation on the work of the Working Group Blockchain / ICO", August 2018, where the Group represented that "clarifying the regulatory framework—both, with respect to civil law as well as financial regulation issues—shall contribute to maintaining Switzerland's position as an

attractive location for blockchain/ICOs, with high standards in the area of market conduct".

117. In particular, it recalls Goanta, C. 2018. "How Technology Disrupts Private Law: An Exploratory Study of California and Switzerland as Innovative Jurisdictions" *Stanford-Vienna TTLF Working Paper No. 38/2018* with respect to the evidence that "Law generally reacts to such developments only if there are circumstances (e.g. case law) showing how existing legal categories might not adequately accommodate these technological developments".

See also Gurrea-Martínez, A. and Remolina, N. 2019. "The Law and Finance of Initial Coin Offerings" *Ibero-American Institute for Law and Finance Working Paper No. 4/2018*, which represented that "securities regulators are addressing this issue in a very different manner across jurisdictions: while countries like the United States, Switzerland and Singapore are requiring companies to comply with existing securities rules only when a company issues 'security tokens', other jurisdictions, such as China and South Korea, have prohibited ICOs, and Mexico subject any issuance of tokens to a system of full control ex ante".

118. In the end, some authors regard the blockchain as nothing more than an overly complex and expensive method of sending information, whose sole actual benefit lies in evading regulation; see Haney, B. S. 2019. "Blockchain: Post-Quantum Security & Legal Economics", *SSRN Research Paper no. 3444695*.

119. Furthermore, see Flick G. M., 1988. "Informazione bancaria e giudice penale: presupposti di disciplina, problemi e prospettive" *Banca borsa e titoli di credito*, fasc. 4–5, pt. 1, p. 441 ff., which anticipates the current debate on the disagreement between judges and banks in the field of information management, and the risks of its radicalization. The prospects and possibilities of overcoming this contrast should be found within the framework of the new techniques of the fight against crime and the management of banking information. Hence, the author questioned the assumptions and the current structure of the so-called banking secrecy in criminal matters, in the perspective of a balance between the requirements of transparency, confidentiality and efficiency that it involves.

120. Among the most recent and remarkable ones, it is possible to quote the crash affecting the Dow Jones index on 6 May 2010 and the one occurred to the pound sterling on 7 October 2016.

121. This is pursuant to Reg. (EU) 648/2012, commonly known as the *European Market Infrastructure Regulation* (EMIR).

122. It is worth mentioning Taskinsoy, J. 2019, "Facebook's project Libra: Will Libra sputter out or spur central banks to introduce their own unique cryptocurrency projects?", *SSRN Research Paper 3423453*.

123. Therefore, by analysing their social media behaviour, Facebook would find relatively easy to collect data on the clients' financial habits, well in advance of Libra's establishment; in turn, this would allow the company to get unduly advantaged from a competitive standpoint, too raising significant antitrust concerns. In summary, upon the commencement of Libra, the company headquartered in Menlo Park would gain a dominant position and get financial benefits from its exploitation, based upon a much larger and more complete dataset vis-à-vis both other social media companies and cryptocurrency minters as well.

124. On the one hand, the fact that Libra will be promoted by an MNE whose core business consists of big data should help overcome the diffidence over the possibility to regard such crypto-ones as traditional currencies, for the level of public trust in Libra would be significantly higher vis-à-vis that experienced by other cryptocurrencies: in turn, this would enhance all three major functions of money. On the other hand, it would raise some unescapable legal questions. First, over the degree in which privacy legislation may be enforced: even in the management of its social network, the company has consistently shown little regard for it, even with consequences at a geopolitical level: see Trautman, L.J. 2014, "Virtual currencies; Bitcoin & what now after Liberty Reserve, Silk Road, and Mt. Gox?" *Richmond Journal of Law and Technology*, p. 1 ff.

125. Perhaps surprisingly, the absence of trust in banks is cited very often as a reason for self-exclusion from the banking circuit, as long as an overall majority of these people, in the United States as of 2017, has actually never considered to open a bank account (Taskinsoy, op. cit.). The paper presents the findings of an enquiry conducted biennially by the Federal Deposit Insurance Corporation (FDIC).

126. Thus, a credible commitment should be taken by regulators well before the academic debate on the nature of cryptocurrencies build any consensus.

127. Also, the issue deals with access to finance for large crowds of "unbanked" subjects, either natural or juridical persons, which are actually experiencing—or will potentially experience—a surge in their financial viability by transacting cryptocurrencies.

128. Whether this occurs, the oversight of subjects might well fail to make all the "sunk" part of the iceberg come to surface, for it would impair the economic meaning of such transactions and, thus, alter both the market structure and the business of those subjects, in their conduct and their performance as well.

129. It remarks the considerations of Ferri G. B. 1982. "Persona e privacy" *Rivista del diritto commerciale* fasc. 1–4, pt. 1, p. 75 ff. on the data protection as an individual right.

130. It clearly needs something more: and this is needed in a way which possibly preserve the benefits of a high degree of privacy and a good degree of integrity, ensured by blockchain in spite of the all the operational risks associated with every ICT technology. It just needs a consistent regulation to address the dangers, rather than any "retaliatory" approach against crypto-users who have benefitted from the positive aspects of said innovation.

131. This ignores fiscal issues: also, because they largely depend upon the regulatory categorisation.

132. The monetary history of the twentieth century shows that systems of fixed exchanges based on determining specific narrow bands wherein exchange rates may float—such as the 'gold exchange standard' designed in Bretton Woods, or the European ERM with its predecessors—may suffer greatly if threatened by external events, such as oil shocks or speculative attacks; yet they generally manage to ensure very long periods of stability.

133. This means that there is still long way to go. Opportunities and threats encompassed by cryptocurrencies need an even deeper investigation. The landscape is beautiful and appealing, yet its inhabitants are not always the best possible ones, including regulators with their lazy and often wrongheaded approach. In a famous Shakespeare's phrase: *O brave new world / That has such people in't!* (*The Tempest*, 1611; Act 5, Scene 1).

REFERENCES

Allen, M. 2019. "World's first crypto banks seen as game changer for Switzerland", appeared on *Swissinfo.ch* on 27 August.

Alpa, G. 1997. "La normativa sui dati personali. Modelli di lettura e problemi esegetici". *Il diritto dell'informazione e dell'informatica*.

Antonucci, A. 1994. "Gli intermediari finanziari «residuali» dalla legge antiriciclaggio al Testo unico delle leggi in materia bancaria e creditizia", *Rassegna economica*.

Avgouleas, E. and Kiayias, A., 2018. "The Promise of Blockchain Technology for Global Securities and Derivatives Markets: The New Financial Ecosystem and the 'Holy Grail' of Systemic Risk Containment", *Edinburgh School of Law Research Paper No. 2018/43*.

Baily, M. N. and Campbell, J. Y. and Cochrane, J. H. and Diamond, D. W. and Duffie, J. D. and French, K. R. and Kashyap, A. K. and Mishkin, F. S. and Scharfstein, D. S. and Shiller, R. J. and Slaughter, M. J. and Shin, H. S. and Stulz, R. M. 2013. "Aligning Incentives at Systemically Important Financial Institutions" *Columbia Business School Research Paper No. 13-18*.

Baily, M. N. and Campbell, J. Y. and Cochrane, J. H. and Diamond, D. W. and Duffie, J. D. and French, K. R. and Kashyap, A. K. and Mishkin, F. S. and Scharfstein, D. S. and Shiller, R. J. and Slaughter, M. J. and Shin, H. S. and Stein, J. C. and Stulz, R. M. 2011. "Reforming Money Market Funds" *Columbia Business School Research Paper No. 12-13.*

Bank of England 2020 "Central Bank group to assess potential cases for central bank digital currencies", 22 January

Barillà, G. 2015. "Il trasferimento dei servizi di pagamento", *Le Nuove leggi civili commentate.*

Basso, R. 2011. "Informazioni relative alle operazioni di pagamento e ai contanti", *La nuova disciplina dei servizi di pagamento,* Torino.

Baur, D. G. and Dimpfl, T. and Kuck, K. 2018. "Bitcoin, gold and the US dollar – A replication and extension", *Finance Research Letters.*

Bessone, M. 1978. "L'esperienza francese del diritto alla intimità della vita privata", *Politica del diritto.*

Bianca, C.M. 1999. "Esigenza di una disciplina uniforme delle obbligazioni pecuniarie", *Atti del Convegno su Aspetti giuridici dell'introduzione della moneta unica europea,* Roma, 19 May.

Bollen, R. A. 2013. "The Legal Status of Online Currencies: Are Bitcoins the Future?", *Journal of Banking and Finance Law and Practice.*

Brands, S. 1993. "Untraceable Off-line Cash in Wallets with Observers", *Advances In Cryptology-Crypto '93, Lecture Notes In Computer Science.*

Bullmann, D. and Klemm, J. and Pinna, A. 2018. "In search for stability in cryptoassets: Are stablecoins the solution?", *ECB Occasional Paper Series.*

Burchi, A. et al., 2019. "Financial Data Aggregation e Account Information Services", *Consob, Quaderni FinTech.*

Burilov, V., 2019. "Regulation of Crypto Tokens and Initial Coin Offerings in the EU", *European Journal of Comparative Law and Governance.*

Capriglione, F. 1975. "I surrogati della moneta nella vigente normativa del T.U. n. 204 del 1910 sugli Istituti di emissione", *Banca borsa titoli di credito.*

Carli, G. and Capriglione, F. 1981 "Inflazione e ordinamento giuridico", Milano.

Cawrey, D. 2014, "How Economist Milton Friedman Predicted Bitcoin".

Cecchetti, S. G. and McCauley, R. N. and McGuire, P. M. 2012. "Interpreting TARGET2 Balances", *BIS Working Paper No. 393*

Chaum D. and Pedersen T. P. 1992a. "Transferred Cash Grows in Size" *Advances In Cryptology-Eurocrypt '92.*

Chaum, D. 1985. "Security Without Identification: Transactions to Make Big Brother Obsolete" *Computing Machinery.*

Chaum, D. and Pedersen, T.D. 1992b. "Wallet Databases With Observers" *Advances In Cryptology--Crypto '92, Lecture Notes In Computer.*

Chaum, D. et al 1988. "Untraceable Electronic Cash" *Advances in Cryptology-crypto '88, lecture notes in computer science.*

Chohan, U.W. 2018. "Tethering cryptocurrencies to fiat Currencies without transparency: A case study", *SSRN Research Paper No. 3129978*.

Ciocca, P. 1973. "Note sulla politica monetaria italiana", *Lo sviluppo economico italiano*, Bari.

Clarich, M. 1996. "Diritto d'accesso e tutela della riservatezza: regole sostanziali e tutela processuale", *Diritto processuale amministrativo*.

Clarich, M. 2010. "L'armonizzazione europea dei servizi di pagamento: l'attuazione della direttiva 2007/64/CE", *Scritti in onore di Francesco Capriglione*, Padova.

Commission de Surveillance du Secteur Financier (CSSF), 2018. "Warning On Initial Coin Offerings ("Icos") And Tokens".

Committee on the Global Financial System and Financial Stability Board. 2017. "FinTech credit: Market structure, business models and financial stability implications".

Confederazione Svizzera – Working Group Blockchain / ICO 2018 "Consultation on the work of the Working Group Blockchain / ICO", August.

Consob 2018. "Lo sviluppo del FinTech. Opportunità e rischi per l'industria finanziaria nell'era digitale", 1st March.

Consob 2019. "Le offerte iniziali e gli scambi di cripto-attività. Documento per la Discussione".

Consolo, G. 1975. "Informazione, riservatezza e calcolatori elettronici. aspetti sociologici e giuridici", *Amministrazione e politica*.

Costi, R. 1993. "Servizi di pagamento: il controllo sugli enti produttori", *Banca borsa titoli di credito*.

Criscuolo, L. 2003. "Gli intermediari finanziari non bancari", Bari.

Dam, K. W. and Lin, H. S. 1996. "Cryptography's Role In Securing The Information Society" Danvers.

Dang, T. V. and Gorton, G. B. and Holmström, B. R. and Ordoñez, G. 2014 "Banks as Secret Keepers", *NBER Working Paper No. w20255*.

Davies, G. 2019. "How China dodged a trade war recession", appeared on *Financial Times*, 15 September 2019.

Di Maggio, M. and Egan, M. and Franzoni, F. A. 2019. "The Value of Intermediation in the Stock Market", *CEPR Discussion Paper No. DP13936*.

Diamond, D.W. 1984. "Financial intermediation and delegated monitoring", *The Review of Economic Studies*.

Dow, S. C. 2009. "David Hume and Modern Economics" *Capitalism and Society*.

Draghi, M. 2018. "Monetary policy in the euro area", *Speech by the President of the ECB, ECB Forum on Central Banking*, Sintra, 19 June.

Draghi, M. 2019. "Farewell Remarks".

Dyhrberg, A.H. 2016. "Bitcoin, gold and the dollar – a GARCH volatility analysis", *Finance Research Letters*.

EBA. 2019. *Report on crypto-assets*, available at *www.eba.europa.eu*

ECB 2019, "Crypto-assets – trends and implications", Bruxelles

ECB 2020, "Central bank group to assess potential cases for central bank digital currencies", Bruxelles 21 January

Eng, T. and Okamoto T. 1994. "Single-Term Divisib Electronic Coins" *Advances In Cryptology-Eurocrypt '94.*

ESMA. 2017a, "ESMA alerts investors to the high risks of Initial Coin Offerings (ICOs)".

ESMA. 2017b. "ESMA alerts firms involved in Initial Coin Offerings (ICOs) to the need to meet relevant regulatory requirements".

ESMA. 2019. "Advice on initial coin offerings and crypto-assets"

ESMA 2020. "Guidelines on securitisation repository data completeness and consistency thresholds". 17 January

EUCJ, Sec. V, 4 October 2018, n. 191, C-191/17, published in *Giurisprudenza commerciale*, 2019, with the comment of Greco, G. "Il conto che non opera con terzi non è un conto di pagamento. Note critiche alla sentenza C-191/17 della Corte di Giustizia dell'Unione Europea".

EUCJ, sect. III 11 September 2014, C-382/12 P, *Il Foro italiano*, 2015, pt. 4, c. 38 ss. and the comment of Granieri, M. "Diritto europeo. Pagamento tramite carte di credito: rispetto del regime della concorrenza ed applicazione di commissioni interbancarie multilaterali".

FASB. 2017. *Report of the Chairman*; EY 2018, IFRS (#). Accounting for Crypto-Assets, available at www.ey.com

Fenwick, M, and Kaal, W. A. and Vermeulen, E. P.M., 2017. "Regulation Tomorrow: What Happens When Technology is Faster than the Law?", *American University Business Law Review.*

Ferrarini, G. 2000 "Osservazioni in merito alla disciplina della concentrazione degli scambi azionari", *Banca impresa società.*

Ferretti, R. 2018. "Commento sub art. 126-decies", *Commentario al testo unico delle leggi n materia bancaria e creditizia*, Padova.

Ferri, G. B. 1982. "Persona e privacy", *Rivista del diritto commerciale.*

Financial Consumer Authority (FCA). 2017. "Consumer warning about the risks of Initial Coin Offerings ('ICOs')".

Finck, M. 2017. "Blockchains and Data Protection in the European Union" *Max Planck Institute for Innovation & Competition Research Paper No. 18-01.*

Flick G. M., 1988. "Informazione bancaria e giudice penale: presupposti di disciplina, problemi e prospettive", *Banca borsa e titoli di credito.*

Flick, G. M. 1991. "Insider trading: una tappa significativa -anche se controversa- della lunga marcia verso la trasparenza". *Rivista delle società.*

Friedman, M. and Schwartz, A.J. 1987, "Money in Historical Perspective", Chicago.

FSB. 2017a. "Chair's letter to G20 Finance Ministers and Central Bank Governors ahead of their Baden-Baden meeting", 17 March.

FSB. 2017b. "FinTech credit. Market structure, business models and financial sta-
bility implications". Report prepared by a Working Group established by the
Committee on the Global Financial System (CGFS) and the Financial Stability
Board (FSB), 22 May.

FSB 2020. "Global Monitoring Report on Non-Bank Financial Intermediation
2019", 19 January

Fullenkamp, C. and Nsouli, S. M. 2004. "Six Puzzles in Electronic Money and
Banking" *IMF Working Paper*.

G7. 2019. "Biarritz Strategy for an Open, Free and Secure Digital Transformation".

Gambaro, A. 1981. "Falsa luce agli occhi del pubblico", *Rivista di diritto civile*.

Ganguly, M. and Delaney, M. 2018. "Unregulated Financial Markets and the
Shadow Banking Narrative: China, India and the United States", *Market Express*.

Garonna, P. 2019. "Ethics from Within: A Paradigm Shift for Financial Ethics".

Stiglitz, J. E. 2017. "Where Modern Macroeconomics Went Wrong" *NBER
Working Paper No. w23795*.

Georgescu, M. and Georgescu, I. E. 2004. "The Emergence of Electronic Payment
Systems for the Growth of E-Business", *International Symposium Economics
and Management of Transformation*.

Goanta, C. 2018 "How Technology Disrupts Private Law: An Exploratory Study
of California and Switzerland as Innovative Jurisdictions", *Stanford-Vienna
TTLF Working Paper No. 38/2018*.

Grey, R. and Dharmapalan, J., 2017. "The Macroeconomic Policy Implications of
Digital Fiat Currency" *'The Case for Digital Legal Tender' Paper Series*.

Gupta, S. and Roy, A. K., 2011. "BRICS at the Gate: Modern International
Monetary System in Conditions of Balanced Uncertainty" *Journal of Emerging
Knowledge on Emerging Markets*.

Gurrea-Martínez, A. and Remolina, N. 2019. "The Law and Finance of Initial
Coin Offerings", *Ibero-American Institute for Law and Finance Working Paper
No. 4/2018*.

Haar, B. 2016. "Freedom of Contract and Financial Stability through the Lens of
the Legal Theory of Finance" (LTF) – LTF Approaches to ABS, Pari Passu-
Clauses, CCPs, and Basel III", *SAFE Working Paper No. 141*.

Haney, B. S. 2019. "Blockchain: Post-Quantum Security & Legal Economics",
SSRN Research Paper No. 3444695

Hansen L. P. 2019. "Reflection on MFR's conference on Cryptocurrencies and
Blockchains".

Hansen, A. H. 1953. "A Guide to Keynes", New York.

Harrod, R. F. 1969. "Money", London.

Hayek, F.A. 1976, "The Denationalization of Money", *Institute of Economic
Affairs*, London

Hayek, F.A. 1978. "Denationalization of Money: The Argument Refined",
Institute of Economic Affairs, London.

Hicks, J.R. 1937. "Mr. Keynes and the "classics"; a suggested interpretation", *Econometrica. Journal of the Econometric Society.*

Hicks, J.R. 1967. "Critical Essays in Monetary Theory", Oxford.

Holmstrom, B. 2015. "Understanding the Role of Debt in the Financial System", *BIS Working Paper No. 479.*

Holmström, B. R. 1989. "Agency Costs and Innovation", *Journal of Economic Behavior & Organization.*

Houben, R. and Snyers, A. 2018. "Cryptocurrencies and blockchain. Legal context and implications for financial crime, money laundering and tax evasion", European Parliament – Policy Department for Economic, Scientific and Quality of Life Policies – Directorate-General for Internal Policies.

Hristov, N. and Hülsewig, O. and Wollmershäuser, T. 2019. "Capital Flows in the Euro Area and TARGET2 balances", *Deutsche Bundesbank Discussion Paper No. 24/2019.*

Hume, D. 1748. "Of Interest", *Essays Moral and Political,* A. Millar, London.

Hussain, H. 2017. "Reinventing regulation: The curious case of taxation of cryptocurrencies in India", *NUJS Law Review.*

IFRS 2018, *IASB update January 2018,* available at *www.ifrs.org*

IFRS 2016, *Summary Note of the Accounting Standard Advisory Forum.*

IMF. 2016. "Virtual currencies and beyond: Initial considerations", *IMF Staff Discussion Note,* January.

Jevons, W.S. 1875. "Money and the Mechanism of Exchange", New York.

Kakushadze, Z. and Liew, J. K. S., 2018. "CryptoRuble: From Russia with Love", *World Economics.*

Kaplow, L. and Shavell, S. 1991. "Optimal Law Enforcement with Self-Reporting of Behavior", *NBER Working Paper No. w3822.*

Kristoufek, L. 2015. "What are the main drivers of the Bitcoin price? Evidence from wavelet coherence analysis", *PLoS One.*

Krugman, P.R. 2018. "Bubble, Bubble, Fraud and Trouble, appeared on *The New York Times,* 29 January.

Law, L. and Sabet, S. and Solinas, J. 1997. "How to make a mint. The cryptography of anonymous electronic cash" *American University Law Review.*

Lemma, V. 2015. "Too big to be popular", *La riforma delle banche popolari,* Padova.

Lemma, V. 2017. "Commento sub articolo 126 quinquies del d. lgs. 385 del 1993" "Codice commentato dei contratti", Padova.

Lemma, V. 2018. "Fintech regulation: The need for a research", *Open Review of Management, Banking and Finance*

Libertini, M. 2011. "Brevi note su concorrenza e servizi di pagamento", *Banca borsa e titoli di credito.*

Lo, S. and Wang, J. 2014. "Bitcoin as Money?", published by Federal Reserve Bank of Boston.

Lothian, T. 2010. "Law and Finance: A Theoretical Perspective" *Columbia Law and Economics Working Paper No. 388*

Lothian, T. 2011. "Rethinking Finance Through Law: A Theoretical Perspective", *Columbia Law and Economics Working Paper No. 412*

Lucantoni, P. 2018. "Commento sub art. 126-octies" *Commentario al testo unico delle leggi n materia bancaria e creditizia*, Padova.

Manaa, M. and others. 2019. "Crypto-Assets: Implications for Financial Stability, Monetary Policy, and Payments and Market Infrastructures", *ECB Occasional Paper No. 223.*

Marchetti, P. 1981. "Le offerte pubbliche di sottoscrizione e la legge 216" *Rivista delle società.*

Markesinis, B and Alpa, G. 1997. "Il diritto alla "privacy" nell'esperienza di "common law" e nell'esperienza italiana", *Rivista trimestrale di diritto e procedura civile.*

Mersch, Y. 2018. "Virtual or virtueless? The evolution of money in the digital age", *Lecture at the Official Monetary and Financial Institutions Forum*, London, 8 February.

Mersch, Y. 2019. "Money and private currencies: Reflections on Libra. Speech by Member of the Executive Board of the ECB", at the ESCB Legal Conference, Frankfurt am Main, 2 September.

Miller, S. M. and Ndhlela, T. 2019. "Money Demand and Seignorage Maximization before the End of the Zimbabwean Dollar" *Mercatus Research Paper no. 3329378.*

Minenna, M. 2019. "The New Eurozone Risk Morphology", *SSRN Research Paper No. 3341540.*

Minsky, H.P. 1986. "Stabilizing an Unstable Economy", New York.

Minto, A. 2017. "FinTech and the Hunting Technique": How to Hit a Moving Target", *Open Review of Management, Banking and Finance.*

Mundell, R.A. 1961, "A theory of optimum currency areas", *The American Economic Review.*

Nabilou, H. and Prum, A. 2018. "Ignorance, Debt and Cryptocurrencies: The Old and the New in the Law and Economics of Concurrent Currencies" *Journal of Financial Regulation.*

Nakamoto, S. 2008. "Bitcoin: A peer-to-peer electronic cash system", available at *www.bitcoin.org/bitcoin.pdf.*

Nelson, B. 2018. Financial stability and monetary policy issues associated with digital currencies, *Journal of Economics and Business.*

Niels, F. 1993. "Single Term Off-line Coins" *Advances In Cryptology-Eurocrypt '93.*

Nou, J. and Stiglitz, E., 2019 "Regulatory Bundling", *Yale Law Journal.*

OECD. 2018. "How to deal with Bitcoin and other cryptocurrencies in the System of National Accounts?" Meeting of the Working Party on Financial Statistics, 5 November.

Ofek, E. and Richardson, M. 2003. "Dotcom mania: The rise and fall of internet stock prices" *The Journal of Finance.*

Okamoto T. 1995 "An Eficient Divisible Electronic Cash Scheme" *Advances In Cryptology-Crypto '95.*

Okamoto, T. and Ohta, K. 1991. "Universal Electronic Cash", *Advances in Cryptology-Crypto '91, Lecture Notes in Computer Science.*

Olivieri, G. 2001. "Appunti sulla moneta elettronica. Brevi note in margine alla direttiva 2000/46/CE riguardante gli istituti di moneta elettronica", *Banca borsa titoli di credito.*

Paganelli M. P. 2006 "Endogenous Money and David Hume" *Eastern Economic Journal.*

Pasquini, N. 1983. "Identità personale e lesione della reputazione: appunti in margine ad alcune recenti sentenze. Nota a Trib. Roma 10 marzo 1982" *Giurisprudenza italiana.*

Peters, G. and Vishnia, G. 2016a. "Blockchain Architectures for Electronic Exchange Reporting Requirements: EMIR, Dodd Frank, MiFID I/II, MiFIR, REMIT, Reg NMS and T2S" *SSRN Research Paper no. 2832604.*

Peters, G. and Vishnia, G. 2016b. "Overview of Emerging Blockchain Architectures and Platforms for Electronic Trading Exchanges", *SSRN: Research Paper No. 2867344.*

Phillips, R.C. and Gorse, D. 2017. "Predicting cryptocurrency price bubbles using social media data and epidemic modelling", *IEEE Symposium Series on Computational Intelligence (SSCI).*

Rispoli Farina, M. 2015. "Informazione e servizi di pagamento", *Analisi giuridica dell'economia.*

Rogers, J. S. 2005. "The New Old Law of Electronic Money" *SMU Law Review.*

Rothbard, M.N. 1963, "America's Great Depression", New York.

Sabett, R. V. 1996. "International Harmonization In Electronic Commerce And Electronic Data Interchange: A Proposed First Step Toward Signing On The Digital Dotted" *American University Law Review.*

Savona, P. 1974. "La sovranità monetaria", Rome;

Sciarrone Alibrandi, A. 2008. "L'adempimento dell'obbligazione pecuniaria tra diritto vivente e portata regolatoria indiretta della Payment services directive 2007/64/CE", "Il nuovo quadro normativo comunitario dei servizi di pagamento. Prime riflessioni", *Quaderni di Ricerca Giuridica della Banca d'Italia n. 63.*

Scitovsky, T. 1969. "Money and the balance of payments", *The Economic Journal.*

Shackelford, J. and Myers, S. 2017. "Block-by-block: Leveraging the power of blockchain technology to build trust and promote cyber peace", *Yale Journal of Law and Technology.*

Shamir, A. 2013. "Quantitative analysis of the full bitcoin transaction graph" "Financial Cryptography and Data Security" Berlin-Heidelberg.

Shavell, S. 2003 "Economic Analysis of the General Structure of the Law", *Harvard Law and Economics Discussion Paper No. 408.*

Shavell, S. 2004. "Foundations of economic analysis of law", Harvard.

Shiller, R. J. 2013 "Reflections on Finance and the Good Society" *Cowles Foundation Discussion Paper No. 1894*.

Shiller, R. J., 2014. "Speculative Asset Prices (Nobel Prize Lecture)" *Cowles Foundation Discussion Paper No. 1936*.

Shiller, R.J. 2000. "Irrational Exuberance", Princeton.

State Secretariat for International Financial Matters (SIF). 2018. "Blockchain/ICO working group established". Bern, 18 Jannuary

Swiss Federal Council, 2014. *Federal Council report on virtual currencies in response to the Schwaab (13.3687) and Weibel (13.4070) postulates*, 25 June.

Taskinsoy, J. 2019. "Facebook's project Libra: Will Libra sputter out or spur central banks to introduce their own unique cryptocurrency projects?", *SSRN Research Paper No. 3423453*.

Tiwari, N. 2018. "The Commodification of Cryptocurrency". *Michigan Law Review*, p. 611 ff.

Trautman, L.J. 2014. "Virtual currencies; Bitcoin & what now after Liberty Reserve, Silk Road, and Mt. Gox?", *Richmond Journal of Law and Technology*.

Troiano, V. 2001. "Gli istituti di moneta elettronica", *Quaderni di ricerca giuridica della Consu-lenza Legale. Banca d'Italia*, Roma.

Troiano, V. 2019. "Gli istituti di moneta elettronica", *Manuale di diritto bancario e finanziario*, Padova.

Tully, E. and Lucey, B. 2007. "A power GARCH examination of the gold market", *Research in International Business and Finance*.

US SEC. 2019 "SEC Orders Blockchain Company to Pay $24 Million Penalty for Unregistered ICO", Sept. 30.

Van Loo, R. 2018. "Making Innovation More Competitive: The Case of Fintech", *UCLA Law Review*.

Venter, H. 2016, "Digital currency – a case for standard setting activity. A perspective by the Australian Accounting Standards Board", AASB, available at *www.aasb.gov.au*

World Bank 2018. "Cryptocurrencies and blockchain", available at www.documents.worldbank.org

Wright, A. and De Filippi, P. 2018. "Blockchain and the Law: The Rule of Code", Harvard Cambridge (MS).

Zalduendo, J., 2006. "Determinants of Venezuela's Equilibrium Real Exchange Rate" *IMF Working Paper*.

Zaring, D. and Bignami, F. 2016. "Comparative Law and Regulation. Understanding the Global Regulatory Process". Northampton, MA, USA.

Zeno Zencovich, V. 1983. "Telematica e tutela del diritto all'identità personale" *Politica del diritto*.

Zeno-Zencovich V. and Zoppini A. 1992. "La disciplina dei servizi telematici nel quadro delle proposte comunitarie di tutela dei dati personali", *Il diritto dell'informazione e dell'informatica*.

CHAPTER 8

Fintech, Regtech and Suptech Towards a New Market Structure

The contents of this chapter aim at highlighting the influence of the regulation of fintech on the credit-transformation processes that find direct execution by means of algorithms and software. This would point out the rules that are transforming the capital market from a place for challenging to a place for unification. Hence, it will focus on the importance of questioning the principles of supervision in the perspective of a new market structure (based on high-tech solutions), where the current regulation intertwines a link between mutualism and competition, whereby the fintech would be able to support the reciprocal influence of sharing economy and financial mercantilism.

Indeed, the findings shown in the previous chapters suggest to focus on the high-tech operational forms that can make the capital digitally circulate from subjects in surplus to others in deficit according to different parameters from those established by prudential supervision (and, more in general, of the traditional public intervention of oversight on credit and money). This would suggest to have regard for the role of the policymakers, regulators and supervisors, given their influence on the fintech business, the market functioning and the relevant transactions. In conclusion, the government seems to be the arbiter that will set the shape that finance is assuming because of fintech, more than the influencer that will lead finance to higher standards of technological efficiency.

© The Author(s) 2020
V. Lemma, *FinTech Regulation*,
https://doi.org/10.1007/978-3-030-42347-6_8

8.1   Overview

Every new beginning comes from some other beginning's end. Bearing in mind the beginning of the deregulation process aimed at entrusting the privates with the duty to manage financial markets, as well as the supervision interventions aimed at preventing any conversation between people that ends in a conspiracy against the public, or in some contrivance to raise prices (Lemma, V. 2016), the current beginning relies on the unveiling of technological mechanisms behind the adoption of choices, even if codified within algorithms and software (FSB 2020).[1] This calls for actions on the supervision of self-decision mechanisms in corporate governance, which is not relying on human decision-making processes, but on self-executing and pre-programmed flows able to collect inputs, move to the next stage and then produce an output (Capriglione F. and Sacco Ginevri, A. 2019). Hence, there is the need for questioning the current supervisors' organizational structures and action plans, as they have been configured in the 'short twentieth century' to supervise human-driven entities authorized to perform reserved activities (Lagarde, C. 2018). Hereafter, it follows the request to policymakers to adopt a new form of supervision customized for fintech, able to control the algorithms and modify their essence by introducing self-executing constraints, limits, controls and security measures.

From a regulatory perspective, this intervention relies on the public duty to protect the fundamental rights from any misconduct, even if executed by artificial instruments.[2] Hence, at this stage of the analysis, it is worth investigating whether the policymaker can consider fintech as a *mere* technological shift able to affect the internal market, the circulation of capitals and the financial operations. As anticipated, all the above is enough to start questioning the regulators' attitude to structure supervisors by mirroring supervised (Lagarde, C. 2020).

In brief, the analysis of the evolution of the European regulation (about the internal market for capitals, banking and financial services) is aimed at verifying whether the relevant rules are suitable for an offering that is the outcome of a chain made by fintech firms; whether any operator may not be able to assess the reliability of the other parties of such chain. This should reflect one of the negative externalities of a high-integrated market, and not only as a consequence due to the absence of an adequate infrastructure and public registers (Lane, P. R. 2020).[3]

Considering the results shown in the previous chapters, the possibility to offer such outputs results from the deregulation process begun in the twentieth century. Hence, the need for recalling the evidences that the fintech environment is becoming an incubator for a large number of firms aimed at playing in the shadow banking system does not surprise. In particular, all the above refers to the need for understanding if and how the internal rules of any supervised entity entitle (or not) the managers to override automatic tools and self-executing processes, and that contingency plans and exit strategies enable (or not) supervised entities to close fintech outsourcing without jeopardizing their business (De Guindos, L. 2019).[4] In the absence of this possibility (of overriding), the human intervention is limited to the initial decision to adopt fintech tools, and then there would be no reason for supervising humans rather than focusing on the algorithms and software. Thus, as anticipated, these findings on the need that the regulator extends the scope of supervision to programmers and coders.

All the above highlights the most relevant reasons for regulating fintech by means of rules aimed at driving any financial operator to the safe and sound management of capitals (Brogi, M. 2019). Indeed, the current regulatory framework does not seem to be sufficient to prevent a new turbulence due to the functioning of the fintech tools (and—as anticipated in the previous chapters—it does not consider the correlation in the decisions adopted by software, the aggregate amount of losses due to high number of small value recurring inefficiencies and the unexpected outcome from intelligent robotics, artificial deep neural networks, machine learning and meta-heuristics optimization) (ESMA 2019).[5]

According to the above, a certain degree of competition is essential to the innovative process among both programmers (in offering fintech solutions) and users (within their final market). This suggests to assume that the competition–innovation link is positive, so that the efficiencies of innovation provide another reason for supporting the need for competition-enhancing reforms.

Consequently, the regulation of fintech would drive to the clarification that this phenomenon must fall within the scope of public intervention, which is required for minimizing the negative effects of market and technical failures. Difficulties in this direction would be related to the costs of the investments required for building the supervisory infrastructure; hence, the need for balancing the principle of prudence (in containing the risks due to innovations) with the will to promote the progress.[6] Moreover, this does not claim for *regtech* or *suptech*, which—as next paragraphs will show better than the previous chapters—would not provide a solution for the efficiency of the public intervention (IMF 2020),[7] and probably would raise the additional question of the accountability of the programmers in charge of elaborating the software required for automated regulation and supervision.

8.2   REGTECH

Shall policymakers restructure the public supervision by mirroring the fintech entities? As remarked above, it is not predicable how firms will exploit AI to fight the next competition for raising capital in the financial market, but it is acknowledged that—after that challenge—firms will fight the following one for trust. It refers to the trust in the capacity of the financial markets to fulfill investors' needs and to enact their rights, by means of efficient infrastructures and mechanisms, provided that supervisors will oversight the micro- and macro-prudential risks (Chatterjee, S. and Jobst, A. A. 2019).

It is worth highlighting that, in the twentieth century, the regulatory intervention did not force the market operators to standardize their practice and to share their innovations, above and beyond the market produced high level of standardization, as a positive externality of constraints, safeguards and backstops (aimed at protecting savers, consumers, welfare and stability). However, such intervention has promoted the application of common methodologies to comply with new requirements (as was the case of the ancillary service undertakers in the context of CRD V and CRR II mentioned in the previous chapters) (EBA 2020a).[8]

That said, it is necessary to verify if there is a regulatory structure that is more efficient than others in supporting the supervision over fintech. In this respect, the analysis should move from the consideration that the application of technology is based on a set of instructions or rules that will help to execute a process, and that this application can also affect both regulation and supervision.[9] Hence the interest for regtech and suptech, for the use of technology to optimize regulatory intervention and make operational processes and controls more effective and efficient (EBA 2020b).

With regard to what has been outlined so far, it is useful to turn the attention to the unstoppable progress of bureaucratic automation.

Moreover, it is not difficult to share the belief that there is nothing in the world that works as precisely as a software.[10] If the analysis looks at a purely technical and efficient administration, at a precise and accurate fulfilment of tasks, as the only purpose of the regulation and supervision, then it will be sufficient to establish an algorithm and a bureaucratic hierarchy that objectively regulates the execution (with precision and without a soul). In this respect, the technical superiority of automatisms is unquestionable when a bureaucratic mechanism is implemented, but neither can the limits of the application of purely technical criteria be questioned. In the regulation of the market, every single intervention is commensurate in a rational calculation and, to an increasing extent, tends towards a type of development that in every point follows exactly this calculation.

Now, regulators are primarily questioning not how something can be changed in the technological development of finance, but what will result from this development.[11]

As anticipated in the previous chapters, the research has approached fintech evolution by considering the positive externalities of the application of its technical foundations to the public intervention, as well as the possibility that its tools would foster both the envisaged financial stability and the concrete market outcome. In this perspective, all the above had begun verifying whether the current institutions can play their part in assessing the main threats of the aforesaid development.

First of all, it has been highlighted that the current set up of competent authorities shows a growing interest for a methodology that mixes economic knowledge, regulatory capabilities and technical skills, but it seems to be far from developing algorithms and moreover to incorporate them in self-executing tools (to be provided by regulators to the market operators or applied by supervisors in their inspections and controls).

All the above leads to focus on regtech solutions based on the most advanced calculation algorithms, the use of artificial intelligence and the ability to obtain real time responses. This is not referring to the use of technology for compliance that predates the financial crisis of 2007 but to radical changes in compliance and supervision work of banks and financial institutions. In this respect, the attention to the widespread use of cloud computing, the increased acceptance of Application Programming Interfaces (APIs) and advances in the fields of Artificial Intelligence and Machine Learning (AI/ML) helps in understanding that the ethical quality of the machine today plays a very important role in these aspects. A question therefore arises as to the type of organization that should prevail:

an expansion of pure business capitalism, a market governed by the human-driven supervisory authorities, or a system ethically correct by a self-executing bureaucracy based on predictive systems.

Focusing on the market for regtech, ESMA showed that, on the one hand, demand is linked to regulatory changes and the need of market participants and supervisors to process large amounts of data; on the other, supply factors primarily focus on advances in technology (ESMA 2018).[12] Moreover, regulators are looking for specific application of data analytics, as the technology underlying fintech can be used to make the output of the regulatory production (*i.e.* the rules themselves) more effective, and then able to improve surveillance and reduce the compliance costs imposed on supervised entities. It is clear that, provided the possibility to exploit automation, any alternative would be more expensive, drive towards a net loss of economic value, and then lead to a market failure.

A regulatory platform is by no means impossible. There is no doubt that the material (social and financial) problems are decisive in its construction and the same presents itself in such an imprecise form that in the beginning it will be possible to devote itself only to marginal operations, of no systemic importance and of a purely technical nature. Hence, the interest goes to the application of AI/ML to perform institutional tasks, by means of software able to run within the operational system of the supervised entities to *detect* any kind of misconduct or fraud. Thus, the need to establish a right of access, as well as a level playing field for open innovation.

The authorities, which are politically unprepared and with resources committed to current activities, are now faced with the task of replacing something new and different from the institutional response to the financial crisis of 1929 and 2009. Although this problem seems to have been defined today, it is useful to repeat a question on the set up of the trading venues as regulated or competitive markets. Considering only the technical aspects of such question, regulation and finance can cooperate by means of a continuous technological exchange of data and rules, both able to self-execute themselves and prevent any firm to breach any rule, as well as any event that is able to adversely affect a number of systemically important intermediaries or markets (including potentially related infrastructures).[13]

8.3   Suptech

The great dichotomy between public and private is at the center of Western political and social thought, through a continuous use of the same to delimit, represent and order the field of investigation. As the first refers to "quod ad statum rei romanae spectat" and the second to "quod ad singolorum unitatem",[14] the supervisors are in front of two spheres, jointly exhaustive and mutually exclusive.[15]

In the legal order, the distinction between public and private reflects the protection of the global society and its individual members, and suggests the affirmation of the supremacy of the first over the second, which is accompanied by the assessment of the "*utilitas*" with respect to the society or to the citizen.[16] Hence, supervisors duplicate this dichotomy by distinguishing between the intervention over *equals* and *unequals*, provided that the market society, in the idealization of classical economists, is usually elevated to a model of a private sphere as opposed to the public sphere, characterized by equal and coordinated relations.

In this context, the application of high-tech mechanisms will lead supervisors' software to control supervised entities' software. And this suggests a new kind of relationship, whereby software-to-software relations will follow the path set by their programmers and coders. Thus, there is a relevant distinction between the sources of the market rules: the law and the contract, but the algorithm too.

This is not questioning if suptech is based on the joint application of two sources (the law and the algorithm), but the different ways in which both come into existence as binding rules of conduct: the law is set by the political authority and the algorithm is the set of operations that a private individual establishes to regulate a flow.[17] The intersection of the two dichotomies public/private and law/algorithm reveals all its explicative force in suptech, for which software becomes the typical form by which authorities and individuals regulate their relations in the market of a civil society (that is the society whose components are held together by an authoritativeness superior to individuals).[18]

In turn, in the fintech environment, the contraposition between supervision and the market—as a contraposition of the behaviours regulated by the law and free contractual relations—passes from the distinction between vigilantes and supervised persons, so that only the law can be taken as the basis of public intervention, because the link that binds the State to its citizens is permanent, immanent and imperative; so that only the State can demand from its citizens a sacrifice of their own individual utilities.[19] Hence, the right to command and be obeyed, whose referral to an automatic mechanism of supervision cannot in any way be interpreted as a renunciation by the public of the control over the private sector.

However, the abovementioned technologies have the potential to reshape the relationship between supervisors and market participants.[20] It refers to the use of innovative technology by supervisory agencies to support human-driven supervision, to develop self-executing controls (by means of machine-learning processes), and to monitor the risk and implement automatic backstops.[21] Indeed, nowadays, suptech concerns both data collection and data analytics, and it is based on the algorithms codified by programmers entrusted by the relevant authorities or acquired in the market for high-tech solutions.[22] This raises an issue related to the lawfulness of such basis, as well as the issue of its justification: even if the supervisor has the power to control the financial entities, is this enough to use algorithms, artificial intelligence and self-executing tools?

This question should have two answers according to its interpretation as a question on what suptech is or what suptech does. In this perspective, effectiveness and lawfulness of suptech refers to the axiological distinction between the entity that programs the software and the one that runs it. Therefore, the usual justification according to which the supreme power (which is the political one) must have an ethical justification recalls principles of legitimacy, that is, of the various ways in which a software can be introduced in the financial market that imposes to command, to those who hold the power of intervention, and to obey, to those who are subjected to it.

Assuming that suptech would increase the efficiency of a regulated market, the possibility to explore the potential benefits of its applications requires data availability and data quality, as well as accountable software and analytical resources. However, an action plan would be useful to inform the market participants on how the supervisors will reach the full implementation of its new form of oversight. Within the framework of a legal approach, considering the regulatory solutions put in place by the regulator and made effective by the supervisors, the issue of the legitimacy of suptech is oriented towards the reasons of its efficiency and effectiveness. In fact, the legitimacy of such a choice derives from the latter. In this direction, suptech can take on a form of legitimate power, as a power that is able to condition the behaviour of market participants by issuing commands whose content is considered as a rule of conduct.

Now it is significant that supervision is considered also as a *regime* characterized by the goals it aims at achieving (Pellegrini, M. 2018; Sepe, M. 2018). Hence, a distinction between a formal suptech and a substantial suptech should be introduced, where the first concerns the form of the high-tech mechanisms used to supervise the market participants and the second refers to its contents.

Moreover, with respect to the form of fintech, it should be considered that according to the current European regulatory framework, a service needs to be provided normally in exchange for remuneration in order to fall within the scope of the definition of electronic communications service.[23] In this respect, the European regulator considered that the digital economy is based on the assumption that any market participant can share information, and this sharing can have a monetary value. In particular, the supervision has to consider that electronic services are often supplied to the end-user not only for money but increasingly and in particular for the provision of personal data or other data. This is not denying that a market participant may be a sort of product himself/herself (any time his/her counterparties accept his/her behaviour as a payment). On the contrary, the relevant doubt refers to the suitability of the concept of remuneration, which should be restated or substituted by another one able to encompass situations where the provider requests and the end-user consents the aforesaid sharing. Obviously, in this perspective, the automation of sharing of certain data (*i.e.* identity, IP address, data volume, …) should be considered as an automation of payments, with obvious effects on the affairs (that would include also the underlying flows that are not placed under the direct control of the providers and the end-users).[24]

Concluding on this point, it is useful to consider the possibility of automation in dispute resolutions. It refers to the development of artificial intelligence, and its applications in the field of predictive justice. In particular, provided the possibility that the policymakers will entrust the competent authorities to develop software to regulate and supervise market participants, it is expected that this would lead to the application of predictive analytics in both understanding the rule applicable to any fact, and gaining reliable predictions on the outcome of the proceedings.

In this respect, the dynamics of algorithms can describe the judgement of the supervisor by implementing a simple path, which begins with the identification of the pertinent precedent, the rule of law, the comparability of the matter considered in that precedent case (with respect to legal foundations, size, externalities, *etc.*), the application of the relevant rule and the prediction of a possible solution to the base question. Obviously, if any of this step does not find a satisfactory solution, the sequence will be repeated. All of the above is under the constraints that a *verdict-decision-judgement-ruling* (or any other outcome is under consideration) is not the result of a mechanistic process.

According to the above, it is possible to rely on this model to describe the foundation of a supervisory decisional procedure that does not reproduce the way 'how judges think', but the path of a predictive analysis that can support the duty of regulation and control that burden over financial supervisors.[25] This suggests to postpone to the conclusion any consideration on the role of artificial intelligence and predictive justice in the financial industry, due to the fact that the possibility to formulate exact expectations on the outcome of a dispute (or a settlement) affects the set of forecasts made by economic operators, on the basis of their own information and intuitions, regarding the trend of economic variables in the future; thus, the effective possibility of 'rational expectations' and then the exact forecast of price movements.[26]

All the above is not going to face the questions on the 'robotic reasoning', nor the ones on the ethics of 'artificial intelligence'; however, it is necessary to understand if the decision of relying on the strict application of rules and precedents complies with the current democratic set-up of justice, and the social role of the judges. *De l'esprit des lois* has marked a line, which has been followed by the scholars who developed the juridical system as it is. Now, the application of technology to the legal reasoning would mark another line, whose direction suggests the development of a technical-scientific *apparatus* within which men are destined to operate.[27]

Indeed, this analysis is questioning that the predictive justice would bring the past into the future, whose needs refer to new paradigms, social behaviours and preferences (affected by the technology itself). The question, in the financial market, is dual because it is the tradition of this environment, and of the relative judicial 'appendix', the mediation of the administrative measure, the expression of a power in the technical sense, which characterizes the relations between operator and regulated market. In this context, the intersubjective relationship is established in view of a transaction (usually in the context of a composite affair) or even after the transaction has been concluded. Consequently, the way in which the power is exercised, including the way in which the decision is taken, is of central importance because of or in view of the decision that the interests of private individuals and the supervisory authorities themselves are organized. And it is on the decision or with a view to a decision that the following predictive judgment takes place.[28]

All the above refers both to the decision on what to do and the decision on what should have been done, provided that in the financial markets there is an administrative intervention ex-ante (e.g. in case of a licensing) and ex-post (e.g. in case of a doubtful business conduct). In both cases, the advantages of automation are evident with reference to serial or standardized procedures (*i.e.* those characterized by a high rate of constraint or based on presumptions significant to a certain requirement).

It is necessary to remember that algorithms govern many market operations based on consensus (in which the parties accept in advance the rules of the game and 'trust' the algorithms). However, the intersubjective relationship between private and supervisor is not based on consensus, which may exist but which is normally extraneous to the structure of the administrative relationship. On the contrary, the supervisory authority is bound to a position of *impartiality* according to fundamental rules and democratic principles (which direct its action towards predetermined ends).[29] In this context, the algorithm at the basis of the robotic decision must first be 'knowable', i.e. 'transparent' in all its steps: from the professionalism of its authors to the reliability procedure used for its design, including the priorities assigned in the evaluation and decision-making procedure and the data selected as relevant.

Finally, the question arises whether the process of constructing the algorithm, and in any case the automated procedure, can be imposed by the legislator—which chooses a given valuable social experience—or evaluated by the supervisors from time to time according to paradigms based on technical discretion.

8.4   FINTECH INNOVATIONS IN BANKING AND BANK'S GOVERNANCE

Analyzing technology as a 'market mover' suggests considering that the challenge in the industry is occurring—not only for capital, raw material or services, but also—for technology and mutualistic connections among banks, financial intermediaries, providers, customers, and so on.[30] Platforms and other developments of the sharing economy show that a firm, in the fintech environment, is not only an organization that transforms inputs into outputs but also an entity that intertwines its relations along networks, webs and any other kind of connections.

At this stage of the analysis, it is clear that networks allow the wide-spreading of both big data and technology, and these networks cross any jurisdiction in order to unbundle and offshore activities that substitute banking and financial servicing. It is also clear that a strict interpretation of the current regulatory frameworks would suggest that technology-enabled innovation does not result in new activities (outside of the scope of the above rules), but refers to the relevant reserved activity (which includes any innovative business models based on applications, processes, or products that go beyond the operative standards of traditional banks and intermediaries), even if the performance of this activity is made by the intervention of various firms, jointly involved in the circulation of capital by means of an open network of entities and relations.[31]

From this perspective, even if all the above is suggesting that a new open form of banking arises, this sort of 'open banking' has to be supervised (as a part of the wider definition of banking).[32] However, this does not compensate the benefits of reserving such activity to an intermediary. In particular, it is worth recalling that unless an intermediary had a legally protected interest in funding and lending from the people, there would be diminished incentive to invest in developing the organizational structure required for assessing the creditworthiness and managing the relevant risks.

Moreover, in regulating 'open banking' it should be bore in mind that users who have access to commonly owned resources, typically tend to misuse them[33]; on the contrary, supervised intermediaries, because of their strict approach to lending, are endowed with the right to deal only with trusty borrowers. Hence, it is easy to understand that 'open banking' requires both incentives to pursue social wealth and constraints to limit risk-taking. Accordingly the current need for transparency regards both the network and the circulation of financial information.

What fintech leads to question is why firms still exist, what determines their number, what they do, will they survive to automation. As anticipated in the previous chapters, 'fintech-ing' one or more business units consists not only in reaching an agreement between a bank and an outsourcer (who wish to establish and regulate their legal relationship for the technical development of certain processes), but also in the exploitation of smart-tools that extends their economic function to areas that goes under the scrutiny of public oversight. Henceforth, in the application of fintech by means of outsourcing strategies, the bank should consider the limits that the supervisory system imposes on the exercise of its activities, in order to compose the interests that qualify this industry, and to reach a voluntary collaboration that is in line with the quantum authorized by the supervisory authority. This places the relevance of fintech between the provision of the 'service' and the negotiation of the relevant 'contract', with duties of conduct that reflects the complexity of the contributions owed by these special service providers.

It is acknowledged that most of the intermediation is going to take place by means of fintech solutions, and the efficiency of the whole capital market may depend to a very considerable extent on the process enwrapped within the relevant algorithms. It is worth recalling that, to its advocates, this wave of innovation promises that customers will get more choice, better-targeted services and keener pricing; at the same time, small- and medium-sized businesses will get access to new credit and banks will become more productive (with lower transaction costs, greater capital efficiency and stronger operational resilience). Indeed, the financial system itself will become more resilient with greater diversity, redundancy and depth (Carney, M. 2017).

Considering the difficulties of retail banking in ensuring safety and providing returns (in terms of interest rates), the competition brought by market-based finance would offer to consumers the possibility to be, at the same time, the customers of a bank and the end-users of a platform supporting peer-to-peer lending (facing risks that retail banks cannot afford). Thus, fintech offers an alternative to traditional banking because it not only reduces the costs of using the price mechanisms and carrying out a market transaction but also allows the access to the shadow banking system.

In this respect, the role of technology in the randomization of returns and risks play a central role. In the functioning of fintech, the machine learning paradigm relies on the adversary's gaining intelligence about one's own mode of play—to prevent his/her deductive anticipation of how one may make up one's own mind, and to protect oneself from any adversary's anticipation (Schelling, T. C. 1980).[34]

According to the above, it should be borne in mind that the events of this period are at the origin of phenomenology of the crisis and suggestive projects of individual and collective emancipation. Effective proposals are put forward to make the credit offered and allowed more inclusive and less risky, as well as circumstantial programme to. In brief, it seems that any credit institution may be forced to escape from the multiple and successive structures that closely support and tighten banking (as a sort of prison and sanctuary at the same time): individual identity, internal organization, the market, the supervision.

8.5   Fintech Innovations in Asset Management

The shadowy role of the financial market refers to both the need of investor to store value and the need of firms to find a source of money alternative to banking. Therefore, at this stage of the analysis, it is possible to summarize the aforesaid findings with respect to the application of fintech solutions to asset management, and their impact on 'open market operations'. Although the use of software refers both to the advisory and the management, it is clear that it affects more the latter, because in the former the final decision remains with the investors, while in the latter the intermediary is responsible for carrying out the choice of any transaction and the timing to execute it.[35]

It is clear that the professionalism of the asset managers and the supervisors has to ensure that 'private fortunes' are safely invested (in manufactures, commerce and other useful pursuits and are not "at the mercy of avaritious adventurers … who burthen all the interchanges of property with their swindling profits, profits which are the price of no useful industry, of theirs", provided that "prudent men must be on their guard in this game", as in an 1814 letter Thomas Jefferson complained and advised about the financial sector of his day) (Jefferson, T. 1814).

Anyone should be aware that exchanging *paper* or *bits* cannot make profits for everyone, and—accordingly to the economists—it is very likely that much of his exchange "represents not the creation of new wealth but the sector's appropriation of wealth created elsewhere in the economy" (Kay, J. 2015). Nonetheless, according to such doctrine, the process of 'financialization' has created a sector that is hypertrophied (in respect of people's needs), abstract (and divorced from the real economy), aimed at multiplying the remuneration of its members (and not at increasing the common welfare). However, the role of public supervision is to avoid these results and maintain finance as a tool to support investors to store value and firms to collect money. All the rest is an externality that has to be managed by authorities, and that has to be regulated, controlled, minimized or banned by the public intervention (as the result of the relevant economic analyses would suggest to policymakers).

In asset management, long-term relationships cannot be reduced to short-term transactions, so open-end funds can invest in liquid assets, as well as closed-end funds can participate in long-term operation of debt, private equity, real estate.[36] The result is that the fund's rules set forth an investment policy and the legislator reserves to one kind of supervised entity (*i.e.* the asset managers) the business of executing it. Obviously, the regulatory framework does not ban a change in the fund's policy, but it requires the consensus of a qualified majority of the fund's participants (Lemma, V. 2015).

Hence, in this perspective, any investment policy is made by a set of instructions that limits the discretion of the manager; such set of instructions can be enriched to become an algorithm, and then it can be executed by software and any machine learning tool would suggest to the investors any specific change (to the investment policy of the fund) that would be useful to improve the possibility to reach the objective of the relevant fund.

It is worth considering that the application of such technology may be direct or indirect, by the use of fintech firms as third-party suppliers. It is acknowledged that the organizational structure of the asset managers generally provides the use of professional outsourcers, and that the internal functions are focused on the financial aspects of the business; however, the power to take any investment decision remains with the board of directors. In this respect, the role of humans reflects the need to fill in the gaps (and understand what in the policies is not written), to make the indivisible actions divisible or incommensurate objects homogeneous.

This analysis is not calling for "flipping coins" or playing "double or nothing" (that also a software is able to do), but it refers to the capacity to use the professionalism to execute the instructions written by the manger and approved by the investors.[37] Henceforth, the automation of such stages requires that every aspect of the investment policy or any other feature of asset manager activities can in principle be so precisely described that a machine can execute it. Thus, this does not refer to the possibility that software can imitate human intelligence (being human-like rather than becoming human), because humans enacting investment policies follow a path (disclosed and agreed with investors at the time of the subscription of the fund's units) and do not exercise their full capacity to invest. Perhaps, it refers to the capability of a machine to imitate intelligent human behaviour of an asset manager, and so to perform the relevant tasks that such asset manager has included in its program of activities.

This leads to a system that can work without figuring out how human reasoning works (a sort of 'weak AI'). Hence, an asset manager seems to be in the position to develop its business by means of machine-learning systems that do not imitate humans but are dedicated to solving cognitive problems commonly associated with investment activities (such as gaining information, problem solving, and pattern recognition), in order to grow their business, improve customer experience and selection, and optimize investment's execution speed and quality.

Obviously, one step behind the aforesaid system, there is the software that supports the human resources of an asset manager, whose tasks are limited to create a smarter environment and an useful support for the people entrusted with the execution of the fund's investment policies. This includes also the open platforms for identifying aspirational suppliers and demanders (as the marketplace for eligible assets does), as well as the structuring of specific vehicles.[38]

Provided that UCITS Directive and AIFMD set out conditions and procedures for the authorization required to operate in this sector,[39] the monitoring of fintech has pointed out a set of innovations that goes under the umbrella definition of 'digital portfolio management', which includes tools for algorithmic trading, digital ID verification, predictive/descriptive/prescriptive analytics, algorithmic trading tools and others.[40] We expect that these innovations may reduce competition (because of the internal features of the relevant software, able to align the output of the firms that use it), hence the need for specific safeguards, in order to prevent market failures and unfair conducts. Moreover, the regulators have to consider the need for greater clarity around the governance and risk-management processes associated with both cyber security and cloud outsourcing, and then have to provide technical standards able to identify a coherent and resilient system of infrastructures and software (that is neutral for the purposes of financial supervision).

This part of the research is within one of the theoretical areas with the highest concentration of problems, which collects and filters—after the great historical fractures introduced on the traditional parameters of banking—the most persuasive arguments in favour of or against modernity and technology. Within it, management strategies for dealing with macroscopic transformations and conflicts not yet identified in their nature and implications are envisaged. From this focal point, ideas and operative forms radiate outwards, proposing alternatives and knots that have yet to be unraveled.

8.6   Fintech Innovations in Regulated Markets and Other Trading Venues

The use of algorithms and technology in financial markets is not surprising, neither the implementation of an algorithm able to organize a process aimed at supporting the execution of frequent-systematic-substantial transactions may be astonishing. Markets and trading venues exist to facilitate exchanges, and—as their operators work for profit—this promotes the improvement of their entrepreneurial activity, as well as the research for an innovation able to develop the relevant production function. However, by definition, the current fintech wave is more than a shift in the production function. However, its success is the driver for an adjustment to the scale of operations, with respect both to the subjects (and the relevant increase due to the inclusive effects of fintech) and the objects (due to the improvements and efficiencies in transactions). Obviously, the market operators are now in the position for considering that traditional markets and trading venues are going to diminish in importance if platforms offer a perfect substitute for circulating capital from investors in surplus to firms in deficit.

As market operators usually regulate trading, fintech innovations offer a solution for the functioning of the exchanges, the efficiency of the regulation and the effectiveness of the supervision. This suggests that, if financial markets approach the perfect competition, fintech will let them get closer and closer to it. However, a new set of rules would be required to avoid any attempt to exercise bargain power or to restrict competition. Indeed, software may tend to produce the same output because they rely on the same set of information or on the same analytics, as well as they execute the same controls; and this case may present the same threats that has been observed in the past when the firms tended to collude.[41]

In other words, in the fintech context, the software used in the business conducts may produce a—direct or indirect—contact among supplier to control the price of the financial service they sell (or to limit their output). This is possible not only because of a direct exchange of information between the machines, but also because of the use of the same data, the same algorithms or the same control mechanisms. Hence, two or more fintechers may choose a software that set its output by considering the output of any other firm using such software.

It is difficult to state that this interaction (among firms using the same software) is a form of contract as the one that the scholars found out at the basis of the anticompetitive practices that would injure others that are not party to such contract (Posner, R. 2007). However, it would not be necessary that the firms expect this contract to make them all better off, provided that all the above may be a basic feature of the software (that cannot be overridden by the firms themselves).

True, every customer may use a comparison software; so that—once again—this is a software-to-software relationship.[42] On one hand, there is a possibility that the customer's software would be able to detect the fairness of the supplier's software and, on the other, that any software may refer to the same programmers or to programmers that collude, as well as they may rely on the same data, algorithms or controls. Hence, in digital negotiations, it does not matter if every customer is in a contractual relationship with one or more of the firms or if he/she is able to shift from one to another; indeed, it is important that software does not prevent arbitrages, does not pay any cost to (digitally) negotiate. In absence of such conditions, it is possible to expect that Courts would refuse to admit the use of such kinds of software—as in the end of the nineteenth-century Americans were refusing to enforce cartel agreements (Posner, R. and Easterbrook, F. H. 1981)—on the ground that they were against the goals of the public policy.

According to the above, the features of the financial markets amplify the effects of the use of software, where such use influences also to the efficient circulation of capital and the effective allocation of risks, provided that the public authorities may intervene on the algorithms underlying this software to maintain the price stability, to protect savings and to ensure competition.[43]

In this context, it is useful to consider that financial markets rely on central securities depositories (CSDs) and central counterparties (CCPs), which contribute to a large degree in maintaining post-trade infrastructures that give market participants confidence that securities transactions are executed properly and in a timely manner, including during periods of extreme stress.[44] In this context, the relevant regulatory technical standards (RTS) show the preference for the use of blockchain technology (or any technology able to support chains of market-based operations that are more efficient than the business of traditional credit institutions, given the same level of safety and soundness[45]). This refers to the executions of buy-ins on chain transactions, on both cleared and un-cleared trades, as well as the need to avoid the underestimation of the new tools and transactions subject to buy-ins (and then the lack of certainty in this stage).

In this respect, sets of technical advice to the European Commission would drive the regulator towards the specification of the criteria to determine whether a technology or a big data are systemically important for the EU or a Member State's financial stability.[46] There is no doubt that new devices and software are important financial market *infrastructures* that play a key role in executing operations and mitigating transactional risks related to clearing, even if it would be based on distributed ledgers. As such, the safety of the financial system requires to capture the risks associated with the algorithms applied in post-trading settlements, either centralized or distributed, provided that the relevant software is able to exploit the current infrastructure without undermining the role of public supervisors (Capriglione, F. 2017).

It is expected that a specific assessment would verify the possibility of a comparable compliance between platforms (based on distributed ledgers technologies) and central counterparties; this assessment will have to evidence how the relevant algorithms satisfy the needs of protection required by the *aquis comunitarie*. In this case, it is likely that the Commission would have to adopt new acts to specify further details on the concept of 'systemically important' in the fintech environment, as any widespread software can be the source of "a risk of disruption to financial services that is caused by an impairment of all or parts of the financial system and has the potential to have serious negative consequences for the real economy" or "a risk of disruption in the financial system with the potential to have serious negative consequences for the internal market and the real economy", provided that "all types of financial intermediaries, markets and infrastructure may be potentially systemically important to some degree".[47]

In addition to the above, there is the risk of the granularity of information, in case of distributed ledgers; however, the management of this risk would not request a burden heavier than what is required to achieve the objective of the current EU regulation. Indeed, the conclusions mentioned in the previous chapters are the ground for a preliminary assumption about software and big data analytics models, which are driving transformation across the market of capital by providing its operators with the capability of conducting extensive analytics rapidly (Masera, R. 2012).

Concluding on this point, the analysis would suggest that the firms running fintech innovations should obtain an authorization, as the activities that are carried out through the application of these technological innovations seem to be a 'perfect substitute' for those activities that regulated markets perform, in a low-tech environment, to support the circulation of capital. When the sensorial apparatus by which humans interpret and construct financial relations and market exchanges undergo profound metamorphosis due to the course of events, legal analysis has a duty to redesign and explore the drift and faults of those symbolic continents on which trading venues rest. It is possible to realize that the trading venues are transformed in a normally slow way, even if inexorable, but that in certain situations they undergo sudden transformations and discontinuities that force to reflect more deeply on what happened.

8.7   Fintech Innovations in Insurance, Pensions and Healthcare Schemes

Interdependencies between the innovation facilitators and supervised entities become more and more strict in the insurance sector, due to the reverse production cycle of insurance companies and information asymmetries: the former adds opacity in identifying the areas where the legislation and licensing requirements need changes and adaptation; the latter has required insurance company to accrue additional reserves to cover moral hazards and opportunistic behaviours of the customers.

Nowadays, it is clear that the technology has an impact across all of the steps of the value chain in the insurance and pension sectors (EIOPA 2019), including through the emergence of firms that—cooperating with the undertakings—can reduce the probability of an event to occur or the size of its effects. Hence, technology provides an opportunity to insurance companies for transforming their business models and the relevant consumer experience.[48]

In other words, the analysis is not only considering the possibility to collect more data and improving the knowledge of the customers or the insured events in order to improve the efficiency of measuring risks and the effectiveness of the actuarial calculation,[49] but also refers to the possibility of introducing high-tech tools to prevent risky conducts, of offering solutions alternative to the mere refund of money, of monitoring the life of the client to develop products that are able to satisfy actual needs of protection.

Underlying these possibilities, there are the values of freedom and equality that are linked to one another, in the insurance market and in the contractual relationships. Freedom means a state, equality means a relationship. Both are rooted in the consideration of the customer as a person. They both belong to the determination of the concept of the human person as a being that differs from all other beings. And the use of algorithms and software cannot undermine these values.

In imagining the evolution of insurtech, affirming freedom and equality as values means that they are desirable, respectively, as a state and as a relationship. These values are the foundation of democracy and market. Therefore, insurtech products must not undermine either one (by imposing inhuman conduct) or the other (by discriminating on the basis of profit alone).[50]

Therefore, in the regulation of such products, the difference between the rule and the exception must be explained by the fact that the latter must be justified. Where freedom is the rule, its limitation must be justified (also with regard to the protection of the health or heritage of the customer). Where the rule is equality, different treatment of customers must be justified. On the contrary: where the rule is the discipline, the exception is the freedom; where the hierarchy regulates the relations, equality is the exception.

However, the most suitable set-up for the insurance industry has to be decided on a case-by-case basis, but it cannot be decided once and for all.[51] Thus, this choice requires the full capacity of the policymakers, and so such a choice cannot be attributed to artificial intelligence. Hence, the application of insurtech finds a clear limit with respect to the freedom of the insured, where any conduct (that is not safe, but lawful) may not be banned but may lead to the breach of the contract.

In addition, underlying the threat that a customer may adopt a detrimental conduct being somewhat under his/her control, there is evidence that decision may be taken by a process that is not entirely predictable, fully under control, or intentionally deliberate. It implies that a customer can get even into a major event somewhat inadvertently, by a decision that is imperfect because it is the response to a contingency and depends on certain random processes, on faulty information/communication, on panic or on any other human failure.

In this respect, the technology may support the human decision-making process or, in certain case, replace it. In particular, the offering of 'digital health insurance' should be considered as a coverage that supports the risk mitigation with the use of high-tech tools. In this respect, this is not a mere contract for exchanging a risk for a premium but a sort of cooperative agreement for managing a perspective threat. Self-care and insurtech are influencing the form and the content of the insurance, as the interests mutually converge towards an equilibrium due to effort (of the insured) and the quality (of the tools provided by the insurer). This is not challenging the equilibrium of welfare and insurance, but the match between individual behaviour and the cost of the management of the risk.[52]

In general, it is worth considering that the offering of insurance policies based on technological innovations does not refer to the mere use of devices aimed at monitoring the client, but it denotes the purpose to support the insured in case of an adverse event that occurs or rather to prevent such events from occurring altogether.

All the above suggests that, in the insurance sector, there are additional aspects that the regulator has to consider in order to manage cyber-risks and to support the development of new products based on the interaction among customers, undertakers, intermediaries, fintechers, algorithms, big data, software, and so on. In this sector, in addition to the problems caused by the qualitative transformations of the contract as a result of the intervention of digital devices,[53] there are those arising from the vulnerabilities of such customers and such devices. This opens up a new field of investigation, no longer only concerning the solvency of companies but also their safety: the latter, on the contrary, appears to be particularly relevant, especially in cases where some operators are authorized to protect customers from the damage that can be caused as a result of inefficient choices (to this end, suggesting alternative and safer options).

Opposite attitudes will have to be adopted in the face of this problem. On the one hand, it must be emphasized that the quest for security is a much greater barrier to moral hazard than that which can be achieved with traditional systems. But, on the other hand, it is evident that the traditional systems—precisely because of their backwardness—opposed a natural resistance to the external limitations of individual freedom.

A formal comparison between contract terms and digital solutions is misleading.[54] The task is different: once the growing application of insurtech solutions has been ascertained, it is necessary to study and develop digital and contractual security devices adapted to the novelty of the technical means used (by the insurance company and by the customer). In other words, this research concludes that the problem brought to the regulator's attention is not limited to the functioning of technological innovations but extends to the contractual schemes needed to implement increasingly efficient security systems: the more security systems are developed, the higher the cost of the research needed for this purpose. At this point, the problem becomes that of verifying whether the negotiation schemes are fully integrated into the overall institutional framework of customer protection. Therefore, it is useful to combine legal technique with the technology of the sector, since—from a legal perspective—it is possible to understand the truthfulness of the problems arising from technological development with respect to fundamental human rights. In conclusion, with extreme formulation, it can be affirmed that it is the law that must provide the means to resolve the problems that arise from the use of technology in the insurance business.[55]

8.8   THE ANTI-MONEY LAUNDERING PERSPECTIVE

The preceding paragraphs have developed and put into a regulatory perspective the intentions, explicit or implicit, contained in the application of fintech and insurtech, which are now deepened and expanded from a different point of view: one of the authorities in charge of the effective implementation of legal, regulatory and operational measures for combating money laundering, terrorist financing and other related threats to the integrity of the international financial system.

There is no doubt that, from this point of view, the policymakers will provide that any disciplinary intervention over fintech should be an integral part of the regulation that guides the fight against illegal activities. However, the policymakers have conceived this intervention as a coordinated response to the technological threats to the integrity of the financial system and helped ensure a level playing field.[56]

Provided that certain technical innovations are not compatible with the current structure of the market (as it is for 'end-to-end encryption' that prevent any public authority to decrypt the relevant data), the Financial Action Task Force (FATF)—an inter-governmental body established in 1989—set the starting point to manage the risks that may arise in relation to (a) the development of new products and new business practices (including new delivery mechanisms), and (b) the use of new or developing technologies for both new and pre-existing products.[57]

From this perspective, the aspects to be taken into account in the regulation should essentially be oriented along specific lines. Firstly, it should be provided that money and financial instruments may circulate only by means of devices equipped with technical requirements that guarantee the most appropriate protection with respect to the various categories of risks indicated above. This provision should be further articulated so as to cover aspects of administrative action and judicial intervention that are particularly relevant to the risks considered here (Tanzi, V. 1996). At the administrative level, the specific competence of an authority to set minimum standards under which a device may be used to execute financial transactions should be provided for. There is nothing to prevent such a requirement from being protected by an appropriate sanctioning system and by an almost objective liability, guaranteeing also a compensation to the subjects damaged by an illegitimate use of these instruments for the transfer of money.

Moreover, to manage and mitigate the risks emerging from virtual assets, FATF suggested that public intervention should ensure that virtual asset service providers are regulated for AML/CFT purposes, and licensed or registered and subject to effective systems for monitoring and ensuring compliance with the relevant measures called for in the FATF Recommendations.[58]

A more complex clarification of the institutional framework requires the choice of the legal technique to be adopted, and this refers to the more specific options of the identification of end-users, the different roles that the law, the administrative act, the intervention of the judge, the regulatory action and the activity of supervision can play.[59] In general, all the above suggests that the use of high-tech devices—to let money circulate according to parameters that may not be under the scrutiny of the public authorities—puts in the right light the meaning of the polemical positions towards an attribution to the jurists of a specific competence to deal with some fundamental socio-economic problems arising from the use of digital devices.[60] Such polemical positions arise, in fact, from the concern to highlight the predominantly political significance of these problems and, therefore, the impossibility of finding a neutral and technical solution. The result is the discontinuation of already known legal instruments and the need to build a renewed regulatory framework by means of a wider application of the sovereignty.[61]

However, the simple observation of the slowness of legislative action and the consequent fracture between a backward order and an advanced technological reality cannot be—in itself—the only reason for the refusal of a legislative intervention. It is worth mentioning that Directive (EU) 2019/1151—amending Directive (EU) 2017/1132 with regard to the use of digital tools and processes in company law—provides the rules on online formation of companies, on online registration of branches and on online filing of documents and information by companies and branches.[62] Such directive considers the use of digital tools and processes to more easily, rapidly and time- and cost-effectively initiate economic activity; hence, it set forth a regulatory framework in order to provide the necessary safeguards against abuse and fraud and, on the other, in order to pursue objectives such as promotion of economic growth by exploiting the high-tech innovations.

Provided that Member States remain free to decide which person or persons are to be considered under national law as applicants (with regard to online procedures, provided that that does not limit the scope and the objective of this Directive), these rules make possible to form companies fully online; however, at this stage, other obligations under Union and national law, including those arising from anti-money laundering, counter-terrorist financing and beneficial ownership rules, should also remain unaffected. In this respect, the identification schemes and means defined Article 3 of Regulation (EU) No 910/2014, whose objectives included the removal of existing barriers to the cross-border use of electronic iden-tification means used in the Member States to authenticate, for at least public services.

All of the above drives to the (almost) full reliance on the aforesaid capacity of big data to self-execute, self-update, self-assess, self-correct, and self-execute again. Once again, it is worth considering the possibility that fighting the misuse of fintech would not lead to establish new prin-ciples but to apply the current ones by means of new rules and practices, able to manage the technical advancements made in the field of algo-rithms, software and hardware.[63]

As the above represents, the shift of attention to the political moment, first, and then to the juridical one, takes on a double meaning: on the one hand, it reaffirms the essence of the modifications in the distribution and exercise of power as a consequence of the use of computers; on the other, it requires adequate institutional instrumentation, which represents the awareness—at the political level—of the impossibility of confining the new problems to the area of pure technology.[64] Indeed, this explains the spe-cific role of computer technicians (*i.e.* programmers and coders), whose indispensable participation in regulatory activity appears to be a possible corrective to the abstraction of the law and to iper-legalizing tendencies, which transpose into inappropriate dimension issues whose solutions can only be technical.

Once it had been stressed that such rules must be laid down by law, given the importance of the interests involved, it was not enough, how-ever, to conclude on this point. In fact, after the legislative indications, there will be technical choices of the instruments to be used to ensure the effectiveness of the public intervention for combating money laundering. What is being sought, in short, is a balance between the rigidity of the legislative requirement and the flexibility of the supervisory action, which—overcoming the concerns of those who refuse any protection that could slow down the movement of capital—seems necessary to implement regulatory techniques appropriate to the complexity of the matter under consideration.

8.9   WHY REGULATE ALGORITHMS?

Concluding by questioning could seem an oxymoron. However, it is worth pointing out that the role of the policymakers concerns the identification of the market failures, provided that all the above narration leads to the doubt that, in quantitative terms, stricter rules should offset the benefits of the expansionary monetary measures enacted by the ECB; hence the need for an immediate extension of the supervisory actions, from the mere monitoring to the impact assessment of fintech innovations, their perspective regulation and the development of such industry.

The common starting point was given by the tacit observation, only apparently obvious, that every innovation is a novelty imitable, and it begins a new business at the center of which newness inevitably arises.[65] At first, however, any innovator finds him/herself in front of a market already made, which is not a simple and welcoming container. It must therefore strive to become a part of this market, inserting itself in a complex and changing order, composed of institutions, powers, knowledge, rules and practices; it must relate to other market participants in a harmonious or conflictual way; it must orient itself through the assumption of ethical and business models that are culturally typical of each sector.

The aforesaid findings concern the effects of two major changes in the public intervention and in the financial industry: a loose monetary policy, pursued by means of non-conventional measures, on the one hand, and the decrease of operational possibilities due to the implementation of a stricter regulatory framework, on the other.[66] Including these effects in long-term macroeconomic analysis would support any experimental approach aimed at understanding the way to improve the common welfare by exploiting automation and freeing humans from repetitive and burdensome tasks. Thus, it will be possible to understand rules and incentives aimed at driving these resources to the development of this wired society.[67]

Hence, the suggestion is to investigate and measure the effects of the envisaged impact of the hypothesis of regulation designed by policymakers and to verify if these effects are correlated with the outcome of the current monetary transactions. In particular, the analysis is willing to assess whether the overall impact of the regulation will reduce the multiplying effect of fintech chains (in creating alternative to money), and if this reduction should lead to a liquidity or credit crunch.

Even if it is expected that any theoretical framework (wherein the regulations of monetary policy and supervision on capital requirements are closely connected) would require big (amounts of) data, it would be possible that the aforesaid effects are (somehow) related, besides the safe-guard set forth in order to avoid any reciprocal influence.[68]

Hence, this asks policymakers to verify if their choices about fintech might lead to looser credit policies, entailing the provision of funds to less creditworthy counterparties, and then to monetary unintended conse-quences of regtech and suptech, which should go beyond offsetting the benefits of monetary policies (in the relevant market).

Empirically, any suggestion refers to modelling all the above in two suc-cessive steps. Over a 2007–2018 time horizon, any supervisor would be able to collect and use data from all the banks domiciled in the EU-28 countries, grouped along with their membership of the Euro Area. This does not involve the use, in the first step, of dynamic panel data, but the regression of both liquidity and capital on their respective determinants (whose results would be useful as a proxy of the Regulatory Impact on Liquidity and the Regulatory Impact on Capital respectively).

In the second step, the estimation goes to profitability and risk. In this respect, any statistically significant differences between Euro Area institu-tions and banks located outside of it would sign a trend that should be verified with the monetary ones. In this respect, certain cut-off points could vary over different model specifications, but they will take into account different regulatory changes of great relevance.

From a regulatory perspective, these results should help in understand-ing the relationship between EU regulation and ECB policies, which have increasingly experienced a loosening on monetary policy and a tightening on asset-quality requirements. In particular, the comparisons among the potentially diverging results of Eurozone *vs.* non-Eurozone countries must be bore in mind, because it shows that the impact of ECB policies would be larger without the constraints set forth by the capital adequacy requirements.

In this respect, regulatory cyber-resilience becomes a new pillar of the supervisory mechanisms. As ICT has become deeply ingrained in this industry, it is hard to imagine a market without it, a society less connected and the economies less differentiated. However, cyber-threats can cost a fortune and can pose a risk to the stability of the financial system. Nowadays, ECB is promoting cyber-resilience by developing "strategies to deal with crisis situations, should an attack occur … together with the EU national central banks to protect the European System of Central Banks—and its data—as a whole" (ECB 2018).[69] Thus is the base for cooperating—with other EU and international institutions—to share information, increase understanding of cyber-risks and develop best practices for handling them.

The contents above refer to the limits that imprison the activity and organization of firms within political, economic and technological constraints that have become a source of *suffering* and *aporias*, especially when the boundaries between territories are crumbling.

In the past, regulation (by activities and by subject) has provided exemplary responses to trends that have torn the market, swinging it between the desire to satisfy the masses and the pretension to flee from them, between synchronization with one's own financial determinants and the separation of personal and collective utility.[70] There is an acute awareness of legal constraints and an increased need to reformulate the rules of financial activity and competitive coexistence, in an attempt to quell the hypertrophic development of intermediaries attracted by ineffability (due to being to big) and independence (from the national governments). The rationalization of such contrasting pressures has produced operative solutions centred on contradictions and dissonances, aimed at achieving the coexistence in the same subject of schemes of actions that—according to the traditional logics—would have to be incompatible, exclude or elude each other and that instead give rise to new types of business conduct.

Despite this, deregulation, globalization and technologization have also generated the unbundling of banking into market transactions that are difficult to control.[71] Since these difficulties start from the observation of the disparity of real power between the subjects of multiple legal relations (in which the unbundling of banking is declined), this disparity frustrates the proclaimed formal equality that should be the foundation of a competitive financial market. In this premise, it is possible to reject a formalistic conception that sees in the market participants an abstract centre of imputation of legal situations, regardless of the way in which such situations are negotiated in the market reality.

One of the main consequences is that it is impossible to consider consensus in itself as an instrument for the defence of those who manifest it and for the control of those who request it, as clarified in the previous chapters (Tene, O. and Polonetsky, J. 2013). There is no doubt that in the fintech environment, consensus cannot fulfil its typical function because it does not correspond, in fact, to a situation of power in itself suitable to balance the power of others.[72] As has been widely remembered, in this matter, it is possible to find both enormous differences in power (which make the reference to the consent of the client illusory) and activities that completely disregard the legal instruments (as happens in the request for consent to continue using the tools chosen by the customer). Without prejudice to the fact that consent can be considered a technically efficient instrument (to continue in the various phases of market operations), regulation must increase the possibilities of intervention by the authorities for the delimitation of the activities that can be performed.[73] Recalling the reasons that lead to the preference for a regulation based on principles, it is useful to highlight the guaranteeing purposes of the public intervention in the financial market, which becomes a suitable instrument to regulate exchanges characterized by increasing dynamism.[74]

Whether traditional banks and fintech serve the same needs, the unity of the legal order and the coherence of its principles rely on the dynamic nature of such system, whose individual legal propositions—although they can also be considered in themselves, in their abstractness—tend to be interpreted as part of new regulatory and supervisory system. Therefore, any regulator must tend to derive all the rules from common principles, and then the supervisory intervention will have to be completed with an inductive procedure starting from the content of the individual technical solutions in order to constitute generally accepted policies (Bobbio, N. 1992).

Only an extreme optimist can imagine that further researches on the regulatory profiles of fintech would bring to light all its tacit assumptions. However, further questions may concern new events, conceptual structures, and business ideas; the answer to these questions are at the end of the bridge that this research tried to build to reduce the distance that currently separates the supervised entities from the sketches of solutions outlined so far. All the above leads us to a point where the view shows that the use of tech-fueled instruments has to comply with the social-democratic principles underlying the protection of individuals, the safeguard of competition and the preservation of the financial stability. And this is sufficient to justify the need for regulating fintech![75]

NOTES

1. It refers to FSB 2020 "Global Monitoring Report on Non-Bank Financial Intermediation 2019", which highlighted that interconnectedness between banks and OFIs through credit and funding relationships has been largely unchanged since 2016. See also FSB, 2017 "Artificial intelligence and machine learning in financial services. Market developments and financial stability implications", 1 November.
2. See Nemitz, P. F. 2018 "Constitutional Democracy and Technology in the age of Artificial Intelligence" *Royal Society Philosophical Transactions.*

3. It is also worth recalling that information and data have been already investigated as both 'raw material' and 'finished goods' of the ICT industry, so the analysis had to recall that the current rules seem to be not yet able to drive the high-tech automatic mechanisms of collection and production of information and data towards the best outcome for the common welfare. Indeed, the understanding did not conclude that the aforesaid rules are suitable for the proper functioning of algorithms and software as cognitive functions of artificial intelligence, provided that big data and artificial intelligence combine themselves without the possibility of supervising their compliance with the liberal, illuminist, social, democratic evolution of the individual rights.

4. It is worth recalling the considerations of Barcellona E. 2019 "Control enhancing mechanisms e governance della società a responsabilità limitata: quali limiti all'autonomia privata?" in *Orizzonti del diritto commerciale*, p. 61 ff.

5. It refers to ESMA 2019 "Report. Licensing of FinTech business models" 12 July.

   In addition, see Arner, D. W. and Barberis, J. N.and Buckley, R. P. 2016 "FinTech, RegTech and the Reconceptualization of Financial Regulation", University of Hong Kong Faculty of Law Re-search Paper No. 2016/035; Berríos, M. R. 2013 "The Relationship between Bank Credit Risk and Profitability and Liquidity" The International Journal of Business and Finance Research.

6. It refers to Banca d'Italia 2017 "FinTech In Italia. Indagine conoscitiva sull'adozione delle innovazioni tecnologiche applicate ai servizi finanziari", Roma; Bank of England, Quarterly Bulletin 2019 Q1, "Embracing the promise of fintech".

7. It refers to IMF's analysis made by Taylor, R. C. and Wilson, C. and Holttinen, E. and Anastasiia M. 2020 "Institutional Arrangements for Fintech Regulation and Supervision", 10 January.

8. It refers to EBA 2020a "Discussion Paper on the future changes to the EU-wide stress test", 22 January.

9. As anticipated in Chap. 3, the development of fintech activities within the shadow banking system poses new challenges for supervising and monetary authorities. Hence, the relevant concluding remarks on the impact of fintech refer to the perspective of 'regtech' and 'suptech'. Regardless of the choice to postpone these topics until the following chapter on the evolution of supervision, it is worth highlighting now that the use of algorithms will boost the capacity of public authorities to develop a software to be used for compliance and reporting requirements, able to drive the business analytics of the supervised entity (so-called regtech tools) and verify if this soft-ware has been properly installed and run by the supervised entity (so-called suptech tools).

10. It is worth recalling the approach of Weber, M. 1998 "Scritti Politici" (Italian ed.), p. 56 ff.
11. All the above is in line with the current analysis of Alpa, G. 2019 "Fintech: un laboratorio per i giuristi" Contratto e impresa, 2019, p. 377; Barbagallo C. 2019 "Fintech: ruolo dell'Autorità di Vigilanza in un mercato che cambia" *Bancaria*, p. 10 ff.
12. In particular, it refers to ESMA 2018 "Developments in RegTech and SupTech", Paris, 27 November, ESMA71-99-1070.
13. It refers to the concept of ECB 2006 "Identifying large and complex banking groups for financial stability assessment", *Financial Stability Review*, December 2006.
14. It is worth recalling Corpus Iuris, Istitutiones, I, I, 4; Digesto, I, I, I, 2.
15. It remarks Bauguess, S. W. 2017 "The Role of Big Data, Machine Learning, and AI in Assessing Risks: A Regulatory Perspective" *SEC Keynote Address: OpRisk North America* who highlighted that SEC has made recent and rapid advancements with analytic programs that harness the power of big data (a.k.a "SupTech"). This is driving SEC surveillance programs and allowing innovations in many market risk-assessment initiatives. These remarks are intended to highlight many of the promises—but also the limitations—of machine learning, big data and AI in market regulation.

    See also EBA 2018 "The EBA's fintech roadmap. Conclusions from the consultation on the EBA's approach to financial technology (fintech)". 15 March.
16. On this point, see Gambaro, A. 2019 "Interessi diffusi, interessi collettivi e gli incerti confini tra diritto pubblico e diritto privato" *Rivista trimestrale di diritto e procedura civile*, p. 779 ff.; Alpa, G. 2018 "Diritti, libertà fondamentali e disciplina del contratto: modelli a confronto", *Giustizia civile*, p. 5 ff.
17. In addition, in refers to Tsang, C. Y. 2019 "From Industry Sandbox to Supervisory Control Box: Rethinking the Role of Regulators in the Era of FinTech" *Journal of Law, Technology and Policy* who proposes that the proper use of supervisory technology (suptech) allows regulators to turn current initiatives such as industry sandboxes into the supervisory control boxes to effectively regulate fintech-era collaborations and shift current practices into a new paradigm of technology-enabled regulation.
18. It is worth considering the 'Conjecture of Kate Bush', whose conclusion states that if π (Pi) is a normal number, it has in it any sequence of numbers, any string, any sentence. Even this endnote, all the endnotes of this book and this book itself may be included in Pi. Hence, algorithms and software may exploit this and other characteristics of math and calculation to support negotiations, business analytics and, in general, the conduct of the firm.

19. It is in line with the analysis of Capriglione, F. 2018 "Non luoghi. Sovranità, sovranismi. Alcune considerazioni" *Rivista Trimestrale di Diritto dell'Economia*, p. 5 ff.

20. It recalls Auer, R. 2019 "Embedded Supervision: How to Build Regulation into Blockchain Finance" *BIS Working Paper No. 811* on the case for embedded supervision: a regulatory framework that provides for compliance in tokenized markets to be automatically monitored by reading the market's ledger, thus reducing the need for firms to actively collect, verify and deliver data.

21. In particular, see Basel Committee on Banking Supervision, Sound Practices Implications of fintech developments for banks and bank supervisors, February 2018.

22. It is worth highlighting that supervisory agencies initiate and organize their suptech activities in several ways. Applications used for data collection tend to be management-initiated projects, while those used for data analytics usually start out as research questions, but in a few cases may also be suggested by supervision units. A number of supervisory agencies, particularly those active in exploring data analytics applications, have recently created dedicated units. A few others leverage their existing research units. Supervisory agencies also use both internal and external resources in developing suptech applications. In addition, some are partnering with academic institutions, particularly in the area of data analytics, to keep track of the latest developments and learn how to build state-of-the art algorithms; see Basel Committee on Banking Supervision, Sound Practices Implications of fintech developments for banks and bank supervisors, February 2018, p. 1.

23. See Recital 16 Directive (EU) 2018/1972 establishing the European Electronic Communications Code.

24. It refers to Acquisti, A. and Taylor, c. R. and Wagman, L. 2016 "The Economics of Privacy" *Journal of Economic Literature* on connections among diverse streams of theoretical and empirical research on the economics of privacy. The authors focus on the economic value and consequences of protecting and disclosing personal information, and on consumers' understanding and decisions regarding the trade-offs associated with the privacy and the sharing of personal data. This highlights how the economic analysis of privacy evolved over time, as advancements in information technology raised increasingly nuanced and complex issues associated with the protection and sharing of personal information.

   See also Agostino R. M., 218 "Big data e nuovi beni tra modelli organizzativi e controllo dell impresa" *Rivista di diritto dell'impresa*, p. 58 ff.

25. In addition, it recalls Brummer, C. J. 2011 "How International Financial Law Works (and How it Doesn't)" *Georgetown Law Journal* who presents

an alternative theory for understanding the purpose, operation and limitations of international financial law, by positing that international financial regulation, though formally "soft," is a unique species of cross-border cooperation bolstered by reputational, market and institutional mechanisms that have been largely overlooked by theorists. As a result, it is more coercive than classical theories of international law predict; see also Posner, R. 2008 "How Judges Think", Harvard, explaining the nine intellectual approaches to judging that he identified.

26. Let us recall a set of authors that shows our approach to expectations, see Keynes, J. M. 1936 "The General Theory of Employment, Interest and Money"; Friedman M. 1968 "The Role of Monetary Policy" *American Economic Review* 58; Nerlove M. 1958 "Adaptive Expectations and Cobweb Phenomena", *Quarterly Journal of Economics*; Muth, J. 1961 "Rational expectations and the theory of price movements", *Econometria*; Lucas, R. E. Jr. 1972 "Expectations and the Neutrality of Money" *Journal of Economic Theory*; Sargent, T.J. 1994 "Bounded Rationality in Economics", Oxford; Benabou, R. & Tirole, J. 2001 "Willpower and Personal Rules," *Princeton, Woodrow Wilson School—Public and International Affairs*; Sims, C.A. 2003 "Implications of Rational Inattention". *Journal of Monetary Economics 50(3)*.

27. In this respect, we follow the approach of Severino, E. 2006 "La filosofia futura", Milano on the foundations of such apparatus.

28. Moreover, see Billio, M. and Lo, A. W. and Getmansky Sherman, M. and Pelizzon, L. 2011 "Econometric Measures of Connectedness and Systemic Risk in the Finance and Insurance Sectors" *MIT Sloan Research Paper No. 4774-10* who propose several econometric measures of connectedness based on principal-components analysis and Granger-causality networks, and apply them to the monthly returns of hedge funds, banks, broker/dealers and insurance companies.

29. Furthermore, see Auer, R. 2019 "Embedded Supervision: How to Build Regulation into Blockchain Finance" *BIS Working Paper No. 811* who—after sketching out a design for such schemes—explores the conditions under which distributed ledger data might be used to monitor compliance. To this end, a decentralized market is modelled that replaces today's intermediary-based verification of legal data with blockchain-enabled data credibility based on economic consensus.

30. It is also worth considering the conclusions of Castronova, E. 2002 "On Virtual Economies" *CESifo Working Paper Series No. 752* on the evidence that the nature of games as a produced good suggests that technological advances, and heavy competition, will drive the future development of virtual worlds.

31. It recalls both Argentati, A. 2018 "Le banche nel nuovo scenario competitivo. Fin-Tech, il paradigma Open banking e la minaccia delle big-tech companies" *Mercato concorrenza regole*, p. 441 ff.; see also Rossano, D. 2015 "La crisi dell'Eurozona e la (dis)unione bancaria", *Federalismi. it* p. 31 ff.

32. It refers Zachariadis, M. and Ozcan, P. 2017 "The API Economy and Digital Transformation in Financial Services: The Case of Open Banking" *SWIFT Institute Working Paper No. 2016-001* who—by exploring the fundamental properties and various applications of open application programming interfaces (APIs) mentioned in extant literature—highlights the relevant theories that give rise to the new organizational structures and platform business models observed in the digital age.

33. It remarks the need for going deeper in the topics highlighted by several authors: Paracampo M. T. 2019 "FinTech tra algoritmi, trasparenza e algo-governance" *Diritto della banca e del mercato finanziario*, p. 213 ff.; Minto, A. "Le valutazioni della Vigilanza bancaria (e su queste, quelle dell'eventuale sindacato giurisdizionale) sottostanti la "previsione di gravi perdite patrimoniali" ai fini dell'assoggettamento ad amministrazione straordinaria. Nota a TAR LA sez. III 22 giugno 2011, n. 5567", *Il Diritto fallimentare e delle società commerciali*, p. 220 ff.

34. It specifically recalls the conclusions of Schelling, T. C. 1980 "The strategy of conflict", Harvard-Cambridge-London. On this topic see also Brozzetti, A. "I nuovi "standard" per fronteggiare la crisi dei colossi finanziari di un mercato globale" *Diritto della banca e del mercato finanziario*, p. 203 ff.

35. In addition, see Maume, P. 2018 "Regulating Robo-Advisory" *Texas International Law Journal* who argues that robo-advisory is essentially different from traditional financial advice. Nevertheless, it demonstrates that current regulation, in particular the European Union framework for financial intermediaries, is able to address most of the resulting issues. His core conclusion suggests that, in applying the existing rules to robo-advisors, the rules should not be interpreted to create a level playing field for all market participants.

36. Related to the effects of fintech on the collective portfolio management, there is also a need to clarify how rules concerning safekeeping, and the manner and the means required for custodians, would apply for digital assets funds, crypto-assets and cryptocurrencies; see ESMA 2019 "Report. Licensing of FinTech business models" 12 July 2019 | ESMA50-164-2430, p. 18.

In addition, it is worth mentioning the need for creation of new regulated activities such as the brokerage and asset management related to crypto-assets. There are no doubts that the current principles do not ban the management of crypto-assets under a discretionary mandate or provide brokerage services in crypto-assets, while there is the need to classify and regulate the activities that do not fit with the existing rules, such as "social trading" (as mentioned by ESMA in the document above).

37. In particular, see Jin, D. and Kacperczyk, M. T. and Kahraman, B. and Suntheim, G. 2019 "Swing Pricing and Fragility in Open-End Mutual Funds" *IMF Working Paper No. 19/227* who—using unique data on investor transactions in UK corporate bond funds—show that swing pricing eliminates the first-mover advantage arising from the traditional pricing rule and significantly reduces redemptions during stress periods.

38. It recalls the conclusions of Lamandini, M. 2008 "Alternative investment vehicles & (self)—regulation (Veicoli di investimento alternativi e (auto)-regolazione)" *Rivista di diritto societario*, p. 18 ff.

39. Including the conditions for taking up business activities, the application procedures, conditions for granting authorization, initial capital and own funds requirements as well as the rules relating to changes or withdrawal of authorization; these provisions are based on technical advice provided by ESMA to the European Commission (ESMA/2011/379).

40. It should be noted that there is no standard definition of each of these innovations, so FinTech firms can combine different elements of these differing innovations. It also means that the same firm might have been reported under more than one innovation business model; see ESMA 2019 "Report. Licensing of FinTech business models" 12 July 2019 | ESMA50-164-2430, p. 14.

41. Moreover, see Ezrachi, A. and Stucke, M. E. 2017 "Artificial Intelligence & Collusion: When Computers Inhibit Competition" *University of Illinois Law Review*, who address the abovementioned developments and consider the application of competition law to an advanced 'computerized trade environment'. After discussing the way in which computerized technology is changing the competitive landscape, the authors explore four scenarios where AI can foster anticompetitive collusion and the legal and ethical challenges each scenario raises.

42. It is worth recalling an analysis made by an Italian perspective, see Ammannati, L. 2019 "Il paradigma del consumatore nell'era digitale: consumatore digitale o digitalizzazione del consumatore?" *Rivista Trimestrale di Diritto dell'Economia*, 2019, p. 8 ff.

43. It is worth recalling again the conclusion of Annunziata, F. 2018 "La disciplina delle trading venues nell'era delle rivoluzioni tecnologiche: dalle criptovalute alla distributed ledger technology" Orizzonti del diritto commerciale, p. 40 ff. on the current set-up of this industry.

44. See Regulation (EU) No 909/2014 on improving securities settlement in the European Union and on central securities depositories and amending Directives 98/26/EC and 2014/65/EU and Regulation (EU) No 236/2012.

45. In this respect, the analysis may extend to consider Zeno-Zencovich, V. 2017 "Dati, grandi dati, dati granulari e la nuova epistemologia del giurista" *La rivista di diritto dei media*, p. 7 ff.; Grippo, E. 1999 "Financial Services and Markets Bill" *Rivista del diritto commerciale e del diritto generale delle obbligazioni*, p. 787 ff.; and Antonucci, A. 1996 "L'accesso diretto delle imprese al mercato del capitale di credito" *Banca borsa e titoli di credito*, p. 619 ff.

46. It recalls Zetzsche, D. A. and Arner, D. W. and Buckley, R. P. and Weber, R. H. 2019 "The Future of Data-Driven Finance and RegTech: Lessons from EU Big Bang II" *European Banking Institute Working Paper Series 2019/35* who highlighted strict data-protection rules reflecting European cultural concerns about dominant actors in the data-processing field.

47. It refers to the definitions of BIS 2010 "Systemic risk: how to deal with it?", Basel and article 2, Regulation (EU) No 1092/2010.

48. In addition, see Berti De Marinis, G. and Degl'Innocenti, F. and Marcello, and Pistelli, F. 2018 "Diritto, robotica e nuove frontiere tecnologiche", *Diritto del mercato assicurativo e finanziario*, p. 194 ff.

49. It refers to Acquisti, A. and Taylor, c. R. and Wagman, L. 2016 "The Economics of Privacy" *Journal of Economic Literature* who highlight three themes that connect diverse insights from the literature. First, characterizing a single unifying economic theory of privacy is hard, because privacy issues of economic relevance arise in widely diverse contexts. Second, there are theoretical and empirical situations where the protection of privacy can both enhance, and detract from, individual and societal welfare. Third, in digital economies, consumers' ability to make informed decisions about their privacy is severely hindered, because consumers are often in a position of imperfect or asymmetric information regarding when their data is collected, for what purposes, and with what consequences.

50. It remarks the conclusions of Lin, L. and Chen, C. C. 2019 "The Promise and Perils of InsurTech" *NUS Centre for Banking & Finance Law Working Paper 19/03* who highlight the development of InsurTech with corresponding risks and regulatory concerns, by focusing on potential risks associated with the application of InsurTech, and concludes with a discussion of various possible responses or regulatory approaches to InsurTech applications.

    See also Borselli, A. 2018 "Insurance by Algorithm" *European Insurance Law Review*, on the role of artificial intelligence and machine learning, whose contents focus on the possible application of artificial intelligence and smart contracts to this sector, highlighting the need to ensure transparency and accountability of automated decision-making.

51. It refers to Posner, E. A. 2000 "Agency Models in Law and Economics" *University of Chicago Law School, John M. Olin Law and Economics Working*

Paper No. 92 in which a simple example is used to illustrate the basic trade-off between incentives and insurance when a principal is unable to observe an agent's level of effort.

52. See Ricks, M. 2010 "Shadow Banking and Financial Regulation" *Columbia Law and Economics Working Paper No. 370* who showed that, under plausible assumptions, an insurance regime (supplemented with ex-ante risk constraints to counteract the effects of moral hazard) is efficiency-maximizing.

53. See Werbach, K. and Cornell, N. 2017 "Contracts Ex Machina" *Duke Law Journal* who show certain potential and limitations of smart contracts, by concluding that smart contracts offer novel possibilities and may significantly demand new legal paradigms.

54. It is worth considering Raskin, M. 2017 "The Law and Legality of Smart Contracts" *1 Georgetown Law Technology Review* who introduces a distinction between strong and weak smart contracts, as defined by the costs of their revocation and modification.

55. In particular, see Baran, P. 1965 "Communication, Computer and the People", Santa Monica (California - US), p. 14 that started a discussion against the position above mentioned.

56. In addition, see the conclusion of Castaldi, G. 2019 "Servizi di pagamento e moneta elettronica: la disciplina antiriciclaggio dei collaboratori esterni" *Rivista Trimestrale di Diritto dell'Economia*, p. 18 ff. who pointed out that the Italian legislation on external collaborators of payment institutions and electronic money institutions is excessive and confusing. Hence, it suggests that this confusion hinders the adoption of rational and efficient organizational solutions and forces many operators to establish their headquarters in other EU countries. Therefore, the authorities must intervene to clarify and simplify the rules.

57. It refers to FATF 2012 "International Standards on Combating Money Laundering and the Financing of Terrorism & Proliferation—the FATF Recommendations", Paris, 16 February.

58. See FATF 2012 "International Standards on Combating Money Laundering and the Financing of Terrorism & Proliferation—the FATF Recommendations", Paris, 16 February.

59. It is worth considering Rubel, A. P. and Castro, c. and Pham, A. 2019 "Agency Laundering and Information Technologies" *Ethical Theory & Moral Practice* who argues that when agents insert technological systems into their decision-making processes, they can obscure moral responsibility for the results.

60. See Rose, K. J. 2019 "De-Risking or Re-Contracting the Way around Money Laundering Risks" *CBS LAW Research Paper No. 19-37* who shows a rising concern towards the derisking of certain sectors/actors due to the increased anti-money laundering regulation.

61. It is worth considering Morrone, A. 2017 "Sovranità" *Rivista AIC*, p. 108 ff. on the supreme legislative power (and its extension), and the separation of powers guarantee against arbitrariness in power.
62. It remarks the conclusions of Peluso M. P. 2019 "Le nuove norme antiriciclaggio: i presidi aziendali alla prova del rischio di riciclaggio" *Bancaria*, p. 5 ff.; Zonile, C. 2019 "La regolamentazione internazionale ed europea di contrasto all'uso di valute virtuali da parte della criminalità transnazionale" *Rivista di diritto internazionale*, p. 137 ff.
63. See Zachariadis, M. and Ozcan, P. 2017 "The API Economy and Digital Transformation in Financial Services: The Case of Open Banking" SWIFT Institute Working Paper No. 2016-001 who exposes some of the findings around the key challenges and opportunities that open APIs pose for the banking sector in the UK and the EU following the introduction of the Open Banking Working Group (OBWG) and Second Payments Services Directive (PSD2) regulatory frameworks.
64. See Maume, P. 2018 "Regulating Robo-Advisory" *Texas International Law Journal* and Gürcan, B. 2019 "Various Dimensions and Aspects of the Legal Problems of the Blockchain Technology" *Comparative Law Working Papers* who examines certain legal problems of the blockchain services relevant to understand the abovementioned issue.
65. See Acquisti, A. and Taylor, c. R. and Wagman, L. 2016 "The Economics of Privacy" *Journal of Economic Literature*, who conclude by highlighting some of the ongoing issues in the privacy debate of interest to economists.
66. See Auer, R. 2019 "Embedded Supervision: How to Build Regulation into Blockchain Finance" *BIS Working Paper No. 811* whose key results set out the conditions under which the market's economic consensus would be strong enough to guarantee that transactions are economically final, so that supervisors can trust the distributed ledger's data. The paper concludes with a discussion of the legislative and operational requirements that would promote low-cost supervision and a level playing field for small and large firms.

    See also Pellegrini, M. 2009 "Da un riscontro di regolarità alla "supervisione". La svolta disciplinare degli intermediari finanziari non bancari" *Banca borsa e titoli di credito*, p. 59 ff. on the effects of a stricter supervision; and Rangone, N. 2006 "Impatto delle analisi delle regolazioni su procedimento, organizzazione e indipendenza delle Autorità" *Studi parlamentari e di politica costituzionale*, p. 79 ff. on the regulatory impact analysis as a tool for independent regulatory reform; Desario, V. 1984 "Il sistema creditizio italiano, la supervisione bancaria e i rapporti con le altre istituzioni" *Banca borsa e titoli di credito*, p. 505 ff.
67. See the approach of Kremer, M. and Rao, G. and Schilbach, F. 2019 "Behavioral Development Economics", *Handbook of Behavioral Economics,*

who examines the existence of high rates of return without corresponding growth.

68. It recalls Stemler, A. 2016 "Chasing Unicorns: The Rise, Power, and Regulatory Challenges of Tech Monopolies" *Kelley School of Business Research Paper No. 16-83* on antitrust and Internet laws that fail to address platforms' threats to privacy and fair competition.

69. It refers to ECB 2018 "Why is cyber resilience important?", 10 April. It is worth considering that as a regulator for market infrastructure—for example, payment and settlement systems—ECB sets rules and best practices to ensure that individual institutions and providers have a strong level of cyber resilience, and in its role as banking supervisor, asks the largest euro area banks to report significant cyber incidents as soon as they detect them.

Indeed, it is a practice that identifies and monitors trends in cyberattacks, which helps in reacting more swiftly to a potential crisis caused by a cyberattack, but it is expected that specific ICT risk-management tools may be implemented as a form of regtech and suptech.

70. See Farhi, E. and Tirole, J. 2017 "Shadow Banking and the Four Pillars of Traditional Financial Intermediation" *NBER Working Paper No. w23930* who provides a rationale for the covariation yielding the quadrilogy, and analyses how prudential regulation must adjust to the possibility of migration towards less regulated spheres.

71. Reference is made to Hirsch, D. and Bartley, T. and Chandrasekaran, A. and Parthasarathy, S. and Turner, P. and Norris, d. and Lamont, K. and Drummond, C. 2019 "Corporate Data Ethics: Data Governance Transformations for the Age of Advanced Analytics and AI" SSRN research paper no. 3478826 who provide useful ideas for the pursuing of data ethics.

72. It remarks the approach of Bessone, M. 1972 "Progresso tecnologico, prodotti dannosi e controlli sull'impresa", *Politica del diritto*, p. 203 ff.

73. It is worth considering the analysis of Rodotà, S. 1973 "Elaboratori elettronici e controllo sociale", Napoli (2018 Ed.), p. 43 ff.

74. See Tirole, J. and Lerner, J. 2000 "The Simple Economics of Open Source" *HBS Finance Working Paper No. 00-059* on open source software development that involves developers at many different locations and organizations sharing code to develop and refine programs. These authors analyse the behaviour of individual programmers and commercial companies engaged in open source projects and make a preliminary exploration of the economics of open source software. It refers to their evidences on the difficulties to predict the relevant effects with 'off-the-shelf' economic models.

75. See Graham, S. and Frank, G. 1958 "Beloved Infidel: The Education of a Woman", New York.

References

Acquisti, A. and Taylor, C. R. and Wagman, L. 2016. "The Economics of Privacy", *Journal of Economic Literature*.

Agostino R. M. 2018. "Big data e nuovi beni tra modelli organizzativi e controllo dell impresa", *Rivista di diritto dell'impresa*.

Alpa, G. 2018 "Diritti, libertà fondamentali e disciplina del contratto: modelli a confronto", *Giustizia civile*.

Alpa, G. 2019. "Fintech: un laboratorio per i giuristi", *Contratto e impresa*.

Ammannati, L. 2019. "Il paradigma del consumatore nell era digitale: consumatore digitale o digitalizzazione del consumatore?", *Rivista Trimestrale di Diritto dell'Economia*.

Amorosino, S. 2016. "I modelli ricostruttivi dell'ordinamento amministrativo delle banche: dal mercato "chiuso" alla "regulation" unica europea", *Banca borsa e titoli di credito*.

Annunziata F. 2018. "La disciplina delle trading venues nell'era delle rivoluzioni tecnologiche: dalle criptovalute alla distributed ledger technology", *Orizzonti del diritto commerciale*.

Antonucci, A. 1996. "L'accesso diretto delle imprese al mercato del capitale di credito", *Banca borsa e titoli di credito*.

Argentati, A. 2018. "Le banche nel nuovo scenario competitivo. Fin-Tech, il paradigma Open banking e la minaccia delle big-tech companies", *Mercato concorrenza regole*.

Arner, D. W., Barberis, J. N.and Buckley, R. P.. 2016. "FinTech, RegTech and the Reconceptualization of Financial Regulation", *University of Hong Kong Faculty of Law Re-search Paper No. 2016/035*;

Auer, R. 2019. "Embedded Supervision: How to Build Regulation into Blockchain Finance", *BIS Working Paper No. 811*.

Banca d'Italia. 2017. "FinTech In Italia. Indagine conoscitiva sull'adozione delle innovazioni tecnologiche applicate ai servizi finanziari", Roma.

Bank of England. 2019. "Embracing the promise of fintech", *Quarterly Bulletin 2019 Q1*.

Baran, P. 1965. "Communication, Computer and the People", Santa Monica (California - US).

Barbagallo C. 2019. "Fintech: ruolo dell'Autorità di Vigilanza in un mercato che cambia" *Bancaria*.

Barcellona, E. 2019. "Control enhancing mechanisms e governance della società a responsabilità limitata: quali limiti all'autonomia privata?" *Orizzonti del diritto commerciale*.

Basel Committee on Banking Supervision. 2018. "Sound Practices Implications of fintech developments for banks and bank supervisors", February.

Bauguess, S. W. 2017. "The Role of Big Data, Machine Learning, and AI in Assessing Risks: A Regulatory Perspective", *SEC Keynote Address: OpRisk North America*, June 17.

Benabou, R. & Tirole, J. 2001. "Willpower and Personal Rules," *Princeton, Woodrow Wilson School – Public and International Affairs.*

Benvenuti, M. 2018. "Democrazia e potere economico" *Rivista AIC.*

Berríos, M. R. 2013. "The Relationship between Bank Credit Risk and Profitability and Liquidity", *The International Journal of Business and Finance Research.*

Berti De Marinis, G. and Degl'Innocenti, F. and Marcello, and Pistelli, F. 2018 "Diritto, robotica e nuove frontiere tecnologiche", *Diritto del mercato assicurativo e finanziario.*

Bessone, M. 1972. "Progresso tecnologico, prodotti dannosi e controlli sull'impresa", *Politica del Diritto.*

Billio, M. and Lo, A. W. and Getmansky Sherman, M. and Pelizzon, L. 2011. "Econometric Measures of Connectedness and Systemic Risk in the Finance and Insurance Sectors", *MIT Sloan Research Paper No. 4774-10.*

BIS. 2010. "Systemic risk: how to deal with it?".

Bobbio, N. 1992. "Teoria generale del diritto", Torino.

Borselli, A. 2018. "Insurance by Algorithm" *European Insurance Law Review.*

Brogi, M. 2019. "Governo societario e Risk management, le nuove sfide" *Bancaria.*

Brozzetti, A. "I nuovi "standard" per fronteggiare la crisi dei colossi finanziari di un mercato globale", *Diritto della banca e del mercato finanziario.*

Brummer, C. J. 2011. "How International Financial Law Works (and How it Doesn't)", *Georgetown Law Journal.*

Capriglione, F. 2017. "La nuova finanza: operatività, supervisione, tutela giurisdizionale. Il caso "Italia". Considerazioni introduttive", *Contratto e impresa.*

Capriglione, F. 2018. "Non luoghi. Sovranità, sovranismi. Alcune considerazioni", *Rivista Trimestrale di Diritto dell'Economia.*

Capriglione, F. and Sacco Ginevri, A. 2019. "Metamorfosi della Governance Bancaria", Milano.

Carney, M. 2017. "The Promise of FinTech – Something New Under the Sun? Speech given by the Bank of England Chair of the Financial Stability Board Deutsche Bundesbank G20 conference on Digitising finance, financial inclusion and financial literacy", Wiesbaden 25 January.

Castaldi, G. 2019. "Servizi di pagamento e moneta elettronica: la disciplina antiriciclaggio dei collaboratori esterni" *Rivista Trimestrale di Diritto dell'Economia.*

Castronova, E. 2002. "On Virtual Economies", *CESifo Working Paper Series No. 752.*

Chatterjee, S. and Jobst, A. A. 2019. "Market-Implied Systemic Risk and Shadow Capital Adequacy", *Bank of England Working Paper No. 823.*

Corpus Iuris, Istitutiones, I, I, 4; Digesto, I, I, I, 2.

De Guindos, L. 2019. "Financial innovation for inclusive growth: a European approach. Speech by the Vice-President of the ECB, at the conference Financial Integration and Inclusive Development – A View from the Mediterranean Countries, jointly organised by Banco de España, OECD and European Institute of the Mediterranean (IEMed)" 13 December.

Desario, V. 1984. "Il sistema creditizio italiano, la supervisione bancaria e i rapporti con le altre istituzioni", *Banca borsa e titoli di credito.*

EBA. 2018. "The EBA's fintech roadmap. Conclusions from the consultation on the EBA's approach to financial technology (fintech)", 15 March.

EBA. 2020a "Discussion Paper on the future changes to the EU-wide stress test", 22 January.

EBA. 2020b "EBA Report on big data and advanced analytics", January.

ECB. 2006. "Identifying large and complex banking groups for financial stability assessment", *Financial Stability Review*, December.

ECB. 2018. "Why is cyber resilience important?", 10 April.

EIOPA. 2019."Report on best practices on licencing requirements, peer-to-peer insurance and the principle of proportionality in an insurtech context", 27 March.

ESMA. 2018. "Developments in RegTech and SupTech", Paris, 27 November.

ESMA. 2019. "Report. Licensing of FinTech business models" 12 July.

Ezrachi, A. and Stucke, M. E. 2017. "Artificial Intelligence & Collusion: When Computers Inhibit Competition", *University of Illinois Law Review.*

Farhi, E. and Tirole, J. 2017. "Shadow Banking and the Four Pillars of Traditional Financial Intermediation", *NBER Working Paper No. w23930.*

FATF. 2012. "International Standards on Combating Money Laundering and the Financing of Terrorism & Proliferation – the FATF Recommendations", Paris, 16 February.

Friedman M. 1968. "The Role of Monetary Policy", *American Economic Review.*

FSB. 2017. "Artificial intelligence and machine learning in financial services. Market developments and financial stability implications", 1 November.

FSB. 2020. "Global Monitoring Report on Non-Bank Financial Intermediation 2019".

Gambaro, A. 2019. "Interessi diffusi, interessi collettivi e gli incerti confini tra diritto pubblico e diritto privato", *Rivista trimestrale di diritto e procedura civile.*

Graham, S. and Frank, G. 1958. "Beloved Infidel: The Education of a Woman", New York.

Grippo, E. 1999. "Financial Services and Markets Bill", *Rivista del diritto commerciale e del diritto generale delle obbligazioni.*

Gürcan, B. 2019. "Various Dimensions and Aspects of the Legal Problems of the Blockchain Technology" *Comparative Law Working Papers.*

Hirsch, D. and Bartley, T. and Chandrasekaran, A. and Parthasarathy, S. and Turner, P. and Norris, d. and Lamont, K. and Drummond, C. 2019. "Corporate Data Ethics: Data Governance Transformations for the Age of Advanced Analytics and AI" *SSRN research paper no. 3478826.*

IMF. 2020. "Institutional Arrangements for Fintech Regulation and Supervision", edited by Taylor, R. C. and Wilson, C. and Holttinen, E. and Anastasiia M., 10 January.

Jefferson, T. 1814. "To Wolter Jones", Monticello, 10 January.

Jin, D. and Kacperczyk, M. T. and Kahraman, B. and Suntheim, G. 2019. "Swing Pricing and Fragility in Open-End Mutual Funds" *IMF Working Paper No. 19/227.*

Kay, J. 2015. "Other People's Money".

Keynes, J. M. 1936. "The General Theory of Employment, Interest and Money";

Kremer, M. and Rao, G. and Schilbach, F. 2019. "Behavioral Development Economics", *Handbook of Behavioral Economics.*

Lagarde, C. 2018. "How Policymakers Should Regulate Cryptoassets and Fintech", *Finance & Development, IMF*, March.

Lagarde, C. 2020. "How can a united Europe meet the challenges it faces today? Opening remarks by Christine Lagarde, President of the ECB, during a dinner on "Uniting Europe" at the World Economic Forum".

Lamandini, M. 2008. "Alternative investment vehicles & (self) – regulation (Veicoli di investimento alternativi e (auto)-regolazione)", *Rivista di diritto societario.*

Lane, P. R. 2020. "Policy Frameworks and Strategies for an Open Economy. Bank of England Workshop: The Future of Inflation Targeting" 9 January.

Lemma, V. 2015. "Collective portfolio management", *Italian law on banking and financial markets*, London.

Lemma, V. 2016. "The Shadow Banking System. Creating Transparency in the Financial Markets", London.

Lin, L. and Chen, C. C. 2019. "The Promise and Perils of InsurTech" *NUS Centre for Banking & Finance Law Working Paper 19/03.*

Lucas, R. E. Jr. 1972. "Expectations and the Neutrality of Money", *Journal of Economic Theory.*

Masera, R. 2012. "CRAs: problems and perspectives (Le agenzie di "rating": problemi e prospettive)", *Analisi giuridica dell'economia.*

Maume, P. 2018. "Regulating Robo-Advisory" *Texas International Law Journal.*

Minto, A. 2011. "Le valutazioni della Vigilanza bancaria (e su queste, quelle dell'eventuale sindacato giurisdizionale) sottostanti la "previsione di gravi perdite patrimoniali" ai fini dell'assoggettamento ad amministrazione straordinaria. Nota a TAR LA sez. III 22 giugno, n. 5567", *Il Diritto fallimentare e delle società commerciali.*

Morrone, A. 2017. "Sovranità" *Rivista AIC.*

Muth, J. 1961, "Rational expectations and the theory of price movements", *Econometria.*

Nemitz, P. F. 2018. "Constitutional Democracy and Technology in the age of Artificial Intelligence", *Royal Society Philosophical Transactions.*

Nerlove M. 1958, "Adaptive Expectations and Cobweb Phenomena", *Quarterly Journal of Economics.*

Paracampo M. T. 2019. "FinTech tra algoritmi, trasparenza e algo-governance", *Diritto della banca e del mercato finanziario.*

Pellegrini, M. 2009. "Da un riscontro di regolarità alla "supervisione". La svolta disciplinare degli intermediari finanziari non bancari", *Banca borsa e titoli di credito.*

Pellegrini, M. 2018. "La Banca d'Italia e il problema della sua autonomia (dalla traslazione della sovranità monetaria alla perdita della supervisione bancaria?)", *Rivista Trimestrale di Diritto dell'Economia.*

Peluso M. P. 2019. "Le nuove norme antiriciclaggio: i presidi aziendali alla prova del rischio di riciclaggio" *Bancaria.*

Posner, E. A. 2000. "Agency Models in Law and Economics", *University of Chicago Law School, John M. Olin Law and Economics Working Paper No. 92.*

Posner, R. 2007. "Economic Analysis of Law", New York.

Posner, R. 2008. "How Judges Think", Harvard.

Posner, R. and Easterbrook, F. H. 1981. "Antritrust cases, economic notes and other matherials".

Rangone, N. 2006. "Impatto delle analisi delle regolazioni su procedimento, organizzazione e indipendenza delle Autorità" *Studi parlamentari e di politica costituzionale.*

Raskin, M. 2017. "The Law and Legality of Smart Contracts", *Georgetown Law Technology Review.*

Ricci, O. 2018. "InsurTech: Una nuova frontiera per il settore assicurativo?" *Bancaria.*

Ricks, M. 2010. "Shadow Banking and Financial Regulation" *Columbia Law and Economics Working Paper No. 370.*

Rodotà, S. 1973. "Elaboratori elettronici e controllo sociale", Napoli (2018 Ed.).

Rose, K. J. 2019. "De-Risking or Re-Contracting the Way around Money Laundering Risks" *CBS LAW Research Paper No. 19-37.*

Rossano, D. 2015. "La crisi dell'Eurozona e la (dis)unione bancaria", *Federalismi.it.*

Rossi, E. 2019. "La regolamentazione attuale e prospettica del settore Fintech", *Bancaria.*

Rubel, A. P. and Castro, c. and Pham, A. 2019. "Agency Laundering and Information Technologies" *Ethical Theory & Moral Practice.*

Sargent, T. J. 1994. "Bounded Rationality in Economics", Oxford.

Schelling, T. C. 1980. "The strategy of conflict", Harvard-Cambridge-London.

Sepe, M. 2018. "Supervisione bancaria e risoluzione delle crisi: separatezza e contiguità", *Rivista Trimestrale di Diritto dell'Economia.*

Severino, E. 2006. "La filosofia futura", Milano.

Sims, C. A. 2003. "Implications of Rational Inattention". *Journal of Monetary Economics.*

Stemler, A. 2016. "Chasing Unicorns: The Rise, Power, and Regulatory Challenges of Tech Monopolies", *Kelley School of Business Research Paper No. 16-83.*

Taylor, R. C. and Wilson, C. and Holttinen, E. and Anastasiia M. 2020. "Institutional Arrangements for Fintech Regulation and Supervision", 10 January.

Tanzi, V. 1996. "Money Laundering and the International Financial System" *IMF Working Paper No. 96/55.*

Tene, O. and Polonetsky, J. 2013. "Big Data for All: Privacy and User Control in the Age of Analytics" *Northwestern Journal of Technology and Intellectual Property.*

Tirole, J. and Lerner, J. 2000. "The Simple Economics of Open Source" *HBS Finance Working Paper No. 00-059.*

Tsang, C. Y. 2019. "From Industry Sandbox to Supervisory Control Box: Rethinking the Role of Regulators in the Era of FinTech" *Journal of Law, Technology and Policy.*

Weber, M. 1998. "Scritti Politici" (Italian ed.).

Werbach, K. and Cornell, N. 2017. "Contracts Ex Machina" *Duke Law Journal.*

Zachariadis, M. and Ozcan, P. 2017. "The API Economy and Digital Transformation in Financial Services: The Case of Open Banking", *SWIFT Institute Working Paper No. 2016-001.*

Zeno-Zencovich, V. 2017. "Dati, grandi dati, dati granulari e la nuova epistemologia del giurista", *La rivista di diritto dei media.*

Zetzsche, D. A. and Arner, D. W. and Buckley, R. P. and Weber, R. H. 2019. "The Future of Data-Driven Finance and RegTech: Lessons from EU Big Bang II", *European Banking Institute Working Paper Series 2019/35.*

Zonile, C. 2019. "La regolamentazione internazionale ed europea di contrasto all'uso di valute virtuali da parte della criminalità transnazionale", *Rivista di diritto internazionale.*

CHAPTER 9

Conclusions

9.1 The Ends of the Market and the Last Bankers

As this book began by questioning the role of policymakers, it would be expected in the conclusion that the forthcoming regulation would correct the main market failures of fintech in a way that protects individual rights of end-users. However, this research has uncovered questions concerning the role of the law under the combination of globalization, financialization and digitalization. Indeed, it has identified significant changes in the structure and the dynamics of the market for capital, whose effects project financial operators towards new paradigms for the provision of financial services, exploiting models that—by means of platforms and sharing-economies—increase direct transactions and minimize the role of intermediaries.

Focusing on fintech, the foundations of cryptography, distributed ledger technology and big data have been investigated as the target of a public intervention aimed at safeguarding savings, competition and the stability of the financial industry. From the perspective of an intense transition from banking to new high-tech services, the need to *urgently* overcome the uncertainties that characterize a far-reaching change in the circulation of capital is clear. These new forms of market trading can be managed by software and business analytics, with the effects of placing the parties of the business transaction on a different level playing field; human reasoning and artificial intelligence do not consider the same set of data, and so there will be a relevant information asymmetry. Even if both parties

© The Author(s) 2020
V. Lemma, *FinTech Regulation*,
https://doi.org/10.1007/978-3-030-42347-6_9

rely on software to negotiate, the mechanics of such dealings will rely on the accuracy of the algorithms, the completeness of the data (and the equal access of both parties to it), and the integrity of the software (meaning the impossibility of the AI tools colluding due to their programme).

In this respect, the current regulatory options can be identified in the multiple explanations of decision-making autonomy within the boundaries predetermined by the traditional supervision schemes, and they seem inadequate to support the development of fintech. Hence, all of the above leads to the call for new decisions that align political directions and economic developments, which are both increasingly disconnected from shared economic models and the needs of the wired society. Indeed, the study suggests that the market is not going through a transitory and temporary (and therefore unfinished, incompetent and temporary) phase of transition, but is instead moving towards a new operating condition that arrives at a destination different from the current model of society: the policymakers propose themselves as representatives of the general dissatisfaction, but they do not relate to the people to discuss the new dimension of needs; the regulators try to reduce the pollution of production, but they do not contain harmful, superfluous or useless consumption; the supervisors promote models of sustainable finance, but they do not control the correlation between investments and economic policies.

Today, more so than in the past, the two terms of the regulatory problem—fairness and efficiency—appear more than a dichotomy, an inseparably bound couple in a dialectical relationship: it was the search for fairness that triggered the regulation of the market in a competitive sense; the resulting competition has reached higher levels of efficiency since then. Globalization, financialization and digitization have not been an opponent of the market functioning but a consequence of it. And it was the liberal nature of the market that produced the alternatives to banking and finance.

In the financial environment, if there is anything that makes it possible to distinguish between the human and artificial phases of the circulation of capital, it is precisely the change in the nature of the need for public intervention in the economy.

9.2   New Challenges on the Road to the Capital Markets Union: Regulation, Predictive Analytics and Justice

Addressing the definition of fintech and its fundamental elements, it has been possible to understand that the modernization of the environment would affect the construction of the Capital Markets Union, where the business innovation of European supervised entities is supporting new forms of supply and demand in the internal market. In this respect, the directions provided by international bodies (FSB, G20, etc.) have suggested that policymakers will consider the impact of fintech in setting up the public intervention aimed at correcting market failures and protecting individual rights. This has led to the consideration of the role of artificial intelligence and the usefulness of predictive tools (that aim at formulating exact expectations of the outcome of an event related to an agreement, a transaction, a dispute or a settlement) and to verify whether the policymakers have to set up a supervisory system centered on a principle-based legislation and automatized mechanism of regulation and control (i.e. *regtech* and *suptech*).

According to this way of structuring the Capital Markets Union, the regulatory policy has to evolve in order to enact a system that will not add new rules to the post-crisis reforms but will instead provide new tools for strengthening the soundness of the financial system. This required the consideration of the impact of fintech on the economics of market-based financing, taking into account the opportunity that technology-enabled innovations offer a perfect substitute to banking and finance.

According to the above, the European approaches to financial innovation outline that, apart from the efforts in the European Commission's Action Plan on FinTech, a uniform legal framework applicable to fintech has not yet been established in either the European Union or the G20's countries. Indeed, the EU regulator does not consider fintech to be a new industry, so the European Central Bank has been called upon to ensure that fintechers are properly authorized and have in place 'risk control frameworks'. In addition, evidence from Switzerland has shown that an advanced democracy should enact the principles of freedom, independence and self-determination, and provide a safe haven for such firms. However, the unbundling of the intermediation process into chains of transactions is leading banking and financial activities outside the scope of supervision. Thus, the fintech applications do not appear to be regulatory-neutral.

The following stage of the research has shown that networks widely distribute both big data and fintech applications, allowing fintech firms to execute their activities all around the world. Both the 'acts of fintech' and the responsibility of individuals in developing network of operations came into consideration, concluding by assessing the current need for transparency, with regard to both the circulation of financial information in the market and the mitigation of the bargaining power in bilateral transactions.

The fintechers that supply business analytics and high-tech services to supervised entities in order to understand the possibility of unbundling banking and finance have been taken into account. The relevant outcome showed a relevant number of alternative solutions for savers, lenders, borrowers or investors (such as the management of web-based platforms supporting individuals in trading credits or sharing financial opportunities). It also highlighted the risks arising from the business of fintech banks and the need to strengthen oversight and control over fintechers, programmers and coders (at least, as relevant ancillary service undertakers, and as such subject to licensing requirements).

All of the above suggest to envision the impact of regulation on fintech and its effects on the credit-transformation processes enacted by means of algorithms and software. In this respect, the focus on the possibility of high-tech regulation and supervision over such operational forms suggested that regulators should be arbiters influencing the shape finance is assuming because of fintech, more than an influencer leading finance to higher standards of technological efficiency.

As the president of the ECB remarked on 12 December 2019, the massive technological changes that democratic societies are facing includes aspects of inequality that are certainly rising in developed economies, and—with respect to such evidence—ECB will address such change with a view toward how banking and financial businesses are affected and how ECB can better respond to its mission: serving the euro area citizens and delivering on the mandate of price stability. According to the above, it has been argued that the current regulatory framework is not designed to avoid a fintech crisis, as it is not aimed at preventing turbulence due to the negative externalities of technology and software-to-software relationships. Thus, there is a need for supervisory mechanisms able to avoid asymmetries, reduce risks and promote financial stability, by supervising conducts and transparency in a market that will be driven by automatic tools and self-executing processes.

In this context, the market operators would exploit the possibility of automation in dispute resolutions by means of artificial intelligence and its applications in the field of predictive justice. This refers to both understanding the rule applicable to any fact, and gaining reliable predictions on the outcome of the proceedings, provided that an algorithm can begin with the identification of the pertinent precedent, the relevant rule of law and then a prediction of a possible solution. In this perspective, it seems possible that financial disputes will find a solution that does not refer the jurisdictional approach to these matters but can minimize the predictable costs of its enforcement.

9.3   FINAL REMARK

Now consider what would be likely to happen if rule-makers aim at discovering the possibility of working together in a different way, increasing well-being. If the denial of this possibility is the primary cause of the failure of any regulator and its policymakers, the discovery of new regulatory solutions does not predetermine—in itself—their use. Indeed, this discovery is not the end of public intervention, but its beginning. What technological development makes clear is that there are now two ways to regulate the use of technology in the financial market: one *committed* and one *neutral*. Taking a neutral position between technology and market is a vain attempt to deny the preference of programmers for an impact on human actions, individual or joint, able only to achieve the purpose of abdicating a responsibility of choice that every other supervised entity faces daily.

From this point of view, in Europe, regulation is an all-too-predictable reaction to the accelerated digitization of the financial industry. While the level of private autonomy is constantly restricted by licensing procedures and regulatory models, the level of market security is falling rapidly. In general, the volume of risks is increasing at a rate unprecedented for postconflict generations, while overall welfare is not growing. If the principle of sovereignty is in crisis with respect to the digital dimension of the most recent finance, this appears to be related to the problems of political freedom of the national legislator, which is undermined by the characteristics of fintech: extraterritoriality, immateriality, speed. Thus, the replacement of a *world of national legislators* with a *single global order* is one of the possible scenarios (and, in light of the results of the research above, it is not one of the most likely), while another scenario would reflect the precariousness of *public intervention*, and the regulation of the financial transactions would be downgraded from the level of hard law to the one of soft law. In this context, what unites the financial market would be the utilitarian sacrifice made to keep the circulation of capital together, where the absence of a public link between the legitimate market players has the downside of exposing everyone to the full market power of others.

Index

© The Author(s) 2020
V. Lemma, *FinTech Regulation*,
https://doi.org/10.1007/978-3-030-42347-6